Show Business
Homicides

Show Business Homicides

An Encyclopedia, 1908–2009

DAVID K. FRASIER

Foreword by JIMMY MCDONOUGH

McFarland & Company, Inc., Publishers
Jefferson, North Carolina, and London

LIBRARY OF CONGRESS CATALOGUING-IN-PUBLICATION DATA

Frasier, David K., 1951–
Show business homicides : an encyclopedia, 1908–2009 / David K.
Frasier ; foreword by Jimmy McDonough.
p.   cm.
Includes bibliographical references and index.

ISBN 978-0-7864-4422-9
illustrated case binding : 50# alkaline paper ∞

1. Performing arts — Biography — Dictionaries.   2. Celebrities —
Biography — Dictionaries.   3. Entertainers — Biography — Dictionaries.
4. Murder victims — Biography — Dictionaries.   I. McDonough,
Jimmy.   II. Title.
PN1583.F68   2011   791.092'2 [B]   2010038405

British Library cataloguing data are available

Front cover: John Lennon, 1968 (Photofest)

Manufactured in the United States of America

*McFarland & Company, Inc., Publishers
Box 611, Jefferson, North Carolina 28640
www.mcfarlandpub.com*

For two who mattered:
Otis Layne, Jr.,
and
Dr. Samuel Eugene Stetson

R.I.P., Old Friends

Acknowledgments

While writing is a blessedly solitary process, the support of the following individuals and institutions was essential and most welcome:

Dr. Kenneth Anger, film director and cinema historian, whose *Hollywood Babylon* books did more to form my interests than even I like to admit. Thanks for your repeated kindness and generosity to me and mine during the nearly 30 years of our friendship. Dr. Samuel Eugene Stetson, a dedicatee of this book, whose support and friendship irrevocably changed my life. I miss you, pal. This one's for you. Otis Layne, this tome's other dedicatee, whose friendship was, and memory is, central to my being. The biggest "character" I ever met, nothing in life has since come close to the sheer unadulterated fun I had in your company. Michael Newton, true crime author and treasured friend, a writing machine in human form whose expertise in everything from serial murder to white supremacist groups to cryptozoology, has made him the ideal drinking and luncheon companion for nearly 25 years. Best selling author Jimmy McDonough, a late addition to the Frasier Death March, who was kind enough to write the foreword for this effort. Thanks, buddy. Harold Fiscus, my near daily luncheon companion for the last five years. A man of class, honesty, and integrity. Believe it.

And then there is the Indiana University–Bloomington contingent. I owe a debt of gratitude and thanks to my former colleagues in the Wells Library Reference Department: Jeffrey Graf, no need of titles here, just ask a question if you need the correct answer. A trusted sounding board, Jeff is the class in any field. I miss you. Thanks as well to Anne "not too long now" Haynes, Sarah "Normal for Norfolk" Mitchell, Anne "free at last" Graham, Kelly "life after death" Prill, and Jennifer "I wanted this" Laherty. Other denizens of the I.U. Library world who have contributed to this book include Robert U. Goehlert, Angela and Mike Courtney, John Pate, Sr., Jeff Ray, Judy Quance, Andrea Singer, Roger Beckman, Sherri Michaels, Betty Davis, Mr. Thomas Bullard, Dennis "hold on" O'Brien, Luis González, Akram Khabibullaev, Wook-Jin Cheun, and Peter "go Red Sox" Kaczmarczyk. Lest I forget, I owe a very special debt to two former I.U. librarians who have since gone on to greater triumphs at other institutions. J.B. Hill, director of public services, University of Arkansas at Little Rock, stuck his neck out for me and I'll never forget it. Dr. Frank Quinn, director of Ryan Library at Point Loma Nazarene University, a colleague for 20 years and a friend for more. Thanks for your tireless support and faith in my work. A special thanks and acknowledgment must be given to the interlibrary loan department, which thrives under the unsleeping eye of Rhonda Long. She is just the best. Her co-workers Ron "David Crosby" Luedemann, Diana Somes, and Isabel Planton are the unheralded engine that drives the I.U. Library system. Last, but never least, is my dear friend Hugh Barbry. To him I award my highest accolade, I trust this man. Also, this project was supported by an Indiana University Librarians Association Research Incentive Grant as well as by an I.U. sabbatical and a University Libraries Research Leave. Thank you.

My new colleagues at the Lilly Library are especially deserving of my thanks and gratitude. I had forgotten that such a "brave new world" could exist and that it could have "such people in it." Breon Mitchell, head of the Lilly, and Joel Silver, curator of books, gave me a shot when they were absolutely under no obligation to do so. My boss, Rebecca Cape, head of reference and public services, makes showing up to work every day fun and interesting. Becky has unfailingly supported my research and I owe her. Erika Dowell and Sue "the fun blonde" Presnell, fellow reference colleagues, have unstintingly shared with me their time and expertise. They are never too busy to help. The rest of the crew: Whitney "the comic book queen" Buccione, Lori "much too generous" Deykdtspotter, Andrew "ALFmeister" Rhoda, Elizabeth "the Roadhouse" Johnson, Penny "more postcards" Ramon, Jim "Where's the Wire" Canary, Jillian "the Puzzle" Hinchliffe, Mary "America's sweetheart" Uthuppuru, Cherry "Nashville bound" Williams, Lydia "Paladin" Stewart, Stephen "send me no flowers" Cape, Marty "so this is retirement" Joachim, Valerie "keep it down" Higgins, Elizabeth "you never leave" McCraw, Virginia "unusual deaths are fun" Dearborn, Doug "I met you once" Sanders, and my soul brother Lewis "let there be rock" Johnson. Also, a warm thanks to retired Lilly staffer Saundra "Stompanato" Taylor, the original L.A. Lady. Two friends and Lilly employees are especially essential to my brief sojourn on this planet. Zach Downey, duplication guru, did the image scans for this book and ranks high among the most decent people I've ever met. Zach proves daily that it is possible to be both virtuous and unbelieving. What can you say about Gabriel Swift, reference associate? I've known this guy for 12 years during which time he has served in the unenviable role of my "Father Confessor." Gabriel was involved in every aspect of this book and supplied much needed computer and word processing support.

Hey pal, when the phone rings it'll probably be me. Please continue to pick up.

Among the "fugitives" who have helped in one way or another in the writing of this book: Professor William Sands, the first teacher who ever expressed an interest in me. It has meant everything. Professor Harry Geduld, the man who created the film studies program at I.U., lest anyone forget. Rob Branigin, thanks for Kid Thomas. Bobbi Tannehill-Liell, one of the best and a true survivor. Paul Donnelley, a British writer and obituarist, whose books are well worth a careful read. Derek Tague, independent researcher, for the mountains of clippings. John Waters, filmmaker and author, who for some inexplicable reason likes my work and sends me Christmas cards. My thanks.

Lastly, I owe an incalculable debt to my wife, Mary, the woman I've fallen through time with for the last 30 years, for her love and support. As she often reminds me, I'm "no day at the beach," yet she has chosen to overlook my failings on the way to creating an atmosphere in which I can meaningfully live and work. She deserves better and I know it. Thanks for having "legs," Kiddo. Finally, my son Hayden. Thanks for the heads up on the rock people in this book and for your uncanny knack of making each new day one filled with the threat of new adventure. You are a sometimes frustrating "work in progress," but one I could not possibly love more.

Table of Contents

I like being around celebrities. It makes you feel better than other people.

–Bonny Lee Bakley,
murdered wife of actor Robert Blake

Foreword

BY JIMMY MCDONOUGH

I wish I could write like David K. Frasier. I'm too out of control. Not Frasier. He crafts his words with the cool, detached authority of a pathologist inspecting a diseased liver. There is nothing extraneous, no flights of fancy. Too bad Jack Webb kicked the bucket. A Frasier audiobook cries out for the voice of Joe Friday.

Frasier has written four books — *Murder Cases of the Twentieth Century*, *Russ Meyer — The Life and Films*, *Suicide in the Entertainment Industry*, and the tome you now hold in your hands. I wrote a book about Russ Meyer, and I consider the 25-page essay from Frasier's book ("Russ Meyer, Auteur") the best thing ever written on the man. Consider this passage on *Faster, Pussycat! Kill! Kill!*: "One never gets the impression that a larger world exists beyond this emotionally supercharged microcosm. The operatic, primal passions of Meyer's characters, like the physical endowments of the women, are too big — so big they overshadow the lesser emotions of reality." Dave evokes more in those two sentences than anything I managed to spew forth in over four hundred pages.

My favorite among his books remains *Suicide in the Entertainment Industry*, an alphabetical encyclopedia of all the notable suicides from 1905 to 2000. What a title, what a book. Where else will you find the gruesome details on the demise of such luminaries as George Sanders, Albert Dekker, Bella Darvi, Peg Entwistle, Lupe Vélez and Hervé Villechaize? I mean, how did Frasier even *dream up* such a concept? Did he just wake up one day and say to himself, "Hmmm, I think I'll write a book cataloguing Hollywood *hara-kiri*? Yes, that's the ticket!"

A detail man, Frasier reports the contents of any suicide note left or last words uttered. He reveals that before newscaster Christine Chubbuck shot herself on-air, she stared into the camera and said, "In keeping with Channel 40's policy of bringing you the latest in blood and guts, and in living color, you are going to see another first — an attempted suicide." (Chubbuck succeeded.) Frasier informs us that after nude, distraught thespian Peter Duel pulled the trigger on his .38, "the bullet exited the actor's head, went through a window, and landed on the floor of a carport across the street." Frasier is not afraid to express a bit of pathos. When sometime cinematographer and talent agent Harold "Hal" Guthu took his final exit, Dave notes that soon after "Max, his beloved pet macaw, was found dead from smoke inhalation under some furniture in the office."

Suicide in the Entertainment Industry sports two appendixes: one that breaks down the deaths by occupation ("Clowns and Mimes," "Porn Performers," "Showgirls"), then by method ("Gas," "Gun," "Knife/Razor/Scissors," and my favorite, "Airplane"). I think this book should be required reading for anyone contemplating a show business career. Frasier understands the tawdry, transient nature of life, show biz or otherwise. And yet there is a glimmer of humor every now and then. I wouldn't call it hope, however.

With the opus you now hold in your hands Frasier does for murder what he previously achieved for suicide. *Show Business Homicides* covers nearly three hundred cases. All your favorites are here: Marilyn Monroe, George Reeves, Spade Cooley, Bob Crane... And how about the Kid Thomas, hmmm? The down-on-his-luck blues rocker accidently ran over and killed a 10-year-old child, then was shot down by the kid's father before a court appearance.

1

Thomas died, Dad got three years probation, and Dave Frasier supplies all the wretched details.

Now, if you expect such an author to look like some surly, head-shaven outcast swathed in black and sporting numerous piercings plus a large tattoo of a bat on his neck, guess again. Frasier is a regular Joe. Deceptively so. He might be the guy sitting in the next seat on the bus, or standing behind you at the grocery. Nothing about him shouts "creative type," and I'm certain he prefers it that way. I got to know the man when I was thinking about undertaking my own book on Russ Meyer. Frasier not only encouraged me to go forward with the project during that very first phone call, he let me have his 1,148-piece archive of Meyer articles he'd spent years obtaining.

Since that project Dave has assisted with all my books, and he is a hellacious researcher.

If it exists on microfilm or a piece of paper somewhere, Dave will go to the ends of the earth to nab it. That's the kind of guy Frasier is — the one you want next to you in the foxhole. I could go on and on about Frasier the person. There are his unusual relationships with Meyer, Kenneth Anger, and John Wayne Gacy, not to mention the mini–Algonquin table he runs at his local Bloomington, Indiana, Wendy's, a monthly gathering mainly consisting of insanely prolific author Michael Newton opposite Frasier himself. But allow me to save any further information for *The Grim Researcher*, my tell-all Frasier biography.

In the meantime, let me assure you that David K. Frasier is just the right guide to take you by the hand and lead you into the Tinseltown night. Expect no mercy. Just the facts, ma'am.

Jimmy McDonough is the author of Tammy Wynette: Tragic Country Queen; The Ghastly One: The Sex-Gore Netherworld of Filmmaker Andy Milligan; Big Bosoms and Square Jaws: The Biography of Russ Meyer, King of the Sex Film; *and* Shakey: Neil Young's Biography. *He lives in Portland, Oregon.*

Preface

Okay, I admit it. My fascination with show business folk has always been a guilty pleasure, but I'm not alone. The public at large shares a seemingly endless hunger for information about the lives ... and deaths of those it chooses to elevate to the level of celebrity. Why not? Celebrities just seem to lead more interesting lives than the rest of us. They make more money, get to hang out with intriguing people, live in better houses, drive more expensive cars, and often have their choice of attractive sex partners. An overly simplistic fantasy? Perhaps, but try to imagine a world without the wall-to-wall "legitimate" newspaper coverage of celebrity foibles, not to mention the sensational reportage of their bastard progeny — the supermarket tabloids, celebrity TV gossip shows, or the omnipresent internet specters TMZ and the Smoking Gun. Divorce, have an affair, beat your wife, drive drunk, commit suicide ... or murder, and THEY will come. And guess what? I won't be far behind. If you're reading this, I suspect you won't be hard to find either. But let's cut to the chase. We're both too busy for trivialities. Follies and foibles are part and parcel of all our lives, but are writ large for those in show biz. Their misadventures serve but a single purpose in this tome ... to "swell a scene," to serve as props to the final curtain close — the act of unnatural death at the hands of another.

In 2002, I published the book *Suicide in the Entertainment Industry* that documented 840 cases of self-slaughter committed by business–related persons during the twentieth century. Like this effort, it was a hopefully interesting and entertaining encyclopedia of cases selected for their notoriety, fame, or appeal to the author. Call it an "underground history" of show business inspired by Kenneth Anger's *Hollywood Babylon* books. The present work is a companion volume to *Suicide* chronicling nearly 300 cases of broadly defined "celebrity" homicide in which the person under discussion is either the actual or suspected perpetrator or victim of a homicide. In these pages you'll find a lineup of the usual and not so usual suspects — actors (Bob Crane, Sal Mineo, Dorothy Stratten), directors (Pier Paolo Pasolini, Theo van Gogh), disc jockeys (Alan Berg, Nan Wyatt), dancers (Sampih, Jennifer Stahl), musicians and singers of all stripes (Spade Cooley, John Lennon, Tupac Shakur, Michael Jackson), porno people (John C. Holmes, the Mitchell Brothers), record executives and producers (Joe Meek, Phil Spector), and many more. Check out the "Occupations" appendix for various groupings of individual "perps" and "vics." Some cases defy description. For instance, who really knows the true nature of the deaths of Paul Bern, Thomas H. Ince, Marilyn Monroe, George Reeves, and Thelma Todd? Rappers occupy an exalted place in the pantheon of violent death, but no more so than the *narcocorridos*, Latino balladeers who sing at their own risk of the exploits of drug cartels. While the arrangement of this encyclopedia, is alphabetical, I have given the *narcocorridos* pride of place in Appendix 1. Their entries are chronologically arranged to give the reader a sense of the unfolding horror of this unique and deadly show business phenomenon. Suspected killers are included even if they were acquitted (Robert Blake, O.J. Simpson) as are those who were never charged with taking another life even though their actions resulted in the death of another (Wole Parks, Kid Thomas). The following shorthand is employed in the entries: M=murderer, V=victim, M-S=murder-suicide. This notation is maintained throughout the work although it is often qualified, i.e., M-suspected, M-acquitted, M-not charged, V-suspected, etc. Quite simply, for the purpose of this encyclopedia if the law found a defendant "not guilty," he didn't "do it." Of course, you're free to make up your own mind. Who you won't find in this encyclopedia — Elizabeth "the Black Dahlia" Short, whose horribly mutilated body was found dumped in a vacant lot in Los Angeles on January 15, 1947. Like crime fiction writer James Ellroy said in his 2007 Zocalo lecture, "L.A.: Come on Vacation, Go Home on Probation," Elizabeth Short "was not a sulky succubus or a porno actress or a *film noir* goddess, she was a pie-faced Irish girl with bad teeth and asthma." Dreams of stardom, no matter how tragically they turn out, don't qualify for inclusion. However, if I did leave out a personal favorite "perp" or "vic," maybe next time.

Finally, this book is targeted at two audiences — the general reader who is fascinated by violent "celebrity" death and the serious researcher interested in plumbing the murkier depths of show biz history. For them, each entry concludes with *Further Reading* as well as separate sections for *Notes* and a *Bibliography* of monographs and videos. Both readerships should be entertained and edified. Okay, I admit it. I hold dual citizenship in both worlds along with fellow-natives Kenneth Anger, Jimmy McDonough, Michael Newton, Paul Donnelley, and John Waters. Care to visit? Consider this book and *Suicide* your passport. Safe travels.

THE CASES

Abbott, Darrell ("Dimebag") (V)

Universally recognized by music critics as the preeminent thrash metal band of the early to mid–1990s, Pantera was formed in Texas in 1981 and included lead guitarist Darrell Abbott (born in Dallas on August 20, 1966, and known first as "Diamond Darrell" then "Dimebag"), his older brother drummer, Vincent ("Vinnie") Paul Abbott, vocalist-guitarist Terry Glaze (later known as "Terrence Lee"), and Rex Rocker (nee Brown) on bass. The sons of a Dallas, Texas, recording studio owner, the Abbott brothers were early exposed to the country music of clients Buck Owens and Freddy Fender. Both learned to play by picking up instruments lying around the studio with Darrell playing drums into his early teens before handing the kit off to Vinnie to focus on guitar. Huge fan of bands like Black Sabbath, Led Zeppelin, Deep Purple, Kiss, and Van Halen, the brothers formed Pantera in the early 1980s, but initially sounded like a variety of other so-called "hair metal" groups. By 1983 with the release of their first album *Metal Magic*, Pantera was becoming increasingly well-known through touring in support of headlining metal bands like Dokken, Quiet Riot, and Stryper. Three other albums on the independent Metal Magic label appeared (*Projects in the Jungle*, 1984; *I Am the Night*, 1985; *Power Metal*, 1988) before the group reinvented and reinvigorated itself with a new line-up and a distinctive sound.

In 1988, singer Phil Anselmo replaced Glaze (Lee) and the band's glam-rock image changed to a harder, more heavily tattooed look with the music evolving into its trademark thrash metal sound. "Diamond Darrell" became "Dimebag" (a reference to the price of a bag of dope) while his brother Vincent became known as "Vinnie Paul." In 1990, the band signed with major label Atco/Atlantic and released *Cowboys from Hell* fol-lowed in 1992 by the highly regarded *Vulgar Display of Power* on the East/West label. The latter album's intensely bleak and depressive lyrics underscored by the adrenalized sonic rage of Dimebag's explosive riffs served as the template for the band's frenetic live shows. By the mid–1990s Pantera had earned a place in the pantheon of heavy metal bands alongside Metallica and Megadeth. The group continued through four albums and many years of legendary post-concert parties highlighted by Dimebag's drinking and Anselmo's increasing reliance on drugs, especially heroin. By the late 1990s, however, Anselmo's interest in projects away from Pantera led to an acrimonious and very public split with the band in 2003. Describing the breakup in February 2004, drummer Vinnie Paul told an interviewer, "Me and Dime planned on doing Pantera together forever. That was our life. We put 1,000 percent of our energy into it. But the other guys had other agendas and things they wanted to do, and that didn't include Pantera." Anselmo, quoted in the magazine *Metal Hammer* in 2004, made the split personal by flatly stating that Dimebag "deserves to be severely beaten." The fiery front man formed Superjoint Ritual while Dimebag with Vinnie Paul, bassist Bob Zilla (real name Bob Kakaha), and vocalist Patrick Lachman formed Damageplan in 2003. The band's Elektra debut in February 2004, *New Found Power*, was a hit with most of Pantera's huge fan base, with one fatally notable exception, and the group toured extensively throughout the year.

Nathan Miles Gale, "Crazy Nate," as he was known to his steadily shrinking circle of friends, once described himself as Pantera's "Number 1 fan." That was prior to the band's bitter split and his unwarranted belief that it was Dimebag Darrel's fault. At 6'3" and 250 pounds, Gale was an imposing and threatening figure in his hometown of Marysville, Ohio, some 25 miles northwest of

Columbus. A one-time offensive lineman for the semi-pro Lima Thunder football team, Gale psyched himself up in the locker room with a pre-game ritual of listening to Pantera full blast on headphones. He served with the 2nd Marine Division at Camp Lejeune in North Carolina until November 2003 when he was discharged after fulfilling less than half of his four year hitch. According to his mother, Gale was discharged because he suffered from paranoid schizophrenia. Friends were accustomed to Gale's quiet social awkwardness, but became increasingly estranged from him as his behavior veered toward the bizarre. He began talking and laughing to himself and once appeared to be holding an imaginary dog. More disturbing, Gale showed up at a musician friend's house with songs he claimed to have written and demanded to sing with the band. Upon closer examination, the tunes turned out to be sheets of Pantera lyrics that Gale had laboriously copied. When this was pointed out, Gale quietly insisted Pantera had stolen the lyrics from him and he planned to sue the band. The group was also attempting to steal his identity. At a Marysville tattoo parlor hangout, the former Marine began to frighten customers by staring at them long enough to engage them in lengthy conversations about heavy metal music. On the afternoon of December 8, 2004, Gale argued with a worker at the tattoo parlor over some equipment he wanted them to get him, and angrily stormed out of the shop to go the Damageplan show at the Alrosa Villa nightclub at 5055 Sinclair Road on the northwest side of Columbus.

Shortly after 10:00 P.M. a tall heavyset bald man wearing a Columbus Blue Jackets home jersey and jeans approached the band's bus parked behind the popular heavy metal nightspot and asked Aaron Barns, the group's sound man, if Dimebag and Vinnie Paul were on board. Told they were already in the club, the man walked off. Eighteen minutes later, Damageplan was forty seconds into "New Found Power," their first song of the evening, when Nathan Gale forced his way in through the back door of the club past security and walked onto the stage. A crowd of over 400 people watched as Gale crossed the stage, grabbed Dimebag, and pumped three shots from a Beretta 9mm handgun into the guitarist's face, killing him instantly. While many club-goers initially thought the scene was part of the act, reality quickly set in as the gunman sprayed the stage and crowd killing Nathan Bray, a 23-year-old fan, Erin A.

Halk, a 29-year-old security man at the club, and Jeff "Mayhem" Thompson, a 40-year-old Damageplan crew member from Waxahachie, Texas. Chris Paluska, the band's tour manager, and drum technician John Brooks were wounded. Vinnie Paul, another target in the attack, was remarkably unhurt. As pandemonium reigned and terrified patrons stampeded to the exits, some had the presence of mind to call 911 and describe the horrific scene on their cell phones. Columbus Police Officer James D. Niggemeyer had just begun his shift and was two miles from the Alrosa when he got the call. Two minutes later, armed with a Remington 870, 12-gauge shotgun, Niggemeyer entered the rear of the club shortly after 10:20 P.M. Onstage, Gale had a man in a headlock with a gun pressed to his head. The officer worked his way around a stack of amplifiers and from twenty feet away killed the crazed gunman with a single shotgun blast. It was later determined that Gale had fired over 20 bullets in the three minutes of carnage and had 35 rounds remaining. Patrolman Niggemeyer was honored by the National Rifle Association as the Law Enforcement Officer of the Year 2005.

Numerous tributes from fans and fellow-guitarists followed in the wake of Dimebag's murder. Days after the tragedy, former Pantera frontman Phil Anselmo issued a tearful statement in which he professed his love for the fallen guitarist and reached out to survivor Vinnie Paul. Despite his overture, Anselmo was blocked by the Abbott family from attending Dimebag's funeral. Ironically, the mother of killer Nathan Gale told authorities that prior to her son's diagnosis of paranoid schizophrenia she had bought him the 9mm semiautomatic in pride over his military service. To date, Dimebag has been immortalized by limited edition custom guitars, collectible figurines, and an official clothing line. In the aftermath of the shooting, several Texas and heavy metal bands have refused to play the Alrosa Villa out of respect to the memory of Dimebag. Two concertgoers in attendance at the club on the night of the shooting have since filed a lawsuit against the establishment alleging that inadequate security was provided by the venue. In January 2008, Vinnie Paul broke his silence about the moments leading up to his brother's murder. "The last thing that really matters to me is the last thing we said to each other before we went on stage," Vinnie told the British magazine *Metal Hammer*. "Our code word to let it all hang out and have a good time was 'Van Halen.' And that's the last two words we ever said to each other. I said, 'Van Halen' and he said, 'Van Halen' and we high-fived each other and went on the deck to do our thing. And a minute and a half later I'll never see him again."

Further Reading

Arnold, Chris. *A Vulgar Display of Power: Courage and Carnage at the Alrosa Villa.* Crystal River, FL: MJS Music, 2007.

Crain, Zac. *Black Tooth Grin: The High Life, Good Times, and Tragic End of "Dimebag" Darrell Abbott.* Cambridge, MA: Da Capo, 2009.

Futty, Bob. "What Happened at Alrosa Villa the Night a Gunman Killed 'Dimebag' Darrell Abbott and Three Others?" *Columbus Post Dispatch,* January 16, 2005, sec. A, p. 1.

Adamson, Al (V)

Often unfairly compared to Hollywood hack, Edward D. Wood, Jr. (*Glen or Glenda,* 1952; *Plan 9 from Outer Space,* 1956) as one of filmdom's worst directors, Adamson is regarded in certain circles as a competent schlockmeister who, by economic necessity, worked in the sub-genres of biker films (*Satan's Sadists,* 1969), horror (*Dracula Vs. Frankenstein,* 1972), sexploitation (*The Naughty Stewardesses,* 1973), and blaxploitation (*Black Samurai,* 1977). Born Albert Victor Adamson, Jr., in Hollywood, California, on July 6, 1929, the future director had a film pedigree of sorts. Under the stage name "Denver Dixon," Adamson's native New Zealander father (Victor, Sr.) starred in (*The Last Roundup,* 1929) and directed (*The Lone Rider,* 1922; *Lightning Range,* 1933) several low-budget silent and early sound features for Poverty Row producers. Following service in the Navy, Al Adamson promoted nightclub acts prior to making his screen debut under the name "Rick Adams" in the forgettable 1961 film, *Halfway to Hell,* produced and directed by his father. Adamson's directing career began in 1965 with *Psycho A Go-Go* (a.k.a. *Echo of Terror*). Scripted by Adamson, the low-budget feature was shot by future Academy Award winning cinematographer William (Vilmos) Zsigmond (*Close Encounters of the Third Kind,* 1977) in and around Los Angeles. In a move that served as the *modus operandi* for his career, the filmmaker added footage featuring aged actors (in this case, John Carradine) and re-released the film under a different title, *The Fiend with the Electronic Brain,* in September 1966.

Adamson's career took off in late 1968 after forming Independent-International Pictures Corporation with producer-distributor Sam Sherman. His debut film for the new distribution company, *Satan's Sadists,* is regarded by many of the genre's aficionados as the best low-budget outlaw motorcycle gang movie ever made. Shot in ten days in 1969 for $60,000, the film starred Russ Tamblyn (then suffering a post–*West Side Story* career slump) as the drug-taking psychopathic biker, "Anchor," who rapes and kills anyone who gets in his path. The film's publicity cashed in on the hysteria surrounding the Charles Manson Family infamy by loudly declaring on its posters, filmed "on the actual locations where the Tate murder suspects lived their wild experiences..." *Satan's Sadists* ultimately grossed between $15 million to $20 million world-wide in drive-ins, theatres, and video sales. During the shoot, Adamson met Regina Carrol, a buxom blonde who played the film's "freak-out girl." Carrol became a mainstay in Adamson's production company, and the pair married in 1972, remaining together until the actress's death from cancer on November 4, 1992. The success of *Satan's Sadists* established a formula for the remainder of Adamson's film career: make cheap films, exploit the currently popular genre (horror, sex), use (when possible) name stars at the end of their careers, continually add stock footage and then retitle the films, and target the drive-in crowd where quality takes a back seat to entertainment value. Adamson's films include *Five Bloody Graves* (1970, starring John Carradine), *Horror of the Blood Monsters* (1970, a.k.a. *Space Mission of the Lost Planet, Creatures of the Prehistoric Planet,* among an estimated 13 other titles), *Dracula Vs. Frankenstein* (1972, the first horror spoof featuring Lon Chaney, Jr., and J. Carrol Naish in his last role), *The Female Bunch* (1972, Chaney, Jr.'s final role), *Blazing Stewardesses* (1975, with Yvonne De Carlo), and *Nurse Sherri* (1978).

In the late 1970s, Adamson's film career fell victim to the death of the drive-in, killed by the combination of sky-rocketing land prices and the burgeoning home video market. "The industry changed," Adamson told an interviewer in 1988. "The majors (studios) started making the same films we were making; they'd steal all our stories and ideas ... they started spending $10 million on pictures we spent $100,000 on. So it forced my retirement." Except for the occasional film assignment during the 1980s and 1990s, Adamson was largely out of the industry and earning a comfortable living managing his real estate holdings in California and Utah. In 1994, the director was residing in Las Vegas when the buyer of a property he had recently sold in Indio, California defaulted on the sale. Adamson moved into the dilapidated ranch-style home with Fred Fulford, a 46-year-old independent contractor he had brought with him from Las Vegas to remodel the property. The arrangement lasted ten months until Ken Adamson, the filmmaker's brother, grew suspicious when Fulford never put his brother on the phone when he called. On July 26, 1995, Ken Adamson reported the filmmaker missing after not having seen or spoken to him in five weeks. Shortly before his disappearance, Al Adamson told his brother Fulford had run up $4,000 in unauthorized charges on his (Adamson's) credit card. Indio police delved into Adamson's phone bills and credit cards and discovered Fulford had recently paid for a cement truck delivery to the property with a check pre-signed by the director.

On August 2, 1995, Ken Adamson escorted police into the empty house where he was surprised to find his brother's beloved Jacuzzi cemented over and covered with Mexican floor tile. Police and forensic specialists labored 18 hours digging out the circular four foot pit before unearthing a scene worthy of one of Adamson's B-grade horror films. A badly decomposed body (identified through dental records as Adamson's) was found wrapped in a comforter. A shaken Sam Sherman, friend and co-partner with Adamson in Independent-International, told the press, "Although we did a lot of horror movies, the kinds of pictures we made were not like this. Our pictures were never this grisly." The autopsy revealed the director died as a result of four blows to the head from a blunt instrument. The date of death (later fixed by the prosecutor as June 20) was estimated between June 19 and 22, 1995. A murder warrant was issued for prime suspect Fred Fulford. Indio police followed a trail of credit card receipts to Florida where the 46-year-old contractor was arrested in a St. Petersburg hotel room on August 7, 1995. One week before Adamson was reported missing, Fulford had driven to Florida with his wife and two-year-old daughter. In the Sunshine State, Fulford sold four of Adamson's cars, used the dead filmmaker's credit cards and checking account, wore his suits, and attempted unsuccessfully to secure a passport. At trial, the deputy district attorney depicted Fulford as a cold, calculating killer who bludgeoned the 65-year-old filmmaker to death after Adamson threatened to expose the contractor's credit card fraud. A jury needed only one hour to find Fulford guilty of first-degree murder on November 17, 1999. On March 3,

2000, the contractor was sentenced to 25 years to life in prison. At the time of his murder, Adamson was making *Beyond This Earth*, a docudrama about extraterrestrials for Independent-International. As the subject of periodic film festivals combined with the increasing availability of his work on DVD, Al Adamson will no doubt continue to attract a small, but fiercely loyal following much in the same vein as fellow-director Ed Wood, Jr.

Further Reading

Albright, Brian. "Bikers, Blood Monsters and Black Samurai: A Final Interview with Al Adamson." *Filmfax* 53 (November-December 1995): 48–54.

Konow, David. *Schlock-O-Rama: The Films of Al Adamson*. Los Angeles: Lone Eagle, 1998.

Akeman, David ("Stringbean") (V)

An accomplished banjo player credited with resurrecting the instrument's use in bluegrass and country music, Akeman will be best remembered as the gangly, banjo playing comedian on the late 1960s, early 1970s hit television show *Hee Haw*. Born in Annville, in Jackson County, Kentucky, on June 17, 1915, Akeman was surrounded by music from an early age. His father, a farmer, played the banjo at local dances and Akeman was further influenced by area musicians like B.F. Shelton, Buell Kazee, and Lily May Ledford. At seven, he built his first banjo out of a shoebox using thread for strings, and at 12 traded two roosters for his first commercially made banjo. The teen developed a regional reputation playing dances, but caught his first break when he won a talent competition judged by Asa Martin, a popular country singer, guitarist, and skilled musical saw player. Akeman joined Martin's band in the 1930s, and earned his lifelong nickname "Stringbean" when the bandleader, unable to remember the lanky teen's name during a performance, introduced him to the crowd as "String Beans." Akeman's role as the group's banjoist soon expanded into singing and doing comedy routines after another performer missed the show. Throughout the late 1930s, the banjoist-comedian continued to build a strong following by constant touring with Martin and radio broadcasts out of Lexington, Kentucky. A fine athlete, Akeman was playing baseball when he was noticed by bluegrass legend Bill Monroe. Monroe, in addition to having the top bluegrass band around, also owned a semi-pro baseball team and was always looking for talent. The fact that Akeman was also a clawhammer banjo player extraordinaire was a plus. He signed with Monroe and from 1943–1945 appeared on the group's recordings like "True Life Blues" and "Footprints in the Snow." After leaving Monroe in 1945 (he was replaced by Earl Scruggs), Akeman married Estelle Stanfill, and formed a partnership with Lew Childre. The pair played tent shows throughout the South and became regulars at the Grand Ole Opry.

Under the tutelage of resident Opry banjoist and comic Uncle Dave Macon, Akeman put the finishing touches on his Stringbean persona. Dressed in a shirt down to his knees ending in belted trousers, Stringbean's Opry act consisted of telling corny hillbilly jokes and downhome stories in between traditional banjo playing and country songs. When Macon died in 1952, Akeman essentially took his place as the Opry's resident banjo playing comic. Thanks to the Grand Ole Opry, Stringbean was nationally known in country music circles by the 1950s. Although he had appeared on Bill Monroe's albums, Akeman had yet to define himself as a solo performer until signing with Starday in 1961 to release *Old Time Pickin' and Singin' with Stringbean*, an entertaining rehash of his Opry act. Over the next few years, Stringbean released six other well received country music albums on the label (*Kentucky Wonder*, 1962; *Salute to Uncle Dave Macon*, 1963), before recording his final LP for Starday, *Way Back in the Hills of Old Kentucky*, in 1964. Akeman would have remained just a popular Opry star with regional appeal if not for the CBS television show *Hee Haw*. A countrified *Rowan & Martin's Laugh-In*, *Hee Haw* featured black out comedy sketches, running gags, and plenty of country music. Stringbean and fellow-banjoist and Opry star Grandpa Jones (Louis Marshall Jones) were among the first to join the cast which included Buck Jones and Roy Clark. The banjo playing comedians first met in 1946 and were best friends, later living next to one another on adjacent farms outside of Nashville. The hour-long variety show premiered in 1969, and though savaged by critics, was loved by a legion of nationwide fans. Stringbean, his onscreen persona honed to perfection from years on the road and the Opry stage, was among the most popular performers on the show. His bit, "Letters from Home," in which he pulled a humorous letter from his bib overalls and read it aloud to gales of laughter was a cast and fan favorite. The show made the toothy banjo playing comic with the forlorn expression instantly rec-ognizable even to non-country fans. A star of both the Grand Ole Opry, country music's most venerable institution, and a hit television show, David "Stringbean" Akeman was at the pinnacle of his career.

On November 10, 1973, Stringbean did his second show at the Grand Ole Opry between 10:15–10:30 P.M. singing two songs, "Y'All Come," and "I'm Going to the Grand Old Opry and Make Myself a Name." Akeman, 57, and wife Estelle, 60, said their goodbyes to friends and left the Ryman Auditorium at around 10:40 P.M. for the half-hour drive back to their modest three-room red farmhouse between Goodlettsville and Ridgetop on Baker Station Road in northwest Davidson County. Estelle drove the brand new 1974 green Cadillac, non-driver Stringbean's one concession to celebrity. Returning home around 11:15 P.M., Stringbean noticed his homemade burglar alarm, a piece of fishing line stretched across the driveway, was broken. He walked to the door of the darkened cabin, fished a .22-caliber pistol out of the tote bag containing his stage clothes, and opened the door. The banjo player fired at a shadowy form, and in the ensuing struggle was fatally shot just inside the doorway. Estelle, terrified at the sound of gunshots, began to run from the car, but a gunman ran her down outside on the grass, stopping her with a bullet to the back which exited through her chest. The woman kept running until another slug hit her in the arm. The killer finished her with a shot in the back of the head at close range. At 6:30 A.M. the next morning, Louis Marshall ("Grandpa") Jones, Stringbean's neighbor, Opry colleague, and best friend, arrived at Akeman's isolated farmhouse north of Nashville to begin a planned hunting trip together in Virginia. He saw Estelle's body first lying face-down in a fetal position in a patch of turnip greens some forty yards from the house. The keys to the couple's Cadillac were still clutched in her hand. Stringbean's body was found face-down on the living room floor near the fireplace. Jones called the State Highway Patrol, and their subsequent investigation determined the farmhouse had been ransacked, the telephone line cut, with empty beer cans and cigarettes (Stringbean only smoked a pipe) recovered from the kitchen. Apparently, the killer(s) had listened to the Opry, and waited in the dark for the Akemans to arrive. The couple's other car, a green 1972 Ford Torino station wagon, was found abandoned on the road about 1½ mile from their 142 acre farm. Items (later revealed to be about $250 in cash, a chain saw, and some of Stringbean's guns) were taken from the car and the farmhouse. Ironically, the robbers missed $3,182 in cash in a pocket of Akeman's overalls, and $2,150 hidden in Estelle's bra. This money was found by a funeral home employee preparing the bodies for burial.

Despite the incompetence of the assailants, police immediately focused on robbery as the motive for the homicides. Most connected with the Grand Ole Opry knew of Stringbean's distrust of banks based on his experience of the Depression. While the banjo player used them (at the scene police found seven bank books with assets totaling over $500,000), stories of how he flashed large wads of cash were legendary. If Stringbean carried large sums of money on his person, it was not a stretch to think he might also keep money hidden in his cabin. On November 13, 1973, Opry stars and fans stood quietly together as the Akemans were buried side-by-side beneath a single grave marker in Forest Lawn Memorial Gardens in Goodlettsville, Tennessee. Four days after the shooting, the District Attorney for Davidson County received a phone call from Felix Elliott, a truck driver being held in jail on an arson charge, with information on the killing. In exchange for consideration on a reduced charge, Elliott told the D.A. days before the murder he overheard three men talking about robbing the popular performer. Police questioned brothers Marvin Douglas Brown (called Doug) and Roy Brown, residents of nearby Greenbrier, Tennessee, for six hours, and released them for lack of evidence. The brothers and their cousin, John A. Brown, however, became prime suspects based on their weak alibis, and were placed under close police surveillance. From their command post in Stringbean's cabin, authorities played a waiting game, convinced solid police work combined with the $30,000 reward offered by friends of the Akemans would result in a solid lead. In late November their patience paid off. James Morris, a coworker with Doug Brown at American Marine Company, a fiberglass boat fabricating business, stepped forward anxious to claim the reward. Morris told police that while at American Marine he overheard Doug Brown and co-worker William Edward Downey, planning a home burglary that would net them in the range of $20,000–$30,000. To bolster his claim, Doug Brown flashed a .32-caliber pistol. Police contacted Downey and convinced the frightened boat worker to gather information on Brown. During weeks of "undercover work," Downey milked the talkative Brown for details about the murder, and where some of the loot from Stringbean's cabin could be recovered. Doug Brown talked endlessly of how he and his cousin, John "Tootsie" Brown, had heard that Stringbean kept $25,000 in cash in his farmhouse, and how they had waited for the banjo player to return from the Opry on the night of the murders. According to Brown, it was cousin John who pulled the trigger on the couple.

On January 16, 1974, John A. Brown, 23, and his cousin, Doug Brown, 23, were arrested at their residences in Shady Acres Trailer Park in Greenbrier. Remarkably, eight months later the garrulous Doug Brown relived the "agonizing moments" of the Akeman murders in a jailhouse confession with reporter Larry Brinton published in the *Nashville Banner* on July 23, 1974. What started as a robbery initiated by rumors Stringbean kept $25,000 in his house ended in murder when John Brown shot Stringbean as the banjoist scuffled with Doug inside the cabin. John Brown chased down the fleeing Estelle Akeman in the yard and shot her three times. He told his cousin, "I'll never forget what the last words she said, 'Please don't kill me.'" In addition to two handbags that were in Stringbean's possession when he approached the house, the men used pillow cases to load up their loot—$208 in cash, some guns, and a chain saw. What the Browns failed to keep, use, pawn, or sell, they placed in another pillow case, weighted it down with rocks, and tossed it into a brackish, snake-infested pond in Greenbrier. "It wasn't my intention for anybody to get hurt," the remorseful Doug Brown told Brinton. "I don't see why he shot them because I just about had the gun away from Stringbean when he was shot. I wish it all hadn't happened. If I had wanted to kill, I could have blowed Stringbean out of his house with that shotgun I had." Acting on information supplied by Brown, reporter Brinton and his photographer, Jack Gunter, retrieved the zippered bag containing Stringbean's stage costume, $3,300 in uncashed Opry checks, and *Hee Haw* scripts from the slimy pond.

In late October 1974, the Browns were tried simultaneously on first-degree murder charges with different counsels representing them. As Tennessee did not have a death penalty law in place when the killings occurred, the defendants faced unlimited prison time if convicted. Fearful fans of the dead performer and his wife would feud with members of the Brown family, security was tight. Observers were treated to the incongruous spectacle of elderly country stars like Grandpa Jones and Roy Acuff being patted down by sheriffs before they were permitted to enter the courtroom. Numerous witnesses, the most damning of which was Bill Downey, stepped forward to testify both Browns spoke openly of killing the country couple. *Nashville Banner* reporter Larry Brinton was allowed to testify regarding Doug Brown's published confession and the defendant's statements that led to the recovery of Stringbean's bag (the murder weapon was never recovered). No one expected any surprises when the nine-man, three-woman jury filed back into the courtroom on November 2, 1974, after deliberating only two hours and thirty-five minutes. During closing arguments, John Brown had even written "99" twice on a slip of paper and passed it to Doug. Both Browns were found guilty on two counts of first-degree murder with each count carrying a 99 year prison term. Overruling the jury's sentencing recommendation that the terms run concurrently, Judge Allen R. Cornelius, Jr. imposed consecutive prison terms. Instead of 99 year sentences, the Browns each faced 188 years in the penitentiary unless paroled.

In late 1996, the mystery of what happened to Stringbean's stash of money, the motive for the murders of the country star and his wife, was finally solved. The occupant of the house was seated in front of the fireplace when he noticed bits of paper falling into the grate from the chimney. Summoned to the house, police found several thousands of dollars hidden in the chimney stonework long since chewed by mice into worthless scraps of nesting confetti. On January 8, 2003, Doug Brown, 52, died of natural causes at the Brushy Mountain Correctional Complex in Morgan County. Doug's cousin and triggerman, John Brown, was turned down for parole in 1993. Ten years later, Brown, 52, was again denied parole after the State Board of Pardons and Paroles ruled against his petition on July 15, 2003. The Board in a 2–0 vote was unmoved by the appearance of Tommy Cash, brother of country legend Johnny, who spoke in favor of John Brown's parole, reasoning, "I think he's helping people and to keep him incarcerated would not serve any purpose." Brown, 57, was again denied parole in August 2008 by a vote of 4–2 despite his insistence he had been a model prisoner and attended Alcoholics Anonymous meetings and anger management courses. The Board recommended his case be reviewed in July 2011.

Further Reading

Causey, Warren B. *The Stringbean Murders*. Nashville: Quest, 1975.
Eder, Bruce. "Stringbean." www.allmusic.com.
Paine, Donald F. "Hillbilly Homicides: The 'Stringbean' Murder Trial." *Tennessee Bar Journal*, 40(12) (December 2004): 20–22.
Riese, Randall. *Nashville Babylon: The Uncensored Truth and Private Lives of Country Music's Stars*. New York: Congdon and Weed, 1988.

Albrecht, (Jeffrey) Carter (V)

The keyboardist for the rock band Edie Brickell and the New Bohemians since October 1999, Carter Albrecht, 34, was well-known in the Dallas, Texas, musical community where he also played guitar, keyboard, and sang for the popular local band Sorta. In what authorities called a "perfect storm" of tragic events, the talented musician was accidentally killed in the early morning hours of September 3, 2007. After a night of partying in East Dallas, a drunken Albrecht engaged in a physical altercation with his girlfriend before she managed to lock him out of her house. Albrecht then apparently began shouting, kicking, and pounding the back door of her neighbor's home. Ironically, the neighbor, William Logg, was a local blues guitarist known as "Smokey" who had recorded several albums. Logg's wife was on the phone to 911 as the terrified man first attempted to verbally warn the intruder away, then fired an intentionally high warning pistol shot through the locked door. The 6'5" Albrecht was fatally struck by the bullet. Logg escaped charges as the shooting occurred two days after the enactment of the state's "Castle Doctrine" that gave Texans a stronger legal right to defend themselves with deadly force in their homes, cars, and workplaces. Ryann Rathbone, Albrecht's girlfriend, blamed her lover's uncharacteristically abusive behavior on his bad reaction to a combination of alcohol and hallucinations he suffered from taking the prescription anti-smoking drug Chantix. Described as "friendly" and "quiet" by friends, Albrecht had no prior history of violence.

Further Reading

Weber, Paul J. "Dallas Police Believe Shooting of New Bohemians Keyboardist was Self-Defense." Associated Press, September 4, 2007.

Alfaro (Pulido), Jesús Rey David *see* Appendix 1

Allen, Marcus *see* **Boham**, Timothy J.

Anand, Dinesh (V)

The 35-year-old Hindi character actor's bullet-riddled body was found in his car by a passerby at a junction in the Sanjay Gandhi National Park in the Mumbai suburb of Borivali on February 14, 2001. Fifteen minutes prior to the grisly discovery, witnesses observed two unidentified persons force Anand into the passenger seat of his car and drive away. Police speculated that the minor actor, last seen in *Kuch Khatti Kuch Meethi* (2001), was the victim of warring factions within the Indian Mafia, a confederation of criminal groups that industry sources estimate finance 60 percent of all Bollywood films. Investigators theorized that Anand's sudden rise to prosperity was bankrolled by the Chhota Shakeel gang, bitter rivals of the Abu Salem gang. The actor, suspected of switching loyalties from one group to the other, was murdered in retaliation. To date, Anand's execution-style killing remains unsolved.

Further Reading

"Film Artist Dinesh Anand Was Found." Press Trust of India, February 15, 2001.

Aquino, José Luis *see* Appendix 1

Arbuckle, Roscoe "Fatty" (M-acquitted)

The most famous film comic of the early silent era, Roscoe "Fatty" Arbuckle's precipitous fall from grace due to an ill-advised booze party over Labor Day weekend in 1921, has the elements of a Greek tragedy. In the wake of these contested events lay the death of a 25-year-old actress, the personal ruin of a film legend's career, public outcry over the lack of Hollywood's morals, and the film industry's frantic creation of a self-imposed censorship office designed to soothe the ruffled feathers of society at large. Born Roscoe Conkling Arbuckle in Smith Center, Kansas, on March 24, 1887, "Fatty" (a hurtful name he detested) was seemingly pre-destined to bear the hated moniker. He weighed 14 pounds at birth. His physically abusive father, a farmer who drifted in and out of his life, moved the family to Santa Ana, California, when Arbuckle was two then left them to prospect for gold. Raised by his mother, the youngster was soon cutting school to hang out at a local theatre, the Grand Opera House. There in the summer of 1895 he was pressed into replacing

Disproving the adage "Everyone loves a fat man," the public and Hollywood turned on Roscoe "Fatty" Arbuckle, the popular silent screen comedian, in the deadly aftermath of a wild booze party on Labor Day weekend 1921. Arbuckle was pilloried in the press as a rapist-killer and, although acquitted of all charges after a third trial, was personally and professionally ruined. He died of a heart attack in 1933 while attempting a film comeback.

a missing cast member in a comedy sketch performed by the Frank Bacon Stock Company. A modest success, he was paid 50 cents a week, but more importantly became a fixture at the theatre through 1899 filling in whenever visiting acts needed a juvenile replacement. Arbuckle was 12, and tipping the scales at 215 pounds, when his mother died and he moved to Watsonville, California, to live with his father, and later, stepmother. He performed at the city's Victory Theatre, prior to moving again with the family to San Jose, California, where his father opened a restaurant. When not helping out in the family business, Arbuckle made the rounds of amateur contests in local venues like the Unique Theatre where he impressed all with his pleasant singing voice. In 1904, the teenager was working in the restaurant when showmen Jesse Lasky and Sid Grauman, Jr., dropped by and someone requested that he sing. Grauman's father was so taken with

Arbuckle's voice that he hired him at $17.50 a week to croon illustrated songs at the Unique Theatre, which he owned. An impromptu singing performance orchestrated by Grauman, Sr. led to Arbuckle's hiring by theatre owner Alexander Pantages to perform at his Portola Café in San Francisco for one year and also to tour the West Coast on the Pantages Circuit. Ironically, Pantages was arrested in 1929 and charged with the rape of a 17-year-old vaudeville dancer, Eunice Pringle, in the office of his Pantages Theatre in Hollywood. Convicted and sentenced to 50 years, Pantages was acquitted in a second trial, but was ruined emotionally and financially.

In 1906, Arbuckle was earning $50 a week singing at the Star Theatre in Portland, Oregon when a fateful meeting with Australian comedian and theatre owner Leon Errol led to an invaluable career opportunity. Although Arbuckle took a pay cut to sign with the Errol Company, what he lost in salary was more than made up for in professional experience. Touring with the company throughout the United States and Canada, the rotund performer learned every aspect of performing from burlesque comedy to stage craft to make-up. By 1908 when the 20 year old signed with the Elwood Tabloid Musical Company, he was a polished performer who moved with amazing physical grace for a man weighing 266 pounds. In Los Angeles with new wife Minta Durfee, an $18 a week vaudeville dancer he married in August 1908, Arbuckle agreed in July 1909 to appear in the celluloid one-reeler, *Ben's Kid*, for William Selig, the first film producer to set up in Hollywood. Arbuckle made a few more short films for Selig, but spent most of his career until 1913 traveling with various companies in the U.S., Japan, and China. In April 1913, the baby-faced comic performer joined the Keystone Film Company run by comedy legend Mack Sennett. The film pioneer had made a small fortune grinding out frenetic comedy shorts combining slapstick ("Keystone Kops") with pretty girls ("bathing beauties") all directed to an audi-

A former chairman of the Republican National Committee and U.S. postmaster general in President Harding's administration, Will H. Hays owed his $100,000-a-year career as a Tinseltown censor to a public long tired of the lack of morals portrayed in Hollywood films and those associated with them. The Arbuckle scandal was the tipping point in the decision by studio czars to appoint Hays the head of the Motion Picture Producers and Distributors of America, Inc., an "in-house" organization set up to regulate the moral content of films through a production code. One of Hays' first acts was to blacklist Arbuckle. Will Hays stepped down in 1945 although the Code remained remain relatively unchanged until 1966 (courtesy Lilly Library, Indiana University, Bloomington, Indiana).

ence he felt possessed the average intelligence of an 11 year old. Beginning with his first Keystone one-reeler in May 1913, *The Gangsters*, Arbuckle expanded his comedic range especially in a series of shorts (*Passions, He Had Three*, 1913; *For the Love of Mabel*, 1913; *A Misplaced Foot*, 1914) opposite first-rate comedienne Mabel Normand. In 1914, Arbuckle directed his first film, *Barnyard Flirtations*, a one-reeler in which he also starred. By the end of his association with Keystone (and its variant Keystone-Triangle) in 1916, Arbuckle had appeared in, written, and directed numerous shorts alongside top flight comedic talent like Charlie Chaplin, Chester Conklin, and Ford Sterling. Like most performers in the Mack Sennett stable, Arbuckle was woefully underpaid. A major star by 1916, the now accomplished filmmaker had risen from a $5 a week player to the $200 a week backbone of the Keystone studio. In August 1916, he left Keystone and formed his own production company, the Comique Film Corporation, underwritten by Paramount Pictures, with its films to be distributed through Famous Players–Lasky. Under the agreement, Arbuckle was given total artistic control over his films, a salary of $1,000 a day, and a guarantee of 25 percent of the profits. Remarkably, the contract guaranteed Arbuckle an annual income of over $1 million. Now his own man, Arbuckle entered into his most productive period as writer-performer-director offering an unknown vaudevillian, Buster Keaton, a place in his stock company. Together the comic geniuses and loyal friends made some 15 films together including *The Butcher Boy* (1917), *Fatty at Coney Island* (1917), *Out West* (1918), *Moonshine* (1918), and *The Hayseed* (1918).

When Arbuckle made his first feature film in 1919, *The Round Up*, he was already an international star who was unable to venture out in public without being mobbed by adoring fans. Despite the popularity of Arbuckle's movies and films in general in the late Teens and early 1920s, however, there was a strong feeling in the country that both the content of Hollywood's films and the private lives of its stars was somehow morally lacking. Prohibition took effect in January 1920, but onscreen drinking was portrayed as glamorous while "flappers," good-time girls seemingly engaged in an unending party, became a stock character in many motion pictures. In the Hollywood community, the private lives of the stars were found to be wanting by many Americans. Mary Pickford, "America's Sweetheart," divorced husband Owen Moore in March 1920, and waited only 25 days before marrying another iconic movie star, Douglas Fairbanks. Top film director William Desmond Taylor (see entry) would be murdered on February 2, 1922 and the fallout from the unsolved crime would claim the blossoming career of actress Mary Miles Minter, and destroy Mabel Normand, already established as a top-flight film comedienne. Another top Paramount star, he-man matinee idol Wallace Reid, would die a morphine addict in a private sanatorium in 1923. The Roscoe "Fatty" Arbuckle scandal of 1921, however, proved to be the flashpoint for public outrage against the so-called excesses of Hollywood that were to follow. More historically important for the U.S. motion picture industry, the whole shocking affair ushered in the studio moguls' appointment in 1922 of Will H. Hays, a former Postmaster General under President Warren G. Harding. As head of the Motion Picture Producers and Distributors of America, Inc., Hays was charged with improving the tattered image of the industry in the face of public outcry for some form of outside censorship. In 1930, the organization then known as the Hays Office created the Motion Picture Production Code, Hollywood's official code of what was and was not permissible to be depicted in motion pictures.

While anti–Hollywood feeling was simmering in the country as it prepared to celebrate Labor Day weekend in 1921, it had yet to touch the beloved comic who had six feature films as well as 21 shorts currently running in Los Angeles alone with another three unreleased features in the can for Paramount. On Saturday, September 3, Arbuckle, with buddies director Fred Fischbach and actor Lowell Sherman, drove his $35,000 custom-made Pierce-Arrow from Hollywood to San Francisco to celebrate his success with a weekend party in a twelfth-floor suite in the city's famed St. Francis hotel. The next day, Arbuckle contacted a local bootlegger and ordered several bottles of bourbon and gin for an all-day party. Despite Prohibition being the law of the land, booze parties were so common in the luxury hotel that employees, bribed with alcohol or money, turned a blind eye to the practice. Across town in the Palace Hotel, the other principal in the impending tragedy, 25-year-old actress Virginia Rappe (Rappay), was with her manager, Al Semnacher, and a friend, Bambina Maude Delmont. Rappe, a beautiful one-time nude model, was generally regarded in the film colony as an opportunistic wannabe of questionable morals. By the time the aspiring actress was sixteen she had already weathered at least five abortions. In Hollywood in 1917, Rappe caught the eye of producer-director Henry "Pathé" Lehrman who cast her in a few films including *A Twilight Baby* (1920). Although she rebuffed his proposal of marriage, Rappe allowed the director to use his influence to keep her name in movie magazines. Minta Durfee, Arbuckle's wife and anything but a disinterested observer, later told anyone who would listen Mack Sennett twice had to shut down his studio "because she was spreading lice and some sort of venereal disease." According to those close to Semnacher and Rappe, the actress was in San Francisco that Labor Day weekend to undergo yet another abortion.

On Sunday, September 4, at least 15–20 of the comic's friends dropped by Arbuckle's suite to drink and listen to the Victrola including Semnacher, Rappe, Maude Delmont, and two showgirls, Alice Blake and Zey Prevon. As the party escalated throughout the afternoon, Delmont, overheated from downing ten scotches in an hour, changed into a pair of Lowell Sherman's pajamas. While every writer who has since chronicled the events in Rooms 1219, 1220, and 1221 agree that what actually occurred there can never truly be known, there is some general consensus. Rappe, who knew Arbuckle, quickly became drunk and probably passed out in one of the bedrooms. Arbuckle maintained when he left the company to look after Rappe in the bathroom she was painfully vomiting into the toilet. Thinking Rappe would just sleep off the booze and be okay, Arbuckle placed her in his bed in Room 1221, changed out of his pajamas, and rejoined the party. Sometime later, Rappe awoke screaming in agony and, tearing off her clothes, loudly maintained she was dying. Interestingly, several people familiar with the woman acknowledged Rappe habitually tore her clothes off when drunk and usually accused someone of attacking her. Accounts vary as to the methods used to treat the hysterical Rappe — she was placed in a tub of cold water, Arbuckle applied ice to her thigh or vulva (perhaps the source of the rumor the comic used ice or another foreign object to violate the woman). Arbuckle called the front desk for the house doctor, Arthur Beardslee, and when he could not be found the management sent up Dr. Olav Kaarboe. When Kaarboe arrived, Rappe had been moved down the hall to Room 1227 away from the ongoing party in Arbuckle's suite. Kaarboe asked Rappe if she was injured and when she replied in the negative decided she was just drunk. Dr. Beardslee checked on Rappe hours later and found her in severe abdominal pain. Asked if she had been attacked by Arbuckle or anyone else, Rappe responded emphatically, "No." The next day when Beardslee examined her he found a copious amount of blood in her urine.

Arbuckle was back in Los Angeles celebrating the debut at Grauman's Egyptian Theatre of his new smash, *Gasoline Gus*, when after three days languishing in the St. Francis, Rappe was transferred to the Wakefield Sanatorium. The aspiring actress died there on September 9, 1921 from what the medical report characterized as peritonis brought on by a bladder ruptured by an "extreme amount of external force." Again, controversy surrounds the death. An autopsy revealed Rappe had recently undergone an abortion partially responsible (with the presence of venereal disease) as the cause of a "running abscess in her vagina for upwards of six weeks." Learning of Rappe's death, reporters questioned employees of the St. Francis and were stonewalled. Maude Delmont was more cooperative maintaining Arbuckle had openly lusted after Rappe for many years and forced himself on her in the bedroom of the St. Francis. According to Delmont, Rappe accused the comic of attacking her. Based on Delmont's testimony, Roscoe "Fatty" Arbuckle, Hollywood's biggest comedy star, was returned to San Francisco on September 10, 1921 and later charged with manslaughter. Publishing magnate William Randolph Hearst saw in Arbuckle's misfortune the perfect avenue by which to sell a ton of newspapers. Both Hearst papers, *The Los Angeles Examiner* and *The San Francisco Examiner*, printed sensationalized editorials basically implying Arbuckle was a sex killer. Church and civic groups throughout the country cried for the screen star's blood and by extension criticized the excesses of the entire film community. Bowing to the power of the press and public opinion, Paramount withdrew the comedian's films from circulation and systematically distanced itself from him. Filmdom's ultimate betrayal of Arbuckle would come later on April 18, 1922 when following the exoneration of the funny man, Will Hays acting as a front man for the studios used the power of his office to ban Arbuckle from the screen.

In the meantime, San Francisco District Attorney Matthew Brady faced a serious problem. His star witness, Bambina Maude Delmont, was a liar and a fraud. None of her wildly damning accusations against Arbuckle could be substantiated either by other party-goers or the physical evidence. In fact, her claims that Rappe told her Arbuckle had "hurt" her were contradicted by various doctors who had been told by the dying woman he had not. In fact, "Delmont" was just one of numerous aliases along with "Montgomery" and "Rothenberg." By the time of Arbuckle's arrest (based largely on Delmont's fabricated testimony), the woman had already faced fifty charges on crimes like bigamy, fraud, racketeering, and extortion. The self-described "gown model" was better known to police in L.A. and San Francisco as a con woman who was on hire by unscrupulous attorneys to help them obtain compromising photos to use in divorce cases and blackmail. Brady, realizing the case against Arbuckle and his own future political aspirations would be irrevocably compromised, decided to arrest Delmont on a charge of bigamy thereby making her ineligible to testify. The testimony of doctors disputing the woman's assertions (and by extension casting doubt on Arbuckle's guilt) he simply suppressed.

Arbuckle's first trial for manslaughter began in San Francisco Superior Court with jury selection on November 14, 1921. The comic's defense team introduced evidence Rappe, portrayed by Brady as an innocent, had in fact undergone several abortions and had been repeatedly treated for venereal disease and chronic cystitis, a possible causal factor in the infection that claimed her life. Model and party guest Betty Campbell testified Brady threatened to jail her should she refuse to testify against Arbuckle. Any pro–Arbuckle momentum gained by these revelations, however, was negated by the prior announcement in the press that the film star would also be prosecuted for violating the Volstead Act, the Prohibition law, stemming from the booze party in the St. Francis. After 43 hours of deliberation and 22 ballots the jury hopelessly deadlocked on December 4, 1921 voting 10 to 2, in favor of acquittal. Trial two for manslaughter began on January 11, 1922 and this time the jury deliberated for 44 hours and voted 13 times prior to returning with a deadlocked verdict of 10 to 2, *for* conviction. Trial three began on March 6, 1922 and when the jury received the case six days later they needed only five minutes to acquit with the following note read to the court:

"Acquittal is not enough for Roscoe Arbuckle. We feel that a great injustice has been done him. We feel also that it was only our plain duty to give him this exoneration, under the evidence, for there was not the slightest proof adduced to connect him in any way with the commission of a crime. He was manly throughout the case, and told a straightforward story on the witness stand, which we all believed. The happening at the hotel was an unfortunate affair for which Arbuckle, so

the evidence shows, was in no way responsible. We wish him success, and hope that the American people will take the judgement of fourteen men and women ... that Roscoe Arbuckle is entirely innocent and free from blame."

It did not happen. Arbuckle, already $750,000 in debt from the trial, was targeted by the Internal Revenue Service for $100,000 in back taxes, and forced to sell his estate. Additionally, the government garnished any future earnings until the debt was repaid. Exonerated in the courts, Arbuckle was anxious to return to work in order to pay off the IRS as well as friends like Buster Keaton who loaned him money throughout his long legal ordeal. Then on April 18, 1922, Will Hays blacklisted Arbuckle in the film industry. While the ban was officially rescinded nine months later, Arbuckle was damaged goods in the eyes of a public still largely believing the Hearst-fed hype about his immorality. Friends like Keaton stepped in permitting Arbuckle to work as a writer and director under assumed names like "William Goodrich." After announcing he was through with acting, Arbuckle signed a deal with Reel Comedies to produce and direct 13 uninspired comedies for which he received no film credit. The former superstar kept busy performing in vaudeville and ill-advisedly investing in a hotel and supper club just before the Depression. In 1932, studio head Jack Warner offered Arbuckle a series of six Vitaphone two-reelers in which he was slated to appear *in front* of the camera.

Hey, Pop!, released November 12, 1932, marked the first time in nearly a decade Roscoe "Fatty" Arbuckle appeared under his own name in any type of motion picture. On June 28, 1933, Arbuckle, 46, finished shooting *In the Dough* earlier in the day and celebrated his one year wedding anniversary with third wife Addie McPhail and friends in a New York City restaurant. Afterwards, he retired to his suite in the Park Central Hotel where he died peacefully asleep in his bed from a heart attack around 2:15 A.M. the next morning. Stalwart friend Will Rogers, would eloquently eulogize, "Those who demanded their pound of flesh finally received their satisfaction. Roscoe "Fatty" Arbuckle accommodated them by dying, and from a broken heart. He brought much happiness to many, and never wronged a soul. The Lord will pass on his innocence or guilt now, and not the reformers." On June 30, 1933, a public wake attended by thousands of mourners was conducted at Frank E. Campbell's Funeral Church on Broadway and 66th Street, the site seven years earlier of the Rudolph Valentino wake. The unfairly maligned comedy giant was cremated in accordance with his wishes and the ashes scattered by his widow Addie McPhail over the Pacific Ocean off the coast of Santa Monica on September 6, 1934. In 1975, *The Wild Party*, a feature film "inspired" by the events of the 1921 scandal was released starring James Coco as a character suggested by Roscoe "Fatty" Arbuckle.

Further Reading

Chermak, Steven, and Frankie Y. Bailey. *Crimes and Trials of the Century*. 2 vols. Westport, CT: Greenwood, 2007.
Edmonds, Andy. *Frame-Up! The Untold Story of Roscoe "Fatty" Arbuckle*. New York: W. Morrow, 1991.
Guild, Leo. *The Fatty Arbuckle Case*. New York: Paperback Library, 1962.
Oderman, Stuart. *Roscoe "Fatty" Arbuckle: A Biography of the Silent Film Comedian, 1887–1933*. Jefferson, NC: McFarland, 1994.
www.mary-miles-minter.com.
Yallop, David A. *The Day the Laughter Stopped: The True Story of Fatty Arbuckle*. New York: St. Martin's, 1976.
Young, Robert. *Roscoe "Fatty" Arbuckle: A Bio-Bibliography*. Westport, CT: Greenwood, 1994.

Arcady, John (V)

"It was a senseless, horrible thing that happened. They don't carry much money," said the owner of Cincinnati's Towne Taxi regarding the murder of driver John Arcady. On September 27, 1999, the 49-year-old's body was found slumped over the wheel of his idling cab at 4802 Winneste Avenue in the Cincinnati suburb of Winton Terrace. Killed instantly by a single gunshot wound to the back of the head, Arcady still had a toothpick in the corner of his mouth and a foot on the brake. Arcady, a former touring drummer with the groups the Platters, Los Bravos, and the Hager Twins, often drove double shifts to support himself while still drumming for the Cincinnati-based Mary Ann Kindel Band.

Police, acting on eyewitness accounts, searched for three blacks seen fleeing the scene. A few days later, brother and sister Lemar Goss, 19, Andrea Goss, 18, and their relative Denise Lipscomb, 26, were arrested and charged with aggravated murder during the commission of a robbery. Another suspect, Sion Graham, 21, was later arrested and charged with complicity in supplying the gun to Lipscomb, and in driving the getaway car. On the night of the murder, Arcady picked up the trio and drove them to a spot near Lipscomb's apartment where the woman shot him in the head during a robbery attempt. In exchange for their tes-

timony against Lipscomb, the Goss siblings pleaded guilty to reduced charges of robbery and involuntary manslaughter, and were sentenced to prison terms of 23 years each. In October 2000, Lipscomb was found guilty of aggravated murder, but avoided the death penalty when a jury recommended life in prison without the possibility of parole for at least 43 years. Lipscomb will be 69 years old before her first parole hearing. Sion Graham, Lipscomb's boyfriend, pleaded guilty to involuntary manslaughter and to using a gun to commit aggravated robbery, and received a 23-year prison sentence.

Further Reading

Campbell, Laurel. "Cab Driver Found Shot to Death." *Cincinnati Post*, Sept. 29, 1999, sec. A, p. 1.

Bachemin, Johnnie (V)

During five years of playing Tuesday through Saturday nights at the French Quarter Royal Sonesta Hotel and its popular nightclub, the Mystick Den Lounge, the Johnnie Bachemin Trio built a strong local and tourist following performing Broadway tunes and jazz. Group leader and pianist Johnnie Bachemin was the main attraction at the Bourbon Street landmark. In the early 1970s while an understudy to Sammy Davis, Jr., in the Broadway show *Mr. Lucky*, Bachemin suffered an onstage fall during rehearsal that ended his dancing career. Turning to piano, Bachemin twice appeared on *The Ed Sullivan Show*, and reached a career peak when the Louisiana Symphony Orchestra honored him in November 1997 by performing the world premiere of his composition "Pyramids: A Classical Jazz Rhapsody." Orchestrated by Jay Weigel, director of the New Orleans Contemporary Arts Center, plans were set with Bachemin to record a CD of the piece in August 1998. Liberace, the jazz pianist's friend, bequeathed Bachemin a signature candelabrum. At the time of his death, Bachemin was finishing up another collaboration with Weigel, "Millennium Suite."

On Tuesday, June 9, 1998, friends became concerned when the 74-year-old pianist failed to appear for his gig at the Bourbon Street lounge. The next morning around 9:00 A.M. they went to his apartment in the 1700 block of Pauger Street in the Faubourg Marigny district of New Orleans and found Bachemin, hands and feet bound, dead in his bedroom from a slit throat and numerous hammer blows to the head. Although there were no signs of forced entry, the apartment had been tossed in an apparent robbery scenario. Bachemin's white 1998 Pontiac Bonneville was missing, but police recovered the vehicle a couple of days later after a motorist reported seeing a car burning in a sugar cane field along Bayou Lafourche north of Thibodaux. Earlier in the day, Southland Mall security guards in Houma, Louisiana notified authorities after two men used the dead man's stolen credit card the day before. When the pair, accompanied by two women, returned to the mall the next day for more purchases, security took them into custody. The men, one a white man with gold teeth, escaped with the women in Bachemin's Bonneville. County sheriffs recognized the description of the men and after witnesses in the mall were able to identify them from a photo lineup arrest warrants were issued for Gary "Duck" Harrall, a 21-year-old white man, and black 18-year-old Travis "Sugar" Johnson. As days passed without an arrest, New Orleans police alerted the Big Easy's gay community that the men, and others, could be targeting the city's homosexual population. Houma lounge owner Curtis Moon was murdered on May 31, 1998 in circumstances similar enough to Bachemin's to cause authorities to strongly suspect the cases were connected.

Instead of hiding out in an out-of-the way locale, Harrall and Johnson finally landed in Hollywood, California. While cops scoured the country for the suspected murderers, "Duck" and "Sugar" visited Disneyland and Knott's Berry Farm where they were thrown out by amusement park security while trying to slip in without paying. In Anaheim, California, the pair's repeated attempts to pawn jewelry to purchase guns prompted the owner to call police. Harrall and Johnson, asleep on a Greyhound bus bound for Las Vegas, were arrested by FBI agents at a bus station in Henderson, Nevada on June 25, 1998. Travis "Sugar" Johnson escaped a possible death sentence in Bachemin's slaying by accepting the prosecutor's offer of an automatic life sentence. In his 80-page confession, Johnson admitted to helping "Duck" Harrall murder Curtis Moon for money to support their drug habit. On September 7, 2000, Harrall also took a prosecution deal of life imprisonment in lieu of a near certain death penalty conviction.

Further Reading

Philbin, Walt. "Orleans Musician Found Murdered at Apartment," *New Orleans Times-Picayune*, June 11, 1998, sec. A, p. 1.

Bacon, David G.G. (V)

Bacon (born March 24, 1914, in Jamaica Plain, Massachusetts) acted in small roles in the films *Ten Gentlemen from West Point* (1942), *The Boss of Big Town* (1942), *Crash Dive* (1943), *Gals, Incorporated* (1943), and *Someone to Remember* (1943). The 29-year-old actor had just finished appearing as "Bob Barton" the title character's alter ego in the 1943 Republic serial, *The Masked Marvel*, when he died under mysterious circumstances in the Venice section of Los Angeles on September 12, 1943. A witness saw the British car Bacon was driving weave across Washington Boulevard near Thatcher Avenue, jump a curb, and stop in a beanfield. Another witness rushed to the scene and found Bacon, clad only in denim shorts, lying on the ground between two bean stacks "kicking and squirming" from a 6-inch deep stab wound in his back. The good Samaritan pulled a sweater from the car and placed it beneath the dying man's head as a pillow. The actor died at the scene unable to identify his killer. The police investigation revealed that Bacon kept a personal telephone book filled with encrypted notes and phone numbers. Since late August 1930 the actor had been paying rent on a small apartment about a mile from the Hollywood Hills home he shared with his pregnant wife, former concert singer Greta Keller. Bacon told his Austrian-born wife the apartment was for a handyman he planned to hire to maintain their home. Based on witness descriptions of a man seen riding with Bacon in his car earlier on the day of the murder, and the fact that the sweater was too small to fit the victim, police launched a manhunt for a "slight young man" about 21 years of age. A few days later the investigation was derailed after Blakely Christopher Patterson, a 22-year-old slightly built hospital orderly, admitted he had fabricated a story in which he claimed to have been a witness to a third party extortion attempt on the actor. Asked by detectives why he created the elaborate fiction, Patterson responded, "I thought I could get into the movies if I had my picture in the paper." Patterson was sentenced to 90 days in the L.A. City Jail for making a false police report, but all but the ten days already served were suspended on condition he return to his home in Hibbing, Minnesota. Next, Charles R. White, a 23-year-old Santa Monica man, drunkenly confessed to Bacon's murder and then recanted. Twice arrested by police, White was ruled out as a suspect after authorities determined he could only supply details of the crime already disclosed in press accounts. Bacon's murder was never solved.

Further Reading

"Author of Hoax Story in Bacon Murder Jailed." *Los Angeles Times*, Sept. 21, 1943, sec. A, p. 2.

Baloi, Gito (V)

One of South Africa's leading jazz musicians, Baloi was born in Maputo in the war-torn country of Mozambique in 1964. Learning to play music on discarded paraffin tins and water reeds, Baloi was 14 when he borrowed a bass guitar for his first public concerts. He toured extensively in Mozambique with the band Afro 78, and formed Pongola in 1986 ultimately settling in South Africa to escape the strife in his home country. In 1987, the bassist-vocalist co-founded the jazz/jive fusion trio Tananas with drummer Steve Newman and guitarist Ian Herman. Combining Baloi's knowledge of traditional African music with the co-members' innovative jazz fusion background, Tananas became a hit with both black and white South Africans. The group signed with independent South African label Shifty Records in 1988 and later that year released their revolutionary self-titled debut album, *Tananas*. A skillful blend of several musical styles (jazz, township jive, Mozambican salsa), the record cemented the group's cult status in South Africa, and led to tours on the African continent as well as in Japan, France, and Sweden. Other successful albums on different labels followed (*Spiral*, 1990; *Time*, 1992) prior to the group's disbanding in 1994 to pursue different musical paths. Tananas briefly reformed with its original members in 1996 to release the album *Seed*, but Baloi spent most of the 1990s as either a solo performer, a founder and encourager of other groups, or in collaboration with international artists like Sting and Tracy Chapman. In 1992, the bassist toured France with musicians from Zaire and Mali, and formed the bands (Skabenga and Somewhere Else. Baloi's first solo album, *Ekaya*, was released in 1996 and peaked at Number 2 on the Johannesburg Metro Radio charts. Albums *Na Ku Randza* and *Herbs and Roots* followed in 1997 and 2002, respectively.

Baloi, 39, was returning from a poorly attended show with Landscape Prayers' Nibs van der Spuy in Pretoria's Lucit Candle Gardens to his home in the Kensington district of Johannesburg when he was shot at three times by two gunmen in a central street in that city in the early morning hours of April 4, 2004. Struck in the neck, the musician managed to drive his car fifty yards before getting out, staggering a few feet, then collapsing dead on the pavement. The robbers took Baloi's wallet, but left his instruments in the car. South Africa, long known as the murder capital of the world, has a crime rate estimated at eight times the overall homicide rate of the United States. A spokesman for the African National Congress Youth League characterized the dead musician as "an icon for millions of young people" who contributed "to the creation of a free South Africa through art." Acting on a public tip in late April 2004, police arrested four men (ages 21–28) in connection with the murder and confiscated three guns, two of them unlicensed. As of May 2005, however, no one has been charged with Baloi's murder and the case remains open.

Further Reading

"Tributes for Slain Bass Player." SAPA (South African Press Association), April 5, 2004.

Bany, Michael W. (V)

Bany (pronounced Baney), bassist for the Cincinnati-based band The Goshorn Brothers, was a self-taught musician who had been active on the local music scene for more than 25 years. Around 2:30 A.M. on December 29, 1995, the popular 41-year-old bassist was walking to his car after completing a gig at Tommy's on Main, a nightclub in the Over-the-Rhine section of near north downtown Cincinnati, when he was approached by an armed man and his lookout companion. Bany handed over $60.00 in cash to the robber, but failing to respond quickly enough to the question, "Is your car automatic or stick shift?" was shot once in the back of the head. Both men fled the scene on foot.

Less than one week passed before an anonymous tip led to the capture of gunman Walter L. "Fatman" Raglin, an 18-year-old career criminal who had been arrested 15 times since November 1994 on various charges (carrying a concealed weapon, resisting arrest, disorderly conduct). Convicted on a concealed weapons charge in September 1995 and placed on two year probation, Raglin was living in the Turning Point, a fifty bed residential drug treatment facility, when he walked away from the halfway house on October 6, 1995. Raglin's accomplice, 15-year-old lookout man

Darnell "Bubba" Lowery, was arrested and charged as an adult on charges of aggravated murder and robbery.

Tried separately, Lowery was convicted of the charges on October 10, 1996, and sentenced to the maximum prison term of 33 years. At his trial, Raglin admitted spending several hours drinking and smoking marijuana prior to going out to rob someone for more drug money. "We was (sic) desperate for money," Raglin said in an interview with police. "I'm like, 'come on,' let's rob this man ... I fired the gun at him. I didn't know where I hit him at. I wasn't trying to kill him or nothing like that." Convicted of aggravated murder on October 16, 1996, Raglin was later sentenced to death. An appeal for a new trial based on prosecutorial misconduct was rejected in June 1999. The Michael W. Bany Scholarship Fund set up by the murdered musician's family and friends established the annual "Cincinnati Area Music Awards" (CAMMYS), an event recognizing the accomplishments of local musicians while bestowing a lifetime achievement award on a recipient in Bany's name.

Further Reading

Horn, Dan. "'Panicked' Raglin Fired Deadly Shot." *Cincinnati Post*, October 16, 1996, sec. A, p. 13.

Barrett, Carlton (Lloyd) (V)

As a child, "Carly" Barrett (born Kingston, Jamaica, on December 17, 1950) fashioned his first drum kit out of empty paint cans. With older brother, bassist Aston ("Family Man") Barrett, he formed the Hippy Boys in 1967, later graduating to session work before forming The Upsetters. At producer Lee "Scratch" Perry's studio in Kingston, the Barretts backed reggae star Bob Marley on his pioneering 1969 albums *Soul Rebels* and *Soul Revolution*. While a member of Marley's group, The Wailers, Barrett developed a signature "One Drop" style of drumming which emphasized every fourth beat. With Aston, Barrett formed the driving rhythm section of The Wailers and helped Marley achieve international stardom. In addition to being the most influential reggae drummer in history, Carly Barrett co-wrote the Wailers' songs "Them Belly Full (But We Hungry)" and "Talkin' Blues." Following Bob Marley's death from brain cancer in 1981, Barrett and other members of The Wailers were paid a flat fee by the Estate as a settlement against any future royalties from the star's music. Barrett received a

check for $42,000, and later toured with a version of The Wailers.

Late in the evening of April 17, 1987, Good Friday, the 36-year-old drummer parked his car in front of his Kingston home after returning from a grocery run to buy chicken. Barrett was walking across the courtyard to the front door when an assailant walked up behind him and pumped two bullets execution-style in the back of the drummer's head. His wife, Albertine "Tina" Barrett, 35, was inside the house watching television with their three children when she heard the gunfire. Barrett, who had just returned from a concert in Miami and was set to tour Europe with The Wailers beginning on May 14, was pronounced dead at the scene. Days later, Albertine Barrett, and her lover, Glenroy Carter, a 34-year-old Jamaican taxi cab driver from Brooklyn, New York, were arrested and charged with the murder. According to the police theory of the crime, the couple paid Junior Neil, a 41-year-old mason, $1,123 to kill Barrett because he had beaten his wife Tina out of jealousy. In custody, Neil admitted to receiving some of the money, but denied killing Barrett. In October 1991, Albertine Barrett was sentenced to 7 years in prison along with her confederates for conspiracy to commit murder. (See entries Junior Brathwaite and Peter Tosh).

Further Reading

Talevski, Nick. *The Encyclopedia of Rock Obituaries*. London; New York: Omnibus, 1999.
White, Timothy. *Catch a Fire: The Life of Bob Marley*. Rev. and enl. ed. London: Omnibus, 2006.

Barsi, Judith (V)

In show business since the age of four, the blonde and blue-eyed Barsi (born Judith Eva Barsi on June 6, 1978) had logged over 50 television commercials and numerous appearances on TV shows like *St. Elsewhere*, *Punky Brewster*, *Cagney & Lacey*, and *Growing Pains* by the time she was ten. A pituitary gland problem for which she received hormone injections to spur growth made the child look much younger than age her and, consequently, a casting director's dream. Barsi was six years old when she portrayed "Kimberly," the three-year-old daughter of convicted murderer and former Green Beret doctor Jeffrey MacDonald, in the made-for-television movie *Fatal Vision* (1984). Theatrical motion pictures, however, were the future and in 1987 she appeared in *Slam Dance* and *Jaws IV: The Revenge*. At the time of the tragedy, Barsi's final role (voice work in the animated feature *All Dogs Go to Heaven*, 1989) had yet to be released.

While young Judith's career blossomed, her parents' marriage disintegrated into a daily round of frightening threats issued by Joseph Barsi, a 56-year-old self-employed plumber, against his wife, Maria. Neighbors reported the couple often argued. Urged by a friend to leave her moody alcoholic husband, Maria Barsi confessed she was afraid to do so because he had threatened to kill her and Judith then torch the house. Joe Barsi confided to an associate that he was dissatisfied in the marriage, considered his wife a lousy housekeeper, and darkly intimated that she was driving him crazy. As time passed, life in the Barsi home at 22100 Michale Avenue in northwestern Los Angeles County became increasingly intolerable. Uneasy neighbors commented among themselves about Joe's over-protectiveness concerning his daughter and how he never let her go anywhere alone because he was afraid she would run away. Even the young actress' agent at the Harry Gold Talent Agency knew of the domestic discord in the Barsi household.

On Friday, July 22, 1988, Maria Barsi had endured enough. Despite Joe's past threats of violence, she informed him of her plans to divorce him immediately. She rented a $700 a month apartment for herself and Judith and planned to cash her daughter's $12,000 tax refund check before he could get his hands on it. Five days later on July 27, a neighbor heard a loud bang at 8:30 A.M. and thought, "He's done it." Minutes later smoke began billowing out of the Barsi home. Neighbors fought the blaze with garden hoses while awaiting the arrival of the fire department. Inside the house, authorities made a series of grisly discoveries that were all too easy for case hardened forensics experts to reconstruct. Joe Barsi had made good on his threat. He shot daughter Judith in the head as she lay in her bed and murdered Maria as she fled down the hallway in terror. He doused both bodies in gasoline, splashed the bedroom and hall, lit it then went into the garage where he shot himself in the head. The killer was found clutching a .32-caliber handgun, the empty gas can three feet away. The cap of the can was discovered in Judith's bedroom. According to her entry on the findagrave website, Judith and her mother share a grave in Forest Lawn Memorial Park in the Hollywood Hills. The young actress' plot remained unmarked for 16 years before dedicated fans purchased a marker through a Memorial Fund in 2004. The marker reads: "In Memory of the Lovely Judith Eva Barsi — 1978–1988 — Our Concrete Angel — Yep! Yep! Yep!"

Further Reading

"Child Actress, Mother Shot and Set Afire." United Press International, July 28, 1988. www.findagrave.com.

Beasts of Satan (M)

On January 17, 1998, Chiara Marino, 19, and her boyfriend Fabio Tollis, the 16-year-old lead singer for Beasts of Satan, were last seen together leaving Midnight, a heavy metal rock club in Milan, Italy, with other members of the death metal band. The couple's disappearance remained a mystery for six years until a bizarre confession from a fellow-band member implicated in another murder led shocked Italian authorities and a concerned Vatican to seriously examine the societal influence of Satanism and the occult, especially on young people. On January 25, 2004, Italian police were called to a chalet in the woods near Somma Lombardo on the northwest outskirts of Milan where they discovered in the greenhouse hair and fingers curling out of the earth. The body belonged to Mariangela Pezzotta, a 27-year-old local woman whose bedroom was found to be outfitted with black candles, goat's head skulls, and other satanic paraphernalia. Inquiries led to the arrest of her ex-boyfriend, Andrea Volpe, 27-year-old guitarist for Beasts of Satan, who quickly offered details of the grisly murder in exchange for information and the possibility of leniency in the six year old case involving the disappearance of Chiara Marino and Fabio Tollis. According to Volpe, he invited Mariangela Pezzotta to the secluded chalet where he met her with his current girlfriend. Volpe shot Pezzotta point-blank in the mouth, fearful that she would implicate him in the couple's 1998 disappearance. Volpe then contacted fellow-band member Mario Maccione, 16, who helped him bury the woman. Forensics later determined that Pezzotta had most likely been buried alive.

In a plea deal negotiated with Italian prosecutors in May 2004, Volpe filled in the grisly details surrounding the 1998 disappearances of Marino and Tollis. Fuelled by drugs and alcohol, Volpe and other Beast of Satan band members chose the petite 19-year-old Chiara Marino to personify the Virgin Mary in a ritual satanic sacrifice. Marino and the unsuspecting Tollis were driven to the secluded wood northwest of Milan. Under a full moon Volpe plunged a knife into the young woman's heart. When Tollis attempted to intervene, he was beaten to death with a hammer, and buried alongside Marino. Afterwards, Volpe, Maccione, and fellow-band member Pietro Guerrieri concluded the ritual by urinating on the grave. The occult-inspired killings fascinated Italy where, despite being home to the Vatican, an estimated 5,000 people (most between the ages of 17 and 25) are thought to be members of satanic cults. As sociologists conjectured whether the rise in Satanism was perhaps tied to the breakdown of traditional family values, the Vatican responded by offering priests a two-month long course on diabolical possession and exorcism at the Pontifical University Regina Apostolorum in Rome.

Under Italian law, defendants like Volpe who co-operate with authorities can have their cases placed on a "fast track," a procedure that allows for a speedy trial and the possibility of a drastically reduced sentence. At trial in February 2005, Volpe, the "mastermind" of the so-called occult murders, hoped for a reduced sentence of 20 years for the three murders in exchange for his testimony against other Beast of Satan members. He was disappointed. Volpe, the former guitarist who dressed in black clothes festooned with patches featuring the devil and the number 666, was sentenced to a 30 year prison term. Pietro Guerrieri, Volpe's accomplice in the double homicide, was given a 16½ year sentence while Mario Maccione, a juvenile at the time of the murders, was acquitted. Maccione, however, was tried in juvenile court in April 2005 and sentenced to 19 years. Five other members of the Beasts of Satan with links to the three killings were subsequently imprisoned on sentences ranging from 23 years to life.

Further Reading

Baker, Al. "2 Murders in Italy Linked to Satanism: Pit in Woods Yields Teenagers' Bodies." *The New York Times*, June 21, 2004, p. 3.

Behrmann, Dimitri (M-S)

Following the 1994 release of *Law-Town*, an album based on his experiences in Lawrence, Massachusetts, the 25-year-old Haitian immigrant and aspiring rap artist told an interviewer that music served as an outlet for his anger as a black man. Recently, however, Behrmann complained of insomnia and seemed depressed over his stalled music career. On June 5, 1998, the rapper picked up 27-year-old Beverly Cora, his longtime girlfriend and mother of his 5½-year-old son, at the apartment they shared in Haverhill, Massachusetts. Behrmann appeared to be in good spirits as they left for a drive around 2:30 P.M., but his mood did not last. Less than an hour later as they were driving on Route 495 near the Route 13 exit in Methuen, Massachusetts, Behrmann fired a round from a 9mm Glock semiautomatic handgun into Cora's head before shooting himself. The Toyota sedan veered off the road at 70 miles per hour, snapped a tree, and flipped over. Both victims were alive when rescuers arrived, but each died after being taken to separate hospitals. Cora's parents, who loved Behrmann and refused to blame him for their daughter's murder, requested the couple be buried together.

Further Reading

Lazar, Kay. "Highway Murder — Suicide Baffles Victims' Kin." *Boston Herald*, June 6, 1998, p. 11.

Bender, Christopher L. (V)

The youngest of six children raised by his mother in the Brockton, Massachusetts projects, Bender, 19, had a well-documented history of arrests for offenses ranging from disorderly conduct, trespassing, to possession of, and trafficking in, cocaine. He was scheduled to appear in court in December 1991 (one month prior to his murder) on four drug-related complaints including possession with intent to distribute crack within 1,000 feet of an elementary school. According to family and friends, however, Bender's interest in music signaled a dramatic turnaround in the troubled teen's life. Dropping out of school at 16, Bender recorded an album, *Baby Doll*, for Epic in 1989. Though not a success, the record drew enough industry attention to mark him as a rising star in rhythm and blues laced hip-hop. In 1991, Bender signed a $500,000, seven album recording contract with East/West Records America, a subsidiary of Atlantic Records. His album, *Draped*, was released in July 1991, and the rapper planned to travel to New York City to shoot a video for it when, many believed, jealousy in the ghetto community over his success led to the singer's murder.

At 2:20 A.M. on November 3, 1991, Bender was shot four times in the face and chest as he sat behind the wheel of his 1983 Mercedes-Benz in front of the Crescent Court housing project in

Brockton where his mother and family lived. He died a few hours later at Brockton Hospital. Also in the car, Bender's 17-year-old cousin, Jessie Starks, was uninjured, and told police that three black males wearing hooded sweatshirts approached the vehicle, fired, then fled on foot. Police reported that at least 18 shots from three different pistols had been pumped into the car. Bender's funeral service in Brockton's Full Gospel Tabernacle Church drew 500 relatives and friends. On September 2, 1993, Timothy Lucas, a 21-year-old gang member, was convicted of second-degree murder in Bender's death, and sentenced to a minimum of 15 years imprisonment. The murder was apparently the culmination of a series of altercations between rival youth groups in the projects.

Further Reading

Walker, Adrian. "Slain Brockton Singer Heard the Call of Conflicting Worlds." *Boston Globe*, Nov. 10, 1991, p. 31.

Bennison, Louis (M-S)

In films since 1914 (*Damaged Goods*), Bennison was a minor Western star in several programmers including *Oh, Johnny!* (1918), while also appearing in the title roles of two 1919 features, *Sandy Burke of the U-Bar-U* and *Speedy Meade*. By the early 1920s, however, Bennison's alcoholism had all but destroyed his motion picture career. He appeared briefly on the New York stage in legitimate theatre and vaudeville before traveling with a road company on a tour of Australia in the mid–1920s. In Australia, Bennison met the beautiful actress Margaret Lawrence, a stage veteran who had earned excellent reviews for her work in Chicago and Broadway. When the pair returned to New York City, they were already embroiled in a tempestuous love affair that estranged Bennison from his wife and child. Like Bennison, Lawrence also suffered from a drinking problem that affected her work. In the late 1920s, the producers of the Broadway play *Possession* sued the actress when they suspected that she was a no-show at a performance because she was drunk. In March 1927, the lovers worked together in a play, *The Heaven Tappers*, which closed after a brief run. Another pairing in a 1929 vaudeville sketch called "She Made Up Her Mind," was a similar disaster.

Compounding the disappointment and depression both felt in their stalled careers was Bennison's insane jealousy. The 40-year-old actress was still a strikingly handsome woman, and it maddened Bennison to see her chatting with men in nightclubs. To placate the 45-year-old actor, they often stayed home together and drank in

A minor Western star in silent films including *High Pockets* (1919), Louis Bennison saw his career destroyed by alcoholism. In the mid–1920s he met stage actress and fellow alcoholic Margaret Lawrence while they toured with a road show company in Australia. On June 9, 1929, Bennison murdered his lover, penned a poetic suicide note, then shot himself in their New York City apartment.

Lawrence's penthouse apartment on the roof of 34 East Fifty-first Street in New York City. On June 9, 1929, a concerned friend dropped by the apartment to check on her. In a visit with the actress just a few days before, their conversation had been interrupted when Bennison stormed into the room waving a gun, yelling, "This will finish us both." Alarmed when no one answered the door, Lawrence's friend notified the police, who forced entry. Inside, the apartment was littered with 40 empty liquor bottles and several glasses. A note, scribbled on the back of an envelope and found pinned to the door leading from the living room to the kitchenette, read: "The sunset has a heart. Look for us up there." Signed "Tianna," authorities later determined the script had been written by Bennison. Another note written by the actor on white correspondence paper read: "Please notify Mr. Mussen at the Lambs Club at once." In the bedroom, police found Lawrence's night gown-clad body lying in bed with her arms folded across her breast, dead from a single gunshot wound to the chest. Sprawled on the floor in a half-sitting, half-lying position with his head resting on the side of the bed was Bennison, also dead from a similar wound. The pistol lay between them on the bed. Fully dressed, except for his shoes and socks, the actor was carrying $900 in cash.

Detectives theorized that a drunken Bennison shot Lawrence while she slept, then himself. An autopsy confirmed that both victims had blood alcohol levels four times higher than the legal standard for intoxication. Interviewed at the Lambs Club, Mussen recalled that Bennison was subject to fits of depression and two years earlier after a bout of heavy drinking at the club had threatened to commit suicide.

Further Reading

"Margaret Lawrence Slain by Louis Bennison, Actor, Who Ends Life in Her Home." *The New York Times*, June 10, 1929, pp. 1, 3.

Benson, Lyric (V)

Described by her agent as the "prototypical young, struggling actress in New York," the 21-year-old blue-eyed blonde was just beginning to crack the big time with a small role in the NBC television hit, *Law & Order: Criminal Intent*, when she was murdered in April 2003. Graduating from Yale in 2002 with a bachelor's degree in theatre studies, Benson did some voice-over work in commercials, and was the featured face on American Express' Tribeca Film Festival billboards around New York City. While awaiting her "big break," the aspiring actress supported herself as a hostess at Balthazar, a trendy SoHo bistro. Shortly after graduation, Benson moved into an apartment in the Greenpoint section of Brooklyn with boyfriend, Robert Ambrosino. The 33-year-old former merchant mariner had earned some college credits and, although recently certified as an emergency medical technician, was several months from being hired as a firefighter. Known as "Fast Bobby," the unemployed Ambrosino claimed to be a former C.I.A. agent, bragged he had once shot a man, but was reticent about telling friends how he managed to pay for his expensive clothes and partying. Citing a "religious reawakening," Benson broke off their engagement in February 2003, and relocated to a third-floor apartment at 211 East Broadway in Manhattan's Chinatown district.

Ambrosino refused to accept the split and relentlessly stalked the terrified young actress. After having dessert at Balthazar with friends in the early morning hours of April 24, 2003, Benson returned to her apartment building, and rang for her mother, Deborah Janicke (visiting from North Carolina), to come downstairs and let her up. Janicke opened the door of the vestibule in time to see Robert Ambrosino come up behind her daughter, tap her on the shoulder, and as Benson turned, shoot her once in the eye with an unlicensed .45-caliber Starfire pistol before fatally shooting himself between the eyes. Benson died the next day at Bellevue Hospital surrounded by loved ones. In Ambrosino's apartment, authorities found eight handwritten notes to family and friends in which he said he loved them, and that his decision to murder Benson and himself was not "premeditated." Less than two months after her senseless killing, Benson's *Law & Order: Criminal Intent* episode aired. In it, she played a restaurant worker trying to help police catch the killer of a woman in the prime of her life. The episode ended with a brief tribute that read, "In Memory of Lyric Benson."

Further Reading

"Shattered Dreams an Actress Murdered." *ABC News: Primetime Thursday* (transcript), May 1, 2003.

Berg, Alan (V)

In 1983, Denver, Colorado radio "shock jock" Alan Berg told an interviewer, "I stick it to them and they love it. Hopefully, my legal training will prevent me from saying the one thing that will kill me." His murder on June 18, 1984 was not only tragic in a personal sense, but also served to focus national attention on the role of so-called "insult deejays" in defining the limits of the constitutionally guaranteed right of free speech. A former Chicago lawyer, Berg debuted on Denver radio in 1971 and over the next decade parlayed his persona as "the last angry man" into the highest ratings in town. The *Alan Berg Show* ran from 8:00 P.M. till midnight on Clear Channel radio station KOA and reached into 38 states with a listenership of over 200,000. Like fellow-shock jocks Howard Stern and Don Imus, Berg was an equal opportunity insulter firing thoughtful barbs at ethnic groups, gays, and other minorities. His most trenchant comments were reserved for callers or in-studio guests whose intelligence failed to impress him. Lucky was the caller that Berg only hung up on sparing them a caustic diatribe on their stupidity. Berg's blunt opinionated "in your face" broadcast style both attracted and alienated listeners. The Jewish deejay routinely argued with racists and anti–Semites refusing to be intimidated by their hatred. In 1979, a man later identified as a Ku Klux Klan member showed up while Berg was on-air waving a pistol and threatening to kill the deejay. If death threats were part of the job for Berg, decidedly more listeners, however, were challenged by the former attorney's outspoken views on various social issues and they readily followed him in February 1984 to his new 9:00 A.M. to 1:00 P.M. time slot.

Shortly after 9:30 P.M. on June 18, 1984, the 50-year-old talk show host was getting out of his Volkswagen in the driveway of his Denver townhouse at 1445 Adams Street when he was repeatedly shot in the face, torso, and neck. Police arrived in minutes and found Berg's lifeless body, his right leg still in the car, his burning cigarette nearby. Forensics determined Berg was shot 13 times with a .45-caliber automatic weapon at a range of between five to eight feet. Authorities were initially faced with a daunting list of suspects, i.e., almost any mentally unstable listener of the *Alan Berg Show* might possibly have had a reason to kill the shock jock. The case finally broke on October 18, 1984, after FBI agents investigating The Order of the Silent Brotherhood, a white supremacist neo–Nazi group dedicated to the radical overthrow of the United States government, went to arrest member Gary Lee Yar-

brough, 29, at his home ten miles north of Sandpoint, Idaho. Inside the house, agents found a cache of automatic weapons and ammunition, Nazi literature, and the action plan for The Order outlining a campaign of hatred against Jews and other minorities. More importantly for the Berg case, the raid yielded the Mac-10 submachine gun used in the murder of the talk show host. Yarbrough escaped capture, but FBI agents acting on information supplied by an informant arrested the man and other members of the neo–Nazi group at a hotel in Portland, Oregon on November 25, 1984. The unrepentant racist denied any involvement in the assassination of the Jewish deejay and, when pressed by reporters to name the killer, responded, "God." Yarbrough and nine other members of The Order were ultimately convicted of various multistate racketeering charges and sentenced in February 1986 to prison terms ranging from 40 to 100 years.

Citing insufficient evidence, the Denver district attorney declined to prosecute four members of The Order named in the racketeering trial as having been involved in the murder of Alan Berg. Instead, the Justice Department charged the group under a little used 1968 civil rights law. The defendants (Bruce Carroll Pierce, 33; David E. Lane, 39; Richard Scutari, 40; Jean Margaret Craig, 54) were accused in 1987 of violating the civil rights of Berg, a Jew, when they murdered him on June 18, 1984. The government asserted the group targeted Berg because he was seen as an outspoken threat to the Aryan race. Each racist had a clearly defined role in the assassination. Craig scouted the talk show host's movements for weeks prior to the killing, Scutari was the lookout, Lane the wheelman, and Pierce pulled the trigger. Robert Jay Mathews, the leader of The Order who was earlier killed in a shootout with federal agents on Whidbey Island, Washington in December 1984, was also identified by prosecutors as having participated in the murder. Another convicted member of the white supremacist group, Robert Merki, testified Berg was just one of several influential Jews on The Order's hitlist which included industrialist Armand Hammer and the recently deceased New York Senator Jacob Javitz. Zillah Craig, the former mistress of The Order's leader Robert Jay Mathews, testified under a grant of immunity that Berg was marked for death because he ridiculed two white supremacist preachers during a phone interview with them on February 13, 1984. On November 17, 1987,

Bruce Pierce and David Lane were convicted of violating Berg's civil rights and were each sentenced to prison terms of 150 years with parole eligibility after 50 years served. Jean Craig, the stalker, and lookout Richard Scutari were found not guilty. In August 1989, a federal appeals court upheld the civil rights convictions against the two racists rejecting arguments that they participated in Berg's killing because they hated him, not because he was a Jew. In 1988, monologist-actor-director Eric Bogosian incorporated elements of Alan Berg's murder into his film, *Talk Radio*, a tale of an acerbic deejay murdered by a white supremacist.

Further Reading

Singular, Stephen. *Talked to Death: The Life and Murder of Alan Berg.* New York: Beech Tree, 1987.

Bern, Paul (V-suspected)

On September 5, 1932, the nude body of MGM production supervisor Paul Bern was found dead from a supposed self-inflicted gunshot wound to the head in the home he shared with his movie star wife Jean Harlow, in the Benedict Canyon section of West Los Angeles. Bern's passing, shrouded in controversy and innuendo, stands with the controversial 1935 suicide or accident or murder of screen star Thelma Todd (see entry) and the 1959 suicide or murder of George ("Superman") Reeves (see entry) as among Hollywood's most suspicious deaths. Born Paul Levy on December 3, 1889, in Wandsbek, Germany, a suburb of Hamburg, the future film executive emigrated to America when he was nine with his father Julius, a candy maker, mother Henrietta, and his 17 siblings. Settling in New York City, the family endured continual financial hardships compounded by the death of Julius Levy in 1908. At 18, Paul Levy was forced to put aside his childhood dream of becoming a psychiatrist in order to support his family as a commercial stenographer. In September 1909, however, he was accepted in a two-year acting course at the prestigious American Academy of Dramatic Arts and Empire Theatre Dramatic School. Levy quickly changed his name to the less Semitic sounding "Paul Bern" and became an American citizen.

In February 1911, Bern made his acting debut onstage at the Empire Theatre in *Friends of Youth*. In the company was an attractive young actress named Dorothy Millette, with whom Bern lived in a common-law wife relationship for several years. Over the next decade, he developed a professional resume that made him an ideal candidate for the movie business. Bern acted on Broadway, toured with an East Coast stock company, wrote film scripts, and managed a movie theatre in Manhattan owned by Joe and Nick Schenck prior to their involvement in United Artists and Loew's. In 1920, Bern was living with Millette (registered as "Mrs. Paul Bern") in the Algonquin Hotel and doing writing assignments for the Samuel Goldwyn Company, then making films in New York City. Bern was in the initial stages of relocating to Hollywood when two tragedies delayed his plans. On September 15, 1920, his 72-year-old mother drowned herself. Though the death was ruled accidental, Bern confessed to friends that it was suicide. In 1921, Dorothy Millette suffered a mental breakdown and was institutionalized at the Blythewood Sanitarium in Greenwich, Connecticut. Advised by doctors that Millette's schizophrenia was irreversible, Bern made arrangements for her long-term care and moved to Hollywood in 1922. Millette spent a year at the sanitarium then moved back into the Algonquin Hotel. Bern continued to support her with monthly checks of $350 channeled through his brother, Henry Bern.

In Hollywood, Bern's talent and versatility made him in constant demand as a director (*Head Over Hills*, 1922; *Worldly Goods*, 1924; *The Dressmaker from Paris*, 1925; *Flower of Night*, 1925 with Pola Negri), scenario writer (*The Christian*, 1923; *Lily of the Dust*, 1924; *The Marriage Circle*, 1924; *The Great Deception*, 1926; *The Beloved Rogue*, 1927), and film supervisor (*Geraldine*, 1929; *Noisy Neighbors*, 1929; *Square Shoulders*, 1929). While working at Pathé in 1926, Bern met Irving Thalberg, the "Boy Wonder" at MGM who was that studio's highly successful vice president and supervisor of production. Thalberg hired Bern that year as his personal production assistant (producer) and story consultant. Although MGM producers were not given screen credit, Bern supervised the studio's productions of *New Moon* (1931), *The Prodigal* (1931), and *Grand Hotel* (1932). At MGM Bern's impeccable manners, taste, and compassionate treatment of others earned him universal respect and admiration. Known as "Hollywood's Father Confessor," the sensitive production supervisor was renowned throughout the industry for helping anyone in need.

During his years in the entertainment capital,

Bern had also earned a reputation as a ladies' man. In 1932, the 42-year-old producer fell passionately in love with 21-year-old actress Jean Harlow while pushing her for the sexy leading role in the film *Red-Headed Woman*. Harlow got the part and overnight became the biggest star on the MGM lot. Less than two weeks after the film premiered, Harlow married Bern on July 2, 1932, in a private ceremony at her father's home. The next day, MGM's top brass assembled for a garden party at the Benedict Canyon home Bern had built two years earlier at 9820 Easton Drive. As a wedding gift, the producer gave his new bride the deed to the Bavarian-style house. Outwardly, the couple appeared blissfully happy. Bern maintained a dizzying work schedule while Harlow told a close friend that all she wanted to do was "sit at Paul's feet and have him educate me." Unknown to the glamorous superstar, however, her husband was maintaining Dorothy Millette, a.k.a. "Mrs. Paul Bern," in a hotel back East. Millette read of her common-law husband's marriage to Harlow in a fan magazine and started pressuring him to let her come to Hollywood. Bern played for time telling the mentally unbalanced woman he was too busy to see her. Finally relenting, he installed Millette at the Plaza Hotel in San Francisco on May 4, 1932. He was overseeing the production of *Red Dust* starring Harlow and Clark Gable when the complicated situation reached its crisis in September 1932.

While the truth of the matter can now never be known thanks to a probable studio cover-up, conflicting accounts of key events, and the accumulated force of innuendo built up over 75 years, Paul Bern did die in his Benedict Canyon home on Easton Drive on Labor Day, September 5, 1932, days after he took out a life insurance policy naming Harlow as his beneficiary. The evening before the tragedy, Bern and Harlow apparently argued (other accounts say they did not). The blonde superstar chose to stay across town at her mother's (others say she went to dinner with friends), leaving Bern alone in the house. At 11:30 A.M. the next day, the producer's butler, John Carmichael, arrived at the house and found Bern's naked body lying on the floor in a puddle of blood half out of a walk-in closet off the bedroom. A gaping wound in Bern's right temple two inches in front of his ear had been inflicted by a .38-caliber Colt revolver still clasped in his right hand. The gun was initially unseen by Carmichael because it was obscured under the right side of his

employer's body. The bullet exited the left side of Bern's head and lodged in the wall of the closet.

Carmichael phoned Harlow's mother who (instead of notifying police) called MGM head Louis B. Mayer at his Santa Monica beach house. Acting quickly, Mayer contacted Whitey Hendry, head of MGM studio's police, and Howard Strickling, MGM's head of publicity who specialized in "fixing" personnel problems at the studio. They met at the death house shortly after noon and combed the premises for clues before calling the police. On a table near Bern's body Strickling found a second .38-caliber revolver belonging to the dead man next to his morocco-bound guest book containing the names of several celebrities. On page 13 Strickling discovered a cryptic message written in Bern's hand that read: "Dearest dear, Unfortunately this is the only way to make good the frightful wrong I have done you and to wipe out my abject humiliation. I love you. Paul. You understand that last night was only a comedy." Louis B. Mayer wanted to destroy the note, but Strickling convinced him that without it Bern's suicide had no motive and Harlow might be suspected of killing him. Strickling replaced the book opened at page 13 on the table. At 2:30 P.M., four hours after the discovery of Bern's corpse, the police finally arrived at the scene after Irving Thalberg reported the death. Told of her husband's death, Harlow became hysterical and had to be sedated. When later questioned about the possible meaning of the note's reference to the "frightful wrong" committed against her by Bern, Harlow could provide no explanation. Mayer and the MGM publicity machine, however, could.

Anxious to protect the studio's biggest money-maker from any blame in the death and to ensure the public's sympathy for her, Mayer orchestrated a smear campaign against "Hollywood's Father Confessor." Studio doctor Edward B. Jones, conveniently unavailable for the subsequent inquest, issued a press statement in which he announced Bern had a medical problem that caused him to be impotent. Dr. Jones later told the press, "Bern's suicide was due to an acute melancholia and nervous strain which developed into a mania." Fuelled by MGM's publicity machine, it became common "knowledge" that Bern's genitalia were so undersized he could not engage in sexual intercourse. The cryptic lines in Bern's suicide note referring to the "frightful wrong" and the mysterious "last night was only a comedy" could then be interpreted as guilt, embarrassment, humiliation, and frustration over his inability to sexually satisfy his wife, who also happened to be the most desirable woman in movies. Harlow, not Bern, was the offended party. Sam Marx, a story editor for Irving Thalberg and Paul Bern's friend, offered an alternative theory of the case in his important book, *Deadly Illusions: Jean Harlow and the Murder of Paul Bern* (1990), which accounts for many of the facts initially given to police by witnesses later hushed by MGM. In the early morning on the day Bern died, a neighbor reported seeing a woman being picked up by a car at 9820 Easton Drive. The woman was subsequently identified as Dorothy Millette. The night before, neighbors heard raised voices and Bern scream, "Get out of my life!" According to the "murder theory," Bern orchestrated an argument with Harlow to get her out of the house so Millette could visit him. Millette arrived and Bern entertained her near the pool before the evening ended in an argument. Bern was removing his swim trunks in the walkin bedroom closet when Millette picked up one of the two guns in the room and fatally shot him in the head at point-blank range. Appearing at the scene later, MGM security chief Whitey Hendry placed the gun in the dead man's hand to make the murder appear like a suicide. Murder, it seems, could hurt Harlow's career as much as suicide. A woman's wet bathing suit (not Harlow's) was found near the producer's body. The undated "suicide note" (positively identified as written by Bern) was in actuality an apology to Harlow for the reemergence of Millette back into his life. The "comedy" of "last night" referred to the argument he staged in order to get her out of the house so he could meet Millette. An MGM driver later told several people he had driven a woman back to the Plaza Hotel in San Francisco. The charge for the trip was even billed to Bern's estate.

The next day, September 6, 1932, Millette checked out of the Plaza Hotel and purchased a round trip ticket on the *Delta King*, the overnight ferry to Sacramento. The press, informed of her existence by Bern's brother, Henry, was frantically searching for the woman when a Japanese fisherman found her badly decomposed body floating in the Sacramento River at the Georgiana Slough on September 14, 1932. The coroner's inquest determined the "38-year-old Dorothy Millette came to her death on the 7th of September, 1932, by asphyxiation by drowning." Jean Harlow reportedly paid the $250 needed to bury her dead husband's common-law wife in Sacramento's East Lawn Memorial Park under a headstone that read, "Dorothy Millette Bern." On September 9, 1932, 2,000 mourners and sightseers attended Paul Bern's funeral services at the Grace Chapel in Inglewood. Following the service, the much maligned suicide or murder victim was cremated and his ashes interred at the Golden West Mausoleum in Inglewood Park Cemetery. Jean Harlow died of uremic poisoning at the age of 26 on June 7, 1937.

Further Reading

Fleming, E. J. *Paul Bern: The Life and Famous Death of the MGM Director and Husband of Harlow*. Jefferson, NC: McFarland, 2009.
Golden, Eve. *Platinum Girl: The Life and Legends of Jean Harlow*. New York: Abbeville, 1991.
Marx, Samuel, and Joyce Vanderveen. *Deadly Illusions: Jean Harlow and the Murder of Paul Bern*. New York: Random House, 1990.
Shulman, Irving. *Harlow, an Intimate Biography*. New York: Bernard Geis, 1990.
Stenn, David. *Bombshell: The Life and Death of Jean Harlow*. New York: Doubleday, 1993.

Bhatt, Urmilla (V)

The sixtyish actress appeared in several Hindi films (*Koshish*, 1972; *Dhund* (a.k.a. *Fog*), 1973); *Geet Gata Chal*, 1975) and most recently appeared on the Indian television serial *Zee Horror Show*. In the program, Bhatt's character had her throat slit. On February 22, 1997, Bhatt was found with her throat slit on a blood-soaked bed in her residence in Mumbai. Police theorized that her involvement in a shady stock deal in which wealthy film and television investors lost more than eight million rupees may have served as a motive in her killing. Hours before her death, Bhatt received a threatening phone call, and family members reported that she had "lived in constant fear of her life." To date, no arrest has been made in the case.

Further Reading

Thayil, Jeet. "Murder Copy of Actress' Role in TV Serial." *South China Morning Post*, February 28, 1997.

Big L (V)

Born May 30, 1974 in a section of uptown Harlem known as "The Danger Zone," Lamont (Big L) Coleman parlayed a natural wit and ability to rhyme into a hip-hop career that promised better things to come. In 1995, Big L caught the eye of major label Columbia Records and released *Lifestyles Ov Da Poor and Dangerous* containing the tracks "MVP" ("Most Valuable Poet"),

"8 Iz Enuff," "All Black," and "Da Graveyard" featuring the then unknown Jay-Z. Unable to capture Big L's street smart style, Columbia dropped him after the record tanked. Loved by the hip-hop underground, Big L joined the Bronx-based group D.I.T.C. (Diggin' in the Crates) in the summer of 1998 and appeared in concerts in Amsterdam and Japan. Back in New York City, he had recently released the single "Ebonics" on his own Flamboyant Entertainment label when the talented and likable 24-year-old was gunned down just three blocks from his home in Harlem. At 8:30 P.M. on February 15, 1999, Big L was walking near the corner of Lenox Avenue and 139th Street when a man approached him and pumped nine shots into the rapper's face and chest killing him instantly. As neighbors and fans created a makeshift memorial to the MC at the spot where he fell at 45 West 139th Street, detectives discounted the murder as a continuation of the East Coast and West Coast rap wars suspecting instead that the motive for the hit stemmed from a street beef between Big L's incarcerated brother, "Big Lee," and the gunman. In May 1999, Harlem resident Gerard Woodley, 29, on the lam from a federal drug indictment, was arrested in the Bronx and charged with murdering the rapper. Woodley, a childhood friend of the Coleman brothers, was later released due to insufficient evidence. At the time of this book's publication, no one has been arrested for Big L's murder.

Further Reading

Ankeny, Jason. "Big L." www.allmusic.com.
Jasper, Kenji. "Of Mics and Men in Harlem." *Village Voice,* 44(27) (July 7–13, 1999):51–52.

Big Lurch (M)

On April 10, 2002, a naked black man, his mouth, chest and abdomen smeared with blood, was arrested running down a street in southeast Los Angeles. Antron Singleton, a 27-year-old gangsta rapper known as "Big Lurch," was charged with murder after police found the grisly remains of his roommate Tynisha Ysais, 21, in their nearby second-floor apartment at West 108th and South Figueroa streets. Ysais' neck and jaw were broken, an eye socket fractured, her chest hacked open and a lung removed and partially eaten. Bite marks on her face matched Singleton's teeth and pieces of her lung were found in the rapper's stomach. Singleton pled innocent by reason of insanity to charges of capital murder argu-

ing he was high on PCP, a psychedelic drug known for giving it users superhuman strength and paranoid delusions, at the time of the incident. Under California state law, however, a defendant is barred from using an insanity defense if the mental illness is drug-induced or caused by drug addiction. A jury took less than one hour on June 25, 2003, to convict Big Lurch of murder and aggravated mayhem. He was subsequently sentenced to life in prison without the possibility of parole. The victim's mother, Carolyn Stinson, filed a "wrongful death" suit against Singleton, Death Row Records (headed by rap mogul Marion "Suge" Knight), Stress Free Records, and two employees claiming the label had provided Big Lurch with PCP "to encourage (him) to act out in an extreme violent manner so as to make him more marketable as a 'Gangsta Rap' artist." Death Row Records (later called Tha Row) was dropped from the civil suit in April 2003 after Knight proved he had no connection with Singleton. A Big Lurch CD, *It's All Bad*, was released in 2004 by Black Market Records.

Further Reading

"Death Row Says No Link to Rapper in Murder Case." Reuters News, April 14, 2003.

Big Stretch (V)

Randy Walker, a.k.a. Big Stretch or Stretch, was in the rap group Live Squad, which released the EP *Heartless/Murderahh* on Tommy Boy Records in 1993. Two years earlier, Big Stretch (so named because of his 6' 8" height), met Tupac Shakur (see entry) and the rappers became inseparable friends and companions. Stretch appeared on several of Tupac's tracks including "Crooked Ass Nigga," "Tha' Lunatic," "Strugglin'," "5 Deadly Venomz," "Stay True," "Under Pressure," and "God Bless the Dead." The relationship ended abruptly, however, on the night of November 30, 1994. The gangsta rapper was walking into the lobby of the Quad Recording Studios in Times Square with Big Stretch and manager, Freddie Moore, when two gunmen ordered Shakur to hand over his jewelry. Tupac refused and was shot five times in the hand, head, and groin with Moore shot once in the abdomen. Big Stretch was unharmed. The gunmen escaped with the rapper's large diamond ring and several gold chains valued at $45,000. Although Tupac survived the unsolved attack, he suspected Big Stretch was somehow involved.

At 12:30 A.M. on November 30, 1995, exactly one year and five minutes after Tupac Shakur had been wounded in Manhattan, Big Stretch, 27, was shot to death in Queens. The rapper was on his way home when a black car with three men inside began a high speed chase with his 1992 Mazda minivan at 112th Avenue and 209th Street. Stretch was shot at least four times (two through his back) forcing his car to glance off a tree, strike a parked car, and flip. The rapper was pronounced dead at the scene. Although the timing of the attack suggested a clear link between Tupac's shooting and a "payback hit," the case remained "cold" until April 2007. As part of a federal probe into the unsolved 1995 murder of hip-hop icon Jam Master Jay (see entry), investigators named Ronald "Tenad" Washington, 43, as a suspect in both the murders of Jay and Big Stretch. Fingered by former girlfriend Lydia High, a receptionist in the Queens studio where Jam Master Jay was murdered, Washington denied involvement in either murder claiming his ex was reacting to extreme pressure by investigators. Convicted on April 5, 2007, on six counts of armed robbery and facing life for the crimes that occurred just after Jay was murdered, Washington was named in federal court papers as one of three men from the Queens-based Hollis Crew who, mistaking Stretch for his brother, shot the rapper in a drive-by execution. During the chase, Washington allegedly fired a bullet out of the back window of the car in which he was riding, striking and killing Stretch. The theory of mistaken identity, if proved, would posthumously clear Tupac of ordering a retaliatory "hit" on his former friend and place the murder in the realm of unbelievable coincidence. As of this writing, "Tenad" Washington has yet to be tried for either murder.

Further Reading

McPhee, Michele. "Court: Rapper's Slay Case of Mistaken ID." *Boston Herald*, Apr. 18, 2007, p. 20.

Biggie Smalls *see* **Notorious B.I.G.**

Blackburn, Ronald (V)

Prior to forming the Oakland-based multimedia company Ronlan Entertainment in 1999 with childhood friend Landis Graden, Blackburn managed nightclubs and produced concerts in the Bay Area. At Ronlan, Blackburn focused on finding and signing talent while Graden ran the business side of the entertainment venture. On Oc-

tober 5, 1999, Ronlan released its first album, rapper Silk-E's *Urban Therapy*. Although the company was not affiliated with prominent Bay Area hip-hop artist Money-B, Blackburn, 31, attended the "by invitation-only" release party for the rapper's new album, *Talkin' Dirty*, held at San Francisco's Glas Kat Club on April 19, 2000. According to more than 25 witnesses later interviewed by police, the evening was uneventful until the club's doors closed at 2:00 A.M. the next morning, and patrons were ushered onto Welsh Street, a short dead end alley between Brannan and Bryant streets near a side entrance to the Glas Kat. Several unrelated fights broke out among the crowd culminating in Blackburn being shot twice from a parked Ford SUV that he was standing near. He died at 3:41 A.M. at San Francisco General Hospital. To date, no arrests have been made.

Further Reading

Delgado, Ray. "Man Slain at Hip-Hop Party was a Quiet Recording Exec." *San Francisco Examiner*, April 21, 2000, sec. A, p. 2.

Blake, Robert (M-acquitted)

Dominick Dunne, the *Vanity Fair* journalist best known for his coverage of high profile celebrity trials, used a Hollywood analogy to place the Robert Blake murder case into Tinseltown perspective when he observed, "O.J. was like an MGM Grand movie. This is like a B movie from Republic Pictures." The 1998 meeting of Robert Blake, a faded actor of undeniable talent, and Bonny Lee Bakley, a celebrity wannabe willing to pay any price for "fame," set the stage for a sordid tale of failed dreams, obsession, and murder played out in splashy tabloid headlines. By his own questionable account, Blake, born Michael James Vijencio Gubitosi on September 18, 1933, in Nutley, New Jersey, endured a childhood haunted by an abusive alcoholic father and a weak uninvolved mother who was terrified of enraging her husband. As one of "The Three Little Hillbillies," Blake (with his parents and two siblings) performed song and dance routines on the streets of Depression-era Nutley and at local fairs. "Mickey," an adorable child with dark hair and eyes, was a crowd favorite. Looking to cash in on his son's talent and appealing looks, the elder Gubitosi relocated The Three Little Hillbillies to Hollywood around 1936. The group auditioned in casting offices around the city and Blake was able to find occasional day work in the movies.

In 1939, the youngster (then known by his birth name Michael Gubitosi) was at MGM as an extra on the studio's popular "Our Gang" series when a child actor with a speaking line was unable to perform. Blake boldly stepped forward and nailed the scene. Studio brass, impressed with the five year old's moxie, gave him a recurring role as "Mickey," a part he played until the age of ten when the series ended in 1944. According to Blake, he was essentially supporting his family on the $100 a week he earned on the series and in small uncredited roles in feature films, but it seemingly did little to improve his life at home. In an interview Blake gave to *Playboy* in June 1977, the actor (who was well-known for storytelling if it built up his tough guy image) recounted horrific childhood incidents in which his father locked him in a closet for days, forced him to eat on the floor, and sexually abused him. By the time the man committed suicide (his death certificate listed heart disease as the official cause of death) at 50, Blake had severed all connections with him. In the mid–1940s, the young actor snagged the role of "Little Beaver" in the *Red Ryder* serials and began appearing in small roles in feature films including *Andy Hardy's Double Life* (1943; billed as "Bobby Blake"), Jack Benny's *The Horn Blows at Midnight* (1945), and as the Mexican orphan boy who sells Humphrey Bogart the winning lottery ticket in *The Treasure of the Sierra Madre* (1948). After graduating from the studio high school at 16, Blake left home and appeared on TV shows including *The Adventures of Wild Bill Hickok* and *The Cisco Kid*.

In 1952, the 19-year-old actor entered the Army and was stationed in Alaska as part of an experimental infantry unit testing cold weather gear for use in the Korean conflict. Blake, a muscular 5'4" and unafraid to buck authority, was not an ideal candidate for military life. He proved a constant disciplinary problem and after suffering an emotional breakdown spent a month in the mental ward of the base hospital. Released, he soon got in trouble for stealing gas and was sentenced to three months in a stockade. An understanding priest won Blake's release after a month and pulled strings to have him transferred to a Special Services unit in Anchorage where he spent most of his remaining hitch writing and directing musicals featuring the officers' wives. Mustering out at 21, Blake quickly realized no acting career awaited him in Hollywood and fell into a crippling and suicidal depression. He turned to heroin and co-caine and supported himself as a low-level pusher running dope to Las Vegas and Mexico. Blake's downward spiral ended when a friend introduced the actor to mental health counseling. Over years of therapy he was able to end his drug dependency and regain the confidence to pursue acting. Blake worked continuously throughout the mid–1950s and 1960s in television and films including *Rumble on the Docks* (1956, as "Robert Blake"), *The Tijuana Story* (1957), *Revolt in the Big House* (1958), *Battle Flame* (1959), *Pork Chop Hill* (1959), *The Purple Gang* (1960), *Town Without Pity* (1961), *The Connection* (1962), *PT-109* (1963), *The Greatest Story Ever Told* (1965), and *This Property Is Condemned* (1966). In 1967, the 34-year-old actor gave a career-defining performance as real-life killer Perry Smith in the Richard Brooks production of *In Cold Blood* based on Truman Capote's riveting account of the murder of the Clutter family in Holcomb, Kansas in 1959. Suddenly a "hot" property after nearly two decades in the business, Blake starred in a succession of motion pictures (*Tell Them Willie Boy Is Here*, 1969; *Corky*, 1972; *Electra Glide in Blue*, 1973; *Busting*, 1974) that were commercial flops despite some fine performances. As his career tanked, Blake became increasingly confrontational on set and colleagues were wary of his wild mood swings often punctuated by physical and emotional outbursts. After *Busting* bombed, the actor suffered a debilitating emotional breakdown brought on by binge drinking, pill popping, and heroin use. Blake was hospitalized for two weeks and after his discharge was willing to lower his sights (in his opinion) and focus on television roles.

In mid–1974, Blake was signed by ABC to star in *Baretta*, a mid-season replacement for the series *Toma*. *Baretta* debuted in January 1975 and was an immediate hit with audiences who loved Blake as the street-savvy detective with the cockatoo, "Fred." On the series, the actor introduced catchphrases like "You can take that to the bank" and "That's the name of that tune" that quickly became part of American popular culture. In 1975, Blake won an Emmy as Best Actor in a Series for *Baretta*, but the series was doomed by the $35,000 a week star's relentless perfectionism and abrasive personality. Blake micromanaged the entire show, demanded more control in every phase of production, and argued with everyone including producers, writers, directors, and other actors. A frequent guest on *The Tonight Show*, Blake regaled host Johnny Carson with colorfully phrased tales in which he put overpaid network executives ("the suits") in their place. However, as soon as the show began to lose popularity and was cancelled in 1978 after its third season, it became apparent the actor's prima donna posturings had marked him in industry circles as someone just too difficult to have around. For example, director William Friedkin briefly considered Blake for the lead in his 1977 feature film *Sorcerer*, but gave the role to Roy Scheider. The spurned actor took out a prominent ad in a Hollywood trade paper directed at Friedkin that read, "Put the *Sorcerer* where the sun never shines. Peace & Love, Robert Blake." Under an existing deal with Universal, the actor served as executor producer and starred in three NBC movies-of-the-week as the character "Joe Dancer," a fictional L.A. private detective, and enjoyed strong roles in two 1981 television movies *Of Mice and Men* and *Blood Feud* playing Teamster boss Jimmy Hoffa. Now, however, Blake's well-known drug abuse had forced insurance companies to add a series of humiliating riders to his contracts. Blake's fee would be released only if he did not use drugs during production, caused no on-set problems, and completed his work on time. By 1985 when Blake agreed to star in the series *Hell Town* about a crusading priest the actor was off heroin, but still gobbling pills and harboring thoughts of suicide. Unable to confront the rigors of a series, Blake pulled the plug after only seven episodes (it was cancelled in December 1985) and entered into a self-imposed eight year exile marked by depression, binge drinking, and more drugs. He returned to show business in 1993 with a critically lauded performance in the made-for-television movie, *Judgment Day: The John List Story*, playing the true-life title character who murdered his entire family in 1971. In 1997, Blake appeared as the creepy "Mystery Man" in David Lynch's *Lost Highway*, a role that marked the end of his acting career. Essentially a pariah in the show business industry and largely forgotten by the public, the 64-year-old actor (a multimillionaire from astute real estate investments) lived a comfortable semi-reclusive existence on his poetically named Mata Hari Ranch at 11604 Dilling Street in Studio City, California.

There was never a time in the life of Bonny Lee Bakley that she did not either want to *be* a celebrity or else to bask in the reflected glow of fame by marriage to one. Born into a working class family on June 7, 1956 in Morristown, New Jersey, Bakley's earliest dreams were of fleeing small town life and the father she alleged sexually abused her at age seven. She later claimed that the man died before she became old enough to kill him. Throughout high school, Bakley clung to her dream of stardom and after dropping out in her sophomore year went briefly to New York City to pursue an acting career under the name "Leebonny." She never landed a part, but in June 1977 *Hustler* published a photo of her in "Beaver Hunt," a regular feature of the sex magazine dedicated to below-the-waist snapshots of readers' submissions. Bakley's mother was not amused when she saw her own name, Marjorie Carlyon, next to the explicit photo of her daughter. Months later in November 1977, Bakley again shocked her family by marrying first cousin, Paul Gawron, a 27-year-old laborer. Gawron, who fathered two children (Glenn and Holly) with Bakley, fully understood that his wife's ultimate goal was to marry a celebrity. Though he claimed not to like it, Gawron was also a willing participant in Bakley's principal moneymaking scam — a mail order business targeting lonely older men. Bakley placed ads in regional swinger magazines in which she charitably described herself as young, single, pretty, lonely, and willing to travel in order to meet. Once a mark responded, she sent the man a nude photograph (often not of herself) and asked for money to get her car fixed so she could come to visit him. Next, she would consult a map to determine the median distance between her location and his and telegram the mark her car had broken down and she needed money, or better yet, a credit card number to effect repairs. Bakley used numerous aliases and Social Security numbers of every woman she knew. While Bakley was on the road setting up a network of post office boxes for her scam, Gawron stayed at home copying and addressing "hot" form letters written by his wife to her respondents. If they paid a fee, he enclosed an explicit photo. Occasionally, Bakley met with some of the men if she liked the photo they supplied. By 1980, the business was thriving and Bakley briefly included her sister, Margerry, in the scheme. In 1982, she obtained a Mexican mail order divorce from Gawron after meeting Robert Stuhr, a wannabe rock star from Palisades Park, New Jersey, with minor connections to the movie industry. Through her new husband, Bakley was able to land a gig as an extra in the 1985 film *Turk 182* starring Timothy Hutton and Robert Urich. Although the "part" did not lead to a Hollywood career, Bakley was not too disappointed. Stuhr ran a small music company called Norway USA and recorded her as "Leebonney Bakley" on the tracks "Rock-A-Billy Love" and "Tribute to Elvis Presley." The marriage ended when Bakley realized Stuhr lacked the show business clout to advance her career.

The lucrative mail order sex scam never prevented Bakley from pursuing her ultimate goal of seducing then marrying a celebrity. Around 1990, she relocated to Memphis determined to snag her idol Jerry "the Killer" Lee Lewis. Bakley had targeted Lewis since the mid–1980s and while the star's sister, Linda Gail Lewis, knew the woman to be a gung ho groupie, still liked and associated with her. Bakley used the connection to get close to Lewis who reportedly had never been known throughout his seven marriages to turn down free sex from a young adoring female fan. "The Killer," however, had never met a groupie as determined as "Leebonney." Bakley loudly declared in the tabloid press that she was pregnant with the star's child and when a daughter was born on July 28, 1993, she named her Jeri Lee Lewis. The paternity case against the rock star was tossed out of a Memphis court after Jerry Lee's passport proved he was out of the country during the time Bakley conceived. Paul Gawron, now her administrative assistant in the scam that was generating thousands of letters a month to various drop boxes, later claimed he fathered the child. Undeterred, the con artist deposited the infant with Gawron (also in charge of her two other children) and continued her criminal activities which now expanded to include several illegal marriages. Bonny Lee Bakley, however, had been on police radar since 1989 when she was arrested in Memphis on a misdemeanor drug charge and fined $300. In September 1994, the 38-year-old was arrested for misrepresentation of the value of property after attempting to pass two bad checks for $600,000 and $2,000 drawn on the account of a Memphis record company. The charge was pleaded down and she escaped serious jail time with a $1000 fine and a sentence of three years performing weekend work on a penal farm. In February 1996, Bakley was picked up in Arkansas in possession of seven driver's licenses, 16 stolen credit cards, and five Social Security cards all bearing different names. The false identification came in handy when renting post office boxes around the country for her mail order scam. The case did not go to court for 17 months, but in February

1998 she was placed on probation for three years and forbidden to leave the state without permission except to see Paul Gawron and her children in Memphis.

Perhaps the rapid approach of age 40 made Bakley more than ever determined to bag a celebrity husband. Although her mail order business was thriving and post office drop boxes around the country were clogged daily with money-laden letters from rubes in America as well as their horny counterparts in places as far-flung as Canada, Hungary, India, and Pakistan, she still yearned for the status, security, and respectability that a Hollywood marriage would offer. Bakley initially targeted Christian Brando (see entry), the oldest son of acting great Marlon, who was finishing up a prison term on a manslaughter conviction stemming from the shooting death of Dag Drollet, his sister Cheyenne's lover, in 1990. Prior to Brando's parole from the penitentiary in January 1996, Bakley struck up a postal correspondence with the prisoner and baited the hook with some of the provocative photos she sent to her other marks. After Brando was paroled, Bakley's pursuit of the 32-year-old ex-con intensified. She hired a private investigator to determine where he lived and continued to pepper him with spicy mail. However, before she could set up a meeting Brando received permission from parole authorities to move out of state necessitating her private eye to ultimately track him down in the remote logging town of Kalama, Washington. Bakley arranged a meeting and the pair was soon engaged in a sexual relationship. The only potential drawbacks — Brando suffered from paranoid delusions and had shown a propensity for violence.

In August 1998, Bakley, 42, met Robert Blake, nearly 65, in Chadney's, a steak house and jazz club in Burbank across from NBC where *The Tonight Show* was filmed. Impressed by Blake's celebrity, Bakley was all over the actor who was clearly interested in the younger woman. They left the club together early and drove in Blake's SUV to the Beverly Garland Holiday Inn in downtown Hollywood. The amorous couple did not even take time to check in opting instead to have sex in the back of the actor's car. Afterwards, they exchanged phone numbers and Blake called her a few weeks later. The actor was intrigued by Bakley's tales of her mail order business and the pair continued to have sex. Concerned Blake might not be as well off as he bragged, Bakley ran an asset check on the actor that revealed he owned a portfolio worth $8 million in real estate and business holdings. When the grifter turned up pregnant in late 1999 she faced an important decision as to which celebrity (the younger and handsomer Brando, or, the older, but better known and financially secure Blake) to pressure into marriage. Unknown to everyone, Bakley had for years secretly taped all of her phone conversations. In one with an unidentified associate she discussed the relative merits of each prospective candidate suggesting the child could be used as a bargaining chip in negotiations with the men. Brando, though unconcerned with the pregnancy, was a tad too savvy to think the impending child was his (the timing just did not add up) besides Bakley had decided the older, richer actor was a better catch. She wrote Blake from Memphis informing him of the pregnancy and received a blistering phone call in response. The actor told her under no circumstances to have the child and ordered her to get an abortion. Blake realized he had been played by the grifter just like the thousands of other rubes she had burned in her mail order sex scam. The 67-year-old actor refused to accept Bakley's calls and when the baby, a girl, was born on June 2, 2000, at the University of Arkansas Medical Service in Little Rock, she named her Christian Shannon Brando. Throughout the summer of 2000 Bakley maintained her pressure on Blake sending him photos of the child whose dark features were a mirror image of his own. Delinah, Blake's adult daughter by his failed first marriage to actress Sondra Kerr, desperately wanted a child and this may have been a factor in the actor agreeing to take a DNA test in August 2000. The test confirmed Robert Blake was the father of Bonny Lee Bakley's child. According to press reports, the actor agreed "to do the right thing" and planned to marry the woman.

Bakley, at Blake's invitation, violated her probation in Arkansas and in September 2000 flew with the infant to Los Angeles to meet with her fiancé. Blake was instantly smitten with the baby and his ill will toward the woman was seemingly forgotten. The reunited family was dining at a café near Blake's home when two policemen arrived and placed her under arrest for parole violation. Blake remained calm informing Bakley that he would take care of the baby until he could notify his lawyer and straighten out the problem. In the car on the way to the police station one of the officers offered Bakley a deal. He was just one week shy of retirement and did not want to go

through the hassle of filling out the paperwork on her violation. If she agreed to return to Little Rock that day and report to her parole officer he would forget the entire incident. Bakley readily accepted the deal and back in Arkansas reported the details of her recent adventure to her parole officer. The man told her a private investigator hired by Blake had already called to inform him that his client was out of state and in violation of her parole. The "cops" were fakes hired by "Baretta." Bakley, for once on the receiving end of a con, was placed under house arrest for the remainder of her sentence. The infant was now in Blake's custody and Bakley would never again interact with her except for the occasional hour or so under strictly supervised conditions. Blake placed the baby with his childless daughter Delinah who would ultimately adopt her. Fuming, Bakley obtained permission from authorities to return to Los Angeles and on October 1, 2000, presented Blake with an ultimatum. They could either marry or he could pay $7,500 a month in child support and further risk having the whole story of the "childnapping" be made public. Blake agreed to marry the woman, but only upon condition she sign one of the most unusual pre-nuptial agreements in the annals of show business history. In the agreement formalized on October 4, 2000, Bakley basically gave up any rights she had to the child (since renamed Rose Lenore Sophia Blake) as well as any claim to anything Blake owned (real estate, pension funds, retirement benefits). Bakley could retain her sole assets and continue her porno lonely hearts mail order scam as long as she refrained from conducting business on Blake's property or involving him in any way. Bakley was also forbidden to associate with known felons while with their child and instructed to keep the infant away from any drug use or other illicit activities. Family and friends could visit Bakley at Blake's Mata Hari Ranch *only* with his written permission. Under the terms of a temporary custody agreement, the child would be held by Delinah until Bakley finished her probation in Arkansas in January 2001. The pre-nuptial was signed by both parties and Bakley dropped the pending child-stealing charges against her fiancé. Bakley obtained permission from her probation officer to marry her movie star boyfriend at his home on November 19, 2000, but immediately after the ceremony had to return to Arkansas to serve out the final three months of her probation. If Bakley felt Blake's attitude toward her would soften during her absence she was in error. She arrived on her husband's doorstep a free woman in March 2001, but instead of being warmly greeted by Blake was installed in a guest house behind the main residence where he resided. Bakley demanded to see her daughter Rosie, but was permitted to do so only occasionally for 1½ hours under the strict supervision of a hired supervisor. Bored and blocked by the pre-nup from touching Blake's money, Bakley began operating her porno business from the guest house. As the relationship between the couple deteriorated Bakley phoned a friend on April 30, 2001, and discussed a plan she was considering to kidnap Rosie and take her back to Memphis.

According to Robert Blake's account of the events of May 4, 2001, the 67-year-old actor and his wife Bonny Lee Bakley, 44, decided to go out to dinner and discuss their marriage with an eye towards doing whatever was best for their child, Rosie. Blake felt their relationship was improving and planned to allow the woman to move into the main house with him. Bakley, fearing someone was stalking her, insisted her husband carry one of his pistols to protect her. Blake made reservations at Vitello's Italian Restaurant on 4349 Tujunga Avenue in Studio City, an eatery five minutes from his home. The actor, it was later revealed, had frequented Vitello's at least two or three times a week for the last twenty years without making a reservation. Instead of using the establishment's valet parking service (his usual routine), Blake parked his 1991 black Dodge Stealth on Woodbridge, a side street 1½ blocks from the restaurant, beneath a burned-out street lamp next to a dumpster near a vacant house under construction. The couple walked the short distance to the restaurant arriving at around 8:30 P.M. Although he had been a regular for two decades and even had a dish named after him (*fusilli a la Robert Blake*), the actor made a point of introducing Bakley (she had often dined there) to co-owner Joseph Restivo as "his wife." Restivo and the rest of the staff never realized until then that Blake was married. Rather than taking his usual corner booth, the actor asked to be seated in a booth near the back of the restaurant, but still visible to other diners. Bakley was on her third glass of wine when Blake excused himself and went to the rest room. Another patron later told police he observed the actor vomiting into a waste can, mumbling to himself, and pulling his hair. Other patrons volunteered the celebrity looked shaken and ill as he walked back to the booth to pay his bill. The couple left between 9:30 and 9:40 P.M. and strolled the short distance back to the car. Bakley was seated in the front passenger side of the Stealth when Blake realized he was missing his .38-caliber handgun. It apparently had fallen out of his waistband into the booth. According to Blake, he returned to the restaurant, retrieved the gun, asked for two glasses of water, drank them, then left. The actor returned to the car and discovered his unconscious wife slumped over in the passenger seat and badly bleeding from a head wound. Blake ran to a house behind Vitello's parking lot across the street from the car and rang the doorbell. Its owner, a filmmaker named Sean Stanek, answered and Blake told him to call 911. Around 9:40 P.M. while Stanek remained at the car with the mortally wounded Bakley, an agitated Blake returned to Vitello's for help. Paramedics arrived seven minutes after the call, but were unable to revive the woman who had been shot once behind the right ear and once in the shoulder. Throughout their attempts to resuscitate his wife, Blake never went near the woman and witnesses at the scene later testified that his grief seemed ingenuine. Bonny Lee Bakley, the scam artist who realized her dream of marrying a celebrity, was pronounced dead on arrival at St. Joseph's Medical Center in Burbank.

It did not take long for case-hardened detectives to uncover major inconsistencies in the actor's account of the evening's tragic events. Joseph Restivo, co-owner of Vitello's, told detectives that Blake returned only once to the restaurant and that *after* his wife was shot to ask for help. At that time the actor requested water and drank two glasses. No other patron or employee remembered witnessing Blake's earlier return to the restaurant to retrieve his missing firearm. Also, within two minutes of the actor's departure with Bakley their table was bussed and no weapon was found. Logically, Blake's alibi for the time of the shooting was contingent on establishing his initial return to Vitello's to recover his gun. Without witness corroboration placing him in the restaurant during the time the shooting most likely occurred, Blake could have shot Bakley, summoned assistance from a nearby resident, then returned *once* to Vitello's (corroborated by witnesses) to report the shooting. Burned by a recent string of high profile fiascos in the investigation of celebrity murder cases (see O.J. Simpson entry), LAPD's top cops, the Robbery-Homicide unit, moved very deliberately in amassing evidence against

Robert Blake. During an initial five-hour interview the actor refused to take a polygraph test claiming that while he was innocent the results might point to deception because he once dreamed of killing Bakley and felt responsible for her death because he left her alone in the car. A later gunshot residue test (GSR) proved inconclusive as a positive result could be explained as being produced by the gun Blake carried for protection. The murder weapon, a Nazi-era .38-caliber Walther PPK, was quickly found in a trash bin near where the actor parked his car, but criminalists were unable to lift prints from the freshly oiled weapon. The day after the killing, police armed with a search warrant entered Blake's white stucco ranch-style house on Dilling Street and seized the clothing he wore the night before and other items. Harland Braun, the one-time star's high-power attorney best known for his involvement with LAPD beating suspect Rodney King, immediately launched a media offensive. He revealed Bakley's disturbing mail order scam, hired private investigators to pore over her business records recovered in the guest house at the Mata Hari Ranch, and released audiotapes to various press outlets in which the con artist was heard talking to a friend about how best to "play" the birth of her child vis-à-vis her dealings with Christian Brando and Robert Blake. Braun maintained that while the Bakley-Blake union was not a typical example of normal love, the couple's relationship had been improving at the time of her murder. Someone from Bakley's past, possibly any of a hundred or more men she scammed for money and unfulfilled promises of sex, was responsible for her killing, not Blake. Police, as in the O.J. Simpson case, were focusing only on the actor and not following up on any of the numerous leads supplied by her lonely hearts correspondence. In fact, this was not true. The LAPD conducted interviews in twenty states and ran down numerous leads involving threats made against Bakley by unhappy clients. All the potential suspects were cleared.

Bonny Lee Bakley's family hired attorney Cary Goldstein to present an alternative view of the victim in the national media. Half-brother Peter Carlyon told the press Blake had recently threatened his sister's life. During a particularly heated phone argument, the actor allegedly advised Bakley not to let life get her down because he "had a bullet with her name on it." Contrary to Blake's claim, his sister was terrified of guns and did not want him to carry one. Marjorie Lois Carlyon,

Bakley's mother, accused the actor of being abusive and identified the infant, Rosie, as a continued source of friction between the couple. Blake was seemingly obsessed with the child and appeared ready to do anything within his power to keep her away from Bakley and her family. Carlyon advised her daughter to give the baby to the actor and for her own safety get away from him as fast as possible. Still, the family faced a monumental challenge in rehabilitating Bakley's tarnished image especially as many of them were aware of her illegal activities while some were active participants. Bakley's image continued to suffer in the media as the full extent of the mail order sex scam and her fixation on celebrities emerged. Once again, as with the O.J. Simpson ordeal, investigators were faced with the daunting prospect of trying to build a circumstantial case against a celebrity suspected of killing a largely unsympathetic victim.

On April 18, 2002, nearly one year after the shooting, Robert Blake and his bodyguard-handyman Earle Caldwell, 46, were arrested at the Mata Hari Ranch. The actor was held without bail in the Men's Central Jail on a charge of first-degree murder and conspiracy to commit murder while Caldwell, charged with conspiracy, was released on a $1 million bond posted by Blake. The charge against Caldwell was dismissed although he would later figure prominently in the civil proceedings against his employer. In the maelstrom of media coverage following the actor's arrest, O.J. Simpson offered Blake sage advice on the syndicated television show *Extra*— do not take a lie detector test (the football great had and failed miserably). Harland Braun resigned in November 2002 after Blake pursued media interviews against his advice. Jennifer Keller replaced Braun and lasted until January 2003 before leaving for the same reason at roughly the same time Bakley's family filed a "wrongful death" suit against Blake and his handyman, Earle Caldwell. The actor continued to talk. On February 17, 2003, Blake conducted a memorable jailhouse interview with Barbara Walters in which he maintained his innocence, called Bakley's family "monsters," and spoke movingly of his daughter, Rosie. Keller's replacement, Thomas Mesereau, Jr., negotiated bail in the amount of $1.5 million on March 14, 2003, and the actor, outfitted with an electronic monitoring device around his ankle, awaited trial under house arrest at his Mata Hari Ranch on Dilling Street. During pre-trial hearings, however,

Mesereau announced on February 5, 2004 that he was resigning as Blake's attorney due to "irreconcilable differences" with his client. Those close to the case speculated that Mesereau had grown weary of Blake's ongoing contact with the media and constant second-guessing. Mesereau moved on to another celebrity client, Michael Jackson (see entry), representing the singer in his child molestation case. The attorney's abrupt departure put the impending trial on indefinite hold while Blake sought to find new counsel willing to spend months wading through 60,000 pages of evidence in order to come up to speed for what promised to be a lengthy criminal proceeding. On March 1, 2004, Blake found his man, M. Gerald Schwartzbach, a Mill Valley, California attorney with over 35 years of criminal trial experience.

Facing a September 1, 2004, trial date, Schwartzbach quickly took the offensive presenting a pretrial motion in which Christian Brando was fingered as the principal in a conspiracy involving friends to have Bakley killed. In one of Bakley's secretly recorded phone conversations, Brando told the woman that she would be lucky if one of her duped clients did not put a bullet in her head. In a major setback for the defense, the judge ruled the Brando conspiracy theory could not be introduced at trial. On December 1, 2004, a jury of seven men and five women (and six alternates) ranging in age from 24 to 78 were sworn in after weeks of selection. Unlike the O.J. Simpson case, the Blake jurors were not sequestered, but were instructed not to watch news reports, read papers or magazines, or discuss the case with anyone. Press coverage of the trial was restricted to 25 reporters in the courtroom, one or two still cameras, and one video camera to transmit opening and closing arguments and the verdict, but not witness testimony. The next day, Schwartzbach reported his computer containing the majority of his notes on the case had been stolen from his apartment. Police recovered the computer the same day at a pawnshop in Los Angeles (two teens would later be arrested for the theft). The trial began on December 20, 2004, with the 71-year-old actor facing life imprisonment if found guilty on the charges of first-degree murder and soliciting others to commit murder. As outlined by assistant district attorney Shellie Samuels, the case against Robert Blake was stunning in its simplicity. The actor despised Bonny Lee Bakley and wanted her away from their baby, Rosie, with whom he had become obsessed. After failing in his attempts to

persuade hitmen to kill the woman, Blake shot her to death on the evening of May 4, 2001, near Vitello's in Studio City. Schwartzbach for the defense countered that there was no physical evidence (DNA, hair, fiber, fingerprints) of any kind to tie Robert Blake to the murder. Without such concrete evidence, he argued, the prosecution's case was built entirely on the testimony of two demonstrable drug abusers prone to hallucinations. While the couple's marriage was a non-traditional one of convenience, each got something from it they wanted — Blake, a child he adored; Bakley, a celebrity husband. Someone burned in the woman's mail order porno scam was responsible for her death, not Robert Blake.

Prior to calling their star witnesses (the two stuntmen who told authorities Blake had approached them on separate occasions to kill Bakley) the prosecution called William Welch, a former police detective who, beginning in 1988, periodically did private investigatory work for the actor. Welch testified that in 1999 Blake requested a meet to discuss a woman he had recently met in a jazz club. The pair had a one-night stand, the woman turned up pregnant, and now he wanted something done about it. The former detective recommended paying her off, but Blake responded he tried and it did not work. The actor then offered Welch a "blank check" if he would kidnap the woman and force her to have an abortion. If that failed, he was to "whack her." Welch naturally refused to have any part of the plan and Blake called him the next day to report he had dropped the idea. Months passed and Blake called Welch to report Bakley had given birth and he wanted to get the baby away from her. Welch ran a background check on the woman and learned she was violating her parole in Arkansas by leaving the state to come to California. He suggested Blake notify authorities and her have violated, but the actor told him it would not work because she was allegedly having sex with her probation officer. Welch refused to participate in Blake's idea of planting dope in Bakley's hotel. Unable to shake the former detective's testimony, Schwartzbach was only able to get Welch to say he did not feel Blake was referring to murder when he used the word "whack." Sondra Blake Kerr, divorced from Blake since 1982, testified that when they chanced to meet in January 2001 he told her that while the marriage to Bakley was all "smoke and mirrors" the baby was "real." Lead detective Robert Ito, an 18 year veteran of the LAPD, admitted under questioning by Schwartzbach that he failed to order a GSR test of the restaurant booth or the carpet where the actor claimed to have found his gun after returning to Vitello's to look for it. Schwartzbach claimed Ito's failure to investigate a key element of Blake's alibi underscored the fact authorities never seriously considered anyone but the actor to be a viable suspect, not even the victims of Bakley's mail order lonely hearts scam. However, Detective Ito did order a GSR test to be conducted on Blake's hands and clothes even though departmental rules state not to do so if a person has been known to be carrying a firearm.

The prosecution's case against Blake despite the testimony of others at the murder scene or those the actor allegedly spoke to about Bakley rested on the testimony of two stuntmen, Gary McLarty and Ronald "Duffy" Hambleton. McLarty, 64, a stuntman on *Baretta*, said Blake offered him $10,000 to "pop" Bakley and had taken him on a tour of her living quarters in the guest house. In one scenario, Blake said the murder could take place by a river in Laughlin, Nevada. No money ever changed hands only the insinuation that Blake wanted her dead. Under Schwartzbach's intense cross-examination, McLarty admitted he was a heavy cocaine user subject to paranoid delusions. In one particularly vivid delusion, McLarty believed satellites were being used to keep track of him. Both the man's wife and son testified for the defense portraying McLarty as a delusional paranoid constantly high on coke. In 2004, he was hospitalized with mental health problems. The stuntman had also killed a man a few years earlier, but was not charged when it was ruled self-defense.

Ronald "Duffy" Hambleton, a recovering methamphetamine addict, promised to be a more compelling witness for the prosecution. Hambleton, 68 and suffering from leukemia, knew Blake from his stunt work on *Baretta*. In March 2001, the two men were reunited by a mutual friend who informed the stuntman Blake might have a role for him in a movie about dirt bike racing he was planning to produce. Hambleton and the actor met in a restaurant in the San Fernando Valley and after briefly discussing the movie treatment, Blake turned to the real topic of conversation. He wanted Bonny Lee Bakley "snuffed." The woman was "evil" and he refused to let his child grow up around her or her trailer-trash family. According to Hambleton, he met with Blake three times in the desert town of Pearblossom and once in another location to discuss the details of the

murder. In true Hollywood fashion, Blake offered several dramatic scenarios for the hit including a murder set against the majestic backdrop of the Grand Canyon. In one, Blake suggested he and Bakley camp on a lonely road and Hambleton drive-by on a motorcycle and shoot her. When the stuntman pointed out the potential drawback of Blake being present at every hit, the actor assured him that he was more than capable of playing convincing grief scenes. Blake drove the elderly stuntman around the vicinity of Vitello's in Studio City and was exasperated when Hambleton refused the job. The actor allegedly told Hambleton if he would not kill Bakley, he would even if it meant getting caught. No way was his daughter going to grow up in the unhealthy environment surrounding Bakley and her family. Unlike McLarty's account, Hambleton testified that no mention of a money offer was ever made to him by the actor. Like his fellow-stuntman, however, Hambleton suffered from major credibility issues. Schwartzbach pointed out that when first questioned by police he had not only denied knowing of a plot to kill Bakley, but denied being solicited by Blake to commit the murder. Hambleton only changed his story six months after being subpoenaed to testify before a grand jury and by then had been exposed to the sensationalized coverage of the case in the tabloids. The stuntman, however, refused to change his basic story that Blake had approached him to kill Bakley. The defense called witnesses to refute Hambleton's claim he quit using methamphetamine in 1999, two years before his meeting with the actor. As late as 2002 Hambleton was reportedly cooking meth in his home and once suffered from a drug-induced delusion in which people dressed up as sagebrush were sneaking up around his house. In the final analysis, the prosecution could not overcome the lack of physical evidence tying Blake to the murder, their dubious "star witnesses," and perhaps, most importantly, a tremendously unlikable victim. On March 16, 2005, the jury returned to the courtroom after nine days of deliberation and announced Robert Blake was "not guilty" of Bonny Lee Bakley's murder or of one of the two counts of soliciting her murder. The second solicitation charge was dismissed by the judge when it was learned the jury had voted 11–1 in favor of acquittal. A triumphant Blake borrowed a pocket knife and cut off the electronic monitoring bracelet from around his ankle. Always good for a quote, the actor quipped to reporters, "If you want to know how to go through $10 million in five years ask me," adding, "I'm broke. I need a job." In a post-acquittal interview with Barbara Walters Blake admitted the public was still unsure of his innocence, but maintained his wife's killer was probably connected with her sketchy past. Smarting from yet another expensive celebrity prosecution ending in embarrassing failure, District Attorney Steve Cooley called the Blake jurors "incredibly stupid."

The 71-year-old actor was a free man, but like O.J. Simpson before him, faced a "wrongful death" suit with potentially devastating financial consequences. The suit, filed by attorney Eric Dubin on behalf of Bakley's four children, asserted Blake intentionally caused or plotted to cause their mother's death. Also named in the suit was the actor's former handyman, Earle Caldwell, identified as Blake's co-conspirator. Ironically, listed among the other Bakley children (two adults, Holly and Glenn Gawron; and one minor) suing for monetary damages was little Rosie currently in the custody of Blake's grown daughter, Delinah. Unlike a criminal trial in which a unanimous verdict is needed to find culpability or guilt, the burden of proof in a civil proceeding is significantly lower. If 9 of the 12 jurors determined the claims against Blake were more likely than not to be true he would be held liable and ordered to pay restitution. In April 2002 when the case was filed the actor attempted to settle out of court for $250,000, but after the punitive cost of his criminal trial was now unable to tender the same offer. The pre-trial depositions taken in Irvine, California, in May 2005 offered an interesting glimpse into Blake's psyche. Not compelled by law to testify at his criminal trial due to a defendant's natural presumption of innocence, the actor would enjoy no such luxury in the civil proceeding. During his eight hour deposition Blake was combative, abusive, and repeatedly told Eric Dubin, attorney for the Bakley children, to "shut up." Ex-wife Sandra Blake Kerr reported that after she and Blake separated in 1976, the actor put out a contract on her and then boyfriend, Steve Railsback, who was at the time playing the role of Charles Manson in the made-for-television movie, *Helter Skelter*. Kerr testified Blake planned to blame Manson's followers for the killings.

On September 1, 2005, opening statements in Robert Blake's "wrongful death" suit began in a Burbank courtroom. The actor's attorney, Peter Ezzell, described the couple's marriage as one of convenience, but nevertheless one Blake was determined to make work because of the child Rosie. Dubin outlined in great detail Blake's various plans to kidnap the infant and have her mother arrested and killed. Bakley was a flawed woman, but still loved her children and provided for them. Blake, on the stand for seven grueling days, was probably his own worst enemy during the proceedings. Argumentative, overbearing, and combative, the actor claimed to be dyslexic and repeatedly cited his age of 72 as the reason his memories of the night of the murder seemed to differ in every retelling. He loved Bakley even though she had once allegedly offered him her teenaged daughter for sex. Admitting he tried to harangue the woman into aborting their child, Blake said he was an old man and given Bakley's criminal past did not think anything good could come of having a baby with the woman. Asked why he purchased a phonecard he thought was untraceable and called Ronald "Duffy" Hambleton 56 times in the weeks leading up to the killing, Blake responded that he wanted to talk to the stuntman regarding security concerns about people lurking outside his house. The highlight of the proceeding was the appearance of Christian Brando, Bakley's other celebrity lover and a man who loathed Robert Blake for attempting (unsuccessfully) in the criminal trial to implicate him as the woman's real killer. On the stand, Marlon Brando's troubled son repeatedly invoked his Fifth Amendment right against self-incrimination, but did identify his voice on two secretly recorded tapes in which he cautioned Bakley about the dangers of her mail order scam. It was later determined through interviews with jurors that as Brando left the stand he made gestures toward the jury and mouthed the words "guilty" and "he did it" followed by an expletive. Brando would later be found guilty of contempt and fined $1,000 on May 27, 2006. At that time Brando told the judge, "This has been going on for five years. I had absolutely nothing to do with this. I meant no disrespect for your honor or the court. I have to watch my mouth." Leaving the courthouse after his testimony at Blake's civil trial, a reporter asked Brando if he had any idea who may have killed Bonny Lee Bakley. He smiled, shook his head, and replied, "probably sitting up in the room there," a reference to the courtroom. On November 18, 2005, following eight days of deliberation jurors determined by a 10–2 vote that Robert Blake "intentionally caused the death" of his wife. The panel decided handyman Earle Caldwell had not collaborated in the murder. The actor was assessed a whopping $30 million in damages. The jury foreman told reporters that Blake's belligerent and unprofessional behavior on the stand manifested by his calling opposing counsel "chief," "sonny," and "junior" had not helped his case.

On February 4, 2006, Blake filed bankruptcy claiming he owed $1.5 million in federal and state taxes against assets of around $600,000. The actor was so hard up attorney Peter Ezzell wrote off $200,000 in fees. Eric Dubin was not buying the story claiming Blake had spread his assets around in numerous corporations to avoid paying the judgment. Blake had long since sold his beloved Mata Hari Ranch and now lived alone in a rental apartment in the San Fernando Valley on pensions from Social Security and the Screen Actors Guild. At least daughter Rosie was safe and living with her adoptive mother Delinah Blake. In May 2006 the 72-year-old actor told a bankruptcy trustee at a debtor hearing that the costs involved in his criminal ($450,000 per attorney) and civil ($250,000) trials had left him without funds. Although Blake's motion for a new civil trial was rejected without explanation in April 2006, an appeals court in April 2008 ruled the jury's $30 million award was excessive and cut the judgment in half. Bakley attorney Eric Dubin was unconcerned by the reduction since a $15 million award with interest would still amount to about $24 million in damages that he planned to start collecting immediately. M. Gerald Schwartzbach, back on board as Blake's principal attorney, saw little reason for Dubin's optimism, telling reporters, "If Robert had any money he would be paying me." Blake, 77 at the time of this writing, has not worked as an actor since his brief appearance in 1997 as the "Mystery Man" in the David Lynch film *Lost Highway*.

Further Reading

King, Gary C. *Murder in Hollywood: The Secret Life and Mysterious Death of Bonny Lee Bakley*. New York: St. Martin's, 2001.

McDougal, Dennis, and Mary Murphy. *Blood Cold: Fame, Sex, and Murder in Hollywood*. New York: Onyx New American Library, 2002.

"Playboy Interview: Robert Blake." *Playboy*, 24(6) (June 1977):77–78, 80, 82–83, 86, 89, 92–94, 96, 98, 100–101.

Boham, Timothy J. (M)

Under the pseudonym "Marcus Allen" Timothy "John" Boham appeared in 13 hard-core gay films between 2003 and 2005 including *A Body to Die for 3* (Studio 2000), *Ripe* (All Worlds Video), *Never Been Touched* (Rascal Video), and *Through the Woods* (Falcon Studios). The handsome porn performer was also featured on the covers of the gay-oriented publications *Mandate* and *Freshmen*, a magazine targeted at the 18 to 25-year-old market. Boham was voted "Freshman of the Year" in a 2003 annual readership survey and appeared on the cover of the June 2003 issue. In a possible attempt to cross-over into straight porn, Boham was featured on the cover of the November 2006 "campus hunks" issue of *Playgirl* magazine. In the accompanying pictorial, "John" of Denver (Boham) was described as having a "smooth body and 'softer' side." By 2005, the 25-year-old porn performer was making $1,500 to $2,000 a night as an escort servicing both sexes. In late 2005, Boham had the first of several paid sexual encounters with John Paul Kelso, a wealthy 43-year-old Denver businessman and president of Professional Recovery Systems, a collection agency in the "Mile High" city. Boham briefly worked twice for Kelso at the agency during the 11 months they knew each other. On November 13, 2006, Boham (in a statement he would later refute at trial) "got visited by a spirit that told me to go over and rob J.P." The gay escort had a pregnant girlfriend and was behind in rent and payments on his car and motorcycle. Convinced that the safe Kelso kept in his residence contained $400,000 in cash, Boham drove to the man's home in the 3600 block of East Seventh Avenue Parkway on the pretext of engaging in sex. Boham handcuffed the naked man's wrists, perhaps part of their sexual routine, and then abruptly demanded that he open the safe. When Kelso refused, Boham shot him in the head with a .40-caliber semiautomatic pistol. The former porn actor placed the body in the bathtub where he cleaned it of fingerprints. After repeatedly scouring the scene to eliminate evidence, Boham gathered jewelry, clothes, the shell casing, bedding and other items, and tossed them into a creek. The items were recovered a few days later by a construction crew working in the area. Boham used a power saw to cut open the safe, but instead of finding a stash of cash, it contained only two car titles. That night, Boham took his girlfriend out to dinner at the California Pizza Kitchen then caught a show at Comedy Works. Afterwards, he went to his mother and confessed that he had shot someone. Unable to keep his mouth shut, Boham phoned a Denver detective from Arizona the next day and admitted shooting Kelso. He was apprehended three days later at a U.S. Customs and Border Protection station in Lukeville, Arizona, attempting to cross over into Mexico. Boham informed CBP officers that he was wanted on a first-degree murder warrant issued the previous day by Denver authorities.

Tried in a Denver District courtroom on charges of first-degree murder and aggravated robbery in June 2009, Boham, 28, faced the daunting task of negating the raft of confessions he earlier made to various individuals (his mother, sister, pregnant girlfriend, detective). Susan Strong, Boham's mother, told the 9 woman, 3 man jury that she called police after he confessed killing Kelso. In phone conversations between Strong and her son recorded in the Denver County Jail Boham talked about his "craziness" in fabricating stories about the murder, reasoning that "If I get one juror to hold out, I will get a hung jury. Two or three hung juries, and I may get a deal for six to 10 years." Taking the stand in his own defense (always a sure sign that things are not going well for a defendant), Boham maintained that everything he told his mother was a complete fantasy designed to make it appear as though he had flown off the handle and murdered Kelso. The reality according to Boham? Together, they devised a plan to make his (Kelso's) suicide look like a murder-robbery so that the businessman's life insurance would pay out to his beneficiaries. Kelso, a chronic alcoholic whose blood alcohol level at the time of his death was more than four times the legal limit, shot himself in a depressed state over the recent breakup of two relationships. On June 9, 2009, the jury needed less than five hours to reject Boham's fantastical story and find him guilty of all charges. "Marcus Allen" was subsequently sentenced to the mandatory term of life imprisonment without the possibility of parole.

Further Reading

McPhee, Mike. "Collector's Killing Goes to Jury: The Accused Calls it Suicide, but His Mom Says He Confessed." *Denver Post*, June 6, 2009, sec. B, p. 2.

Bornais, Claude (V)

On the morning of August 24, 2000, horrified neighbors of Canadian-born Claude Bornais, 65, and his 51-year-old Dominican wife, Carmen, witnessed the knife-wielding woman chase the big bandleader-jazz musician out of their home, and down the street of a gated community in Boca Raton, Florida. When Claude Bornais finally crumpled to the pavement he had been gravely wounded from at least 20 slash marks and stab wounds ranging from the top of his head downwards. The tip of the knife blade broke off in his body. Bornais died the following day and Carmen was charged with second-degree murder. She told police her husband of eight months had been abusive, and that she had merely acted in self-defense after Bornais had attempted to stab her. A sheriff's report, however, indicated the wounds on her left arm looked to be self-inflicted. Although the marriage appeared outwardly tranquil according to the bandleader's professional associates, a note found in Bornais' car after his death listed 21 domestic problems with his wife. Bornais wrote, "(she) Cannot fill out job application," "(her) closets and drawers (are in) total disarray," and complained that she spoke little English, and was unable to read street signs or music. The laundry list of complaints closed with the cryptic entry, "Don't let others destroy me!"

Attorneys for Carmen, a hairstylist in Boca Raton, mounted a "battered spouse defense" arguing Bornais was such a controlling tyrant that he forced his wife to give him all her money while physically punishing her for offences as minor as bringing him the wrong brand of beer. Insanely jealous by Carmen's account, the bandleader barred her from taking English lessons because he feared she might meet Latin men. Often, she claimed, Bornais dragged her by the hair, slapped her, and afterwards begged her not to leave him. The prosecution countered this image of the battered spouse justifiably driven to protect herself from an abusive husband, by casting Carmen as a "weeping-but-wily" woman attempting to manipulate events to stay out of prison. On February 13, 2002, a jury rejected Carmen's battered spouse claim and found her guilty of second-degree murder. After hearing the verdict, she fell to her knees and prayed. In June 2002, Carmen Bornais was sentenced to the minimum prison term of 20½ years and, following her release, ordered placed on probation for another 20 years.

Further Reading

Pacenti, John. "Band Leader's Turbulent Marriage Led to His Stabbing Death, Records Show." *Palm Beach Post*, October 13, 2000, sec. B, p. 3.

Bourn, Verlon (V)

Known as JahBuddha, the 35-year-old African-American guitarist specialized in reggae, new age jazz, and world beat music in the Oakland, California, area. His self-released CD, *Seven Chakras: Kundalini Meditation*, was offered on the Internet through Inersha Entertainment. On May 13, 2002, Bourn argued with his roommate Andre Scott, 38, over the division of a $1,000 electric bill, at the home they shared in Oakland at 1001 Chester Street. The dispute ended when Scott fatally shot Bourn five times. In the basement, police found fifty mature marijuana plants, dozens of smaller seedlings, and several powerful lights used to grow them. While awaiting trial, Scott hanged himself with a bed sheet in his cell at the Santa Rita County Jail on May 17, 2002.

Further Reading

Zamora, Jim Herron. "Musician Who Grew Pot in His Basement Is Gunned Down by Roomie, Cops Say." *San Francisco Chronicle*, May 15, 2002, sec. A, p. 1.

Brancato, Lillo, Jr. (M-acquitted)

Brancato, born in Bogotá, Colombia, on August 19, 1976, was adopted at the age of four months by an Italian-American couple and raised in Yonkers, New York. In the summer of 1993, the 17-year-old was hanging out with his brother at Jones Beach when he was noticed by a casting agent for the film *A Bronx Tale*, written by Chazz Palminteri and directed by Robert De Niro. Brancato, aided by his crooked nose good looks and "dese" and "dose" manner of speaking, won the agent over by his spot on impressions of De Niro and fellow-tough guy Joe Pesci. He was cast in the 1960s coming of age story set in an Italian neighborhood of the Bronx as the son of honest, hard working Robert De Niro attracted to the lifestyle of local mobster Chazz Palminteri. Brancato received good reviews for his performance and his acting future looked bright. Success went to the teenager's head. The principal at his local Catholic high school asked Brancato to leave after he continued to pick fights with other male classmates irregardless of their size. At home, he frequently lashed out at his adoptive parents screaming that they were not his real mother and father. Professionally, Brancato kept busy with roles in a string of motion pictures including *Renaissance Man* (1994), *Crimson Tide* (1995), *Enemy of the State* (1998), and *The Adventures of Pluto Nash*. On television, he played the character of wiseguy wannabe "Matt Bevilacqua" in a six episode story arc of *The Sopranos* during the 1999-2000 season. Following a failed attempt to whack "Tony Soprano's" cousin, "Christopher," Brancato's character whimpered "Mommy" as the mobster shot him execution-style in the head. In 2000, he was cast as "Lucky" in the short-lived CBS series *Falcone*, based on the life of undercover FBI agent Joseph D. Pistone, whose infiltration of the Bonnano crime family and subsequent book inspired the 1997 film *Donnie Brasco*.

What was becoming increasingly apparent to casting agents, directors, and fellow-actors, however, was already well-known to his friends. Lillo Brancato had a major league drug habit that was inexorably destroying his career and personal life. Sometime in 2003 Brancato met Steven Armento, a 46-year-old ex-con who was at one time a low-level associate of the Genovese crime family until he was tossed out of the mob for drug addiction. Armento's rap sheet included a history of 13 arrests on weapons, drug, burglary, and other charges. In March 2004, a woman in Armento's Yonkers neighborhood filed an order of protection against him after he fired a gun at her passing van and sicced his pit bull on her fiancé. Brancato and Armento were drug buddies, but there was another attraction for the now struggling actor — Armento's beautiful, but anti-drug daughter, Stefanie. Brancato met Stefanie Armento in 2003 at a gym in Yonkers where she worked. The pair began a tempestuous 1½ year relationship punctuated by frequent breakups instigated by his escalating drug use. Stefanie Armento tried often to break with the drug addicted actor, but her father always interceded on his friend's behalf. By 2005, Brancato's drug use started showing up on police radar. In March 2005, he was arrested in Hermosa Beach, California after officers noticed he was hanging around a suspected drug dealer outside a bar. Brancato's rapid speech and dilated eyes were enough probable cause for officers to suspect he was high, a suspicion confirmed by a urine test that revealed traces of cocaine, marijuana, Valium, and other opiates in his system. He was arrested and released on bail. In June 2005, Yonkers police arrested the 29-year-old actor after discovering four glassine bags filled with heroin in his car during a routine traffic stop. Shortly after the arrest, in the summer of 2005, Stefanie Armento broke with her troubled boyfriend. Brancato tried to get himself clean through drug rehab programs, but the siren call of drugs was too strong. Two weeks after returning from a drug treatment program in Los Angeles, Brancato showed up at Stefanie Armento's home in Yonkers on December 8, 2005, demanding to see her. When Armento refused, he smashed in her front door then stood in the yard screaming abuse at the terrified woman cowering within the house. Police arrived to find Brancato sitting in the middle of the road blocking traffic and shouting, "Don't you know who I am?" The out of control actor was issued a summons for harassment and disorderly conduct.

The next night, December 9, Brancato and Steven Armento, 49, walked into the Crazy Horse Cabaret, a strip club on Boston Post Road in the Bronx. Brancato, despondent and upset over the break with Stefanie, was again using narcotics and the men spent most of the evening drinking and figuring out where they could score more drugs. Brancato suggested a visit to the apartment of Kenneth Scovotti, a 63-year-old Vietnam veteran who regularly supplied him with prescription drugs like Valium. Although Brancato had repeatedly stolen drugs from Scovotti's residence at 3119 Arnow Place in Pelham Bay, the starstruck veteran allowed the actor to crash at his place whenever he was too stoned to drive to Yonkers. Armento and Brancato left the Crazy Horse at 4:00 A.M. on the morning of December 10 and drove to Scovotti's apartment unaware the man had died several months earlier in July 2005. Two days prior to their early morning raid the apartment had been cleaned out and no longer contained Valium. Arriving at the basement apartment and unable to arouse Scovotti, a drunken Brancato kicked in a window and entered the vacant apartment while Armento, too large to squeeze through the window, waited outside. Finding nothing after a hasty search, Brancato and Armento left the scene and drove to the nearby home of Joseph Borelli, the actor's main drug dealer. Borelli, despite the gun Armento brandished in his face, refused to supply the dope sick men and told them to get lost. The return of the jonesing pair to Arnow Place to renew their interrupted search of Scovotti's apartment set into motion a deadly sequence of events. The earlier sound of breaking glass had awakened the next door neighbor at 3117 Arnow Place, Officer Daniel Enchautegui, who had just turned in after working a 4:00 P.M. to midnight shift at the 40th Precinct in the Bronx. A three-year veteran of the force, the 28 year old quickly dressed, placed his police shield around his neck, armed himself with his eight shot off-duty Kahr semiautomatic, and went outside to investigate. Enchautegui called 911 on his cell phone for backup and informed the dispatcher what he was wearing so as not to be mistaken for one of the criminals. The police officer followed procedure to the letter and would have been wearing a bulletproof vest had he had one at home. Investigating the broken window, Enchautegui confronted the two men walking down an alley between the buildings around 5:20 A.M. and loudly identified himself as a police officer. Armento opened fire with a .357 Smith & Wesson fatally striking Enchautegui once in the left side of the chest piercing his aorta. Although mortally wounded, the off-duty officer emptied his pistol at the suspects and, remarkably, made every shot count. Gunman Steven Armento was hit six times; three in the right leg and once each in the stomach, groin, and left arm. Brancato, unarmed, was shot twice in the chest. The wounded actor managed to climb into Armento's Dodge Durango, but was immediately taken into custody by officers responding to Enchautegui's 911 call. Police spotted the armed Armento limping down the street and he collapsed to the street when told to halt. Enchautegui was pronounced dead at Jacobi Medical Center at 6:09 A.M. while in the same facility Brancato and Armento were listed in serious, but stable condition. Officer Daniel Enchautegui, heralded as a hero by the mayor and police commissioner, was the second NYPD officer killed in the line of duty within two weeks. He was posthumously promoted to the rank of detective and in his honor a Pelham Bay street-corner was renamed Detective Daniel Enchautegui Way.

On December 11, 2005, Armento was charged with first-degree murder and his unarmed accomplice with murder in the second-degree. Both men were also charged with criminal possession of a weapon and second-degree burglary. While awaiting trial on Rikers Island, Brancato overdosed on heroin on November 11, 2006 in what was reported as a suicide attempt. The actor was rushed by ambulance to Elmhurst Hospital Center and returned to Rikers the next day. The drug incident earned Brancato a stint in solitary confinement, his third visit to the "hole" since being incarcerated. As the trial date approached, Daniel Enchautegui's father died in May 2007 and was buried next to his son. Top New York attorney Joseph Tacopina, hired by Brancato after his first attorney died, was an effective and aggressive advocate. In October 2007, Tacopina had Brancato's post-arrest statements tossed out after he convinced a judge that his client had already retained an attorney and should not have been questioned by police outside of counsel's presence. In September 2008, he was able to have the cases severed so that his client could be tried separately from the acknowledged gunman. Armento was tried the next month, quickly found guilty of first-degree murder, and sentenced to life imprisonment without the possibility of parole. In November 2008, nearly three years after the killing of Officer Daniel Enchautegui, the 32-year-old actor faced a possible 25 years to life sentence if convicted of charges of second-degree murder and second-degree burglary. Tacopina characterized Brancato as a drug addict who was simply in the wrong place at the wrong time with the wrong person. Brancato did not have a gun, was unaware Armento was armed, and did not burglarize the residence of Kenneth Scovotti because the man had given the actor an open invitation to visit at any time. Brancato had only kicked in the basement window in a bid to attract the veteran's attention. Joseph Borelli, the actor's principal drug supplier, testified for the prosecution that during the pair's early morning visit to his home to obtain drugs Brancato witnessed Armento pull a handgun. Finally, Brancato took the stand and admitted that while he was a junkie, he was no murderer. He was high on heroin and crack that night and unaware his friend was carrying a handgun. Brancato offered no explanation for the latex gloves recovered by police at the scene (compelling evidence of a planned burglary) although experts testified that both men's DNA was on them. On December 22, 2008, a formerly deadlocked jury cleared the one-time actor of the murder and weapons charges, but found him guilty of first-degree attempted burglary. Brancato was subsequently sentenced to 10 years in prison, but having already served more than 3 years since his arrest could be out in 5. Chazz Palminteri, the actor-screenwriter who first gave the inexperienced teen a shot at stardom in 1993 by casting him in *A Bronx Tale*, summed up the entertainment industry's prevailing sentiment regarding Brancato when he told a reporter, "This kid had so much natural ability but did nothing with it. Nothing. Zero."

Further Reading

Wilson, Michael, and Janon Fisher. "An Actor, a Thief and a Shared Path Downhill." *The New York Times*, December 16, 2005, sec. B, p. 1.

Brando, Christian (M)

In 1957, Marlon Brando, Hollywood's most famous actor, was introduced to Anna Kashfi, an exotically beautiful 22-year-old Anglo-Indian actress Paramount had just cast in *The Mountain*, a Spencer Tracy vehicle co-starring Robert Wagner. The actor, notorious for his affairs with a string of actresses ranging from France Nuyen to Rita Moreno, was intrigued by Kashfi's dark beauty and, informed she was pregnant with his child, married the actress that same year. Disastrously for the newlyweds, Brando immediately learned that Kashfi's official studio biography was almost pure fantasy. Enterprising reporters discovered that while Kashfi may have spent time in Darjeeling, neither of her parents was Indian nor had she had been educated in a French convent. Instead, she was Joanna Mary O'Callaghan, the daughter of a dark-skinned Frenchwoman and an English railroad worker who once worked on an Indian railroad. O'Callaghan worked as a waitress and runway model in London prior to changing her name to Kashfi, constructing a biography, and arriving in Hollywood and a movie role. By all accounts, Brando's knowledge that Kashfi was in essence a fraud irreparably damaged the marriage although he bought them a 12-bedroom estate at 12900 Mulholland Drive in Bel Air. On May 11, 1958, Christian Devi (Sanskrit for "goddess") Brando was born to parents whose relationship was already imploding. Weeks after his son's birth, Brando left the marriage to continue uninterrupted a string of serial sexual affairs. Kashfi was granted an uncontested divorce in 1960 and was awarded sole custody of Christian, a payout of $444,000 over the next decade for her maintenance, and $1,000 a month for child support.

In the 12-year custody battle which ensued, among the most rancorous in Hollywood history, Christian Brando was psychically destroyed by his parents' legal wrangling. Dragged in an out of courtrooms, the young boy heard his mother brand his father as a "morally unfit" parent who physically abused her. Brando counter-charged that Kashfi was also a batterer who was, quite simply, a drug addict and drunk. In 1966, a judge withdrew custody of the youngster from Kashfi declaring her reliance on drugs and alcohol fuelled her uncontrollable temper. Sent by the court to live with Brando's older sister, the boy was already irreparably damaged. Moody, withdrawn, and painfully underweight, Christian vented his anger by physically lashing out against animals, his mother, and classmates. Like many children of divorce, Christian learned to manipulate circumstances to his advantage. Undisciplined and unruly around everyone except his father, Christian was always on his best behavior around Brando. In 1974, Kashfi cancelled her final lawsuit against her ex-husband claiming he was cooperating in visitation rights. From that time forward, Marlon Brando loosely supervised his son with mixed results. Even the actor, however, ultimately realized his teenaged son had problems with drugs and alcohol. Refusing to confront the problem directly, Brando told Christian that while he disapproved of the behaviors, he should at least confine them to binging on days he was visiting the house on Mulholland. Over the next several years, Christian was in-and-out of various private schools, but dropped out when he reached 18. Brando continued to pay his son's bills, buy him cars, and at one point enrolled with him in a correspondence course to earn their high school degrees together. The plan ended when neither wanted to study.

Christian married childhood friend Mary McKenna, a cosmetician, in 1981, but they divorced a year later. McKenna later reported the disturbed man had threatened her mother with a gun. Working as a tree surgeon in Beverly Hills and as a welder, the 29-year-old Brando was offered the role of a hitman in a proposed 1987 Italian film, *La Posta in Gioco* (*The Stake Is High*), but the movie was never made. Two years later, trade publications reported he and drug guru Timothy Leary planned to collaborate on *Trippers, LSD '66*, but that movie was not made either. Brando's filmography consists of brief appearances in *Unmasked Part 25* (1988) and *Wishful Thinking* (1990). In 1988 at the age of 30, Brando received the first installment of his trust fund, $100,000, but quickly squandered it on booze, drugs, and freeloading friends.

By May 1990, Christian Brando was a 32-year-old largely unemployable misfit with a multi-year history of behavioral problems and substances abuse living rent-free in his father's Mulholland Drive mansion. Marlon Brando, 66, shared the home with his common-law wife, Tarita Teriipia, the Tahitian actress he met while filming *Mutiny on the Bounty* in 1962. Also in residence was their 20-year-old daughter, Cheyenne, and her lover, 26-year-old Tahitian-born Dag Drollet. Cheyenne Brando, eight months pregnant with Drollet's child, had recently come from Tahiti at her father's request to have the baby in the United States. Perhaps even more emotionally unstable than her half-brother Christian, Cheyenne had endured years of neglect from her famous father descending into drug addiction in the bargain. Drollet, tired of his lover's jealous rages and drug abuse, sought to end the relationship even after learning she was pregnant with his child.

On the evening of May 16, 1990, Christian and Cheyenne went to dinner together at Musso & Frank Grill on Hollywood Boulevard. During the course of the meal, Christian consumed at least three drinks while his half-sister informed him that Drollet had slapped her around (an allegation never proven). Returning to the Mulholland Drive manse, Christian (by his initial account) angrily waved a pistol in the face of the 6' 3", 270-pound Tahitian while denouncing the man's abuse of Cheyenne. During their ensuing struggle on the couch, the gun discharged striking Drollet in the face. Marlon Brando, in another part of the house at the time of the shooting, attempted to resuscitate Drollet, but he had been killed instantly. At the death scene, a talkative Christian allegedly told police, "I shot him man, but not on purpose ... I wasn't crazy about the guy, but what was I going to do? We were rolling around on the couch. He was trying to shoot me. I don't know who was trying to shoot who. He grabbed me, and the [expletive] thing shot him in the head." The evidence, however, failed to fit Brando's account of the crime. Drollet was shot while lying on the couch on his back. In one hand, investigators found the dead man holding a pack of cigarette papers, a pack of tobacco, and a lighter while in the other he clasped a television remote control. Tested three hours after the shooting, Christian Brando's blood alcohol level was .24, three times the legal limit to operate a motor vehicle in California. A key witness to the event, Cheyenne was hastily sent to Tahiti to avoid being called as a potential witness against her half-brother at trial. One month after the killing, Marlon Brando's severely depressed and drug addicted daughter gave birth to Drollet's son, Tuki. The infant was immediately placed in a detoxification unit. Her lover's death shattered what little mental stability the young woman still possessed. As the international legal battle raged over her potential extradition to Los Angeles to testify at Christian's trial, she overdosed on tranquilizers and antidepressants on November 1, 1990. Ten days later she tried to hang herself from a tree with a dog chain.

Half a world away, Christian Brando faced his own problems. After initially hiring civil rights attorney William Kunstler to defend his son, Brando retained Los Angeles attorney Robert Shapiro, later to achieve fame as a member of the "Dream Team" purchased to defend football star turned actor O.J. Simpson (see entry) in a double homicide. Shapiro began immediately earning his massive fee. Noting the millionaire's son had not been informed by police that counsel could be provided him at no cost, Shapiro convinced the judge to toss out the "confession" his client had made shortly after police arrived on the scene and later reiterated under questioning at the station. As Shapiro worked behind the scenes to block the D.A.'s attempt to extradite Cheyenne to Los Angeles, the usually reclusive Marlon Brando took center stage with the media in support of his son. The first-degree murder case against Brando fell apart after the court ruled Cheyenne's "fragile mental condition" precluded her from traveling to Los Angeles to offer testimony at her half-brother's trial. Shapiro negotiated a plea of voluntary manslaughter for Christian in January 1991 and during the subsequent sentencing hearing the prosecution pressed for the maximum 16 year sentence. Psychiatrists offered analysis of Christian both pro and con, but the most compelling testimony came from Marlon Brando in a scene eerily reminiscent of Lana Turner's appearance in court nearly 33 years earlier in defense of her daughter, Cheryl Crane (see entry). In what many considered his greatest performance, Brando told the judge he blamed himself and Anna Kashfi for the emotional damage done to Christian by their multi-year feud. The actor tearfully accepted responsibility for any mistakes he had made, but added he had done the best he could. Christian later took the stand and apologized to Drollet's parents who were in the courtroom. On February 28, 1991, Brando was sentenced to 10 years in prison (6 on the manslaughter charge; 4 on aggravating circumstances, i.e. use of a gun) with parole eligibility after serving 5 years.

Christian did his time at the California Men's Colony in San Luis Obispo, about 180 miles northwest of Los Angeles, where he earned his high school G.E.D. and trained as a machinist. Fellow-inmates described the son of the iconic actor as quiet, depressed, and giving the impression that he was sorry to have disgraced his father. The prison waived its policy against no Monday prisoner visits to accommodate Marlon Brando who was driven in a limo every week to visit his son. Christian Brando, 37, was released from prison on January 10, 1996. Time earned for good behavior and participation in educational classes had reduced his 10 year sentence to slightly less than 5 years of actual incarceration. Under the terms of his release, Christian remained under 3 years supervised parole in the Los Angeles County area and was forbidden to drink alcohol. Brando immediately had his parole transferred to New Hampshire reporting monthly to an officer in Brentwood while residing in Derry. He took classes at the New Hampshire Technical Institute in Nashua. Christian transferred out of the area on January 24, 1997 relocating to the small town of Kalama, Washington about 35 miles northwest of Portland, Oregon. The residents liked and respected the quiet welder and carefully guarded his identity against rubberneckers and reporters. In turn, Brando often told friends that it was one of the few places on earth he felt accepted and at peace.

Christian Brando might have lived out the remainder of his life in relative obscurity save for the occasional divorce or odd alcohol-drug charge if not for his involvement with Bonny Lee Bakley and her ill-fated husband, actor Robert Blake (see entry). Bakley, an operator of a mail order sex scam targeting lonely men, decided early in life that if she could not be a celebrity she would marry one. Bakley first set her sights on Christian Brando and the pair had a sexual relationship in late 1999–early 2000. Brando, however, was not so much interested in marrying the scam artist as in having regular sex. Bakley, 44, next targeted 67-year-old actor Robert Blake best known as the star of the popular 1970s television series *Baretta*. Like Brando, Blake was also interested in having sex with Bakley, but not in a permanent relationship. Bakley, however, played her trump card—she was pregnant and informed both men that one of them was the father. Brando, unlike Blake who felt he had been duped, was unconcerned about the forthcoming child. Bakley named the female infant "Christian Shannon Brando" when she was born on June 2, 2000. Robert Blake demanded she take a DNA test and when results confirmed the infant was his decided to "do the right" thing and married Bakley. Nevertheless, the actor was openly resentful of the woman he felt had used the innocent child to trap him. The marriage lasted until the evening of May 4, 2001 when Bakley, out for dinner with husband Blake, was shot to death outside of an Italian restaurant in the Studio City section of Los Angeles. Blake was arrested and charged with the murder and his defense team used the nearly 3½ years prior to the case going to trial on December 20, 2004 to find an alternative theory of the crime that did not make their now 71-year-old client look so incredibly guilty. Bakley routinely (and illegally) audiotaped and cataloged her telephone conversations without the knowledge of Christian Brando and many others. In one tape recorded in October or December 1999, Brando warned Bakley about her dangerous scamming. "You better get a handle on that," he cautioned, "and really think what you're doing, running around sending letters to guys, embezzling money from these idiots. Think about it. It gets close. You're lucky — not on my behalf— but you're lucky somebody ain't out there to put a bullet in your head." Blake's lawyers argued in pre-trial hearings that the taped conversation strongly suggested Brando was deeply involved in a conspiracy to murder his former lover. In October 2004, the presiding judge in the case ruled jurors would not hear the tapes. Brando's comments were simply irrelevant. Blake, however, did not need the tapes to be included. He was acquitted of Bakley's murder on March 16, 2005.

The Bakley-Blake-Brando legal merry-go-round did not end with the actor's acquittal. The dead woman's family filed a multimillion dollar wrongful death suit against Blake and, this time, the septuaganerian's defense team could include, and did, Brando's "damning" audiotape. Called to the stand on October 25, 2005, Christian repeatedly invoked his Fifth Amendment against possible self-incrimination. As he was leaving the witness stand, Brando made the mistake of pointing to Blake and mouthing the words "He did it" and an expletive to the jury. Questioned later by reporters if he had any idea who might have killed Bakley, Brando smiled and said, "probably sitting up in the room there," a pointed reference to Blake seated in the courtroom. Robert Blake was found liable in November 2005 for Bakley's death and ordered to pay $30 million in damages. In May 2006, Christian was found in contempt of court for his crack to the jury and fined $1,000 for his courtroom outburst. "Your honor," Brando addressed the judge, "This has been going on for five years. I had absolutely nothing to do with this. I mean no disrespect for you or the court. I have to watch my mouth. When I'm overwhelmed I lose it sometimes. I'm taking medication for that."

While still embroiled in the Bakley-Blake murder drama, Brando's homelife unraveled. In December 2005, Deborah Brando, a woman he met in 1990, married in October 1994, and divorced in 1995, filed suit against him charging that shortly after Marlon Brando's death on July 1, 2004, Christian often abused and threatened to kill both her and her 11-year-old daughter from a previous marriage. Court papers filed by the woman painted a dark picture of a troubled marriage. One month after the actor's death, the Brando family moved into the Mulholland Drive manse scene of the Drag Drollet killing. According to Deborah Brando, Christian beat and forced her to have sex under threat of being suffocated with a pillow. Once in a rage, he chased his stepdaughter threatening to dismember her. In January 2005, Brando pleaded guilty to charges of spousal abuse, and was sentenced to two months of drug and alcohol rehab, a spousal-abuse prevention program, and three years probation. On February 6, 2007, the day jury selection was set to begin for Christian's trial on charges including violation of civil rights, assault, domestic violence, battery and emotional distress, the battling Brandos settled out of court for undisclosed terms.

Almost as a blessing, the 49-year-old's tragic, emotionally devastated life began winding down on January 11, 2008, when he was admitted into Hollywood Presbyterian Medical Center with a diagnosed case of pneumonia. Though his attorney predicted a full recovery, Brando died on the morning of January 27, 2008. Based on the troubled man's past history with drugs, Brando's family requested the coroner's office conduct an autopsy that included a toxicology analysis (it came back negative with the official cause of death ruled pneumonia). Two days after Christian's death, ex-wife Deborah Brando sued the executors of Marlon Brando's estate asserting she was the victim of professional negligence, fraud and deceit. The woman claimed that as part of her February 2007 settlement with Christian, she would become assignee of her ex-husband's rights and claims in the estate. Christian Brando was buried on February 19, 2008, at the Kalama Oddfellows Cemetery following an hour-long service conducted at a chapel in nearby Longview and attended by fifty people. Brando had often remarked that Kalama was one of the few places he felt accepted and at peace. His mother, Anna Kashfi, whom he had not seen or spoken to in 25 years, and first wife, Mary, announced their intention to be buried next to him in the small southwest Washington town. Brando's girlfriend, Leah Donna Geon, filed suit in January 2009 claiming ownership of all his property (power tools, music equipment) based upon her lover's assertion that he would provide for her after his death. Anna Kashfi, 74, administrator of her son's estate, disputed Geon's claims. However, in May 2009 both parties agreed to mediation to settle the dispute which remains unresolved at the time of this book's publication.

Further Reading

Higham, Charles. *Brando: The Unauthorized Biography*. New York: New American Library, 1987.
Kanfer, Stefan. *Somebody: The Reckless Life and Remarkable Career of Marlon Brando*. New York: Alfred A. Knopf, 2008.
Schickel, Richard. *Brando: A Life in Our Times*. New York: Atheneum, 1991.

Brathwaite, Junior (V)

The third member of the Jamaican reggae group The Wailers and its various incarnations to die violently (see entries for Carlton Barrett and Peter Tosh), Franklin Delano Alexander Brathwaite, better known as "Junior," was born in Kingston, Jamaica on April 4, 1949. With neighborhood friends Bob Marley, Peter McIntosh (Tosh) and others he was co-founder in 1963 of The Wailers, a popular island vocal group. Generally acknowledged as having the best voice (a high tenor) in the group, Brathwaite sang lead on the songs "It Hurts to Be Alone," "Don't Ever Leave Me," "Habits," and "Straight and Narrow Way." In the summer of 1964, Junior left the band and immigrated to Chicago to join his family, hoping to realize a medical career that never happened, later settling in Wisconsin. Twenty years after exiting his home country, Brathwaite returned to Jamaica to appear on *Never Ending Wailers*, an album of reworked songs initiated by Peter Tosh and released to a lukewarm reception in 1991. Over the next several years, the singer tried unsuccessfully to restart his career. On June 2, 1999, Brathwaite, 47, and friend Lawrence ("Chadda") Scott, 49, were at Scott's home on Rose Avenue in the Duhaney Park section of Kingston. According to published reports, three men emerged from a car, entered the house, and shot both men who were later pronounced dead on arrival at the Kingston Public Hospital. Police believe the unsolved murders were part of a gangland drug war in which Scott was the intended target and Brathwaite just collateral damage.

Further Reading

Katz, David. "Junior Brathwaite; The Original Lead Vocalist for Bob Marley's Wailers." *The Guardian* (London), June 23, 1999, p. 18.
Steckles, Garry. *Bob Marley: A Life*. Northampton, MA: InterlinkBooks, 2009.

Brish, Jerome *see* **Haskel**, Presley

Buckland, Wilfred, Sr. (M–S)

Born in 1866, Buckland was a stage director for David Belasco before entering films in 1914 as an art director for Famous Players–Lasky. As the first bona fide art director in the motion picture industry, he was credited with widening the scope of films by freeing them from the scenic limitations of the stage. An innovator, Buckland was the first to build architectural settings for films, and introduced artificial lighting into movies through the use of klieg lights. Buckland, often uncredited, served as the art director for several films directed by Cecil B. DeMille. These include: *The Squaw Man* (1914 and 1918 versions), *The Call of the North* (1914), *The Ghost Breaker* (1914), *The Virginian* (1914), *The Warrens of Virginia* (1915), *The Trail of the Lonesome Pine* (1916), *The Devil Stone* (1917), *We Can't Have Everything* (1918), *For Better, For Worse* (1919), and *Adam's Rib* (1923). At 60, Buckland reached the pinnacle of his phenomenal career as "Hollywood's first art director" by creating the castle setting for the 1922 Douglas Fairbanks epic *Robin Hood*, directed by Allan Dwan. Buckland was 80 years old and in poor health when he decided he could not chance leaving the care of his 36-year-old mentally ill son, Wilfred Buckland, Jr., to strangers. In 1940, shortly after the death of his mother, the younger Buckland had suffered a mental breakdown. The next year, the one-time Princeton student was committed to the Camarillo State Hospital for the Insane. Discharged, he suffered a second breakdown in 1944. In early July 1944, Buckland, Jr., quit his job in a studio prop department because of "increasing nervousness." On July 18, 1944, Buckland, Sr. entered his son's bedroom in the home they shared at 2035 Pinehurst Avenue in Hollywood, fired one shot from a .32-caliber Mauser automatic pistol into the sleeping man's head, and turned the gun on himself. The art director died in an ambulance en route to a hospital. In a note disposing of his possessions and naming William DeMille, the producer-brother of former colleague Cecil B. DeMille, as executor of his estate, Buckland wrote, "I am taking Billy with me."

Further Reading

"Film Pioneer Buckland Kills His Son and Himself." *Los Angeles Times*, July 19, 1944, sec. A, p. 1.

Bugz (V)

The MC Bugz (born Karnail Paul Pitts on January 5, 1997) was a highly regarded rapper in Detroit and an early member of the group D12 (Dirty Dozen) along with Proof (see entry). Bugz, also known onstage as Robert Beck, had just turned 21 and his future in the rap world looked bright. D12 had recently signed with Eminem's label Shady Records and a debut EP was in the works. On the evening of May 21, 1999, the group was set to perform in Grand Rapids, Michigan as part of the Eminem tour when the promising talent became just another victim in rap's bloody history. That afternoon, Bugz, his cousin, and a female friend were picnicking on Detroit's Belle Island when a man sprayed the woman with a high powered water gun. She took offense, angry words were exchanged, and a fistfight broke out. Bugz sought to intervene and a friend of the man with the water gun drew a rifle from a Ford Expedition and shot the rapper three times at close range, striking him in the neck and chest. The assailants drove over Bugz as they fled the scene. An ambulance was called, but due to heavy traffic on the bridge to Belle Island it took thirty minutes to reach the wounded MC. Bugz died without regaining consciousness in a nearby hospital. The deadly incident, captured on the park's security video and shown on local news, generated no leads and to date no arrests have been made in the case. Thanks to D12, material unreleased at the time of the young rapper's death was made available on *These Streets EP*. The group's members and Eminem have "Bugz" tattooed on their wrists in remembrance of their fallen friend. In the 2004 album, *D12 World*, the songs "Bugz 97" and "Good Die Young" honor his memory.

Further Reading

www.deadpoetz.com.

Burmeister, Christoffer (V)

The Bush Pilots, a jazz fusion band that described its music as "klezmer-Viking-punk-funk," was formed in northern Denmark in 1990. Relegated to playing high schools and small bars in Scandinavia, the group decided in 1997 to come to New York City where their perseverance was rewarded with an upcoming gig on March 7, 1997, at Wetlands, a trendy Manhattan nightclub. On February 23, 1997, bandmembers Matthew Gross and Christoffer Burmeister, a 33-year-old guitarist and expectant father, were topping off a day of sightseeing in the city with a trip to the Empire State Building. The pair was on the building's 86th floor observation deck when Ali Hassan Abu Kamal, a 69-year-old Palestinian, randomly opened fire with a .380-caliber semiautomatic Beretta pistol. Prior to turning the gun on himself, Kamal shot Burmeister in the head while critically wounding five others, including American-born Bush Pilots guitarist Matthew Gross. Kamal's shooting spree was not politically motivated, but prompted by the Palestinian's recent loss of $300,000 in life savings amassed over a fifty-year career teaching English to private students. Days later, metal detectors were installed at the Empire State Building. In March 2004, a New York State Appeals court dismissed a multimillion dollar lawsuit filed against the Empire State Building on behalf of Burmeister and the five survivors of the shooting declaring, in effect, the building's management had taken sufficient security precautions prior to Kamal's murderous rampage.

Further Reading

Pyle, Richard. "Gunman Kills Tourist and Self, Wounds Others in Empire State Spree." Associated Press, February 24, 1997.

Burton, Roderick Anthony, II *see* Dolla

Byard, Jaki (V)

Acknowledged as one of the most versatile pianists in jazz, Byard (born John Arthur Byard on June 15, 1922, in Worcester, Massachusetts) came from a musical family (his father was a trombonist in marching bands, his mother a church pianist) and he played his first professional engagement at the age of 16. Following a stint in the army during World War II, Byard left the military in 1944 with the ability to play almost any instrument with equal facility. An early bebopper in New York, the musician returned to his home base of Boston in the mid–1940s recording with jazz saxophonist Charlie Marinaro and later touring with R&B great Earl Bostic. In the early 1950s, Byard distinguished himself as the leading musical teacher in Boston laying the groundwork for that city's preeminence in the field of jazz education. As the years past, he worked with some of the leading artists in the field including playing tenor sax with Herb Pomeroy's orchestra, piano with Maynard

Ferguson's big band, and a particularly rich association with Charles Mingus from the 1960s until the early 1970s. Signing a recording contract with Prestige in 1961, Byard released a string of quality albums (*Out Front!*, 1961; *Freedom Together!*, 1966; *Sunshine of My Soul*, 1967; *Jaki Byard with Strings*, 1968) highlighting his musical eclecticism. While with Prestige, he won the *Down Beat* Jazz Poll for most promising musician of 1966. His 21 piece group, the Apollo Stompers, was voted the Best House Band in the "Big Apple" in 1979 while playing Ali's Apple in downtown Manhattan. Continuing to perform with distinction in various groups throughout the 1980s and 1990s, Jaki Byard also demonstrated an unrivalled commitment to jazz education. A faculty member at Boston's prestigious New England Conservatory of Music from the early 1970s to the 1980s, the musician (in addition to an unbroken allegiance to private instruction) also taught at institutions including the Hartt School of Music, the Alma Lewis School of Fine Arts (Boston), the Brooklyn Conservatory of Music (Flushing), the Manhattan School of Music, and Harvard.

At 11:45 P.M. on February 11, 1999, paramedics responding to a 911 call found the 76-year-old jazz great dead on the couch at the two-story home he shared with his two daughters at 192-54 Hollis Avenue in Queens. Emergency personnel initially told the family that it appeared Byard had suffered a fatal stroke, but an autopsy conducted the next day revealed the musician had been shot once through a nostril. The bullet tore through his skull exiting his neck. Byard had last been seen by his family around 6:00 P.M. Adding to the mystery, no weapon was recovered nor were there any signs of forced entry, robbery, or a struggle. The daughters, in different parts of the house at the time of the shooting, heard nothing nor did neighbors. Police suspected, but never proved, that Byard was murdered by a relative over a money dispute. To date, no charges have been filed in the homicide.

Further Reading

Blumenthal, Bob. "Jaki Byard, 1922–1999: Jazzman was Versatile, Eccentric." *Boston Globe*, February 16, 1999, sec. C, p. 3.
www.jakibyard.org.

C-Murder (M)

A member of the gangsta rap group Tru along with brothers Percy "Master P" Miller, president and founder of No Limit Records, and Vyshonn

"Silkk the Shocker" Miller, C-Murder (Corey Miller) was a vibrant part of the Louisiana rap scene since the mid–1990s. Following two No Limit CD releases with Tru (*True*, 1995; *Tru 2 da Game*, 1997), C-Murder released his solo debut, *Life or Death*, on March 17, 1998. The CD sold well as did his 1998 follow-up, *Bossalinie*. It was not until 2000, however, that C-Murder became a key player in the world of rap with the release of *Trapped in Crime* and its hit single, "Down with My N's," featuring Snoop Dogg and Magic. The success of the CD helped the rapper to launch his new label, Tru Records, and production company, Deadly Soundz. *Trapped in Crime* proved to be the last record C-Murder would make under "normal" studio conditions or without the omnipresent threat of criminal prosecution.

C-Murder's first widely reported trouble with law enforcement began in March 1998 when the 27-year-old was arrested in St. John the Baptist Parish for speeding on Interstate 10. A computer check revealed the truck had been stolen and during the pat down state troopers pulled a semiautomatic handgun from C-Murder's waistband and noted he was wearing a bulletproof vest. Barred from carrying a gun due to a prior felony record, the rapper was arrested for a variety of charges including speeding, driving without a license, unlawful possession of a firearm, unlawful use of body armor, and possession of stolen goods worth over $500. In January 1999, C-Murder, with noted O.J. Simpson (see entry) defense attorney Johnnie Cochran at his side, pleaded guilty to carrying a concealed firearm and was given a six-month suspended jail term and a $500 fine. In exchange for the plea, the district attorney dropped the charge of unlawful use of body armor. The rapper paid an $81 speeding ticket and the charge of driving without a license was dropped as was possession of stolen property after he proved he had bought the truck at auction. C-Murder's next brushes with the law would not be so easy to resolve.

On June 14, 2001, C-Murder allegedly forced his way into the Baton Rouge home of a man he had argued with earlier in the day and held one person at gunpoint while he searched for his target. Baton Rouge police were holding warrants for the rapper on counts of aggravated burglary and aggravated assault with a firearm when they responded to an incident at Club Raggs at 2605 Plank Road on August 14, 2001. The problem started when security guard Daryl Jackson asked to search the rapper for a gun before letting him into the nightclub. C-Murder asked to speak to the club's owner, Norman Sparrow, who also refused his request to enter the premises without being searched. The rapper allegedly grabbed Sparrow's arm, pulled a gun and fired at the club owner, but the firearm jammed. C-Murder cleared the jam, the live round falling to the floor, then again tried to fire, but the weapon malfunctioned a second time. No shots were fired during the altercation (captured on a four-minute security video) and C-Murder left the scene. In addition to being wanted by police on two counts of attempted murder, he also faced a lawsuit filed by Sparrow and others in the club charging severe emotional anguish. Also charged in the suit were No Limit Records and various other corporate entities associated with the rapper.

While out on bail for the Club Raggs confrontation, C-Murder was involved in a deadly shooting in Harvey, Louisiana. On January 12, 2002, the 30-year-old rapper was in the Club Platinum in the 900 block of Manhattan Boulevard with 300 other patrons, when an argument with 16-year-old Steve Thomas (in the club illegally) ended when C-Murder allegedly pulled a handgun and shot the unarmed teen once in the chest. Thomas was pronounced dead on arrival at the West Jefferson Medical Center. C-Murder, who exited the scene before authorities arrived, was arrested by New Orleans police six days later at about 1:00 A.M. following a disturbance at the House of Blues in the French Quarter where he had previously been barred from entering the club. The rapper was booked on a second-degree murder charge while authorities pieced together what had occurred at the Club Platinum. Witnesses, as usual in most cases involving a rapper, were initially reluctant to step forward, but several later fingered C-Murder as the shooter. In April 2002, a state judge revoked the rapper's $2 million bond after prosecutors expressed concern over the safety of potential witnesses who might testify against him at trial. Guards at the Jefferson Parish Correctional Center had discovered a smuggled cell phone in C-Murder's possession allegedly used to call friends to possibly harm or influence witnesses. Later, the rapper and two sheriff's deputies were indicted on 13 felony counts including conspiracy to introduce contraband into a correctional facility and conspiracy to commit public bribery in connection with the smuggled

cell phone. The contraband indictment was later tossed. While awaiting trial, *True Dawgs* was released on April 30, 2002, and although the rapper was paired on the album with guest stars including Snoop Dogg, Master P, Bizzy Bone, and da Brat, it sold only a disappointing 95,000 units.

In September 2003, the unfortunately named defendant's second-degree murder trial began in the Jefferson Parish Courthouse in Gretna with the rapper denying any involvement in the deadly shooting. According to prosecutors, C-Money and his entourage first beat Steve Thomas before the rapper took it to the next level and shot the teen. A security guard, living out of state since the shooting, testified he had witnessed the rapper shoot Thomas, who ironically had illegally entered the club that night in hopes of seeing his idol whose posters and pictures plastered his bedroom walls. Another witness told the court that she heard the rapper tell Thomas, "You don't know who the fuck I am," to which the teen responded, "I don't care who you are." The ensuing beat down by at least 15 of the rapper's associates culminated with C-Murder producing a gun and shooting the youth in the heart. Defense witnesses, however, countered that they were certain C-Murder had not fired a weapon corroborating the rapper's contention that he was talking to the club's disc jockey at the time of the shooting. On September 30, 2003, a jury deliberated 3 hours and 40 minutes before returning a verdict of guilty which carries a mandatory life prison sentence in Louisiana. Days later prior to the formal sentencing, jurors were called back into the courtroom for a closed door session in which it was determined that the prosecution had withheld information that several of its key witnesses had criminal records. In April 2004, state judge Martha Sassone ordered a new trial for C-Murder, but rejected his request to post a $2 million bond to secure his freedom because he was still facing a trial for the Baton Rouge nightclub incident in August 2001. In March 2006, the Louisiana Supreme Court upheld the lower court ruling and scrapped the rapper's second-degree murder conviction clearing the way for a new trial.

While awaiting trial, C-Murder was placed on $500,000 bond, outfitted with an ankle monitor, and placed under house arrest in his residence in Kenner. Under the conditions of his bond, the rapper was barred from drinking alcohol and agreed to both a house curfew of 10:00 P.M. to 6:00 A.M. and the further condition that he remain in Jefferson and Orleans parishes at all other times. He was released from the home incarceration program in July 2006 over the objections of prosecutors who noted numerous instances when his monitoring gear lost track of him. C-Murder's limited freedom lasted one month before an appeals court ruled that the judge who removed him from home incarceration had done so improperly. His home incarceration privileges were revoked in March 2009 when it was discovered the rapper had violated the terms of the order and he was ordered to remain in the Jefferson Parish Correctional Center until his retrial for the murder of Steve Thomas. Remarkably, during the years C-Murder spent awaiting trial he was able to release three albums (*The Truest $#!@ I Ever Said*, 2005; *The Tru Story*, 2006; *Screamin' 4 Vengeance*, 2007) all extolling the gangsta lifestyle.

C-Murder, however, still had to face trial on the two counts of attempted murder stemming from the August 2001 incident at the Club Raggs in Baton Rouge. On May 27, 2009, one day after jury selection began and over eight years since he attempted to shoot the club's owner and the security guard, the 38-year-old rapper pleaded no contest on May 27, 2009 and under a plea deal accepted a sentence of 10 years in prison. Under the terms of the agreement, C-Murder was to be given credit for time served in jail and under house arrest in the Thomas case meaning the rapper's punishment in the Club Raggs case could be completed in months. Meanwhile, the court ordered a stay in the club owner's civil suit against C-Money. Finally, in August 2009 Corey "C-Murder" Miller was retried for the Thomas murder of January 2002. Once again the bouncer at the now-closed Club Platinum testified that he saw the rapper shoot the teenager as some 15 men beat and kicked him. Another witness, his credibility shaken upon admitting under defense questioning that he cut a deal with prosecutors to dismiss a carnal knowledge charge against him in exchange for his testimony, told of seeing a beaten Thomas balled up on the floor as C-Murder stood over him and fired at point-blank range. Shortly before 2:00 P.M. on August 12, 2009, a jury in a 10–2 vote found C-Murder guilty of second-degree murder after deliberating for more than 13 hours over two days in contentious sessions marked by jurors yelling, crying, and becoming physically ill. At one point, 9 of the 12 jurors voted for conviction, one vote short of a legal verdict in Louisiana. Their impasse continued and threatened to end the trial in a hung jury before the judge asked them to continue their deliberations. C-Murder was automatically sentenced to life in prison. The rapper's attorney in both trials, unpaid for over three years, split with his client after the verdict necessitating C-Murder to hire another lawyer for the inevitable appeal. In late August 2009, the rapper was formally sentenced to 10 years for the attempted murder of the nightclub owner and bouncer in Baton Rouge with the term to run concurrent with his life sentence.

Further Reading

Erlewine, Stephen Thomas, and David Jeffries. "C-Murder." www.allmusic.com.
Purpura, Paul. "Chaotic Jury Vote Caps Rapper's Trial; C-Murder Convicted of Murder in 10–2 Vote." *New Orleans Times-Picayune*, August 12, 2009, p. 1.

Cabot, Susan (V)

Typecast by her dark haired sultry good looks into playing ethnic roles in B-grade movies for major studios in the 1950s, Cabot's most entertaining and enduring work was done at the end of her career for independent producer-director Roger Corman. Born Harriet Shapiro in Boston, Massachusetts on July 9, 1927, Cabot spent a troubled childhood in a series of eight foster homes. It was while attending high school in New York City that she joined a dramatic club and began singing nights at Manhattan's Village Barn. Cabot appeared as an extra in the 1947 crime drama *Kiss of Death* shot in New York, but her big break did not come until Max Arnow, a casting director at Columbia, caught her performing at the Village Barn. In 1950 she was cast as the islander "Moana" opposite Jon Hall in the B-grade South Seas crime adventure film, *On the Isle of Samoa*. Veteran actor Jon Hall, later to gain television fame in the early 1950s in the title role of the syndicated show *Ramar of the Jungle*, committed suicide in December 1979 to escape a lingering death from bladder cancer. In 1951, Cabot's promising performance in the small role of Indian maiden "Monahseetah" in *Tomahawk* starring Van Heflin prompted Universal to sign her to an exclusive contract. At Universal, the young actress was relegated to exotic roles in costume dramas and Westerns. Cabot's films for Universal (released through Universal-International) include *Flame of Araby* (1952), *Son of Ali Baba* (1952, as "Tala"), *The Battle at Apache Pass* (1952), *The Duel at Silver Creek* (1952), *Gunsmoke* (1953), and her final film for the studio, *Ride Clear of Diablo* (1954).

The one-time lover of King Hussein of Jordan, Susan Cabot could not escape typecasting in exotic roles until B-movie king Roger Corman cast her in five exploitation films including her most memorable performance as the title character in *The Wasp Woman* (1959). Seen here as "Moana" in her 1950 motion picture debut, *On the Isle of Samoa*, the ill-fated actress shares an onscreen kiss with co-star Jon Hall, who committed suicide in 1979. Cabot was murdered by her son, the suspected love child of the Jordanian king, in December 1986.

Fed up with the limited roles being offered to her in Hollywood, Cabot left the movies and returned to New York City to appear in the off Broadway stage production *A Stone for Danny Fisher*. The play (based on a Harold Robbins novel) opened at the Downtown National Theatre on October 21, 1954 to lukewarm reviews. Cabot received fourth billing in the production and was not mentioned in *The New York Times* review the following day. Prior to returning to films in 1957, the actress made her television debut on June 10, 1957 in the controversial *Kraft Television Theatre* production of "The First and the Last," a dramatization by Morton Wishengrad of a John Galsworthy story depicting suicide as an acceptable solution for human problems. Back in Hollywood, Cabot began a six film association with

independent B-movie producer-director Roger Corman that effectively constitutes what film legacy she enjoys today. Corman immortalized the actress in a series of exploitation films covering the topics teen music (*Carnival Rock*, 1957), sex (*Sorority Girl*, 1957), gangsters (*Machine-Gun Kelly*, 1958, co-starring Charles Bronson), sword-and-sorcery (*The Saga of the Viking Women and Their Voyage to the Waters of the Great Sea Serpent*, 1958), and science fiction (*War of the Satellites*, 1958; *The Wasp Woman*, 1959). As the title character in *The Wasp Woman*, Cabot's most memorable screen role, she injected herself with the extract of the royal jelly of wasps to prevent the aging process with predictably disastrous results. According to Cabot, she enjoyed working with Corman—"He gave me a lot of freedom, and also a chance to play parts that Universal would never have given me." Following the cult favorite *The Wasp Woman*, Cabot left the movies (although she continued to find some minor television and stage work) to devote herself to fundraising for film education and preservation programs.

On the personal front, Cabot's life was as turbulent and erratic as her motion picture career. In 1944, the 18 year old married Edwin Sacker in Washington, D.C., but they separated in early 1951. Cabot next married businessman Michael Roman, but they too divorced. In April 1959, Cabot was a 32-year-old divorcee when she met Jordan's King Hussein at a Beverly Hills dinner party thrown by oil millionaire Edwin W. Pauley. The actress called Hussein, 24, "the most charming man I've ever met" and began a private (though highly publicized) multi-year relationship with the divorced Jordanian king that ultimately ended because Cabot was Jewish. In 1964, the unmarried Cabot gave birth to Timothy Scott Roman giving rise to speculation the child was not the offspring of former husband Michael Roman, but rather the son of King Hussein. If so, the child would be a half-Jewish, half-Arab direct descendant through the Hashemite Dynasty of the prophet Muhammed. Court papers introduced after Cabot's death showed that she received a monthly stipend of $1,500 from the Keeper of the King's Purse, Amman, Jordan, that could be interpreted as child support for Hussein's bastard son. Also presented were copies of letters from Cabot to the king in which she discussed the health of her son. Timothy Scott Roman suffered from dwarfism and from 1970 through 1985 was a participant in a federal program in which he was treated with an experimental growth hormone. The program was discontinued after certain batches of the hormone were found to be infected with a virus, Creutzfeldt-Jakob, a disease causing degeneration of the central nervous system. The experimental growth hormone was later found to have caused neurological damage in some patients.

Roman was a 22-year-old art student at Pierce College sharing a dilapidated home in Encino, California, with his 59-year-old mother when he called police on the night of December 10, 1986, to report a horrible crime. Investigators arrived on scene to find the former actress savagely bludgeoned to death in her plush master bedroom. According to her son, an assailant dressed in a Ninja warrior robe entered the house and knocked him

out. When he regained consciousness, Roman discovered his mother's body beaten with a steel shaft from a dumbbell and $70,000 in cash missing. Police immediately suspected Roman, a rabid martial arts movie fan with a fascination for Ninja weapons, who reportedly had a long-standing feud with his mother. Discrepancies in his account of the crime led to his arrest on December 15, 1986, and a charge of first-degree murder. Under advice of counsel, Roman pleaded innocent by reason of insanity citing the side effects he allegedly suffered as a test subject in the experimental drug hormone therapy study. In a brief filed with the court to move Roman to a jail closer to the site of his trial in Van Nuys, the defense attorney introduced the Hussein-Cabot connection that suggested the 22-year-old accused murderer was the love child of the Jordanian king. The deputy district attorney called the motion "really glamorous," but maintained it had nothing "to do with [Roman] killing his mother."

Roman's first trial ended in a mistrial after his attorney became ill. With new counsel, he was retried in a non-jury trial in a Van Nuys courtroom in October 1989. This time, Roman changed his plea from "not guilty by reason of insanity" to "not guilty" to avoid being institutionalized if convicted. Medical testimony supported the defense's contention that Roman could have suffered brain damage (including memory loss) from the experimental growth hormone, and established his reasoning skills as those of a young child. Blood tests recorded prior to the killing showed a high thyroid count which could have produced confusion and disorientation. More telling, however, was the testimony given by Cabot's physician and psychiatrist. Her therapist for seven years portrayed the former actress as a suicidally depressed woman severely disturbed by an abusive childhood. Prior to the slaying, Cabot manifested irrational fears about her health, was bedridden, and disoriented. Roman testified that on the night of the murder he became frightened by his mother's hysterical screaming and tried to call paramedics despite her warnings not to contact anyone. Cabot appeared confused, and failing to recognize her son, demanded "Who are you?" She came at him with the barbell rod, he grabbed it from her, but could not remember striking his mother. He confessed to lying about the Ninja-clad intruder who struck him and admitted stealing the money because he was frightened. On October 10, 1989, Roman was convicted of the lesser charge of involuntary manslaughter by Van Nuys Superior Court Judge Darlene Schempp because she believed he did not plan to kill his mother. Cabot's son was subsequently given a three-year suspended sentence and placed on probation. Everyone, including Roman's grandparents, was satisfied with the ruling because it thoughtfully considered medical problems suffered by both Cabot and Roman that may have contributed to the killing.

Further Reading

"Alleged Killer May Be Son of King Hussein." *San Francisco Chronicle*, April 14, 1989, sec. A, p. 30.
Weaver, Tom. *Interviews with B Science Fiction and Horror Movie Makers: Writers, Producers, Directors, Actors, Moguls, and Makeup.* Jefferson, NC: McFarland, 1988.

Camoflauge (V)

Speaking of his celebrity in his hometown of Savannah, Georgia, the rapper known as Camoflauge told reporters, "Everyone knew it was going to happen. I just wanted to be like the boys I saw on the corner — with gold teeth and fancy cars." Born Jason Johnson in 1982 in a Savannah housing project, Camoflauge logged a series of arrests on drug possession charges and, in 2000, spent three weeks in jail charged with the murder of 17-year-old Kenneth Capers. He was released after a grand jury failed to indict. The same month as Capers' murder, the rapper released his first album, *I Represent*, on the label R&d. The album, with songs like "Head Bustin," "17 Shots," and "Bring da Pain," peaked at Number 58 on the *Billboard* Rhythm and Blues/Hip Hop Chart. Major label Universal Records signed the rapper for his sophomore effort, *Strictly 4 Da Streets: Drugs, Sex & Violence, Vol. 1*, but dropped him soon after its release in 2001. Despite Johnson's reputation as a "gangsta," many in Savannah looked upon him as a role model. Local area high schools invited him to pep rallies and in 2001 he was asked to appear at a city-sponsored Father's Day celebration. Dressed in a red suit and beard at Christmas, "Camo Claus" drove around town in a Ford Expedition with his name and face painted on the side handing out turkeys, gifts, and money. In August, 2002, Camoflauge released what would be his final album, *Keepin' It Real*, on Pure Pain Records, an independent label based in midtown Savannah. Around 4:30 P.M. on May 19, 2003, the 21-year-old rapper was walking with his 16-month-old son, Yadon, on West 37th Street outside Pure Pain when he was shot. He died later

that day. His son was unhurt. Police suspected the rapper's murder was tied in with three separate slayings in Savannah during a two week period. All the victims knew one another and had criminal records. At the rapper's funeral service at Temple of Glory Community Church, the Reverend Matthew M. Odum, Sr. told the standing room only crowd of 2,000 that it was never too late to turn away from violence. "You can get saved with crack in your pocket," preached the reverend. "You can get saved while you finish up a six-pack." Johnson was buried in a blue athletic jersey wearing a necklace with a gold cross. In February, 2004, the rapper's mother successfully petitioned a court to order Pure Pain Records to stop selling her son's records until the company submitted an accountant-certified financial statement of sales. No arrests have been made to date.

Further Reading

"Rapper Camoflauge Fatally Shot." Associated Press, May 21, 2003.

Campbell, Margaret (V)

In films since 1919 (*Please Get Married* and *The Price of Innocence*), Campbell was a second female lead and character actress in at least 24 films including *Their Mutual Child* (1920), *Legally Dead* (1923), *The Lady from Hell* (1926), *Children of Divorce* (1927), and her last documented appearance, *Take the Heir*, in 1930. By 1939, the 56-year-old mother was employed as a W.P.A. elocution instructor at Los Angeles City College, and served as secretary of the Spiritual Assembly of the Baha'i. On June 27, 1939, the manager of the Hollywood rooming-house at 7058 Hawthorne Avenue where the former actress lodged with her 25-year-old son, Campbell McDonald, became alarmed when, after not seeing her tenant for two days, noticed a key hanging above the door of Campbell's room. Entering, she found Campbell's half-nude body sprawled across an unmade bed, her head shattered by multiple blows from a bloody claw hammer nearby on a pillowcase. Campbell's night clothes were disarranged and two bloody handprints were found on her thighs. Placed carefully near the body were a candle, a whistle, a key, and a Bible tract. A forensics team determined Campbell had been dead for two days. A statewide manhunt for the woman's missing son, a former crossing guard and a student of spiritualism last seen on the night before the murder, led to Campbell McDonald's arrest two days later in Santa Monica. McDonald, who spent the days since his mother's death sleeping on park benches in the area, readily admitted to murdering the woman. However, as police continued interrogating the soft-spoken, well-mannered suspect they began to doubt his sanity. Those who knew Campbell and McDonald painted a disturbing portrait of the mother and son relationship. A sickly child, McDonald spent only three weeks in school before his overly protective mother took over tutoring him for the rest of his education.

Taken to the still bloody scene of the crime, an unemotional McDonald informed police, "I feel soiled. I want to shave and put on a clean shirt, if I may." After being permitted to do so, he related how his mother had returned late from a religious meeting on the night of the murder. She warned him that reading too much would lead to another nervous breakdown (he suffered one two years earlier) and threatened to commit him to a mental asylum if he did not obey her. Later that night after they went to bed, McDonald could not sleep. Looking down into the murder bed, he calmly told police: "I stood here ... I'm left-handed. I remember it was moonlight enough so I didn't turn on any lights. Everything seemed like a dream. It does now, it is all hazy like, but I remember she didn't scream. I hit her first on the forehead. Then some more. I know my hands were bloody and sticky so I washed them. Then I found her pocketbook. It had $10 all together. It was just getting dawn when I left the house." McDonald dimly remembered placing the candle, whistle, key, and Bible tract near the body, but insisted they held no symbolic significance. Though McDonald was arraigned for the murder and insisted that he was mentally competent to stand trial, three court-appointed psychiatrists disagreed. The judge, citing that no sane man could fail to shed a tear over the death of his own mother, ruled on September 5, 1939, that McDonald was insane, and sentenced him to the Mendocino State Hospital until such time as he was ruled psychologically fit to stand trial for the murder.

Further Reading

"Death Scene Fails to Shake Young Slayer of His Mother." *Los Angeles Times*, July 1, 1939, sec. A, p. 2.

Cantat, Bertrand (M)

At 8:00 A.M. on July 27, 2003, Marie Trintignant, 41-year-old daughter of French cinema legend Jean-Louis Trintignant and a major film star in her own right, arrived by ambulance at the Vilnius University Hospital located in the capital city of Lithuania. Trintignant, in Vilnius since early June to shoot the joint French-Lithuanian telefilm *Colette*, the biography of the nineteenth century French novelist, was already in a deep coma and being kept alive by life support as the result of what appeared to be a vicious beating administered to her face and skull. Her lover, rock star-poet Bertrand Cantat, 39, of the French megagroup Noir Desir, was admitted to the same hospital two hours later suffering from a suspected overdose of drugs ingested in a failed suicide attempt. It was later determined that Cantat, the band's central creative force, had downed only two packets of vitamin C and a couple of depressants. For months, the pair's love affair had been played out under the merciless glare of the French press. Trintignant, famous for playing brutalized, but defiant women condemned by society in such films as *Une Affaire de Femmes* (1988) and *Betty* (1992), had very publicly left her current lover and father of two of her four children, film director Samuel Benchétrit, to be with the rock star after they met in the summer of 2002. Cantat, often called the "French Jim Morrison," was regarded in Gallic rock circles as an icon for France's anticapitalist youth, a pacifist and supporter of various humanitarian causes ranging from anti-racism to the environment. The day after Cantat's wife, Kristina, gave birth to their son in September, the rock star left her to be with Trintignant, his apparent "soul mate."

From the first, the relationship seemed to be obsessive on the part of Bertrand Cantat. In the summer of 2003, he followed Trintignant to Vilnius where she was starring in the title role of the made-for-television movie *Colette* directed by her mother, Nadine Trintignant. Normally outgoing with the film crew, the actress now spent all of her off-camera time alone with her lover in their three-room suite, Number 35, at the Domina Plaza hotel in downtown Vilnius. On the day of the tragedy, a neighbor in the hotel reported hearing a loud argument followed by the sound of a crashing chair. As Trintignant lay in a death-like coma at the hospital, her lover initially told authorities that he slapped her only once across the face during a drunken argument and she fell awkwardly striking her head on the floor. Attending physician Dr. Robertas Kvascevius performed emergency surgery on the actress to relieve pressure on her brain caused by cerebral hemorrhage, but afterwards pronounced that she had literally no chance to survive. At the request of the French government, neurosurgeon Stéphane Delajoux was flown to Vilnius to perform a "last chance" operation to save the brain dead actress. Delajoux, however, concurred with his colleague's prognosis, informing the press, "Medically there is no more we can do. We can make her comfortable, but it is not necessary. She is in a state where there is no suffering, neither moral nor physical." As Cantat was held in a pretrial detention facility on a preliminary charge of suspicion of causing bodily harm, Trintignant was flown back to Paris in a private jet so she could die on French soil in accordance with the wishes of her parents. The popular actress expired on August 1, 2003, five days after the assault, of cerebral edema, and was buried amid great fanfare near the grave of rock legend Jim Morrison in the Cimitière du Père Lachaise in Paris. The results of the autopsy failed to support Cantat's claim that he struck Trintignant once and she then hit her head on the floor. The beautiful actress had suffered multiple facial trauma including nose fractures, a hemorrhaging of the optic nerve, and cerebral lesions nearly identical to those found in shaken babies.

Failing in his bid for extradition to France for trial, Cantat faced a Lithuanian legal system that did not recognize the mitigating French concept of a "crime of passion." If the crime was found to be the result of "extreme emotion," the rock star could do as little as six years prison time possibly to be served in a French penitentiary. Held initially on a charge of manslaughter (later upgraded to murder), Cantat maintained that Marie's death was a "tragic accident" and kept fit in his single-bed cell in Lukiskiu Prison by doing yoga and reading his voluminous fan mail. In France, the death of Trintignant polarized the public into those who viewed Cantat as a violently jealous abuser of women (he allegedly once struck his wife), or, a tragically romantic figure who just got carried away by a fit of jealousy during a night of heavy drinking. Supporters of the rock star met at the trendy nightclub Café de Paris in Vilnius in a show of strength to both raise Cantat's spirits and to pay tribute to the dead actress. Trintignant's family was outraged when they learned that during the festivities excerpts of the actress's films were projected onto the walls of the club. Meanwhile, an unidentified arsonist torched Cantat's home in the south of France burning it to the ground. Nadine Trintignant, Marie's mother,

took a more direct route in blaming the rock star for her daughter's death. In October 2003, the director published her book, *Ma Fille, Marie* (*My Daughter, Marie*), overcoming a legal challenge by Cantat's attorney that its publication would undermine his client's right to be presumed innocent. Though Trintignant never referred to Cantat by name in the book, no reader encountering the term "murderer" 85 times in the text could fail to understand who she meant. The book became a best seller in France where the public was hungry for any information about the sensational case.

An international press corps of over 200 journalists packed the Vilnius District Court as Cantat's trial began before a three-judge panel on March 16, 2004. Under Lithuanian law, the rock star did not have to enter a plea, but faced a maximum 15 year sentence if found guilty of manslaughter. In the course of the three day trial, the events leading up to the tragic incident unfolded as several witnesses, including Cantat and Nadine Trintignant, testified before the spellbound courtroom. According to testimony, on July 26, 2003, Cantat and Trintignant attended a wrap-party for *Colette* at the Vilnius Literary Club, leaving together at 9:50 P.M. to drop by the home of Andrus Leligua, the film's third assistant director. Earlier in the day, Cantat became enraged when Trintignant received a text message from former lover and father of two of her children, Samuel Benchetrit, signed *bisou* ("little kisses.") As the pair continued to drink and smoke pot with Leligua, a jealous Cantat challenged the actress to sever all contact with her former lovers, proving his sincerity by phoning his estranged lover, Kristina, to dramatically inform her that "I no longer want us to have close relations." When Trintignant failed to respond in kind, the rock singer threw a glass across the room, wrenched the seated actress to her feet, and shoved her down. The tense atmosphere persisted after the pair returned to Suite No. 25 at the Domina Plaza shortly after midnight. According to Cantat's emotional testimony, Trintignant slapped him in the face as they argued about her relationship with Benchétrit and their sons. Cantat angrily responded by slapping (*not* punching, he insisted) her four times across the face with the flat of his hand. "Perhaps Marie hit her head on the door frame," he told the court, "I'd had enough of all that and wanted to shut her up." Cantat put the unconscious woman to bed allegedly unaware of the severity of her injuries.

Vincent Trintignant, Marie's brother, arrived at the suite at 7:30 A.M., and unable to rouse his comatose sister, frantically phoned for an ambulance. The forensic evidence contradicted Cantat's "four slap" account strongly suggesting that Trintignant had endured 19 blows to her head, shattering her nose and causing brain swelling. Cantat concluded his testimony by addressing Nadine Trintignant, Marie's mother who had characterized the rock star as an "assassin" without regret, from the stand: "I want to tell you this even if you are incapable of hearing it. I want you to know I loved Marie." Asked by the court if she wanted to respond to Cantat, she said, "I've heard too many lies and if I had to speak, I would express myself poorly."

On March 29, 2004, Cantat was sentenced to 8 years for voluntary homicide escaping the maximum penalty of 15 years. The popular musician dropped his plan to appeal the sentence on the assurance that he might possibly be able to serve his time in a French prison. While awaiting the decision on his petition to transfer to a penitentiary in France, Cantat gave an hour-long acoustic guitar concert to an overflow crowd of fellow-inmates in Lukiskiu Prison. The next month, he was transferred to a French prison to serve out the remainder of his term. In a final twist on this tragic case, Stéphane Delajoux, the French neurosurgeon who performed the second operation on Trintignant in Vilnius, was found guilty of fraud in 2005 after attempting to bilk an insurance company out of $80,000 by pretending to be paralyzed as the result of a skiing accident. In addition to his suspended prison sentence, Dr. Delajoux was banned for at least six months (possibly three years) from performing any surgeries.

Further Reading

Trintignant, Nadine. *Ma fille, Marie*. Paris: Fayard, 2003.
_____. *Marie Trintignant*. Paris: Fayard: 2004.

Caux, Claude (M-S)

A native of Abbeville, France, and a one-time colleague of mime Marcel Marceau, Caux, 57, taught drama for 17 years at the University of Houston where his works were performed at the Wortham Theatre and the Houston Ballet. On July 22, 1991, Caux and local actress Mary Avery Chovanetz quarreled in Memorial Park over her refusal to respond to his romantic advances. To the horror of onlookers, the mime stabbed Chovanetz 15 times in the chest, abdomen, and legs. Caux then stabbed himself in the stomach and begged the witnesses to "please let us die." Chovanetz did so at the scene, but the professor survived. Freed on $50,000 bail, Caux stabbed himself in the stomach on October 7, 1991, but was found in time by his wife crumpled on the patio of their Houston home. A suicide note written in French was discovered at the scene. Caux again recovered. However, on January 10, 1992, Caux's body was found by his wife and son hanging from the staircase leading to the second-floor of his condominium in the 5300 block of Richmond in southwest Houston.

Further Reading

"Drama Professor May Have Slain Actress Because She Rejected Him." *Dallas Morning News*, July 25, 1991, sec. A, p. 26.

Cavlar (V)

Leval (Cavlar) Lyde, a resident of the rough Bedford-Stuyvesant section of Brooklyn, honed his rap skills while serving time on an assault and weapons charge in the Arthur Kill Correctional Facility on Staten Island. Released in the early 2000s, the aspiring rapper became associated with the independent label Earthquake Camp Records and the "Step Your Game Up" underground DVDs which featured interviews and videos with top hip-hop stars. In 2004, he toured with Lil Jon and the Ying Yang Twins and was featured on WBLS' *Wendy Williams Show*. Interestingly, Cavlar frequently appeared on homemade underground "beef" videos in which rappers engaged in a particularly noxious variation of the dozens in which threats are rapped to beat, rob, and kill one another. Readily accessible on YouTube, one Cavlar video features the rapper and rival Uncle Murder in a heated exchange. Whether such viral showdowns factored into the father of three's violent death on March 25, 2008, in Fort Greene, Brooklyn, is pure speculation. According to differing press reports, the 36-year-old Cavlar, a regular at Fish & Crustaceons Quality Seafood, left the restaurant around 5:00 P.M. eating a sandwich and was shot once in the chest as he walked to his parked car. Another account had the rapper engaged in a confrontation on the street with a gunman and two of his friends who all fled after the shooting. Cavlar died at Brooklyn Hospital Center. One anonymous web poster to the "Save Brooklyn Now" blog wrote, "[Cavlar] ran across the same type of individual that he himself was and he got caught with a sandwich instead of a gun in his hand. Don't get it twisted, it could easily have been the other three people who approached him that could've been left on the ground." Tragically, Nancy Williams, a 27-year-old mother of three, was fatally shot on March 30, 2008, while handing out "In Remembrance of Cavlar" buttons at a makeshift memorial and Irish wake for the murdered rapper in an outside courtyard in his Bed-Stuy neighborhood. The woman was struck when a lone gunman aimlessly fired 12 shots from an automatic weapon through the yards behind the Bedford Stuyvesant Garden Houses, a housing complex, into the public gathering. To date, no arrests have been made in either case.

Further Reading

Louis, Errol. "For Thug Violence and Hip Hop, the Bloody Beat Goes On." *New York Daily News*, March 30, 2008, p. 31.

Chediak, Almir (V)

The son of Lebanese immigrants born on June 21, 1950, in Rio de Janeiro, Chediak was revered by Brazilian musicians and composers for his tireless efforts in making their music available to a world audience through his book and CD publishing company Lumiar Discos & Editora established in 1988. After studying guitar with famed virtuoso Dino Sete Cordas, and music theory with Ian Guest, Chediak began instructing Brazilian music stars like Cal Costa and Moraes Moreira in guitar method and music theory. It was however, as a meticulous researcher and publisher of some 18 songbooks and sheet music featuring standard chord notation that the publisher popularized, and many performers maintained, *saved* Brazilian music so it could be studied by scholars and students. Songbooks and CDs published by Chediak include the works of Carlos Jobim, Carlos Lyra, Edu Lobo, Gilberto Gil, and Caetano Veloso. Additionally, in the 1980s the music producer wrote influential books on harmony and musical theory that became standard texts for the study of Brazilian music.

On May 26, 2003, Chediak, 52, and his girlfriend, Samy da Costa Alves, were kidnapped at gunpoint by two unknown assailants and taken from his home in Petropolis, forty miles outside of Rio de Janeiro. The kidnappers forced the couple into Chediak's car and drove to a remote spot where they shot the musician to death before releasing the woman unharmed. The killers dumped Chediak's body by the roadside and torched his car. Police speculated that the two would-be robbers broke into Chediak's country home thinking that the arranger-publisher had returned to Rio. Chediak was murdered after recognizing his assailants. Generino Pedro da Silva and a man known as "Mr. dos Prazeres" were arrested days later, but to date no one has been convicted of Almir Chediak's murder.

Further Reading

Holston, Mark. "Noteworthy Guardian of Brazil's Music." *Americas*, 55(5) (Sept./Oct. 2003): 58–59.

Childs, Evelyn (V) (M-S)

Lawrence S. Mueller, 32, a sign painter-artist from the California desert town of El Centro, married New York showgirl Evelyn Childs (real name Evelyn Pearl Tatum) on March 26, 1927. The 25-year-old performer soon tired of life away from the footlights and, on May 26, went to Los Angeles following a quarrel with her husband. Checking into the Rosegrove Hotel at 532 Flower Street, Childs made the rounds of Hollywood studios and theatrical agencies looking for work. Distraught and anxious to save their marriage, Mueller sent a flurry of letters and telegrams addressed to his "golden girl" begging her to come back. Childs advised him not to come to Los Angeles on the pretext that it might discourage producers from casting her. In a final letter before driving to Los Angeles, Mueller pleaded with his wife for "one week of happiness" together during which time he would look for work in the city and, if they still proved incompatible, would accept a position in Chicago. On the morning of May 30, 1927, the maid at the Rosegrove let herself into Childs' room to clean. The young showgirl, clad only in a flimsy pink nightgown, lay on the bed strangled to death with a bedsheet. Mueller's nude, lifeless body was found a few feet away suspended by a bedsheet wound tightly about his neck attached to a closet door lintel. The record "All for Love" was on a running phonograph beside the bed. Among numerous letters chronicling the buildup to the tragedy was a picture of Mueller with the following written across the corner: "To Pearl, my perfect pal. Yesterday, today, and I hope, forever."

Further Reading

"Double Killing Romance's End: Artist Strangles Showgirl Bride, Hangs Self." *Los Angeles Times*, May 31, 1927, pt. II, p. 2.

Church, Hubert ("Kyle") *see* **Mr. Cee**

Clarke, Rowan (V)

The road manager for legendary reggae singer Gregory Isaacs, Clarke, 39, co-owned two restaurants in Harlem, the Hot Pot Caribbean and Mr. Jerk. On the evening of April 2, 2007, Clarke and his girlfriend were at his apartment on St. Nicholas Avenue when two gunmen pushed their way into the residence. Shouting, "Where's the money?," one assailant shot Clarke in the back and armpit as he pushed his girlfriend out of the way. The road manager died nine hours later at Harlem Hospital. To date, no arrests have been made in the case.

Further Reading

Burke, Kerry. "Bizman Shot Dead in Harlem Break-In." *New York Daily News*, April 5, 2007, p. 34.

Clary, Wilton Werbe (M)

Best known for a one-year stint on Broadway as Curly in the Rouben Mamoulian directed Rodgers and Hammerstein musical *Oklahoma!* in the 1947-1948 season, Clary also appeared on the New York stage in *The Desert Song* (1946), *The Barrier* (1950), and *Three Wishes for Jamie* (1952). He later sang in nightclubs in Miami and Palm Beach before retiring to teach private voice lessons in the Asheville, North Carolina area. On February 7, 1981, the body of 16-year-old Pamela Denise Durham, a voice student of Clary's, was found face-down one hundred yards off a road in the fashionable community of Flat Rock, about twenty miles south of Asheville. The East Henderson High School honor student was shot twice with a small caliber pistol. Clary, 64, and his handyman, Richard Amico, 38, were arrested later that day in Flat Rock. On April 27, 1981, Clary pleaded guilty to first-degree murder following a judge's ruling that the retired Broadway performer's confession made at the time of his arrest could be used against him at trial. Though no motive for the murder was made public, Clary told his attorney that he had planned to kill Durham because "it was the only way out." With Amico, Clary drove to a meeting with Durham in Flat Rock, walked over to her car, and shot her twice at close range. Police found the murder weapon, a .38-caliber pistol, and a pair of gloves hidden in his garage. Over the loud protests of several courtroom observers demanding the death penalty, a judge sentenced Clary to life imprisonment.

Further Reading

McCrary, Elissa. "Actor Sentenced to Life After Pleading Guilty to Murder." Associated Press, April 28, 1981.

Cleaves, Robert Weldon (M)

Road rage turned to murder in Los Angeles on September 30, 1998, when the 79-year-old retired film and television actor argued with Arnold William Guerriero, a 39-year-old furniture mover. Around noon, Guerriero and two men with him in his car took a lunch break from a moving job at the J. Paul Getty Museum. The 250 pound ex-New Yorker reportedly honked at Cleaves to move his 1972 Ford Maverick out of their way. An argument ensued, obscene gestures exchanged, and Cleaves recklessly pursued Guerriero as the furniture mover sped past. Not realizing how angry the elderly man was, the furniture movers shared a laugh as Cleaves chased them through the streets honking his horn and screaming for them to get out of their car. After several blocks, Guerriero stopped his Ford Taurus and approached Cleaves' auto. According to eyewitness accounts, Cleaves gunned his engine and drove into Guerriero flipping the man's body onto the hood of the car. As horrified onlookers watched, Cleaves sped over the victim and, when his body fell to the pavement, pushed him 350 feet with the car. The former actor then put the car into reverse and again ran over Guerriero's body all the time laughing. "As the car sped off, I heard a whooping sound, a guttural sound ... it was chilling," one witness reported. At trial, Cleaves testified that he accidentally ran over Guerriero when the man pointed a gun at him (no weapon was ever found). Jurors also learned that in 1987 the actor bashed in a female motorist's windshield with a baseball bat following a traffic incident. On March 23, 2000, Cleaves was convicted of second-degree murder, and later given the maximum possible sentence of 16 years to life in prison. Ironically, the actor had appeared in small roles in the films *The Born Losers* (1967), *Targets* (1968), the made-for-television movies *Pursuit* (1972), and *Death Scream* (1975), as well as on the television show *Dragnet*.

Further Reading

"Deadly Road Rage: Widow Grieves for Husband Dragged to Death Beneath Car." Associated Press, October 7, 1998.

Codona, Alfredo (M–S)

Codona, born in Laredo, Mexico, in 1895 to trapeze star parents, was once considered among the world's top trapeze artists. His first wife, Danish aerialist Lillian Leitzel, died in a fall in Copenhagen in 1931 during a performance of The Flying Codonas. Vera Bruce joined the act and they married the next year. Codona's career was cut short in 1933 when he missed a triple somersault and fell 60 feet from a flying trapeze during a performance of the Ringling Bros.-Barnum & Bailey Circus at New York's Madison Square Garden. When the aerialist's shattered shoulder failed to heal, he became the manager of the troupe and traveled for a year with Tom Mix's Circus as an executive to the cowboy star. In 1937, Codona purchased a garage in Long Beach, California, and was employed there when his wife was granted a divorce on July 1 on grounds of mental cruelty. On July 30, 1937, the Codonas, accompanied by Vera Bruce's mother, were in an attorney's office in Los Angeles discussing the division of household effects when Codona, 42, asked the lawyer to leave for a few moments. When he did, Codona calmly lit his wife's cigarette, locked the door, and said, "Vera, this is all you've left for me to do." Pulling an automatic pistol from his pocket, Codona pumped four rounds into his ex-wife before killing himself instantly with a head shot. Vera Bruce, 32, died the next day.

Further Reading

"Codonas in Dual Tragedy." *Los Angeles Times,* July 31, 1937, pt. I, p. 3.

Colby, Barbara (V)

The daughter-in-law of Broadway superstar Ethel Merman, Colby (born July 2, 1940 in New York City) was an accomplished stage actress whose credits included supporting roles in *The Devils* (1965, New York's Broadway Theatre), *Murder in the Cathedral* (1966, American Shakespeare Festival Theatre, Stratford, Connecticut), *Murderous Angels* (1970, Mark Taper Forum, Los Angeles), *The House of Blue Leaves* (1973, American Conservatory Theatre, San Francisco), *Richard III* (1974, New York Shakespeare Festival), and *A Doll's House* (1975, New York Shakespeare Festival) featuring the New York stage debut of Swedish actress Liv Ullmann in the role of "Nora." In films, Colby played small roles in *Petulia* (1968), *California Split* (1974), *The Memory of Us* (1974), and *Rafferty and the Gold Dust Twins*

(1975). In 1971, the actress appeared in the premier episode of the Peter Falk television series *Columbo,* and later added guest shots on *The FBI, McMillan and Wife,* and the 1973 made-for-television movie, *A Brand New Life,* to her list of small screen credits.

Colby, however, will be best remembered for two standout appearances as the good-natured hooker, "Sherry," in Season 5 of the classic CBS comedy series *The Mary Tyler Moore Show.* In episode number 97, "Will Mary Richards Go to Jail?," aired on September 14, 1974, Colby played the prostitute Mary converses with while in jail for refusing to reveal a news source. The episode won an Emmy in the category of Outstanding Writing in a Comedy Series. Colby was so good in the episode, that "Sherry" was brought back on February 8, 1975, in episode number 117, "You Try to be a Nice Guy," this time to enlist Mary's aid in helping the ex-hooker to promote her new career as a fashion designer. Grant Tinker, president of MTM Productions, quickly signed the actress for the role of "Julie Erskine" in *The Mary Tyler Moore Show* spinoff, *Phyllis,* starring Cloris Leachman as the titular character.

The 36-year-old actress had filmed only three episodes of the series when she was senselessly gunned down shortly before midnight on July 24, 1975, in the Palms district of West Los Angeles. In tandem with New York stage actor James Kiernan, 35, Colby taught acting classes at a drama school on Ellis Street. The pair was walking across the parking lot to their car after class when a van approached and two young armed black men emerged. Colby and Kiernan obeyed the robbers' order to raise their hands, but were shot anyway. The talented actress sustained a single gunshot wound that passed through her left arm and into her chest fatally perforating a lung. She died at the scene. Kiernan was shot near the heart, but managed to live long enough to explain to police what happened, and to give a description of the assailants. Ambulanced to Brotman Memorial Hospital in Culver City, the actor who had one guest shot on the CBS series *Rhoda* to his credit, died an hour-and-a-half later. Six youths suspected of being involved in the murders as well as in robberies and burglaries in the area were arrested, but to date no one has ever been charged in the crime.

MTM executives and co-workers on *Phyllis* were stunned by Colby's murder. A moving eulogy to the dead actress delivered by Cloris

Leachman was filmed, and was to run at the conclusion of the show's third episode, but CBS brass fearing the segment would be a downer nixed the spot and it never aired. In it, Leachman told viewers: "As some of you may know, shortly after we filmed tonight's episode last July, Barbara Colby, who has played the part of Julie, was tragically killed. She was a superb actress and one of the most joyful and giving people I have ever known. The loss of Barbara left those of us involved in the production of *Phyllis* a number of alternatives. We could have redone the episodes in which she appeared without her. But to those of us who knew Barbara, this was unthinkable. We could have 'written' out the character, Julie — had her move somewhere and sell the photography studio — but this would not have fooled you, and more important, it would not have fooled us. And so beginning next week, the part of Julie will be played by another actress [Liz Torres]. This will mean that some episodes will be shown out of their logical sequence, but we hope you will bear with us. It was not easy to replace Barbara Colby as an actress, and it is impossible to replace her as a person."

Further Reading

Rovin, Jeff. *TV Babylon*. Updated ed. New York: Signet, 1987.

Coleman, Lamont *see* Big L

Colwell, Timothy (V)

A respected jazz saxophonist who played with the British musical institution Kenny Ball & His Jazzmen in the 1960s, the 65-year-old musician continued to receive regular BBC airplay with his group, Tim Colwell's Jazzfriends. On the evening of September 19, 2003, Colwell was at home in his ground-floor flat in Lymington, Hants when someone outside began shouting and banging on his windows. The musician had been a target of verbal taunts, graffiti abuse, and violent threats for months since phoning police to report truants congregating in a park near his home. His practice of sometimes photographing the neighborhood toughs led the youths to falsely brand him as a pedophile. Two weeks earlier, someone (later identified as Richard Harris) crashed a tractor tire through his living room window. When Colwell left his apartment on what proved to be the final night of his life and walked to the nearby playground to investigate the disturbance, Richard Harris, 20, and Daniel Newham, 17, knocked the elderly man to the ground, and repeatedly punched and kicked him. Neighbors intervened, but Colwell collapsed as he walked back to his flat. Shortly afterwards, he died in hospital without regaining consciousness. While Colwell had a previous heart condition, it was ruled that the assault was so brutal that it could have caused a heart attack in a healthy 65-year-old while the kicks to his head were sufficient to have killed a 25-year-old.

Harris, who boasted of liking to hurt animals and acting like a vigilante, was on parole for two earlier violent assaults at the time of his attack on Colwell. Conversely, Newham had no previous convictions and apparently came from a decent, supportive family. At trial in February 2005, both men were cleared of murder charges, but found guilty of manslaughter. At a hearing in London in April 2005, Mrs. Justice Harlett sentenced Richard Harris to life imprisonment with a recommendation that he serve a minimum of three years before being considered for parole. "It is clear that, whether or not you are mentally disordered," the judge told Harris, "your personality is such that you are likely to remain a danger for many years to come, possibly forever." Daniel Newham was sentenced to five years youth custody.

Further Reading

Taylor, Mike. "Men Jailed for 'Heart Attack' Killing." The Press Association, April 7, 2005.

Cooke, Sam (V)

The man credited with inventing soul music was born Samuel Cook (the "e" would be added later) in Clarksdale, Mississippi, on January 22, 1931. The fourth child of Charles Cook, a houseboy for a millionaire cotton farmer and a reverend in the Church of Christ (Holiness), the future superstar's roots were firmly grounded in gospel music. The Reverend Cook established his church as a "Ministry of Music" with services featuring gospel quartets whose performances often moved their listeners to ecstatic visions. When the Depression bankrupted his employer, the Reverend migrated with his family to the impoverished Bronzeville section on the South Side of Chicago. The elder Cook worked as a day laborer in the Stockyards and, after a year in the city, was appointed pastor of the Christ Temple Church (Holiness) in Chicago Heights. Home to 90 percent of Chicago's blacks, Bronzeville was a musical melting pot for gospel, electric blues, and urban dance music. Young Sam heard and absorbed it all. By the age of four, Sam and his siblings were billed as the Singing Children and performed gospel tunes before their father's sermons and in other area churches. Sam sang alone for pocket change on street corners. Underaged, he sneaked into bars where electric blues held sway singing stool-to-stool for handouts. While a sophomore in high school, Sam joined the Teenage Highway QCs, a gospel group popular on the area's church quartet circuit. Already the possessor of a beautiful tenor voice and melting good looks, Sam's charisma was unquestionable and dangerous. Women loved him, he loved women. This attraction would serve as the wellspring of many of the problems that plagued the talented performer throughout his short, tragic life.

Shortly after graduating high school in 1948, Sam had his first brush with the law. Inadvertently leaving some pornographic material at a girlfriend's house, he was arrested on a morals charge after the girl's younger sister took the material to school. He spent his 90 day sentence in Cook County Jail organizing a gospel group. By late 1948, the QCs were making a name for themselves touring the country on the gospel circuit, but essentially earning little money after expenses. Frustrated, Sam began writing music rightly discerning that financial security ultimately depended upon owning a song's publishing rights. In mid–1950, the talented tenor caught his first big break when R.H. Harris, the legendary lead singer of the country's most popular gospel group, the Soul Stirrers, retired. Though only 19 in a group where everyone else was over 40, Sam was chosen as Harris' replacement. With the Soul Stirrers, the singer developed what his biographer, Daniel Wolff, called Sam's "charismatic quaver ... almost a yodel" consisting of the trademark "whoah-whoah-whoah." The singer also began exploiting his good looks by targeting his performances to the younger female members of the congregation. These women, swept away by feelings of religious ecstasy unleashed by the handsome gospel singer, would be replaced by sexually excited screaming fans when Sam made the transition into pop music. In 1951, the Soul Stirrers signed with Specialty Records. Their March 1951 recording session in Los Angeles produced the smash gospel hit "Jesus Gave Me Water" and Cooke's own composition, "Until Jesus Calls Me Home."

In April 1953 while Sam was on a grueling 101 city tour with the Soul Stirrers his grade school sweetheart, Barbara Campbell, quietly gave birth to their daughter, Linda, in Chicago. Sam acknowledged the child as his own, sent Campbell $35 a week, but did not marry her. That same month, Marine Sommerville of Cleveland, gave birth to Sam's daughter, Denise. As before, the singer recognized the child as his own, sent money, stayed in touch, but did not marry the woman. The pattern, however, was broken on October 14, 1953 when the 22-year-old idol of the gospel music world married Dolores Mohawk in Chicago. The marriage lasted until mid–1958 hastened, no doubt, by a paternity suit filed against the singer by a woman he had impregnated in New Orleans. Sam paid Mohawk $10,000 and presented her with a new car in exchange for her promise not to contest the divorce. She died drunk in a car wreck in Fresno, California in March 1959.

By 1956, Sam had reached the pinnacle of success in the niche arena of gospel music and was anxious to crossover into the highly lucrative field of rhythm and blues then enjoying a boom in popularity. Wary of the maxim that a performer could not be both R&B and religious, Sam obtained permission from his father before launching into the world of pop music. In December 1956, Sam entered a studio in New Orleans under the name "Dale Cook" and recorded his first pop single for Specialty — "Lovable" (B-side "Forever"). The ballads, aimed squarely at the white teenaged girl market, failed to generate much excitement, and the "Dale Cook" subterfuge fooled no one. Sam's smooth voice and phrasing were unmistakable. On June 1, 1957, Sam Cooke (now adding the "e") was born. Two months after leaving the Soul Stirrers without a goodbye, Cooke entered a recording studio and cut his own composition, "You Send Me." Released by Keen Records after some legal wrangling with Specialty, the song charted Number One and sold 1.7 million copies. On the strength of "You Send Me" Cooke got national exposure on *The Ed Sullivan Show* on an abbreviated performance on November 3, 1957, and then a two song set featuring his hit and his new release, "For Sentimental Reasons," on December 1, 1958. Just as his pop career seemed to be taking off, Cooke was slapped with a paternity suit that led to his arrest in Philadelphia on May 30, 1958. The singer settled out of court for $10,000, quickly divorced wife Dolores Mohawk, and surprised his inner circle by becoming secretly engaged to Barbara Campbell, the mother of his daughter Linda, in the fall of 1958. Cooke saw the opportunity to perform in 1958 at New York City's prestigious Copacabana nightclub as a chance to appeal to white middle-class America, much in the same manner as the wildly popular Sammy Davis, Jr. had done in Las Vegas. The show was a disaster with Cooke performing "square" songs like "Begin the Beguine" and "Canadian Sunset." A savvy businessman, Cooke founded KAGS Music, his own music publishing company, in November 1958. A first for a black performer, KAGS allowed the songwriter to reap the majority of profits from the hits he continued to write. In late 1959, Cooke introduced another innovation when he became the first rock 'n' roller of any color to own his own label, SAR Records. The label signed gospel groups like the Soul Stirrers and, for the first time, recruited gospel singers like Johnnie Morisette, Kylo Turner, Patience Valentine, and the Womack Brothers into pop.

On January 6, 1960, the man many believed possessed the best voice in the world signed with RCA Records joining Elvis Presley as the label's top pop attraction. Left relatively free to write, arrange, and produce his own music, Cooke unleashed a creative torrent of pop masterpieces including "Wonderful World" (1960), "Chain Gang" (1960), "That's It — I Quit — I'm Movin' On" (1961), "Cupid" (1961), "Twistin' the Night Away" (1962), "Bring It On Home to Me" (1962), "Another Saturday Night" (1963), and posthumously, "A Change Is Gonna Come" (1964). It was in live performance, however, that Cooke electrified audiences particularly women who began the practice of throwing their panties onstage. Driven by the belief he could be an even a bigger star than he was, Cooke toured relentlessly, cut albums, and devoted himself to developing talent at SAR Records. On the personal front, Cooke and wife Barbara had reached an "understanding" by early 1963 that their marriage would be "open." In July 1963, the couple's 18-month-old son, Vincent, drowned in the family's pool, essentially ending their marriage in all but name. The grief-stricken singer blamed Barbara and those closest to him noted a sea change in his personality characterized by moodiness and an increase in his drinking. Under new manager Allen Klein, Cooke returned to the Copa on June 24, 1964, and in a wonderfully received show erased his most humiliating professional failure of six years previous. After the career-defining show, the

singer planned to do a limited tour on the nightclub circuit, devote more time to the civil rights movement, and concentrate on the business side of his many music ventures.

Late on the evening of December 10, 1964, Cooke, 32, met friends for drinks at Martoni's, a restaurant favored by show business folk located on Cahuenga above Sunset. There, he was introduced to Elisa Boyer, an attractive 22-year-old woman of English-Chinese descent. The pair left together around 1:30 A.M. and Cooke drove his cherry red Ferrari to the Hacienda, a remote $3 a night motel at 9137 S. Figueroa Street near the airport that he often used for sexual liaisons. The manager of the Hacienda, a 55-year-old black woman named Bertha Lee Franklin, later told police Boyer did not appear to be an unwilling participant when Cooke signed the guest register as "Mr. and Mrs." Theories abound as to what next occurred between Cooke and the woman inside the cheap motel room around 2:30 A.M. The singer had been drinking for hours (a half-bottle of Scotch was recovered from his car) and may have frightened Boyer with his sexual advances. According to the woman, Cooke tore away her clothes leaving her only in bra and panties. Boyer entered the bathroom hoping to escape from the window only to find it painted shut. When she emerged, Cooke was already undressed. He used the bathroom and when he emerged found Boyer gone and most of his clothes missing. Enraged that he had been played for a fool and ripped off, Cook threw on an expensive sport coat and a pair of shoes and stormed out of the room to find the woman. Possibly believing she had gone to the manager's office unit, he jumped in his Ferrari, drove to Bertha Lee Franklin's room, and began banging on the door demanding she produce the woman who stole his clothes. Franklin told the angry singer she was alone in the unit, but Cooke knocked the door off its hinges with his shoulder, stormed into the room and conducted a frantic search. Failing to find Boyer, Cooke shook Franklin's shoulders demanding she give him more information. According to Franklin, they struggled and she was able to reach a .22-caliber pistol that she kept as protection in her job as manager of a seedy motel. The first shot harmlessly struck the ceiling, but as a second, then a third bullet ripped through his lungs and heart, he reportedly told Franklin in disbelief, "Lady, you shot me." Cooke still posed a threat, according to Franklin's police statement, so she struck him repeatedly over the head with a broom handle breaking it in two. As the singing idol of millions lay dead on the floor of a hot sheets motel, Elise Boyer was calling the police from a phone booth less than a block from the scene to report that she had been "kidnapped" by Sam Cooke. Minutes later, police received a related call, this one from the owner of the Hacienda, reporting that her manager had just informed her of a fatal shooting on the premises. At the Hacienda, officers found Cooke's body clad only in a sport coat and wearing one shoe slumped against a desk.

Few in the black community believed Cooke died in the scenario described by Elisa Boyer and Bertha Lee Franklin. Those close to the singer also refused to believe that the man they knew would ever kidnap a woman for purposes of forced sex no matter how inebriated. Boyer and Franklin, however, did pass lie detector tests. Rumors that the 22-year-old Eurasian "receptionist" was in fact a hooker who may have been working with a confederate to "roll" Cooke (only $108 and no credit cards were found at the scene) were given some credence when it was learned she had once been arrested in a Hollywood motel for offering sex to an undercover police officer. The charge was later dropped on a technicality. Amid lingering doubts, a coroner's jury exonerated Bertha Lee Franklin in Cooke's shooting returning a verdict of "justifiable homicide." In February 1965, the motel manager sued the Cooke estate for $200,000 claiming physical injuries from Cooke's unprovoked attack. The case was settled out of court for a $30,000 payout.

As a testament to Cooke's popularity, the singer was given two funeral services. The first conducted in Chicago's Tabernacle Baptist Church filled the 2,000 seat facility while another 2,000 mourners shivered outside in the cold of winter. Among those paying respects to the fallen superstar were Muhammad Ali, the Soul Stirrers, and comedian Dick Gregory. The second at the Mount Sinai Baptist Church in Los Angeles was highlighted by an impromptu performance by Ray Charles who offered a heartrending rendition of "Angels Keep Watching Over Me" when the scheduled soloist was too overwhelmed with grief to perform. Cooke was buried in Forest Lawn Memorial Park–Glendale under a marker which reads (in part) "Until the Day Break—And the Shadows Flee Away." Two months after her husband's violent death, Barbara Cooke shocked the family by wedding her husband's best friend and protégé Bobby Womack. Years later, Womack admitted the marriage had greatly hurt his career. In 1986, Sam Cooke was inducted into the Rock and Roll Hall of Fame. As of the publication of this book, the long anticipated biopic of the singer's life has yet to be filmed.

Further Reading

Guralnick, Peter. *Dream Boogie: The Triumph of Sam Cooke*. New York: Little, Brown, 2005.
Wolff, Daniel. *You Send Me: The Life and Times of Sam Cooke*. New York: William Morrow, 1995.

Cooley, Spade (M)

In a life equaling the lyrics of the most improbable and melancholy country and western song, the saga of Spade Cooley, the self-proclaimed "King of Western Swing," ranks among the most tragic. Born Donnell Clyde Cooley on either February 22, 1910, or December 17, 1910 (sources vary), in either Pack Saddle Creek or Grand(e), Oklahoma (sources vary), he inherited his musical ability from his grandfather and father, both skilled fiddlers. "Spade," so named because he once held three consecutive winning poker hands in that suit, received classical instruction on the violin as a child, and was soon making a name for himself fiddling at local dances in Oregon where the family moved in 1914. According to Cooley, he moved to Los Angeles in 1934 with only "his violin and 6 cents in his pocket" determined to make it in country music. That same year his physical resemblance to Roy Rogers landed him work as the western star's stand-in in several Republic Studios films. Throughout the 1930s Cooley stayed busy touring as a fiddle player with Rogers and occasionally singing with the Riders of the Purple Sage and standing-in with other bands.

In 1942, Cooley got his big break when he took over leadership of Jimmy Wakely's house band at the Venice Pier Ballroom in Santa Monica, California. Cooley's orchestra, featuring multiple fiddle players and a harp combined with crooner-style vocalists like Tex Williams, represented a much lusher sound than previously heard in western swing music. The bandleader, resplendent in elegant western-style regalia, held sway at the Venice Pier Ballroom for 18 months prior to moving to the more prestigious Riverside Rancho Ballroom in Santa Monica where he played to overflow crowds from 1943 to 1946. In 1945, Spade Cooley and His Orchestra scored the first of six consecutive Top Ten singles on *Billboard*'s

Spade Cooley, the self-proclaimed King of Western Swing (pictured here with wife Ella Mae and his band, the Barn Dance Boys), was popular during the 1940s, but saw his career wane in the late 1950s. An abusive alcoholic, Cooley tortured and murdered Ella Mae in front of their teenaged daughter in April 1961. The killing was so brutal and shocking that crime fiction novelist James Ellroy has featured Cooley as a character in several of his novels.

country chart. "Shame on You," featuring a Tex Williams vocal, debuted on March 3, 1945, peaked at Number One, and stayed on the charts for 31 weeks. The tune became Cooley's theme song, and introduced a spate of best sellers with titles like "A Pair of Broken Hearts" (1945), "I've Taken All I'm Gonna Take from You" (1945), and "Crazy 'Cause I Love You" (1947), a tune that would take on a portentously sinister meaning in light of the bandleader's impending troubles. During this period, Cooley expanded into other media appearing in Western films like *The Singing Sheriff* (1944) and *Texas Panhandle* (1945). By 1945, the bandleader's future looked limitless. That year, he left the Riverside Ballroom, leased the spacious Santa Monica Ballroom, and formally dubbed himself the "King of Western Swing." On December 9, 1945, the 34-year-old divorced Cooley married Ella Mae Evans, a 21-year-old singer with his band, in a secret ceremony in Las Vegas, Nevada. In 1947, he added "television star" to his already impressive list of accomplishments. The Hoffman Company, a regional television set manufacturer, offered him the role of musical host on its variety show, *The Hoffman Hayride* (renamed *The Spade Cooley Show*). Broadcast on Saturdays from the Santa Monica Ballroom on station KTLA, the show was a huge hit drawing an estimated 75 percent of all viewers in Los Angeles until it ended after almost six years on-air in 1952. By the mid–1950s, however, Cooley's popularity was waning, a casualty of the changing musical and television tastes of the American public.

Without a recording contract or a television show to occupy his time, Cooley's heavy drinking blossomed into full-blown alcoholism. By the late 1950s even Cooley realized he was no longer in show business and began referring to himself as a "land developer." In March 1961, he unveiled an ambitious plan to develop a $15 million amusement park and recreation center near his ranch in Willow Springs, California, on a 1,000 acre site overlooking Antelope Valley in the Techachapi foothills above the Mojave Desert. "Water Wonderland" would include three man-made lakes, an amusement park, a bowling alley, a hotel and motel, a Western and Indian Village, four restaurants, an 18 hole golf course, and a 20,000 square foot ballroom where Cooley planned to televise his show. On March 24, 1961, just weeks after publicly announcing his development plans, Cooley filed for divorce from Ella Mae after 15 years of marriage charging incompatibility, and seeking custody of their two children, Melody, 13, and Donnell, 11. "Ella Mae has moved out and I'm heartsick, but there isn't a chance of a reconciliation," he told reporters.

Convinced Ella Mae had been unfaithful, Cooley hired Hollywood private investigator William ("Billie") Lewis on April 1, 1961 to keep tabs on her. In taped telephone conversations between Cooley, Lewis, and his wife conducted on April 3, 1961, the morning of the day of the murder, Ella Mae admitted to having an affair. Melody and brother Donnell were staying at the home of family friend A.P. McWhorter in nearby Rosamund, when Cooley phoned that evening and asked Melody to meet him and her mother at the family ranch. She arrived at 6:20 P.M. to witness a scene of unfolding horror. "When I went inside," she later told a coroner's jury, "I started crying. I knew what was going to happen because my father was always beating my mother. My dad was on the phone... He was real sweaty and his pants were splattered with blood. He was saying, 'Don't call the police... Don't call the police.'" Cooley hung up the phone, grabbed his daughter by the arm, commanding, "Come in here. I want you to see your mother. She's going to tell you everything's she's done." Melody heard the shower running as Cooley marched her into the bathroom off the master bedroom. There, she saw her mother's nude inert body sprawled on the floor of the shower stall. When she did not move, Cooley grabbed his wife's hair with both hands, dragged her out of the shower, and banged her head twice against the floor. Laughing, Cooley stormed out of the room. Melody tried to revive her mother with cold water, but although "I could hear a rattling noise in her throat when she breathed," the woman was unconscious. Cooley returned, said, "We'll just see if you're dead," and repeatedly stomped his wife on the stomach, then burned the woman's breasts with a lighted cigarette. According to the stunned teenager, her father said, "You're going to watch me kill her, Melody. If you don't, I'll kill all of us." Cooley took the girl into the living room and had her sit on his lap as he calmly smoked a cigarette. After twenty minutes, the girl ran hysterically screaming from the house. A pathologist's report revealed Ella Mae had sustained numerous bruises and abrasions to her body, signs of forceful strangulation, with death resulting from a split in the abdominal aorta (the main artery from the heart) consistent with injuries associated with stomping.

Over two quarts of blood were found in the victim's abdomen. Injuries to Ella Mae's vagina and anus (cited in the death certificate, but not in the media) suggested she had been raped with a broom handle found at the scene.

As his wife was quietly buried in the Oakdale Cemetery in Glendora, Cooley passed the pretrial time composing songs inspired by her ("Everything I write is about her," he told reporters) in the Kern County Jail in Bakersfield.

Cooley's trial for first-degree murder began in Bakersfield, California on July 14, 1961. The six-week proceeding, the longest criminal trial to that time in Kern County history, was a media free-for-all punctuated by near daily bombshell revelations, and twice interrupted after the bandleader suffered minor heart attacks. Although four court-appointed psychiatrists agreed Cooley was currently sane and was so at the time of the murder, the bandleader pleaded "not guilty by reason of insanity." According to psychiatric reports, Cooley told doctors that on the day of the murder Ella Mae had confessed that she had an affair with two men at a trailer park and a motel. She loaned money to one. In a tape recording played in open court made on the morning of the day of her death, Ella Mae admitted to private investigator William Lewis that she did have an affair with a man in October 1960. Allegations were also made that the dead woman once had an affair with Roy Rogers, a claim vigorously denied by the cowboy star.

No defense offered by the former media star, however, could undo the damage done to his case by Melody Cooley's tearful description of her mother's sadistic maltreatment at the hands of her father, a person, she told the 10 man, 2 woman jury, that she disowned and "stopped calling ... 'daddy' when this happened." As a last resort, the defense put Cooley on the stand. He testified "rockets ran through my brain" when Ella Mae admitted her sex play with two men, and then informed him she planned "to join them in the 100-member free love cult they were forming." Cooley admitted striking his estranged wife, but then remembered nothing else except standing in front of her in the bedroom with a lighted cigarette. Saying repeatedly, "I'm not worth it, Spade," Ella Mae took the cigarette from her husband, opened her blouse, and burned her breasts with it. Cooley acknowledged knocking Ella Mae unconscious and taking her into the bathroom to revive her. "She went into the shower alone. I didn't push or shove her. Then the next thing that happened, I'll remember as long as I live. There was a terrible thud ... the glass breaking. I didn't go in there right away." Although he did not remember phoning his daughter, Melody did help him take her out of the shower. "I rubbed her wrists, breathed in her mouth, put cold towels on her head—and I prayed." According to Cooley, his daughter was lying out of spite about the so-called "murder by torture" because he had been recently forced to discipline her. Regrettably for the bandleader, none of the injuries sustained by Ella Mae could be explained by a fall in the shower. The jury needed only 10 hours and 14 minutes on August 20, 1961, to return a guilty verdict against the "King of Western Swing." The subsequent sanity phase of the trial ended after Cooley unexpectedly withdrew his insanity plea to avoid "reliving the tragedy and horror of another trial." Waiving his right to a jury hearing, Cooley threw himself on the mercy of the court. On August 22, 1961, the trial judge sentenced the former star to life imprisonment. Under California law, Cooley would be eligible parole in 7 years. A request for a new trial based on prejudicial errors in the first was rejected by the Fifth District Court of Appeal in December 1962, and upheld by the California Supreme Court in February 1963. A model prisoner, Cooley spent his time in prison studying gems and minerals and teaching music and crafts to fellow-inmates. In August 1968, his first year of parole eligibility, Cooley was turned down. He was, however, set to be granted a full parole on February 22, 1970, when a perversely Hollywood-type finale brought the curtain down on the former western music star. Temporarily freed on a 72-hour supervised furlough from the Vacaville State Medical Facility, the 59-year-old Cooley performed at a benefit show for the Alameda County Sheriffs Association in Oakland, California on November 23, 1969. He had just left the stage after performing a three-song set to a standing ovation from 2,000 fans when he suffered a massive heart attack backstage and died. Cooley is interred in the Chapel of the Chimes Memorial Park in Hayward, California in a wall crypt with a panel bearing his name, dates, and the legend, "Beloved Father."

Further Reading

Ankeny, Jason. "Spade Cooley." *All Music Guide to Country*, p. 102. San Francisco: Miller Freeman, 1997.
"Cooley Held for Murder; Describes Killing." *Los Angeles Times*, April 14, 1961, pt. I, pp. 2, 23.

Gilmore, John. *L.A. Despair: A Landscape of Crimes & Bad Times*. Los Angeles: Amok, 2005.

Henstell, Bruce. "How the King of Western Swing Reached the End of His Rope." *Los Angeles*, 24(6) (June 1979):126, 128–130, 132, 134–136.

Jones, Daniel C. L. "Cooley, Spade." *American National Biography*. Vol. 5, pp. 413–415. New York: Oxford University Press, 1999.

Riese, Randall. *Nashville Babylon: The Uncensored Truth and Private Lives of Country Music's Stars*. New York: Congdon & Weed, 1988.

Tosches, Nick. *Country: The Biggest Music in America*. New York: Stein and Day, 1977.

Cortéz, Angel (V)

On Saturday night, April 1, 1995, the 23-year-old L.A. based anti-gang organizer and rapper was in Salt Lake City, Utah, with his group, South Central and Celebrity Boys, to perform at a "peace dance" at El Centro Cívico Mexicano, a Latino cultural center at 155 S. 600 West. As Cortéz and the group performed inside the center before a largely teen crowd of over 200, hired security guards outside patted down and scanned concert goers with metal detectors before admitting them into the auditorium. Trouble began when suspected gang members refused to be searched, and one pulled a gun and fired through the center's glass doors at rival gang members. Cortéz, in town to rap the message of non-violence, was struck in the back and killed. Friend and fellow-band member, Francisco Dueñas, sustained a minor leg wound. Not surprisingly, only six of the more than 200 people attending the concert came forward to supply information about the shooting despite the $2,000 reward offered by the Salt Lake City Police Department.

More than two years passed before the department identified 21-year-old gangbanger Issac Cirillio González as its prime suspect based on information supplied 1½ years after the event by Mario Cortéz, the victim's cousin, who admitted returning gunfire during the shooting before fleeing the scene. Arrested, González was initially charged with first-degree felony murder, but due to witness problems was allowed by prosecutors to plead guilty to a charge of third-degree felony homicide by assault. In February 1998, the gang member was sentenced from 0 to 5 years in prison with a consecutive 5 year gun enchancement term tacked on, and ordered to pay over $22,000 in restitution to the victim's family. While González took responsibility for escalating the violence at the concert, he insisted that he was not responsible for firing the gun that killed Cortéz and wounded Dueñas. According to González, the incident at the cultural center had been precipitated two weeks earlier when a rival gang shot and paralyzed his friend. On the night of the peace concert, gunfire broke out when the two gangs saw each other. Angel Cortéz was merely an innocent casualty. In offering the plea bargain agreement to González, Deputy District Attorney Judy Jensen conceded that available, but conflicting, evidence strongly suggested that someone else did the shooting.

Further Reading

Hunt, Stephen. "Gangster Gets Up to 10 Years for His Role in S.L. Killing." *Salt Lake Tribune*, February 24, 1998, sec. B, p. 2.

Crane, Bob (V)

Known in "television land" as the wisecracking "Colonel Robert Hogan" in the popular CBS sitcom *Hogan's Heroes*, Bob Crane will be forever remembered (thanks to director Paul Schrader's 2002 film *Auto Focus*) as the sex-addicted actor who was brutally murdered in a motel room in Scottsdale, Arizona, in 1978. Born Bob Edward Crane on July 13, 1928 in Waterbury, Connecticut, the future television star began life as the cliched "All American Boy." Raised by loving parents in a stable Roman Catholic family, the youngster showed an early interest in big band music and dreamed of becoming a drummer like his idol Gene Krupa. Crane, a good looking and likable teenager with a mischievous personality, dropped out of high school at 15 to develop his musical skills. The next year he landed a job as a drummer with the Connecticut Symphony Orchestra, but was fired two years later for a lack of seriousness. Crane hit the road drumming for several East Coast bands before serving in the Connecticut National Guard from 1948–1950. In 1949, he married his high school sweetheart, Anne Terzian, and the couple would have three children (Robert David, Deborah Ann, Karen Leslie).

In 1950, radio station WLEA in Hornell, New York, hired Crane as an announcer at $37.50 a week. Crane's talent and hard work led to a better job with WICC in Bristol, Connecticut where his off-the-wall style, witty banter, and general likability made his morning radio show a ratings favorite. In 1956, CBS-owned radio station KNX in Los Angeles was in the market for a replacement personality for its morning show. According to show biz legend, Crane (now earning $500 a week at WICC) was recommended to KNX by a

New York radio executive at WCBS who wanted the popular performer out of the East Coast market. Crane took over the 6:00–10:00 A.M. slot and was a smash hit earning the nickname the "King of the L.A. Airwaves." Seldom playing records, the entertainer wowed the radio audience with his brash, irreverent humor, ad libs, skits, and interviews with stars like Marilyn Monroe (see entry), Bob Hope, and Frank Sinatra. With customary energy, Crane promoted himself on the L.A. banquet circuit making some 256 appearances in one year. Graduating to the coveted 5:00–9:00 P.M. drive time slot, Crane was an established radio personality knocking down a six-figure salary in a major market, but felt at a career dead end. He had accomplished all his goals in the medium, and feared being typecast. In order to realize his dream of becoming the next Jack Lemmon, Crane expanded his career aspirations to include film and television. To that end, he subbed for Johnny Carson on *Who Do You Trust?*, played drums on *The Ed Sullivan Show*, and appeared in small roles in television programs including *The Twilight Zone* ("Static," air date March 10, 1961) and *General Electric Theater* (October 15, 1961).

Crane might have continued indefinitely guesting on various TV shows except for a career changing meeting with Carl Reiner in 1962. Interviewed on Crane's KNX radio show, Reiner gave the aspiring actor a guest spot on his television comedy hit *The Dick Van Dyke Show*. Crane's appearance in the episode "Somebody Has to Play Cleopatra" aired on December 26, 1962, and led directly to a one-shot appearance on the wholesome ABC television sitcom, *The Donna Reed Show*. Crane was so good in the episode, that he was signed as a regular on the show in 1963 as Reed's next door neighbor "Dr. Dave Kelsey." For the next two seasons (1963–1965), Crane maintained a breakneck pace, doing his morning radio show, then shooting his television series in the afternoons and evenings. Though never comfortable with his square, old-fashioned role on the family-oriented sitcom (he saw himself as a hip con man), Crane was disappointed and hurt when the show's producer dropped him rather than meet his demand for a modest pay raise. At 36, Crane was ready to be the star of his own television series. In late 1964, CBS (parent company of KNX) shopped around for a television property that could cash in on the popularity of their top-rated radio personality. They found it in the un-

likely half-hour series, *Hogan's Heroes*, a slapstick version of the 1953 motion picture *Stalag 17* set in a World War II Nazi prisoner of war (*not* concentration) camp for allied military personnel. The role of U.S. Air Corps "Col. Robert Hogan," the wisecracking mastermind of the weekly prison breaks, perfectly suited Crane. Produced by Bing Crosby Productions, *Hogan's Heroes* debuted on September 17, 1965 and was an instant smash. No one in the cast worked harder than Crane who was often the first person on, and last person off, the set. Each weekly half-hour show took four intense days to shoot, and he continued at KNX until leaving the station after *Hogan's Heroes* was deemed a bona fide hit. Crane's hard work paid off with an Emmy nomination during the show's first season, but he lost to friend Dick Van Dyke. Still, Crane loved the celebrity the series gave him, and became a regular on TV talk shows.

Friends and co-workers, however, began to notice a change in Crane's personality following the success of *Hogan's Heroes*. Known in show business circles as a devoted husband and family man, Crane early moved his family to Tarzana, a suburb of Los Angeles, because it provided a better atmosphere in which to raise his three children. While "King of the L.A. Airwaves," Crane did not drink, smoke, do drugs, or conduct sexual affairs. As late as 1963, he reportedly refused to take his mother to see the film *Tom Jones* deeming it too racy. A self-confessed electronics nut, Crane documented the growth of his children on 16mm film, often writing, then casting them in his self-shot home movies. Perhaps to escape the pressures of shooting the series, Crane began dropping by strip bars and nightclubs after work to play drums with the house band. Sometime during the early years of *Hogan's Heroes*, co-star Richard Dawson brought his friend, John Henry Carpenter, to the set. Dawson, who was turned down for the lead in the series, openly disliked Crane, but shared a common passion with the star for electronics and cameras. Carpenter, of American Indian descent, worked for Sony USA demonstrating the newly emerging technology of home video equipment to wealthy customers, and had set up systems for Dawson, Alfred Hitchcock, and Elvis Presley. Crane bought the then clumsy, top-of-the line black & white beta video equipment from Carpenter, and found he had more in common with the man than just an interest in electronics. Like Crane, the video equipment salesman loved cruising bars to pick up women often taping himself having sex with his one-night stands. Crane and Carpenter entered into what many have characterized as a symbiotic relationship — Crane attracted sexually willing, starstruck women while Carpenter, content with the celebrity's castoffs, supplied the video equipment and expertise to record their conquests.

As Crane's sexual addiction took precedence over his career, his 19-year marriage to high school sweetheart Anne Terzian suffered. In the first year of *Hogan's Heroes*, Crane began an affair with Cynthia Lynn, the striking blonde who played the role of "Helga," the secretary of the camp's commandant "Col. Wilhelm Klink" (Werner Klemperer). The relationship ended in 1966 after Lynn broke off the affair, quit the series, and reconciled with her husband. She was replaced without missing a beat in either the series or Crane's sex life by buxom, pigtailed blonde Sigrid Valdis (real name Patti Olsen) who was cast at the beginning of the season's second year as Klink's new secretary, "Hilda." Crane's affair with the voluptuous actress effectively ended his marriage to Terzian. On May 13, 1969, one week before their 20th wedding anniversary, Terzian filed for divorce from the 40-year-old actor. Shortly after their divorce was finalized, Crane married Olsen on October 16, 1970 in a ceremony conducted on the set of *Hogan's Heroes* attended by the show's cast. The marriage to a glamorous actress and the birth of a son, Scott, in 1971 did little to curtail Crane's sexual activities with his "shadow" John Carpenter. The video salesman routinely altered his work schedule to hang out after hours with his TV star friend. Videotapes, some obviously taken without the knowledge of the women involved, showed Crane alone with a woman, or sometimes with Carpenter engaged in a threesome with their pickup. It is believed that Crane, strictly heterosexual, knew that his friend was bisexual, though with a strong preference for young women.

In a move designed to save money and field a schedule more appealing to a younger, more urban viewing demographic, CBS unceremoniously cancelled *Hogan's Heroes* at the end of the 1970–1971 season. The still popular series ran for six seasons and produced 168 episodes. For the first time since the late 1950s, Crane was unemployed. While the enforced respite afforded the out-of-work actor more time to indulge his sexual ramblings with Carpenter, Crane was anxious to work, and needed the income (residuals from *Hogan's Heroes* would not be sizable until 1976).

Crane had done uncredited parts in a few films (*Return to Peyton Place*, 1961; *Man-Trap*, 1961; *The New Interns*, 1964), and a credited role in the 1968 Elke Sommer bomb, *The Wicked Dreams of Paula Schultz*, but was still regarded in the industry as a television actor. Following the failure of the 1972 pilot made-for-television movie, *The Delphi Bureau*, to be picked up as a series, Crane optioned the rights to *Beginner's Luck*, a two-act sex farce in 1973. The actor toured the lucrative dinner theatre circuit where unsophisticated audiences still looked upon "Col. Robert Hogan" as a major star. On the road with the omnipresent Carpenter in tow, Crane used the travel opportunities to exploit his celebrity and meet more sexual partners. Post-show autograph sessions in the theatre lobby became the means by which the charming actor often selected his companion for the evening. The starstruck woman almost always had a friend for Carpenter and, after dinner and drinks, the foursome often ended up in Crane's two-bedroom motel digs. Many women did not find the video camera aimed at the bed or couch offensive, and permitted Crane to photograph them during sex. The woman who failed to wind up with the television star either left, or, had sex with Carpenter in the spare bedroom.

In 1973, Crane landed his first starring movie role in the ironically entitled Disney generation gap comedy, *Superdad*. Shot largely in San Francisco, when not on-camera the actor prowled the city for "alternative sex" (group, S & M). Released in 1974, the movie flopped, and Crane was once again relegated to television guest shots on shows like *Ellery Queen* and *Channing*. NBC, hoping to cash in on the actor's likability factor, bankrolled *The Bob Crane Show* in March 1975. In the half-hour sitcom, Crane played a fortyish insurance executive who quits his job to enter medical school with comedic results. Panned by critics, the series ended in June 1975 after just 13 episodes. To add insult to injury, in 1976 he appeared in a secondary role opposite stars Don Knotts and Ed Asner in another poorly reviewed Disney film, *Gus*, the story of a football kicking mule. When rumors of Crane's sordid off-screen antics reached Disney executives, the studio terminated their relationship with the actor. On the home front, Patti Olsen finally had enough of her husband's philandering (although she had at one time apparently been a willing participant in his sexcapades), and filed for divorce in December 1977. Frustrated in his television and movie career,

Crane always had *Beginner's Luck* to fall back on. If the actor felt dinner theatre was a professional step down, his ego must have been salved by the fans of "Col. Hogan," especially female, still flocking to see him play in the sticks. When not onstage in various towns, Crane continued to feed his addiction for sex by cruising bars and/or his audience for sex partners. The result — the actor's cache of homemade sex tapes grew as did his collection of self-photographed and processed 35mm sex photos.

In June 1978, *Beginner's Luck* was booked into the Windmill Dinner Theatre in Scottsdale, Arizona. The production opened to bad notices, attendance was down, and was set to be cancelled one week early. Crane, 49, was staying in the city at the Winfield Apartments at 7430 East Chaparral on the corner where it intersects Miller Road. The actor's two-bedroom ground floor apartment, Room 132-A, was routinely booked by the Windmill Theatre for the stars of their shows. The apartment was crammed with videotape cameras, VCRs, boxes of videos, editing equipment, even a mini-dark room lab for developing still photos jerryrigged on the back of the bathroom commode. Crane's sexual predilections were no secret to his cast mates. Often, he invited them to his apartment for screenings of the black-and-white Beta sex tapes, and to view the erotic photos he took of his one-night stands (including pictures of his estranged wife, Patti) displayed in a white binder. One tape featured Crane and John Carpenter engaged in three-way sex with a female, a common practice Crane once admitted to an associate.

On June 25, 1978, Crane picked up John Carpenter, 50, at the local airport. Carpenter, now the national service manager for AKAI Equipment Limited in Compton, California, was in town to hang out with his friend and score women, the pair's usual routine. Unlike on other occasions, however, Carpenter did not stay with Crane at his two-bedroom flat in the Winfield Apartments. On this visit, Crane booked his friend a room in the Sunburst Motel, a modest facility a half-block from the Winfield Apartments. During the following days, the men continued their usual symbiotic sexual relationship (Crane attracted the women, Carpenter taking the star's leftovers), but with no apparent success for the video equipment troubleshooter. On the evening of June 28, 1978, Carpenter was in the audience for *Beginner's Luck* with plans to hang out with the actor after the show. Both men secured dates and went their separate ways around 1:00 A.M. Crane's date, possibly aware of the actor's reputation, refused to accompany him to his digs at the Winfield, and went home alone. Carpenter was somewhat luckier. He was able to get his date back to his room at the Sunburst, but failing to bed her, drove the woman to her home around 2:30 A.M. According to Carpenter's later statement, he then returned to his motel.

Shortly after 2:00 P.M. the next afternoon, June 29, Victoria Ann Berry, a 21-year-old cast-member in *Beginner's Luck*, arrived at 132-A for a scheduled appointment with Crane. The actor, who had twice bedded the young Australian actress, had promised to dub her voice over a scene in a videotaped copy of the play. When no one answered her repeated knocks, Berry tried the door and found it uncharacteristically unlocked. It was well known to anyone familiar with Crane that he always locked the door to prevent theft of his video equipment, tapes, photos, or perhaps to even guard against the intrusion of irate husbands and boyfriends. Entering the darkened apartment, the actress found the rooms cluttered with video equipment, tape boxes, and papers. Opening a blind, she saw an unrecognizable male body on the double-sized bed. The bloody form was lying on its right side with knees slightly bent in a semi-fetal position. The left hand was tucked under the chin, the right arm stretched down the length of the body. Blood from a head wound was everywhere, soaking the mattress, and spattered on the wall above the head. A black plastic camcorder cord was tied around the throat with a twist knot. The man was dressed only in boxer shorts. Scottsdale police arrived on the scene around 2:30 P.M. and were investigating when the telephone rang at 3:15 P.M. Acting under orders from lead detective, Ron Dean, Berry answered the phone. It was Carpenter calling to report he had left Scottsdale that morning and was back in Los Angeles. Dean took the phone, identified himself as a Scottsdale Police Department officer, and informed Carpenter he was investigating "an incident at the Crane apartment." Carpenter did not solicit more information about the type of crime, and told Dean he had left Crane around 1:00 A.M. that morning (later revising the time to 2:45 A.M. in a call to the detective the next day). He returned to his motel, collected his things, drove his rental car back to the airport, then caught his flight back to Los Angeles. Meanwhile, the body in the bloody bed had been identified as Bob Crane. Death, as the actor slept, had resulted from two hard blows to the left temple from a blunt object. The violence of the attack combined with the force of the blows led police to suspect the killer to be a male. The murder weapon, never recovered, was believed by police to have been a tripod for a video camera. The SPD immediately suspected Crane, a notoriously light sleeper, had known his victim. There were no signs of a struggle, the door was unlocked, and nothing appeared to have been taken except for the white binder containing Crane's collection of homemade 35mm sex photos. Authorities confiscated boxes of homemade porn videos along with pictures and negatives found in the makeshift photo lab in the bathroom.

For many, the subsequent investigation by the Scottsdale Police Department served as a textbook case of how not to process a crime scene, and moreover, what can happen when various branches of law enforcement fail to cooperate. In the late 1980s, Scottsdale averaged only two homicides a year, not enough to merit funding a separate homicide unit. In the absence of such a trained department, a small-time police force could well expect to be overwhelmed by such a high profile case. The County Attorney's Office, miffed by the SPD's failure to bring them quickly into the case, charged that SPD investigators had failed to secure the crime scene. Victoria Ann Berry was allowed to answer the phone before it was dusted for prints (denied by the SPD), evidence was tainted when it was indiscriminately dumped into one garbage bag (denied by the SPD), and the actress was allowed to chain smoke at the scene. Cops were also permitted to rest their radios on table tops. Most damning, however, was the fact that both Crane's business manager, and son, Robert, Jr., were allowed the next day to remove items from the apartment before they had been checked for fingerprints. Also, although immediately focusing on John Carpenter as their prime suspect based on his past seamy relationship with Crane and subsequent behavior, police had failed to search his room at the Sunburst Motel in a timely fashion. Inexplicably, a blob of semen or KY jelly found on Crane's left thigh was never analyzed.

Another problem facing police—too many suspects. Crane, despite his charm and sociability, left a swath of emotional destruction in his wake. The murderer could be one of the many women he had videotaped (sometimes surreptitiously), or, their irate boyfriends or husbands. Estranged wife Patti, the chief beneficiary of Crane's insurance policy, engaged in a loud phone argument with her wandering husband on the night before the murder. She was briefly considered a suspect until it was determined she had an airtight alibi. A fellow one-time cast member in *Beginner's Luck*, also cleared by police, had threatened Crane a few months earlier. Still, Carpenter seemed the most likely suspect to the SPD, especially after Robert Crane, Jr. told them his dad had recently intimated to him that the video equipment dealer was becoming "a bit of a pain in the ass." According to Crane's eldest son, "My dad expressed that he just didn't need Carpenter kind of hanging around him anymore." Another red flag to the SPD—the fact Carpenter had not, as usual, bunked with Crane in his two-bedroom apartment pointed to a possible rift between the men. The actor's recent unease with Carpenter was underscored by the testimony of a waitress who saw the two men together in a restaurant the night before the murder. While they did not argue, there did appear to be a palpable tension between them. The SPD theorized that Carpenter killed the actor when he realized their relationship was over and he would no longer have sexual access to the women Crane attracted. Carpenter's behavior on the morning of the murder was also viewed by police as suspicious. He left the hotel in a hurry, dropped off his rental car (a 1978 Chrysler Cordoba) complaining that it need to be serviced, and arrived at the airport well before his flight was due to depart. An examination of the rental car revealed specks of dried blood on the interior of the passenger door along with a 3" scratch line of dried blood on the padding near the door top. Police determined no one had bled in the car, and tests revealed the sample to be Type-B (a type shared by one out of every 7 people). Crane's blood was Type-B, but the sample pulled from the Cordoba was insufficient to determine if it was the actor's (DNA testing was not available at the time). Cops surmised that the scratch line was caused by the murder weapon being tossed from the car. Carpenter (Type-A blood), was subsequently interviewed, denied killing his friend, and readily offered to take a polygraph or sodium pentothal test. He was given neither because police felt he possessed the psychological make-up to beat the machine and the drug.

The County Attorney's Office, still peeved over

its perceived exclusion from the case by the SPD, duplicated the department's efforts with its own investigators. County Attorney Charles Hyder, openly critical of what he perceived as the SPD's incompetent handling of the crime scene and their fixation on Carpenter as the only viable suspect, called a press conference on July 20, 1978 to announce that the evidence amassed by the local police department was "insufficient to file a complaint or even to show probable cause." In the next couple of years the Crane case became a hot political campaign issue in Scottsdale. In 1980, Phoenix attorney Tom Collins ran against Hyder with a pledge to take another, unbiased look at the case. Collins unseated Hyder, but upon reviewing the sensational murder, decided against pursuing an indictment on Carpenter. The case languished for a decade, ten years in which Carpenter endured the strain of being an unindicted murderer while the SPD smarted under the publics' perception of the department as incompetent. In the late 1980s, Richard Romley was elected to replace Collins, and vowed to finally solve the Crane murder. In June 1989, the new county attorney appointed a team of prosecutors and investigators to review the complex case. Nearly 12 years after the murder, DNA testing had reached a level where it was possible to determine if the blood inside Carpenter's rented Cordoba belonged to Bob Crane. Unfortunately, the test proved inconclusive — the dried blood was too old after 11 years, and there was not enough of a sample. The case appeared permanently stalled until county investigator Jim Raines found the proverbial "smoking gun" inside a storage room in the Maricopa County courthouse. Overlooked by past investigators and prosecutors, Raines uncovered a color photo of an irregularly shaped $1/16$" in diameter dark speck on the door panel of Carpenter's rental car. The speck was not preserved, but various experts who examined the photo determined the spot was "probably" brain or fat tissue.

On June 1, 1992, 14 years after the Bob Crane bludgeon murder, John Carpenter, now a 63-year-old national service manager at Kenwood USA, was arrested in the Los Angeles suburb of Carson, California. While awaiting trial, the stereo component representative remained free on $98,000 bond still adamant that he did not kill his best friend. The March 1993 preliminary hearing used to establish probable cause exposed the many weaknesses of the county's case against Carpenter. The Department of Public Safety, the organization that photographed the inside of Carpenter's rental car in 1978, did not have the tissue speck. In fact, the DPS had destroyed all its reports on the case in 1988, including the negatives of photos documenting the inside of the car. Further, the DPS was unable to produce any written record that had noted the tissue in the car. No one at the DPS was even able to identify who took the photos in 1978. At trial in September 1994, the problems of winning a murder conviction against Carpenter based on shoddy police work and forensic conjecture became even more glaringly apparent. The photo evidence disputed, if not totally discredited, the prosecution played a videotape in which Crane, Carpenter, and an unidentified woman were engaged in three-way sex. It proved nothing other than Crane and Carpenter enjoyed having sex with an apparently willing female. The defense countered that the homemade videotape suggested a universe of other possible suspects with a motive for murder — jealous boyfriends, incensed husband, perhaps even the women sometimes unknowingly captured on the black & white tapes. On October 31, 1994, a jury acquitted Carpenter after deliberating two days. The verdict was a clear rejection of the prosecution's claim that Carpenter had killed his friend in a fit of rage over the actor's desire to end their relationship, thereby cutting off the video equipment salesman's access to women attracted by Crane's celebrity. As Carpenter told an interviewer in 1993, "I never even had a fight with Bob. He was my friend. And he was the goose who laid the golden egg for me, in terms of meeting ladies." Jury foreman, Marine Sgt. Michael Lake, told the press after the verdict, "There wasn't any proof. What was the speck? Nobody knows what it was, not even the doctors." Carpenter, a destitute social pariah reduced to working part-time in a stereo repair shop, died of a heart attack at the age of 70 on September 4, 1998, at the Little Company of Mary Hospital in Torrance, California.

The Crane murder case hit the headlines again in 2002 with the release of Paul Schrader's film, *Auto Focus*, starring Greg Kinnear as Bob Crane, and Willem Dafoe as John Henry Carpenter. The critically acclaimed motion picture chronicled the actor's transformation from an ordinary guy with a family into a deluded, emotionally sterile sex addict, and strongly implied that Carpenter was his murderer. Crane's son from his marriage to Anne Terzian, Robert, Jr., served as a consultant on the film and was paid $20,000. Scotty Crane, the actor's son by second wife Patti Olsen, damned the film as "Auto Fiction," accusing Schrader of "destroying my dad's reputation in the world." To counteract the screen portrayal of his father as a seedy, sex-obsessed creep, Scotty, a former Seattle radio shock jock, launched a website (www.bob crane.com) on June 1, 2001, where for a 30 day fee of $19.95 subscribers could view the infamous homemade sex tapes and photos shot by Crane. Deflecting one reporter's criticism that the site served merely as "a disturbing repository of his dad's porn," Scotty insisted it portrayed his father as a "sexual rebel." "I think if my father were alive," said Scotty, "he'd be running the site himself." According to Crane's youngest son, the site logged 5.6 million hits during the first week it was up. Both sons, however, agreed that their father showed them pornographic videotapes when they were youngsters. To date, the Bob Crane murder case remains officially open, but inactive. Members of the Scottsdale Police Department remain convinced that John Carpenter was the killer, he just got away.

Further Reading

Clark, Denise M. "Cold Case: The Murder of Hogan's Hero." (http://crimemagazine.com.bobcrane.htm).
Graysmith, Robert. *The Murder of Bob Crane.* New York: Crown, 1993.
Rovin, Jeff. *TV Babylon.* Updated ed. New York: Signet, 1987.

Crane, Cheryl (M–acquitted)

The only child of cinema sex goddess Lana Turner, Cheryl Crane serves as the classic Hollywood cautionary tale of what can occur when a celebrity parent is more interested in their own fame and sex life than in their child's welfare. Dubbed the "Sweater Girl" after taking her memorable walk in the form fitting garment in director Mervyn LeRoy's 1937 film *They Won't Forget*, the curvaceous Turner became a star in 1941 after dyeing her hair blond to play a showgirl in MGM's *Ziegfeld Girl*. Under contract at the studio, she solidified her image as a sex symbol in *The Postman Always Rings Twice* (1946) and projected an image of elegance laced with promiscuity in a series of carefully crafted costume dramas and melodramas including *The Three Musketeers* (1948), *The Bad and the Beautiful* (1952), *The Flame and the Flesh* (1954), and later in films for other studios (*Peyton Place*, 1957; *Imitation of Life*, 1959; *Portrait in Black*, 1960).

Turner's personal life, however, was more dramatic than any role she ever played during her 42 year career in motion pictures. By January 1972 when she finally got off the marriage-go-round, the star had been wed eight times to a total of seven different men: bandleader Artie Shaw (1940), restaurateur Stephen Crane (1942–1943; 1943–1944), millionaire businessman Bob Topping (1948–1952), actor Lex Barker (1953–1957), Fred May (1960–1962), Robert Eaton (1965–1969), and Ronald Dante (1969, separated 6 months later, divorced 1972). Turner was 22 and already a fixture in the Hollywood club scene when she eloped to Las Vegas with 45-year-old wannabe actor turned restaurateur, Stephen Crane, on July 17, 1942. Crane, however, was still technically married to a woman in Indiana from whom he had obtained a divorce less than a year earlier. Embarrassed, pregnant, and illegally married to a bigamist in the eyes of the law, Turner had the union annulled on February 4, 1943. The couple legally remarried on March 14, 1943 and some five months later their only child, Cheryl Christina Crane, was born in Hollywood on July 25, 1943. The marriage limped along for a year before ending in divorce on August 21, 1944. Lacking any natural instinct for mothering, Turner abdicated the raising of her daughter to a series of nannies and her own mother (known to the child as "Gran"). More interested in her career and sex life than in providing a stable emotional atmosphere for her child, Turner paraded a string of star lovers like Tyrone Power, Turhan Bey, Fernando Lamas, and numerous others through their home. The star instructed her daughter to refer to her ever changing cast of sex partners as "Uncles" or mother's "gentlemen friends."

Following her bitter divorce in December 1952 from third husband, Bob Topping, Turner married actor Lex Barker on September 7, 1953. Barker, destined to be best remembered for playing "Tarzan" in five minor films from 1949 to 1953, allegedly began sexually abusing 10 -year-old Cheryl Crane sometime around March 1954. The abuse, sexual and physical, continued for three years with Barker threatening to send the girl to Juvenile Hall should she tell anyone of their encounters. Finally around March 1957, Crane worked up the nerve to tell her mother of the abuse after first confiding in her grandmother. That day, Turner threw Barker out of their home at gunpoint. The next morning the stunned star drove her daughter to the Beverly Hills Clinic for a gynecologic examination that verified the teenager had been violently and repeatedly entered over time. The decision not to prosecute Barker as a child molester was largely made by the studio to protect the career of its biggest female star. In April 1957, just weeks after Crane's shattering admission, Turner accused her teenaged daughter of flirting with her new "gentleman friend." Crane interpreted the accusation as proof that her mother actually believed she had seduced Lex Barker and caused the ruin of her marriage. Later that day, Crane ran away in downtown Los Angeles after being dropped at a train station for the trip back to yet another of the boarding schools in which she spent much of her youth. The teenager was recovered less than five hours later wandering in the city's Skid Row district. To avoid negative publicity, the papers were fed a story that Crane had bolted because she "hated school."

During the filming of *Peyton Place* in mid–1957 Turner began an intense sexual relationship with John Stompanato, a darkly handsome Latin type for which the actress always held a particular weakness. Born in Woodstock, Illinois, on October 19, 1925, Stompanato graduated military school and served with the Marines in the Pacific during World War II. After the war, Stompanato drifted out to Hollywood where his good looks and easy manner soon made him popular, especially with women. "Johnny," as he was known to his friends, was working as a greeter-bouncer in a bar owned by Mickey Cohen, a notorious Los Angeles mob boss, when the gangster hired the ex-Marine as one of his $300-a-week bodyguards and bag men. Well known to police under a variety of aliases ("John Holliday," "Jay Hubbard," "John Valentine," "John Steele," "John Truppa") Stompanato was arrested six times, but never convicted, on charges ranging from vagrancy to suspicion of burglary. To cover his criminal activities, the small-time hood sold cars, pets, flowers, and furniture. Women, however, were Stompanato's main source of income. Prior to meeting Lana Turner, he had been married at least four times often to older women who financially supported him. During divorce proceedings, one ex-wife accused Stompanato of attempting to strangle her mother to death because she had mislaid his handkerchiefs. A police file on the criminal characterized Stompanato as a con man who frequented expensive nightspots to meet wealthy women, let them lavish presents on him for a while, and moved on to another once their money was gone. Stompanato opened the Myrtlewood Gift Shop, a "front" business in Westwood, with $8,150 bor-rowed from a widow. Nicknamed "Oscar" after the Academy Award statuette, the physically well-endowed con man carried an address book filled with the private numbers of female movie stars like June Allyson, Zsa Zsa Gabor, and Anita Ekberg. Turner, 38, fell heavily for Stompanato who, lying to the actress, claimed to be 43 years old when, in fact, he was a decade younger. Stompanato ("John Steele" when they first met) also assured Turner his mob connections were a thing of the past pointing to his gift shop in Westwood as proof he was a legitimate businessman. Turner showered Stompanato with gifts and wrote torrid love letters filled with frank sexual innuendo and Spanish endearments calling him "my love and my life" usually signed "Lanita." Daughter Cheryl Crane, nearly 14 when she met the hood, immediately liked Stompanato because he spent more time with her than her own mother.

Cracks in the Turner-Stompanato love affair began to emerge in November 1957 when the actress traveled to England to shoot the film *Another Time, Another Place* opposite screen newcomer Sean Connery. Stompanato followed "Lanita" to England where they quietly rented a house together in suburban Hampstead. Barred from the set, Stompanato became enraged when rumors reached him that Turner was reportedly having an affair with her handsome co-star. The small-time hood angrily forced his way onto the set, loudly confronted Connery in front of the cast and crew, and was unceremoniously knocked out by one punch thrown by the future "James Bond." Humiliated, Stompanato pressed Turner to finance a screenplay he was trying to option thinking that in addition to producing the film, he might even act in it. When Turner informed him around Christmas 1957 of her hard and fast rule *never* to mix business with pleasure, Stompanato lashed out, knocked her around, held a razor to her face, and was smothering her with a pillow when the actress broke free and was saved by a hotel maid who heard her terrified screams. Turner told a studio friend about the assault, Scotland Yard was notified, and Stompanato was expelled from England that same day. After wrapping the film, Turner (followed by Stompanato) checked into the Villa Vera in the Mexican beach resort of Acapulco on January 21, 1958. Accounts vary widely as to what happened between the pair in Mexico. The Villa Vera's manager later told reporters that Stompanato "wouldn't let her alone for a moment." Turner characterized the time spent there as an uneasy armed truce marred by recurring violent arguments. Stompanato reportedly struck the actress and held a gun to her head when she refused to have sex with him. The pair, however, was photographed in clubs together and neighbors near their bungalow in the Villa Vera complained of their noisy and boisterous lovemaking sessions. Turner, fearing negative career repercussions, cringed whenever the press described Stompanato as a "mob figure" with connections to top L.A. gangster Mickey Cohen. Arriving back in Hollywood after their six-week stay in Acapulco, Turner took the dangerous step of informing Stompanato that he would not be attending the Academy Awards with her. Nominated for Best Actress for *Peyton Place*, Turner instead chose to take her daughter and mother in a move carefully calculated to present her to the world as a committed family woman. According to Turner, Johnny Stompanato was awaiting her when she returned with Cheryl to the star's rented two-story Colonial-style home at 730 North Bedford Drive in Beverly Hills after the ceremony on Good Friday, April 4, 1958.

While accounts vary widely as to the exact chronology of events that occurred inside the house on North Bedford Drive, the scene was set for a deadly confrontation. Turner, evidently learning earlier in the evening that her abusive lover was not 43, but in reality 10 years younger, was panic-stricken. As an aging star of 38 whose sexploits were already grist for the papers, Turner was panic-stricken that the Hollywood press would present her as a has-been star forced to "pay" younger men for sex. The actress informed her 14-year-old daughter that she was breaking up with Johnny. That night, Stompanato cursed Turner to the point that she asked Crane, watching television in her upstairs bedroom, not to pay attention to the tirade. The heated exchange continued in the star's bedroom directly across the landing from daughter Cheryl's. Turner accused Stompanato of lying and, though terrified of the hoodlum, demanded he leave. Turner later described the unfolding scene to a coroner's jury: "All I kept saying was, 'There's no use discussing it any farther: that I can't go on like this, and I want you to leave me alone.' He grabbed me by the arms, and Mr. Stompanato grabbed me by the arms and started shaking me and cursing me very badly, and saying that, as he had told me before, no matter what I did, how I tried to get away, he would never leave me, that if he said jump, I would jump; if he said hop, I would hop, and I would have to do anything and everything he told me or he'd cut my face or cripple me. And if— when— it went beyond that he would kill me, and my daughter and my mother. And he said it did not matter what he would get me where it hurt the most and that would be my daughter and my mother." Turner turned and saw that her daughter, concerned her mother was in grave danger, had opened the door of the room. The actress told Crane to go back to her own bedroom and not to listen to any of the hateful exchange. Instead of doing so, the frightened girl raced downstairs to the kitchen and picked up an 8" butcher knife purchased earlier that day by Turner and Stompanato.

Inside the bedroom, according to Turner's testimony, the angry actress confronted her lover— "That's just great, my child had to hear all of that, the horrible—and—I can't go through any more.'" Stompanato kept up a steady stream of verbal abuse and turned to the closet to pick up a suit on a hanger, in Turner's mind, to use to strike her. "Don't—don't ever touch me again. I am—I am absolutely finished. This is the end. And I want you to get out," Turner said and moved to the bedroom door with Stompanato close on her heels. "I opened it," the star tearfully testified, "and my daughter came in. I swear it was so fast, I—I truthfully thought she had hit him in the stomach. The best I can remember, they came together and they parted. I still never saw a blade. Mr. Stompanato grabbed himself here (abdomen). And he started to move forward, and he made almost a half turn, and then dropped on his back, and when he dropped, his arms went out, so that I still did not see that there was blood or a wound until I ran over to him, and I saw his sweater was cut, and I lifted the sweater up and I saw his wound. I remember only barely hearing my daughter sobbing and I ran into my bathroom which is very close and I grabbed a towel. I didn't know what to do. And then I put the towel there, and Mr. Stompanato was making very dreadful sounds in his throat of gasping, terrible sounds..."

One-half hour after the killing, Dr. John B. McDonald arrived on scene and attempted to jump start the dead man's heart with an injection of adrenaline. The doctor wisely suggested Turner phone noted attorney Jerry Giesler, famous in Hollywood for winning acquittals for both Erroll Flynn and Charlie Chaplin in their statutory rape trials. In 1959, Giesler was briefly hired by the mother of George ("Superman") Reeves (see entry) to investigate her son's mysterious death. A few minutes later, an ambulance arrived followed by police who had picked up the emergency call on their scanners. One hour after the stabbing, Beverly Hills Police Chief Clinton B. Anderson visited the death house to find a mob of people including celebrity columnist James Bacon and Jerry Giesler who was already in firm control of the situation. An autopsy revealed the 8" knife (which had been inserted upside down with the sharp edge facing up) had fatally punctured the abdomen, kidney, and struck the backbone with such force that it curved up into the heart. Death, in any event, would have resulted in five minutes. Interestingly, the autopsy revealed Stompanato suffered from an incurable liver disease that would have certainly claimed his life within ten years. As Cheryl Crane cooled her heels in Juvenile Hall booked on suspicion of murder, the press crackled with stories about the case. Mickey Cohen stepped forward to claim Stompanato's body telling any reporter within earshot that he was not satisfied with the way the case was being handled by authorities and suggesting Turner herself might in some way be responsible for Johnny's death. Cohen's thugs broke into Stompanato's apartment and retrieved a stack of explicit love letters written by Turner to Stompanato at the height of their tempestuous romance. The gangster turned these over to the *Los Angeles Examiner* to prove the star was actually, at one time, deeply in love with the man she called "Daddy" and "Honey-Pot." The Hearst paper ran the embarrassing letters splayed across its pages to the mortification of Lana Turner. Later, a roll of film shot by Stompanato was quietly turned over to Turner's attorneys. The film contained shots of Stompanato having sex with various women and photos of the naked Turner asleep on a bed. The obvious inference was that Stompanato or his gangster friends could one day use the material to blackmail Turner or her studio. Cohen also footed the bill for his friend's funeral and burial with full military honors in Oakdale Cemetery in the hood's hometown of Woodstock, Illinois.

On April 11, 1958, the much anticipated coroner's inquest into the death of John Stompanato was held in the Hall of Records in Los Angeles minus Cheryl Crane. Earlier, the wily Jerry Giesler had successfully argued that the juvenile had suffered enough and had previously given a full statement of the affair to authorities at the time of her arrest. Lana Turner, one of the world's biggest stars, was to be the key witness at the inquest. Mickey Cohen, in attendance to make sure the proceedings were above board, was called as the first witness. Asked if he had been able to identify Stompanato's body, the gangster remarked, "I refuse to identify the body on the grounds I may be accused of this murder." Cohen was dismissed after spending only two minutes on the stand. All eyes were on Turner when she was finally called to testify. For 62 drama-filled minutes the star (often seemingly on the brink of collapse) dramatically described the fatal incident. When finished, many observers called Turner's testimony the greatest performance of her career. Less than twenty minutes after the case went to the ten man, two woman jury they returned with a verdict of "justifiable homicide" in a ten to two vote. Cheryl Crane had protected her mother from a potentially dangerous man. Next day, an editorial in the *Los Angeles Times* essentially called Lana Turner an unfit mother guilty of parading a series of questionable men through her daughter's life. The piece concluded with the damning observation, "In the Turner case Cheryl isn't the juvenile delinquent; Lana is."

Cheryl Crane may well have escaped being tried for murder, but afterwards became the flash point for a series of soul killing custody battles between her mother and father, Stephen Crane. As the Stompanato family announced they were filing a $750,000 "wrongful death" suit against Turner on behalf of the dead man's 10-year-old son, Cheryl Crane appeared in a Juvenile Court in Santa Monica. An earlier case report had been unkind to both Lana Turner and Stephen Crane who were found to be exercising "a lack of proper parental control and supervision" over their daughter. While Cheryl Crane would legally be a ward of the court until 18, the hearing would determine who would gain physical custody of the troubled 14-year-old girl. Unwilling to offend either parent, she asked the judge to allow her to live with her grandmother. Over the next few years, as Turner and her ex-husband periodically sparred over her in court, Cheryl Crane continued to make news by running away from reform schools, consorting with questionable company, taking drugs, or being admitted to the Institute for Living, a psychiatric facility in Hartford, Connecticut. Crane finally "escaped" institutionalization for good in April 1962 after Turner signed her 19-year-old daughter out of the Hartford facility. Turner, who settled the "wrongful death" suit with the Stompanato clan out of court for $20,000, survived the scandal and subsequent bad press to achieve career success in films like *Imitation of Life* (1959) and *Madame X* (1965) that oddly mirrored her turbulent personal life. Cheryl Crane worked for her father for 15 years at his trendy restaurant, the Luau, learning the business from the ground up, even attending the restaurant management school at Cornell University. In *Detour* she describes her committed lesbian relationship of 15 years and has since enjoyed great success in the field of California real estate. Lana Turner, the MGM love goddess destined to be forever known as filmdom's "Sweater Girl," died of throat cancer at the age of 75 on June 29, 1995. Mother and daughter had long since reconciled.

Further Reading

Crane, Cheryl, and Cliff Jahr. *Detour: A Hollywood Story.* New York: Arbor House/William Morrow, 1988.
Jones, Jack. "Jury Clears Cheryl after Lana's Story." *Los Angeles Times,* April 12, 1958, sec. A, pp. 1, 3, 6.
"Lana Love Letters Show She Wooed Johnny." *Los Angeles Examiner,* April 9, 1958, sec. 1, pp. 1, 3.
Turner, Lana. *Lana—The Lady, the Legend, the Truth.* New York: Dutton, 1982.

Crittenden, T. D. (V)

Born in Oakland, California, on September 27, 1878, the character actor appeared in several silent films (*Jewel*, 1915; *Love Never Dies*, 1916; *Polly Put the Kettle On*, 1917; *The Devil's Wheel*, 1918; *The Hottentot*, 1922; *The Fast Worker*, 1924) under the names "T. D." and "Dwight" Crittenden (Crittendon). Long retired from acting, the 60 year old was a deputy city marshall in Los Angeles when he was killed in the line of duty in that city on February 17, 1938. Crittenden and his partner, Leon W. Romer, 60, were serving a $67.50 eviction notice on George Farley, a 57-year-old black laborer, when the man fired a large caliber rifle through the door of the small frame house at 1741 East 23rd Street. The bullet struck Romer full in the chest killing him instantly. A retreating Crittenden was able to gain the street before he was dropped by a bullet in the head. Summoned by neighbors, police surrounded the house and for an hour pumped volleys of bullets and tear gas into the structure. Detectives cautiously entered the home to find Farley slumped on his face in a rear room severely wounded five times in the thighs, arms, and chest. The laborer survived, and was convicted on two counts of manslaughter in June 1938. Farley, unsuccessful in his insanity de-

fense, was ordered to serve two consecutive 5 to 10 year terms in San Quentin.

Further Reading

"Two Officers Die in Battle with Maniac." *Los Angeles Times,* February 18, 1938, pp. 1, 6.

Cunnane, Barry (V)

A native of Ballinteer, Dublin, and a graduate of the University of Wales at Aberystwyth, the fledgling actor appeared in several theatrical productions in Ireland before coming to Chicago to immerse himself in that city's "vibrant theatre culture." Cunnane worked days as an insurance sales specialist with the American Medical Association while performing nights on piano and guitar at a local club, Wise Fool's Pub, and acting with amateur theatre groups. A participant in the actors' workshop at Roosevelt University and a member of the St. Sebastian Players at St. Bonaventure's Church, he had recently acted the role of "Antonio" in Shakespeare's *Twelfth Night*. On May 24, 2003, Cunnane, 27, and a friend were walking around 1:30 A.M. in the 1900 block of West Leland in the relatively crime-free neighborhood of Ravenswood on Chicago's Northwest Side when they passed two men walking in the opposite direction. According to the part-time actor's friend, one of the men said something like "What's up?" as he passed, then quickly turned and shot Cunnane point-blank in the back of the head. The friend (on condition of anonymity) told police, "They weren't trying to engage us in conversation... And as soon as it happened they disappeared. It wasn't a robbery. It was, 'I'm going to kill, to kill somebody for no reason.'" Cunnane was pronounced dead at 3:45 A.M. at the Advocate Illinois Masonic Medical Center. Police characterized the motiveless random-killing as possibly related to a gang initiation rite. Michael Moore, director of the 2002 anti-gun documentary, *Bowling for Columbine*, sent a wreath to Cunnane's funeral. As of March 2005, no person has been charged with the murder despite a $15,000 reward offered by the Chicago-based "Justice for Barry" campaign.

Further Reading

"Police Have No Clues in Aspiring Actor's Shooting Death." Associated Press, May 26, 2003.

Cupit, Jennifer (M)

In the 184-year history of the Centenary Operatic and Dramatic Society of Warrington,

Cheshire, the amateur acting group never put on a production more packed with the elements of lust, betrayal, and violence than the true-life drama involving the murder of Kathryn Linaker by Jennifer Cupit. Linaker, the mother of two young children and her husband, Chris, a 34-year-old computer training consultant, were active members of the dramatic society where Kathy had scored leading roles in several musicals including *Gigi*. Through their involvement in the theatrical group, the couple met the Cupits, Jennifer and Nick, in 1996 and became close friends. Unlike her talented leading man husband, Jennifer, a former hairdresser, was a perennial member of the chorus unable to land any of the company's starring roles. Craving attention, the 24-year-old wannabe actress with a dream of stardom, faked fainting spells during rehearsals and was recognized by other cast members as an outrageous flirt. By 1997, the Cupit marriage had all but ended helped along by Jennifer's bulimia, depression, and self-inflicted razor mutilations. Unknown to their respective spouses, Chris Linaker and Jennifer Cupit began a torrid affair in January 1997 shortly after returning to Warrington from a trip to London with society members. During the next 16 months, the lovers had sex in a variety of places including each other's homes, the Delamere Forest, and car parks. At the suggestion of Chris Linaker who learned from Jennifer that it was one of her "fantasies," the pair spiced up the sex by first videotaping themselves, then staging "three-ways." Remarkably, Nick Cupit, unaware his wife actually enjoyed an ongoing adulterous relationship with friend Chris, was an enthusiastic participant, as was Linaker's brother-in-law. For Chris, the clandestine meetings were purely about sex, but for Jennifer the relationship offered at the least a way out of a loveless marriage. In early 1998, the frustrated actress began pressuring Linaker to leave Kathy and run away with her to Canada where they could start a new life together. In April 1998, Chris finally told his lover he was not leaving his wife, or their two children, Matthew, 2, and four-month-old Holly. To add insult to injury, he informed the stunned woman that Kathy was in the early stages of pregnancy.

On April 17, 1998, one day after she and Chris had sex in a public car park, Jennifer Cupit purchased a heavy glass bottle and a 4" kitchen knife with a serrated edge in a local grocery store. She carried her purchases in a handbag to Kathy Linaker's home in Penketh, Warrington, where

the 33-year-old deputy head of St. James's Church of England Primary School at Haydock, Merseyside, was alone with her infant daughter, Heather. The jealous woman slugged Linaker eight times in the head with the decorative glass bottle and, as the wife of her lover stumbled into the living room, stabbed her in the back with the kitchen knife, snapping the blade off in Kathy's spine. Cupit left the dying woman on the floor, fetched a carving knife from the kitchen, and finished the slaughter by repeatedly stabbing the woman in the stomach all in sight of her rival's daughter. She waited two hours before notifying authorities and when emergency personnel arrived to find a gruesome scene straight out of a grade-B horror film, Cupit was cradling the blood-smeared Heather in her arms. At the scene, the failed actress initially told detectives she was in the kitchen drinking coffee with her friend when a male skinhead intruder broke in and attacked Kathryn while she, Cupit, bravely protected the baby. The woman briefly fainted when leaving the house for the hospital, but "miraculously" revived when a dubious ambulance driver told her to open her eyes. When formally arrested by police (who instantly discounted her tale of the knife-wielding skinhead), Cupit changed her story to one of self-defense. In the revised version, Kathy Linaker attacked Cupit with a carving knife after she informed the school teacher of the affair. Cupit was forced to defend herself with the knife she had presciently purchased hours before the deadly confrontation.

At trial in January 1999, Cupit denied murdering Linaker instead pleading manslaughter due to diminished responsibility. The British tabloid press had a field day reporting on the "chorus line killer" with every new day filled with fresh revelations of Cupit's history of eating sawdust, self-mutilation, gobbling Prozac, and three-way sex. Insisting she was never jealous of Kathryn Linaker, Cupit stuck with her claim of self-defense until it was largely discredited by a friend who testified that less than a week before the murder, the bit actress had confessed to her that she "hated Kathy" because she "had a perfect family" while own husband Nick "never paid her any attention." A seven-woman, five-man jury quickly found Cupit guilty and a judge sentenced her to life imprisonment. Weeks after the sentence, the British tabloid *Daily Mirror* printed an explosive story detailing how the "sex-crazed killer" had continued to fantasize about "kinky sex" during the pre-trial period she was held in a bail hostel. According to a male inmate of the facility who handed over his sexually explicit correspondence with Cupit to the tabloid, the woman orally serviced him and, without his knowledge, two other men in a secluded area of the center. Her betrayed lover concluded, "She is a lying, cruel killer who cannot be trusted."

Further Reading

Byrne, Paul. "I Close My Eyes and See Kathy Lying There Dying. All I Can Hear." *Daily Mirror*, February 27, 1999.
Carter, Helen. "Accused Lover, 'Hated Victim's Perfect Family.'" *The Guardian* (London), January 30, 1999, p. 7.

Da Prato, Emilia (V)

"I have killed my sweetheart," Umberto Giusti, 37, told San Francisco police moments after he surrendered to them following the fatal shooting of Emilia Da Prato, his 26-year-old girlfriend, on December 19, 1933. Da Prato, a promising opera singer, was one of two winners in the Western district of the Atwater Kent national radio audition contest in 1927. She later placed second in the New York City portion of the contest. According to Giusti, an employee of a dry cleaning establishment, he fell in love with Da Prato two years earlier and acted as her booking and press agent. Giusti financed her career and was buying his lover a car when he learned that Da Prato was seeing another man, and planned to leave the Bay area for an audition with the Metropolitan Opera Company in New York City. On the day of the killing, Giusti called at the Da Prato family home in South San Francisco and angrily confronted the woman, shooting her three times in the back. He turned the gun on himself, but the weapon jammed and he walked away in a daze. Shortly afterwards, Giusti gave himself up at a local police station. Neighbors and relatives of the dead woman shouting "Lynch him" attempted to mob the self-confessed killer at the South San Francisco jail prompting authorities to hastily transport Giusti to the county jail at nearby Redwood City. At trial in February 1934, the jealous dry cleaner turned opera impresario pleaded "not guilty by reason of insanity," but a jury needed less than two hours to convict him of first-degree murder with a recommendation of leniency that carried an automatic life sentence.

Further Reading

"Radio Singer Slain by Jealous Suitor." *The New York Times*, December 20, 1933, p. 44.

Davidson, Quentin ("Footz") (V)

Nicknamed Footz in recognition of his energetic drum playing, Davidson was one of the founders of the pioneer Washington, D.C., go-go band Rare Essence. Formed in the mid-to-late 1970s, Rare Essence (named after the transposed name of a perfume) was the District's premier exponent of go-go, a frenetic highly percussive form of driving music wildly popular among the area's teens and young adults. Though gaining national attention in recent years with albums like *Work the Walls* (1992), the band remained loyal to local nightclubs like Deno's where they had played every Friday night for nine years. In what, perhaps, became a presentiment of darker things to come, Davidson, 33, was abducted by three men from his home in Clinton on June 29, 1994. Forced at gunpoint into the backseat of his car, the handcuffed and blindfolded drummer was driven around by the men who threatened to kill him if he did not hand over the band's receipts from a previous concert. Davidson was released unharmed after convincing the kidnappers that he did not have the money. On Sunday, September 18, 1994, Davidson's mother reported her son missing after he uncharacteristically missed a Saturday night show. She was unaware that police had already found an unidentified body that night (September 17) dumped a few feet from the Exit 6 ramp off Route 50 to Corporate Drive in Landover, Maryland, in Prince George's County. The man, later identified as Davidson, was shot at least once in the upper body and left for dead. The case was never solved although police felt that it may have been linked to the earlier kidnapping attempt. The drummer's 16-year-old son, Quentin Maurice Davidson, Jr., was murdered in Prince George's County on April 5, 1999.

Further Reading

Jeter, Jon. "Go-Go Music Pioneer Footz Davidson Is Found Shot to Death on P.G. Road." *Washington Post*, September 20, 1994, sec. B, p. 4.

Davis, Eric DeSean (V)

Nicknamed Magic, Davis worked several odd jobs after graduating high school in Killeen, Texas, before deciding to rap full-time. His debut CD, *Playa's Dynasty*, was scheduled to be released in June 2002. On the evening of April 1, 2002, the 20-year-old rapper was standing on the street outside his apartment in Killeen when he was approached by a vehicle containing three intoxicated service personnel from the nearby Fort Hood Army base. Their brief interaction ended when one of the men fired a single 9mm gunshot that passed through Davis' arm fatally lodging in his chest. Davis, a father of three, had married only six days earlier. Hours after the murder, a service couple living on the Fort Hood base answered a late-night knock at their door. Seconds later, a gunman fired into the home's doorway wounding a 39-year-old woman. The case broke after detectives linked the shootings to the earlier rape of an 18-year-old member of the 21st Replacement Company at Fort Hood on January 9, 2002. The woman was violated in her barracks at knifepoint by an unknown assailant who videotaped the assault. On February 4, 2002, the victim and her mother appeared (anonymously) on Houston television station KPRC and criticized the Army's handling of the case. They maintained the military had failed to compare the DNA evidence collected in the rape investigation with the Army's DNA repository of samples taken from all soldiers. An Army spokesman countered declaring that such a comparison was both impossible and constitutionally illegal. While a repository of military DNA exists in the event that a soldier dies in combat and cannot be otherwise identified, there is no searchable, computerized database of analyzed DNA. Under the Army's system, a suspect's name would be needed prior to searching the collected DNA of Fort Hood's 43,000 soldiers.

One day after the murder of Davis, Spc. Christopher M. Reyes, 21, was arrested in his barracks and charged with murder (Davis), two counts of attempted murder (the Fort Hood couple), and burglary, rape and sodomy (the 18-year-old soldier). Also arrested were Reyes' companions in the vehicle on the night of the Davis killing, fellow-members of the 1st Cavalry Division Pvt. Gregory Payton and Spc. Vance Rogers. Both men unhesitatingly fingered Reyes as the shooter. As local authorities ceded jurisdiction of the case to the military, all three men faced court-martial on charges of premeditated murder and conspiracy to purchase drugs in the Davis death. With Reyes, the two soldiers also faced attempted murder charges for allegedly trying to kill the Fort Hood soldier and his wife. In January 2003, Reyes, the gunman, was convicted of all charges (murder, attempted murder, rape) at a court-martial hearing and sentenced to life in prison at Fort Leavenworth, Kansas without the possibility of parole.

Further Reading

Osborn, Claire. "Man Killed in Killeen was Newlywed with First CD." *Austin American-Statesman*, April 9, 2002, sec. B, p. 2.
www.armytimes.com.

Davis, Myra (V)

In a bizarre twist of fate, Davis, one of the stand-ins for star Janet Leigh in the infamous shower murder scene in Hitchcock's classic 1960 film *Psycho*, was also the victim of violent death. Born in Albuquerque, New Mexico, in 1917, Davis studied dance before migrating to Los Angeles in the 1930s to look for studio work. As "Myra Jones," her maiden and professional name, Davis appeared as a dancer in MGM's 1935 musical *Folies Bergère*. In 1947, she was a telephone operator in *The Perils of Pauline*, and in 1956 appeared in a cameo role in the star-studded epic *Around the World in 80 Days*. It was, however, as Janet Leigh's stand-in and double in *Bye Bye Birdie* (1963), and most notably, *Psycho*, that she became a tragic footnote in film history. In Hitchcock's Davis' masterpiece, Davis is not seen nude in the shower, those shots are either of Leigh wearing strategically placed flesh-colored moleskin patches, or, model Marli Renfro. It is Davis' hand holding the plunging knife, and at the film's climax she appears as psycho "Norman Bates'" mother seated in the rocking chair in the fruit cellar. Some film historians also credit Davis as the voice of "Norman Bates'" mother. In one of her final film "appearances," Davis's scream is heard at the opening of the 1977 Diane Keaton movie *Looking for Mr. Goodbar*.

On July 3, 1988, the decomposing body of the 71-year-old was found by her granddaughter in the bedroom of the former actress' Cheviot Hills home in the 2900 block of South Beverly Drive in West Los Angeles. The position of the body on the bed (face-up, legs bent with feet on the floor) and her disarranged clothes suggested rape (later confirmed). Death was caused by strangulation, Davis' nylon panties twisted to the point of suffocation by a pot scrubber handle still in grisly evidence around her neck. There was no sign of a break-in although the dresser drawers had been ransacked. Semen recovered by the rape kit was preserved and stored. During the two year period immediately following the murder of Myra Davis, six rapes occurred in the Cheviot Hills area as well as a spate of bizarre sexual attacks in which the perpetrator fondled women on sidewalks in broad daylight. It would take ten years and another rape-murder before police would close the Davis case.

On March 29, 1998, the naked body of 60-year-old Jean Orloff was found face-down on the bed in her home on Bentley Avenue two miles away from the site of the Davis murder. Although blood was visible around Orloff's head, a coroner's investigator initially ruled the death due to natural causes, perhaps a heart attack. However, after the mortuary encountered administrative problems with the death certificate, another coroner's investigator was summoned to examine the body. This official instantly recognized the telltale deep purple furrow around Orloff's neck and ruled the death a homicide by strangulation. Like Davis, Orloff had been sexually assaulted. Understandably, the dead woman's family was unimpressed by the "professionalism" of the Los Angeles County coroner's office. Orloff's sister told the press, "I know people make mistakes. But this wasn't a mistake. This was gross negligence." In the subsequent investigation, detectives discovered a link between the Davis and Orloff rape-strangulation murders: Kenneth Dean "Sonny" Hunt. The 31-year-old handyman had not only lived next door to Davis at the time of her murder, he had also done repair work in Orloff's home. The son of an abusive alcoholic father, Hunt was a product of the California Youth Authority where he spent most of his adolescence doing time on a laundry list of offenses including assaults to commit rape, burglary, and grand theft. On March 6, 1992, Hunt was viciously beating his dog in Cheviot Hills when Bernard Davis, 67, attempted to intervene. Hunt struck the elderly man who remained in a coma until dying three weeks later. The career criminal was sentenced to six years in state prison on a negotiated plea of voluntary manslaughter in July 1992, and paroled in November 1995. After beating up his girlfriend in 1996, Hunt was bounced back to prison on a parole violation, earning release on July 12, 1997. In April 1998, detectives anxious to question Hunt in the murders of Davis and Orloff picked him up on yet another parole violation. He was charged with both murders (and forcible rape) after his blood genetically matched semen samples recovered from the bodies of the victims.

Convicted in March 2001 on dual counts of first-degree murder and forcible rape, Hunt faced either the death penalty (under the special circumstances of multiple murder, rape, burglary) or, life in prison without the possibility of parole

to be determined by a jury during the trial's subsequent penalty phase. After deliberating two days, the jurors announced they were hopelessly deadlocked at a vote of 11–1 in favor of the death penalty. Under the law, a mistrial was declared and the option given to the prosecution to either retry the penalty phase of the trial with a different jury, or, allow the default sentence of life imprisonment without the possibility of parole to be automatically imposed. A retrial in July 2001 ended in the same result — a deadlock, but this time with a 10–2 vote in favor of execution. Shortly afterwards, the district attorney's office decided not to retry the case, issuing the statement, "The chances are getting less and less that you'll get a different decision. The more you retry a case, you get diminishing returns." Hunt was automatically sentenced to life without parole. The convicted killer's sentence was upheld by a California state appellate court on February 24, 2004.

Further Reading

Lasseter, Don. *Body Double.* New York: Pinnacle, 2002.

Del Fierro Lugo, Roberto Ignacio *see* Appendix 1

Del Mar, Claire (V)

On January 10, 1959, the mutilated body of 57-year-old Clara Eloise Mohr was found in the home she shared with her aged bed-ridden mother in Carmel, California. According to the investigating sheriff, the woman was struck over the head outside the house then carried into the bedroom where she was sexually assaulted and butchered with a steak knife. Scrapbooks and photographs on the wall identified Mohr as one-time silent screen actress Claire Del Mar who had appeared uncredited in the films *The Four Horsemen of the Apocalypse* (1921, dancing with star Rudolph Valentino), *The Jazz Singer* (1927), *The Grain of Dust* (1928), and *The Wedding March* (1928). A marriage to Hollywood cameraman Hal Mohr in 1926 (with Erich von Stroheim as best man) ended in divorce in 1929. To date, the case remains open.

Further Reading

"Sadist Hunted in Killing of Film Actress of 20s." *Los Angeles Times,* January 12, 1959, p. 7.

Diehl, Mary Louise (V)

A lyric soprano, Diehl (real name Marilouise Paoli) made her New York debut in Lincoln Center's

Tully Hall on April 5, 1975, performing a recital of arias by Handel and Mozart, and the world premieres of Paul R. Goldstaub's three *Tempest* songs after Shakespeare and two songs by Vincent P. Zito to poems by Mirko Tuma. While a *New York Times* review of April 7, 1975 by Peter G. Davis described the program as "ambitious and interestingly planned," he generally dismissed Diehl's voice as lacking "coloristic variety" with a tendency "to thin out at the top." While she was a "thoughtful interpreter" of the composer's intentions, her sense of pitch was "not always absolute." A divorced mother of three children who resided with their father in New Jersey, the 45-year-old soprano was sharing a third-floor apartment at 317 West 108th Street in New York City with actor-singer Michael McFarlane when she was found dead there on August 22, 1980. Shortly before 7:00 P.M. that day, McFarlane went to the upper West Side apartment and noticed the door was ajar. Fearing a burglary in progress, he locked the door, left the area, and flagged down a police car in the street. Investigating officers noticed no signs of forced entry on the door and the immediate interior of the apartment had not been ransacked. However, the alcove adjoining the bathroom was covered in blood. In the bloodsmeared bathroom, police discovered Diehl's fully-clothed body in a partially filled bathtub. The victim bore defensive stab wounds on her hands with death apparently resulting from a blow to the head. Diehl had been dead for several hours. To date, the killing remains unsolved.

Further Reading

Horsley, Carter B. "No Suspects Found in Slaying of Singer, Police Say." *The New York Times*, August 24, 1980, p. 40.

Dimebag Darrell *see* **Abbott**, Darrell ("Dimebag")

Dismukes, George (M)

Given up for adoption in Brownsville, Texas, at age five by his Mexican mother, Dismukes was a teenager when he left his adoptive parents and crossed the border to search for his birth parent. He worked on a bull-raising ranch outside of Monterrey and by 14 was bullfighting under the name "Jorge Meija." A conversation with a film producer at a party in Madrid in 1962 opened the "show business door" to the eighteen year old. Told by one of the producers of *Hatari!*, a 1962 John Wayne vehicle shot on location in Africa, that the crew was having trouble handling a rhino in the film, Dismukes offered to help. In Africa, he redrafted the scenes featuring the rhino and consulted on the animal's filming. This, according to newspaper reports, led to an eight film association with John Wayne and Dismukes' involvement in the long-running television series, *Gunsmoke*. If the former matador was involved in any of the Duke's movies, he was not credited.

Dismukes, variously described as a handyman, writer, producer and director of public service films for local public television, was living in the heavily wooded Country Village Estates subdivision southeast of Conroe, Texas, in the early 1990s. Reacting to the escalating problems of deer poaching, illegal trash dumping, and trespassing in the area, the neighborhood association developed a Crime Watch with residents taking turns patrolling the subdivision. By all accounts, Dismukes, 49, a co-founder of the program, took the job of enforcing neighborhood security very, very seriously. Known for his heavy-handed confrontations with motorists who drove through Country Village Estates, Dismukes routinely stopped and questioned anyone he did not recognize. Neighbors, however, were already aware that the writer-producer was tightly wound. In January 1990, he punctuated a dispute with the Country Village Homeowners' Association with a terse letter to the group, warning—"I can be a good and caring neighbor or I can be a formidable enemy, the choice is up to you at this point. Push me, and I will take that choice away." Dismukes told other neighbors that he had mined his property (set back away from the road behind a locked gate) to discourage trespassers and thieves.

Around 4:45 P.M. on December 24, 1991, Dismukes spotted Richard Orville Tyson, a 43-year-old oil company storage employee and married father of two teenagers, driving his blue pickup in the Country Village Estates. Tyson, who lived about a mile away, was possibly in the area to look at lots. According to the police reconstruction of the crime, Dismukes was on patrol and, failing to recognize Tyson as a resident, trailed the man's truck into a cul-de-sac. Dismukes confronted Tyson, an argument ensued, and witnesses reported hearing a single gunshot. Tyson's body was later found face-down in a pool of blood near his still running truck, dead from a single point-blank .38-caliber bullet wound to the forehead. Dismukes, who claimed not to own a gun, was arrested less than a week later after police found a pistol cleaning kit in his home, and recovered .38-caliber ammo from his ex-wife's Houston residence where he occasionally stayed. Although Dismukes passed a lie detector test, traces of Tyson's blood were found on the driver's door handle of the writer's pickup.

At trial in Montgomery County in October 1993, the murder case against Dismukes was largely circumstantial. After eight days of testimony in which the Crime Watch volunteer was portrayed as an overbearing vigilante, Dismukes testified that he had paid little attention to Tyson's pickup while making his rounds. "With God as my witness," he told jurors, he did not shoot Tyson. On November 5, 1993, Dismukes collapsed in the courtroom and had to be rushed to a hospital after he was found guilty of second-degree murder and sentenced to 16 years in prison. Still loudly protesting his innocence, Dismukes reportedly has been a model prisoner whom psychiatrists assess as posing virtually no threat to society. Despite co-writing the parole manual for the Texas Inmate Families Association, Dismukes has been denied parole three times as of May 2001. Some feel his chances for early release have been hurt by his outspokenness in the press. In a May 2, 1994 *Newsweek* article, "What It's Like to Live in Prison," Dismukes roundly criticized the minimum security county holding unit where he was housed, and cautioned: "I say to you, the smug and contented: watch out. As one return for your indifference, our numbers are enlarging, our costs are rising swiftly. Building bigger and better or, alternatively, more degrading prisons does not begin to start resolving the reasons behind the problems and madness. It only makes the gibbering louder and the eventual consequences more awful for everyone when they finally occur. I find this situation to be humorous when I don't marvel."

Further Reading

McKay, Paul. "Self-Appointed "Vigilante" a Suspect in Bizarre Slaying." *Houston Chronicle*, January 6, 1992, p. 9.

Dolla (V)

The rapper Dolla, born Roderick Anthony Burton II in Chicago in 1988, endured a nightmarish childhood that included a twin sister who died at birth, and a father who committed suicide in front of him when he was five years old. Following his father's death, the family moved to Atlanta where the 12-year-old Dolla formed Da Razkalz Cru with two cousins. The trio signed with Elektra Records in 2000, but was dropped three years later after their single, "So Fly," tanked. The disappointing experience did afford Dolla a valuable opportunity to work with Akon, a rising hip-hop star and producer who would figure prominently in the young MC's future. The Elektra exposure also brought Dolla to the attention of the multi-faceted Sean "Diddy" Combs. Diddy featured the rapper as a model for his Sean Jean clothing line in a huge billboard above the Hyatt Hotel in Los Angeles. Returning to music as a solo performer, Dolla's song, "Feelin' Myself," appeared on the soundtrack of the 2006 movie, *Step Up*. Akon signed Dolla to his label, Konvict Muzik, and in early 2007 the single, "Who the Fuck Is That," was released.

The 21-year-old rapper's future looked bright as he arrived in Los Angeles on May 18, 2009 to put the finishing touches on his debut album, *Another Day, Another Dolla*. He would die that same day, a victim of a tragic coincidental meeting that had its roots in a bar brawl nearly two weeks earlier in another state. On May 6, 2009, Dolla and Aubrey Louis Berry, a 23-year-old events promoter, were involved in an altercation at the Platinum 21 Adult Entertainment strip club in Atlanta. The fight spilled out into the parking lot where both men threatened each other and shouted out their gang affiliations. As fate would have it, 12 days later Dolla was in the restroom of P.F. Chang's China Bistro in the Beverly Center Mall in West Hollywood when he ran into Berry. According to the events promoter, Dolla threatened him and, with two others, followed him out of the eatery to the mall's valet area where his rented Mercedes-Benz SUV was parked. Dolla and his "crew" continued shouting abuse at Berry who believed that the rapper was reaching to his waistband to pull a weapon. The concert promoter pulled his own 9mm semiautomatic and shot the 21-year-old rising hip-hop star in the head in a hail of gunfire. Dolla was pronounced dead at nearby Cedars-Sinai Medical Center. As mall shoppers and Dolla's friend and fellow-rapper, D.J. Shabbazz, dove for safety, Berry sped off, but not before his vehicle's license plate was recorded. Police arrested the promoter without incident three hours later at 6:15 P.M., the 9mm tucked in his waistband, in the waiting area of Terminal 1 at Los Angeles International Airport. Hundreds of mourners dressed in white clothing with white scarves draped around their heads honored Dolla at a funeral service at the World Faith Love Center in East Point, Georgia. Following the ceremony, the up and coming rapper was buried in Atlanta's Westview Cemetery. Berry, charged with two counts of assault and Dolla's murder, pleaded not guilty and insisted the shooting was in self-defense. At the time of this book's publication the case had not come to trial.

Further Reading

Fausset, Richard. "Rapper May Have Had Dispute with Man Suspected in His Death." *Los Angeles Times*, May 20, 2009, pt. A, p. 3.
Jeffries, David. "Dolla." www.allmusic.com.

Door, William H. (V)

"Man, Nude Woman Found Murdered" ran the titillating page two headline in the November 20, 1963 issue of the *Los Angeles Times*. Five days earlier the fully clothed body of William Door, 46, the owner of Fax Records, a company producing "risqué recordings," and an individual well-known to police as a porn distributor, was discovered face-down with his feet bound on the dining room floor of his home at 7671 Fountain Avenue. Door had been shot once in the back of the head and once in the hand, a telltale sign of a defensive wound inflicted as the pornographer struggled with his killer. In a bedroom, the nude body of his lover and roommate for the past year, 30-year-old Ernestine Ellen Criss, was found face-up, her head covered by a pillow, splayed across a king-sized bed. Criss was shot once in the mouth, but spared the brutal beating inflicted on Door prior to his execution. Large sums of money were found on the pornographer and his new Thunderbird was still parked outside the bungalow, obviously ruling out robbery as a motive for the double slaying. Police theorized that Door and his lover were possibly the victims of a grudge killing meted out by associates in the skin trade due to what the *Los Angeles Times* article naively suggested as retribution for his "rough handling of female models" in the films he produced. More likely, Door owed some bad people big money. In a career dotted with arrests for obscenity, possession of lewd literature, and income tax evasion, Door was also listed as the owner of the Crescendo nightclub on L.A.'s famed Sunset Strip.

As authorities continued their investigation, more lurid details about the pornographer and his lover emerged in the headlines of the *Los Angeles Times*. On November 2, 1963, the article "Slain Man's Love Lair Discovered," though relegated to page 34, still offered up readers some juicy details of Door's lifestyle. Describing his secluded hideaway in the Santa Monica Mountains at Malibu Lake as containing "wall-to-wall beds," homicide detectives reported that the walls of the love nest were covered with photos of nude women, and that the "smut merchant" often let his friends use the place for wild parties. Shortly after the double murder, two teenagers broke into the two-bedroom dwelling in what police described as their misguided attempt to help them crack the case. Both teens were briefly questioned and released. In his will, Door left Fax Records to his secretary and, ironically, $1,000 to Ernestine Ellen Criss, his murdered lover. The remainder of the estate was put in trust for his six-year-old son. The killings, undoubtedly related to Door's porn rackets, to date remain unsolved. (See Paul E. Rothenberg entry.)

Further Reading

"Man, Nude Woman Found Murdered." *Los Angeles Times*, November 20, 1963, p. 2.

Dorsey, Leslie (V)

The son of a Barbadian social worker, Dorsey was born in the South Bronx in 1944. Educated at the High School of Music and Art in Manhattan, Dorsey became a professional musician over the objections of his mother who insisted that he would never be able to earn a living as a musical artist. In 1976, the basso performed the role of "Lawyer Frazier" in a European tour of the musical *Porgy and Bess*. Three years later the multi-talented singer toured for a year with folksinger Judy Collins, later working with Roberta Flack and the Gregg Smith Singers. Though never able to fully support himself as a performer, Dorsey continued to sing and play clarinet in several genres of music including opera, pop, jazz, and rhythm and blues. When not serving as the associate chorister with the New York City Opera the divorced 44 year old drove a gypsy cab at night to support his three children. On Labor Day 1988, Dorsey was shot point-blank in the back of the head by one of the three black youths he had picked up as a fare in New York City. The robbers stole his money and personal papers, postponing for a week the identification of his body by family members. Friends of the slain musician established a scholarship in his name at the Mannes College of Music in Manhattan. To date, no one has been convicted of Dorsey's murder.

Further Reading

Lyall, Sarah. "Requieum for a Victim: A Singing Cabby." *The New York Times*, September 19, 1988, sec. B, p. 1.

Duarte, Pablo (M–S)

The dance team of "Ricardo and Georgiana" (Duarte, 41, and his 28-year-old wife), performed in minor New York City nightspots, but were planning to return to their native Cuba when a deadly argument erupted in their one room ground floor apartment at 44 West 65th Street on July 16, 1949. Later that day, Georgiana's brother arrived to help the couple pack and smelling gas, notified the building's super and several neighbors. Breaking into the gas-filled apartment, the group found a classic scene of murder-suicide. Duarte, near death from the fumes, had fatally butchered his wife with an 8" carving knife. Removed to Roosevelt Hospital, the dancer died of asphyxiation three hours later.

Further Reading

"Dance Team Found with Fatal Stabs." *The New York Times*, July 17, 1949, p. 41.

Dube, Lucky (V)

Dube (pronounced "Doo-Bay") was at the height of his international fame as South Africa's first and foremost reggae performer when was shot to death in a botched carjacking in 2007. Born August 3, 1964, into a Zulu family in Ermelo, Eastern Transvaal, South Africa, a town 90 miles west of Johannesburg, the sickly infant was named "Lucky" by parents surprised that he survived. As a nine-year-old growing up in Johannesburg, Dube's love of reading earned him a job as an assistant in his grade school's library and it was there that he first read in an encyclopedia about Rastafarianism and its association with reggae. Dube, who began singing in church and school choirs the year before, used the money he earned to purchase albums by Peter Tosh (see entry), the only reggae artist whose music was then available in South Africa. Upon completion of high school, he moved to Durban then enrolled at the University of KwaZulu-Natal where he completed a bachelor of science degree. Dube enrolled in Wits University in Johannesburg to begin a medical degree, but dropped out in 1982 at the age of 18 to join the band, The Love Brothers. Founded by his cousin, record producer Richard Siluma, the quintet played *mbaqanga*, or "Zulu pop," a musical fusion of soul and pop merged with tradi-

tional Zulu music first introduced to America by Paul Simon in his landmark album, *Graceland*. Siluma, the group's manager and arranger, worked in Johannesburg for Teal Records which ultimately became a part of Gallo, the largest recording company in South Africa. Promoted by Siluma as Lucky Dube and the Supersoul, the group released five *mbaqanga* albums on the Gallo label over the next few years.

Lucky Dube, however, had become increasingly attracted to the Rastafarian lifestyle, despite refusing to smoke marijuana or drink alcohol, and saw in reggae a powerful, universal, and commercial vehicle by which to address important social issues like apartheid confronting blacks in his own country. Without the knowledge of the Gallo Record Company, Dube and his band went into the studio in 1985 and recorded *Rastas Never Die*, a four-song EP which marked the first attempt to introduce reggae into South Africa. Heavily influenced by reggae great Peter Tosh, Dube played all the instruments on the album which sold a disastrous 4,000 units at a time when *mbaqanga* records were selling on average 30,000. Gallo's anger with Dube over the shift in his musical direction was exacerbated by the banning of the album as subversive by government radio broadcaster SABC. Undeterred, Dube introduced reggae into his live shows and slowly began winning over his base audience to his new sound and message. The singer-songwriter's second reggae album, *Think About the Children* (1986), was a minor hit, but it was not until the 1987 release of *Slave* that Lucky Dube and his renamed backup band, The Slaves, experienced a breakthrough. The album sold more than 500,000 units worldwide aided by its release in France on the Celluloid label and a distribution deal with New Jersey-based Shanachie Records. In Johannesburg, crowds at concerts of Lucky Dube and the Slaves swelled to over 50,000. Released in 1988, *Together as One* openly called for all South Africans, black and white, to unite. Though the Pretoria government banned the album in 1989 due to its use of the word "apartheid," state run radio bowed to unprecedented popular demand and played the record's title track. Now a commonplace, Dube became the first black artist to be played on white radio. Building on the success of his albums, Dube routinely played to crowds topping 65,000 and became internationally recognized as a new and powerful voice in reggae. Buoyed by his popularity as a singer, Dube appeared opposite John

Savage in the 1989 motion picture *Voice in the Dark*. *Prisoner*, released in 1989, achieved double platinum status in five days, and in 1991 Dube became the first South African ever to perform at the prestigious Sunsplash Festival in Jamaica. An electrifying performer, Dube wowed the discerning reggae crowd and earned the further distinction of becoming the first and only artist ever to be recalled to the stage for a 25 minute encore. Recognized as the preeminent non–Jamaican performer of reggae, Lucky Dube and the Slaves shared world-wide stages with other international artists concerned with social justice like Peter Gabriel, Sinead O'Connor, Sting, and Midnight Oil.

On the evening of October 18, 2007, moments after dropping off his 16-year-old son and 15-year-old daughter at the gate of his brother's home in Rosettenville, a suburb south of Johannesburg, three carjackers shot the 43-year-old singer at close range as he sat in his Chrysler. Mortally wounded, Dube was able to drive off, but the car hit a parked vehicle, jumped a curb, and smashed into a tree. The carjackers fled the scene in a blue Volkswagen Polo leaving Dube dead at the scene behind the wheel of his car. The popular singer-songwriter who had recorded some 21 albums and had received over twenty local and international awards was survived by a wife and seven children. The killing of arguably the country's most heralded star refueled public outrage and debate over the South African government's inability to curb violence at a time when the country was logging an astounding fifty murders a day. As many South Africans called for the reinstatement of the death penalty, a crack squad of detectives was assigned to quickly resolve the highly visible case. Three days after the shooting, police arrested five suspects (two were later released) and recovered two handguns and the car believed to have been used in the crime. Herded into a magistrate's court in Johannesburg jammed with hostile members of Dube's family and fans, three men (Sifiso Mlanga, 32, Julius Gxowa, 30, from Mozambique, and Mbofi Mabe) were charged with murder and held without bail awaiting trial. Meanwhile as condolences and testimonials from artists around the world were printed in the international press, Dube was buried on his Ingogo farm near Newcastle in a ceremony attended by thousands who had been touched by his music and personal generosity. At trial (delayed by a seemingly endless series of postponements), all three men were found guilty of Dube's murder on March 31, 2008, and subsequently sentenced to life imprisonment.

Further Reading

Katz, David. "Obituary: Lucky Dube: South African Reggae Star Famed for his Energetic Stage Shows and Lyrics of Daily Life." *The Guardian* (London), October 22, 2007, p. 32.
www.luckydubemusic.com.

Dunne, Dominique (V)

Dominque Ellen Dunne (born November 20, 1959, in Santa Monica, California) possessed a family pedigree that suggested she could become a first-rate theatre, television, and motion picture actress. The daughter of novelist and film producer Dominick Dunne (*The Boys in the Band*, 1970; *The Panic in Needle Park*, 1971), Dominque's older brother, Griffin Dunne, had already appeared in the 1981 horror spoof *An American Werewolf in London*. She was also the niece of author-screenwriter John Gregory Dunne and his wife writer Joan Didion. Dunne studied acting at Milton Katselas' Los Angeles Workshop and appeared in stage productions of *Mousetrap*, *West Side Story*, *A Man for All Seasons*, *A Black Comedy*, *My Three Angels*, and *The Centi*. On television, the dark-haired actress appeared on episodes of *Lou Grant* (1980), *Hart to Hart* (1981), *Fame* (1982), *St. Elsewhere* (1982), and *Hill Street Blues* (1982). A veteran of four made-for-television movies (*Diary of a Hitchhiker*, 1979; *Valentine Magic on Love Island*, 1980; *The Day the Loving Stopped*, 1981; *Louis L'Amour's "The Shadow Riders,"* 1982), Dunne had just made her promising big screen debut in the 1982 ghost story, *Poltergeist*, produced by Steven Spielberg and directed by Tobe Hooper. Cast in the role of eldest daughter to actors JoBeth Williams and Craig T. Nelson, her most memorable line in the film occurred when she screamed, "What's happening?" At the time of her death, Dunne was in discussions to appear in the ambitious television mini-series *V*.

As Dunne's professional career took off, she attempted to put her troubled personal life in order. Roughly a year before the attack on October 30, 1982, that led to her death, the actress met John Sweeney, 26, a night chef for six years at the exclusive Ma Maison restaurant. Sweeney, the abused son of an alcoholic father, worked his way through culinary courses at Luzern Community College, and impressed Ma Maison owner Patrick Terrail enough to foot the bill for his training in

Paris for two years under master chef Louis Out-heir. The pair fell in love and set up housekeeping in an apartment in Beverly Hills. Dunne, 22, by all accounts, chafed under her lover's possessive behavior and their relationship was already in serious trouble when it flared into violence on September 26, 1982. The couple spent the early evening dining and drinking with friends Bryan Cook and his date, at Ma Maison before continuing the party at the apartment shared by Dunne and Sweeney. The couple went into their bedroom and moments later Cook reported hearing the pair argue loudly, then a "thud (and) bang," followed by silence and the sound of someone gasping for air. The actress shouted, "Bryan, please help me." Dunne ran out of the room crying and told Cook, "He just tried to kill me. Can't you see the marks on my neck?" The actress later escaped the scene by crawling through a bathroom window and driving off in her car. Sweeney, however, heard her start the engine and jumped on top of the moving vehicle as she sped away. According to Sweeney's later trial testimony, the argument started over his concern that Dunne and her friends were doing drugs in his home. "Dominique was walking around the bedroom, raising her voice and saying I was being over-protective of her," Sweeney testified. "I grabbed her around the neck from behind ... I never let go of her. I pulled her toward me. She fell over the bed and on to the floor." Whatever the provocation for the attack, Dunne was through with the mercurial Sweeney. At her insistence, he moved out of the apartment, but continued to press for a reconciliation. Dunne told family and friends that Sweeney's possessiveness (bordering on obsession) was terrifying.

On October 30, 1982, the chef was still attempting to reconcile with his former lover now living alone in a house at 8723 Rangely Drive in West Hollywood. Earlier in the day, Sweeney sent the 22-year-old actress two boxes filled with Halloween presents from Ma Maison. One box contained four pumpkins, the other her face meticulously carved in chocolate and three pink flowers. That evening when Sweeney drove over to the house on Rangely Drive, Dunne was discussing a script with friend and fellow-actor, David Packer. According to Packer, soon after Sweeney pulled up in the driveway, he knocked on the door and told Dunne, "We have to talk about this." Dunne tried to get Sweeney to leave and, when he refused, let him in and introduced him to Packer. Sweeney and Dunne went outside on the front porch and

several minutes later Packer heard them quarreling. Packer later testified he heard Sweeney yell, "...but this is my house also." Packer could not hear Dunne's reply delivered in a sobbing voice, but soon afterwards heard a "banging" noise followed by screams. He looked outside and saw Sweeney in the driveway on his knees with his back towards the street. When their eyes locked Sweeney told the terrified actor to call the police. Packer did not see Dunne, but sheriff's deputies responding to his emergency call around 9:45 P.M. found the actress unconscious, but still clinging to life, at the foot of the driveway. Sweeney, standing in front of the residence when authorities arrived, told arresting officers, "I killed my girlfriend." Only later did David Packer remember that during the height of his terror he had phoned a friend and left a message on the answering machine — "If I die tonight, it was by John Sweeney." Rushed by ambulance to Cedars-Sinai Medical Center, Dunne was placed on life support in the fifth-floor intensive care unit. The purpled bruises from Sweeney's hands were still clearly visible on the actress' throat as doctors ran tests to determine if the comatose young woman would suffer permanent brain damage from lack of oxygen should she miraculously survive the assault. On November 5, 1982, five days after the attack, Dominique Dunne died without regaining consciousness. Her heart had stopped before the family was forced to make the painful decision to remove her from life support. Dunne's organs were donated and her body turned over to the coroner for an autopsy. The procedure determined that the actress suffered "brain death caused by strangulation." Remarkably, the strangulation itself was estimated to have lasted over 4 minutes. On November 6, 1982, some 500 mourners attended a funeral service at the Church of the Good Shepherd where 22 years before the actress had been christened. Afterwards, Dominque Dunne was buried in a private ceremony in Westwood Memorial Park.

Charged with first-degree murder and assault to commit great bodily injury, Sweeney awaited trial in the Men's Central Jail in Los Angeles. The jockeying for legal advantage began immediately. Public defender Mike Adelson, assigned Sweeney's case, told reporters that "When all the facts of that tragic evening are known you will find a mind with as little control as an electrical appliance with the plug pulled out." Informed that the prosecution would not be seeking the death penalty or life imprisonment without the possibility of parole in the proceeding, Sweeney pleaded innocent to all charges. On December 14, 1982, the prisoner attempted to commit suicide in his cell by slashing the inside of both wrists with the blade from a disposable razor. The wounds, deemed "superficial" by jail staff, required a total of 13 stitches to close and barely bled. On July 21, 1983, Judge Burton S. Katz listened outside the presence of the jury to a prosecution witness, Lillian Pierce, to determine if her testimony detailing her past relationship with Sweeney was to be admissible as evidence. Pierce, an attractive woman in her thirties, testified that on ten separate occasions during her two-year relationship with Sweeney the man had beaten her. Hospital records documented Pierce had twice been admitted for extended stays for treatment for a broken nose, a punctured eardrum, and a collapsed lung all inflicted by Sweeney. Katz ruled the testimony (effectively establishing Sweeney as a classic serial abuser of women) was too prejudicial to the defendant's case and did not allow the jury to hear it. While Pierce recounted approved parts of her nightmarish association with Sweeney, the defendant suddenly jumped up, tried to escape through the rear doors of the courtroom, and had to be forcibly restrained by the bailiff. Weeks into the trial, Judge Katz dealt another crippling blow to the case for the prosecution when he ruled it had not presented sufficient evidence to support a charge of first-degree murder. However, while there was no evidence that Sweeney's attack was premeditated or deliberate, Katz maintained there was strong enough evidence to support second-degree murder, a charge carrying a hefty 15 years to life sentence. The jury's other option could be for a reduced charge of manslaughter.

Near the end of the seven week trial, Sweeney took the stand and explained what he called his "loving" and "romantic" relationship with Dunne. On the night of October 30, 1982, the chef arrived at Dunne's West Hollywood home on Rangely Drive certain they were going to reconcile, marry, and have children. After the actress angrily accused him of being obsessive and flatly stated she would not be sharing her life with him the discussion escalated into a screaming match. While Sweeney claimed he could not remember the exact moment he started to choke her, he testified, "I just lost my temper. I remember just like exploding ... I just lunged at her. I only know from the point where I stopped. When we were in the driveway ... I remember the feeling of Do-minique underneath me. I saw Dominique's face ... at that time I knew I had my hands around her neck. Sometime thereafter I picked her up and tried to make her walk. I'm sure I picked her up because I dropped her. I was shaking her and talking to her. I don't remember what I said. She wasn't responding, and at some point in time I dropped her."

On September 12, 1983, the case went to the eight man, 4 woman jury charged with determining whether Sweeney, who admitted choking Dunne to brain death over a 4 minute period of manual strangulation, was guilty of second-degree murder or the lesser crime of manslaughter. Because of Judge Katz's earlier ruling, the jury was unaware Sweeney's violence against Dunne was not an isolated event, but part of an ongoing pattern of abuse against women. One week later, the jurors reported being deadlocked over legal questions in the case, most notably, the distinction between murder (cold blood) and manslaughter (heat of passion). Judge Katz asked them to reconsider and on September 21, 1983 they found Sweeney guilty of voluntary manslaughter in Dunne's death and of misdemeanor assault in an earlier September 1982 choking incident involving the actress. The maximum sentence for manslaughter was 6 years with 6 months tacked on for the misdemeanor assault. Sweeney, who had found God during his ordeal, listened quietly to the verdict with his hands folded over the Bible in his lap, while friends and family of the dead actress groaned and burst into tears. As Judge Katz was thanking the jury for their efforts telling them "justice was served," Dominick Dunne, the dead woman's father, could no longer contain himself. "Not from our family, it wasn't," he told the shocked judge who informed Dunne that he would have time to speak to jurors at the sentencing. "Too late then," Dunne countered, "You withheld important information from this jury about this man's history of violent behavior." Jurors later admitted that had they known of Sweeney's past pattern of abusive behavior against women they would have found him guilty of second-degree murder. After sentencing Sweeney to the maximum prison term of 6 years on November 10, 1983, Judge Katz seemingly tried to placate the shattered Dunne family by criticizing the jury's verdict. "I am convinced this was murder," he told the panel, "I am convinced that John Sweeney did not kill Dominique Dunne in the heat of passion, but rather that he killed her because his ego could not stand rejection." Then to Sweeney, "You hung onto this fragile, beautiful and vulnerable woman and squeezed and squeezed and squeezed the oxygen from her while she flailed for her life. This is an act that is qualitatively not of manslaughter, but of murder." With credit for time served and good behavior in prison, Sweeney was released after serving 2½ years. The violent death of Dominique Dunne in 1982 coupled with the untimely passing of her co-star in the first *Poltergeist* film, Heather O'Rourke, in 1988 during intestinal surgery at the age of 12, has since given rise to the so-called *Poltergeist* curse. Dominick Dunne, 83, died of bladder cancer at his home in Manhattan on August 26, 2009.

Further Reading

Dunne, Dominick. *Justice: Crimes, Trials, and Punishments.* New York: Crown, 2001.

Echevarria, Lydia (M)

Luis Vigoreaux Presents, hosted by the titular star described in a *New York Times* article dated September 12, 1984, as a "Puerto Rican television mixture of Johnny Carson and Arthur Godfrey," was the island's most popular weekly variety show. Co-hosting with the tall, handsome Vigoreaux was his wife of 22 years, radio soap opera star Lydia Echevarria. A seeming model of marital bliss, the Vigoreaux-Echevarria union started to unravel in 1981 at about the same time as their production company went bankrupt. Amid gossip column reports that Vigoreaux, 54, was seeing a younger woman, the fiftyish Echevarria abruptly quit their television program. Soon afterwards the gossip press confirmed that the likable television host was involved with 26-year-old Nydia Castillo. Over Echevarria's objections, Vigoreaux filed for a divorce and announced plans to marry his young lover.

On January 17, 1983, one day before the divorce was to be granted, Vigoreaux left a meeting with Echevarria and their lawyers that settled the couples' financial matters. The television star was not seen again until the next day when his body was found in the trunk of his burnt out Mercedes-Benz in an isolated area outside of San Juan. An autopsy determined that Vigoreaux was beaten with a metal object, stabbed 11 times with a sharp instrument (either a barbecue fork or ice pick), and more disturbingly, was still alive when the car was torched. Echevarria joined in the national outpouring of grief over the loss of her husband

and was witness to the hundreds of thousands of people who lined the road to the cemetery where he was buried. Alone for the first time in over two decades, the grieving widow lost herself in work appearing in several plays and in two television soap operas.

Twenty months after the murder, amid press reports that a witness had stepped forward to implicate Echevarria in a murder-for-hire scheme with Pablo Guadalupe, 64, and two of his sons, the three men were arrested on September 2, 1984. Murder charges were also filed against Echeverria, but she was not taken into custody until the next day when authorities traced her to the home of a friend. In May 1986, following nearly four month trial, the actress was found guilty of first-degree murder by a 9–3 jury vote (a unanimous verdict is not required in Puerto Rico). In a 10–2 vote, the actress was also found guilty of kidnapping and two counts of conspiracy. Echevarria was sentenced to 208 years in prison, but in January 2000, the 68-year-old diabetic was granted clemency by a parole board (acting on the recommendation of Puerto Rican Governor Pedro Rosello) for health reasons.

Further Reading

"Puerto Rican Star Is Held in Murder." *The New York Times*, September 12, 1984, sec. A, p. 27.

Elizalde, Valentín *see* Appendix 1

Elmore, Belle (V)

A would-be music hall performer in Britain, Belle Elmore (real name Kunigunde Mackamotzki, but also known as Cora Turner) is today remembered only as the victim of her infamous husband, Dr. Hawley Harvey Crippen. His transAtlantic flight from justice and subsequent capture marked the first time radio technology was utilized in the apprehension of a killer. Hawley Harvey Crippen (known as "Peter") graduated from the University of Michigan and by age 25 had taken a medical degree at the Homeopathic Medical College in Cleveland, Ohio. After the death from apoplexy of his first wife in January 1892, Crippen remarried Cora Turner (Mackamotzki/Elmore) in Jersey City on September 1, 1892. Turner, known professionally as Belle Elmore, was reportedly a profoundly untalented music hall singer who entertained artistic pretensions of becoming a grand opera diva. In this endeavor, Crippen supported her both emotionally and financially while undergoing a series of stunning career reversals. By 1897 when they moved to London, Crippen had descended into the nether regions of medical quackery selling medicine on commission for the Munyon Patent Medicine Company, co-partnering the Yale Tooth Company, and later working for an ear care business called the Aural Remedy. Meanwhile, Belle Elmore tried unsuccessfully to launch a music hall career, and had to content herself with entertaining performers at No. 39 Hilldrop Crescent, the Crippens' home in the Kentish Town District of North London. Blaming Crippen for her professional failure, Elmore began drinking and publicly humiliated him by indiscreetly taking a series of lovers. The 50-year-old Crippen turned for solace to his secretary of four years, Ethel Le Neve, and the two began a clandestine affair marked by deep affection and respect.

On January 31, 1910, Elmore disappeared after hosting a dinner party in their home. To cover her absence, the diminutive doctor explained to those asking after her that she had died while visiting friends in California. Eyebrows were raised, however, when Ethel Le Neve began openly living with Crippen at Hilldrop Crescent on March 12, 1910. After the secretary was seen wearing the missing woman's jewelry, suspicious friends contacted Scotland Yard. One week later, Chief Inspector Walter Dew interviewed Crippen. The doctor readily admitted that he had concocted the story of his wife's death in order to avoid the inevitable scandal that would result if people were to learn that she had really run off with another man. Dew's search of the premises revealed nothing amiss and Crippen may very well have escaped justice had he not panicked and fled with Le Neve on July 10, 1910. Learning of the doctor's flight, Dew revisited Hilldrop Crescent on July 13, 1910. After finding nothing buried in the garden, the inspector went down to the coal cellar and tested the crevices in the brick floor with a poker. When a few bricks yielded, he dug the area up with a spade and discovered a reeking mass of flesh wrapped in a pajama top and covered with lime. The head, arms, legs, and genitals had been removed so all that remained was an unidentifiable torso from which the bones and several organs had been removed with surgical-like precision. Though the fate of the missing limbs and organs was never determined, it was conjectured that some were burned in the kitchen grate while Crippen had tossed the head overboard in a handbag

during a trip to Dieppe. A later autopsy confirmed that the remains contained a lethal dose of the drug hydrobromide of hyoscine. Belle Elmore's remains were buried in the Saint Pancras and Islington Cemetery in East Finchley, Greater London.

Crippen and Le Neve, posing as "Mr. John Philo Robinson" and his young son, "Master Robinson," were in Antwerp, Belgium, waiting to ship out on July 20, 1910, aboard the *S.S. Montrose* bound for Quebec when arrest warrants were issued for them three days after the grisly discovery in the cellar. Police handbills and newspaper accounts of the pair featured their photographs beneath the bold face heading "Murder and Mutilation." To avoid detection, Crippen shaved off his moustache and Le Neve cut her hair and wore boy's clothes. The *S.S. Montrose* was at sea two days when Captain Harry Kendall used the ship's Marconi wireless to send a message to authorities reporting that he had identified the "Robinsons" as the wanted fugitives. On July 23, 1910, Inspector Dew sat sail from Liverpool aboard the *Laurentic*, a faster ship that would arrive in Quebec on July 30, 1910, one day ahead of the *Montrose*. Crippen, isolated aboard the ship, was unaware that the chase was front page news in every paper in England. On July 30, Dew arrived at Father Point, Canada, one day ahead of Crippen. Backed up by a contingent of Royal Canadian Mounted Police, Dew boarded the *Montrose* the next day and arrested Crippen and Le Neve.

Amid enormous negative publicity, Crippen's trial opened at London's Old Bailey on August 28, 1910. Instead of admitting to killing his wife during a heated argument (a tactic that certainly would have reduced the murder charge to manslaughter), Crippen unwisely maintained his innocence in the face of damning forensic evidence. Sir Bernard Spilsbury identified the mutilated remains as those of Belle Elmore by connecting a scar found on the torso with that produced by an operation she had to remove an ovary. A chemist testified that days prior to the woman's disappearance, he sold Crippen five grains of hyoscine and produced the poison book containing the doctor's signature. Dr. Spilsbury had previously testified that large traces of the deadly drug had been found in the remains. Crippen was found guilty and sentenced to death on October 22, 1910, after the jury deliberated only 27 minutes. Ethel Le Neve was tried three days later as an accessory after the fact of murder, but due largely to Crippen's insistence that she had no involvement in the affair combined with a brilliant legal defense, she was acquitted. While awaiting execution, Dr. Crippen was a model prisoner who won the respect of all with his continued allegiance and devotion to Le Neve. Hanged at Pentonville Prison on November 23, 1910, Crippen was buried with a photograph of Le Neve and her letters in accordance with his last wish. Le Neve subsequently sold her story to the press, changed her name, married, and died in Dulwich in August 1967 at the age of 84.

Further Reading

Cullen, Tom. *Mild Murderer*. London: Bodley Head, 1977.
Goodman, Jonathan, comp. *The Crippen File*. London: Allison & Busby, 1985.

Engels, Virginia (M-acquitted)

Voted "Miss Streamline" out of field of 250 Pacific Coast lovelies at San Francisco's Golden Gate International Exposition in April 1940, the striking blonde's other beauty titles included "Miss Los Angeles, 1940" and "The Orchid Queen." As official hostess for the San Francisco Fair, Engels caught the attention of motion picture producer Joe Pasternak who cast her in a microscopic uncredited role in Universal's 1940 Deanna Durbin vehicle, *It's a Date*. In fact, Engels was destined to become nothing more than uncredited "eye candy" in most of her 26 other feature appearances for studios like Universal, RKO and MGM in films like *Arabian Nights* (1942) as a "harem girl," *From This Day Forward* (1946) as "girl in the window," and her final role, "woman on trial," in MGM's 1952 *Just This Once* starring Janet Leigh. Ironically, she had just appeared as an uncredited "inmate" in the 1950 Warner Bros. prison drama *Caged* when she was booked into a Hollywood police station on August 16, 1950 on suspicion of misdemeanor drunk driving.

Engels was effectively "out of the business" when she was arrested for the knife murder of her 47-year-old husband, Charles H. Brown, on June 8, 1954. According to the 37-year-old former actress, her marriage to Brown, a parking lot attendant, was "hell." Once married to radio store operator James Robert Dennis in 1946, she divorced him the next year. Introduced to Brown by friends, Engels married him in 1950, but soon had cause for regret. According to the one-time beauty queen, Brown "had a lot of meanness in him" that violently manifested itself in once a month beat-

ings of his unhappy wife. Engels walked out five times, but always came back after he promised to change. The beatings continued and in November 1953 she was admitted to a Hollywood hospital with a broken shoulder after Brown knocked her down and stomped her. One month before his death, the parking lot attendant slugged his wife in the mouth with a bottle.

At 12:45 A.M. on June 8, 1954, Brown returned home to their apartment at 6027 Barton Avenue in Hollywood after a night of drinking. The couple argued, Brown hit her once in the face with his fist, then went after Engels' father who had been living with them for a week while looking for another place to stay. According to Engels, she picked up a 5" paring knife from a table to frighten Brown away when her drunken husband rushed her like a "madman." She lashed out, Brown grabbed his chest, reeled into the bathroom, then moments later stumbled back out into the living room and, asking his wife to call a doctor, fell to the floor. Engels called an ambulance, but Brown died around 1:00 A.M. at Hollywood Receiving Hospital without making a statement. Following a coroner's inquest that ruled the former actress was "probably criminally responsible" for Brown's death, Engels was formally charged with murder and bail set at $5,000. At the time of his death, Brown's blood alcohol content was .15 percent, well above the legal level of intoxication. A first trial ended on November 6, 1954 after a jury deadlocked 8–4 for acquittal. Engels was acquitted in January 1955 after the jury in a second trial needed less than an hour to rule that she had acted in self-defense. In what has since become almost a Hollywood cliché for beauty queens turned failed actresses, Engels lived alone and forgotten until making the news one last time. Concerned that she had not seen her tenant for a couple of days, Engels' landlady let herself into the flat at 5200 Marathon Street on December 5, 1956, to find the former actress lying on the floor beside her bed. "Miss Los Angeles, 1940" had died of meningitis hours earlier.

Further Reading

"Ex-Miss Los Angeles Held on Charge of Slaying Mate." *Los Angeles Times*, June 9, 1954, p. 2.

Ethridge, LaJean (V)

Ethridge, professionally known as "LaJean Guye," was a member of the touring company Names-Townsend Players when the group of six was signed by Hollywood star John Wayne to appear in small roles in his directorial debut, *The Alamo*. Bit players were assigned lodging in bunkhouses in Spofford, Texas while the film's main cast (actors Wayne, Richard Widmark, Laurence Harvey, Richard Boone) stayed in better accommodations on the Shehan Ranch in nearby Bracketville. Initially signed for $75 a week and given one line of dialogue, the 26-year-old actress was thrilled when Wayne, impressed by her ability, gave her a page of dialogue and a salary bump to $350.00 a week. More dialogue, however, meant that Ethridge needed to relocate from Spofford to Bracketville to be closer to the set. On October 11, 1959, Ethridge was in the process of moving out of the bunkhouse she shared with five male members of the Names-Townsend Players, when her actor-boyfriend, Chester ("Chet") Harvey Smith, 32, became distraught that she was leaving him. They argued and Smith stabbed Ethridge in the chest with a butcher knife. A fellow-actor found the tearful Smith on the floor cradling the dead woman's body in his arms. As he was led away by police, Smith said, "I couldn't stand being without her." Despite maintaining that he blacked out and could not remember the incident, Smith was convicted of murder and sentenced to 30 years in prison, but was paroled after serving less than 8 years.

Further Reading

Munn, Michael. *The Hollywood Murder Casebook*. New York: St. Martin's, 1987.

Europe, James Reese (V)

Considered by many musical authorities to be among the most important African-American musical leaders of the early twentieth century, Europe championed black American musical expression in all its forms, and was successful in bridging the gap between black and white audiences. A seminal figure in the transformation of orchestral ragtime into what would later be termed "jazz," the man who friend and collaborator Eubie Blake dubbed "the Martin Luther King of black American musicians" was born on February 22, 1880 (some sources state 1881), in Mobile, Alabama, among the first generation born in the South after Reconstruction. Europe showed early musical ability on the piano and violin, and was fascinated by the military brass bands that played in the port city. The budding musician was still a child when the family relocated to Washington, D.C., in

1889. In the nation's capital, Europe studied with concert violinist Joseph Douglass, grandson of Frederick Douglass, and Enrico Hurlei, assistant director of the U.S. Marine Corps Band. In 1894, the 14-year-old gave his first public recital on violin also winning a prize for composition later that year.

Following the death of his father in 1903, Europe, 23, moved to New York City then a ferment of musical activity for African-American musicians. An accomplished pianist and violinist, Europe began working with Ernest Hogan, a major black entertainer, in 1905. The collaboration led Europe to assume the role of musical director in several notable black musical comedy theatrical productions including *A Trip to Africa* (1904), *The Black Politician* (1904–1908), *Shoo-Fly Regiment* (1906–1907), *Red Moon* (1908–1909), and *Mr. Lode of Koal* (1909). Recognizing the high demand for black entertainers in theatre and high society functions, Europe organized and became the president of the Clef Club in 1910. The first of its kind organization in New York City, the Clef Club served as a combination gathering place and booking agency for African-American musicians. In his quest to promote the black musical community, Europe created the Clef Club Symphony Orchestra, an orchestral group composed of singers, over 100 hundred instruments, and 11 pianos. On May 2, 1912, Europe conducted the orchestra in a "Symphony of Negro Music" before an enthusiastic, soldout audience in Carnegie Hall. He further popularized the musical compositions of African-American composers like Will Marion Cook, Ford Dabney, Henry Creamer *et al.* in a series of concert tours performed before both black and white audiences in several major Eastern cities.

Europe may have remained just an East Coast musical phenomenon if not for a chance meeting at a high society party in 1913 with Vern and Irene Castle, the husband and wife dance team who were then the toast of vaudeville and Broadway. The couple loved dancing to the bandleader's heavily syncopated music, hired him as their musical director, and toured the country dancing to music provided by Europe's Society Orchestra. During the dance craze that swept America prior to World War I, the Castles were the preeminent demonstrators of new dance steps (Fox-Trot, etc.). In December 1913, the couple opened the doors of its New York City–based dance school, the Castle House, with a composition by Europe composed to commemorate the event, "Castle House Rag." Over the next few years, Europe continued to pen heavily syncopated dance numbers for the couple including "Castle Walk," "Castle Innovation Tango," "Castles' Half and Half," and "Castles' Lame Duck Walk." Through the dance team, Europe and his complement of talented African-American composers and musicians became well-known in high society often playing in the homes of the wealthy, and at swanky venues like the Tuxedo Club, Delmonico's, and the Hotel Biltmore.

More importantly, his successful collaboration with the Castles led to a recording deal with the Victor Talking Machine Company, the first time an African-American was signed by a major label to lead his own band. In two sessions (December 29, 1913, and February 10, 1914), Europe and his Society Orchestra recorded eight tunes which featured dances like the Turkey Trot, the Maxixe, the Boston, and the Two-Step. The unique instrumentation featured in the compositions (mandolin, banjos, drums) earned Europe the nickname "the Paderewski of syncopation." By 1914, Europe was a major force in the African-American musical community. Sheet music sales of his waltzes and tangos were selling well, he continued to compose marches, dances, and songs in collaboration with other black composers (Noble Lee Sissle, Eubie Blake), and served as a booking agent for black musicians playing the high society circuit. The orchestra leader was set to accompany the Castles on a European tour when war was declared in late 1914. Europe enlisted in the 15th Infantry Regiment (Colored) of the New York National Guard (the first black unit organized in the state) on September 18, 1916, apparently for no other reason than he felt it would set a good example for other African-Americans. As in other areas of American society at the time, blacks were poorly treated in the military. Segregated into "blacks only" regiments, the African-American soldier was by military tradition barred from joining U.S. combat divisions, routinely ridiculed by white troops, and assigned the most menial duties.

Colonel William Hayward, the white commander of the 15th Infantry Regiment, realized Europe's musical ability would be wasted if he remained just another private in a machine gun company. After Europe passed the officer's exam and was scheduled to become a first lieutenant, Col. Hayward called him in to discuss the forma-

tion of "the best band in the U.S. Army." Initially reluctant to forego actual fighting, Europe was won over by Hayward's argument that the band could be useful in building morale. When Europe was unable to recruit enough talented black musicians in New York, Daniel G. Reid, director of U.S. Steel Corporation and American Can Company, instituted a $10,000 fund to canvass the country for suitable players. Within the year, the 15th Regimental Band under Europe's baton was playing concerts in the States. In December 1917, the 15th Infantry Regiment was shipped out arriving on New Year's Day in France, the first African-American combat unit to ever set foot on French soil. Barred from fighting alongside white American army troops, the 15th Infantry saw combat only after being renamed the 369th U.S. Infantry Regiment and assigned to the 16th Division of the French Army. In April 1918, the 369th was stationed with French divisions on the front line trenches in the town of Maffrecourt. In France, Europe became the first African-American officer in World War I to lead troops into combat. The 369th Infantry fought so well during the campaign they were given the name "Hellfighters." Europe, the leader of a machine gun company, was gassed during the conflict and sent to a field hospital behind the lines. While painfully recuperating, he wrote the song "On Patrol in No Man's Land." In August 1918, Lt. Europe was officially ordered away from front line combat, and charged with devoting himself full-time to conducting the 15th's band, now officially renamed the 369th U.S. Infantry "Hellfighters" Band. Credited with introducing orchestrated ragtime and a precursor of jazz to France, the band became a sensation playing before thousands in camps, hospitals, and in special concerts attended by French dignitaries and U.S. military brass like General John J. Pershing. Following the Armistice in November 1918, Europe and his men earned the distinction of being among the first African-Americans to enter Germany.

Jim Europe and the Hellfighters were already famous when they arrived by ship in New York City in February 1919. Dubbed by U.S. newspapers as "America's first 'Jazz King,'" the popular bandleader was discharged from the Army on February 25, 1919. Less than two weeks after returning from the war and prior to embarking on a multicity tour with the Hellfighters, Europe and the group signed a contract with the New York–based Pathé Frères Phonograph Company to record the songs that captivated France during the war. In two sessions (March and May 1919), the Hellfighters recorded "On Patrol in No Man's Land" (with battle sound effects provided by the band), "Memphis Blues," "All of No Man's Land is Ours," "My Choc'late Soldier Sammy Boy," and, among others, "Jazzola."

On May 9, 1919, two days after the band's final recording session, Europe and the Hellcats were in Boston, Massachusetts, for a concert at Mechanics Hall. While accounts of the ensuing tragedy vary, the concert was in progress when one of the band's drummers, 24-year-old Herbert Wright, angrily confronted Europe backstage as the bandleader was talking to Noble Sissle, the group's tenor soloist, in their shared dressing room. Wright was apparently upset because he felt Europe was critical of his drumming while oblivious to the mistakes made by another drummer in the band. Newspaper accounts reported Wright became enraged when Europe told him not to cause a disturbance in the performance by walking on and off the stage while other acts were working. What is known is that Wright left Europe's dressing room only to burst in again moments later clutching a small pocket knife in his fist and screaming, "I'll kill anybody that takes advantage of me. Jim Europe, I'll kill you." Europe attempted to hold Wright off with a chair, but the drummer pushed it aside and stabbed the bandleader in the neck. The 39-year-old former army lieutenant who had survived the horrors of World War I trench warfare was pronounced dead at 11:45 P.M. at City Hospital. As newspapers around the world praised the bandleader as a patriot, race leader, and composer, Europe lay in state at the Paris Undertakers in Harlem as thousands of whites and blacks filed past to pay their final respects. On May 13, 1919, the "Jazz King" was given the first public funeral procession ever accorded an African-American in New York City. The next day, he was buried with full military honors at the National Military Cemetery in Arlington, Virginia. Herbert Wright was subsequently allowed to plead guilty to a charge of manslaughter after the state psychiatrist reported that while the drummer was not insane, he was "of such (a) low type of mentality that there was a question as to his entire responsibility" in the killing. He was sentenced, without trial, to a prison term of 10 to 15 years. Wright was paroled from the Massachusetts State Penitentiary on April 1, 1927, after serving only 8 years.

Further Reading

Badger, Reid. *A Life in Ragtime: A Biography of James Reese Europe.* New York: Oxford University Press, 1995.
Gracyk, Tim. "James Reese Europe with His 369th U.S. Infantry 'Hellfighters' Band." (A 44-page booklet accompanying the CD *James Reese Europe with His 369th U.S. Infantry 'Hellfighters' Band: The Complete Recordings.* Memphis, TN: Memphis Archives, 1996).
"Jim Europe Killed in Boston Quarrel." *The New York Times,* May 10, 1919, p. 1.
"Lieut. Europe's Funeral." *The New York Times,* May 14, 1919, p. 17.

Evans, Mal *see* Lennon, John

Forrester, Rhett (V)

The Brooklyn-based heavy metal rock band Riot was formed in 1976, but Forrester did not join the group until 1982 when he replaced departed front man Guy Speranza as lead vocalist. Forrester appears on two of the band's albums, *Restless Breed* (1982) and *Born in America* (1984). When the group disbanded in 1984, Forrester relocated to Atlanta to front the local group Mr. Dirty. At 6:00 A.M. on January 22, 1994, the 37-year-old rocker left his DeKalb County apartment and drove to Techwood Homes, a crime-ridden public housing project in northwest Atlanta. Two black men approached Forrester as he sat in his parked car at the intersection of Lovejoy Street and Merritts Avenue. An argument ensued and one of the men pulled a pistol and shot the musician in the back. As the pair sped away in an older model Cadillac, Forrester managed to stumble from his car, flag down a police cruiser, and relate the incident before dying at the scene. Police theorized that the musician was likely in the area to buy drugs. Forrester's mother: "He had no business being where he was or doing what he was doing. But he didn't deserve to be murdered." The case remains unsolved.

Further Reading

McDonald, R. Robin. "Son's Slaying Haunts Mom: Case Is Among 70 Unsolved Last Year." *Atlanta Constitution,* March 20, 1995, sec. B, p. 2.
Talevski, Nick. *The Encyclopedia of Rock Obituaries.* London; New York: Omnibus, 1999.

Forsberg, Florence (V) (M-S)

Five weeks prior to her murder, the 25-year-old Canadian joined the cast of the Broadway musical *Wonderful Town* as a singer and understudy to Edith Adams in the role of "Eileen." On July 16, 1953, the body of Lester Johnsen, a 25-year-old Korean War veteran, was found in the New York City apartment he shared with his mother and sister at 255 West 108th Street. Johnsen, a tie and candy salesman, had killed himself with a rifle. A note found at the scene led authorities across town to Forsberg's apartment at 34 West 69th Street where they found the singer dead from multiple stab wounds. While Johnsen's note supplied no motive for the murder-suicide, it indicated that he spent the evening drinking in her apartment prior to stabbing his acquaintance of five years to death shortly before 4:00 A.M. Returning to his apartment, he shot himself at around 7:15 A.M.

Further Reading

"Veteran Kills Singer and Commits Suicide." *The New York Times*, July 17, 1953, p. 36.

Foth, Steven M. (V)

Foth, 35, co-wrote the 1994 song "Hitchhiker Joe" with Steve Poltz of the Rugburns, and for years played guitar with the San Diego–based joke-folk band C.L.A. (Carnivorous Lunar Activity), before opening Rocket Records, a small independent record and zine store on Ninth Avenue in San Francisco's Sunset District. Rocket Records established itself as the hub of the city's underground music scene until the chain Amoeba Records opened a huge store in the nearby Haight district. As his business disintegrated, Foth turned to crack cocaine and to what associates characterized as a fondness for dangerous sex. Concerned friends staged an "intervention" and, as part of Foth's recovery, convinced him to hang out with musician friends in San Diego. Foth had been in that city for three weeks when on September 29, 1999, he borrowed a friend's black 1997 Audi so he could first visit Steve Poltz at the musician's home in La Jolla, then meet other friends for dinner back in San Diego. After a brief visit with Poltz, Foth made a fatal error. On the way to his dinner date, the record store owner attempted to score sex and crack cocaine from a prostitute in City Heights, a seedy part of San Diego. Foth's naked body was found the next day near a pumpkin patch just south of the Lake Hodges reservoir in Rancho Bernardo. The musician-songwriter had bled to death from 83 stab wounds to his neck, face, and chest. The burned out Audi was recovered in City Heights.

On October 14, 1999, Willard James Hall, 19, Ronnie Jermaine Sherrors, 25, and 22-year-old prostitute, Lena Renee Hixon, were arrested for Foth's murder. A conviction under California's special circumstances law (commission of a robbery and murder while in the commission of a kidnapping) meant all faced possible sentences of death or prison without the possibility of parole. Hixon quickly cut a deal with the prosecution — her testimony against Hall and Sherrors in exchange for a 12 year sentence on assault and drug charges. According to Hixon, she was working the corner of 47th Street and University Avenue in City Heights when Foth randomly approached her to buy crack cocaine. She had none, but directed him to a nearby apartment on Wightman Street where Sherrors and Hall lived. Foth and the pair then drove off in the Audi returning in fifteen minutes with only Sherrors and Hall visible in the car. Hixon joined the men and they drove to Lake Hodges where she was told they were going to buy some marijuana. Instead, the two men parked in a remote area and opened the trunk to reveal Foth, his hands bound. The pair proceeded to stab him multiple times forcing her to stab Foth once to "involve" her in the crime. Sherrors and Hall stripped Foth's body and threw it over a barbed wire fence. On September 28, 2001, Sherrors and Hall were sentenced to life in prison without the possibility of parole.

Further Reading

Finz, Stacy. "Violent End to Record Store Owner's Life; S.F. Man's New Vices Led to His Death." *San Francisco Chronicle*, October 18, 1999, sec. A, p. 1.

Frachet, Eric (V)

Frachet, 33, had acted in small roles in a few films (*La Cible*, 1997; *Le Déménagement*, 1997; *Vidangel*, 1998) and in several television commercials in his native France. In 1997–1998, he worked as a high speed stunt driver on director John Frankenheimer's film *Ronin*, starring Robert De Niro. After spending the day of June 30, 1998 visiting his grandparents in Nouyaery, the actor boarded a train at Grenoble bound for Lyon on his way to Paris to audition the next morning for a television commercial. Unfortunately for Frachet, who had no interest in soccer, a World Cup game between bitter rivals England and Argentina was being played that evening in nearby St. Etienne. Sitting opposite the Frenchman in the train car was Paul Birch, a 43-year-old self-employed engineer from the Isle of Dogs, East London. Birch, though not on file with Scotland Yard as a known soccer hooligan, was an ardent England supporter and was in France to attend the match. He apparently believed Frachet was an Argentinian and felt the man was smirking at him and mocking the English team. When the train arrived at the village station of St. Andre-le-Gaz, Birch pulled out a hunting knife, plunged it into Frachet's stomach, and fled across a field. The Frenchman bled to death en route to the hospital from the 3 inch deep wound in his gut. The next day, French police responding to a disturbance in a hotel in Grenoble arrested Birch for attacking a knife porter with a broken bottle. Under questioning, he admitted knifing Frachet after the "Argentine" mocked England's soccer team (England later lost the match to Argentina on a penalty kick). Prophetically, at the time of his arrest authorities felt Birch was "mentally deranged."

On July 3, 1998, the Briton was formally charged with murder and faced a 30 year prison sentence for the unprovoked attack. One year later, the prosecutor's office stated that psychiatric tests conducted while he was in custody established that Birch was suffering from "psychic problems" that significantly hindered his judgment and limited the control he had over his actions. While French authorities repeatedly sought cooperation from the British Government to determine whether the engineer had a documented history of mental illness before ultimately deciding his case, Birch managed to smuggle a letter out of prison to Frachet's family. In it, he stated that he killed Frachet under orders from a neo–Nazi gang of English fans who wanted to insure that England would stage the World Cup in 2006. In February 2000, a French appeals court upheld the lower court ruling that Birch was mentally unfit to stand trial. Outraged, the victim's family and friends marched through the streets of Grenoble carrying banners demanding "Real Justice for Eric, the forgotten dead of the World Cup 1998." Birch was returned to England in December 2001 and removed to a mental institution in London at the request of French authorities.

Further Reading

"English Killer of Frenchman During World Cup Returns Home." Agence France-Presse, December 19, 2001.

Fragson, Harry (V)

Born Leon Phillipe Pott in London on July 2, 1869, Fragson spent most of his early life in Belgium learning the yeast trade from his salesman father, Victor. Equally adept in speaking English and French, Fragson did not touch a piano until 1889. Two years later, the 20 year old was wowing Parisian audiences with a cabaret act in which the elegantly dressed singer-comedian accompanied himself on the piano. A perennial favorite in the *Folies Bergère*, Fragson performed almost exclusively in France until 1905 when he appeared in a role specifically written for him in the pantomime *Cinderella* at London's Drury Lane Theatre. In London, Fragson appeared in the musicals *Castles in Spain* (1906) performing his composition, "Hello! Hello! Who's Your Lady Friend?," *Sinbad the Sailor* (1906–1907), and in *The Babes in the Wood* at the Drury Lane during the 1907-1908 season. In 1913, Fragson, 45, was at the height of his career and earning $750.00 a week in various revues when his relationship with music hall actress Paulette Franck led to tensions between the entertainer and his 83-year-old father, Victor Pott. Quarrels between father and son became more frequent after the actress moved into the Paris home they had happily shared for many years in the Rue Lafayette. Concerned by his father's violent threats against him and his lover, Fragson consulted a doctor who recommended that the elderly man be placed in a rest home. The entertainer was evidently in the process of arranging to do so when the senile Pott learned of the plan. On the evening of December 30, 1913, Fragson returned home after dining with friends to find the door locked. He rang the bell for several moments before his father answered the door. The singer complained of the delay, a bitter quarrel ensued, and Pott shot his son once in the back of the head as the entertainer stormed past him. Fragson died without regaining consciousness. Pott later told police: "I more than once wanted to commit suicide. That is the reason why I had the revolver. Life had become a burden to me. The woman whom my son imposed on me under my roof was the cause of frequent quarrels between us. I often made representations to my son about this cohabitation, but he would never listen to me. This evening, after the first angry word from my son addressed to me, I intended to kill myself before him. I produced the revolver which I was holding in my pocket. I do not know what happened. Instead of putting a bullet through my head I fired in the direction of my son. I cannot explain why I did so." Public opinion against the filicide ran high. Ten thousand mourners and gawkers brought traffic to a stop as the funeral procession fought its way to Montmartre Cemetery. Souvenir hunters ripped apart floral tributes to the dead entertainer and one bystander, mistakenly thought to be Victor

Musical comedy star Harry Fragson earned his reputation in France in the early twentith century before establishing himself as a name draw in London musicals and revues in the Drury Lane Theatre. Fragson, 45, was at the height of his popularity when he was shot to death by his 83-year-old senile father in Paris on December 20, 1913, following a series of escalating arguments centered on the entertainer's relationship with a French music hall actress.

Pott, had to be protected by police. Pott, medically diagnosed in the latter stages of senile dementia, died in prison on February 17, 1914 awaiting trial.

Further Reading

Lamb, Andrew, and Julian Myerscough. *Fragson: The Triumphs and the Tragedy*. Croydon: Fullers Wood Press/Music Hall Masters, 2004.
"Murder of Mr. Harry Fragson — Shot by His Father in Paris." *Times* (London), December 31, 1913, p. 32.

Franklin, Melvin B. (V)

Unrelated to The Temptations singer of the same name, Franklin sang bass with the Boston-based R&B band the Energetics in the 1970s. The five-man band renamed themselves Planet Patrol in 1982 and had two dance-pop chart hits ("Play at Your Own Risk," 1982; "Cheap Thrills," 1983) before disbanding in 1984. Franklin returned to Boston where he grew up and worked various blue-collar jobs including 13 years as a doorman at the Westin Hotel. In 1994 the former singer took a job as a skycap for Northwestern Airlines at Logan International Airport. In the late night hours of October 15, 1996, Franklin, 39, was on his way home from the airport when he was shot once in the chest less than one-tenth of a mile from his home at 88 Woodrow Drive in the suburb of Dorchester. Franklin was found in the gutter, his pockets turned out, and an estimated $200 in cash missing. Married for ten years, Franklin and his wife had recently converted a pantry in their home to a one-room "come as you are" church that they hoped would draw troubled teens. In November 2009 Boston police reopened the case. At that time, Franklin's widow vowed that a headstone would not be placed on her husband's grave until the case was solved and some type of peace restored to the family.

Further Reading

Kahn, Ric. "Murder Victim was '70s R&B Star, Religious Family Man." *Boston Globe*, October 17, 1996, sec. B, p. 4.

Freaky Tah (V)

Raymond Rogers, known under the nom de rap, Freaky Tah, was highly regarded as one of hip-hop's most socially committed rappers. Born in New York in 1972, Rogers began rapping with his relatives in-between classes at school and at block parties in his Queens, New York neighborhood of South Ozone Park. After high school, the friends all took jobs at JFK Airport, but quit the same day determined to make it big with their hip-hop group Lost Boyz, named after the 1987 teenage vampire film, *The Lost Boys*. While struggling to make it in the early 1990s, the group's members turned to small-time drug pushing, but decided to go straight after witnessing a fellow-drug dealer get shot. Lost Boyz (comprised of Freaky Tah/Raymond Rogers; Mr. Cheeks/Terrence Kelly, Rogers' brother; and his cousins Pretty Lou/Eric Ruth; DJ Spigg Nice) was signed by Uptown/Universal in 1995 following the success of their first single, "Lifestyles of the Rich and Shameless." The track appeared on the group's 1995 debut breakout album, *Legal Drug Money*, described by some as a morality tale about ghetto life. Their second album, *Love, Peace & Nappiness* (1997), debuted at Number 2 and sold more than 500,000 copies.

Unlike the majority of hip-hop groups, Lost Boyz (and particularly Raymond Rogers) demonstrated a keen social consciousness. Committed to revitalizing their neighborhood in South Jamaica, Queens, the group converted an abandoned building into a barber shop in a bid to get local kids interested in starting up legitimate businesses. The group formed their own production company, LB Family Entertainment, for the purpose of finding and developing undiscovered musical talent from Queens. Lost Boyz also hosted barbecues for local youth at Rosedale Village Park and an area video arcade. Rogers, idolized by the neighborhood kids, preached hard work and nonviolence. According to his father, Linford, "He checked their report cards. He bought them sneakers and jackets. He always told them, 'You do the right thing, and I'll do the right thing.'" A father of two, with another child on the way, Rogers' professional career also appeared bright with the group's third album, *LB IV Life*, set for release in June 1999.

Around 4:30 A.M. on March 28, 1999, the 27-year-old rapper was leaving a party at the Four Points Sheraton Hotel a few blocks from his home in South Jamaica, Queens, when a gunman wearing a ski mask ran up behind him and shot him once execution-style in the back of the head. The killer fired several shots into the air to freeze the group surrounding the fallen rapper prior to fleeing the scene on foot. Rogers, who was not wearing a bulletproof vest or carrying a weapon, was pronounced dead at Jamaica Hospital. With robbery ruled out as a motive, investigators looked into the rivalry-revenge factor that seemingly hangs like an omnipresent cloud over the world of rap. On April 6, 1999, an anonymous tip led to the arrest of Rasheem Fletcher, 22. Less than a week later, Kelvin Jones, 29, and Ryan Frith, 24, were picked up as Fletcher's partners in the murder. Police speculated the hit on Raymond stemmed from a late 1998 incident in which Lost Boyz member, Mr. Cheeks (Terrence Kelly), was robbed at gunpoint. In possible retaliation for the robbery involving Rogers' brother, Mr. Cheeks, a gunman opened fire on a street corner in Queens in December 1998, killing Michael Saunders, the half-brother of murder suspect, Kelvin Jones. Jones, a member of the Hell Raisers, a group of wannabe rappers and their posse based in South Ozone Park, Queens, killed Rogers out of revenge. On July 16, 2001, Kelvin Jones admitted to being the triggerman in the killing and was sentenced to a prison term of 15 years to life. Frith, the driver of the getaway van, pleaded guilty to criminal facilitation and was given 15 years. Fletcher pleaded guilty to the lesser charge of manslaughter and received a 7 year prison sentence. Three days after the murder of Freaky Tah, Roderick Padgett, connected to rival hip-hop group Hell Razor Pham, was shot execution-style in what appeared to be a retaliation hit. Corey Bussey, a 27-year-old "gofer" for the Lost Boyz, was tried and convicted on April 12, 2003 of the killing and sentenced to 15 years to life. It was later learned that Padgett had nothing to do with Freaky Tah's murder. A state appeals court unanimously overturned Bussey's conviction in April 2004 citing incompetent representation. In August 2005, the wannabe rapper cut a plea deal and was sentenced to 10 years with the possibility he could be released from prison in 2 years. Under the terms of the agreement, Bussey admitted shooting Padgett and requested through his attorney that he be permitted to serve the remainder of his sentence at the Eastern Correctional Facility where he had already spent the last 6 years.

Further Reading

McPhee, Michelle. "'Good Guy' Rapper's Slaying a Mystery." *New York Daily News*, March 30, 1999, p. 6.
www.allhiphop.com.
www.sohh.com

Frodl, Helmut (M)

Frodl, 36, an Austrian television producer-director of children's television programs, documentaries, and travel films, was enraged when his friend, 46-year-old sound studio owner Fritz Koeberl, exposed illegal deals that Frodl had made with government officials to fund his overpriced films from state subsidies. In a scheme reminiscent of an Alfred Hitchcock thriller, Frodl enlisted his girlfriend and another accomplice in a plot to murder Koeberl and take his studio. The television producer duped 32-year-old Hungarian Bica Novakov into believing that he was a C.I.A. operative and instructed her to seduce Koeberl. Mission accomplished, she was ordered to lure the sound studio owner from Vienna to Budapest where they were to discuss marriage plans with her family. In May 1992, Koeberl was given schnapps laced with barbiturates in a flat in Budapest. Frodl then emerged from a back room and shot the drugged man four times in the back of the head with a 9mm pistol. The director chain sawed the body into 17 pieces and scattered the remains in trash cans around the city. Frodl later disguised himself and used the dead man's passport to fly to London where he duped the Austrian Embassy into signing over Koeberl's £2 million studio to Gabor Pesti, a fellow "C.I.A. operative," in reality, his tax adviser. Frodl, Pesti, and Novakov (later exonerated) were arrested after a tramp looking for food found a body part in a trash can. Viennese police linked the body part and others to a missing persons report on Koeberl and determined that Frodl had introduced the dead man to his bride-to-be. Frodl and Pesti were subsequently found guilty of murder on December 22, 1993 and sentenced to life and 20 years in prison, respectively. In his 1993 book, *Außer Kontrolle. Im Netz der Agenten* (*Out of Control: Caught in the Agents' Net*), Frodl maintains that a Russian KGB agent murdered Koeberl.

Further Reading

"Film Director and Accomplice Jailed for Hitchcock-Style Murder." Agence France-Presse, December 23, 1993.

Fula, Yafeu (Kadafi) *see* Shakur, Tupac

Fuller, Bobby (V-suspected)

The rock star, born Robert Gaston Fuller on October 22, 1942, in Goose Creek, Texas (some sources report one year later in Baytown, Texas), made his first independent label recording, "You're in Love," in 1961. In the summer of 1963, the guitarist-vocalist moved from his home base in El Paso to Hollywood, California where the Bobby Fuller Four, with their fusion of rockabilly *a la* Buddy Holly with the newly emerging British sound, became a sensation on the local club scene.

In January 1966 their cover of the Crickets' "I Fought the Law" on the Mustang Records label charted at Number 9 on the *Billboard* charts. When their follow-up single in April 1966, the Buddy Holly–penned "Love's Made a Fool of You," peaked at Number 26 everyone agreed Fuller was on his way to stardom. Despite the group's success, the musician was moody and withdrawn. A perfectionist who oversaw every detail in the studio, Fuller, 23, was rankled that the group's biggest hit had not been written by him, and that he had yet to faithfully record the sound he heard in his head.

Despite Fuller's moodiness, however, few believed that he took his own life. During the late afternoon of July 18, 1966, the rocker's mother, Lorraine, found her son's body lying across the bloodstained front seat of her car parked in a lot adjacent to the Hollywood apartment he shared with brother and fellow-bandmate Randy Fuller at 1776 N. Sycamore Avenue. The doors were unlocked, the windows closed, and no key was in the ignition. Fuller's friends and family told authorities that the vehicle was not parked there three hours earlier when they searched the area for him. On the car's front floorboard, Hollywood police found a box of matches, and a gallon can of gasoline, with a plastic hose leading from it into the musician's hands. His hair and clothes reeked from gasoline which was also found in his body. Additionally, dried blood was detected on Fuller's chin and right eyebrow, and his chest and face exhibited bruises as though he had sustained a recent beating. Initially ruled a suicide, months later Bob Keane, owner and president of Mustang Records, persuaded authorities to change the report to "accidental death due to inhalation of gasoline." A rumor persisted that the insurance company would not pay off Fuller's $1 million life policy if he had taken his own life.

At best, however, the subsequent police investigation was sloppy. The death car was never dusted for fingerprints, and detectives at the scene inexplicably discarded the gas can in a nearby trash bin. In the years since Fuller's "suicide," several alternative theories have been advanced speculating on the actual cause of the rock 'n' roller's death. In one, Fuller is said to have been executed on the orders of Eddie Nash (see entry John C. Holmes), a jealous club owner with major drug and gangland connections, after he paid too much attention to the man's prostitute-girlfriend. In another scenario supported by the dead man's

mother, Lorraine, Jim Reese, a guitarist with the band (now deceased) is alleged to have killed Fuller out of professional jealousy motivated by the 75 percent royalty split enjoyed by the band's leader.

Further Reading

Dudick, J. Mark. "Was the Law Just Plain Wrong?" *Orange County Register*, October 13, 1996, sec. F, p. 21.

Gaye, Marvin (V)

With Sam Cooke (see entry) Marvin Gaye ranks among the greatest soul singers in the history of popular music. A protean talent, Gaye's personal life was marred by drug addiction, failed marriages, and a complicated relationship with his father ultimately ending in a tragedy of biblical proportions. Marvin Pentz Gay, Jr., was born on April 2, 1939, in Washington, D.C. His father, the Rev. Marvin Gay, Sr., was a minister in the House of God, an ultra-strict religious sect combining elements of Pentecostalism with orthodox Judaism, and his mother, Alberta, a cleaning woman. The second of four children, Gay (he later added the "e" to escape ridicule over the homosexual connotation of his surname) began singing in his father's church at age 3 quickly becoming a soloist in the choir and attracting a wide following with his beautiful tenor voice. Singing (later playing drums and piano) afforded Gaye his only release from a bizarre and harrowing domestic life lorded over by his deeply troubled father. An unyielding disciplinarian in accordance with a faith that demanded strict religious observance from Friday night to Sunday morning, the Reverend Gay insisted his children call him "Father" and never question his authority. Reared in an atmosphere forbidding movies and television, the children were terrified of Father who dispensed Old Testament-style punishment on their naked bodies with a leather belt. By the time Gaye was 12 there was not an inch of his body that had been spared welts and bruises from Father's near daily beatings. Although known as a ladies' man who engaged in numerous affairs, the Reverend's ambiguous sexuality caused comment in the community. Soft-spoken and effeminate, Father often wore wife Alberta's clothes favoring flamboyantly colored silk blouses, nylon stockings, and straight-haired wigs. He encouraged women parishioners to believe that by serving him they were serving God. Alberta, dedicated to her husband and the church's teachings, accepted her husband's eccentricities and provided the lion's share of financial support for the family by working as a cleaning woman. Resentful he was not the principal bread-winner in the family, the Reverend Gay abused his wife physically and verbally in front of their children.

Marvin, who both loved and feared his father, was eager to earn his respect and affection. He never did. From the outset, the Reverend Gay disliked Marvin and each of his son's accomplishments only seemed to underscore his own lack of talent and resultant failure. The Reverend sang, but Marvin was a truly gifted singer that people came to the church to see and hear. Resentment grew as Marvin aged and chafed under his father's church-inspired discipline. Mother Alberta often interceded on Marvin's behalf, but managed only to earn some of the beatings dished out to the son. Totally devoted to his mother, Marvin's relationship with Father became more complicated as he felt the need to confront and challenge the man he increasingly realized he could never please. Looked upon as "weird" by non-church goers at school, Marvin was painfully shy around girls although they were instantly attracted to his handsome features, respectful attitude, and more importantly, his incredible voice. As his repeated attempts to earn his father's love met with rebuffs, Marvin saw music as his only way out of the family nightmare. While at Cardozo High School in 1953, the teenager formed his first group, the D.C. Tones. By 1956, Gaye, unknown to his father, was cutting school to appear in matinee shows at the Howard Theatre where he rubbed shoulders with black performers like Jackie Wilson, the Dells, James Brown, and the Platters. Against his father's wishes, Gaye quit high school that summer a year from graduating and joined the Air Force reasoning the military would get him out from under the Reverend's roof and afford him an opportunity to sing. Instead of learning to pilot airplanes, Gaye spent most of his time performing menial duties, and was honorably discharged in June 1957 after Air Force brass judged him unable to submit to regimentation and authority. Gaye's one accomplishment in the military seems to have been losing his virginity to an overweight black hooker in Salinas, Kansas while stationed at nearby Schilling Air Force Base.

Deemed a failure by Father, Gaye wisely chose to stay with friends back home in D.C. rather than with his family while hustling to begin a musical career. With friends, he formed the doo-wop group the Marquees and soon became known locally to adoring female fans at area dances and school assemblies. Through Bo Diddley, the Marquees were introduced to the Okeh label, a division of Columbia Records in New York, and recorded the novelty tune "Wyatt Earp." Okeh offered the group a contract, but true to form Marvin Gay, Sr. refused to co-sign for his under-aged son, and threatened his wife if she attempted to do so. The issue was resolved when a co-member of the group co-signed for the young singer. The Marquees recorded several singles, all failures, forcing Gaye to support himself in Washington as a laborer and dishwasher. His career stalled, Gaye caught a break when the popular Chess Records recording group the Moonglows fronted by Harvey Fuqua arrived in D.C. on December 29, 1958, for a week-long stand at the Howard Theatre. Internal dissension within the group was signaling an end to the Moonglows when Fuqua replaced the old with the new, offering the Marquees the chance to become the new Moonglows. Relocating to Chicago in 1959, the 19-year-old singer with Harvey and the Moonglows recorded several singles with Chess, all of which flopped. Nonstop touring on the "chittlin' circuit" (a grueling series of one-nighters in towns with large black populations in segregated venues) re-exposed Gaye to the blatant racism he had endured in the military. During a 1961 tour of the Midwest, the group played Detroit where Fuqua, convinced Gaye's easygoing sexual allure and three-octave range could make him a standout solo performer, introduced him to Berry Gordy, Jr., president of Motown Records. Gordy's signing of Gaye to the label in 1961 began a tempestuous relationship that would produce some of the finest soul music ever recorded.

At first, however, the 20-year-old Gaye was just another fledgling wannabe artist in a recording stable that featured up and coming acts like Smokey Robinson and the Miracles, the Marvelettes, Martha and the Vandellas, and The Temptations. In the highly competitive world of Motown, artists submitted songs to a panel of reviewers whose ratings determined if, and when, they were ever made. Gaye began his association with the label as a $5 a session drummer with the Miracles, but his prospects dramatically improved after catching the eye of Anna Gordy, sister of Motown's owner. While some at the label cynically viewed Gaye's relationship with the 47-year-old Anna Gordy as the 20-year-old newcomer's way of circumventing the established pecking order at Motown, the pair, at least initially, were devoted to one another and married on January 8, 1961. Gaye's early singles failed and his dream of becoming the "black Frank Sinatra" placed him radically at odds with Berry Gordy's successful track record of producing a hybrid form of R&B targeted to white teenagers. The album, *The Soulful Moods of Marvin Gaye*, released in June 1961 immediately tanked. Gaye's first modest success came in July 1962 with the single "Stubborn Kind of Fellow" followed in December 1962 with "Hitch Hike" and in April 1963 with the Top Ten hit, "Pride and Joy." During this period, Gaye earned a paltry $60 a week as part of the Motown stable of stars bus tour featuring "Little" Stevie Wonder, the Marvelettes, the Supremes, and Mary Wells.

Still unsure of his position within the Motown label and constantly at odds with Berry Gordy's plans for his career, Gaye spent 1964 churning out singles like the now-classic "How Sweet It Is (To Be Loved by You)" and his first charting album, *Together*, a series of duets with Mary Wells. 1965 was even more productive with Gaye reaching Number 8 with singles "I'll Be Dog-Gone" and "Ain't That Peculiar." In December 1966, Gaye teamed with Kim Weston for the Top Twenty hit, "It Takes Two." That same month, Motown paired Gaye with Tammi Terrell, a 20-year-old former member of the James Brown revue, and the chemistry was instantaneous. Together, they recorded a string of classic hits including "Ain't No Mountain High Enough" (April 1967), "Your Precious Love" (August 1967), "If I Could Build My Whole World Around You" (November 1967), "Ain't Nothing Like the Real Thing" (March 1968), and "You're All I Need to Get By" (July 1968). The beginning of the end, however, occurred on October 14, 1967, when Terrell collapsed into Gaye's arms onstage at a Homecoming concert at Hampton Sydney College in Farmville, Virginia. Diagnosed with a brain tumor, Terrell endured multiple career ending operations prior to dying at the age of 24 on March 16, 1970. His close friend and musical collaborator's long illness and death profoundly affected Gaye, who now became more interested in making serious music that commented on the country's social problems like racism, the Vietnam War, and environmental pollution. Motown, leery of alienating its core audience of white teens, continued to have Gaye record "safe" records with a real chance of mass appeal. The unhappy artist complied, producing the chart topping hit "I Heard It Through the Grapevine" (October 1968), "Too Busy Thinking About My Baby" (April 1969), and "That's the Way Love Is" (August 1969).

Gaye's artistic struggles with Motown over the direction of his music no doubt added to the problems in his personal life. By 1967, Gaye was supplementing his daily pot habit with heavy cocaine use. Despite the arrival of a child in November 1965, his marriage to Anna Gordy had been in trouble for several years with each engaging in the occasional affair. A religious man, Gaye reportedly assuaged his guilt over adultery by sometimes opting to watch female prostitutes perform with one another. As his success grew on the back of hit singles, Gaye's forced touring exacerbated his lifelong stage fright. Soon, drug use and performance anxiety combined to make him a notorious "no show" at several concerts. Promoters, unsure if he was going to make the gigs, began not to book him. Looming over all, the Internal Revenue Service was dogging the entertainer for unpaid back taxes. Questioning the validity of his Motown output in light of a society plagued with racism and an ongoing war, and well on his way to drug addiction, Gaye, 30, went into virtual seclusion in 1970 and performed publicly only twice until January 1974.

Inspired by the Vietnam horror stories related by his brother, Frankie, and his own experience of racism, Gaye began work on a concept album in mid–1970 that would not only address social problems (drug abuse, ecology), but also express the religiosity that was a major component of his psyche. Recorded in five days in June–July 1970, the single "What's Going On" marked a radical departure from what Gaye viewed as the musical irrelevancy of the current Motown product. Self-produced by the singer, the heavily jazz–influenced song was greeted with confusion by Motown which felt the track was too overtly political and the company was in no hurry to release it. Gaye, refusing to record any other music until it was, spent the next six months reading self-help literature, New-Age philosophy, working out, and doing drugs. Berry Gordy relented and "What's Going On" was released in January 1971 peaking at Number 2 on the *Billboard* chart. A hit single demanded a supporting album. Gaye launched into a period of unprecedented artistic control writing and producing every track on the album, *What's Going On*. Released in May 1971, the landmark LP was a critical and commercial smash rising to the top of the R&B chart and to Number 6 on the *Billboard* pop chart. Though snubbed at the Grammys, Gaye was presented an Image Award by the National Association for the Advancement of Colored People for being "the nation's most significant entertainer" and voted by *Cashbox* as its Male Vocalist of the Year. The entertainer changed direction in 1972 and produced a primarily instrumental soundtrack for *Trouble Man*, a 20th Century–Fox blaxploitation thriller starring Robert Hooks. Of note, on May 1, 1972 the city of Washington, D.C. honored its native son with a "Marvin Gaye Day." The singer performed "What's Going On" at his old high school, was feted at a V.I.P. reception, and presented the key to the city by Mayor Walter Washington. Later that evening, Gaye performed before an adoring soldout crowd at the Kennedy Center which included his parents. Gaye remarked at the time, "At least on this one day I felt like I made Father proud."

The ongoing multi-year disintegration of the Gaye-Anna Gordy marriage while accelerated by the success of *What's Going On* was irreparably shattered by the events inspiring the content and the recording of Marvin's next single and album, *Let's Get It On*. If *What's Going On* delved deeply into the religious side of the artist, *Let's Get It On* was Gaye's sexual manifesto. While in the studio recording the album, the 34-year-old singer became deeply infatuated with Janis Hunter, a barely 17-year-old friend of one of Gaye's musical collaborators. The single topped the U.S. and U.K. charts, but by the time the hit album was released in August 1973, Hunter had dropped out of high school and was living with Gaye. The couple had a child in September 1974 and another in November 1975. Anna Gaye formally filed for divorce on March 25, 1975, demanding $11,000 a month in support for herself and son, Marvin, and other payments totaling roughly $35,000. Gaye, whose crippling stage fright had prevented him from touring for several years, was nearly broke and owed the IRS $165,000. After the release of another frankly sexual album, *I Want You*, in March 1976 failed to brighten his financial picture, Gaye agreed to a concert tour of the U.S. and Europe. Instead of paying off the tax man and Anna, the singer spent most of his payout on drugs, cars, and the purchase of a house for his parents in the middle-class black Crenshaw district of Los Angeles. Humiliated by Gaye's re-

lationship with Hunter, Anna continued to apply legal pressure periodically dragging him into court. Ultimately, a unique settlement was devised to payoff the ballooning $600,000 settlement he owed her. Along with other considerations, Gaye agreed to give his soon to be ex-wife of 12 years the profits of his next album appropriately titled, *Here, My Dear*. As an aural document of the painful dissolution of a marriage (Anna Gordy briefly considered filing suit for invasion of privacy), the poorly selling LP stands as a unique musical offering. The divorce was finalized in March 1977.

Marvin Gaye married Janis Hunter in October 1977, but the relationship was already irreparably damaged. Years of living with the singer had turned her into a junkie, and to fuel her husband's sexual fantasies Janis had taken lovers like Rick James. When she moved in with singer Teddy Pendergrass, Gaye, still obsessed with her, drifted to Hawaii where he lived in a trailer and spent his time taking drugs. Compounding his problems with Janis, Gaye declared bankruptcy and agreed to a June 1980 European tour to help pay off a $2 million tax bill. Gaye's performances were erratic with the tour soon degenerating into an orgy of sex and drugs. While in England, he formed an odd relationship with Eugenie Vis, a 24-year-old Dutch woman who served as little more than a live-in sex slave to the older man. Like Anna Gordy, Janis Hunter now sought to dissolve her marriage with the out of control singer. In the November 1982 divorce, Gaye lost custody of his children and was ordered to pay $4,500 a month in support.

The one ray of hope in the singer's spiraling life, however, had occurred earlier following a fortuitous meeting with Freddy Cousaert, a 42-year-old Belgian concert promoter and club owner, while on a tour of England in 1981. Gaye, reeling from drug addiction and battling with Motown over their unauthorized release of his album *In Our Lifetime*, was near rock bottom. Cousaert convinced the singer to live with him and his family in Ostend, a windswept Belgian seaport, where Gaye could regain his health and desire to once again make records. Profiting from the emotional stability afforded by this nurturing environment, the singer dramatically reduced his drug intake and began taking care of his health, embarking on a physical fitness regimen that included bicycling and running on the beach. While in Ostend, Gaye severed his relationship with Motown after

CBS purchased his contract for $1.5 million from Berry Gordy, Jr. Rejuvenated, Marvin went back in the studio and recorded the song, "Sexual Healing," suggested both by the singer's belief in the spiritually regenerative powers of sexuality and the stacks of sadomasochistic magazines littering his apartment. Released as a single in October 1982, "Sexual Healing" became the fastest rising soul single of the past five years and stayed atop the R&B chart for five months. The subsequent album, *Midnight Love*, released the next month peaked at Number 7 on the charts. On the strength of "Sexual Healing," Gaye triumphantly returned to America after a self-imposed exile of nearly three years performing a memorable rendition of "The Star Spangled Banner" at the 1983 NBA All-Star game. Less than a week later, the singer was honored with two Grammys for Best Male Vocal and Best Instrumental Performance in the R&B categories. Removed from his support system in Ostend, Belgium, Gaye lapsed back into freebasing cocaine and was consumed by the drug-induced fear that some unknown assassin was planning to attack his family. In early 1983, Gaye instructed his bodyguard to purchase an unregistered .38-caliber Smith & Wesson and give it to Father. The Reverend Father Gay kept it under his pillow at the $300,000 house on Gramercy Place in Los Angeles his son had given him.

Midnight Love had been out four months and CBS expected Gaye to tour in support of the album even though concert promoters (burned in the past by the singer's "no shows") were cautiously optimistic. The Midnight Love Tour commenced with two dates in San Diego on April 15–16, 1983 and lasted over four months with 60 shows in 40 cities. Backed by 25 musicians and assorted supporting vocalists, the ambitious shows lasted two hours and included costume changes. Badly timed (the album had been out too long and Michael Jackson's *Thriller* was at the top of the charts), the tour degenerated into a maelstrom of drugs, lurid sex, and paranoia. Death threats made against Gaye early in the tour convinced the "black Sinatra" that he was going to be shot onstage. Fueled by cocaine binges, Gaye instructed his bodyguards to carry a small arsenal of weapons including a submachine gun. To confuse would-be assassins, he had family members who looked like him accompany him through airports and other public places. He wore a bulletproof vest and upon leaving the stage had his security staff lead him by circuitous routes out of the building. The fundamental split in Gaye's psyche between the religious and the sexual became even more pronounced as his drug use escalated out of control. Hookers were kept in one room while in another nearby he would have a minister on call. Throughout the tour, Gaye yo-yoed between the two extremes. By tour's end in August 1983, Gaye had taken to stripping down to leopard skinned bikini briefs at the conclusion of "Sexual Healing." The tour, a dismal financial failure that often played to half-filled halls, left the 44-year-old singer depressed, broke, and hopelessly addicted to cocaine.

More than $300,000 behind in back alimony to ex-wives and terrified he would murdered, Gaye retreated to his parents' home on Gramercy Park he had purchased for them 11 years earlier. Father Gay, 70, recently returned from months of preaching in Washington, D.C., had sold the family home there, but refused to share any of the proceeds with his 71-year-old wife, Alberta. Long simmering tensions between father and son were daily intensified within the emotional pressure cooker of the house as both men battled crippling addictions — Marvin with drugs, Father with alcohol. Keeping them apart was Alberta, a woman suffering a debilitating kidney ailment that kept her shuffling back and forth from the house in the Crenshaw district to the Cedars-Sinai Medical Center. Drug sick and suffering from uncontrolled paranoia, Gaye spent his days in his upstairs bedroom. Physically symbolic of the woman's place in the dysfunctional family, Alberta's bedroom was situated between that of her son and Father's. A virtual prisoner in his own room, the singer sat in bed with his back to the wall to prevent an unexpected attack. Down the hall, Father holed up in his room drinking vodka and nursing a festering resentment that his famous son, not he, was now the principal breadwinner in the family. Outside, drug dealers, hangers-on, and women tried to get at Marvin Gaye. The singer attempted to work on a new album as his family did their best to keep the drugs away, but it was an impossible situation. Gaye refused professional help and continued to experience wild mood swings as he snorted and smoked huge quantities of cocaine. The man whose faith prohibited suicide talked openly of taking his own life and once had to have a gun wrested from the side of his head. On another occasion, he threw himself out of a car going 60 miles an hour, but suffered only superficial injuries. Casting a pall over all, the looming presence of the elder Gay and his son's resentment fed by memories of daily beatings received as a youth under his Father's roof. As tensions mounted within the family and verbal clashes between Marvin and Father increased, the preacher repeated the threat he had made since his son was a child, "If he touches me, I'll kill him."

Shortly before noon on Sunday morning, April 1, 1984, one day before Marvin Gaye's 45th birthday, Father Gay made good his threat. Gaye and Alberta were upstairs quietly talking in Marvin's room when Father, downstairs, angrily shouted about some insurance documents he could not locate. Father continued to scream at his wife and Gaye shouted to the man to come upstairs where they could talk to him. The 70-year-old man entered Marvin's room, shouted again at his wife, prompting Gaye to order him out of the room. When Father refused, Marvin shoved his father into the hallway and began punching and kicking the elderly man. Gaye returned to his room to discuss the incident with his mother. A few moments later, Father returned to Gaye's room, walked up to his son seated on the bed, leveled the .38-caliber pistol his son had purchased for him, and fired a bullet from a range of 4" to 6" into the singer's heart. As Marvin slumped to the floor, his mother looking on in horror, Father approached the dying man and pumped a bullet into his son's left shoulder. Alberta begged the man not to kill her as well, but Father Gay was done. He calmly walked down the stairs, sat on the front porch, tossed the Smith & Wesson in the yard, and waited for the police to arrive. Speculation on whether the drug addicted and financially ruined entertainer orchestrated his own death by knowingly striking a man who repeatedly threatened to kill him should he ever do so was ultimately beside the point. At 1:01 P.M., just hours before his 45th birthday, Marvin Pentz Gaye, Jr., was pronounced dead on arrival at the California Hospital and Medical Center. The "black Sinatra" died owing the IRS more than $1 million, the State of California $600,000, and the ex-wives more than $300,000 in back alimony.

Marvin Gaye, outfitted in the military style uniform he had worn onstage during *The Midnight Love Tour*, was remembered at a service conducted at the Hall of Liberty Chapel in Forest Lawn Memorial Park–Hollywood on April 5, 1984. Prior to the service, some 10,000 fans, many waiting in line for several hours, had filed past the coffin. The service was attended by 500 mourners including his family, ex-wives and children, Smokey Robinson, Stevie Wonder, and Berry Gordy, Jr. Comedian-social activist Dick Gregory performed the eulogy and asked the mourners to forgive Father Gay, housed in the L.A. County Men's Jail on a murder charge. After the service, Gaye was cremated and his ashes taken aboard a yacht and scattered in the Pacific Ocean. The Reverend Gay pleaded not guilty and in an interview with a local newspaper a week after the killing admitted to the reporter he had fired the weapon in self-defense thinking the gun was only loaded with pellets. A psychiatric examination of the elderly man led to the discovery of a large tumor on his pituitary gland, a possible mitigating factor in the murder. The tumor was surgically removed on May 17, 1984. Father Gay was judged competent to stand trial, but as the result of a plea bargain which took into account several variables (his advanced age and medical condition as well as visible signs of bruises caused by Marvin's attack) the prosecution's initial charge of first-degree manslaughter was reduced to voluntary manslaughter. The Reverend Gay subsequently pleaded no contest, and on November 2, 1984, was sentenced to a 6 year suspended sentence and placed on 5 years probation. As part of the sentence, Father was prohibited from drinking alcohol or owning any type of deadly weapon and ordered to continue psychiatric counseling. Alberta Gay, the long suffering wife and mother, filed for divorce ending their 49 year marriage. She died of cancer in 1987. Following the 5 year probation period spent at the Inglewood Retirement Home, the Reverend Gay moved into a home in Long Beach, California where he lived until his death at 84 on October 17, 1998. Marvin Gaye was enshrined into the Rock and Roll Hall of Fame in 1987, and in February 1986 posthumously honored with the Lifetime Achievement Award from the National Academy of Recording Arts and Sciences at the 38th annual Grammy Awards. On February 27, 2001, the 30th anniversary of its original release, Gaye's landmark album, *What's Going On*, was issued as a two-disc edition including alternate takes and a memorable 1972 live performance. In 2008, it was announced that Jesse L. Martin, "Detective Ed Green" on the television series *Law & Order*, had signed to portray Gaye in a biopic tentatively titled *Sexual Healing* loosely based on Steve Turner's 1998 biography, *Trouble Man*.

Further Reading

Cahill, Tim. "The Spirit, the Flesh and Marvin Gaye," *Rolling Stone*, 158 (April 11, 1974):40–44.
Dyson, Michael Eric. *Mercy, Mercy Me: The Art, Loves, and Demons of Marvin Gaye.* New York: Basic Civitas, 2004.
Gaye, Frankie, and Fred E. Basteen. *Marvin Gaye, My Brother.* San Francisco: Backbeat, 2003.
Ritz, David. *Divided Soul: The Life of Marvin Gaye.* New York: McGraw-Hill, 1985.
Turner, Steve. *Trouble Man: The Life and Death of Marvin Gaye.* London: M. Joseph, 1998.

Gelman, Eric (V)

An aspiring actor who left Florida for Los Angeles, Gelman appeared as a paparazzo in two episodes of the Tony Shalhoub USA Network television series, *Monk*, in 2004–2005. While waiting for other acting gigs, the 32-year-old worked as a waiter in the Marmalade Café in the city's Fairfax District. Around 10:00 P.M. on April 17, 2005, Gelman completed his shift and was walking to his car in the 7900 block of West First Street when he was accosted by a person witnesses described as a 35 to 40-year-old bearded black man approximately 6' tall and weighing 180 pounds. In what appeared an attempted robbery, the assailant stabbed the actor multiple times and fled leaving a dollar bill and a 16-inch knife at the scene. Responding to a 911 call, paramedics rushed Gelman to Cedars-Sinai Medical Center where he was pronounced dead.

Although police papered the apartment-dense area with fliers following the attack it still took over two hundred tips before an arrest was finally made at Pan Pacific Park in late December 2005. Eyewitnesses identified Kim McMurray, a 43-year-old transient with a criminal record dating back to 1983 for grand theft and drug charges, as the man they saw stabbing Gelman a half-block from The Grove shopping center. McMurray's first trial for murder in March 2007 ended in a mistrial with the jury deadlocked 11–1 in favor of convicting the homeless defendant. After yet another mistrial, McMurray was finally found guilty of second-degree murder in September 2007 and, still maintaining his innocence, was sentenced to 20 years to life. Gelman's parents established a scholarship fund in their son's honor at Baltimore's Goucher College from which he graduated in 1995.

Further Reading

"Transient Charged in Stabbing Death of Aspiring Actor." City News Service, December 29, 2005.

Glahn, Rebecca (V)

The 24-year-old disc jockey (known variously as "Rebecca Fox" and "Madison") had been the daytime personality on Memphis radio station Q107.5, WHBQ-FM for six months when co-workers on Monday, April 12, 2004, became concerned when she missed her shift. Friends visited the deejay's residence at the Gayoso House at 103 South Front Street in downtown Memphis to discover Glahn's body in her apartment on the building's fourth-floor, a victim of rape and manual strangulation. Residents informed authorities that on the night of Saturday, April 10, a man slipped past security cameras and randomly knocked on several doors on the fourth-floor of the apartment house. Glahn apparently opened the door to the knock allowing the killer to force himself past her into the apartment. Less than twelve hours after the rape-homicide Memphis police arrested three individuals when items stolen from the deejay's apartment were traced back to them. Stanley Andrews, 23, was charged with first-degree murder in the perpetration of a rape while Lontrell Williams, 27, and Marquita Thomas, 19, were charged with forgery and as accessories after the fact to murder. Andrews, arrested in 2003 for the aggravated assault of his girlfriend, received a suspended three year sentence after pleading guilty to the attack. Of more interest to police, however, was the contention by Andrews that he had once lived in the same apartment as Glahn before she moved from Jackson, Mississippi, to Memphis five months prior to their deadly meeting. Andrews initially told authorities that Glahn was an acquaintance with whom he had shared sex and drugs on the night of the incident. He choked the woman in self-defense after they got into a "tussle," but did not kill her. Confronted with additional police evidence, Andrews admitted that he did not know Glahn, but did force his way into her apartment and raped and strangled her when she would not be quiet. He could not be certain if she was still alive when he left with her DVD player, credit cards, and other property. Faced with a death penalty trial in September 2006, Andrews cut a deal with prosecutors in which he pled guilty to first-degree murder and aggravated rape in exchange for a sentence of life imprisonment plus 20 years. At press time for this book, Lontrelle Williams and Marquita Thomas remain out on bail awaiting trial as accessories after the fact.

Further Reading

"Memphis Radio Personality Found Slain in Apartment." Associated Press state and local wire, April 14, 2004.

Gobert, Dedrick (V)

An aspiring actor, Gobert, 22, appeared in small roles in three films directed by his friend John Singleton: *Boyz N the Hood* (1991), *Poetic Justice* (1993; starring fellow-murder victim Tupac Shakur), and *Higher Learning* (1995). In the early morning of November 19, 1994, Gobert was among several participants and spectators at an illegal drag race on Etiwanda Avenue in Loma Linda, California. Violence erupted after an intoxicated and angry Gobert looked for a man he felt had cut him off in an earlier race among a group of people congregated in the parking lot of a nearby pizza parlor. Gobert and his friend, Ignacio Hernandez, 19, were beaten and fatally shot. Hernandez's 16-year-old girlfriend, Jennifer Hyon, was shot in the throat attempting to help the men. The teenager survived, but was permanently paralyzed. Authorities, acting upon a tip from an informant, located the getaway car spotted at the scene of the shooting and arrested its driver, 22-year-old Sonny Enraca, without incident at his residence in the La Sierra area of Riverside, California on December 12, 1994. Enraca, a member of the predominantly Filipino street gang Akrho Boyz Crazzy (known as ABC), confessed to the shootings in a videotaped police interrogation, but pled extenuating circumstances. According to Enraca, Gobert and Hernandez walked into a group of ABC gang members and then the actor tried to bluff his way out of danger by claiming an affiliation with the Crips, a Los Angeles–based black street gang. The men were allegedly beaten after Gobert made a disparaging remark about the Bloods, a rival black street gang to which the ABC was connected. Enraca maintained he shot the men because he thought Gobert had a gun. More difficult to explain, however, was the fact that both had been shot execution-style as they lay beaten into unconsciousness on the street, or, why Hyon, an unarmed teenager, had also been targeted. On May 5, 1999, a jury found Enraca guilty on two counts of first-degree murder and on one count of assault with a deadly weapon. Under the "special circumstances" proviso in California law the jury was limited in their sentencing options to either life without parole or execution. The convicted killer was subsequently sentenced to death. At his formal sentencing on November 19, 1994, Enraca told the mothers of the victims, "Your boys died like soldiers ... with respect." Hyon, sentenced to life in a wheelchair, told the gang member, "I do forgive you for all the pain you've caused me. I know I'll see you in heaven where we can be brother and sister, you and I."

Further Reading

Kataoka, Mike. "Killer Gets Death, and Forgiving Poem." *Press Enterprise*, July 24, 1999, sec. B, p. 5.

Gomez, Audrey (V)

The all-time leading scorer at Saint John Vianney High School in Holmdel, New Jersey, the 5'9" point guard graduated in 1991 after leading her team to the all-state Tournament of Champions title in her senior year. Heavily recruited, Gomez was awarded a full scholarship to Notre Dame, but transferred to the University of Southern California after her sophomore year. The high school standout was an occasional starter at USC during the 1994-1995 season before a knee injury following her junior year ended her dream of a WNBA career. In 2000, she appeared as a player in the film *Love & Basketball*. Around 6:00 A.M. on August 25, 2001, a park warden making rounds at the Murphy Park Ranch in Whittier noticed a Mazda 626 parked in a lot. Surprised to see it there seven hours later, he took a closer look and saw a body under a blanket in the backseat. Police found Gomez, 28, dead from two gunshot wounds to the chest. An L.A. County Sheriff's bloodhound led investigators from Gomez's car directly to the South Whittier home of Angela Marie Shepard, 37, some four miles away. Shepard was an LAPD patrol officer from August 1989 until her termination in December 1995 after she pleaded "no contest" to threatening to kill a female co-worker. Afterwards, she became the program director at the Girls and Boys Town facility for troubled youth in mid-city Los Angeles where Gomez had worked for 13 months as a dayshift supervisor. Shepard was arrested after her fingerprints were found on the door of Gomez's vehicle and two handguns and ammunition were retrieved from her house. Friends of the dead woman told investigators that Gomez complained that the older woman was "weird" and "obsessed" with her. Although initially maintaining her innocence, Shepard cut a deal on November 8, 2001 and pleaded "no contest" to second-degree murder in exchange for a sentence of 15 years to life. While the motive for the killing remained unclear, Shepard's attorney reported that the two were romantically involved. A heated argument between the pair in Shepard's South Whittier home in the

15100 block of Hornell Street on the evening of August 24 prompted the older woman to shoot the former basketball star, drive the dead woman's car to the park, and walk home. In January 2002, the Audrey Gomez Memorial Scholarship was established at Saint John Vianney High School by her former teammates, classmates, and their parents.

Further Reading

Werner, Erica. "Former USC Basketball Player Murdered; Boss Arrested." *Associated Press*, August 28, 2001.

Gómez, Javier Morales *see* Appendix 1

Gómez, Sergio *see* Appendix 1

Gonzalez, Israel Chappa (M-S)

Known as "Gargoyle" to friends and associates in the porn industry, Gonzalez, 28, worked variously as a set designer, editor, cameraman, and even performed onscreen sex under the names "Max DeNiro" and "Max Ren." Gonzalez joined Elegant Angel, a hard core video production company, in late 1996 after serving seven years as art director for porn director John T. Bone. During their association, Gonzalez shot and appeared in several amateur videos for the director. More recently, "Gargoyle" started Columns, Smoke, and Chains, a Glendale, California–based movie prop company outfitted from material he pulled from the dumpsters of legitimate film studios.

On May 27, 1997, Mischelle Bowen told her lover of eight years that she was ending their relationship. Gonzalez, already stressed out over a pending $10,000 tax bill, attacked Bowen with a taser gun, tied her up, stuffed a rag in her mouth to stifle her screams, and repeatedly slammed her head against the bathtub before leaving the scene. Acting on information supplied by the battered woman that Gonzalez often stayed in his loft office at the Elegant Angel warehouse located at 9801 Variel Avenue, just south of Lassen Street in Chatsworth, California, Glendale detectives Charles Lazzaretto, 30, and his partner Art Frank drove to the building. As Lazzaretto, a ten year veteran and father of two small children, entered the darkened warehouse filled with porn movie props, Gonzalez fired a fatal shot into the detective's head. Throughout the night and early morning, Los Angeles police and a SWAT team exchanged gunfire with Gonzalez while periodically lobbing teargas and flash grenades into the building. Two LAPD officers were wounded attempting to rescue their fallen comrade.

At 6:00 A.M., police entered the building during a lull in the gunfire and found the set designer dead from a gunshot wound. An autopsy determined that Gonzalez placed the muzzle of a semiautomatic handgun in his mouth and pulled the trigger. The act fulfilled "Gargoyle's" oft-stated desire to friends that he wanted to "go out in a blaze of glory." More than 1,000 friends, fellow officers, and Glendale citizens attended Lazzaretto's funeral and donated more than $170,000 to his family.

Further Reading

Ross, Gene. "Elegant Angel 'Employee' Dies in Police Gun Battle." *Adult Video News*, 13(7) (July 1997):28.

Gordon, Jim (M)

Most likely to be remembered as the co-writer (with guitarist Eric Clapton) of "Layla," the 1971 Derek and the Dominos hit, James Beck Gordon, the "only living metronome," was one of the finest rock drummers of the 1960s and 1970s. Taking up drums when he was eight, a teenaged Gordon was already making a name for himself in 1961 playing clubs with a fake ID in Hollywood and West Los Angeles in the band Frankie Knight and the Jesters. Gordon turned down a music scholarship to UCLA to focus on studio work and quickly caught the eye of the bass player with the Everly Brothers. Gordon toured Europe with the group in 1963–1964 returning to Los Angeles to establish himself as the town's most sought after session drummers. Over the next few years, the 6' 3" musician with the All-American good looks earned top wages working in the studio with Bobby Darrin, Gordon Lightfoot, Glen Campbell, and the Righteous Brothers. Seemingly happy and successful, Gordon had suffered since early childhood with what doctors later diagnosed as "acute paranoid schizophrenia." As a child, he was lonely, withdrawn, and often binged on food for comfort. More ominously, Gordon was continually plagued by audio hallucinations. A 1964 marriage to a dancer ended in 1969 shortly before he left for England on a summer tour with Delaney and Bonnie featuring guitarists Eric Clapton and ex–Beatle George Harrison. Gordon's association with the group ended in 1971 after he left to play with Joe Cocker on the British rocker's infamous Mad Dogs and Englishmen Tour, a series of dates legendary in the annals of rock and roll for its unfettered indulgence in alcohol, drugs, and sex. Gordon, who prior to the tour was known as a straight arrow, began abusing a laundry list of drugs including heroin, cocaine, acid, and mescaline. Despite his prodigious drug use, the drummer never appeared impaired and continued to impress everyone with his professionalism. While on tour, Gordon began a close relationship with singer Rita Coolidge which ended abruptly when he socked her in the eye without provocation. Gordon's violence toward women re-emerged in 1973 when, suffering under a delusion that "a magic triangle" appeared on the floor of his house, he punched his second wife out, leading to their divorce after only six months of marriage. At the conclusion of the tour, Gordon appeared on George Harrison's classic album, *All Things Must Pass*, prior to joining Eric Clapton's short-lived band, Derek and the Dominos, in 1971. The sessions that produced the achingly beautiful song "Layla," co-written by Clapton and Gordon, were also noteworthy for rampant heroin abuse. When the group broke up in 1972, Gordon briefly joined the group Traffic, and in 1973, the Souther-Hillman-Furay Band.

In Los Angeles, tales of Gordon's drug-addled behavior and violence against Coolidge were making the rounds. Still in high demand as a session drummer, Gordon temporarily swore off drugs replacing them with alcohol. Though later exchanging booze for speedballs (cocaine laced with heroin), Gordon continued to be the consummate professional, although friends began noticing a change in his personality. Always quiet and polite, the session drummer now spent his breaks in the studio standing alone in a corner muttering to himself. Gordon holed up for days in out-of-the-way hotels listening to the non-stop voices in his head (most often his mother's) tell him to eat only half his food. During a recording session for Johnny Rivers in 1977, Gordon accused a guitarist of mentally controlling his drum beat. As news spread that the drummer's behavior was becoming increasingly aberrant the session work dried up. Soon the competing voices in his head fused into one — his mother's. Former nurse Osa Marie Gordon was, by all accounts, a loving mother and nothing in her relationship with her son would warrant Gordon's hate-filled obsession with her. Over the next 6 years, Gordon checked himself into 16 mental hospitals always leaving prior to treatment under orders from his mother's voice. Over time the voice instructed Gordon on what

to wear, when and how much to eat, and where to work. The voice commanded the drummer to drink excessively and to destroy his equipment and gold records. If Gordon disobeyed, he felt intense pain in his jaw and shoulder. To still the voice, he drank even more. By 1980, the drug-addicted alcoholic was essentially unable to work as a professional musician. The co-writer of the rock classic "Layla" spent days alone sleeping, watching old movies on television, drinking, and obsessing on his mother's voice. Convinced she had murdered Paul Lynde and Karen Carpenter, Gordon moved from apartment to apartment stocking freezers with food against the coming Apocalypse. On October 22, 1982, Gordon checked himself into a hospital complaining he was "dying of hate." By July 1, 1983, Gordon was convinced the only way to still the voice in his head was by killing his mother. At 9:30 P.M. that night he called the woman's apartment to complain that "you're bugging me again" and threatened to kill her. The terrified woman immediately reported the death threat to the LAPD and was advised to leave her light on and wished luck. Two hours later, Gordon called and repeated the death threat. The next morning, Osa Gordon phoned the city attorney's office to initiate a restraining order, but frustrated by the process, gave up. In the meantime, her son had settled on a course of action to "silence" the voice.

On the afternoon of June 3, 1983, Gordon packed a hammer and an 8¼" butcher knife into a leather valise and drove from his condominium in Van Nuys to the North Hollywood triplex where his 72-year-old mother was living prior to relocating to Seattle in a few weeks. Discovering she was not at home, the drummer drove the five miles back to his apartment and waited. Shortly before 11:00 P.M. he returned and knocked on his mother's front door. When she opened it, Gordon struck the woman four times in the head with the hammer then, as she was slumped on the floor, stabbed her three times in the chest, leaving the weapon sticking dead center in her body. Afterwards, he went to a bar then home where he drank himself into insensibility with a fifth of vodka. The next morning police sent to the apartment to notify Gordon of his mother's murder found him crying, but coherent, face-down on the living room floor. He confessed, "I had no interest in killing her. I wanted to stay away from her. I had no choice. It was so matter-of-fact, like I was being guided like a zombie. She wanted me to kill her, and good riddance." On May 22, 1984, Gordon, 38, was found guilty of second-degree murder, and "sane" despite the testimony of five psychiatrists who diagnosed one of rock's most memorable drummers as an "acute paranoid schizophrenic." Sentenced to 15 years to life, Gordon appears unlikely to ever be released from prison. Of note, on February 4, 1993, Gordon was awarded a Grammy with co-writer Eric Clapton for "Layla," re-released in 1992 as part of the guitarist's *Unplugged* album. In Clapton's acceptance speech for his acoustic version of "Layla" he failed to mention that his writing partner was incarcerated in the California Men's Colony at San Luis Obispo.

Further Reading

Booe, Martin. "Bang the Drum Slowly: The Tragedy of Jim Gordon, Percussionist, Songwriter, Paranoid Schizophrenic, Murderer." *Washington Post*, July 3, 1994, sec. F, p. 1.
Des Barres, Pamela. *Rock Bottom: Dark Moments in Music Babylon.* New York: St. Martin's, 1996.
Rehfeld, Barry. "When the Voices Took Over," *Rolling Stone*, 449 (June 6, 1985):17–18, 20, 22, 64, 66, 68.

Gray, King David (V)

At noon on June 30, 1938, a pedestrian walking by a parked car outside the Hollywood post office at 1615 North Wilcox Avenue noticed a man slumped in the vehicle's front seat. The driver, dead from a single .32-caliber gunshot wound to the chest, was identified as studio cameraman, King D. Gray, active in films since 1915 when he shot *The College Orphan* for Universal Film Manufacturing Company. Born in Danville, Virginia, on March 9, 1886, Gray photographed over 50 films (*The Mark of Cain*, 1916; *The Scarlet Car*, 1917; *Forgive and Forget*, 1923) in a twenty year career. From 1932, he worked exclusively for Universal Pictures as either a camera operator (*The Invisible Man*, 1933) or as second cameraman (*The Black Cat*, 1934). When found, the 52-year-old married father of two was holding a letter in his right hand postmarked from New Castle, Pennsylvania bearing the salutation, "Dear Daddy." Police established the identity of the letter writer as Frances Bleakley, a 29-year-old University of Southern California student once employed in the art department of a Hollywood department store, but now living in Pennsylvania. During their four year relationship the cameraman passed himself off as unmarried and rented a secret post office box to hide the deception from his family. Although baffled police ultimately settled on the theory that Gray was shot during a robbery attempt no valuables were taken from the dead man or his car. The death weapon, a .32-caliber automatic, was retrieved a few days later from a vacant lot at Santa Monica Boulevard and El Centro Street eight blocks from the murder scene. Ex-convict Joseph L. Chester, considered a suspect in the Gray murder, committed suicide to avoid capture on an unrelated matter on July 20, 1938, following a high speed car chase with authorities in Ventura County.

Further Reading

"Hollywood Film Cameraman Found Slain in Automobile." *Los Angeles Times*, July 1, 1938, p. 1.

Griffin, Phillip Tyrone *see* Priceless Game

Gunter, Cornell (V)

One of the most critically acclaimed doo wop acts of the mid–1950s to early 1960s, the Coasters perfectly blended music with serio-comic lyrics (often penned by the producing team of Jerry Leiber and Mike Stoller) in a series of R&B hits like "Searchin'" (1957), "Yakety Yak" (1958), "Charlie Brown" (1959), "Along Came Jones" (1959), and their final Top 30 *Billboard* chart hit, "Little Egypt" (1961). Former Flairs singer Cornell Gunter joined the Coasters in 1957 and was the featured lead vocalist on many of their hits before exiting the group in 1961. Gunter, a year-round Las Vegas resident, toured in the late 1980s with a version of the Coasters known as Cornell Gunter and His Coasters to distinguish them from other incarnations of the group formed by past members. Gunter was scheduled to perform with his ensemble at the Lady Luck Hotel in Las Vegas when he became the second member of the legendary doo wop group to die violently in the vicinity of the gambling mecca. Nathaniel ("Buster") Wilson (see entry), a much later addition to the Coasters, was set to perform in Vegas when he was murdered, and his body dumped in the desert outside of Modesto, California, in April 1980.

At midday on February 26, 1990, Gunter, 52, was stopped at the intersection of Berg Street and Bourbon Way in a residential block of the city of North Las Vegas when initial eyewitnesses observed him apparently arguing with a thin black man standing on the driver's side of the car. The man fired through the windshield of the car and as he fled on foot into the surrounding desert tossed away his gray warm-up jacket. Gunter managed to drive his 1979 Chevrolet Camaro a block before crashing into a wall. The Coasters front man was found slumped over the steering wheel dead from two point-blank chest shots. In May 1990, North Las Vegas police arrested 19-year-old Kinnie Deon Poole and charged him with Gunter's murder based upon eyewitness testimony and physical evidence (minus the gun) found at the scene. According to the police theory of the crime, the teenager shot the pop singer during a failed robbery attempt. At trial in December 1990, Poole, a self-described "street hustler," told the court that he spent the days before the shooting drinking hard liquor and smoking rock cocaine with Gunter and another man, "Little" George Thomas. The trio went to the North Las Vegas neighborhood to score more cocaine when Gunter and Thomas began arguing. Gunter slammed on the brakes and pulled a pistol from beneath the seat. Poole: "I freaked. I ran. I know bullets ain't got no name on them." He turned to see Thomas firing several rounds inside the car. Witnesses backed up Poole's claim that he had asked several of them to use their phone to allegedly call for help. Also, the gray warm-up jacket found discarded near the crime scene did not appear to fit Poole when he tried it on in court. George Thomas testified that he was not even with Poole or Gunter on the morning of the shooting although he did admit to past drug usage with the men. After deliberating less than three hours, a jury acquitted Poole of murder on December 7, 1990. To date, no arrests have been made in the murder of Cornell Gunter. The Coasters were among the first inductees into the Rock and Roll Hall of Fame in 1987.

Further Reading

Bates, Warren. "Gunter Slaying Suspect Admits Partying with Singer." *Las Vegas Review-Journal*, December 7, 1990, sec. B, p. 6.

Hagnes, Helen (V)

On the morning of July 24, 1980, the nude and bound body of Helen Hagnes (birth name Mintiks), a 30-year-old Canadian-born free-lance violinist, was found at the bottom of a ventilating shaft in New York City's famed Metropolitan Opera. Hired for 11 days to accompany the visiting Berlin Ballet, the Juilliard graduate was last seen the previous day around 9:40 P.M. during an intermission prior to her performance in *Miss Julie*. When Hagnes failed to make her curtain call, employees searched the labyrinthine maze of backstage corridors beneath the 3,700 seat opera house before notifying police. Their search of the facility revealed evidence of a sexual assault conducted in a lower level stairwell. Investigators searching the sixth-floor roof of the Met discovered Hagnes' broken body around 8:30 A.M. on a steel ledge in an airshaft at the rear of the opera house. The musician had been stripped, possibly blindfolded, gagged, and her hands tied behind her with rope and rags matching those found in a crate on the roof. An autopsy determined that Hagnes was alive when hurled the sixty feet down into the fan pit. Death resulted from skull fractures and other injuries.

Dubbed by the press "The Phantom of the Opera Murder," the homicide investigation conducted by the NYPD was one of the largest in New York City history. A task force of fifty detectives systematically questioned five hundred Met employees and performers who were backstage on the night of the killing. The rope and the knot (a clove hitch) were typically used backstage by stagehands to secure scenery and provided authorities with a starting point for their investigation. Police photographed, printed, and had each stagehand fill out a detailed questionnaire charting their activities at the time of the murder. Suspicion fell on well-liked 21-year-old stagehand Craig Stephen Crimmins as inconsistencies in his questionnaire began to emerge when compared with those of his co-workers. "Crimmie" at first insisted that he did not miss any cues on the night of Hagnes' disappearance. However, when a search party composed of stagehands reported being unable to locate him during the second half of the show Crimmins changed his story and said he was passed out drunk backstage. He later convinced a fellow-stagehand to corroborate this alibi. Initially nervous and uncooperative when asked to supply prints, Crimmins finally did so and police quickly matched his palm print to a partial lifted from a pipe on the roof. Further inconsistencies in his story emerged during a grueling 16-hour interrogation session conducted on August 17, 1980. Though not held, the prime suspect's movements were closely monitored by authorities. Crimmins was picked up for questioning outside his apartment building on August 29, 1980, after his stagehand friend admitted lying to police in support of his alibi.

In a videotaped confession given later that day,

Crimmins admitted murdering Hagnes ostensibly to cover up an unsuccessful rape attempt. On the day of the murder, Crimmins drank two dozen beers, popped diet pills, and smoked marijuana. He encountered the violinist on a backstage elevator during the intermission and crudely propositioned her. Hagnes responded by slapping him across the face and saying something "snotty and loud." He threatened Hagnes with a hammer and forced her to undress in the lower levels of the building. After trying unsuccessfully for five minutes to rape her in a stairwell Crimmins admitted rubbing himself to orgasm on her body. He herded the violinist to the roof, tied her with rope, and was leaving the scene when she worked herself free. Recapturing her, Crimmins cut the woman's clothes off with his knife, threw them down the fan shaft, and bound and gagged her with rags found on the roof. The stagehand was again in the process of leaving when the sounds of her struggling caused him to panic. According to his statement, he "went back and kicked her off."

Crimmins' family and friends reacted with shock to the arrest of the popular young man described by those who knew him well as a "regular guy." Born in Manhattan in 1959, Crimmins did not walk until age three and was not toilet trained until five. Diagnosed with a learning disability, the young boy struggled in school and was still in the fifth grade although 13 years old. Crimmins was later admitted to a vocational high school, but dropped out before graduating. Through his father, a backstage worker at the Metropolitan Opera House, Crimmins landed a $20,000 a year union job as a stagehand. Engaged to a woman studying veterinary medicine, his future looked bright. The so-called "Phantom of the Opera," however, had alcohol and drug problems. Crimmins routinely filled the long hours between shows at the Met drinking in local bars, smoking dope, and popping diet pills. Still, few believed him capable of a sexually motivated murder and several coworkers and childhood friends pooled their money to post his $50,000 cash bond.

On April 27, 1981, opening arguments began in a Manhattan courtroom where Crimmins pleaded innocent to charges of second-degree murder and attempted rape. Prior to the start of the trial, the defense unsuccessfully sought to exclude Crimmins' videotaped confession as well as the "enhanced" testimony of a witness police had hypnotized. Under hypnosis a dancer in the Berlin Ballet identified Crimmins as the man she had last seen on the Met elevator with Hagnes prior to the musician's disappearance. The thrust of Crimmins' defense was an attack on police investigators who in their haste to get a quick arrest presented false evidence and "cut corners." The prosecution called 33 witnesses in support of a case made nearly airtight by the defendant's confession. After receiving instructions from the judge not to consider the uncorroborated rape charge, the jury received the case on June 3, 1981. The next day after deliberating nearly 12 hours, they found Crimmins guilty of the lesser charge of felony murder, i.e. the stagehand had killed Hagnes in the commission of another crime (sexual assault). While awaiting sentencing, Crimmins was held in the infirmary at Rikers Island where his only companion was Mark David Chapman, the murderer of former Beatle John Lennon (see entry). Neither "media murderer" liked the other. Crimmins derided Chapman as a "nut case" while the stagehand's chain smoking finally drove Chapman berserk and into a transfer to the Ossining Correctional Facility. On September 2, 1981, Crimmins received a sentence of 20 years to life. Appeals filed on behalf of Crimmins to the appellate division of the state supreme court (1984) and to the New York court of appeals (1985) were rejected. Since being first eligible for parole in 2001, the "Phantom of the Opera" has been turned down three times. Noting that Crimmins, 45, had used heroin in 2001, the parole commissioners flatly told the killer in 2004, "Releasing you to the community would make a mockery of the criminal justice system."

Further Reading

Black, David. *Murder at the Met*. Garden City, NY: Dial, 1984.
Fried, Joseph P. "Freedom Is Denied to the Opera House Killer." *The New York Times*, June 27, 2004, sec. N, p. 25.

Harger, (Solon) Bert (V)

As one-half of the ballroom dance team of Harger and Maye, the 39-year-old dancer appeared with great success before the crowned heads of Europe. Currently billed at New York City's Biltmore Hotel as "the dancing toast of the continent," the team previously performed at the St. Regis Room and the Cotillion Room of the Hotel Pierre. Harger was last seen on August 19, 1945 by his lover, Walter H. Dahl, Jr., a 30-year-old Pennsylvania Railroad freight representative, at the apartment they shared at 43 West 46th Street. Police suspected Dahl in the disappearance, but could make no headway in the case until a dismembered torso was found floating in the Hudson River off Rockaway Beach. Dahl examined the body part in the morgue and declared it not to be Harger's because it lacked an identifying birth mark. Immediately afterwards, he made a hasty trip to Philadelphia to post telegrams under Harger's name to himself and the man's dance partner, Charlotte Maye, informing both that he planned to leave the business. In late August 1945, Dahl notified police that he was in receipt of a letter from Harger with a Chicago postmark in which the dancer wrote that he was going to visit his brother in California. Police checked with Harger's brother who had heard nothing from the man. After Dahl moved from the apartment on West 43rd street, detectives scoured the rooms and found minute blood splotches on the bathroom floor. Taken into police custody on October 6, 1945, Dahl finally confessed to killing Harger with a hammer when the dancer attacked him with an ice pick during an argument. Afterward, Dahl dismembered his lover's body with a razor and butcher knife in the bathtub then dropped the packaged arms and legs off the Weehawken Ferry and the bundled torso off the Staten Island Ferry. On April 26, 1946, Dahl pleaded guilty to first-degree manslaughter and was sentenced to 20 years in prison. The lesser plea was accepted after the district attorney declared that it would be difficult to convict the killer on a charge of first-degree murder.

Further Reading

"Room-Mate Is Held in Dancer Slaying." *The New York Times*, October 7, 1945, p. 37.

Harrison, Danny (V)

Harrison left a career as a psychologist to enter the music business, first as a stagehand, and later as the tour manager for rock stars like Paul Simon, Billy Joel, Dan Fogelberg, Boz Scaggs, and the Eagles. In 1980, he managed Joel's Glass Houses Tour, and reached the pinnacle of his success as the driving force behind Paul Simon's 1981 Central Park concert attended by over 400,000 fans. Harrison also managed Simon's famous anti-apartheid Graceland Tour, but was fired in 1997 after the performer caught him stealing money. Most recently, he produced some episodes of the cooking show *Iron Chef* for the Food Network. The thrice married, twice divorced father-stepfather of five grown children was coming off a bad breakup

with a former girlfriend when he met Kathleen Connors, 37, in the summer of 2005. Connors boasted a rap sheet dating back to 2001 that included four arrests for prostitution (the most recent in May 2005) and worked sporadically for a man who ran a small escort service. Harrison met Connors through a friend and was never a client. In October 2005, he let the woman move into his sixth-floor Upper Eastside studio apartment at 530 East 89th Street less than a block from Gracie Mansion, home of the mayor of New York City.

According to Kathleen Connors' later police statement, she spent the morning of November 20, 2005, with Harrison in the apartment celebrating his 57th birthday by freebasing cocaine when they began to argue. Neighbors reported hearing 15 to 20 minutes of shouting, bodies slamming walls, and furniture being tossed about before someone finally called 911. A police officer arrived shortly after 1:00 P.M. and was met at the door by Connors with an assurance that "everything is fine." However, looking past her into the apartment the cop saw the bloody body of a man lying on a bed, a blood-smeared butcher knife on the sofa, and a scene reminiscent of an abattoir. The former tour manager was pronounced dead at New York University Medical Center. Connors, arrested and charged with second-degree murder and weapons possession, told authorities the argument began when Harrison complained about the messy apartment and began striking her in the head with his hand. She stabbed him twice in the chest in self-defense. The woman did sport fresh bruises on her back and head, but police found no drugs in the apartment. Connors plead guilty to a reduced charge of first-degree manslaughter and was sentenced to 23 years in prison in January 2008.

Further Reading

Italiano, Laura. "'Slay' Hooker a Bloody Liar: Cops." *New York Post*, November 22, 2005, p. 20.

Hartman, Brynn (M-S)

Born Vicki Omdahl in Thief River Falls, Minnesota, in 1959, the future wife of *Saturday Night Live* and *Newsradio* star Phil Hartman dreamed of leaving the small Midwestern town for a career in Hollywood. Dropping out of high school, she quickly married and divorced Doug Torfin, a local telephone operator, while carving out a modest modeling career in Minnesota. Omdahl, moving to Tinseltown in her 20s, changed her name numerous times (Vicki to Vicki Jo Brindon to Brynn) and developed a major cocaine and alcohol addiction that lasted through most of the 1970s. While an acting career proved elusive, a reportedly drug-free Omdahl was working as a swimsuit model for the Catalina Sportswear Company when she met Canadian-born television star Phil Hartman on a blind date in 1986. The couple married on November 27, 1987, and produced two children, Sean and Birgen. Hartman, a gifted impressionist and actor, was hitting his comedic stride and was cast in increasingly meaty roles in television (he would later be the voice of the washed up B-movie star turned pitchman, "Troy McClure," on *The Simpsons*) and movies (*Blind Date*, 1986; *Greedy*, 1994; *Jingle All the Way*, 1996; *Small Soldiers*, 1998). In 1994, he left *Saturday Night Live* and moved to Los Angeles with his family.

According to friends, Brynn was jealous of her husband's success and frustrated by her inability to have a career. During Hartman's *SNL* years the closest she came to appearing on the popular show was a brief shot of the back of her head in the opening credits. Brynn was the blonde sitting next to Hartman. In 1994, a bit part in Rob Reiner's flop film *North* failed to lead to any other acting assignments. She could not even convince her husband to get her a guest shot on his television series *Newsradio*. Struggling as an actress, Brynn (with Sheree Guitar) wrote the screenplay for the proposed film *Reckless Abandon*. The script was rejected by Showtime. Brynn's lack of self-esteem prompted her to undergo a series of cosmetic surgeries in a confused attempt to become the perfect "Hollywood wife." By spring 1997, however, the troubled woman was again doing cocaine and undergoing treatment in various drug rehabilitation centers. Her emotional insecurity fueled by substance addictions and jealousy over her husband's career led to frequent domestic quarrels. According to Hartman's ex-wife, Lisa Strain-Jarvis, Brynn routinely screamed at and slapped the actor during arguments. Hartman, the emotional polar opposite of his volatile wife, dealt with the situation by simply going to bed. This coping strategy failed in the early morning hours of May 28, 1998.

The previous evening, Brynn, 40, had drinks with a female friend at a restaurant in Encino, California, a block from her home. Shortly after 10:00 P.M. she visited an old friend, Ron Douglas, at his home in Studio City. Sometime during the night, Brynn used cocaine and consumed more alcohol on top of Zoloft, a powerful prescription antidepressant. Studies suggest Zoloft taken in concert with alcohol and drugs, can cause violent mania and blackouts. Around 1:00 A.M. Brynn returned to the Ponderosa, the $1.4 million home at 5065 Encino Boulevard named by Phil Hartman. Police theorize that she argued with Hartman while her children (son Sean, 9, and daughter Birgen, 6) slept in another part of the house. The 49-year-old actor, dressed in boxer shorts and a tee shirt, ended the confrontation by going to bed. Around 2:00 A.M. Brynn removed a .38-caliber pistol from a locked safe and pumped three shots into him as he slept. Leaving her sleeping children alone in the house, Brynn drove to Ron Douglas' home, confessed the murder, and fell asleep. Douglas, though initially disbelieving his friend's account, removed the pistol from her handbag. Shortly after 6:00 A.M. Brynn and Douglas drove back to the house on Encino Boulevard in separate cars. After confirming that Phil Hartman was dead, Douglas called 911 to report the murder.

By the time a police SWAT team entered the house 20 minutes later to remove the children, Brynn had barricaded herself in the bedroom containing her husband's body. Moments before shooting herself in the head, she called her sister with a message for her children — "Tell (them) that I love them more than anything and I always loved them, and Mommy doesn't know what happened, and she's just very sorry." After hearing the shot, police cautiously entered the bedroom to find Brynn, dressed in a two-piece pajama outfit, in bed next to Hartman. Lying face-up, her upper body was supported by pillows leaning against the headboard. The gun was still in her hand. Hartman, shot twice in the head and once in mid-torso, was found lying in a fetal position on his left side. A toxicology report verified that Brynn's body contained trace elements of cocaine and the antidepressant Zoloft, and registered a blood alcohol content of .12 percent. Under California state law a driver is considered to be under the influence with a blood alcohol level above .08 percent. In accordance with their wills, man and wife were cremated. The actor-comedian's ashes were scattered at Emerald Bay, Catalina Island. The custody of their children was given to Brynn's sister in Eau Claire, Wisconsin.

Further Reading

Fleming, Charles. "Death in the Valley." *TV Guide*, 46(29) (July 18, 1998):24–25, 33–37.

Harvey, Bryan (V)

Singer-guitarist Bryan Harvey and drummer Johnny Hott formed House of Freaks in their hometown of Richmond, Virginia, in 1986 thereby becoming one of the first blues and folk rock groups not to carry a bassist. Named from a blurb on an old circus poster, House of Freaks relocated to Los Angeles where they quickly signed with Rhino Records, and in 1987 released their first single, "Bottom of the Ocean." Two popular albums on Rhino followed (*Monkey on a Chain Gang*, 1988; *Tantilla*, 1989) with the group signing with major label Giant (a Warner Bros. affiliate) to release *Cakewalk* in 1991. The album tanked, Harvey and Hott put House of Freaks on hold, and joined the band Gutterball for a couple of years. *Invisible Jewel* (released as an EP in 1993 on indie label Brake Out) proved to be the final House of Freaks material with the band officially calling it quits in 1995. Tired of the grind of touring, Harvey returned to Richmond to occasionally play guitar with local group NrG Krysys and work in technology for the Henrico County school system.

Harvey, 49, and his 39-year-old wife Kathryn, well-known in the local business community as the owner of an offbeat toy and gift shop called the World of Mirth, lived with their two daughters, nine-year-old Stella and four-year-old preschooler, Ruby, in the middle-class neighborhood of Woodland Heights, a ten minute walk from downtown Richmond. On December 31, 2005, Harvey played a New Year's Eve show with NrG Krysys at the Doubletree Hotel near the Richmond International Airport. The next day, the Harveys invited friends to their home at 812 W. 31st Street for a New Year's Day chili party to begin at 2:00 P.M. Johnny Hott and his daughter arrived at the residence around 1:40 P.M. to help his friends set up the party. Entering the home through the unlocked front doors, Hott was immediately engulfed in smoke. After calling out for the family and checking that there was nothing burning on the stove, he ran from the house and yelled across the street to a neighbor to phone 911. Firefighters responded and found the bodies of Harvey, his wife, and their two children in the fire-damaged basement bound and gagged with duct tape, their throats cut, and beaten with a blunt, hammerlike object. A seasoned detective said the crime scene was the worst he had ever seen. Reconstructing the morning of the crime,

authorities spoke to a friend of the Harveys who dropped off their daughter Stella from a sleepover at 10:00 A.M. Stella went directly to the basement where the family usually congregated and as the friend and her daughter attempted to follow they were met at the top of the basement steps by a noticeably shaken Kathryn Harvey. Kathryn informed her friend that she felt unwell and made a circular motion with her finger to indicate that things were crazy at the moment. The friend left believing that she could get further details a few hours later at the chili party. Unknown to her, the killers were already in the basement holding the Harveys hostage.

While Richmond authorities were investigating the quadruple murder, they were confronted five days later on January 6, 2006, with a triple homicide in the city's Broad Rock neighborhood barely a mile from the Harvey residence. The concerned sister of 47-year-old Mary Baskerville-Tucker notified police after she was unable to contact her sibling. Authorities broke down the door of the home on East Broad Rock Road that Baskerville-Tucker shared with husband, Percyell Tucker, 55, and 21-year-old daughter, Ashley Baskerville. The place had been ransacked and in separate rooms the bodies of the family were found bound, gagged, and viciously stabbed. Acting on information supplied by the surviving sister, local authorities contacted Philadelphia, Pennsylvania, police. The next day, a SWAT team arrested Ray Joseph Dandridge and his uncle, Ricky Jovan Gray, both 28. The criminal association of Dandridge, nicknamed "The Terminator" by family and friends, and Gray began in October 1995 when the pair was part of a group who robbed five people at gunpoint in locations in Northern Virginia and the Georgetown section of Washington, D.C. Gray was released in 2002 after serving six years for robbery, and possession of firearms and cocaine. Dandridge did 10 years for the robberies and was released from the James River Correctional Center in October 2005. During his prison stint, "The Terminator" began an internet relationship in mid–2005 with a then 19-year-old Ashley Baskerville released that March after serving time in a nearby correctional center on a federal drug conviction. Upon release, Dandridge lost little time in hooking up with Ricky Gray. The results were tragically predictable. On November 4, 2005, the pair was visiting Gray's wife, Treva, in Washington, Pennsylvania, when a man who lived two blocks away from the woman's home was the victim of a home-invasion robbery. The next day, police discovered Treva Terrell Gray's beaten body covered by leaves in a wooded area of town. Death was ruled as due to asphyxiation.

Around 8:30 P.M. on New Year's Eve as Bryan Harvey was preparing for the NrG Krysys show at the Doubletree Hotel, Gray and Dandridge were in Arlington, Virginia, viciously stabbing a 25-year-old man with kitchen knives during a robbery. The assault was so frenzied pieces of the knives broke off and were recovered at the scene. Afterwards, Dandridge contacted his old internet "pen pal," Ashley Baskerville, who drove to Arlington to meet the criminals. According to the police reconstruction of the Harvey massacre, the trio spent New Year's morning cruising the streets of South Richmond looking for a house to rob when they settled on the Harvey place. Dandridge and Gray entered the unlocked home around 9:00 A.M. while Baskerville waited in the car as a lookout. Richmond authorities discovered the duo's work later that day after responding to the emergency call initiated by Johnny Hott. Two days later, Dandridge and Gray, with Baskerville's help, struck again, this time invading the home of Roy Mason, 75, and his wheelchair bound wife in Chesterfield County. The Masons escaped a beating, but were robbed of computer equipment and money from a recently cashed Social Security check. Then, on January 6, the pair ended their six day killing spree with the murder of accomplice Ashley Baskerville, ostensibly to "shut her up," as well as the young woman's mother and stepfather. The sister of Mary Baskerville-Tucker, aware of her niece's connection with ex-con Dandridge, supplied authorities with enough details to finally end the horror.

At trial in Richmond in August 2006, only Ricky Jovan Gray was charged with the murders of the Harvey family. Ray Joseph Dandridge was tried separately for the January 6 killings of the Tuckers and one-time accomplice Ashley Baskerville. Facing the death penalty if convicted of the quadruple murders, Gray entered a "not guilty" plea. Jurors, fighting back tears, and weeping courtroom observers listened as the district attorney described in graphic detail the final moments of the lives of the Harvey family. Gray hogtied Bryan and Kathryn Harvey with duct tape and their two daughters with electrical extension cords prior to stabbing them all then slitting their throats with an 8-inch kitchen knife. When they

failed to die, he bashed in each victim's head with a claw hammer. Before leaving with the proceeds of the robbery (a computer, a wedding ring, a basket of cookies), Gray used bottles of wine to start a fire to cover up the crime. A jury needed just 30 minutes to find the ex-con guilty of the heinous murders. In a separate penalty phase of the trial, Gray told of being sexually abused as a child, his lifelong drug addiction, and admitted that he was high on PCP at the time of the slaughter. Unmoved, the jury recommended the death penalty for the murders of the two children, and life sentences for the killing of their parents. The judge agreed, and Gray was sentenced to death. By comparison, admitted accomplice Ray Dandridge received a remarkably lenient sentence due largely to a psychological assessment that ruled he was borderline mentally retarded. As part of a plea agreement, Dandridge was allowed in September 2006 to plead guilty to the Tucker and Baskerville murders in exchange for a term of life imprisonment.

Further Reading

Deming, Mark. "House of Freaks." www.allmusic.com.
Noland, Jim. "Seven Days in January." *Richmond Times-Dispatch*, January 16, 2006, sec. A, p. 1.

Harvey, Gerald (M-S)

The vice-president of programming at the Z Channel, a popular Santa Monica, California–based pay television service, Harvey had been off work for a week complaining of health problems when on April 10, 1988, he fatally shot his wife before turning a handgun on himself in their Westwood home in the 200 block of South Thurston Avenue. Though Los Angeles police said the 39-year-old suffered from a "mental disorder," they could provide no motive for the murder-suicide. A public memorial service for the murdered woman, 39-year-old Frederica ("Deri") Rudulth, publisher of the *Westwood Insider*, was subsequently held at the Westwood Playhouse. The 2004 documentary, *Z Channel: A Magnificent Obsession*, chronicles the history of this important television service which was among the first to show uncut motion pictures in their proper aspect.

Further Reading

Boyer, Edward J. "TV Executive and Wife Die in Murder-Suicide." *Los Angeles Times*, April 11, 1988, pt. 1, p. 23.

Haskel, Presley (V)

The acknowledged father of the punk rock and New Wave music scene in Milwaukee, Wisconsin,

Haskel (real name Jerome Brish) formed the punk band The Haskels in the late 1970s naming it after the ingratiatingly duplicitous character "Eddie Haskell" in the television series *Leave It to Beaver*. In addition to rendering inspired covers of standard rock classics, The Haskels established their name as one of Milwaukee's premiere punk bands by playing their own compositions like "Liberace's Coming" and "Baby Let's French" in several clubs on the East Side. Influenced by musicians like Pete Townshend of the Who and Keith Richards of the Rolling Stones, the guitarist left The Haskels and formed other bands like In a Hot Coma, and his most recent, Wilderness of Pain. Haskel, characterized by friends and bandmates as a one-time energetically self-destructive alcoholic, had cleaned up his act in recent years and began speaking out against drinking and drugs. Prophetically, in describing to a friend about how well his live was going, Haskel added, "Watch, I'll probably die."

The 39-year-old guitarist was putting up posters advertising an upcoming Wilderness of Pain gig when he was found lying face-up and unconscious on a sidewalk in the 1600 block of N. Humboldt Avenue around 2:00 A.M. on Saturday, May 18, 1991. Haskel died later that day from head injuries at Froedtert Memorial Lutheran Hospital in Wauwatosa. While an initial autopsy failed to determine whether the musician's death was accidental or intentional, the Milwaukee County Medical Examiner later ruled it a homicide. Skull fractures and numerous bruises to the dead man's brain, face, and mouth pointed to a severe beating. On June 3, 1991, a 15-year-old boy was charged with second-degree reckless homicide in Haskel's death. According to the suspect's testimony, he encountered the guitarist on the street and punched him in the face after the man directed a racial slur at him. Haskel fell backwards from the blow and hit his head on the pavement. In July 1991, a circuit court found the youth guilty on a lesser charge of battery causing great bodily harm. Haskel was inducted into the Wisconsin Area Music Industry (WAMI) Hall of Fame in 1994.

Further Reading

Skalitzky, Lori. "Ex-Punker Rocker Dies as Dream Within Reach." *Milwaukee Sentinel*, May 20, 1991, p. 1.

Hassan, Muzzammil ("Mo") (M)

In the wake of 9/11, Hassan, a 44-year-old Pakistani businessman, and his third wife, Aasiya Zubair Hassan, 37, founded cable station Bridges TV in 2004 to counter the negative stereotypical images of Muslims as bomb throwing terrorists and religious fundamentalists. Located in the upscale village of Orchard Park, New York, the station developed news and opinion shows that were distributed by satellite to cable networks around the U.S. and Canada. As the first English language cable station targeted to the Muslim demographic, Bridges TV received numerous high profile endorsements from American Muslims like Muhammad Ali, but by 2007 was financially strain. "Mo" Hassan was actively seeking new investors from Saudi Arabia with capital of over $5 million while also battling with cable carriers for access to a larger audience and more potential revenue.

Outwardly, the Hassan marriage appeared to be a happy union between equals. After the events of 9/11, Hassan left a lucrative position at M&T Bank at his wife's urging to found Bridges TV. Aasiya, a university trained architect in Pakistan, passionately believed that a moderate Muslim message needed to be broadcast while her husband was seemingly more interested in the business aspects of the cable station. Unknown to all but a few close friends and police departments in Texas and Orchard Park, however, the Hassan marriage was a living nightmare for Aasiya. Fearful that exposure of her husband's controlling and violent behavior would destroy their business, the woman endured physical and psychological maltreatment for years. Over the course of two years she had called Orchard Park police more than a dozen times for violent domestic issues ranging from a black eye and split lip to sleep deprivation in which Hassan poured water on his wife when she appeared to being nodding off. In 2006, Aasiya confided to local police that the abuse had been going on for the last 6 years. A July 2007 visit to her husband's family in Flower Mound, Texas turned ugly when the couple quarreled and Hassan sat on his wife's chest and pinned down her arms and legs. Aasiya reported the incident to authorities who pressed her to file assault charges, but she left the state without contacting them. In Orchard Park, the cycle of violence was ongoing. From February 2006 through March 2007, the battered woman filed three separate orders of protection against Hassan, but always refused to sign the complaint that would have jailed her abuser. Finally, Aasiya could no longer endure her husband's mistreatment even if it jeopardized the business they had both sacrificed to make a reality.

After eight years of marriage, she filed for divorce and obtained a protection order on February 6, 2009 barring Hassan from their home on Big Tree Road. Discussions continued regarding custody arrangements for their children, ages 4 and 6, as well as for two older children, ages 17 and 18, from a previous marriage.

At 6:20 P.M. on February 12, 2009, six days after being legally barred from his home, Muzzammil Hassan walked into the headquarters of the Orchard Park Police Department and announced that his wife was dead at their television station on Thorn Avenue. Police entered Bridges Television to discover Aasiya's bloody body in a hallway off a row of offices. The woman's decapitated head was found near her body. An autopsy determined that Aasiya was stabbed multiple times with hunting knives which were also used to sever her head. Undetermined was whether she was alive or dead at the time of her decapitation. Hassan, who did not confess to murdering his unhappy wife, pleaded not guilty to a charge of second-degree murder. In the state of New York, first-degree murder is reserved for a range of special circumstances like torture or the killing of a police officer. The murder made a mockery of Aasiya's vision to present Muslims in a more moderate light in a post–9/11 world despite the efforts of Hassan's attorney to explain the horrific killing as a just another domestic tragedy, not a culturally motivated "honor killing" in which men, in some Islamic countries, feel justified in punishing their insubordinate women. At the time of this book's publication, "Mo" Hassan was being held in jail without bond awaiting trial.

Further Reading

Tan, Sandra. "A History of Abuse: Aasiya Hassan Endured Years of Violence and Controlling Behavior from Her Husband While Keeping Up the Façade of a Stable Marriage." *Buffalo News*, February 22, 2009, sec. A, p. 1.

Hedderel, Rivet (V)

"I've got to get out of New Orleans ... I'm going to be murdered here," the 61-year-old actor told a friend in the summer of 1996 weeks before planning to retire and relocate to Natchez, Mississippi where he owned an historic home. As "Robert Lans" Hedderel appeared in the original 1960s off–Broadway production of *The Fantasticks* and sang and danced in the Broadway shows *South Pacific* and *Show Boat*. Equally well-known as a top hairdresser, he created styles for stars Elizabeth Taylor, Alice Faye, and Zsa Zsa Gabor. In New Orleans, the owner of Rivet's Coiffures was a much loved figure who appeared in plays at the Le Petit Theatre du Vieux Carré, Gallery Circle, and the Old Beverly Dinner Playhouse. In Natchez, he reigned as king of the city's Mardi Gras in 1989.

Around 9:00 A.M. on August 19, 1996, a neighbor walking his dog by Hedderel's Creole cottage at 1438 N. Derbigny Street in the city's fashionable Esplanade Ridge section noticed blood puddled on the stoop and smeared on an entranceway. Police found Hedderel in the house dead from a savage beating and multiple knife wounds. Missing was the man's 1994 Plymouth Avenger. Two days later authorities caught a break after the vehicle was found on a street in Chalmette, Louisiana. Mark Jenkins, a 22-year-old ex-con with a fifth-grade education who served time in 1991 for robbing and beating a pizza delivery man, was identified as a suspect in the killing after he used Hedderel's credit card to purchase gas and jewelry. The card was confiscated at a department store in Chalmette, but Jenkins quickly exited the scene before police arrived. Armed with a search warrant, officers found several items of blood-spattered clothing in the suspect's Chalmette apartment. Jenkins was arrested in Jefferson Parish on August 22, 1996, three days after Hedderel's body was found.

At his trial for first-degree murder in January 1998, Jenkins did not take the stand, but the jury heard a tape of an hour-long statement he made to police at the time of his arrest. Jenkins said that he was walking in the French Quarter when Hedderel approached and offered him $100 "just to talk." At the house on Derbigny Street, the actor added $200 to the offer just "to cuddle." Jenkins agreed as long as there would be no sexual contact. A struggle ensued, according to Jenkins, when Hedderel sexually attacked him. The younger man cut his own hand when he grabbed the knife from Hedderel. Jenkins tried to stab Hedderel in the shoulder, but missing slashed the actor's face, and began punching him. Jenkins fled the scene, but later returned to get his clothes. He told police he was forced to defend himself again when Hedderel started running at him and yelling. "I didn't know the guy was dead. I didn't mean to hurt him like that. I just wanted to hurt him so he'd get off me." Prosecutors discounted Jenkin's portrayal of the actor as an intoxicated sexual predator. Not only had Jenkins told several different versions of the deadly encounter since his arrest, bloody marks on the kitchen floor left by Hedderel were strong evidence that he was trying to claw his way to safety, not attack. Jenkins' subsequent use of the dead man's credit cards pointed to robbery as the motive for the murder. On January 16, 1998, Jenkins was found guilty of first-degree murder and sentenced to life imprisonment.

Further Reading

Coyle, Pamela. "Hairstylist's Killer Gets Life Term; Victim Was Stabbed 14 Times." *New Orleans Times-Picayune*, January 17, 1998, sec. B, p. 1.

Hicks, Andre *see* Mac Dre

Hill, Allan (V)

Weeks shy of graduating from Boston's prestigious New England Conservatory of Music, the talented clarinetist had already been offered a position with the St. Louis Woodwind Quintet, a group affiliated with the St. Louis Symphony. On the evening of May 6, 1993, the 21-year-old musician was walking from his apartment in the South End to redeem a box of bottles when he was accosted by two men, stabbed in the chest and belly, and left to die in Sparrow Park. Minutes before the attack, the two criminals had tried to rob Peter Wattles, but he managed to escape. Hill was rushed to Boston Medical Center where surgeons attempted to stitch together severed arteries and veins. Unsuccessful, the musician died two weeks later. Nearly six years passed before half-brothers Herdius Evans, 23, and James Ware, 25, were arrested for Hill's murder and the assault on Wattles. Following a three-week trial in which the defense accused police of planting evidence, the pair was found guilty of first-degree murder and assault on October 23, 1998. Both men were sentenced to mandatory life terms for murder and armed robbery, plus an additional 18 to 20 years for trying to rob Wattles.

Further Reading

Estes, Andrea. "Musician's Accused Killers Go on Trial." *Boston Herald*, September 29, 1998, p. 7.

Hinkley, Ineka Margaret (V)

The discovery of the young rock musician's decomposed body in the Bongil Bongil State Forest 16 kilometers south of Coffs Harbour, New South Wales, Australia, on November 5, 1996, was central in fueling official speculation that a serial killer was active in the area. Hinkley, a 20-year-old bass guitarist-drummer-singer with rock bands like Proteus and Sour Puss, unexpectedly left her home in the Melbourne suburb of Eltham on October 25 without telling her parents where she was going. According to her father, she loved to hitch-hike and often smoked marijuana while doing so. The rock musician's semi-nude body was found by a Road Traffic Authority worker lying face-up in the bush some fifty yards from a Pacific Highway rest area. Naked from the waist down, Hinkley was wearing a purple mohair jumper and matching shoes. Her purple tights were found nearby, and the contents of her pink canvass backpack were strewn about the area. An autopsy determined that Hinkley had been strangled and possibly dead for up to nine days. Information as to a possible sexual assault was not released, but given the position of the body it was highly likely. Authorities began to suspect a serial killer was at large after the body of 16-year-old Lee Ellen Stace was found on October 17, 1997, buried in a grave in the bush at the Yuraygir National Park near the northern coastal town of Yamba. Stace was last seen alive six weeks earlier hitching a ride after work on her way home to Broomshead. On January 8, 1999, Lois Roberts, twin sister of Aboriginal actor Rhoda Roberts, was also found buried in a shallow grave this time outside Nimbin, N.S.W., in the Whian Whian State Forest. Roberts, a mother of two, disappeared six months earlier after accepting a ride from a stranger. Public fears that young women were being stalked in the Coffs Harbour area were further compounded after Rose Howell, 18, disappeared from Bellingen on April 11, 2003. Like the others before her, Howell was last seen accepting a car ride from a stranger. Three months later, 39-year-old Coffs Harbour school teacher Janine Whitty disappeared while taking a stroll around Coffs Creek. Public pressure over the murders and disappearances finally resulted in a coronial inquest in the Hinkley killing in May 2004 ... eight years after the fact. Coroner Peter Rheinberger discounted a woman's claim that her lover at the time, Murray Cavanagh, confessed during a fight with her in January 1997 that he had killed Hinkley. Official conclusion — insufficient evidence to charge anyone in the Hinkley murder. The string of killings and disappearances around Coffs Harbour remain unsolved as of this writing.

Further Reading

Adams, David. "Autopsy Finds Eltham Woman Was Strangled." *The Age*, November 7, 1996, p. 3.

Holmes, John C. (M-acquitted)

Famous, or infamous, for the size of his erect penis (11" to 15" according to conflicting sources), Holmes became the first recognizable male porn star based largely on the strength of his signature character "Johnny Wadd," a private investigator. Holmes served as the basis for Mark Wahlberg's character "Dirk Diggler" in director Paul Thomas Anderson's 1997 film *Boogie Nights*. The hard-core sex career of porn's most prolific stud extended two decades and it is estimated that he appeared in more than 2,200 films including 8mm loops and features. While most of the star's work was male-female, Holmes did some gay loops and performed homosexual sex in *The Private Pleasures of John Holmes* (1983). Like most performers in the porn industry, Holmes created a self-mythology in countless stroke magazine interviews in which he claimed to have lost his virginity at age six to a Swedish nursemaid, earned a university degree, and had sex with some 14,000 women. Reality, however, was not so glamorous. Born John Curtis Estes on August 8, 1944 in Pickaway County, Ohio, the future porn star's father Carl Estes, a railroad worker, was long gone by the time his son was old enough to remember him. His mother Mary, a fire and brimstone Southern Baptist, remarried Edward Holmes, a carpenter by trade and an abusive drunk by nature. John took his surname. The couple divorced when the child was three and Mary relocated Holmes and his siblings to a housing project in Columbus, Ohio. There, she moved in with another divorced woman and lived on welfare for several years. Holmes was eight when she remarried. Harold Bowman, a phone company worker, was an alcoholic whose drinking fuelled a manic depression that manifested itself in progressively bizarre and abusive behavior. Shortly after the family moved into a house on a five acre wooded lot in Pataskala, Ohio, Bowman realized his dream of never having to work again by intentionally jamming his hand into a harvesting machine losing a thumb and three fingers in the bargain. Forced to support her family, Mary secured a line job at a nearby Western Electric plant while her husband stayed at home and drank. Holmes, the favored target of his stepfather's physical and emotional abuse, sought comfort in the woods, but inevitably always had to return to the house. Tension within the home reached a flashpoint when John Holmes turned 15. After years of enduring Bowman's drunken lectures often punctuated by unpredictable backhanded slaps across the mouth, the teen balled up his fist and knocked the man out. Informing his mother he would kill Bowman if he remained at home, Holmes dropped out of high school in his junior year, enlisted in the Army with Mary's signed permission, and served three years in the Signal Corps in Nuremberg, West Germany.

Honorably discharged at 19, Holmes turned his back on his family in Ohio to settle in Los Angeles and work as an ambulance driver. He met Sharon Gebenini, a nurse assigned to a heart transplant team at USC County General, and they married in August 1965. For the next several years, Holmes drifted between jobs variously working as a shoe salesman, a chocolate factory worker in Glendale, a uniformed security guard, and as a forklift driver at a meat packing plant in Cudahy. Daily exposure to the constant temperature fluctuations in the meat lockers resulted in a lung condition that forced Holmes to quit the job. While recuperating in the late 1960s, he spent his time playing cards at a men's club in Gardena, California. During a break at the table, Holmes was relieving himself in the restroom when a man at the stand-up urinal next to him casually glanced over and was dumbstruck by the size of his fellow-gambler's penis. A still photographer by trade, the man told the unemployed Holmes that anyone as well hung as he could make a lot of fast money posing for sex magazines and performing in porno loops. Unknown to wife Sharon, Holmes began appearing unbilled in hard-core sex mag layouts and quickie 8mm porno loops. He ultimately confessed his underground life in porn when she unexpectedly caught him measuring his member with a ruler in the bathroom of their home. Though Holmes tried to convince his shocked wife that he felt nothing for the numerous women he was sexing, Sharon now considered their union as tantamount to being married to a hooker. They continued to live together and share a strong emotional bond, but Sharon ended the sexual dimension of their marriage. Remarkably, as Mike Sager noted in his incisive 1989 *Rolling Stone* article on the case, while Sharon continued to work as a nurse and used her paycheck to meet the rent and grocery bills, Holmes spent his porno money exclusively on himself buying flashy gold and diamond jewelry, outsized gem encrusted belt buckles, and three-piece vested suits. In 1971, Holmes appeared as the title character in the sex feature, *Johnny*

Wadd, a role that spawned a series of lucrative films (*Tell Them Johnny Wadd Is Here* (1976) *et al.*) featuring the well-endowed and passable by porn standards actor as a private eye. His ascendancy in the hard-core sex industry to the exalted rank of the "King of Porn" may have been aided by a 1973 arrest for pimping and pandering. Some have written that in order to avoid prosecution, Holmes agreed to become an informant for the LAPD in their investigation into the world of porn and he may have ratted out his competition. By 1978, John C. Holmes was the top male porn star in the world. Earning a reported $3,000 a day, his popularity in the murky sex film industry was based on the unmatched size of his penis, an unequalled ability to attain an erection almost at will, and more importantly, to unfailingly and repeatedly perform on cue. Holmes' stature in porn led to other moneymaking opportunities. At the height of his career, Holmes was reportedly also knocking down huge fees for sexually servicing wealthy male and female clients in Los Angeles, New York, and Europe.

On the homefront, John and Sharon Holmes continued to live together. In 1974, Sharon became the resident manager of a ten-unit cabana style apartment complex in Glendale owned by the doctor for whom she worked. The couple lived rent-free in an adjacent house on the property and Holmes served as a combination handyman-gardener when not appearing before the camera. Two years later, 15-year-old Dawn Schiller arrived at the Glendale complex in the company of her younger sister and recently divorced father.

Holmes, 31, was taken with the teen and began showering her with gifts. After her family decided to move on, Schiller moved in with Holmes' halfbrother David, and his wife, Karen, who also lived in the complex. Unfettered by any physical attachment to Sharon, the porn star made love to the smitten teenager. Schiller dropped out of high school and when not at her day job in a nursing home was babysitting for David and Karen. In an almost Christ-like act of charity, Sharon had Schiller move into her apartment concerned that her husband's rampant cocaine abuse would destroy the naïve young girl. Holmes had been introduced to the drug in the mid–1970s while shooting a film in Las Vegas. The porn star quickly became addicted to freebasing and was never without his ubiquitous brown Samsonite case in which he carried his works, glass pipe, and related paraphernalia. His porn lifestyle and wholesale need for the drug made it inevitable that Holmes would meet Eddie Nash, one of the most feared and powerful drug dealers in Los Angeles.

Born Adel Gharib Nasrallah in Palestine, his family reportedly owned several hotels in Israel prior to the 1948 creation of the Jewish state. In the 1950s, Nash arrived in the United States with $7 in his pocket and an inexhaustible energy aimed at getting rich. A naturalized American citizen, he opened Beef's Chuck, a hotdog stand on Hollywood Boulevard where he impressed diners by not only cooking, but also waiting tables. By the mid–1970s Nasrallah had changed his name to "Eddie Nash" and had parlayed his $7 grubstake into 36 liquor licenses and real estate holdings valued well over $30 million. As a nightclub owner, Nash offered something for every personal taste be it sexual (straight, gay), racial (blacks) or musical. The Kit Kat Club featured strippers while the Seven Seas, a joint on Hollywood Boulevard across from Mann's Chinese Theatre, offered Polynesian cuisine, parasol drinks, and bellydancers. Nash's gay clubs permitted same sex dancing and he also owned nightspots catering to blacks. The Starwood, a happening rock music club on Santa Monica Boulevard, logged 25 drug busts a month and it was well-known that Quaaludes were handed out free at the door then sold after patrons returned for more. One of the top drug dealers in L.A., Nash had ties to the Colombian market and was seemingly immune from arrest by higher ups within the police department and local government. Nash, however, was also a heavy taster of his own supply and his incessant freebasing had already cost him part of a sinus cavity and one lung. Increasingly paranoid as his drug intake escalated, the multimillionaire managed his vast criminal empire from his home in Studio City. Soon, the house situated on a cul-de-sac in the 3300 block of Dona Lola Place became a well-known drug destination where an unending narcotics and sex party hosted by the reclusive Nash was always in full swing. Nash, clad only in a maroon silk robe over bikini briefs, restlessly wandered the premises holding a crack pipe and offering free drugs to his guests. Later, if they failed to amuse or offer some financial upside, they would have to pay. Watching over the never-ending drug binges and sex orgies was Gregory DeWitt Diles, Nash's 6'3" black bodyguard whose doglike devotion to his employer had earned him a place at the party. Born in 1948,

Diles was a twice convicted felon who entered into street legend after he once chased a patron out of the Kit Kat Club and emptied his gun into the man's car across six lanes of traffic in broad daylight. A karate specialist, the thug's weapon of choice was either a baseball bat or a lead pipe outfitted with a plastic bicycle grip for better handling.

Eddie Nash loved hanging out with celebrities, although only fringe ones like Liberace's ex-lover Scott Thorson could risk any association with him. Thorson reportedly became a drug addict after undergoing a series of painful plastic surgeries designed to make him look more like his lover. When the dope sick "King of Porn" showed up on his doorstep looking to score, Nash was thrilled. Nash consumed porn like others gobbled breath mints and was known to have invested in sex films and leased office space to the industry. The pair had earlier met in 1978 at the Seven Seas and Holmes was soon installed in Nash's claustrophobic world as his Number One celebrity. The porn star solidified his position with the drug kingpin by supplying girls to Nash to keep the free coke flowing. On Christmas Day 1980, Holmes gave Dawn Schiller to Nash and was rewarded with a quarter ounce of cocaine. Their relationship, however, began to sour as drug addiction sabotaged Holmes' career. By 1980, the porn star's habit of freebasing coke every 10 to 15 minutes and cutting the edge with 50 Valium a day, had made it problematic for him to attain an erection. Unable to earn enough money in porn to support his drug need, "Johnny Wadd" ripped off the apartments of friends, co-workers, and former girlfriends. Even wife Sharon was unspared. Holmes charged $30,000 worth of appliances on her credit card then fenced them for cash. When not breaking into parked cars, he was stealing bags at the airport, and pimping Schiller out to support their mutual drug habit. Nash, losing an estimated $1 million a year as a result of his own drug use, no longer reveled in the company of a washed-up porn star who could not perform. The free drugs once willingly given to his "staff star," Nash now dispensed for cash and favors. In 1980, Holmes and Schiller moved out of the Glendale complex and, when not staying in cheap motels, lived out of Sharon's car. Holmes, looking to score, often left the young woman in the car for days to live off candy bars and soft drinks. Schiller, 20, was busted for prostitution in January 1981 and a couple of weeks later Holmes was arrested, despite being a police informant, for stealing a computer out of a car in Marina Del Rey. Nash bailed him out the next day.

Emaciated and desperate for drugs, Holmes made the rounds of L.A. dope dealers and finally hooked up with Billy DeVerell, 44, a thief and junkie who had been in trouble with the law since the 1950s, and fellow-junkie Joy Audrey Miller, 46. The couple lived at 8763 Wonderland Avenue, a three-story stucco house with two balconies facing the street in the Laurel Canyon section of Los Angeles. The residence was known to neighbors and cops as a drug house with a steady flow of traffic being buzzed through the locked street level security gate at all hours. DeVerell, leader of the so-called "Wonderland gang," agreed to let Holmes be a drug runner for the group while also selling stolen items to Eddie Nash in exchange for drugs. In June 1981, Holmes took a savage beating from Wonderland gang member Ron Launius, a 37-year-old drug smuggler who had done federal time, after he smoked up a couple of the group's deliveries. Threatened with death if he did not replace the drugs, Holmes turned to Nash for assistance, but was told by Greg Diles that he already owed too much money. His employer was not running a charity ward. To make good the debt, Holmes told the Wonderland gang that Nash kept a large stash of cash and drugs in the safe at his home in Studio City and supplied them with a sketched layout of the floor plan. Initially wary of ripping off a man as powerful as Nash, the gang was desperate. They had foolishly sold a pound of baking soda masquerading as cocaine for $250,000 to the wrong people and contracts had been put out on their lives. Without a huge score, they were all as good as dead.

On the night of June 28, 1981, DeVerell, Ronald Launius, Tracy McCourt, and David C. Lind, a 40-year-old biker and member of the Aryan Brotherhood, drove to Nash's home in Studio City. McCourt waited in the stolen car while his three accomplices gained access to the residence through an unlocked sliding door. The pistol-waving David Lind flashed a police badge at Greg Diles and shouted they were under arrest. Nash, on the sofa wearing a pair of bikini briefs, was stunned. The drug don knew most of the cops on the force and had never seen these three before. While attempting to cuff Diles, Launius bumped into Lind causing the gunman's .357-Magnum to discharge. The gun flash burned the beefy bodyguard and the blood flowed. Terrified, the 52-

year-old Nash pleaded on his knees for his life. Lind pressed the gun to the dope dealer's head and demanded the whereabouts of the safe containing the drugs and money. When Nash initially refused, Lind shoved the gun into the kneeling man's mouth and gave him to the count of five. In Nash's bedroom, the robbers found a floor safe containing two large plastic bags of cocaine and a further search of the room resulted in the discovery of a strongbox containing thousands of Quaaludes and more coke. Before leaving the house, the group took guns, a vial of heroin, and an attaché case containing large amounts of cash and jewelry. Lind, the racist, wanted to kill the black bodyguard, but settled instead for just slicing the back of Diles' neck with a hunting knife. Back at 8763 Wonderland Avenue on the afternoon of June 29, the gang split up the proceeds with a disgruntled Holmes reduced to taking only $3,000, a small amount of drugs, and a diamond ring taken from the heist he helped set up.

On June 1, days after the robbery, the dope sick porn star was at a pay phone in a pharmacy in Laurel Canyon setting up a drug buy when he was confronted by Greg Diles. The bodyguard recognized the diamond ring on Holmes' finger as belonging to Nash and dragged the whimpering addict back to the house on Dona Lola Place. Scott Thorson, Liberace's coke addicted ex, was with Nash, but ordered out when Holmes was brought before the enraged drug kingpin. Diles beat Holmes as Nash pistol-whipped and railed against the ungrateful man to whom he had given "everything." Threatening to kill Holmes' entire family, Nash quickly determined from a notebook taken from the drug addict as well as the man's own pleading confession that the gang on Wonderland had been responsible for the robbery and his humiliation. "Go back to that house! Get me my property!" Nash screamed at Holmes. "Bring me their eyeballs! Bring me their eyeballs in a bag and I will forget what you have done to me. Go!"

Around 3:00 A.M. that morning, Holmes led two men armed with a lead pipe and a baseball bat to the three-story house at 8763 Wonderland Avenue. Holmes used the telephone at the front door caged in iron to contact the occupants, identified himself as being alone and having drugs, and a buzzer was pressed unlocking an electronic deadbolt and granting him access. The men pushed Holmes through the upstairs door and followed swinging their clubs in a killing frenzy

as they went room-by-room to exact Nash's deadly retribution. Joy Audrey Miller was bludgeoned to death in an upstairs bedroom, her lover William DeVerell found in a similar broken and bloody condition slumped against a television set. Dead on the living room floor next to a couch lay Barbara Richardson, 29, from Sacramento. In a bed downstairs, Ron Launius, one of the men who had dared to invade Nash's domain, was beaten to death beyond recognition. His wife, Susan, lay in another bedroom. Although repeatedly bludgeoned about the head, her skull had fractured in such a way that the displaced bones kept her from bleeding out. Launius' moans throughout the next morning were finally heard by a moving man working nearby who notified police after entering the bloody scene to find four people dead and one barely clinging to life. Later that day, police investigating what the press dubbed the "Four-on-the Floor" murders received a phone call from David C. Lind, the racist biker boyfriend of victim Barbara Richardson. He would have been killed as well in the massacre had he not been in San Gabriel selling the drugs the gang had ripped off from Nash. Lind had been informed of the killings and in exchange for a deal told police of the gang's connection with John Holmes and Eddie Nash.

An hour after the slaughter on Wonderland Avenue a stunned and blood soaked John C. Holmes showed up at wife Sharon's Glendale residence. Initially explaining his swollen face and bloody clothes as due to a car accident, Holmes bathed then confessed to Sharon about the murders and his unwilling participation in them under Nash's threat to eliminate his entire family. Horrified, Sharon gave him a change of clothes, and ordered him to leave. Holmes drove to the motel in Sherman Oaks where Dawn Schiller had spent days watching television and snacking on junk food awaiting his return. Broke and dope sick, Holmes and Schiller were arrested by police at the motel on July 10, 1981. Along with Schiller and wife Sharon, Holmes was placed in protective custody and shuttled between various hotels for three days while detectives tried to convince him to open up about who was involved in the murders. While the longtime informant was happy to give up the names of various and sundry pimps, prostitutes, and drug dealers he refused to discuss the Wonderland murders unless all three of them were given new identities and placed in a witness protection program, preferably on an island where his fame would go unrecognized. Exhausted by days of grilling the addict, police unwisely released Holmes on his own recognizance seemingly confident he would show up for a court date stemming from his earlier arrest on computer theft. Sharon Holmes, the only innocent in the entire Holmes saga, decided not to go on the lam with her husband and Dawn Schiller. Weeks later, she filed for divorce calling it quits on their rocky 17 year marriage. During months on the run from the police and Nash, Holmes supported their mutual drug habit by breaking into cars and fencing the stolen items. By early November 1981, the pair arrived in Miami, Florida and checked into a cheap motel where they stayed rent-free in exchange for Schiller operating the switchboard and cleaning rooms. The porn star who had once earned $3,000 a day now worked as a painter for a construction company. Informed by Schiller that she no longer wanted to solicit men on the beach for extra drug money, Holmes beat the woman in full view of her friends at the motel. The addict disappeared for two weeks and when he returned on November 30, 1981 he was taken into custody by police for missing various court dates. In reality, the authorities in Los Angeles had decided to charge the 37-year-old fugitive with the Wonderland murders.

Nash, as well, had been on police radar ever since the Wonderland murders. On July 10, 1981, a narcotics raid on Nash's home in Studio City disintegrated into a pitched gun battle between authorities and Nash bodyguards Greg Diles and Amnon Bachshian, 37. No one was injured in the incident, but both men along with Nash were charged with narcotics violations. Diles was later compelled to give hair, blood, and saliva samples to the LAPD for comparison to evidence found at the scene of the Wonderland massacre. On November 25, 1981, police again raided Nash's residence and seized two pounds of rock cocaine with an estimated street value of $1 million. Nash was arrested along with Greg Diles and three other individuals. All were later released after posting $50,000 bail each. Shortly after 37-year-old fugitive John Holmes was arrested in Miami and charged in L.A. with the murders, Greg Diles was arrested at the Seven Seas on December 8, 1991 and booked on suspicion of the murders though not formally charged.

If the authorities thought by charging Holmes with four counts of murder and one count of attempted murder (Susan Launius) they could scare

him into rolling over on Eddie Nash and company they vastly underestimated how terrified the former porn star was of the drug kingpin. The Los Angeles County district attorney's office even threatened Holmes with the death penalty to no effect. Holmes very publicly let it be known that he was not talking and would take his chances at trial. Days after his arrest, Greg Diles was released after the D.A.'s office released a statement saying there was insufficient evidence "at this time" to prosecute him. Though Diles was still considered to be a strong suspect in the case prosecutors lacked the physical evidence to tie him to the killings. On February 2, 1982, Holmes was ordered to stand trial for the murders after a day-long preliminary hearing filled with compelling testimony revealed that a palm print belonging to the actor had been found on the brass headboard just inches from where one of the victims had been bludgeoned to death. David C. Lind and Tracy McCourt told the court that Holmes and others were involved in the planning of the robbery and that it had been the porn star's idea. Ten days after the hearing, Nash and Diles were again in the news. An LAPD SWAT team conducted an early morning raid of Nash's home and found less than two ounces of cocaine, scales, $6,000 in cash, three handguns, and a quantity of Quaaludes. Both Nash and Diles were arrested and charged on suspicion of possessing cocaine for sale and released after posting $30,000 bail each.

In June 1982, nearly one year after the "Four-on-the-Floor" murders, the 37-year-old one-time "King of Porn" faced a possible life sentence at trial in an L.A. County courtroom. David C. Lind gave a detailed chronology of the robbery and its aftermath again asserting that it was Holmes' idea to ripoff Eddie Nash. According to the prosecution, this initial betrayal of Nash led to the robbery and set into motion the drug kingpin's deadly retaliation committed on his order by unidentified agents in the company of John C. Holmes who led them past security into the house on Wonderland Avenue. In an opening statement, the defendant's counsel denied Holmes had willingly participated in the killings, but rather was forced at gunpoint to accompany the killers to Wonderland Avenue. The damning palm print found on the headboard could have been left any time since Holmes in his drug dealings was a frequent visitor to the residence. Susan Launius, the sole survivor of the mass murder, was unable to identify Holmes as one of the three "shadowy figures" who had entered the bedroom and attacked her. The beating had cost Launius a finger, a large portion of her skull, as well as partial paralysis in her left leg. Looking directly at Holmes Launius testified that she could not remember ever having seen him before, not surprising since she had only arrived at the house on Wonderland a day before the incident in an ill-timed attempt at reconciliation with her estranged husband, Ron Launius. In effect, the defense argued, Holmes was the "sixth victim" and asked why the real perpetrators of the crime were not present in the courtroom adding, "You will figure out from the evidence who they are." On June 25, 1982, a jury of eight men and four women ended nearly four days of deliberation by acquitting Holmes of all charges. Holmes' reaction — "Thank God."

The acquitted porn star, however, was not permitted to walk out of court a free man. Moments after the verdict was read, Holmes was taken to the Los Angeles County Jail and held under $50,000 bond on unrelated charges of grand theft and receiving stolen property. While Holmes sat in jail awaiting a July 8 trial on those charges, the L.A. County district attorney's office subpoenaed him to testify before a grand jury about the Wonderland Murders. Because he had been acquitted of the charges under review by the grand jury, Holmes would not be able to plead the Fifth Amendment against self-incrimination and could be jailed for contempt for refusing to disclose what he knew. Still fearful of reprisal against his wife and family, Holmes refused to cooperate with the grand jury and vowed to stay in jail indefinitely. However, on November 22, 1983, the day Eddie Nash was sentenced to the maximum term of 8 years in prison and fined $120,000 for possessing cocaine for sale, John C. Holmes ended his 110 day hold-out and purged himself of the contempt charge by answering all questions put to him by the grand jury. His testimony was not made public and Holmes was released later that day telling reporters he planned to return to films after first enjoying a steak dinner with caviar and wine. Eddie Nash, however, was released from Soledad Prison in November 1984 after a Superior Court judge cut the convicted felon's sentence in half citing the man's model record as a prisoner and immediate need for an operation to remove a sinus tumor. In 1991, Diles and Nash were tried for the Wonderland murders, but the jury hung in an 11–1 vote to convict and a mistrial was declared. Nash later admitted bribing the lone hold-

out juror with $50,000 to secure her vote to acquit. Retried the next year, both men were acquitted. Greg Diles died in 1995. A federal task force was created to bring down Eddie Nash, a viable suspect in several murders and millions of dollars in cocaine trafficking, and in September 2001 he pleaded guilty to racketeering, money laundering, conspiracy to murder four people in the Wonderland killings, and large scale drug trafficking. Under the terms of his agreement with the U.S. Attorney's office, the 71 year old agreed to spend 37 months in prison, 14 of which he had already served, and five years of supervised release upon the expiration of his term. Nash, said to be suffering from advanced cases of emphysema and tuberculosis, reportedly lives in Los Angeles.

Holmes never spoke publicly about the Wonderland murders and once freed from jail on the contempt charge tried to reconnect with Sharon. It was too late. She flatly refused to see him. Likewise, Dawn Schiller had sufficiently covered her tracks making it impossible for Holmes to locate her. Broke and with nowhere to go, Holmes' attorney fronted him a car and $100. Few in the porn industry now trusted Holmes, the memory of the former star borrowing money he never repaid and ripping off their homes still too fresh in their minds. Holmes turned to Bill Amerson, a longtime friend in the industry for whom he had once worked. Holmes, paid by the day like most porn performers, had signed away the rights to his films and Amerson had quickly snapped up the movies and formed John Holmes Productions to market the movies to the then burgeoning video market. With his name plastered across headlines everywhere, Holmes was still a marketable commodity although years of drug abuse had made him an unreliable porn performer. Amerson realized that while the "King of Porn" was no longer a star performer, erotica consumers would still pay to see him if as nothing more than a novelty act. In *California Valley Girls* (1983), Holmes appeared in but one scene with the sex restricted to six women fondling his penis. In 1983, Holmes met 19-year-old actress Misty Dawn, billed as the "Queen of Anal," while shooting *Fleshpond* (some say *Marathon*) in San Francisco. Misty Dawn (real name Laurie Rose) shared no scenes with Holmes, but the two began dating soon after shooting wrapped. Rose weaned Holmes off drugs and the couple lived a relatively normal homelife when not in front of the camera. In late 1984, Bill Amerson hired Holmes as an executive at his company, VCX, to oversee sales, pre-production, marketing, as well to write, direct, and act in some films. When VCX cut off Holmes' salary for failing to noticeably perform any duties, Amerson installed his friend as the head of Penguin Productions and hired Laurie Rose as a secretary. The short-lived arrangement ended when Amerson fired Holmes after suspecting he had embezzled $200,000 from the company.

In the summer of 1985, Holmes tested positive for AIDS, but kept the diagnosis secret to avoid the public stigma associated with the disease. He continued to work in the industry exposing numerous partners to the disease that at the time was a certain death sentence. His final film, *The Rise and Fall of the Roman Empress* (1986), featured Italian Parliament member Ilona ("Ciccolina") Staller. By 1987, Holmes was too sick to work, and explained away his startling weight loss as the effect of colon cancer. Broke and uninsured, Holmes was cared for by Laurie Rose who worked as a computer programmer to pay for rent and medicine. On January 24, 1988, the couple married in Las Vegas, and within weeks Holmes was admitted to the Veteran's Administration Medical Center in Sepulveda, California suffering from AIDS-related encephalitis, a painful swelling of the brain that caused the porn star to bleed from the ears. Holmes was down to 90 pounds and near death when LAPD detectives visited the hospital in one final attempt to convince the actor to name names in the Wonderland murder case. The actor feigned unconsciousness. "Johnny Wadd" passed away on March 13, 1988, at the age of 43. Laurie Rose was at the crematorium to honor his final wish. Moments before the lid to his coffin was fastened down and consigned to the flames she made certain his penis was still intact. The appendage, a source of awe, envy, and entertainment in the porn world for nearly two decades, would not be harvested by a medical school or collector of bizarrities. The ashes of John C. Holmes were scattered over the Pacific Ocean. The porn star's life has been the subject of at least two documentaries (*Exhausted: John C. Holmes, the Real Story* [1981]; *Wadd—The Life and Times of John C. Holmes* [1998]) and Val Kilmer portrayed him in the 2003 feature film *Wonderland* directed by James Cox.

Further Reading

Gilmore, John. *L.A. Despair: A Landscape of Crimes and Bad Times*. Los Angeles: Amok, 2005.

Holmes, John C., and Laurie Holmes. *Porn King: The Autobiography of John C. Holmes*. Albuquerque, NM: Johnny Wadd, 1998.
Sager, Mike. "The Devil and John Holmes." *Rolling Stone*, 554 (June 15, 1989):50–52, 54–55, 61, 150, 152.
_____. *Scary Monsters and Super Freaks: Stories of Sex, Drugs, Rock 'n' Roll and Murder*. New York: Thunder's Mouth, 2003. (Reprint of June 15, 1989, *Rolling Stone* article.)

Holton, DeShaun DuPree *see* Proof

Horner, Mark (V)

The 25-year-old principal trombonist with the San Antonio Symphony enraged local artist Mike Pogue, 47, after the younger man began dating his estranged wife, Susan. Pogue, a fixture in the San Antonio arts community, specialized in outrageous, brilliantly colored sculptural cartoons influenced by *Mad* magazine, tattoos, and "Big Daddy" Roth hot rod drawings. In recent months, he had created the "Chili Man" logo for Taco Cabana and his work was featured at the Edith Baker Gallery in Dallas. On Thanksgiving Day 1998 Susan Pogue asked her husband for a divorce then, shortly afterwards, began dating Mark Horner. Unsettled by the separation, Pogue was unable to sleep and confided to his mother that he wanted to knock out the musician's teeth so he could never again play the trombone. Despite promising his wife that he "wouldn't do anything crazy," Pogue drove to Horner's San Antonio home in the 300 block of Thorman Place on December 14, 1998 and rang the doorbell. Stephen Dumaine, a neighbor and fellow-symphony player who was dining with Horner, answered the door and was speaking to the man who "looked familiar" when Horner walked up. Pogue fired several rounds from a .45-caliber revolver at the trombonist striking him in the abdomen and thigh. Dumaine briefly struggled with Pogue before the artist broke free, fired once at him, and sped away in his car. Horner died later that evening at Brooke Army Medical Center. Police traced the car's license plate to Pogue's address in the 300 block of Kokomo Avenue in nearby Alamo Heights where they found the artist slumped over in the front seat of the vehicle dead from a self-inflicted gunshot wound to the head. A suicide note was discovered inside the house. "Mike said in the note that he loved me and he didn't want to lose me," said Susan Pogue. "He did it to hurt me. I feel really sad about what has happened, but I'm also really angry at Mike. He had no reason to shoot Mark. I feel like I've been doubly widowed."

Further Reading

Hunger, Kate, and Dan R. Goddard. "Musician, Artist Deaths Probed." *San Antonio Express-News*, December 16, 1998, sec. C, p. 1.

Howard, Malcolm (V)

On May 13, 1999, the 29-year-old rapper in the Hartford, Connecticut, based group 4 Black Faces was reported missing by his family. Three days later Howard's body was discovered by a man walking his dog off a wooded stretch of road in Southwick, Massachusetts near the Connecticut border. An autopsy revealed that Howard had died a day or two before from a single gunshot wound to the head. The recovery of the rapper's abandoned and bloodstained car in Hartford on May 18 led to the arrest of 19-year-old Shane O. Moffat in Miami, Florida where he was in jail on an unrelated charge. At trial, a jury in Springfield, Massachusetts rejected Moffat's testimony that he watched another man called "Quentin" shoot Howard during a cocaine deal gone bad, and needed only two hours to find him guilty of first-degree murder. On October 12, 2001, Moffatt was sentenced to a mandatory term of life imprisonment.

Further Reading

"Man Held Without Bail in Murder of Aspiring Performer." Associated Press, January 11, 2000.

Howden, Victoria (M–S)

In pursuit of the dream of a career in acting, the attractive 26-year-old blonde left the British seaside resort of Torquay for Hollywood in 1990. In Tinseltown, the Devon native landed a single line appearance on a November 1990 episode of the NBC sitcom *Dear John*, but found steadier employment as a part-time stripper at private parties. Desperate to remain in America, Howden secured a Green Card by marrying Charles House in a Las Vegas ceremony in December 1990. House, a 40-year-old former cop from Kentucky, was in training to become a police officer with the Los Angeles Unified School District. On May 8, 1991, California Highway Patrol Officer Ronald Webb, 34, shot himself alongside a freeway in the San Fernando Valley after Howden refused to marry him. The next day, Howden went to the home of Webb's estranged wife and threatened to commit suicide. She was subsequently held for 72 hours on a psychiatric evaluation and released. At 2:00 A.M. on June 10, 1991, neighbors heard a gunshot from the apartment Charles House and

Howden shared in the 4600 block of Willis Avenue in Sherman Oaks. Howden called a friend to report House had shot himself, and when paramedics arrived they found the man dead in the dining room from a gunshot wound. In the bedroom lay the body of the actress. The .357-Magnum she used to shoot herself in the chest was recovered near a note in which she apologized for her death and asked to be buried next to her lover Ronald Webb. While police initially believed the event was a double suicide, the coroner's report and forensic evidence proved that Howden shot House in the head while he slept at the kitchen table, placed a phone call to her friend, and took her own life. Immigration authorities noted that Howden had been granted permanent resident status five days prior to the murder-suicide.

Further Reading

Laurence, Charles. "The Life and Death of a 'Wannabe.'" *Daily Telegraph*, June 13, 1991, p. 19.

Huffman, David Oliver (V)

A veteran actor equally at home in films (*F.I.S.T.*, 1978; *The Onion Field*, 1979; *Blood Beach*, 1981; *Firefox*, 1982) and television movies (*Eleanor and Franklin*, 1976), Huffman (born May 10, 1945) was currently appearing in San Diego, California in the Old Globe Theatre stage production, *Of Mice and Men*. On February 27, 1985 the 40-year-old actor was walking in Balboa Park not far from the theatre when a Canadian couple spotted someone rifling their motor home. Huffman gave chase to the intruder, but when he failed to return, the tourists assumed that the prowler escaped and their protector left the park. Later that day, Huffman's body was found in a narrow crevice off a nature trail by a group of school children on a field trip. An autopsy determined that he had been stabbed five times in the chest and abdomen with a screwdriver. The Canadian tourists notified San Diego police after seeing Huffman's photo in a newspaper account of the murder. Their description of the intruder combined with fingerprints left in the motor home led to the arrest of Mexican-born Genaro Samano Villanueva in San Diego on March 11, 1985. Villanueva, a 16-year-old illegal alien living in the city with relatives since November 1984, was ordered to stand trial as an adult. While admitting that he stabbed Huffman to death out of fear that his pursuer would either kill or turn him over to police, Villanueva pleaded for forgiveness insisting he never meant to kill the man. Rejecting a defense motion to place the teenager in the California Youth Authority until the age of 25, Superior Court Judge Norbert Ehrenfreund sentenced Villanueva to the maximum term of 26 years to life on June 2, 1986. In asking the judge for the stiffest possible sentence, Huffman's wife, Phyllis, stated, "I adored that man for 20 years. He was life, not just to me but to all of us. The loss is immeasurable and is impossible to articulate."

Further Reading

"Youth Sentenced in Murder of Actor." Associated Press, June 3, 1986.

Hull, Jay G. (M-S)

Described as "intense," "confrontational," "mean," "eccentric," and "psychologically troubled" by acquaintances, Hull, 39, was an accomplished classical guitarist utterly devoted to his music and environmental-wildlife concerns in Lake County, California. Over the years, Hull became well-known in the area's tight knit arts community performing at numerous local concerts, chamber of commerce functions, and political rallies. However, he was equally well-known as a volatile, verbally abusive troublemaker not averse to threatening anyone he felt was thwarting his will. Hull once threatened to sue the Lake County Parks Department over payment for a performance, and nearly dumped a bag of trash on the desk of the director of the county's Solid Waste Office to protest rising landfill rates. Perhaps frustrated over the area's limited artistic opportunities, Hull immediately clashed with Patricia M. Wiley, executive director of the nonprofit Lake County Arts Council, when she assumed the post in 1990. Over the next five years, the troubled guitarist maintained a nonstop professional dispute with the popular and respected Wiley who, by 1995, confessed to friends that she was terrified of the man.

On March 20, 1995, Hull showed up unannounced at the Arts Council office demanding an audiotape of an interview he had given for the group's publication. Hull, though adamant that he wanted the tape and agitated when it could not be located, was reportedly civil to Wiley's assistant. Early the next morning, Hull phoned Wiley, 56, insisting that they meet at her office. According to the musician, he secured a donation of $35,000 to the Arts Council from a retired guitar player who wanted to fund Hull's program to teach kids to play the instrument at the Lake County Juvenile Hall. The donor wished to deliver the check to the director that morning *before* her Lakeport office opened at 10:00 A.M. Wiley reluctantly agreed to meet with Hull and the anonymous donor then phoned several friends to express her trepidation over the meeting. She asked a couple friends to "check up" on her shortly after the 8:00 A.M. meeting was set to commence. At least three people phoned and Wiley assured them that the meeting with Hull (the donor, if one ever existed, had yet to show) was cordial. After repeated calls went unanswered, however, a friend entered Wiley's office around 10:00 A.M. to find the arts director slumped behind her desk dead from a single bullet wound in her right eye. Meanwhile, around 7:50 A.M., Hull's wife had frantically phoned authorities to report her husband had just left the house packing a .380-caliber pistol and threatening suicide. A sheriff's deputy posted outside their Upper Lake home on Witter Springs Road saw the guitarist rush into the residence after 9:00 A.M., then heard a single gunshot. Ambulanced to a nearby hospital, Hull died hours later from a pistol wound to the head. Commenting on Patricia Wiley's death, a co-worker said, "It's so incredible to have someone snatched away like that, just taken, because someone couldn't cope with life... There are no words for that kind of pain."

Further Reading

Callahan, Mary. "Murder Suspect Known as Volatile." *Press Democrat*, March 23, 1995, sec. B, p. 1.

Icewood, Blade (V)

Variously known by several rap names ("Ruler of tha Great Lakes," "Motor City's Finest," "Mayor of tha Mitten"), Icewood (real name Darnell Quincy Lyndsey) grew up in the 7 Mile-Greenfield area of Detroit. Rap styles and the concomitant rivalries in the Motor City are generally divided between the East and West sides of the city and are believed to have played a significant role in the murders of two rappers, Wipeout and Blade Icewood, who quarreled over the origins and use of a name claimed by the musical groups of both men. Icewood (from the West side of Detroit) joined a rap group called the Street Lordz that laid claim to the name Chedda Boyz. Rival rapper Wipeout (real name Antonio Caddell, Jr.) was a member of the gangsta rap group The East

Side Chedda Boyz. Tensions mounted as both groups claimed the name on the streets and in dueling rap lyrics. Ironically, in mid–2004 Icewood headlined a "Stop the Violence" rally in front of Platinum Records (the Street Lordz label) in which he urged those young people in attendance to create their own non-violent way out of the ghetto. On September 18, 2004, Wipeout, 32, and an innocent bystander were shot to death outside the Candy Bar nightclub at Woodward Avenue and John R in downtown Detroit. Two days later, Icewood was in his apartment in Oak Park when it was invaded by AK-47 wielding gunmen. The rapper was shot seven times, and although surviving the attack was permanently paralyzed from the chest down. True to the code of the streets, however, Icewood refused to cooperate with authorities who credited violence to ongoing tensions over the right to use the Chedda Boyz name.

In 2005, the 27-year-old rapper formed Icewood Entertainment and signed Candi Cane, Balee, and Cash Out to his roster. On April 21, 2005, Icewood was in a wheelchair inside his parked Range Rover at West 7 Mile Road and Faust when another vehicle pulled alongside and a shooter pumped multiple shots into his body. The rapper was killed instantly. The fatal attack took place less than a mile from the site where he had headlined the anti-violence rally seven months earlier. The week before his murder, Icewood had released a song targeting his murdered rival, Wipeout. The rapper's CDs include *Still Spinnin*, *Stackmaster*, and *Blood, Sweat, Tears*. As of the date of this book's publication, no arrests have been made in the killings of Wipeout or Blade Icewood.

Further Reading

"Rapper Blade Icewood Killed in Detroit Drive-By Shooting." Associated Press, April 21, 2005.

Ince, Thomas H. (V-suspected)

Sadly, the film pioneer's numerous contributions to the early history of American motion pictures have been forgotten in the wake of his "mysterious" death in November 1924 stemming from events aboard the luxury yacht of newspaper magnate William Randolph Hearst. Unsubstantiated rumors persist that Hearst accidentally shot Ince in a case of mistaken identity believing him to be Charlie Chaplin, the alleged lover of the tycoon's mistress, Marion Davies. Conflicting media reports and perfunctory investigations conducted at the time by the police and the office of the San Diego District Attorney did little to dispel the rumors that Hearst was responsible for the movie mogul's death rather than the more mundane official ruling that Ince died from a heart attack. Like the other great cases of suspicious death in this book (see entries Paul Bern, Marilyn Monroe, George Reeves, Thelma Todd) the truth will never be known, but does make for interesting speculation as in director Peter Bogdanovich's 2001 feature film reimagining of the case, *The Cat's Meow*. What is certain, however, is that the untimely death of Ince at 42 robbed American cinema of a powerful innovator and entrepreneur who very well may have gone on to take his place among the great studio moguls of the day.

Thomas Harper Ince, the son of show business parents, was born on November 6, 1882, in Newport, Rhode Island. Debuting onstage at 6, Ince worked for years in stock and vaudeville companies perfecting a song-and-dance routine prior to forming his own short-lived stock company in 1905. In 1907, he married Elinor ("Nell") Kershaw, an actress with whom he had appeared in the Broadway show *For Love's Sweet Sake*. Kershaw was a "Biograph" girl and through her connections at the New York City–based film studio, the actor was able to

Largely forgotten today, Thomas H. Ince was a protean figure in the early days of American cinema, writing, directing, and producing hundreds of films including *Civilization* (1916), a pacifistic fantasy that beat D.W. Griffith's epic, *Intolerance*, at the box office. The "mysterious" death of the "Father of the Western" shortly after attending a party on board the yacht of newspaper tycoon William Randolph Hearst in 1924 has spawned numerous murder conspiracy theories and has become an enduring Hollywood legend (courtesy Lilly Library, Indiana University, Bloomington, Indiana).

secure $5 a day movie work beginning in 1910. Ince was not in front of the cameras for long. That same year, he impressed Carl Laemmle, owner of Independent Motion Picture Company, by filling in for another director on the set of *Little Nell's Tobacco*. Ince helmed several films for IMP prior to leaving in 1911 to accept a director's position with the Bison Co., a subsidiary of the New York Motion Picture Co. (NYMP). In November 1911, the director left New York and moved to Edendale (later known as Echo Park) to make films in California. With Bison, Ince became known as the "Father of the Western" co-writing, often directing, and producing films like *War of the Plains* (1912) and *Custer's Last Fight* (1912). At the end of 1911, the heads of NYMP acquired rights to 18,000 acres at the mouth of Santa Ynez Canyon and what is today the Pacific Coast Highway. Known as Inceville, the studio as set up by its creator included stages, labs, offices, props, sets, and commissaries. To add authenticity to his two reel westerns, Ince placed the Miller Brothers' 101 Ranch Wild West Show on retainer. Remarkably, many of the Indians in the show had actually fought in battle. Ince was also a great recognizer of talent and is credited with helping the careers of cowboy star William S. Hart, Japanese actor Sessue Hayakawa, and with the discovery of director Frank Borzage.

It was, however, as an organizer and innovator of motion picture production that Ince made his greatest mark in American film history. Few of the hundreds of films made by Ince during this period have survived, but it is known that he turned moviemaking on its ear by insisting upon the supremacy of the producer over the director and cameraman in a film's production. At Inceville, he controlled every aspect of filmmaking from its inception to production. As the first Director-General (director-producer) Ince introduced the factory-like approach to filmmaking that became the norm in the studio system in the 1920s. He controlled directors, writers, and editors. He rethought the way scripts were written and institutionalized the idea of the continuity script. No longer was a script loosely confined to story, but under Ince's influence became a blueprint for the production filled with directions that translated into a greater efficiency that in turn helped to control costs. In 1914, Ince produced and co-directed his masterpiece, *The Battle of Gettysburg*, a five-reeler employing 800 extras with eight cameras shooting the action from different angles. The filmmaker left NYMP in 1915 and formed Triangle Film Corporation, a production-distribution company, with other industry heavyweights including D.W. Griffith, Mack Sennett, and Harry Aitken. As vice president at Triangle, Ince focused on making feature-length films high on quality and epic drama. His most ambitious film of the period, *Civilization* (1916), was a pacifistic fantasy dedicated to the mothers of soldiers who died in World War I. Ince was credited as the film's producer-director-editor and though largely forgotten today, *Civilization* beat D.W. Griffith's epic *Intolerance* at the box office. Triangle dissolved as a production company in 1918 and its distribution wing failed soon afterwards due to financial mismanagement. That same year, real estate developer Harry Culver offered free land in Culver City to anyone who would build a movie studio there. Ince took the challenge and constructed a second Inceville (to replace the one he had earlier sold) on a 16-acre parcel that became the physical plant for MGM. The filmmaker set up his own production company and released his product through Paramount and Metro. Ince's power in Hollywood was declining hastened by his independent status and an association ending argument over money with his biggest star William S. Hart. In 1919, he joined with other producers and directors including Mack Sennett and Allan Dwan in founding Associated Producer's Inc., an independent releasing company. Unable to function independently, the company was absorbed by First National in 1924. Supplanted by the studio system, the independent producer was still able to make a few important films (*Anna Christie*, 1923; *Human Wreckage*; 1924), but needed stronger financial backing to remain a major player in Hollywood. Enter William Randolph Hearst, the 61-year-old newspaper magnate whose affair with 27-year-old actress Marion Davies had prompted him to form Cosmopolitan Pictures to promote his lover's career. Backed by the publicity power of his chain of newspapers, Hearst believed there was no reason Davies could not be made into a major film star with the proper industry connections. Enter Thomas Harper Ince. Up to that time, Cosmopolitan had shot Davies' films in New York, but with the company's move to Goldwyn Hearst was negotiating with Ince to use his facility in Culver City.

Mixing business with pleasure, Hearst invited Ince to discuss the merger and celebrate his 42nd birthday as guest of honor on board the newspaperman's 280' luxury yacht, *Oneida*, setting sail with a group of select friends from San Pedro, California on Saturday, November 15, 1924. Ince, unable to make the departure because of a movie premiere in Los Angeles, planned to join the party the next day in San Diego. The passage of nearly 70 years and (if one accepts any of the various "murder theories" surrounding Ince's death) a cover-up have obfuscated the facts of the case even down to who was on board the *Oneida* when it left San Pedro for a fun-filled cruise to San Diego and the Baja. Along with Hearst and his lover, Marion Davies, the passengers included: Dr. Daniel Carson Goodman (a licensed, but non-practicing physician who was the head of Cosmopolitan Pictures), novelist Elinor Glyn, film actress Seena Owen, Charlie Chaplin (Davies' alleged lover who later said he was *not* on board), Hearst columnist Louella Parsons (another many say had yet to even set foot in California), and others not central to the tragedy. On the morning of Sunday, November 16, Ince took an early train from L.A. to San Diego and met up with Hearst and company on board the *Oneida* anchored in the bay. Ince suffered from ulcers and a heart problem and allegedly complained of feeling ill on the wharf prior to boarding the yacht. That night at dinner as the happy company toasted Ince's natal day with illegal alcohol and gorged on the fine cuisine prepared by Hearst's private chef, Ince reportedly began to cough up blood and became understandably agitated. The next morning, Sunday, November 17, the 42-year-old film mogul was rushed by water-taxi to the shore after on board attempts by Dr. Goodman failed to lessen the severity of what was initially diagnosed as acute indigestion. Ince, with the doctor in attendance, was initially placed on a train for Los Angeles, but after his condition worsened was taken off at Del Mar and installed in a room at the Stratford Inn. There he was joined by his wife, Nell, and their 15-year-old son, William. Surrounded by doctors and nurses, Ince's condition stabilized and hope was entertained for a full recovery. A private railroad car was engaged and Ince, attended by two specialists and three nurses, made the trip back to Los Angeles on Tuesday, November 18. Ambulanced from the train station to his Benedict Canyon ranch, Ince died in bed at 5:30 A.M. the following morning, November 19, surrounded by his wife, three sons, and two brothers (John and Ralph, both filmmakers). Death was officially attributed to heart disease su-

perinduced by an attack of acute indigestion and Dr. Ida Cowan Glasgow duly signed the death certificate to that effect.

Rumors and innuendo, now the stuff of Hollywood legend, refused to pass away as quickly as did Thomas Harper Ince. All the permutations of the "murder theory" share a common theme — William Randolph Hearst was made insanely jealous by the imagined infidelities of his mistress, Marion Davies, and took decisive, deadly action. In one theory, the tycoon (angered by reportage in non–Hearst papers that Chaplin was keeping company with Davies) invited the "Little Tramp" on board the *Oneida* to determine if the couple had been intimate. The media mogul allegedly caught the pair in a compromising position, retrieved his diamond-studded revolver, and was preparing to shoot Chaplin when Tom Ince intervened, brought to the scene by the overwrought screams of Marion Davies. In the ensuing struggle, the gun discharged accidentally sending a lethal bullet into Ince's forehead. Supposedly, Chaplin's Japanese secretary, Toraichi Kono, saw the bleeding wound in the film mogul's head as he was removed from the *Oneida* in San Diego. A second version of the fatal incident has Hearst mistaking Ince for Chaplin (both had graying curly hair) and shooting the producer as he was innocently below deck in the yacht's ill-lit galley looking for something to relieve his upset stomach. In another version of the incident, Ince replaces Chaplin as Davies' ardent lover and he is shot by the elderly Hearst when he catches them together. Other theories, too elaborate or preposterous to recount, continue to circulate around this Hollywood legend. Several "suspicious" incidents added fuel to the ongoing speculation. Shortly after Ince's death, Hearst awarded Louella Parsons, a supposed witness to the murder, a lifetime contract and she became (with Hedda Hopper) the most powerful gossip columnist in Hollywood. Payment to buy her silence? Nell Ince, the grieving widow, was allegedly given a trust fund by Hearst to ensure her continued cooperation in maintaining the elaborate fiction surrounding her beloved husband's death. In return, she refused to have an autopsy conducted and ordered his immediate cremation to block any future attempt to determine the "true" cause of Ince's death.

On the morning of November 21, 1924, the body of Thomas Harper Ince was placed in an open casket at the Hollywood Cemetery Chapel and for one hour friends and studio employees were permitted to pay their final respects. Following the viewing, a private funeral service was held attended by family and a few close personal friends including Douglas Fairbanks, Mary Pickford, Charlie Chaplin, Harold Lloyd, Mack Sennett, Hal Roach, and Samuel Goldwyn. While Ince was not affiliated with any religious faith, wife Nell was a devotee of Theosophy, had her sons educated at a school run by the religion, and asked John Garrigues, a South Pasadena member of the United Lodge of Theosophists, to deliver the funeral oration. Meanwhile, as hundreds of letters and telegrams of condolence flooded Días Doradas, the mogul's palatial home in Benedict Canyon, and the Ince Studio at Culver City, the funeral service was awash in floral tributes sent by a who's who of Hollywood including Will H. Hays, Charlie Chaplin, Adolph Zukor, Tom Mix, Harry M. Warner, Jesse L. Lasky, Buster Keaton, Pola Negri, and D.W. Griffith. Two days later, filmland paid a final public tribute to Ince at a special memorial service at Grauman's Hollywood Egyptian Theatre where on a darkened velvet-shrouded stage a large portrait of Ince acted as stand-in for his cremated remains.

Still the rumors refused to die prompting San Diego District Attorney Chester C. Kempley to announce on December 9, 1924, an inquiry designed to clear up certain facts in Ince's death, most notably what preceded the producer's attack of indigestion on board the *Oneida*. Miss Jessie Howard, a trained nurse brought in to care for Ince, told investigators the filmmaker attributed his coughing up of bloody sputum to his incessant smoking at the celebration and the bad liquor he consumed on the yacht. Nell Ince informed the press that she knew of no circumstances aboard the *Oneida* that warranted an investigation. The next day the so-called inquiry was abruptly terminated without investigators even questioning the witnesses on board the party yacht. District Attorney Kempley issued the following statement on December 10, 1924:

> I began this investigation because of the many rumors brought to my office regarding the case and have continued it until today in order to definitely dispose of them. I am satisfied that the death of Mr. Ince was caused by heart failure as a result of acute indigestion. There will be no further investigation, at least so far as the county of San Diego is concerned. If there is any investigation of the stories of liquor drinking on board the yacht where

Mr. Ince was a guest it will have to be in Los Angeles where, presumably, the liquor was secured.

The "Father of the Western" left an estate valued at $1.6 million largely in stock in the Thomas H. Ince Corporation to his wife and three children. As previously mentioned, director Peter Bogdanovich (no stranger to personal tragedy — see entry Dorothy Stratten) offered one view of Ince's "murder" in *The Cat's Meow* (2001). In the 2001 film the principals are played by Cary Elwes (Ince), Edward Herrmann (Hearst), Kirsten Dunst (Davies), and Eddie Izzard (Charlie Chaplin). Tragically, Thomas Ince has become an obscure footnote in an American cinema he helped to define in its early years.

Further Reading

Anger, Kenneth. *Hollywood Babylon*. San Francisco: Straight Arrow, 1975.
Kaplan, Margaret Hall. "Inceville: Key Site for Film Pioneers." *Los Angeles Times*, February 12, 1984, sec. P, pp. 1–2, 30, 37, 41.
Munn, Michael. *The Hollywood Murder Casebook*. New York: St. Martin's, 1987.

Isenberg, Caroline (V)

The 23-year-old daughter of a Brookline, Massachusetts, psychiatrist, Isenberg studied acting at Harvard and was a member of the Harvard-Radcliffe Dramatic Club, the Harvard Independent Theatre, and the Lowell House Dramatic Society. Graduating in the fall of 1984, she relocated to New York City to continue her acting studies at the Neighborhood Playhouse School of the Theater. On October 10, 1984, she moved with a roommate into a three-room apartment, 7-C, on the top floor of an Upper West Side building at 929 West End Avenue. The building's security system consisted of a front-door lock and buzzer system that tenants often reported as being in disrepair. Returning home alone at 1:40 A.M. on December 2, 1984 after attending the Broadway production of *Hurlburly* at the Barrymore Theatre, Isenberg was confronted by a knife-wielding intruder and forced into the building's dimly lit 4' × 4' elevator for a ride to the roof. Forced to hand over her valuables ($12 in cash), Isenberg was stabbed nine times after refusing to have sex with the man. Neighbors, hearing the woman's agonized screams, called police who found Isenberg conscious on the tar paper rooftop, but badly injured. At St. Luke's Hospital Isenberg described her attacker as a "male black, light-skinned, with an apparently clean-shaven face and a square jaw."

Prior to dying on the operating room table at 7:25 A.M. she told police, "All this for $12.00. I should have given him the money. I should have let him do it. I should have given in." A massive manhunt for Isenberg's killer led to the arrest on December 6, 1984, of Emmanuel Torres, the 21-year-old son of the building's superintendent. According to police, Torres (a slight black man with a scraggly beard) confessed to the murder. The interview was terminated prior to its videotaping, however, when it was learned that the suspect was already awaiting trial on a charge of assaulting a man in the Bronx with a baseball bat in July 1984. Under recent court rulings the police had to assume that since Torres presumably already had an attorney for the assault he could not be currently questioned unless the lawyer from the Bronx case was present. On June 28, 1985, a jury of eight men and four women needed only six-and-a-half hours spread out over two days to find Torres guilty of second-degree murder. Although Torres maintained his innocence, his oral confession combined with testimony from jail inmates to whom he had bragged about the murder led to his conviction. Terming the murder of "Shakespearean proportions in its foul and tragic dimensions," Justice Stephen G. Crane sentenced Torres on August 5, 1985, to the maximum prison sentence of 25 years to life.

Further Reading

Raab, Selwyn. "Dying Student Called Resisting Rape a Mistake." *The New York Times,* December 4, 1984, sec. B, p. 1.

Ivers, Peter Scott (V)

Ivers, 36, hosted "New Wave Theater," a half-hour segment of the four hour weekly live music and video show *Night Flight* on the USA Cable Network. Described by network executives as a "New Wave Dick Clark," the Harvard graduate began "New Wave Theater" on local public access cable television in Los Angeles in the early 1980s as a forum for local punk rock and New Wave bands. The show was picked up by USA in 1982 and gave early exposure to bands like The Dead Kennedys, X, the Blasters, Wet Picnic, Attila, and the Brainiac. Outfitted in bizarre costumes and hats, Ivers asked each band, "What is the meaning of life?" just to provoke outlandish or rude answers. Earlier in his career, the television host had a recording career with the Boston-based band Beacon Street Union and Street Choir before going solo in 1969. Signing with Epic that year,

Ivers released *Knight of the Blue Communion,* a commercially unsuccessful blending of rock and classical music. In 1974, he released the album *Terminal Love* with Warner Brothers and two years later a self-titled album. Musically, Ivers is destined to be best remembered for composing and performing "In Heaven (The Lady and the Radiator Song)" in David Lynch's 1978 film *Eraserhead* which starred fellow-homicide victim, Jack Nance (see entry.) On March 3, 1983, Ivers was found beaten to death with a blunt object in his sixth-floor studio apartment in Los Angeles. Unable to contact the television host, a concerned neighbor entered Ivers' apartment to discover his battered body lying fully dressed on a bed. Police theorized that Ivers' unsolved murder was the result of an opportunistic burglary gone wrong, rather than due (as many believed) to his involvement in the punk music scene. Calling Ivers a "poet of the new music movement," "New Wave Theater" producer David Jove eulogized (that) "Where many saw new music as angry or dangerous, he made it accessible, healthy and important." In remembrance, Harvard University initiated the Peter Ivers Visiting Artist Program.

Further Reading

"Slain 'New Wave Theater' Host Apparent Burglary Victim." Associated Press, March 7, 1983.

Jackson, Al, Jr. (V)

With organist Booker T. Jones, bassist Donald "Duck" Dunn, and guitarist Steve Cropper, drummer Al Jackson (born November 11, 1934) formed the legendary house band of Memphis-based Stax Records, playing behind that label's roster of stars in the 1960s which included Otis Redding, Wilson Pickett, Sam & Dave, Rufus Thomas, and many other Soul and R&B greats. As Booker T. & the MGs ("Memphis Group") the band released its first Stax single "Green Onions" on August 11, 1962. The cooking instrumental stayed on the *Billboard* chart for 16 weeks, peaking at Number 3, and sold more than a million records. Other notable singles include "Groovin" (1967), "Soul-Limbo" (1968), "Hang 'Em High" (1968), "Time Is Tight" (1969), and a dynamite 1969 cover of the Simon & Garfunkel hit, "Mrs. Robinson." While the group disbanded in 1971, to briefly resurrect without Cropper and Jones in 1973, Jackson spent most of the 1970s working with performers like Al Green and Syl Johnson. In mid–September 1975, Cropper, Jones,

Dunn, and Jackson met to finalize the re-formation of Booker T. & the MGs in January 1976. Record companies Atlantic, Polydor, and Epic were reportedly offering contracts in the half-million dollar range to sign the group credited with almost single-handedly creating the signature Stax sound.

The marriage between Jackson, 39, and wife, Barbara, was on the rocks. In mid–1975, the drummer filed divorce papers, but continued to live with the woman pending the dissolution of their marriage. On July 31, 1975, an argument between the couple in their Memphis home nearly ended in a fatality after she shot Jackson in the chest. Assault and attempted murder charges filed against Barbara Jackson were later dropped after she convinced a judge she had acted in self-defense. The 39-year-old woman maintained her husband had first beaten then thrown her in a flower bed. In mid–September 1975, Jackson applied for a permit to carry a pistol on the grounds that he traveled extensively and often carried large sums of money. The carry permit was pending when, on Tuesday, September 30, 1975, the drummer rented an apartment in East Memphis and purchased home furnishings.

That evening around 11:00 P.M., Barbara Jackson returned home to 3885 Central from a beauty shop appointment to interrupt a burglary in progress. The intruder (later described by her as a black man between the ages of 25 and 35, sporting an Afro and mustache) demanded money from the woman and, when informed there was none, tied her to a chair with a cord torn from an iron, and continued to ransack the house. Al Jackson arrived home at 12:15 A.M. the next morning, October 1, after attending a closed-circuit telecast of the Muhammad-Ali/Joe Frazier fight. Momentarily untied by the burglar to allow her to admit the drummer into the house, Barbara Jackson was re-fastened to the chair and her husband forced at gunpoint to lie face-down on the floor. Jackson, unable to produce the money demanded by the intruder, was shot five times in the back. Soon after the gunman fled the scene, Barbara Jackson freed herself from the chair, and unable to phone for help because of her bound hands, ran into the street and flagged down a motorist. Police determined the burglar had gained access to the house by forcing open a bedroom window, but were unable to confirm the woman's statement that she saw a white man wearing a tee shirt standing near the front door as she fled the house. Barbara Jackson, grilled by police based on her recent troubled domestic history with the deceased, was eventually cleared.

On October 5, 1975, a crowd of grieving family, friends, and admirers overflowed the funeral service conducted at the Mississippi Boulevard Christian Church in Memphis where Jackson had been baptized as a boy. Nearly 200 mourners listened to the service via a public address system installed in a nearby building. Al Green, the singer Jackson had backed on many occasions, sang a moving rendition of "Amazing Grace" in honor of his friend. A shaken Steve Cropper commented, "I went through this with Otis [Redding, killed in a plane crash in 1967] and I thought it was the worst. But now part of my life is gone. He was one of the greatest drummers in the world. It's too much to take." Jackson's murder remains officially unsolved.

Further Reading

Kingsley, Patrick. "Stax/Booker T. Drummer Al Jackson Shot to Death." *Rolling Stone*, 199 (November 6, 1975):14.

Jackson, Michael (V)

One of the most dynamic singing artists and personalities in show business history, Michael Joseph Jackson (born August 29, 1958, in Gary, Indiana) has to date sold an estimated 750 million records world-wide. As a member of the Jackson 5 (with four older brothers), he signed his first recording contract in 1968 at the age of nine. Over the next forty or so years Jackson literally grew up in the media spotlight achieving unparalleled professional heights while enduring catastrophic personal lows largely brought about by his own eccentric behavior and ever-changing appearance. Jackson's collaborations with arranger Quincy Jones (*Off the Wall*, 1979; *Thriller*, 1982; *Bad*, 1987) changed the face of popular music by fusing soul, disco, and pop ballads into albums that appealed not only to fans of the various genres, but also to people who never traditionally purchased music. *Thriller*, the best selling album of all-time, has to date sold an estimated 53 million units while at the time of its release destroyed conventional industry wisdom that dictated only one or two songs on a record could be spun off as singles. Seven of the album's nine tracks entered the Top Ten and *Thriller* stayed on the charts for over two years enjoying 37 weeks at Number 1. The album, however, did more than sell a ton of records and earn the superstar a record eight Grammys in one night. Jackson realized before any of his contemporaries the power MTV possessed to promote his music to a diverse audience. Instead of offering a bland three minute presentation in which he sang the song and danced a little, Jackson expanded the music video into mini-films with elaborate production values and huge budgets. The video for the single "Thriller" (directed by John Landis) ran 15 minutes and featured a story replete with Vincent Price narration, beautifully choreographed zombies, and motion picture quality make-up. Other notable videos spawned by the album include "Beat It," a striking homage to *West Side Story*, and "Billie Jean," remarkable for Jackson's solo dance moves and trademark single sequined glove. MTV played the videos in heavy rotation making the singer a pioneer in opening up the network and the medium to the work of black performers. A media superstar, Jackson introduced his signature dance step, "the Moonwalk," at the Motown 25th anniversary special on May 16, 1983.

The biggest star in music, the self-proclaimed "King of Pop" was ground zero for the media, especially the tabloids that found in him the proverbial "gift from God." Michael Jackson was shy, soft-spoken, a semi-recluse, expressed little interest in the opposite sex, and was constantly in the company of children. Every aspect of the superstar's eccentric life was fodder for the tabloids. It was reported that after seeing the 1980 David Lynch film *The Elephant Man*, the singer attempted to buy the skeleton of Joseph (John) Merrick, the real-life Victorian attraction played by John Hurt. "Wacko Jacko," as he was dubbed in the British tabloids, reportedly slept in the same room as his pet chimpanzee, Bubbles, often in a hyperbaric chamber believing the highly oxygenated atmosphere would prolong his life to the age of 150. In public, he often wore a surgeon's mask ostensibly to ward off germs, but more realistically to cover the ill effects of numerous cosmetic surgeries. As Jackson aged, he became increasingly self-conscious of his looks and more enamored of plastic surgery first having his nose repaired in 1979 after it was broken during a dance routine. Soon, however, the entertainer's entire face began to change (some said in an attempt to look more like his friend and idol, Diana Ross). He had his nose thinned and a cleft put in his chin, but denied having his skin lightened to appear less "black." In 1993, Jackson told Oprah Winfrey he was suffering from vitiligo, a skin condition causing the loss of pigmentation. The superstar denied undergoing extensive plastic surgery, but it was undeniable that his face had changed dramatically over time. In later years, he took to wearing a prosthetic nose piece to cover a small hole surrounded by bits of cartilage.

The public, more specifically the ravenous tabloid press, might have dismissed Jackson's odd behavior and freakish appearance as the eccentricity of genius, were it not for his interest in, and devotion to, children. Jackson, a professional since the age of five, felt he had been robbed of a childhood by a strict father and the entertainment industry. Now among the richest entertainers in the world, the singer attempted to reclaim his childhood while insuring other children did not suffer the loss of theirs. In 1988, Jackson paid around $17 million for a 2,600 acre ranch in Los Olivos, California about 125 miles northwest of Los Angeles. Naming it Neverland after the mythical island in *Peter Pan*, the 30-year-old spent an estimated $35 million in upgrades to the property including the installation of a fifty seat movie theatre, a private zoo, a miniature railway, and a Ferris wheel among other amusement park rides. In short, Neverland was an idyllic sanctuary where Jackson, the evergreen Man-boy could retreat to reclaim a lost childhood surrounded by children whose parents were all-too willing to let their children spend overnights with the superstar (often sharing his bed). In August 1993, Jackson was accused by Beverly Hills dentist Evan Chandler of molesting his 13-year-old son, Jordan, at Neverland and other locations. The singer vigorously denied the charges claiming he was the victim of an extortion plot, but settled out of court in 1994 for an estimated $22 million. (Evan Chandler committed suicide on November 5, 2009). The sex abuse incident cast a lingering pall over the superstar's subsequent career and branded him, fairly or unfairly, as a homosexual pedophile.

In what was viewed by cynics as a transparent public relations move designed to rehabilitate his damaged image, Jackson married Lisa Marie Presley, daughter of Elvis, in the Dominican Republic on May 26, 1994. Their clumsy onstage kiss at the 2004 MTV Video Music Awards show did little to convince skeptics that the union was anything but a PR ploy. The couple divorced amicably in January 1996. In November 1996, Jackson married Deborah Jeanne Rowe, a nurse in his dermatologist's practice, in Sydney, Australia. Rowe, allegedly artificially inseminated, gave birth to two of Jackson's children — son Michael Jackson ("Prince") Jackson, Jr., in February 1997, and daughter Paris-Michael Katherine Jackson in April 1997. The couple divorced in late 1999 with Rowe receiving a generous settlement and Jackson awarded full custody of the children. In 2002, the "King of Pop" added another son, Prince Michael Jackson, II, more popularly known as "Blanket." The identity of Blanket's mother has not been made public. In 2003, British journalist Martin Bashir was given unprecedented access to the entertainer in a series of interviews that must have been imagined by Jackson's handlers as a way to kickstart their client's career. The singer had not released a CD since 1995 (*HIStory: Past, Present and Future, Book I*) and most publicity since that time had not shown the singer in a favorable light. Bashir's television documentary, *Living with Michael Jackson*, aired in February 2003 and was a public relations nightmare for the eccentric superstar. Jackson defended as "loving" his practice of letting young boys sleep in his bed at Neverland. The admission led to increased speculation regarding Jackson's possible sexual interests as well placing him on the radar of authorities in Santa Barbara County.

In November 2003, Neverland was searched by police in response to allegations Jackson, 46, had molested a 13-year-old boy who had spent the night there several times during the year. He was booked on multiple counts of engaging in lewd or lascivious contact with a child younger than 14 and released after handing over his passport and posting $3 million bail. The alleged victim, a cancer survivor, reported Jackson gave him alcohol on several occasions prior to inappropriate sexual touching. Jackson, facing up to 20 years in prison if convicted of child molestation as well as the certain end of a brilliant career, vigorously fought the charges. Following nearly a five month trial, Jackson was acquitted of all charges on June 14, 2005. The superstar was free, but even more suspect in the eyes of all but his most loyal fans. He was also broke. Jackson always lived a lavish lifestyle and loved to shop. In 1999 alone, his personal expenses were $7.5 million while it cost an additional $5 million annually to maintain Neverland. In 1998, Jackson took out a loan for $140 million from Bank of America upping it two years later to $200 million. More loans from other financial institutions followed. As collateral against his massive debt, Jackson put up his share of ATV Music Publishing, a firm holding the

rights to a portfolio of thousands of songs including 259 Beatles tunes written by John Lennon (see entry) and Paul McCartney. Jackson purchased ATV in 1985 for $47.5 million, effectively ending his personal and professional relationship with McCartney, who had earlier told him music rights were an excellent investment. Ten years later the superstar was forced by economic necessity to sell a 50 percent interest in ATV to Sony for $90 million. The joint venture, Sony/ATV, owns a music catalog conservatively valued at over $1 billion. Still, in 2009 creditors were moments away from foreclosing on Neverland after Jackson defaulted on a $24.5 million debt he owed on the property. Neverland was saved after Colony Capital L.L.C. bought the note and entered into a joint venture with the singer. Shortly after his acquittal in 2005, Jackson and his children sought refuge from the press in the Middle Eastern emirate of Bachrain at the invitation of Sheik Abdullah bin Hamad al-Khalifa, son of the king. According to court papers filed by the prince in November 2008, al-Khalifa covered Jackson's living and travel expenses during his year in Bachrain, built him a state-of-the-art recording studio, spent over $300,000 for a motivational guru, and footed a $250,000 cash bill so the singer could entertain friends at Christmas. The sheik, an amateur songwriter and owner of 2 Seas Records, further claimed Jackson reneged on a contract with his label to produce a new CD release in 2007, an autobiography and a stage play, after accepting multimillion dollar advances. The suit for $7 million was settled out of court for an undisclosed sum.

Despite his legal and financial troubles, Michael Jackson was still a world-wide cultural phenomenon with a rabidly loyal fan base. The singer returned to Los Angeles in 2009 from his self-imposed exile abroad determined to stage a comeback tour unlike any other in the history of popular music. The This Is It Tour set to begin in July 2009 and conclude in March 2010 was envisioned as a series of 50 concerts at the 02, an 18,000 seat arena on the banks of the Thames River in eastern London. Amid speculation that this would be the superstar's final tour, 1.6 million people signed up for a chance to purchase tickets. The tickets sold out immediately. Although Jackson stood to earn at least $50 million from the shows, those closest to him stated categorically that money was not the principal motivation for his comeback. Prince, Paris, and Blanket had never seen their father perform live and he wanted to show them why he was considered the "King of Pop." In return for his commitment to do the shows, he demanded the promotion company AEG Live install him and the kids into an English-style country manor where they could ride horses. Jackson also insisted that at tour's end he be commemorated in the *Guinness Book of Records* for some (to be determined) accomplishment. While in Los Angeles rehearsing the elaborate show, the 50-year-old star rented a seven bedroom chateau style mansion in the exclusive Holmby Hills section of the city for a $100,000 a month. Determined to eat healthy, Jackson engaged a full-time chef and began workouts with Lou Ferrigno, the bodybuilder who appeared in the late 1970s–early 1980s television series, *The Hulk*. Most important to the star's health, however, was a doctor he trusted who could be on 24-hour call throughout the tour.

In April 2009, Michael Jackson spoke to several doctors about his chronic insomnia and requested prescriptions for a laundry list of sedatives. The star had battled an addiction to painkillers for years since being badly burned during the filming a Pepsi commercial in 1984. Now, as he pushed his body to the limits during workouts and rehearsals, access to drugs became even more of a priority in his life. The physicians consulted refused Jackson's request for Diprivan, the brand-name version of propofol, a powerful potentially life-threatening anesthetic they cautioned should only be administered by a licensed professional in a hospital setting. In addition to its properties as a sedative, propofol could magnify the effects of other drugs in a patient's system making its unlicensed use even more potentially hazardous. Jackson, however, was no stranger to acquiring drugs. For years he had employed various pseudonyms to get prescription medications including the sedatives lorazepam and midazolam. In May 2009, AEG Live hired Dr. Conrad Murray at Jackson's insistence at an astronomical salary of $150,000 a month. A cardiologist (licensed in California, Nevada, and Texas), Dr. Murray had a three year relationship with the star and Jackson felt a strong "rapport" with him. The doctor was set to travel to England with Jackson and remain on 24 hour call throughout the tour. Given Murray's sketchy personal history he was an odd choice to be the legendary pop star's attending physician. Murray had at least seven children by six different women and always seemed in need

of money. Murray's Nevada practice, Global Vascular Associates, faced more than $400,000 in judgments and two cases were pending. Between 1993 and 2003 he had several tax liens filed against him in California and Arizona in addition to massive credit card debt, delinquent student loans, and late child support payments. Still, the 50-year-old "King of Pop" felt a "rapport" with the 51-year-old doctor.

On the evening of June 24, 2009, Jackson conducted a grueling six hour dress rehearsal of the concert at the Staples Center prior to returning to his Holmby Hills mansion. According to Dr. Murray's later statement to police, he had been treating Jackson's insomnia for the last six weeks by administering 50 milligrams of propofol every night via an intravenous drip. Recently, however, he had grown fearful the music star was becoming addicted to the anesthetic known as "milk of amnesia" (because of its creamy white color) and was attempting to "wean" his patient from the drug by lowering the dosage to 25 milligrams and adding small doses of the sedatives lorazepam and midazolam. Propofol, however, is not addictive or cause cravings. Two days before, the chemical cocktail had worked. The next day, according to Murray, he cut off propofol, and Jackson fell asleep under the influence of just the two sedatives. Around 1:30 A.M. on June 25, Murray began Jackson's nightly sleep ritual by giving the entertainer a 10 milligram tablet of Valium. Around 2:00 A.M. he injected 2 milligrams of lorezapam followed by a 2 milligram injection of midazolam around 3:00 A.M. The injections of lorezapam and midazolam were repeated at 5:00 A.M. and 7:00 P.M., respectively. Still, however, Jackson had not fallen asleep and demanded his "milk." Finally, around 10:40 A.M., Murray relented and administered 25 milligrams of the anesthetic, a small dose, and Jackson fell quickly asleep. Murray stayed with the singer for ten minutes prior to leaving for a two-minute bathroom break. When he returned Michael Jackson was in cardiac arrest, but had a faint pulse. Murray administered CPR and made at least three phone calls on his cell phone between 11:18 A.M. and 12:05 P.M. A 911 call was placed at 12:21 P.M. and when trained paramedics arrived at Jackson's top-floor bedroom five minutes later he was not breathing. They administered CPR at the scene for 42 minutes before ambulancing him to the nearby Ronald Reagan UCLA Medical Center. A team of doctors worked over the superstar for an hour before calling the time of death at 2:26 P.M. The subsequent out-pouring of grief over the shocking demise of the 50-year-old "King of Pop" was unprecedented culminating in a public memorial service at the Staples Center on July 7, 2009 broadcast live to a global audience of over 1 billion. Following months of legal wrangling, Jackson was interred in the Holly Terrace section in the Great Mausoleum in Forest Lawn Cemetery in Glendale on September 3, 2009. The interment site is inaccessible to the public although the flowers delivered daily are reportedly placed near his tomb. Since his death, Jackson's world-wide CD sales have surged topping 29 million units and the film, *This Is It*, cobbled together from rehearsal footage for the 02 concerts, was a box office smash.

The investigation into the death of Michael Jackson was assigned to the Robbery-Homicide unit of the LAPD. Robbery-Homicide had investigated the cases of O.J. Simpson (see entry) and Robert Blake (see entry) with less than stellar results and the L.A. County district attorney's office had consistently demonstrated its limitations in successfully prosecuting high profile cases. Simpson and Blake "walked" while it took two costly trials to finally convict eccentric record producer Phil Spector (see entry) of second-degree murder in May 2009. Anxious to avoid yet another embarrassing public humiliation, the LAPD and D.A.'s office proceeded slowly and methodically in their investigation while the coroner's office conducted an autopsy. Jackson's family had a second private autopsy performed. Dr. Conrad Murray was questioned twice by detectives who focused on the all-important timeline in the superstar's death. As news leaked to the press concerning the cocktail of drugs administered as "sleep aids" by Murray to Jackson, conventional medical opinion was firmly against the man dubbed the "deathbed doctor" by the tabloids. Propofol, an anesthetic, does not induce restorative sleep. The anesthetic was designed for use by trained medical personnel in a hospital setting to induce unconsciousness in patients during medical procedures. On-site resuscitation equipment is mandatory whenever the drug is used because the correct dosage is determined by the weight of the patient (Jackson weighed 136 pounds) and can be tricky. Propofol also depresses breathing, lowers the heart rate, and can magnify the effects of other drugs in the system—a dangerous combination for Jackson who routinely took a cocktail of sedatives ostensibly to battle insomnia.

In late July 2009, it became apparent Dr. Conrad Murray was the target of a manslaughter investigation. Search warrants were issued for his clinic in Houston and a nearby rented storage unit as well as his home and business in Las Vegas. Tellingly, the court documents referred to Jackson as an "addict" and sought information on the doctor's use of propofol. Computers and business papers were seized from the locations, but no propofol was found. Investigators did learn Murray had legally purchased five 100-milliliters bottles of the anesthetic on May 12, 2009, from Applied Pharmacy Services in Nevada and brought the drug with him to Los Angeles. In early August, Murray (hounded into seclusion by the press and the singer's angry fans) uploaded a short YouTube video in which he stated he had told the truth to investigators and insisted the "truth" would prevail. On August 28, 2009, the L.A. County coroner's office released its official report ruling the pop star's death a homicide caused by "acute propofol intoxication." Lorazepam, a sedative sold under the name Ativan, also contributed to his death. Also present in Jackson's system were the sedatives midazolam and diazepam, the painkiller lidocaine, and the stimulant ephedrine. No illegal drugs were found in Jackson at the time of his death. For a man of 50, Jackson was in good health although bed sores were present on his body, a possible holdover from the period following his 2005 acquittal on child molesting charges when he spent long periods in bed. Jackson's good health blocked a potential defense strategy that could argue the singer hid from doctors a serious pre-existing condition that increased the risk of death from drugs he willingly took. The homicide ruling also gave the L.A. County district attorney's office more options if it chose to prosecute. A homicide ruling does not mean a crime was committed while manslaughter is defined as homicide without malice or premeditation. To win a conviction, the prosecution need only prove a doctor acted recklessly and with negligence. On February 8, 2010, some seven months after Jackson's death, the L.A. County district attorney's office charged Dr. Conrad Murray with involuntary manslaughter. The doctor pleaded "not guilty" and posted a $75,000 bail. Deputy Dist. Atty. David Walgren of the major crimes division, also involved in extradition hearings against director Roman Polanski (see Sharon Tate entry), will try the upcoming case.

Further Reading

Andersen, Christopher P. *Michael Jackson: Unauthorized.* New York: Simon and Schuster, 1994.

Boteach, Shmuel. *The Michael Jackson Tapes: A Tragic Icon Reveals His Soul in Intimate Conversations.* New York: Vanguard, 2009.

Fine, Jason. *Michael.* New York: HarperStudio, 2009.

Halperin, Ian. *Unmasked: The Final Years of Michael Jackson.* New York: Simon Spotlight Entertainment, 2009.

Hoffman, Claire. "The Last Days of Michael Jackson," *Rolling Stone,* 1084 (August 6, 2009):44–52.

Huey, Steve. "Michael Jackson." www.allmusic.com.

Jackson, Michael. *Moonwalk.* Rev. ed. New York: Harmony, 2009.

Jefferson, Margo. *On Michael Jackson.* New York: Pantheon, 2006.

Taraborrelli, J. Randy. *Michael Jackson: The Magic, the Madness, the Whole Story, 1958–2009.* New York: Grand Central, 2009.

Jam Master Jay (V)

Hailed by many critics as the "Beatles of hip-hop," the group Run–D.M.C. (Joseph "Run" Simmons, Darryl "D.M.C." McDaniels, Jason William "Jam Master Jay" Mizell) was a seminal hardcore rap group that became the first such act to craft concept albums, enjoy crossover success in mainstream rock, and to earn a Grammy nomination. All natives of the New York borough of Hollis, Queens, rappers Run and D.M.C. enlisted Mizell, an accomplished turntable scratcher, while still in high school and formed the group Orange Crush in the early 1980s. Upon leaving school, the trio changed their name to Run–D.M.C. and began actively circulating demos ultimately signing a deal with Profile Records for a $25,000 advance. Their first single in 1983, "It's Like That" and B-side "Sucker M.C.s," introduced a new rap sound fusing hard drum machine beats and turntable scratching furnished by Jam Master Jay with dynamic literate lyrics and overlapping vocals supplied by Run and D.M.C. "It's Like That" entered into the R&B Top 20 while "Sucker M.C.s" gave rap one of its signature phrases. The group scored other notable singles ("Hard Times," "Jam Master Jay," "Rock Box," "30 Days") all included on their debut album, *Run–D.M.C.,* released in 1984. Viewed as a landmark album in hip-hop, the group's blending of the sounds of hard rock with gritty raps about life on the streets resulted in a gold record, the first in rap's history. In addition to a new sound fusing rock with hip-hop, the group's signature look (three-striped white Adidas shoes, sports clothes, black leather coats, caps) also became an instantly recognizable and widely imitated fashion statement. In 1985, Run–D.M.C. toured relentlessly,

but found time to star in a film, *Krush Groove,* and to release their second album, *King of Rock,* a clear statement of the group's commitment to further explore the union of rock and rap. In this album, Jam Master Jay (Mizell, born in Brooklyn on January 21, 1965) emerged as what music writer Stephen Thomas Erlewine called the backbone of the group and his turntable scratching skills are prominently featured in "Jam-Master Jammin" and "Darryl and Joe."

Mainstream stardom beyond the insular world of hip-hop, however, came in 1986 after producer Rick Rubin signed on to co-produce their third album, *Raising Hell,* with longtime Run–D.M.C. producer and Run's brother, Russell Simmons. The most memorable track on the record paired the hip-hop pioneers with Steven Tyler and Joe Perry of Aerosmith in a rap-rock cover of the rock group's 1975 hit, "Walk This Way." The supporting video became the second most played piece on MTV and helped fuel album sales of over three million units making it the first rap record to reach Number One on the R&B chart and to go platinum. Other "firsts" soon followed. In August 1985, the group became the first rappers to appear on *American Bandstand,* and followed that distinction by being the first of their musical genre to appear on the cover of *Rolling Stone* (December 4, 1986). If musical success was not enough, in July 1986 the shoe giant Adidas signed Run–D.M.C. to endorse its three-stripe sneaker (the first non-athletes ever to be asked) which had long been the group's signature footwear. *Tougher than Leather,* their fourth album released at a time when the group was commanding $100,000 per live performance, also supported a motion picture by the same title directed by record producer Rick Rubin. A 1970s blaxploitation parody starring Run–D.M.C., the film failed to connect with rap audiences who had turned suspicious of hip-hop-rock crossover acts and were now embracing hardcore rappers like Public Enemy, Ice Cube, and Ice-T. Although the album went platinum it failed to yield any hit singles and marked the beginning of the end of the group as rap innovators and top sellers. Three other albums (*Back from Hell,* 1990; *Down with the King,* 1993; *Crown Royal,* 1999), while enjoyable were further proof that the group's glory days were behind them although popular artists of the day (Public Enemy, Naughty by Nature, Q-Tip) openly acknowledged their debt to Run–D.M.C.

Shortly after the release of *Back from Hell* key

elements of the group experienced hard times. Run (Joseph Simmons) was accused of raping a woman after a concert in Cleveland in August 1991 and arrested. While awaiting trial, Run became a born again Christian and had further reason to believe in the almighty after a judge tossed the rape case out of court with prejudice in February 1992. After being cleared, Run stated that he felt no animosity toward his accuser and blamed a life spent taking drugs for most of his problems. Meanwhile, D.M.C. (Darryl McDaniels) was fighting his own personal demons — alcohol and depression. At one point, the rapper's drinking became so bad that he began to embarrass himself onstage slurring words and forgetting rhymes. In 1993, D.M.C. became a born again Christian and quit drinking. Throughout the post–*Tougher than Leather* era Jay just kept working, but faced his own problems. Informed by the Internal Revenue Service that he owed over $100,000 and would soon have a lien placed on his earnings, Jay started his own label, JMJ Records, and produced artists including the Afros (*Kicking Afrolistics*, 1990) and Onyx (*BacDaFucUp*, 1993). When Run–D.M.C. did tour it was no longer to sold-out arenas, although they still commanded a loyal following. Run, however, had recently informed his bandmates that he was leaving the group.

On October 30, 2002, Jay, 37, was in his 24–7 Recording Studio on Merrick Boulevard producing a record for a group called Rusty Waters featuring his friend and business partner Randy Allen. Around 7:30 P.M. the rapper took a break and sat in the second-floor lounge with Uriel "Tony" Rincon, 25, to play a video football game. In addition to the two men, four others were in the studio that night including Allen. While accounts have varied widely over time depending upon who is recounting the events, what remains certain is that two armed men were buzzed into the locked building and climbed the stairs to the second-floor lounge. One stood near the door while the other, a large man wearing a black sweatsuit, approached Jay and embraced him (leading detectives to believe the DJ knew his killer) before producing a .40-caliber pistol. The gunman's first shot missed and struck Rincon, but a second shot fired at point-blank range fatally entered into the left side of Jay's head behind the ear. The intruders escaped down the stairs leaving behind only two empty shell casings. A police canvass of the surrounding area turned up a .380

semiautomatic pistol unrelated to the crime. Rincon was treated for his injury and released from hospital the next day. Authorities were unclear of the motive behind the murder of the popular married father of three who had no connection to the East Coast–West Coast rap rivalry that had already claimed the lives of two of hip-hop's biggest stars, Tupac Shakur (see entry) and the Notorious B.I.G. (see entry). Stymied by the reluctance of witnesses to cooperate, authorities formulated possible theories of the case. The gangsta rapper 50 Cent (Curtis Jackson) was a protégé of Jay's whose mocking raps directed at other performers may have resulted in his mentor's murder. Another theory explained the killing as simply the result of a dispute over money while another looked into Jay's possible involvement in the murky world of drugs. Though unsubstantiated, the drug angle was predicated on Jay's association with Curtis Scoon. Both men had allegedly pooled $15,000 each to purchase cocaine from a dealer in 1993, but after the drugs were sold their pusher took off with the money. Scoon heatedly denied any drug involvement, but did admit that Jay owed him money for a personal loan. Jay's longtime friend and business partner, Randy Allen, also drew official notice when it was learned that both men held personal insurance policies naming the other as beneficiary.

While investigators tried futilely to solve the murder, Hollis, Queens, prepared to bury one of its own. Hours after news of the beloved figure's murder was announced, fans constructed a street memorial outside the studio on Merrick Boulevard comprised of roses, memorial candles, an old turntable, and a single Adidas sneaker bearing the inscription, "R.I.P. JMJ." On November 4, 2002, a wake was held in the J. Foster Phillips Funeral Home in St. Albans, Queens. Outside in the rain under the watchful eye of police, a respectful crowd of three hundred (many wearing laceless Adidas) stretched three blocks down Linden Boulevard waiting to pay their respects to a beloved artist who had never forsaken his community. Jay was unstinting in offering assistance to aspiring rappers listening to and critiquing their demo tapes and helping them to secure record deals. Recently, he founded the Scratch DJ Academy where students could learn D.J. techniques. Inside the mortuary, Jay was laid out in his trademark leather suit, broad-brimmed black hat, gold chains, and the ubiquitous three-striped pair of white Adidas. The next day, the funeral service in the Greater Allen Cathedral in Jamaica, Queens, was attended by hip-hop luminaries including Foxy Brown, Dr. Dre, A Tribe Called Quest, Queen Latifah, and Doug E. Fresh. The pulpit was covered with floral displays fashioned to look like records and a turntable. The centerpiece read simply, "Love. Respect LL Cool J, Student." Both bandmates eulogized their friend, but the highlight of the ceremony came after Run led the congregation through the Prayer of Comfort then added, "[Jason] helped to create this hip-hop nation. Jason walked in grace, in style, and with class. I don't know if I should say this, but I believe this is Jason's biggest hit ever: all the support that has come in, all the people that have cried out across the world." Afterwards, pallbearers wearing matching black leather coats, fedoras, and three-striped Adidas carried the coffin to a white hearse for its ride to Ferncliff Cemetery in Hartsdale, New York. At the cemetery, Jay's wife Terry Corley-Mizell and their three children each released doves. The next day, Run and D.M.C. announced at a press conference attended by Sean "Puff Daddy" Combs, Busta Rhymes, and the Beastie Boys that they would not continue to record as a group in the irreplaceable absence of their friend and bandmate. Also announced was a fund to provide for the immediate needs of the murdered star's family as well as the foundation of a college scholarship for the children. Of the fund, $50,000 was set aside for tips leading to the arrest and conviction of Jam Master Jay's killers.

The murder investigation stalled for years hampered by the understandable reluctance of witnesses to testify against the thugs responsible for the crime. In April 2007, however, career criminal Ronald "Tenad" Washington was identified as an accessory in Jay's murder by an unnamed witness during his trial for six armed robberies committed just weeks after the rapper's murder. Washington was also a prime suspect in the murder of rapper Randy Walker (see entry Big Stretch) in 1995. Washington was convicted of the armed robberies, but denied killing Jay or Walker. "They want to blame me for all the blood in rap," Washington complained. One woman, Lydia High, sister of Jay's business partner, Randy Allen, told authorities that she was near the door of the 24-7 Recording Studio on the day of the murder when Washington forced her face-down on the floor while the second gunman pumped a bullet into the rapper's head. Washington admitted being at the studio that day, but only because Jay had

wanted him there for protection. A few months later, Randy Allen, once considered a suspect in the murder, broke his five year silence and told authorities that while he could not identify the shooter (he was in the recording booth, not the lounge) he had noticed a tattoo on the gunman's neck as he fled the scene. In published newspaper accounts, Allen has stated his belief that the killers are from the Hollis neighborhood and condemns Uriel "Tony" Rincon, wounded in Jay's shooting, for refusing to identify the assailants. It must be noted, however, that as of early 2010 not one individual either named or unnamed in the case has been arrested or charged with the murder of popular DJ. In 2007, MTV.com and VH1 declared Run-D.M.C. the Greatest Hip-Hop Group of All Time and the Greatest Hip-Hop Artist of All Time, respectively. The group credited with bringing hip-hop into the mainstream was inducted into the Rock and Roll Hall of Fame in 2009.

Further Reading

Erlewine, Stephen Thomas. "Run-D.M.C." www.allmusic. com.
Kiersh, Ed. "Beating the Rap." *Rolling Stone*, 488 (December 4, 1986):58–60, 62–63, 102, 104.
Ro, Ronin. *Raising Hell: The Reign, Ruin, and Redemption of Run-D.M.C. and Jam Master Jay.* New York: Amistad, 2005.
Thigpen, David E. *Jam Master Jay: The Heart of Hip Hop.* New York: Pocket Star, 2003.

Januskevicius, Melissa A. (V)

An aspiring country singer from Stevens Point, Wisconsin, Januskevicius performed the national anthem at a few Milwaukee Brewers home games and upon graduating high school in 1997 briefly recorded in Nashville, Tennessee. Recently married with a new job working with Alzheimer's patients at a residential treatment center in Stevens Point, the 20 year old left home on August 13, 1999 with an area record producer to complete her first CD at the independent Omni Recording Studio in Nashville. Recording as Melissa Love, the singer had just finished the final mix of her CD, *Melissa Love Won't Settle for Less*, when illness forced her to change her plans to drive back to Stevens Point with her producer. Instead, she would wait a few days, recuperate, and take a bus back home. On August 16, Januskevicius left Nashville for Stevens Point by way of stops in Louisville and Chicago, but when she failed to arrive as scheduled her parents notified authorities. Two days later, the partially nude and decomposing body of a woman was found in a vacant lot on the western edge of downtown Louisville some five blocks from the Greyhound bus station. The body was identified by dental records as that of the young singer. Januskevicius had been raped and strangled with a belt she had won in 1994 as the queen of the Kellner Rodeo near Wisconsin Rapids. Authorities determined that Januskevicius was last seen alive at the bus terminal around 11:30 P.M. on August 16 while on a one-hour layover for a bus change to Chicago. The outgoing singer had spoken to fellow passengers about her upcoming CD and even sung a few songs. The case remained cold for nearly 4 years until January 2004 when Glenn Isaac Goins, 22, of Johnson City, Kentucky was arrested for the rape-murder of Amanda Wood, a 24-year-old pregnant woman whose body was found in the crawl space of his mother's home. In custody, Goins admitted that he "liked killing people" and confessed to murdering several women in various states including Januskevicius. On the morning of September 25, 2006, Goins was found by guards hanging by a bed sheet in his cell at the Northeast Correctional Complex in Mountain City, Tennessee where he was awaiting a trial date for the rape-murder of Amanda Woods. For Brenda Schmidt, the mother of Melissa Januskevicius, the killer's suicide left forever unanswered the question, "What could have possibly happened in his life that made him want to hurt her?"

Further Reading

"Wisconsin Victim's Mom Says Suspect's Death Doesn't Ease Pain." Associated Press, September 26, 2006.

Jenkins, Ryan Alexander (M-S)

A self-described mega-successful investment banker and real estate developer from Calgary, Jenkins, 32, was a finalist on the VH1 television reality show, *Megan Wants a Millionaire*, in which well-to-do bachelors competed to win the affections of Megan Hauserman. The good-looking Canadian appeared in three episodes prior to being eliminated. Jenkins was also set to appear in the network's upcoming reality series *I Love Money 3*. Had VH1 producers conducted a more rigorous background check on Jenkins it is highly unlikely that he would have been selected to appear on a program in which the object is to marry a woman. In January 2007, the businessman was sentenced in Calgary to 15 months probation for an unspecified assault charge on his then ex-girl-

friend. In addition to imposing a restraining order on Jenkins, the court ordered him to attend a battery of counseling sessions for anger management, domestic violence, and sexual addiction. Shortly after filming wrapped for *Megan Wants a Millionaire*, Jenkins married 28-year-old swimsuit model Jasmine Fiore (birth name Lapore) two days after meeting her in a Las Vegas strip club where she worked. The beautiful blonde dreamed of making it big when she first arrived in Vegas, but instead scored only low-level jobs dealing cards at the Palms Playboy Club, serving cocktails in the MGM Grand, and being bodypainted at parties. Jenkins, the son of a wealthy Canadian architect, valued his net worth at $2.5 million and must have seemed to Fiore like a prize catch. The ill-conceived marriage, however, was troubled from the start. In June 2009, the reality show contestant was charged in Clark County, Nevada, with "battery constituting domestic violence," a misdemeanor, for allegedly punching Fiore in the arm. A non-jury trial was set for December 2009. Both partners cheated on one another, but stayed together even after Fiore changed her last name to "Kinkaid" and relocated to a penthouse apartment in the 800 block of Edinburgh Avenue near Melrose in Los Angeles to start a personal training business.

On August 13, 2009, the couple checked into the upscale resort hotel L'Auberge Del Mar to attend a poker tournament at the nearby San Diego Hilton. According to witnesses at the Hilton, Jenkins argued with Fiore in the hotel's lobby after observing her speaking on a cell phone to an ex-boyfriend. Security tapes at the L'Auberge Del Mar showed him checking out alone around 9:00 A.M. the next day. The next morning, August 15, a man scrounging for recyclables in a dumpster behind a Buena Park apartment complex in the 7400 block of Franklin Street made a grisly discovery of a large gray bloodstained suitcase. Police were summoned and opened the luggage to find the badly beaten nude body of a woman whose fingers and teeth had been removed to hinder identification. An autopsy determined that the woman's nose had been broken and death was fixed as due to strangulation. On the night the body was discovered, however, Ryan Jenkins filed a missing person's report with the LAPD claiming that he had not seen his wife since she dropped him off at their apartment after returning from their trip to San Diego. As police searched for the missing woman, the 32-year-old investment banker spent August 16 packing his car prior to leaving the "City of Angels" for good. By the time authorities identified the dismembered body in the dumpster as that of Jasmine Fiore through a serial number taken from her breast implants, her husband (now facing a first-degree murder charge in Orange County) had a multi-day headstart.

Based on cell phone records and his contact with people (including an attorney) throughout his flight, authorities determined that Jenkins made a 1,000 mile dash to Washington state where it was believed he crossed over into Canada on foot. His speedboat, the Night Ride Her, was discovered by police on a spit of land across from Blaine, Washington. Investigators later found a storage unit in Washington filled with his belongings including a suitcase of clothes. The international manhunt for Ryan Alexander Jenkins ended on August 23, 2009, after the manager of the Thunderbird Motel in Hope, Alberta, 100 miles east of Vancouver, discovered the man's body hanging by a belt from a clothing rack in his room. Three days earlier, Jenkins had arrived with a woman driving a Chrysler PT Cruiser with an Alberta license plate who paid $130 cash for three nights while he sat in the car. The woman drove away and did not return. Her name was not released and any charges against her remained unfiled as of press time for this book. In the wake of the murder-suicide, VH1 suspended the airing of *Megan Wants a Millionaire* after three episodes and cancelled plans to run *I Love Money 3* set to air in January 2010. Critics of reality shows, particularly those based on brokering romance, used the tragedy to demand stricter vetting procedures for contestants.

Further Reading

de Moraes, Lisa. "VH1 Abandons Reality Series After Contestant's Apparent Suicide." *Washington Post*, August 25, 2009, sec. C, p. 6.
Flaccus, Gillian. "TV Show Contestant Delayed Flight After Wife Died." Associated Press, August 28, 2009.

Jerome, Helene (V)

A graduate of the Royal Dramatic Academy in London, Jerome acted on stage in China, but never appeared in films. On August 27, 1958, Jerome's ex-husband, Edwin, became alarmed after the switchboard operator at the Hollywood apartment where the former actress lived informed him that her phone had been off the hook for several hours. Edwin Jerome entered the apartment at 1738 N. Las Palmas Avenue and found Helene's naked body in the rear, a victim of strangulation. Investigating officers discovered a screen torn away from a painted window which allowed the killer access to the apartment. A few days later, Edgar G. McAdoo, a 25-year-old carhop from Texas, was arrested on suspicion of murder due to his resemblance to a police sketch based on descriptions of witnesses who saw a man with the 50-year-old onetime actress in a bar shortly before her death. McAdoo admitted being with Jerome and to escorting her back to the apartment, but insisted he then left. The case against McAdoo collapsed due to a lack of physical evidence and his passing of a lie detector test. Only momentarily deterred, authorities arrested Miller F. Dowdy, 42, on September 6, 1958. The operator of a newsstand on Hollywood Boulevard only a half block from Jerome's apartment on N. Las Palmas, Dowdy admitted briefly dating the woman, but maintained he was at work on the day of the killing. As with McAdoo, the case against Dowdy soon fell apart. The Jerome murder remained a cold case until November 21, 1962, when Michael John Donahue, a 26-year-old shipping clerk from La Puente, California, walked into a Portland, Oregon police station and confessed to the strangulation. Guilt-stricken over the murder, he fled to Oregon to "try and get away from it all." Donahue pleaded guilty to second-degree murder and was sentenced in April 1963 to a prison term of 5 years to life.

Further Reading

"Woman's Killing Here 4 Years Ago Confessed." *Los Angeles Times*, November 22, 1962, sec. B, p. 1.

Johnson, Jason *see* Camoflauge

Johnson, Robert (V)

Now synonymous with the Delta blues and known in myth as the guitarist who sold his soul to the Devil at a rural Southern crossroads, Robert Johnson died in 1938 at age 26 leaving behind just 29 recorded compositions (and 12 alternate versions) that have influenced successive generations of musicians, most notably guitar giant Eric Clapton. The subject of intense interest since black music champion John Hammond belatedly learned of his death while organizing a "From Spirituals to Swing" concert at Carnegie Hall in 1938, Robert Leroy Johnson's biography, as cobbled together by various researchers, is filled with contradictory eyewitness accounts and speculation, although there are some areas of consensus. Johnson's mother, Julia Ann Majors, married

Charlie Dodds, Jr., a landowning farmer and furniture maker, in February 1889. The couple had six daughters with Dodds contributing another two sons to the family from an affair with his mistress. Around 1907, Dodds was forced to leave his home and family following a serious run-in with two prominent white businessmen. He relocated to Memphis under the assumed name "C.D. Spencer" leaving wife Julia Ann Majors with some of their children back in Hazlehurst, Mississippi. On May 8, 1911, future blues great Robert Johnson was born there the product of an affair between Majors and a sharecropper named Noah Johnson. Ultimately, Majors, her legitimate children, and Robert Johnson reunited with Charlie Dodds (now Spencer), their children as well as his mistress and their sons into one large family in Memphis. Julia Majors exited the extended family arrangement in 1914 to work elsewhere leaving Robert Johnson to be raised by his father's mistress, Mrs. Spencer. By 1918 it was apparent to everyone that Johnson was too much for the Spencer family to handle and he was shipped off to Robinsonville, Mississippi to live as "Robert Spencer" with his mother, since remarried to laborer Willie "Dusty" Willis. He lived with them until his late teens, but after being told by his mother of his true parentage began calling himself Robert Johnson. It is uncertain if Johnson ever met his birth father although many of his contemporaries reported that he actively looked for him.

As a young teenager, Johnson began playing a jew's harp later becoming an accomplished harmonica player. During the late 1920s, the aspiring musician switched his focus to guitar which soon became an all-consuming passion. At that time, the Delta was filled with "jook joints" (a.k.a. barrelhouses), usually one-room shanties where rural blacks went to drink "hootch" (distilled corn whiskey), gamble, meet persons of the opposite sex, and dance and listen to itinerant blues players like Willie Brown, Charley Patton, and Son House. The jooks were invariably on the outskirts of town, catered to a rough clientele, and offered poor blacks an alternative to church. Johnson immersed himself in the world of the jooks pestering established blues guitarists like Son House between sets to show him fingerings and chords. House was unimpressed and scolded the young musician for driving away business. Around this time, Johnson married 16-year-old Virginia Travis in February 1929, but the teenager died in childbirth in April 1930. Perhaps to cope with the loss

or to find his birth father, Johnson began a period of wandering that would find him honing his guitar playing and singing in jook joints, lumber camps, and street corners throughout the South. Bluesman Ike Zinnerman took Johnson under his wing and many scholars credit him with transforming the player from just another guitarist into a musical phenomenon that redefined his instrument. Handsome and charismatic, Johnson was seemingly irresistible to women especially when performing. In May 1931, he secretly married Calletta "Callie" Craft, a woman ten years his senior, and fathered three children by her. Craft provided Johnson with an emotional stability that allowed the moody musician to devote himself to practice and performance. Filled with wanderlust, Johnson ultimately deserted the woman, who died a few years later.

After Johnson returned to Robinsonville, Son House and his fellow-performers were amazed by the young man's development as a guitarist-singer. The disparity between the mediocre player the wannabe bluesman was prior to leaving the area and the accomplished performer who returned gave rise to the legend that Johnson had sold his soul to the Devil in exchange for his unrivalled talent. Establishing a base in Helena, Arkansas, Johnson spent the next several years playing throughout the Delta further developing his singing, playing, and compositions. His *modus operandi* was unvarying. Hitting a town, Johnson targeted the homeliest woman he could find, charmed her, and stayed with her before moving on to the next town and woman. Despite his mythic virtuosity, Johnson's legend would have been confined to a small geographic area had it not been for H.C. Speir, a white music store owner in Jackson, Mississippi. Speir, a talent scout for the American Record Company (ARC), specialized in finding regionally established black performers for the major label. To date, he had "discovered" blues greats Tommy Johnson, Charley Patton, and Willie Brown. Speir put Johnson in touch with Ernie Oertle, ARC's salesman for the Mid-South, who set up a recording session with the bluesman in a room in the Gunter Hotel in San Antonio, Texas in November 1936. In sessions conducted on November 23, 26, and 27, Johnson reportedly turned his back on the recordists and other acts in the room choosing to play and sing facing a wall. Speculation as to the reasons for Johnson's eccentric behavior include a case of first time recording-induced nerves, a desire to conceal his technique from the other artists present, or a belief that the acoustics would be better playing into a hard surface. Whatever the reason, the San Antonio session resulted in the recording on 78s of 16 songs including "Cross Road Blues," "Kind Hearted Woman," "I Believe I'll Dust My Broom," "Sweet Home Chicago," and Johnson's signature song, "Terraplane Blues." In June 1937, the guitarist traveled to Dallas for a two-day recording session for ARC that yielded an additional 13 songs, including "Love in Vain," "Hellhound on My Trail," "Me and the Devil Blues," and "From Four Till Late." The success of 78s like "Terraplane Blues" (it sold 5,000 copies) made Johnson a major attraction on the blues circuit, and he expanded his travels to include Chicago, Detroit, St. Louis, New York, and New Jersey, often with fellow-musician Johnny Shines.

In August 1938, the 26-year-old bluesman with fellow-performer Honeyboy Edwards had been in the area around Greenwood, Mississippi, for three weeks playing Saturday nights at a jook joint in Three Forks, some 15 miles outside of town. Following his established pattern, Johnson had flirted with a woman at the joint for weeks, but this time he had made a fatal mistake. The woman, who returned the guitarist's interest, was the wife of the jook's owner. On August 13, 1938, an open-sealed half-pint bottle of whiskey was sent over to Johnson who, against the advice of Honeyboy Edwards, drank from it. Shortly afterwards, Johnson stopped performing, stumbled outside, and vomited. Moved to a friend's home in the area, he began raving, and passing in and out of consciousness. It is now universally believed by scholars that the jook owner laced the whiskey with strychnine. Johnson was sweating out the poison and appeared to be rallying when he contracted pneumonia and died from the combined effects on August 16, 1938. The man later recognized as the embodiment of Delta blues was buried in a pine coffin supplied by the county in an unmarked spot of the Old Zion Church near Morgan City, Mississippi. In 1990, Columbia Records released *Robert Johnson: The Complete Recordings*, a two-CD box set featuring the original 29 master recordings plus 12 alternate takes, with a definitive booklet covering the artist's life and legacy. The set sold an astounding one million units, the first blues recording to top that mark. Eric Clapton, the guitar genius whose band Cream recorded notable versions of the Delta giant's "Four Until Late" and "Crossroads Blues,"

has written, "Robert Johnson to me is the most important blues musician who ever lived. He was true, absolutely, to his own vision, and as deep as I've gotten into the music over the last 30 years, I have never found anything more deeply soulful than Robert Johnson." In 1986, the bluesman was among the inaugural group of five inducted into the Rock and Roll Hall of Fame.

Further Reading

Guralnick, Peter. *Searching for Robert Johnson*. New York: Dutton, 1989.
Pearson, Barry Lee, and Bill McCulloch. *Robert Johnson: Lost and Found*. Urbana: University of Illinois Press, 2003.
Wald, Elijah. *Escaping the Delta: Robert Johnson and the Invention of the Delta Blues*. New York: Amistad, 2004.

Jones, Kenneth Bruce (M-S)

Jones, 32, a member of the Dallas, Texas, branch of the Screen Actors Guild, appeared in television commercials and several local stage productions. On September 20, 1977, ten days before the air date of the ABC made-for-television movie *The Trial of Lee Harvey Oswald* in which he played a policeman, Jones phoned a friend at 2:00 A.M. to report, "I've done it. I have killed Myra and her blond-headed lover. Call the police because by the time they get here I'll be dead." Dallas police rushed to the apartment at 6402 Melody Lane of Jones' ex-wife, Myra Emmanuelli, and kicking in the front door, found Jones lying dead a few feet inside in a hallway. The gun he used to shoot himself in the mouth was still clasped in his left hand. The nude bodies of Emmanuelli and her lover, 27-year-old local business executive Michael L. Crim, were found in a bedroom. The woman sustained gunshots to the face and chest with Crim dead from a head wound. The next day, the secretary Jones dated found a "farewell letter" from him in a satchel on her doorstep.

Further Reading

Ewell, James. "Lovers' Killing Ruled: Actor Shoots Ex-Wife, Man and Self." *Dallas Morning News*, September 21, 1977, sec. D, p. 1.

Jung, Paul (V)

Jung (born 1901 in Dayton, Ohio) was eight years old when he left school for vaudeville to perform an acrobatic act with his brother. In 1916, the 15-year-old quit the act to become a clown with the Ringling Bros.-Barnum & Bailey Circus. Jung stayed with the company until 1924 when he returned to vaudeville ultimately going back permanently to the circus in 1934. Dubbed by his peers "the King of Clowns," the ex-vaudevillian was a "producing clown" who created some of the most funny and recognizable skits ever performed under the Big Top. Jung devised the "Fireman, Save My Child" routine where a bevy of madcap midgets attempted to rescue another midget from a burning building. In his "Adam Smasher" routine, a giant clown is placed in a crusher, the machine started, and six midget clowns in identical outfits emerge. In another circus classic devised by Jung, a fat woman is placed in a reducing machine and a midget emerges. In yet another gag, a midget is stuffed into an outsized cannon and "shot" across the circus floor to float down unharmed from the top of the tent. After sustaining a serious hip injury, Jung turned his permanent limp into laughs by training a duck to waddle after him with a similar gait around the arena. With wife Elise, a former high wire performer, the man described as "a combination of an engineer and a gimmick builder," operated the Laugh Factory in Tampa, Florida. There, Jung created gags and built machinery to rent to circuses and ice shows.

In April 1965, the Ringling Bros.-Barnum & Bailey Circus was performing to standing room only crowds of 18,000 plus in New York City's Madison Square Garden. As he had done for the past eight seasons, the 65-year-old clown stayed at the Forrest Hotel, an unfashionable address at 224 W. 49th Street, one block from the Garden. On the morning of April 21, 1965, fellow-clowns became concerned when the ever punctual Jung failed to show at curtain time. A bell captain, acting upon their request, let himself into Room 1211 and found the body of "the King of Clowns," lying face-up and stretched across a narrow entry way into the bedroom, covered by a blood-soaked bedspread. Jung, clad in pajama bottoms and an undershirt, had his hands tied behind him with a cloth. Death was caused by a vicious bludgeoning about the head and face. The room showed no signs of forced entry and Jung's money and valuables were apparently undisturbed by the killer. Informed in Tampa of her husband's murder, Elise Jung sobbed, "It's that terrible New York City. It's like a jungle." Homicide detectives interviewed some 1,500 persons before charging two Harlem residents, Allen Jones, a 24-year-old unemployed laborer, and his girlfriend, Marian De Berry, 21, with the murder on June 6, 1965. Both had police records, De Berry for prostitution. Detectives maintained they beat Jung to death with

the brass nozzle of a fire hose from the midtown hotel then robbed him of $40.00 and a typewriter to support Jones' narcotics habit. In August 1966, De Berry cut a deal with prosecutors in which she agreed to name Jones as the clown's sole killer in exchange for pleading guilty to a lesser charge of third-degree assault. Damned by De Berry's testimony, Jones was convicted of first-degree murder on October 17, 1967 and sentenced to life imprisonment.

Further Reading

www.clown-ministry.com.

Kallman, Richard ("Dick") (V)

Kallman's movie career lasted a decade in which he acted in *Hell Canyon Outlaws* (1957), *Born to Be Loved* (1959), *Verboten!* (1958), *Back Street* (1961), *It's All Happening* (1963), and *Doctor, You've Got to Be Kidding* (1966). He also wrote the song "Teen-Age Cutie" for the film *Rockabilly Baby* (1957) and "The Cry Baby Killer" for the 1958 movie of the same name (notable for being Jack Nicholson's first starring role.) After dropping out of films, Kallman partnered with designer Joyce Bowen in 1975 to manufacture a line of women's play and party clothes known as the Burton Constable Collection. By 1980, the 46-year-old former actor was a well-known and respected art and antiques dealer in Manhattan who had been recently featured in television and magazine interviews discussing his lavishly furnished duplex apartment at 17 East 77th Street. On February 22, 1980, Kallman's partially-clothed body was found sitting in a chair. His business associate and attorney, Steven Szladek, 26, lay nude in a pool of blood nearby. Both men had been shot in the head. Several paintings, pieces of jewelry, and antiques were missing from the luxury apartment. Charles Lonnie Grosso, 27, was arrested in California, extradited to New York, and on July 28, 1981 convicted of second-degree murder in both deaths. Grosso received the maximum penalty of 25 years to life in prison.

Further Reading

Asbury, Edith Evans. "Antiques Dealer, Assistant Killed on the East Side." *The New York Times*, February 23, 1980, p. 23.

Kanyva (M)

Around March 2004, wannabe rapper Kanyva (real name Juston Michael Potts) entered into a loose business relationship with promoter Shani

Renee Holloway. The 31-year-old promoter was starting her own record label, All in 1 Promotions, and wanted the performer to record music designed to garner air play on local Pittsburg, California, radio stations. Kanyva, however, demanded that his music not be presented in a way that would be considered mainstream. On June 6, 2004, Holloway, her boyfriend, and the 18-year-old rapper discussed his career in a parked car in the 3300 block of Peppermill Circle in Pittsburg. Incredulous that he would not want his music widely promoted on radio, Holloway bluntly told the rapper that his prospects for stardom were not good. Kanyva got out of the car and walked across the street to talk to the occupants of a parked black SUV. He returned to Holloway's car, pulled out a handgun, and shot the woman twice in the head at point-blank range, afterwards fleeing the scene in the black SUV. Holloway died five hours later. Kanyva was arrested the next day and admitted quarreling with Holloway about his career. Following a failed insanity defense, the rapper waived a trial by jury and was subsequently sentenced by a judge to a prison term of 50 years to life for first-degree murder. An appeal in 2008 was denied.

Further Reading

Donaldson, Stan. "Slaying Puts Focus on Pittsburg Rap." *Contra Costa Times*, June 24, 2004, sec. A, p. 1.

Kean, Norman (M-S)

Kean was the general manager of the original New York staging of Kenneth Tynan's controversial show *Oh! Calcutta!* when it first opened at the Eden Theatre on June 17, 1969. That same year, he converted the ballroom in the Edison Hotel into a 499-seat playhouse, the Edison Theatre. The Edison Theatre opened in March 1970 with a poorly received production of *Show Me Where the Good Times Are*, a musical based on Molière's *The Imaginary Invalid*. In 1974, the theatre enjoyed critical success with the Tony Award winning bill *Sizwe Banzi Is Dead* and *The Island*, the first plays to depict life in Black South Africa to New York City theatregoers. On September 4, 1976, *Oh! Calcutta!* opened off Broadway at the Edison Theatre with Kean as its producer. Through his tireless efforts at promotion, the show took on the status of a Big Apple tourist attraction ultimately running for 5,969 performances. In theatrical circles, however, *Oh! Calcutta!* was generally dismissed as a "nudie musical." The

criticism stung Kean who desperately wanted to be taken seriously as a top producer. In 1978, he produced *A Broadway Musical*. It flopped.

While *Oh! Calcutta!* continued to generate income, Kean's personal life was unraveling. In the spring of 1987, he was dismissed as head of the theatre advisory committee at the nonprofit John Drew Theater of Guild Hall in East Hampton, Long Island. At the same time, the 53-year-old producer learned that his wife, the former stage actress Gwyda DonHowe, was having an affair with an advertising executive. Kean and Don-Howe met while doing summer stock in 1957, wed in 1958, and had one child, David. According to a friend, Kean's obsession with his wife throughout their 29 year union was "palpable." In an attempt to save his marriage, Kean spent more time at home, delegating business matters to deputies. In January 1988, however, he learned through a private investigator that Gwyda was still seeing her lover.

Kean now applied the same compulsive attention to detail that characterized his success as a businessman-producer to planning the murder of Gwyda and his suicide. One week before the double tragedy, Kean instructed his attorney to draw up divorce papers. One day before she was to die, Gwyda confessed to a friend, "I want to be free as a bird." On the morning of January 15, 1988, Kean waited until their 14-year-old son David left for school before entering the master bedroom of their luxury apartment on Riverside Drive in Manhattan. Sometime between 7:30 and 8:00 A.M., Kean stabbed his sleeping wife sixty times with a 6" kitchen knife. When the housekeeper arrived at 8:30 A.M., Kean instructed her not to awaken his usually late-sleeping wife. For the next several hours, the producer made business phone calls, left the apartment to drop off material at his attorney, and returned home around 3:00 P.M. After giving the housekeeper $150 in cash, three carboned letters, and a tape recording to place in his son's room, Kean went to the roof of the 15-story building, removed his glasses, and plunged 150 feet to his death into a back courtyard.

David Kean discovered his mother's body when he returned home from basketball practice, and was later called on to identify his father's broken remains. Kean's notes (to police, his son, and housekeeper) contained references to his depression over Gwyda's drinking, the affair, and his love for her. In the audiotape, the producer told his son in a voice devoid of emotion that his college would be paid for and that what had just happened to his parents was much better for him than suffering through a divorce.

Further Reading

Freifeld, Karen. "Murder and Suicide by a Thorough Man." *Newsday*, February 9, 1988, pt. II, p. 4.

Kelly, George Augustus (M-S)

Kelly, a native of Omaha, Nebraska, joined the U.S. Army at the outbreak of World War I, but transferred to the British Air Force where distinguished service in the sky over France gained him a captain's commission. Described as possessing a "magnetic personality," the handsome 30-year-old ex-flyer was acting as the manager of the Palais de Danse in Hammersmith when he met the attractive divorcee and dancer Sophia Erica Taylor, 29, there in 1920. Known as "Babs," Taylor was a chorus girl at the Gaiety Theatre and Hippodrome and was notorious for making the rounds of London nightclubs to dance. The pair became lovers and dance partners, appearing in private exhibition dances in London and its suburbs. Their extravagant lifestyle coupled with Kelly's gambling and addictions to alcohol and drugs soon cooled the relationship. A violent pattern developed. Taylor, looking for a new benefactor, flirted with men while Kelly, drunk and insanely jealous, beat her. Weeks before the impending tragedy (during which time the ex-soldier often disappeared for days) the dancer confided to a friend: "I am very unhappy and Kelly is so strange. He has hit me many times, and threatened me. I do not know what to do." Taylor became intimate with Captain Allan Leslie, formerly in the Gordon Highlanders, and the two arranged to live together in Brighton. Shortly after receiving a notice cancelling his appointment as manager for a circuit of suburban movie houses, Kelly entered Taylor's London flat at 8 St. James Street, Picadilly, W., on December 17, 1920. In the presence of her maid, he attempted to strangle his former lover to death on her bed. The maid broke his grip, but Kelly fired a fatal shot into the fleeing Taylor before shooting himself in the head. Among items found on Kelly's body were a quantity of cocaine and notes to the dead woman. In one he wrote, "Wish we could have fallen in love with each other as we have gotten along splendidly."

Further Reading

"Drama of Love and Jealousy." *Daily Mail*, December 20, 1920, p. 5.

Kelly, Paul (M)

Hollywood, as witnessed by its treatment of Roscoe "Fatty" Arbuckle (see entry) and others who have fallen from grace, is not usually the most forgiving of places. Yet, even Tinseltown can occasionally be moved by a tragic love story. Paul Michael Kelly (born August 9, 1899, in Brooklyn, New York) first appeared onstage in 1907 at the

Paul Kelly, a promising actor in silent films, was convicted of manslaughter after his brutal beating of Ray Raymond in an argument instigated by his attentions to the song-and-dance man's wife, Scottish-born actress Dorothy Mackaye, resulted in the performer's death in April 1927. Proving even Hollywood can have a heart, the film industry welcomed Kelly back into the fold following his release from prison in August 1929. Among the nearly 100 films made by Kelly during his 35-year career was the ironically titled one above, *Not a Ladies' Man* (1942), co-starring Fay Wray of *King Kong* fame.

age of eight in *A Grand Army Man* and continued to perform in stock companies for many years. Signed by the New York–based Vitagraph studio, Kelly appeared in juvenile roles in several silent shorts, before logging his first adult lead in the 1919 feature *Anne of Green Gables* directed by future murder victim William Desmond Taylor (see entry). Kelly's other feature films of the period include *Uncle Sam of Freedom Ridge* (1920) and *The Great Adventure* (1921). In 1917, Kelly met the Scottish-born actress Dorothy Mackaye while both were appearing in legitimate stage roles in New York City. The friendship remained strong even after Mackaye married song-and-dance man Ray Raymond, then her castmate in the Big Apple production of *Blue Eyes* in 1921. Ironically, prior to leaving the New York stage to try his hand in Hollywood, Kelly appeared in a stage production that strangely presaged the impending tragedy. In August 1925, the actor portrayed "Charlie Watts" in *The Sea Woman*. The character, a combination rum runner and lady killer, conspires with a woman to deceive another man. In early 1926, Kelly arrived in Hollywood to appear in the feature film, *The New Klondike*. The athletic actor next appeared in the 1927 baseball film *Slide, Kelly, Slide*, though not in the title role. That "Kelly" was actor William Haines whose career would abruptly end in 1936 amid a homosexual scandal. Another cast member, Karl Dane, would commit suicide on April 14, 1934. For Paul Kelly, his role as a baseball player in the film would later serve only to underscore in the public mind his physical superiority over the man he would be tried for killing.

Raymond and wife Dorothy Mackaye were based in Los Angeles when Kelly arrived to break into motion pictures. Raymond, often on the road in various musical productions, never had to worry that his wife was neglected. Kelly and Mackaye were seemingly inseparable and were often seen at gin parties and taking long car rides together. Weeks before the tragedy, Raymond drunkenly ordered Kelly out of his house and told his wife to end her relationship with the actor. Mackaye insisted that nothing unseemly was happening between them and flatly refused to end the friendship. When the song-and-dance man left on tour with the musical *Castles in the Air*, Mackaye and Kelly continued seeing one another. On Saturday, April 16, 1927, an exhausted Ray Raymond arrived at his home at 2261 Cheremoya Drive in Hollywood following an all night train trip from San Francisco where several hours earlier he had concluded the final performance in *Castles in the Air*. The 33-year-old performer immediately resumed arguing with Mackaye about her 26-year-old "friend" and she left the house on the pretext of shopping for Easter supplies. Mackaye drove across town with a friend to Paul Kelly's apartment where she downed at least two gin fizzes. Mackaye informed her ardent admirer that Raymond had flatly accused them of having an affair. Paul Kelly, enraged and most likely inebriated, angrily phoned Raymond at 7:00 P.M. and told him he was coming over to discuss the matter. Charlotte Ethel Lee, the Raymond's black maid and the only witness (besides the couple's 4½-year-old daughter, Valerie) to the incident told police in her statement:

> I knew he was talking to Paul Kelly, and I heard Mr. Raymond say, "All right, come on over." He told me Paul was coming. Five minutes later Paul knocked at the door. Paul spoke up right away, "I understand you have been saying things about me." He was very angry. Mr. Raymond told him to sit down with him on the davenport. Mr. Raymond then said something to Paul and he struck Mr. Raymond on the jaw. "Where is Mrs. Raymond?" Mr. Raymond asked. "I don't know," Paul replied. "Yes, you do," said Mr. Raymond. Then Paul struck him again. Mr. Raymond remonstrated. He said: "I haven't eaten. I'm a wreck and I can't fight. I'm thirty pounds underweight and have been drinking." "That's your alibi," Paul cried. Paul hit Mr. Raymond three or four times and knocked him down. I went to the kitchen. I begged Paul not to hit Mr. Raymond again. Then Mr. Raymond called him. "I'll beat you," Paul said. He then hit him three or four times. This was in the dining-room. Mr. Raymond got up and Kelly grabbed him and put one hand behind his neck and beat him with the other, and then threw him on the couch. He fell to the floor. "I'm a man and can't take a blow, but I'll fight you," Mr. Raymond said. Kelly kept knocking him down as he got to his feet. His face was cut and bleeding. Finally, with one crushing blow Paul knocked Raymond out.

Kelly left the scene, returned to his apartment, and related the events of the violent confrontation to Mackaye. Raymond was at home nursing his blackened eye and other injuries when Perry Askom, a friend and fellow-cast member of *Castles in the Air*, accompanied by his wife dropped in on him moments after the beating. Askom later related to police that Raymond told him, "Kelly came over and beat (me) up and that (I) never had a chance." Charlotte Ethel Lee would concur in her police statement noting that the 5'6", 140 pound Lee was little more than a "punching bag" for the younger, more athletic 6'0", 190 pound Kelly. The Askoms left shortly after Mackaye returned home. The next morning at 6:00 A.M., Raymond was found by housekeeper Lee lying flat on his back on the bedroom floor near the side of the bed unconscious, breathing unnaturally, and "frothing at the mouth." Dr. Walter Sullivan was called, examined the song-and-dance man, and ordered him rushed to the Queen of Angels Hospital. According to published reports, Mackaye continued to visit Kelly in his apartment up to the moment her husband died without regaining consciousness at 5:20 A.M. on April 19, 1927 — two days after his altercation with the actor. Dr. Sullivan, paid $500 by Mackaye for his two day treatment of Raymond, was poised to sign a death certificate stating the man had died of "natural causes" when the coroner, demanding an autopsy, hurriedly reclaimed the body from the mortuary. The autopsy confirmed that Raymond had sustained a bad beating at the hands of the younger man. Raymond suffered two fractured ribs, cuts on his forehead, a damaged left eye, bruises on his chest, shoulder, arms, and shins, and a serious head injury resulting in a hemorrhage covering the right portion of the brain. The cause of death was officially listed as hypsostatic pneumonia following an extensive subdural hemorrhage on the right side of the brain. Dr. Sullivan's supposed ignorance of the fact that Raymond had been in a fight prior to his death opened the medical man up to allegations that the exorbitant $500 fee he received from Mackaye made him a co-conspirator in trying to cover up the facts of his patient's death.

On April 20, 1927, a grand jury indicted Paul Kelly for the first-degree murder of Ray Raymond. In between fainting spells, Dorothy Mackaye testified she precipitated the fatal meeting between the two men by informing Kelly her husband had accused them of adultery. Continuing to insist that their relationship was purely "platonic," Kelly had angrily phoned the man and stormed over to the house on Cheremoya Drive. The next day, a coroner's inquest sought to fix responsibility for Raymond's death and, more importantly, determine whether Dr. Sullivan and Mackaye had made attempts to conceal the true facts of the case. The doctor insisted that in the absence of information regarding the fight between the two men, he told the autopsy surgeon

A.F. Wagner that the bruises on the dead man's body had been the result of a drunken fall from his bed. Days later, Sullivan and Mackaye were indicted by a county grand jury on charges of "compounding a felony" and with being "accessories after the fact" in an alleged plot to cover-up the details surrounding the beating death of Ray Raymond. The jury interpreted the doctor's "rather high" fee of $500 paid by the grieving widow as an attempt to conceal Raymond's condition and cause of death. Both remained free on $5,000 bond each while the L.A. District Attorney's office built a murder case against Paul Kelly.

Jury selection began in Los Angeles on May 9, 1927, with eight women and four men seated to determine the young actor's fate. When the court was not in session, the jury was "locked down" in a downtown motel to prevent possible intimidation. Although Kelly maintained his innocence (insisting Raymond died of acute alcoholism, not the beating), he faced an uphill battle against a mountain of damning evidence. Autopsy Surgeon A.F. Wagner testified Raymond died of a subdural hemorrhage caused by nothing else than the result of a violent kick or blows, not the drunken fall suggested by the defense. Charlotte Ethel Lee, the prosecution's star witness, was unshakeable in describing Kelly as the aggressor in his confrontation with the "almost helpless" song-and-dance man. Further, during the time Raymond was on the road touring Mackaye spent many nights away from the house. According to Lee, she often located her absent employer by phoning Kelly's apartment the next morning. In riveting testimony, Dorothy Mackaye continued to assert her relationship with Kelly was chaste and platonic. Though present at Kelly's apartment at the time he placed a phone call, Mackaye insisted she did not know it was to her husband, nor did she have any idea where the actor went when he angrily left his apartment. The prosecution next produced its "trump" evidence — love letters and telegrams from Kelly to Mackaye to establish a motive for the premeditated attack. In the letters, Kelly often referred to Mackaye as "my wife" while others were written in a lover's code deciphered by the embarrassed actress for the jury. In one letter dated March 20, 1927, Kelly wrote to Mackaye: "Darling Mine: Oh, I am so terribly in love with you — so terribly — I am miserable here without you — I love you — love you — love you." While Mackaye admitted to often speaking of marriage with Kelly while her husband was on the road, she did so only in a "kidding way." The final nail in the defense's case came when Kelly's Japanese houseboy, Teno Yobu, was called by the prosecution to corroborate parts of Charlotte Ethel Lee's testimony. Known as "Jungles," Yobu stated he served gin drinks on at least half a dozen occasions to Mackaye and Kelly in the actor's apartment. Mackaye sometimes spent the night there and Jungles saw them together in Kelly's bedroom in the morning. When the houseboy was present, the pair often resorted to a "love language" (perhaps Pig Latin) to disguise what they were saying. According to Yobu, Kelly had at least two gin drinks prior to leaving the apartment to confront Raymond. Kelly's appearance on the stand was almost anti-climactic. The actor admitted slapping Raymond twice for vilely insinuating that he had an improper relationship with Mackaye and was forced to defend himself when the song-and-dance man unexpectedly attacked him.

On May 25, 1927, the jury returned after two days of deliberation to find Kelly guilty of the lesser crime of manslaughter. Sentenced to 1 to 10 years in prison, the actor initially vowed to appeal, but soon told his attorney he would "take his punishment like a man and then begin life anew when society's debt had been paid." Transported to San Quentin on July 2, 1927, to serve his posted 5 year sentence, Inmate No. 43,814 became a trusty in the prison library and took voice culture lessons to prepare for a post-prison career in talking pictures. His lover, Dorothy Mackaye, and Dr. Walter Sullivan still faced separate trials for covering up the facts of Raymond's death. On June 29, 1927, a jury needed less than three hours to find the actress guilty. Mackaye was sentenced to a year in San Quentin, her lover's new address. Her appeal denied, Mackaye did her time operating a sewing machine. She was released for "good behavior" on January 1, 1929, after serving only 8 months. Dr. Walter J. Sullivan was the only winner in the ordeal. On October 28, 1927, the case against the Hollywood physician was dismissed after the D.A.'s office determined the evidence against him was "too thin" to win a conviction.

On the strength of his "excellent behavior," Paul Kelly won parole from San Quentin on August 2, 1929, after serving two years and one month of his manslaughter conviction. "I'm going straight to New York," Kelly told reporters. "I'm headed straight for the comeback trail. I've got a job with the New Century Play Company in New York and I'm going to hit it hard." The job, apparently, was as a clerk for the company. On Broadway, however, Kelly earned the dubious distinction of being the lowest-salaried leading man ever to appear in a show on the Great White Way. As a parolee, the actor was limited under California law to earn no more than $30 a week, the salary he was paid in February 1930 to work in the *Nine Fifteen Revue*. On a happier note, Paul Kelly and Dorothy Mackaye married in February 1931 and remained together until she was killed in a car crash near their Northridge, California ranch in 1940. The actor returned to an uncharacteristically forgiving Hollywood in 1932 and worked nonstop amassing credits in some 88 films often in supporting roles in "A" and "B" features as well as the occasional lead in programmers. Kelly's post-conviction films include *Broadway Thru a Keyhole* (1933), *The Song and Dance Man* (1936), *The Roaring Twenties* (1939), *Not a Ladies' Man* (1942), *The Glass Alibi* (1946), *Crossfire* (1947), *The Painted Hills* (1951), *The Square Jungle* (1956), and his final film, *Curfew Breakers* (1957). In a filmic act of self-expiation smacking of gimmick casting, Kelly appeared as Warden Clinton D. Duffy in the 1954 production of *Duffy of San Quentin*, a chronicle of the maximum security prison where the actor spent 25 months of his life in the late 1920s. Kelly also found time to appear onstage (winning a Tony Award as Best Actor in 1948 for *Command Decision*) and in television series guest shots. On November 6, 1956, the 57-year-old actor suffered a fatal heart attack in his Los Angeles home at 1148 Club View Drive shortly after returning from casting his vote at the polls. The actor is buried in Holy Cross Cemetery in Culver City, California beneath a flat marker inscribed, "Paul Michael Kelly —1899–1956 — Rest in Peace."

Further Reading

"Kelly, Guilty, Asks New Trial." *Los Angeles Times*, May 26, 1927, sec. A, p. 1.
"Kelly Is Indicted for Raymond Death." *The New York Times*, April 21, 1927, p. 29.
"Platonic Friendship Given Blame for Tragedy in Hollywood." *Los Angeles Times*, April 20, 1927, sec. A, p. 2.

Kilian, Victor (V)

In a career spanning some seventy years, the tall, heavyset character actor distinguished himself on the stage and in over 130 films, but achieved his greatest popular success as the "Fernwood Flasher" in the mid–1970s television program

Mary Hartman, Mary Hartman. Born to German immigrant parents in Jersey City, New Jersey, on March 6, 1891, Victor Arthur Kilian drove a laundry truck for his father's business and labored as a longshoreman and ditchdigger. In 1908, he joined a small repertory company in New England and Canada and in 1912 toured in the production of *The Red Window.* Kilian's big theatrical break came in 1924 when he was tapped to replace Perry Ivins as "Peter Cabot" in the original Broadway production of Eugene O'Neill's *Desire Under the Elms.* On the strength of that performance, the young actor was continuously employed on the eastern stage during the 1920s and 1930s in *Beyond the Horizon* (1926), *Triple Crossed* (1927), *The Black Crook* (1929), *The Seagull* (1929), *At the Bottom* (1930), *Cloudy with Showers* (1931), and *Riddle Me This* (1932). Though appearing unbilled in the 1929 film, *Gentlemen of the Press,* Kilian's official movie career began in 1932 with *The Wiser Sex.* Over the next thirty years, the lanky, villainous-looking actor appeared almost annually in scores of films including *The Public Menace* (1935), *The Adventures of Tom Sawyer* (1938), *Jesse James* (1939), *The Adventures of Huckleberry Finn* (1939), *Dr. Cyclops* (1940), *Sergeant York* (1941), *Reap the Wild Wind* (1942,

in which he lost an eye during a fight scene with star John Wayne), *The Ox-Bow Incident* (1943), *Meet Me in St. Louis* (1945), *Gentleman's Agreement* (1948), and several Westerns in the early 1950s (*The Return of Jesse James,* 1950; *Passage West,* 1951; *The*

A character actor equally at home on stage or on screen, Victor Kilian worked continuously for 70 years, appearing in numerous plays and more than 130 motion pictures. It is, however, as exhibitionist "Raymond Larkin," the "Fernwood Flasher" on the mid–1970s television program *Mary Hartman, Mary Hartman,* that the actor is destined to be best remembered. Kilian, 88, was bludgeoned to death in his Hollywood apartment on March 11, 1979, in an unsolved murder bearing remarkable similarities to the earlier death of fellow-actor and neighbor Charles Wagenheim.

Tall Target, 1951). Blacklisted from motion pictures during the McCarthy era, Kilian continued to work sporadically onstage in *Look Homeward, Angel* (1957), *The Gang's All Here* (1959), *All the Way Home* (1960), and in the 1964 pre–Broadway tour of *What Makes Sammy Run?* in Philadelphia. The veteran actor, however, will undoubtedly be best remembered for his role as exhibitionist "Raymond Larkin," the notorious "Fernwood Flasher," in the syndicated television soap opera satire *Mary Hartman, Mary Hartman* (produced 1975–1978, released January 1976). On the evening of March 11, 1979, Kilian was sitting in his favorite chair watching television in his rooms in the Lido Apartments at 6500 Yucca Street in Hollywood when an intruder broke in, beat the 88-year-old actor to death, and ransacked the apartment. Five days earlier, 83-year-old veteran character actor Charles Wagenheim (see entry) was similarly bludgeoned to death in his apartment not far from the Kilian residence. Both murders remain unsolved.

Further Reading

"Victor Kilian, Actor, Found Beaten Fatally in Hollywood Home." *The New York Times,* March 13, 1979, sec. B, p. 8.

King, Natel (V)

A native of Newfoundland, the statuesque, busty platinum-blonde saw the adult entertainment industry as a means by which to make a lot of money in a hurry. King's life plan was to use her earnings to finance a psychology degree at Newfoundland's Memorial University, leave the business, then marry and have children all by the age of thirty. At 18, she was living in her parents' home in Mississauga, Ontario, when she originated a softcore internet webcast from her bedroom featuring herself in various naked poses. Under the name "Taylor Sumers" (some sources say "Summers"), the "Sexy Canadian," began advertising herself as a nude model on the internet ultimately earning as much as $1,000 a day on photo and video shoots. Her one rule — no sex with men. In July 2003, the 23-year-old model shot a movie in New York entitled *Naughty College Couples 6* in which she was featured in a solo masturbation scene. King, as "Sumers," also appeared in some bondage and foot fetish videos and did magazine work. Against the advice of both her "straight" friends and associates in the adult industry, however, she insisted on booking her own gigs rather than working through a modeling agency that could offer her a degree of safety by running background and reference checks on photographers. King reasoned that during the time it took a talent agency to determine if a photographer or company was legit, she could be earning a $1,000 a day without having to pay a commission. Schedule permitting, Curtis Shear, King's roommate in Mississauga, often chaperoned his friend on photo shoots. However, he was unavailable to do so in late February 2004 when King agreed to meet photographer Anthony Joseph Frederick, 46, in the Philadelphia suburb of Conshohocken, Pennsylvania.

King and Frederick already had an uneasy history of sorts dating back to December 2003 when she answered a call for nude models posted on his website. She traveled to Allentown, Pennsylvania, to meet with the photographer, but at the last minute Frederick called the hotel where she was staying to say the location for the shoot had been changed to a remote cabin outside the city limits. Alarmed, King phoned a friend in the adult industry who strongly advised her not to meet with the photographer. King returned to Canada, and escaped the fate reportedly suffered by another of Frederick's photo subjects. Sometime earlier, a young model who willingly posed for him in a bondage scene chained to a heater was refused payment. The woman complained, and a police search of Frederick's studio uncovered fake blood, handcuffs, and shackles. The photographer was not charged with any crime.

On February 28, 2004, King drove her red 1992 Saturn from Mississauga to Conshohocken to meet with the photographer. The next day, King met with Frederick at a local hotel and finalized the deal—twenty photos, some featuring bondage, for $900.00. Frederick took some bondage photos at the hotel then informed King that he wanted to do a second shoot at his studio with the aid of his assistant, 29-year-old Jennifer Marie Mitkus. King was nervous about the shoot and cell-phoned her friend Curtis Shear for advice. Shear was not home, but King left a hushed message on the answering machine begging him to call her back as soon as possible because something "weird" was happening. When Shear returned King's call, the woman was already in Frederick's basement studio in a house in a quiet residential area of Conshohocken. Speaking in a soft tone so no one near could hear, King told her friend that the photographer was "kind of weird" and that she was "worried." When Shear

asked if she was worried about "not getting paid" or "getting killed," the model replied, "I don't know, both." Though terrified, King was unwilling to walk away from a $900.00 modeling fee. Shear told her that if she was not paid in the next few minutes to call him back. In any event, he warned her to get out of there. He called back in 1½ hours, but she did not answer. After repeatedly trying to contact King over a period of days, Shear reported her disappearance to Toronto authorities who in turn notified the Conshohocken Police Department. On March 5, 2004, the CPD found King's car near Frederick's studio. Inside the vehicle, they discovered the model's suitcase, laptop computer, but no purse or toiletries. Questioned by authorities, Frederick and Mitkus showed them the photos they had taken of King, but stated they had not seen the model since she left the shoot on her way to a restaurant.

Nearly three weeks passed before King's badly decomposed body was found on March 23, 2004, dumped in a heavily wooded ravine near the Schuylkill River in Whitemarsh County, a short drive from Frederick's basement studio. Naked except for two white socks, the model bore extensive stab wounds to her neck and face as well as defensive wounds to her hands. More disturbing, King was gagged with a leather type dog-collar with a pink rubber ball in the center. The model's body was wrapped in a bloodied drape (a type often used as background in a photo studio) and the makeshift burial shroud had been secured with duct tape. Other bondage paraphernalia located near the body seemed to match devices featured in the photos of King taken by Frederick and Mitkus. Shortly after the grisly discovery, the 46-year-old photographer was arrested and charged with first-degree murder after DNA tests revealed large traces of King's blood in his studio. Also found in the studio was a handwritten poem that read, "Cut with a knife, blood does flow/You may bleed out, death coming on slow...." Mitkus was also arrested and preliminarily charged with lying to authorities and hindering apprehension.

In February 2005, Frederick cut a deal with the prosecution that allowed him to plead guilty to charges of third-degree murder (requires intent to kill with malice, but no specific or planned intent to kill), possession of an instrument of crime (the Colt hunting knife), unsworn falsification (lying to authorities), abuse of a corpse, and criminal conspiracy in exchange for the possibility of parole in the very remote future. In his confession, Frederick admitted killing King because of a dispute over the $900 modeling fee. According to the photographer, King became angry when he told the model that he did not have her entire fee. The model allegedly picked up a hunting knife used as a prop in the bondage shoot and began threatening Frederick. The pair wrestled, the photographer managed to disarm King, and stabbed her with such force that the blade passed through her neck. While he was upstairs wiping the blood from his hands, Mitkus was downstairs cleaning up the crime scene with bleach. According to Frederick's statement, Mitkus admitted to him that she had twice stabbed the woman's lifeless body while he was upstairs. The couple rolled "Taylor Sumers" into the backdrop screen, placed the bundle into the back of Frederick's car, and the photographer dumped the body alone. Unexplained in the photographer's account was how King managed to argue with him while the bondage gag (bearing a telltale knife slit) was obviously in her mouth both pre and post-mortem. In a statement designed to still criticism that the deal was too favorable to the confessed killer, Montgomery County District Attorney Bruce Castor said, "I don't believe the part about her grabbing the knife, but we have separated [Frederick] from the public and he will be spending a long time in prison." In July 2005, Anthony Joseph Frederick was sentenced to 51 years in prison. He will be 71 after serving the minimum 24 years of his sentence before becoming eligible for parole consideration. Mitkus pleaded out to lying to detectives, tampering with evidence (cleaning up the crime scene), and the abuse of a corpse. Sentenced to 23 months incarceration and ordered to undergo psychiatric assessment, she will be eligible for release after serving just six months.

Further Reading

Appleby, Timothy. "Ambition and Death in Porn's Underworld." *The Globe and Mail*, March 25, 2004, sec. A, p. 1.

Knight, Terry (V)

The promotional and marketing force behind the 1970s supergroup Grand Funk Railroad, Knight (born Richard Terrance Knapp in Flint, Michigan, on April 9, 1943), began his musical career as a teenaged disc jockey on hometown radio station WTAC. In a nod to the nocturnal shifts he invariably worked, Knapp changed his name to the cooler sounding "Knight." While at legendary Windsor, Ontario–based station CKLW-AM (800), the deejay became well-known in Detroit for advocating bands like the Rolling Stones while other jocks spun the more sedate Beatles. In 1964, Knight left radio to make his own music first fronting the Jazz Masters that ultimately became Terry Knight and the Pack. Backed by Flint area musicians Mark Farner on guitar and drummer Don Brewer, the Pack's debut single, "Tears Come Rollin'," failed to click with local Detroit area record buyers. The band's first success, a cover of the Yardbirds' "Mr. You're a Better Man Than I," paved the way for a string of regional hits before a cover of Ben E. King's "I (Who Have Nothing)" peaked at Number 46 on the *Billboard* charts. Hopelessly derivative both musically and lyrically, the Pack was not helped by Knight's limited vocal ability. The group dissolved around 1968 with Farner and Brewer continuing as the Fabulous Pack while Knight pursued an unsuccessful solo career.

In 1969, Knight signed with Capitol Records as a consultant and talent scout. The label, anxious to cash in on the power trio gold being mined by Atco with Cream and Reprise with the Jimi Hendrix Experience, listened with interest when the deejay turned minimally successful rock star pitched them on a three-man group he already had under contract through his own company, Good Knight Productions. Knight christened the trio Grand Funk Railroad after Michigan's Grand Trunk Railroad line, and added former Question Mark and the Mysterians bassist Mel Schacher to the existing line-up of Farner and Brewer. A skilled promoter, Knight scored a major coup by managing to have GFR open the Atlanta Pop Festival on July 4, 1969, before a wowed crowd of over 125,000. The supersonically loud blues-rock power trio built on its triumph at the stadium show by near-constant touring and word of mouth from an increasingly growing and rabid fan base. Universally despised by the critics, Grand Funk Railroad, under Knight's brilliant manipulation, was marketed as a "people's band" and targeted at youth who instinctively distrusted anything the mainstream media was trying to sell them. Simply put by Knight, "Critics don't count, the kids do." Not content to just sell millions of records, the producer-promoter made a game out of antagonizing detractors like *Rolling Stone* and *Billboard* by taking out full-page ads in their pages which depicted him flipping them off. From 1968 through early 1972, Knight not only designed

GFR's album covers, produced their million selling albums, encouraged Farner to write songs about contemporary social issues, but also kept the group near continuously on the road. In 1970 alone, the band grossed $5 million. In 1971, GFR soldout the 55,000 seat Shea Stadium faster than the Beatles had done six years earlier. By age 28, Knight had realized his childhood dream of becoming a multimillionaire.

In March 1972, however, three months before his management contract with the group he helped create was set to expire, Grand Funk Railroad unceremoniously fired Knight in a dispute over control of the band's name and a greater share of royalties. Knight immediately filed a $56 million breach of contract suit barring them from recording as Grand Funk Railroad. Farner, Brewer, and Schacher countersued for $8 million. The relationship between the litigants became so rancorous that on one memorable occasion in December 1972, Knight showed up hours before the band was set to perform at a charity concert accompanied by two deputy sheriffs and a court order authorizing him to confiscate the group's equipment. In a 1974 settlement, Knight was awarded more than $1.3 million in cash, various undisclosed investments, plus 50 percent of the publishing royalties to some of the band's topselling albums until 2064. While the group's original name, Grand Funk Railroad, was determined to have been Knight's creation, the settlement allowed the band to be known thereafter as Grand Funk. In a rare 1999 interview for a VH1 *Behind the Music* documentary on the band that would come back to haunt him, Knight openly gloated about the settlement in effect calling the band "stupid" for firing him instead of not just waiting three months for his contract to expire. Farner, Schacher, and Brewer never again spoke to their former friend and mentor.

Dating from his acrimonious split with the band in 1972, Knight's life became an inexorable downward spiral fuelled by rumor, innuendo, and his own increasingly reclusive lifestyle. His fortune, estimated by some after the settlement to be as high as $15 million, was rapidly squandered. In the 1970s he was involved with his Westport, Connecticut, neighbor, actor Paul Newman, on the S.C.C.A. Pro Racing Circuit. Unsuccessfully dabbling in music with his Brown Bag Records label, Knight produced unmemorable records for forgettable bands like Bloodrock, the Jayhawkers, and Mom's Apple Pie. He reportedly left the music business for good in 1974 after turning down the chance to manage a fledgling band, Kiss. By 1981, accounts of Knight's life varied widely with some saying his stay in the Bahamas was spent moving drugs for international gangsters and in developing his own heavy duty cocaine habit. Amid rumors that he was involved with Colombian drug lords, Knight resurfaced in Michigan in 1981 broke, divorced from his first wife (a former stewardess from Sweden), and addicted to drugs. Living off royalties from Grand Funk Railroad, he married a woman 17 years his junior in 1986 and fathered a child, Danielle, in 1988. The family relocated to Yuma, Arizona, where the former rock manager was briefly employed as a manager for a defense contractor testing military equipment at the Yuma Military Proving Ground before turning to selling advertisements. The couple divorced in 1991 and Knight was awarded sole custody of his daughter.

Largely forgotten by rock music, Knight could not resist talking about his lucrative settlement with Grand Funk Railroad when VH1 asked him to appear on an episode of *Behind the Music* detailing the supergroup's rise and fall. Weeks after the program appeared, Knight was accused on July 11, 1999, of attempting to fondle his daughter's 11-year-old female friend at his condominium in Yuma. Included in the seven count felony indictment were charges that he used methamphetamine and threatened his daughter who was present at the time of the alleged incident. Although Knight denied the allegations insisting they were motivated purely by a desire to extort money, he pleaded guilty to a reduced charge of aggravated assault and was sentenced on October 5, 2000, to 36 months of intensive probation. The victim's family quickly filed a civil suit against Knight in an effort to secure his royalty payments from Grand Funk Railroad, then about $100,000 a year thanks to the band's reissue on CD. To protect his assets, the former manager filed bankruptcy in November 2002.

Although Knight had been drug-free for five years, by late 2003 his health had been ravaged by the long-term effects of addiction and diabetes. Now living in Temple, Texas, with his 16-year-old daughter Danielle in order for her to be near her mother, the pair shared an unusual living arrangement in their $1,000 a month condominium in the Chappell Hill Apartments. Fearful that his teenaged daughter would run away if he challenged her on the issue, Knight (with his ex-wife's approval) agreed to let Danielle's lover, 26-year-old unemployed junkie Donald Alan Fair, live with them at Number 1213. Early on November 1, 2004, Fair and Danielle began the day loudly arguing about his five day amphetamine binge. Someone called the police around 8:30 A.M., but they left soon after responding when they found no weapons or injuries. Fourteen hours later, Danielle ran to a neighbor's apartment screaming hysterically that Fair had killed her father and was trying to kill her. The neighbor locked the door and dialed 911. Fair banged on the door, but denied entry fled the scene and was apprehended by police minutes later in the apartment complex covered in blood and still carrying a knife. Knight's lifeless body was found inside the apartment stabbed 17 times in the neck and back.

According to Danielle, the argument over Fair's drug use simmered throughout the day finally exploding as they sat together on the couch watching television. Fair pushed her around prompting Knight who was sitting nearby to shout at his daughter, "How long are you going to put up with this?" Fair jumped up, grabbed a hunting knife, and repeatedly stabbed Knight as the older man begged him to stop. Facing a charge of first-degree murder, Fair maintained he acted in self-defense. Knight, he insisted, regularly beat and cut him, allegations of abuse unsupported by evidence of any kind. Fair's attorney asked that a court-appointed psychiatrist examine his client to determine if he was sane at the time of the murder. Fair insisted that director Oliver Stone was his father, a claim the filmmaker's people denied. The killer's birth father, Michael Oliver Stone, was never involved in his son's life and his whereabouts were unknown. Knight was dead only two days when an Arizona judge approved the settlement with the parents of the girl he had admitted abusing. The girl's family was awarded a $65,000 lump-sum payment plus $110,000 over the next six years. On April 25, 2005, a Bell County jury deliberated less than forty minutes before finding Fair guilty of first-degree murder. He was sentenced to life imprisonment and, under Texas law, must serve at least 30 years before becoming eligible for parole. Knight's remains were cremated and interred at Mount Hope Cemetery in Lapeer, Michigan, where his parents are buried.

Further Reading

Huey, Steve. "Grand Funk Railroad." www.allmusic.com.
Snell, Robert, and Doug Pullen. "Knight's Last Days — The Life and Death of a Flint Rock Icon." (Part 1 of 2). *Flint Journal*, November 14, 2004.
_____. "Knight's Last Days — In the End, Seclusion, Sex Charges, Poetry — and Murder." (Part 2 of 2). *Flint Journal*, November 15, 2004, sec. A, p. 1.
Unterberger, Richie. "Terry Knight." www.allmusic.com.

Knox, Robert Arthur (V)

Knox (born August 21, 1989, in Chatham, Kent) began acting at age 11 and at 13 was featured on British television in the Channel 4 reality show *Trust Me I'm a Teenager*. In 2004, Knox and younger brother, Jamie, briefly appeared in the film *King Arthur*, and following a role in an episode of ITV's *The Bill*, Robert was seen in two installments of the BBC comedy *After You've Gone*. Knox's biggest acting coup (and a sign that his career was taking off) was his signing to play "Marcus Belby," a trainee wizard at Ravensclaw, in *Harry Potter and the Half-Blood Prince*, the sixth film in the wildly popular series. Producers were so pleased with his performance that the 18-year-old was inked to reprise the character in the follow-up adventure, *Harry Potter and the Deathly Hallows*. On May 24, 2008, four days after completing his scenes in *Harry Potter and the Half-Blood Prince*, Knox, his 17-year-old brother, Jamie, and some friends were celebrating the event in the Metro, a bar in Sidcup in south-east London. One week before the celebration, Knox was involved in an ugly physical confrontation with Karl Bishop, 21, a black unemployed window cleaner, over a stolen cell phone. At the time, Bishop told the 6'0" school rugby player and his friends, "I'm going to come back next week and someone's going to die." Bishop showed up at the Metro on the night of the celebration, but was denied entrance. He went home, armed himself with two kitchen knives (11" and 12" long), and returned with friends to the Metro. Outside the bar, Karl Bishop threatened Jamie Knox and when Robert intervened to protect his brother was stabbed five times in the chest, the death blow severing a major artery. Bishop continued frenziedly windmilling the knives in both hands before being overcome by onlookers including some of Knox's friends. During the ninety second rampage Bishop stabbed and slashed five others ranging in ages from 16 to 23. Knox, taken to Queen Elizabeth Hospital in Woolwich, southeast London, was pronounced dead shortly before 1:00 A.M. Dean Saunders, 23, survived a neck wound that severely damaged his spinal cord, and was left with partial paralysis in his legs. Bishop was arrested at the scene and when told by an officer of Knox's death complained that now he was going to miss the televised Ricky Hatton fight.

The murder of the aspiring young actor marked the 28th teenager to have been killed in Britain since the beginning of 2008, and the tenth in London to die from stab wounds in what police termed a gun and knife epidemic. In London, it was estimated that ⅓ of all 11- to 16-year-olds occasionally carried a knife and prosecutions for the crime seldom resulted in the maximum sentence of two years in jail for carrying one in a public place. In the aftermath of Knox's killing, a two week campaign conducted by London police resulted in the seizure of some two hundred knives as well as the convening of a Downing Street summit that lowered the prosecution age for carrying a blade from the age of 18 to 16. Karl Bishop, identified at his February 2009 trial in London's Old Bailey as a habitual knife carrier, had been on the radar of social services since the age of five when his father abandoned him. He received rage counseling as a child and was home tutored after being expelled from primary school. At 16, he was expelled from high school for his angry outbursts and for threatening a man with a knife. The charges were dropped for lack of evidence. Bishop enrolled in a college mechanics course, but quickly dropped out to pursue a life of petty crime, narcotics, and alcohol. In December 2004, Bishop slashed the face of the same man he had earlier threatened and attacked his friend at a taxistand in Bromley after they intervened to stop the thug's harassment of a woman. Convicted of inflicting grievous bodily harm for the incident in May 2005, the habitual offender was sentenced to four years in a young offender institute, but released on license in March 2007. Bishop was out only a year when in March 2008 he was named as a suspect in a knifepoint robbery, but released for insufficient evidence. Two days later, Bishop threatened a man with a knife in an argument over drugs. Metropolitan Police were informed and as a matter of routine should have followed up on the complaint, but did not. Given Bishop's history as a serial knife carrier he would most certainly have been picked up and not on the street to attack Knox and the others in the Metro bar incident. Two police officers were officially disciplined over their handling of the affair. At trial,

Bishop maintained that he had acted in self-defense after Knox and his group attacked him. The prosecution, citing his past record, characterized Bishop as a person who "carried knives like others carried pens in their pockets." Found guilty of murder and of four counts of wounding and stabbing, Bishop refused to attend the court proceedings on March 5, 2009. He was sentenced to life in prison and ordered to serve a minimum of 20 years behind bars.

Further Reading

Bannerman, Lucy. "Parents of Harry Potter Actor Vow to Fight Knife-Carrying Culture After Murder Verdict." *The Times* (London), March 5, 2009, p. 11.
www.robknox.co.uk.

Kupcinet, Karyn (V)

The daughter of famed *Chicago Sun-Times* columnist, Irv "Kup" Kupcinet, Karyn (born March 6, 1941) was nudged into acting by her mother, Esther, a member of a wealthy Near Northside family who had never realized her own dream of becoming a dancer. Known in Windy City nightclub and entertainment circles as "Mr. Chicago," Kup used his considerable professional pull to help position his 13-year-daughter as the understudy to actress Carol Lynley in the 1954 Chicago production of *Anniversary Waltz*. At the prestigious Francis Parker School, the teenager appeared in several stage productions later majoring in drama at Wellesly College. Following a stint at the exclusive Actors Studio run by Lee Strasberg, Karyn Kupcinet migrated to Hollywood in 1960 convinced her talent and father's connections would make her a marketable star. Kup's pal, Jerry Lewis, cast her in a bit part in his 1961 movie *The Ladies' Man*, but following this microscopic role she managed to work only sporadically in television series including the *Red Skelton Show*, *U.S. Steel*, *Hawaiian Eye*, *Surfside Six*, and *The Donna Reed Show*. However, in 1962 she earned strong reviews for her final stage performance in the role of "Annie Sullivan" in the Laguna Beach Summer Theatre production of *The Miracle Worker*.

As Karyn struggled to prove she could make it as an actress independent of favors from her famous father's industry friends, her natural insecurities came to the fore. She underwent a battery of plastic surgeries to her face and battled a weight problem with prescription diet pills. On November 10, 1962, Kupcinet was arrested for shoplifting after walking out of a Pomona department store with two books and a $10.40 pair of green Capri pants. She pleaded guilty and paid a $150 fine. In late 1962, Kupcinet began an intense love affair with 26-year-old actor Andrew Prine, Earl Holliman's co-star in the NBC television series *Wide Country*. According to friends of the couple, Mark and Marcia Goddard, Kupcinet became pregnant by Prine and they paid to have the child aborted in a quickie procedure in Tijuana on July 4, 1963. As the Kupcinet-Prine relationship deteriorated, Karyn's behavior became increasingly erratic. Death threats pieced together from words clipped out of movie magazines and scotch taped to a piece of paper began appearing on the doors of both Kupcinet's and Prine's residences. One taped to Prine's door read:

> You may die without nobody
> Winner of loneliness wants death
> Until
> One someone special cares

In early November 1963, weeks after Prine broke with Kupcinet, he and new girlfriend, 18-year-old actress Anna Capri, were enjoying each other's company in the actor's Hollywood home when they heard noises in the attic. While Capri ran next door to phone police, Prine investigated the disturbance and found Kupcinet hiding in the house. It was later learned she had been spying on her former lover since the breakup and kept detailed notes of her surveillance and feelings in a diary.

On Saturday, November 30, 1963, Mark and Marcia Goddard became concerned after they were repeatedly unable to contact their friend since dining with her on the previous Wednesday. Around 7:00 P.M. the couple arrived at Kupcinet's $135 a month, second-floor apartment at 1127 N. Sweetzer Avenue a few blocks below the Sunset Strip. Several newspapers lay undisturbed outside the door. When ringing the doorbell failed to generate a response, Mark Goddard tried the door. It was open. Inside the modest apartment, the only light came from a television set with the sound turned down. Goddard flicked on the light switch to discover the nude body of the 22-year-old actress lying on its side on a couch. Minute particles of blood flecked her face and the pillow beneath her head. Other than a bowl of cigarettes and a coffee pot that had been knocked to the floor and an overturned lamp, the scene yielded no signs of a life-or-death struggle. Though police were initially uncertain how or when the actress died, an autopsy ruled that death was caused by "asphyxiation due to manual strangulation which fractured the hyoid bone in the throat." Kupcinet was killed shortly after midnight on Wednesday or very early Thursday morning.

Ex-boyfriend Andrew Prine, the last known person to have spoken to Kupcinet on Wednesday evening by phone, was immediately picked up and questioned by Hollywood police. He and three other male friends of the dead woman were administered lie detector tests with results deemed as "inconclusive." Prine admitted that for some time he had been trying to extricate himself from Kupcinet and handed over seven death threats he had found taped to the door of his home. Police later determined the distraught Kupcinet had constructed and posted the threats herself after the crime lab pulled her fingerprint off the scotch tape. Although Prine was quickly ruled out as a suspect, Kupcinet's murder without question blighted a promising career that many felt his talent fully warranted. Another friend of Karyn Kupcinet, 27-year-old actor David Lange, son of actress Hope Lange, briefly became a prime suspect when he stupidly told an acquaintance, "I did it." Lange later insisted he was only "kidding," and was cleared only after several unpleasant rounds of police interrogations. As the investigation continued, Karyn Kupcinet was charitably eulogized as a person "born to be a star" at a funeral service conducted in Chicago's Temple Shalom. Among the more than 1,500 attendees were Illinois Governor Otto Kerner and Chicago Mayor Richard Daley. The troubled actress was buried in Memorial Park Cemetery in Skokie, Illinois. In a 1998 article appearing in *GQ*, true crime novelist James Ellroy maintained Kupcinet's death was either an accidental or intentional suicide. Overdosing on pills, Kupcinet fell against the edge of a coffee table and fractured her hyoid bone. Both police and surviving members of the Kupcinet family dispute the author's claim despite an entry in Karyn's diary found in the death apartment that read, "I'm no good. I'm not really that pretty. My figure's fat and will never be the way my mother wants it. I won't let it be what she wants.... What happens to me — or my Andy? Why doesn't he want me?"

Further Reading

"Actress Found Dead in Hollywood Apartment." *Los Angeles Times*, December 1, 1963, p. 11.
Ellroy, James. "Glamour Jungle," *GQ*, 68(12) (December 1988): 288–300.

Landau, Jack (V)

Active in theatrical set and costume design since the early 1940s, Landau (born January 5, 1925, in Braddock, Pennsylvania) joined the American Shakespeare Festival Theatre and Academy in Stratford, Connecticut, in 1956. That same year, with John Houseman, Landau was associate director for productions of *King John* and *Measure for Measure*. He also directed *The Merchant of Venice* (1957), *A Midsummer Night's Dream* (1958), and at the invitation of President John F. Kennedy, staged a program of Shakespeare at the White House on October 4, 1961. On television, Landau designed the *Curtain Call* series (NBC, 1952), and in 1953 became a staff designer for CBS. In the early 1960s, he wrote, produced, and directed a series of news documentaries culminating in the 1965 Emmy award winning production, *This Is Ben Shahn*, an examination of the life and work of the American artist. In May 1966, Landau joined the National Educational Television Network as a producer of the *N.E.T. Playhouse* series.

On March 16, 1967, a business associate dropped by Landau's Beacon Street apartment in Boston, Massachusetts to find the door uncharacteristically unlocked. Inside, the apartment had been ransacked and Landau's body was found on the bedroom floor. The multi-talented 42-year-old bachelor had been battered, trussed with wire, strangled (with two neckties, a scarf, and a wire still in place around his neck), and stabbed nine times with an 8" carving knife. A neighbor told detectives that early the day before he had seen three youths carrying a portable television, clothing, and other articles out of the building. Days later, Boston and Revere police arrested Eugene C. McKenna, 17, Michael Riley, 19, and Frederick Simone, 16, and charged them with Landau's murder. Riley and McKenna were convicted on January 24, 1968, but the convictions were set aside by the state Supreme Court after it unanimously ruled that Boston police had prevented the youths from talking to their lawyers during questioning. In November 1969, both men subsequently pleaded guilty to the lesser charge of manslaughter and received 12 to 20-year prison sentences. The fate of Simone, a juvenile at the time of the killing, was unreported.

Further Reading

"Ex-Newsman Strangled in Boston Flat." *Chicago Tribune*, March 17, 1967, sec. D, p. 2.

Laney, Barbara Jean (V)

A former actress who did some episodes of the 1950s television series *Sky King*, Laney also modeled and appeared as an Aquabelle in water-ski shows at Cypress Gardens and the Sunshine Springs and Gardens in Sarasota, Florida. While living for years in Hong Kong, she dubbed movies in English. On August 3, 2002, a friend of the 67 year old became curious when he was unable to contact her at her condominium in the Wildewood Springs complex in Bradenton, Florida. He entered the residence and found Laney face-down in a pool of blood on the kitchen floor. The former actress had been beaten and stabbed to death with a large knife. In October 2002, police charged Gary Michael Cloud, 45, with the brutal murder after blood and DNA samples collected at the scene tied him to the crime. In and out of jail 16 times since 1988, Cloud boasted a record filled with arrests for forgery, home invasion, and a ten year prison term for carjacking. Released in March 2001, but required to serve ten years of probation for the carjacking offense, Cloud violated the bail agreement after dropping out of a court-mandated drug treatment program. Laney was a close friend since grade school of Cloud's mother and had loaned the career criminal-cocaine addict $130 to pay a traffic ticket and to pick up some items from a pawnshop. The one-time Aquabelle admitted to acquaintances that she feared the man and would no longer loan him money. According to court documents, Cloud confronted Laney, beat, stabbed, and strangled her, then washed his hands in the sink as the woman bled out on the kitchen floor. Inexplicably leaving behind several pieces of expensive jewelry, Cloud rifled through his victim's purse and stole her wallet. In June 2006, Cloud was convicted of first-degree murder and sentenced to life in prison without the possibility of parole.

Further Reading

Roman, Selina. "Former Actress Stabbed to Death." *Sarasota Herald-Tribune*, August 6, 2002, p. 1.

La Rock, Scott (V)

Often identified as hip-hop's first murder victim, Scott La Rock (born Scott Sterling in the South Bronx on March 2, 1962) shattered the stereotype of the street tough rapper. A high school basketball star with a bachelor's degree in business administration, Sterling was working as a counselor for homeless men at the Franklin

Armory Men's Shelter in the Morrisania section of the Bronx in 1985 when he met day visitor Laurence Krisna Parker. Sterling, a weekend disc jockey known as Scott La Rock while attending Castleton State College in Vermont, was instantly drawn to Parker, a rap artist known as KSR-One. La Rock and KRS-One formed Boogie Down Productions and after releasing their first independent single, "Crack Attack," in 1986 cut a full-length album, *Criminal Minded,* for indie label B-Boy Records in 1987. The album's street-wise lyrics concerning drugs and violence (mainly written by KRS-One) combined with La Rock's DJing attracted a devoted following and is considered by music critic Steve Huey to be an early classic of hardcore rap. Word-of-mouth on the album was so strong that Jive, an affiliate of RCA, signed the duo to a contract. La Rock, 25, would not live long enough to record an album for the major label.

On August 25, 1987, La Rock, 25, learned his friend and BDP associate Derrick (D-Nice) Jones had argued with some older teenagers over a woman in the South Bronx near Highbridge Garden Homes. La Rock, a trained counselor, drove his jeep accompanied by some friends to the housing project to defuse the situation. The teens were not there, but the DJ spoke to their friends in a bid to make peace. He was sitting in the jeep when shots fired from an apartment window across the street struck him in the head and neck. La Rock was first taken to Lincoln Hospital and then to Misericordia Hospital where he died two days later on August 27. In May 1988, two Bronx teenagers were arrested and charged with La Rock's murder. Cory Bayne, 17, was already in custody for allegedly stealing subway tokens from turnstiles. Two confederates implicated in the token thefts fingered Bayne as the shooter. Also arrested and charged with second-degree murder was 18-year-old Kendall Newman. The final disposition of the case remains uncertain.

Further Reading

Huey, Steve. "Boogie Down Productions." www.allmusic.com.
Iverem, Esther. "Violent Death Halts Rap Musician's Rise." *The New York Times,* August 31, 1987, sec. B, p. 1.
Simmonds, Jeremy. *The Encyclopedia of Dead Rock Stars: Heroin, Handguns, and Ham Sandwiches.* Rev. ed. Chicago, IL: Chicago Review, 2008.

Lawes, Henry ("Junjo") (V)

Born circa 1960 in a ghetto area of Kingston, Jamaica, Lawes began singing with the reggae trio Grooving Locks in 1978. Uncomfortable with public performing, he switched to producing in 1979 and worked with such acts as Barrington Levy, the Roots Radic Band, Michael Prophet, Eek a Mouse, and Cocoa Tea. Active with Jamaican deejays Yellowman, General Echo, and Nicodeemus, Lawes pioneered "dancehall," catchy street-style music that initially relied on the organic rhythms of live instruments, but later morphed into computerized reggae. In 1983, the producer developed the Volcano sound system that quickly became the standard throughout Jamaica's top clubs. Scrupulously honest in the payment of royalties to the artists he produced, Lawes's "street credibility" was solidified by his association with Kingston's powerful gangs. Lawes moved to New York in 1985, but was barred from producing after he was imprisoned for associating with criminal groups. Deported back to Jamaica in 1991, he continued to work with Cocoa Tea, Ninjaman, and John Holt, but his earlier success eluded him. In England, however, Lawes continued to remain popular with 42 of his Volcano produced albums released by British-based Greensleeves Records. On June 14, 1999, the 51-year-old record producer left his flat on St. Mary's Road in the shabby Harlesden area of northwest London to buy a pack of cigarettes. The district, riddled with "Yardie" gangs (criminals who illegally entered Britain from Jamaica), was in the throes of a violent turf war to determine control of the area's lucrative crack cocaine trade. Lawes was walking down the street when a car carrying five gang members drew alongside him. The producer was repeatedly shot, but managed to stumble away. Two men got out of the car, tracked the dying man down, shot him to death, and drove away. Police theorized that Lawes' lifelong connection to unsavory elements in both Jamaica and London led to his murder in an escalating drug war between rival dealers.

Further Reading

"Obituary — Henry 'Junjo' Lawes." *The Guardian* (London), July 20, 1999, p. 20.

Lee, Anthony Dwain (V)

"His biggest fear was getting killed by cops, because he's a tall black man," a friend of Lee's commented after the tragic October 2000 shooting of the actor by a Los Angeles police officer focused even more negative attention on the city's beleaguered department. A former member of the

Crips street gang, Lee renounced the gangbanger lifestyle after being stabbed in the back during a fight. The actor moved from Sacramento to Seattle in 1988 where his commanding voice and imposing 6' 4" physical presence helped him win roles in local productions of Shakespeare's *Othello* and Lorraine Hansberry's *A Raisin in the Sun*. Lee was also instrumental in creating a school touring play for the Seattle Repertory Theatre's Outreach Bunch and appeared at the Oregon Shakespeare Festival in Ashland. Relocating to Los Angeles in 1994, Lee appeared in supporting roles on several television programs (*ER*; *NYPD Blue*; *Brooklyn South*) and in the films *American Strays* (1996) and *Liar, Liar* (1997).

In the early morning of October 28, 2000, the promising actor was one of several hundred costumed guests at a Halloween party in a Benedict Canyon mansion in the 9700 block of Yoakum Drive. Several of the partygoers were dressed in LAPD uniforms. Two actual police officers (Tarriel Hooper, 27; another unidentified) responding to a noise complaint were trying to locate the homeowner, when three-year veteran Hooper looked through a glass door and saw Lee allegedly point what appeared to be a real gun at him. Hooper, a black man, fired nine shots through the glass door striking Lee. LAPD spokeswoman Charlotte Broughton stated that Hooper was reacting to what he perceived as a life-threatening situation, but refused to say if the officer identified himself as such before firing.

Amid public charges of racial profiling and police abuse, the LAPD and the District Attorney's office launched separate inquiries into the shooting. At a press conference held two days after the incident LAPD Chief Bernard C. Parks blamed the realistic prop gun (a solid gray rubber replica of an Israeli-made .357 Desert Eagle semiautomatic pistol) for the fatal incident. In 1987, Los Angeles became the first major U.S. city to outlaw the manufacture and sale of realistic toy guns after a television reporter was held hostage on the air by a man wielding a fake pistol. Chief Parks maintained that Officer Hooper had "no time" to either determine if the weapon was real or shout a warning before discharging his own. Hooper, a former University of Southern California football player, was placed on paid administrative leave while authorities continued their investigation. On November 1, 2000, a crowd estimated at 650 people attended a memorial service for Lee in the auditorium of the Buddhist SGI-USA Los Angeles Friendship Center. Meanwhile, Lee's sister, Tina Vogt, retained famed O.J. Simpson (see entry) attorney Johnnie Cochran to represent the family in a $100 million gross negligence suit against the city and the two officers involved in the shooting. Fuel was seemingly added to that charge when an autopsy revealed that of the nine bullets fired at Lee three struck him in the back and one in the back of the head. The report also concluded that cocaine and alcohol had been found in the actor's system. After reviewing an internal investigation report, a five-member Los Angeles Police Commission ruled on October 23, 2001, that Hooper was justified in his use of deadly force. In April 2003, the Los Angeles City Council voted 12–0 without comment to approve a $225,000 settlement with Lee's family.

Further Reading

Lin, Judy. "Friends Outraged Over Police Killing of Halloween Partygoer." Associated Press, October 29, 2000.

Lees, Robert (V)

On June 13, 2004, Morley Hal Engelson, a 67-year-old retired physician, was on the phone with a Southwest Airlines booking agent when the conversation was abruptly ended by a commotion. The agent immediately notified the Los Angeles Police Department and after they arrived minutes later at Engelson's home on Stanley Avenue they spotted his body through a window. Forcing entry, officers verified that Engelson was dead from multiple stab wounds then made the grisly discovery of a severed human head in another room of the house. While examining the scene, investigators received a call from the Los Angeles Fire Department reporting that they had responded to a call at a neighboring house in the 1600 block of North Courtney Avenue belonging to Robert Lees, 91. Lees, who had served in Frank Capra's Army film unit during World War II, was best known as the comedy film writer (often with partner Frederic I. Rinaldo) of scripts for Abbott and Costello (*Hold That Ghost*, 1941; *Buck Privates Come Home*, 1947; *The Wistful Widow of Wagon Gap*, 1948; *Abbott and Costello Meet Frankenstein*, 1948; *Abbott and Costello Meet the Invisible Man*, 1951; *Comin' Round the Mountain*, 1951; and the Dean Martin and Jerry Lewis vehicle *Jumping Jacks*, 1952). The laughter and the scriptwriter's film career, however, abruptly ended on April 10, 1951, when actor Sterling Hayden named him to the House Committee on Un-American Activities

(HUAC). Lees joined the Communist Party in 1939 and steadfastly refused to name names when called before the committee. Blacklisted by Hollywood, the studio attempted to remove his name from the credits of *Jumping Jacks*, but was prevented by the Screenwriters Guild. Lees was working as a maitre d' in the dining room of the Hotel Westerner in Tucson, Arizona, when the Martin and Lewis smash-opened in a theatre up the street. Under the alias "J.E. Selby" Lees wrote episodes for the television programs *Rawhide*, *Flipper*, and ironically given future events, *Alfred Hitchcock Presents*.

Lee's longtime friend, Helen Colton, arrived to pick him up for a social function to discover the scriptwriter's bloody and headless corpse lying under a comforter with a big heavy drawer on top of him. Police theorized that the random killer decapitated Lees, hopped a backyard fence between the properties carrying the writer's head, and murdered Engelson. A massive manhunt in the surrounding Hollywood neighborhood culminated in a televised news conference on June 15 in which police showed a photograph of 27-year-old drifter, Kevin Lee Graff. Within minutes of the broadcast, a security guard at nearby Paramount notified police that a man answering to that description was currently outside the studio's front gate talking to himself and making obscene gestures at passing cars and pedestrians. Graff was quickly taken into custody by LAPD officers, but during subsequent questioning admitted that he was high on methamphetamines and Ecstasy and had no memory of the grisly murders. "If I really did this, man, I just want to say I'm sorry," he told detectives. "I'm so sorry. I know saying sorry isn't enough. It isn't going to do nothing. But I'm no criminal, dude. I'm really a good kid. I don't know how all this happened." Graff escaped a possible death penalty by pleading guilty on February 26, 2008, to two counts of first-degree murder along with eight other charges including torture, mayhem, and burglary. In April 2008, the killer was sentenced to two life terms without the possibility of parole and ordered to pay $9,000 in restitution and court fees.

Further Reading

"Man Gets Life for Hollywood Beheading and Second Murder." Associated Press, April 4, 2008.

Lennon, John (V)

With the exceptions of Marilyn Monroe and possibly Michael Jackson, more has been written about the life and untimely death of John Lennon than any celebrity in this survey. As founder of the Beatles, the most popular and influential group in the history of rock 'n' roll, Lennon (with fellow-bandmate and writing partner Paul McCartney) provided the sound track to much of the 1960s and beyond. The artist's contribution to popular culture is incalculable. As a solo artist with second wife Yoko Ono he actively opposed the Vietnam War and became an outspoken, if eccentric, advocate for peace. Hand in hand with his widely documented commercial success, however, Lennon's personal life was marked by profound human loss, mercurial behavior, periods of intense substance abuse, a search for spirituality and social commitment, and an attempt to redefine himself as a husband and father. At the time of his murder on December 8, 1980 by Mark David Chapman, a schizophrenic former fan, the 40-year-old rock star was triumphantly emerging from a nearly five-year period of self-imposed creative exile. Lennon's death extinguished the promise of new music yet to come including, perhaps, the long cherished hope of Beatles fans for a reunion of rock's greatest band. More tragically, it left a devoted wife without a husband and two children without a father.

John Winston (later Ono) Lennon was born at Oxford Street Maternity Hospital in Liverpool, England during an air raid alert on October 9, 1940. Father Alfred (Freddie) Lennon was a ship's steward and mother Julia Stanley listed her occupation on the marriage register as "cinema usherette" principally because she loved going to movies. As a merchant seaman, Freddie was often away from home and stopped sending support money 18 months after the child was born. Julia, fun-loving and social, wasted no time lamenting over her deadbeat husband and soon became pregnant by a soldier on leave from the war in 1944. The man's name is not known, but Julia gave the unwanted infant up for adoption through the Salvation Army. Julia was employed as a café waitress in Penny Lane when she met John (Bobby) Dykins, a hotel manager, in early 1946. Although still legally married to Freddie Lennon, Julia and five-year-old John moved into the man's one-room flat. The woman's family was scandalized by the immoral living arrangement. As matriarch of the clan, Mary Elizabeth Smith, Julia's oldest sister and John's "Aunt Mimi," demanded that she turn the child over to her to be raised in a more stable environment with her husband,

George, a dairyman in Woolton. Mimi met Julia's curt refusal with a call to social services alerting the agency of the couple's unmarried status and demanding that the child be placed in her care. The social worker investigated the complaint, but saw no grounds worthy of breaking up a loving mother and her son. Undeterred, Mimi learned that John did not have his own room and was forced to sleep in the same bed as his mother. The determined woman placed another call to social services and this time John was taken from Julia and given to his Aunt Mimi until such time as his mother and Dykins could find more commodious living arrangements. Once the devoted couple (they later had two children of their own) found a roomier place, everyone agreed that John should stay with his aunt to avoid the psychic trauma of being uprooted from a stable home.

As if on cue, Freddie Lennon reappeared on the scene to play his role in the roiling domestic drama. In July 1946, Julia took John to Blackpool to visit with his father recently returned to England from a long voyage. Tensions escalated to the point between the troubled couple that Freddie angrily shouted an ultimatum at his five-year-old son — choose between your mother or me. John chose his absentee father, and a heartbroken Julia agreed and left. She was walking down the road when her sobbing son ran up and begged her not to leave him. Julia took John back to Liverpool to live with his Aunt Mimi and Uncle George. Freddie Lennon did not re-enter his son's life for 18 years and then only at the height of Beatlemania when he exposed his relation to the famous rocker in the media. Although understandably suspicious of the man's motives, Lennon was nevertheless cordial, blessed his father's upcoming marriage to a 19-year-old woman, and even bought them a house and put his "stepmother" on the payroll as a secretary. The hurt, however, was just too deep. Lennon and wife Yoko Ono were in primal scream therapy with Dr. Arthur Janov and the seismic event of October 30, 1970, at Tittenhurst Park, the couple's mansion in Ascot, Berkshire, could possibly be explained as a necessary milestone in the healing of the rocker's damaged psyche. On his 30th birthday, Lennon informed Freddie that he was cutting off all financial support and explained in excruciating detail the pain caused by his father's abandonment. John Lennon no longer wanted this man in his life. Father and son would not reconcile until John phoned him shortly before Freddie Lennon died from cancer

in a charity ward at a hospital in Brighton on April 1, 1976.

John Lennon was raised by his Aunt Mimi and Uncle George in their middle-class home, Mendips, at 251 Menlove Avenue, in Woolton, a suburb of Liverpool. Julia, though she remained a vital presence in his life, was relegated to the role of a distant relative while Aunt Mimi supplanted her as the child's mother. Personality-wise, the two strongest female influences in the young child's life could not have been more dissimilar. Julia was warm, outgoing, and quick to show affection. She loved music and as a banjo player taught John his first chords on guitar. John was permitted to play music in the house Julia and Dykins shared with their two daughters, while Mimi insisted he play only on the glassed-in porch at Mendips. Undemonstrative in showing affection, but equally loving in her way as Julia, Aunt Mimi raised the youngster according to strict middle-class values. She encouraged him to read and nurtured his early interest in drawing. Uncle George expressed no such reserve in his love for the child and John adored him. The 14-year-old Lennon was shattered when his beloved uncle died of a brain hemorrhage on June 5, 1955. At five, John attended Dovedale Road Primary and was considered a bright if headstrong student. Even at this early age the seeds of Lennon's inherent distrust of authority were apparent in his unwillingness to be anything but an individual. In September 1952, the 11 year old entered Quarry Bank High School, a state suburban facility. Administrators and teachers quickly identified Lennon as a behavior problem who had no interest in studying or showing respect to authority. He became the class clown and used his bitingly sarcastic wit to lash out at anyone he felt to be weak taking a special delight in tormenting cripples and those with deformities. A talent for art manifested itself in a series of devastating line drawn caricatures of teachers and classmates. Multiple disciplinary canings dished out by school administrators over the years did nothing to curb Lennon's penchant towards disrespect and disruption.

Within months after the sudden death of Lennon's beloved Uncle George at 52 in June 1955, the American film *Rock Around the Clock* played Britain in 1956. The movie featured performances by U.S. rock 'n' roll acts like Bill Haley & His Comets and helped inspire the teddy boy craze in the United Kingdom. Soon, 16 year old boys (including John Lennon) were wearing their hair greased back in a "duck's ass" and dressed in tight stovepipe pants and jackets. While Aunt Mimi opposed the music, Julia bought Elvis Presley's singles and she and John danced to them in her kitchen. Rock 'n' roll gave Lennon the perfect natural outlet for his resentment of authority and love of attention. Inspired by Presley and British musician Lonnie Donegan, Lennon formed a skiffle band (the Blackjacks later changed to the Quarry Men) and purchased his first guitar for £5 from a mail order catalog. Julia later bought her son a £17 model after his cheap guitar fell apart from constant use. The Quarry Men played skiffle (because of its popularity and the simplicity of the music and instruments — washboard, jugs, teabox chest bass) in churches, youth clubs and carnivals in the areas. On July 6, 1957, undoubtedly among the most important dates in the history of rock 'n' roll, the Quarry Men played a garden fete at St. Peter's Church in Woolton. Lennon, nearly 17 and sporting teddy boy gear and slicked back hair, downed a few ales for courage before the show. Though slightly inebriated when he joined the other Quarry Men on an outdoor platform set in a field away from the church he impressed the audience, especially Paul McCartney, with his raw energy and stage presence. McCartney, at 15 a year and eight months younger than Lennon, attended the show with a friend who was eager to introduce him to the leader of the Quarry Men. Unlike Lennon, McCartney was a talented musician who was raised in a musical family. After the show, their mutual friend made the introductions and McCartney instantly impressed the older Lennon by tuning his guitar (a skill John had yet to learn). More noteworthy, McCartney possessed encyclopedic knowledge of the lyrics to dozens of Lennon's favorite songs. A short time later, Lennon through a friend offered McCartney a spot in the band after overcoming his fear that the younger boy's superior musicianship and knowledge of rock 'n' roll might one day prove to be a possible threat to his leadership of the band. Lennon, however, saw in McCartney a powerful ally in moving the Quarry Men away from skiffle to the rock 'n' roll he wanted to write and play. George Harrison, nearly 15, was Paul McCartney's friend and classmate at the Liverpool Institute, and a talented lead guitarist devoted to his instrument. Although eight months younger than McCartney and three years Lennon's junior, Harrison joined the Quarry Men in early 1958.

Not surprisingly given his disdain for academe,

Lennon failed his general certificate education exam, but on the strength of a letter of support from a friendly teacher at Quarry Bank High School was accepted into the Liverpool College of Art in September 1957. Lennon loved the freedom of college life and devoted himself full-time to drinking, womanizing, and wearing teddy boy outfits accessorized by a guitar slung across his back. The charismatic loner went out of his way to offend teachers and classmates alike and was renowned and feared for his witty, sarcastic, and deeply hurtful remarks. One saving grace of the art college was its location just around the corner from the Liverpool Institute where McCartney and Harrison, 15, were students. The pair spent lunch hours with Lennon in a spare room at his school where they played hits of the day and worked on their own songs. On July 15, 1958, the 17 year old suffered the most traumatic event in his life. Mother Julia, 44, and Aunt Mimi were still close and together had raised an anarchic, but loving son. After having tea with Mimi at Mendips, Julia was crossing Menlove Road on her way to the bus stop two hundreds yards away when she was struck by a car and instantly killed. The novice driver, an off-duty policeman, was drunk and inadvertently hit the gas pedal instead of the brake when he saw her crossing. The cop was acquitted at trial and received only a reprimand and brief suspension of duty from the job. Lennon was devastated by the loss, but Paul McCartney well understood the pain of losing a mother. His had died of breast cancer when he was 14. A few months after Julia's death, Lennon met Cynthia (Cyn) Powell in a lettering class he was forced to take by teachers who refused to have him in their classes. The pair started dating and would make love in the one-room flat of Lennon's closest friend and classmate, Stuart Sutcliffe, a brilliant student and artist who dreamed of becoming a painter. Lennon was insanely jealous and possessive of Cynthia and when she informed him years later in July 1962 that she was pregnant he readily married her on August 23, 1962. Their son, John Charles Julian Lennon, was born on April 8, 1963.

The Quarry Men played their earliest shows in places like the Casbah Club, a venue in the cellar of a house in the Liverpool suburb of West Derby owned by Mona Best. The woman set up the non-alcoholic club as a place where her son, drummer Pete Best, could meet and perform with his mates. The group (without a drummer and with stand-in guitarist Ken Brown) played the opening of the Casbah Club on August 29, 1959, in front of a crowd of three hundred. In attendance was Mal Evans later to be the number one roadie (later road manager), gofer, and fixit man for the Beatles until their breakup in 1969. It was Evans, the "6th Beatle," who set off the alarm clock in "A Day in the Life" and banged the anvil on "Maxwell's Silver Hammer." After the group split, Evans lost his identity in a haze of depression. On the night of January 4, 1976, Evans, 40, picked up a .30-caliber rifle and started to chase his 26-year-old girlfriend, Fran Hughes, around the rented duplex they shared at 8122 West 4th Street in Los Angeles. Hughes called the LAPD on her flipped out fiancée and when they responded Evans pointed the gun at them. Four of the six shots fired by the cops struck Evans killing him instantly. On November 15, 1959, the Quarry Men (briefly renamed Johnny and the Moondogs) auditioned at the London Hippodrome for Carroll "the Starmaker" Levis, a local promoter who booked several acts in an around Liverpool. The band lacked a drummer and Levis was unimpressed. Around this time, John Lennon and Paul McCartney formed an agreement that any songs they wrote together or separately would be listed as by "Lennon and McCartney," a tacit understanding of the importance each individual played in the songwriting process. In early 1960, Lennon convinced his art school friend Stu Sutcliffe to join the Quarry Men as a bassist. Sutcliffe, though possessing the good looks of a young James Dean, was a hopeless musician who often turned his back to the audience so they could not see how little he was playing. McCartney, the band's keyboardist, incessantly criticized the amateur and pressured Lennon to sack him.

Allan Williams, owner of the Jacaranda, a club near the Liverpool College of Art, was tied into the local music scene and showcased rising talent like Rory Storm and the Hurricanes, a band that featured Ringo Starr (Richard Starkey) on drums. In late 1959, Lennon and McCartney were changing the group's sound away from skiffle to the rock 'n' roll currently racing up the charts. To go along with the band's new sound, Lennon needed a new name. As an homage of sorts to his idol Buddy Holly and the Crickets, the rocker called his band the Beetles, quickly renamed the Silver Beetles with input from the other members of the former Quarry Men. Through Williams, the Beetles got an audition with Larry Parnes, a local promoter

who had discovered Tommy Steele and Elvis wannabes like Billy Fury, Vince Eager, and Duffy Powell. They failed the audition even with drummer Tommy Moore, a 36-year-old forklift driver, and McCartney was more than ever convinced that Sutcliffe's playing was holding back the Silver Beetles. Parnes, however, offered the group a one-week gig in May 1960 at the sum of £18 each to back up singer Johnny Gentle on a tour of northern Scotland. The tour exposed the weakness of Sutcliffe's playing to the point that Lennon was openly critical of his friend, no doubt to the delight of McCartney who had been lobbying for months to get rid of the artist. Tommy Moore left the band immediately after the tour. Back in Liverpool the group (with Pete Best on drums) was becoming local favorites at £10 a night gigs at the Casbah. On June 2, 1960, the band played a show at the Neston Institute under its new name — the Beatles. The next month, Lennon was officially expelled from the Liverpool College of Art. Desperate to make the band into a career, Lennon pestered Allan Williams for more and better paying gigs. The promoter came through with a six-week engagement at a club in Hamburg, West Germany where British pop acts were enjoying huge popularity. McCartney, now openly at war with Sutcliffe, still played piano in the group, but clearly wanted to supplant Lennon's best friend on the bass. In fact, at this point in the band's career, McCartney could outplay anyone in the group on their instrument. The Beatles (Lennon, 19, McCartney, 18, Harrison nearly 17, with Pete Best and Stu Sutcliffe) arrived in Hamburg in mid–August and played the Indra, a former strip club, on August 16, 1960. The band was moved days later to the larger Kaiserkeller club to alternate sets with Rory Storm and the Hurricanes, Liverpool's biggest group. Onstage from 8:00 P.M. until 2:00 A.M., the Beatles earned only 15 pounds a week each for doing six 45 minute shows a night in front of rough German crowds filled with working class drunks and prostitutes. To keep up with the frenetic pace of performing, Lennon and some other band members gobbled amphetamines just to keep awake. During the so-called "Hamburg experience," the Beatles developed a polish and stage presence with Lennon particularly exuding confidence while shouting insults from the stage at the largely non–English speaking crowd. Word of mouth spread in the city about the English group's dynamic stage performances and the wild man fronting the band. It was in Hamburg that the group changed their hairstyles to their signature mop tops and traded in their teddy boy outfits for black leather jackets with matching turtlenecks. The Beatles played the Kaiserkeller for four months until authorities were notified that George Harrison at 17 was under the legal age of 18 to work in Germany. The lead guitarist was deported back to Britain where the rest of the Beatles joined him in mid–December 1960.

Back in Liverpool the Beatles became a local sensation knocking down £60 a night and were recognized as the second-best group behind Rory Storm and the Hurricanes. Driven by a loud, pulsating beat and dressed in black leather, the group looked and sounded unlike any band in town. On March 21, 1961, the Beatles played the Cavern club in Mathew Street in Liverpool's city center. Formerly a bastion of jazz, the club was forced by economic reality to book rock 'n' roll acts. The Beatles packed fans of the popular new music into the cramped dark cellar and over the next couple of years played there 292 times earning 25 shillings a set for lunch and evening shows. The band was a sensation performing frenetic versions of the popular hits of the day. Though the aloof Lennon was the clear leader and still directed caustic comments to the crowd, McCartney, the popular crowd pleaser, was sharing singing duties and involved in every aspect of the band. Their run at the Cavern club was interrupted by a second trip to Hamburg in the mid-summer of 1961. After the gigs, Stuart Sutcliffe informed the band that August that he would be staying in Hamburg with his German girlfriend to study art. Sutcliffe, Lennon's best friend, would die there on April 10, 1962 at the age of 21 from a cerebral hemorrhage. The Beatles resumed their popular run at the Cavern unaware that their fortunes were about to change dramatically. Brian Epstein, 27, operated his family's record store, NEMS (North End Music Store), located down the street from the Cavern. Epstein, a closeted homosexual, would become closest to Lennon in the band sparking ongoing speculation that the pair was sexually involved. On the advice of a friend, Epstein visited the Cavern at lunch time on November 9, 1961. Though the group was sloppy, raw, and undisciplined onstage, their charismatic stage presence and musical proficiency was undeniable. The group believed Epstein when he told them with his help they would be bigger than Elvis Presley, Lennon's idol. On December 3, 1961 Epstein became the Beatles' manager. Weeks later on Jan-

uary 24, 1962, the band entered into an official management contract with Brian Epstein after agreeing to a list of his non-negotiable ground rules. The band must be punctual and professional at all times (Lennon, Best, and Harrison were late for the initial meeting). The band would limit itself to rigid one hour shows and perform only its best repertoire. No more eating, drinking, or smoking onstage. Lennon was forbidden to curse or verbally abuse the audience. Tee-shirts, jeans, and leather jackets were to be replaced by coordinated suits and ties for a cleaner, more professional image. They could keep their music, he just wanted to package and promote the product. Girlfriends were okay, but Epstein demanded that the lads keep them in the background and not publicize the fact (as in Lennon's case) that they were taken. Female fans needed the illusion that their idols were available. Lastly, Epstein would receive 25 percent of the group's earnings while initially paying all their costs. Epstein relieved drummer Pete Best of his added responsibility of finding bookings for the group. As their new promoter, he held out for better venues and higher fees while trying to land the band a coveted recording contract.

As proof of how hard he would work for the band if they signed an exclusive management contract with him, Epstein had earlier set up an audition for the Beatles at Decca studio on January 1, 1962. The band played none of their own material and waited three months to hear the bad news. The Decca rep did not like the group's sound and besides, guitar bands were on the way out. Epstein kept pressing and in May 1962 he got demo tapes of the group's original compositions "Hello Little Girl" and "Till There was You" to George Martin, a producer at Parlophone, a small label within the EMI empire. A classically-trained musician, Martin agreed to give the group an audition at EMI studio in St. John's Wood in May 1962. In the audition, the band played a mix of its own compositions and popular covers. On Martin's recommendation, the Beatles were signed to a five year deal with Parlophone on June 4, 1962. There was just one stipulation — Martin (sources differ) did not think Pete Best was a steady enough drummer for the group. Fellow-band members welcomed this opportunity to eliminate Best from the group. The darkly handsome drummer looked like a real pop star and his popularity with female fans overshadowed and threatened Lennon and McCartney. Epstein performed the unenviable task of firing Best on August 16, 1962 while the remaining band members avoided him. Two days after the sacking, Ringo Starr (not cursed with Best's good looks) was hired as his replacement. Starr, 22, recently between bands after leaving Rory Storm and the Hurricanes, knew the lads from the Liverpool scene and the Hamburg experience and personality-wise was a perfect unthreatening fit. Epstein told the drummer the only condition of his employment was to wear his hair down like the rest of the band.

Under the management of Brian (the "5th Beatle") Epstein and guided by the production genius of George Martin, the Beatles (already a craze in Liverpool, but virtually unknown outside the port city) would become the biggest rock 'n' roll band in the world within two years of recording their first single, "Love Me Do," on September 4, 1962. The single climbed to Number 17 on the charts. The band's follow-up, "Please Please Me," released in mid–January 1963 was Number 1 by February. The band's debut album, *Please Please Me*, was recorded in one 11 hour session on February 11, 1963, and was a smash hit. Epstein carefully controlled the group's image booking the Beatles on top British television shows and live performances. In one memorable appearance in the Royal Variety Performance at the Prince of Wales Theatre, London on November 4, 1963, Lennon irreverently suggested the wealthy audience members in the expensive seats should just rattle their jewelry instead of applauding. On February 7, 1964, the Beatles launched the "British Invasion" landing at New York's Kennedy Airport amid thousands of screaming fans. Their iconic appearance two nights later on *The Ed Sullivan Show* (in which they played their Number 1 U.S. hit, "I Want to Hold Your Hand") was viewed by an estimated 73 million people and firmly cemented the Beatles status as the most famous rock 'n' roll band in the world. Until their highly publicized breakup in late 1969 the Beatles redefined rock music with classic singles, albums, and three motion pictures (*Hard Day's Night*, 1964; *Help!*, 1965; *Yellow Submarine*, 1968).

In 1968, John Lennon, rock star and multimillionaire, was clearly a restless man searching for some type of personal fulfillment. In August of 1967, his close friend and the band's troubled manager Brian Epstein, 32, died a probable suicide from a drug overdose. Lennon, as well, was abusing alcohol and drugs like LSD, cocaine, and heroin. In February 1968, Lennon, with fellow-band members and an entourage in tow, traveled to India to study advanced meditation techniques with the Maharishi Mahesh Yogi, a guru the rocker had proclaimed to be a "holy man." Lennon's spiritual quest ended in disaster when he learned the Maharishi was allegedly coming on to females in the group. The rock star unceremoniously left India in April and denounced the "holy man" as a fraud in the media. Lennon had first met Yoko Ono (born 1933), a Japanese performance artist, at an exhibition of her work at the Indica Gallery in London on November 9, 1966. Mutually intrigued by one another's intellect the pair kept in touch and became lovers in May 1968. Cynthia Lennon was granted an uncontested divorce on the grounds of adultery on November 8, 1968. For the next decade Lennon did little to see their son, Julian, finally reconciling with him in 1978. Ono became an omnipresent force during the 1968 recording sessions for *The Beatles* [*White Album*] and helped bring to the surface long simmering antagonisms between the band's two main creative elements, Lennon and McCartney. Meanwhile, Lennon and his new lover forged their own creative paths releasing their first collaboration, *Unfinished Music, No. 1: Two Virgins*, in November 1968. In early 1969 during the tortuous filming of *Let It Be* (the album of the same title would be released in 1970) Lennon announced he was through with the Beatles. For the next several years Lennon and McCartney took pot shots at one another in their solo albums while their business empire was contentiously picked over by their attorneys. Freed from the Beatles, Lennon devoted himself to several multi-media events with Ono and used his world-wide celebrity in creative ways ("bed-ins") to speak out against the Vietnam War. The couple married on Gibraltar on March 20, 1969. In 1971, the Lennons moved to New York City, and over the next five years waged a legal battle with the U.S. government to remain in the country. Arrested for cannabis possession in London in October 1968, Lennon (largely because of his outspoken political beliefs) had been classified as an "undesirable alien" and marked for deportation. In July 1976 his application for permanent residency status was approved after years of costly legal wrangling.

By 1973, however, the John and Ono marriage was in trouble. Lennon was abusing alcohol and Ono insisted on a trial separation. In October 1973, the rocker began his legendary "Lost Weekend" in Los Angeles accompanied by May Pang, Ono's secretary and a woman handpicked by the performance artist to serve as her watchdog and Lennon's concubine. For months Lennon caroused with singer Harry Nilsson and broadcasting personality Elliott Mintz and generally exhibited violent drunken behavior that set a new standard for decadent rock star excess. After a nearly two year exile (including a year spent living apart from Ono in a New York apartment with Pang), Lennon returned home to his wife in January 1975. The couple now lived on the sixth-floor of the Dakota, an exclusive apartment building located on Central Park West at 72nd Street. After several miscarriages, Ono gave birth to a son, Sean Taro Ono Lennon, on October 9, 1975, the same month and day as Lennon's birthday 35 years earlier. When the rock star's contract with EMI expired in February 1976 he decided not to renew it. Over the next five years, Lennon entered a period of creative self-exile to devote himself full-time to the care of his son. Lennon, the house-husband, remained at home with Sean while Ono managed their business affairs. During this exile, however, persistent rumors circulated that Lennon was heavy into narcotics, especially cocaine and heroin. In November 1980, the 40-year-old ended his creative exile with the release of *Double Fantasy* on Geffen Records. The collaboration between John and Yoko was an overt reaffirmation of their love and a testament to the importance of the life he shared with his family. Meanwhile, the rock star's refusal to be a prisoner of celebrity was putting his life in jeopardy. Lennon's residence in the Dakota turned the venerable apartment building into a tourist attraction and mecca for his fans, but he still enjoyed relative freedom. The couple loved the ease and convenience of walking together in Central Park across from the Dakota and visiting neighborhood restaurants and bars. In London, glimpsing the former Beatle on the street would have caused a riot. Tragically, Lennon's naïve lack of concern for his personal security would end in his murder at the hands of a deranged former fan who blamed the star for ruining his life.

Mark David Chapman was born on May 10, 1955, at Harris Hospital in Fort Worth, Texas. The relationship between his father, David Curtis Chapman, a Staff Sgt. in the U.S. Air Force, and mother, Diane Chapman, a nurse, was reportedly marred by abuse. As a child, Chapman dreamed of killing the man who made their homelives unbearable. To escape his father's criticism, the youngster created a fantasy world populated with "Little People" subject to his total control. Routinely picked upon at school, the dumpy, overweight youngster vented his frustration by pushing an imaginary button on his sofa tied to explosives. The detonation blew up the homes of the Little People killing hundreds of thousands of them. Chapman's other emotional outlet was music. He worshipped the Beatles, especially John Lennon, and plastered the walls of his room with posters of the band. Discovering drugs in 1969 while a high school student in Decatur, Georgia, the 14 year old routinely dropped LSD and found the kaleidoscopic swirl of lights the acid produced in his head replaced the Little People. Letting his hair grow, playing guitar, and listening to rock music gave the teen an identity. In 1970 he briefly ran away from home and spent time in Miami looking to hook up with "freaks." Within a year of returning to Decatur, Chapman became a born-again Christian through a girl he liked and her friends who played in a Christian rock band. On October 25, 1970, Chapman gave his life to Christ and weaned himself off drugs. In his new persona as religious zealot, the teen turned his back on the Beatles and was especially rankled with John Lennon whose comment in 1966 that the band was more popular than Jesus greatly angered him. Chapman cut his long hair, replaced his Hippie clothes with black trousers, black shoes, and a white shirt, and began handing out Bible tracts. The born-again Chapman was attending two different prayer meetings a week when an incident occurred that ended his commitment to Christianity. The enthusiastic teen was at a meeting and anxious to perform a song he had written about Jesus, but was told there was no time. Chapman closed his Bible, stopped praying, and started listening nonstop to the music of Todd Rundgren, a performer then in the beginning of a well-publicized feud with John Lennon.

For the next six years (1970–1975), Chapman replaced prayer and meetings with a fervent commitment to the De Kalb County Young Men's Christian Association in Decatur, first as a counselor, then as an assistant program director. The kids adored the nerdy man they called "Captain Nemo" (a character in Jules Verne's novel *Twenty Thousand Leagues Under the Sea*), and Chapman's outstanding service earned him a nomination in 1975 to the YMCA's international program. With two other counselors, Chapman was assigned to work a summer in Beirut, Lebanon, then in the midst of a bloody civil war. Within a short time, the workers were evacuated and Chapman found himself back in Decatur, Georgia. As an alternative, the 20 year old was offered a $200 a week position at a YMCA–run resettlement camp at Fort Chaffee, Arkansas, counseling "boat people" displaced by the Vietnam War. Chapman worked 16 hour days helping the refugees and was moved by their suffering. In October 1975, the counselor renewed his acquaintance with Jessica Blankenship, a former grade school classmate he got to know better during his stint as a born-again Christian. The couple became engaged after she visited him at Fort Chaffee and he made plans to join her at Covenant College, a fundamentalist Presbyterian school in Lookout Mountain, Tennessee. A few weeks earlier Chapman, 20, had lost his virginity to a town woman and felt incredible guilt over the episode. As penance, he worked even longer hours at the camp prior to its closing at the end of 1975. In the spring of 1976, Mark David Chapman joined his fiancée at Covenant College and enrolled in classes. Plagued by depression triggered by a class he took on human warfare and the refugee problem he had experienced first-hand at Fort Chaffee, Chapman suffered a nervous breakdown. He dropped out of one class, struggled through the rest, said goodbye to Blankenship, and returned to his old job at the YMCA in Decatur. Chapman quit in the middle of the summer and took a job as a night security guard at the Atlanta airport. Isolated for long stretches of time, Chapman's depression deepened and his sense of identity, never strong, weakened. As a YMCA counselor in Lebanon he had enjoyed prestige and responsibility, now he was just a lowly paid security guard driving alone around an airport at night.

In 1977, Chapman, 22, flew to Hawaii with a single thought in mind — commit suicide in a beautiful tropical setting. He had spent months planning and reading about the islands and upon arrival called Blankenship to say goodbye. Though no longer interested in the unstable man as a future husband, she did not want his death on her head. Chapman returned home just long enough to realize it was over with Blankenship and to argue with his family. He returned to Hawaii this time with a plan to carve out a life in the islands. Once there, however, his attitude quickly changed. Chapman burned through his savings and attempted to support himself in Honolulu by work-

ing a variety of odd jobs including peeling rotten potatoes at a snack food factory. Within two months of vowing to start a new life, Chapman was suicidal. The 22 year old spent his last dollar to rent a compact car and drove to a deserted stretch of beach. He fastened a plastic hose to the car's exhaust, snaked the tubing in through a slightly opened window, turned on the ignition, and waited to die from carbon monoxide poisoning. Chapman would have died and John Lennon lived had only the plastic hose not melted on the car's hot exhaust pipe. Suffering from acute depression, Chapman was admitted to Castle Memorial Hospital in Kalilua on June 22, 1977, and placed under a suicide watch. In less than a week his depression lifted and he was happily playing guitar, chatting up hospital personnel, and leaving the hospital grounds on day passes. Excited about his future, Chapman was discharged on July 5, and hired part-time at the hospital as a housekeeper and maintenance man. Well-liked at the facility, he was accepted by staff and made several friends in the community including the Rev. Peter Anderson, a minister at a local Presbyterian church. The pastor was so impressed with the recovered mental patient that he invited Chapman to take up residence at the home he shared with his wife.

In 1978, Chapman decided he needed a change of pace. He had saved his money for months to go on an around the world cruise and contacted his travel agent, Gloria Abe, a shy 27-year-old Japanese-American. Chapman visited the woman often at her office and showered her with deliveries of flowers. Abe reciprocated his interest. On July 6, 1978, Chapman embarked on his world tour visiting countries like Japan, Thailand, and India. In Geneva, Switzerland he attended the World Alliance of the YMCA returning to Hawaii in August 20, 1978. Gloria Abe was waiting for him at the airport. The pair became inseparable. Abe, aware of Chapman's trouble with depression, was willing to cope with any problems because she found him to be so sensitive and spiritual. In early 1979 the couple's courtship was complicated by the re-emergence of Diane Chapman into her son's life. The 48-year-old woman announced that after nearly 25 years of marriage she was divorcing her husband and moving to Hawaii. After Chapman and Gloria were married on June 2, 1979 in a ceremony conducted by the Reverend Anderson, the woman became a constant, smothering presence in their lives. Gloria complained about the situation and was informed by her new husband that a son's first duty was to his mother. At the end of 1979, Chapman was given a better job at the hospital as a public relations assistant and print shop worker. In his new positions, the former patient conducted hospital tours, photographed visiting dignitaries, and designed and produced brochures. The print shop was situated in the basement of the hospital and Chapman found the work isolating and boring while the constant smell of chemicals gave him headaches. To cope with the twin pressures of work and marriage, he binged on junk food (causing his weight to balloon) and became argumentative and confrontational with staff. In late 1979, a tense interaction between Chapman and a nurse who complained to him about a late printing assignment ended badly when he was given the choice to resign with a glowing recommendation or be fired without one. Chapman resigned and severed all connection with the facility and friends he had known since 1976.

On December 26, 1979, the 23 year old started a new job working nights as an unarmed security guard at a high-rise complex at 444 Nahua Street near Waikiki Beach. In debt, bored, and feeling an extreme sense of isolation, Chapman started drinking heavily and began to converse with the Little People in his head, returned after a multi-year absence. He informed his wife that the Little People would help him reorganize his life and get them out of debt. On October 23, 1980, Chapman quit his security guard job and signed out as "John Lennon." Frustrated, angry, and lacking a coherent sense of personal identity or direction, Chapman only found comfort in his daily visits to the Honolulu Public Library where the ordered rows of books helped him to cope. Sometime in 1980, he remembered having read as a teen J.D. Salinger's coming of age novel *The Catcher in the Rye*. Since its publication in 1951, the book's protagonist, 16-year-old "Holden Caulfield," had become a symbol a teenage alienation and his fight against the phoniness of life had strongly appealed to other "lone gun" type stalkers like John Hinckley, President Ronald Reagan's would-be assassin, and Robert John Bardo, the man who murdered television star Rebecca Schaeffer (see entry) in 1989. Unable to secure the popular book at the library, the 25-year-old bought a copy and instantly reconnected with Holden Caulfield. Over the next months, he became obsessed with the novel re-reading it several times and committing long passages to memory. He bought an extra copy for his wife and inscribed it from "Holden Caulfield." While at the library scanning the shelves, Chapman ran across a copy of Anthony Fawcett's book, *John Lennon: One Day at a Time*, featuring photographs of the rock star on the roof of the Dakota, his New York City residence across from Central Park. The more he read the angrier he became. In true Holden Caulfield–type logic, Chapman concluded Lennon was a phony who had lied to a generation of kids. While Lennon sang a philosophy of imagining no possessions, he was living in a multimillion dollar apartment situated in the middle of some of the most expensive real estate in the world. Lennon was laughing at people like him who had built their entire lives around the lies in his music. The rock star had ruined his life. As Chapman later explained to a prison psychiatrist, "*The Catcher in the Rye* was the stove and the Lennon book was the fire." The tipping point came when he checked Lennon's album *John Lennon — Plastic Ono Band* from the library and gave it a close listen. In the song "God" the rock star flatly stated he did not believe in anything (Jesus, Buddha, the Beatles, etc.) other than himself and wife Yoko Ono. The rock star's lack of religiosity angered Chapman. He could find his identity in a phony world only by killing its preeminent prophet, John Lennon. In conference with the Little People, Chapman meticulously planned the ex–Beatle's murder.

On October 27, 1980, Chapman paid $190 for a .38-caliber Charter Arms Special pistol at a Honolulu gun shop. At the police station, he lied on the gun permit application as to whether he had ever been hospitalized for a mental illness. No computerized background check was run. Chapman, however, did not purchase ammunition reasoning that if he was arrested with an unloaded weapon the punishment would not be as severe. He later learned that New York's gun laws (among the most rigid in America) do not even permit a licensed handgun to be brought into the city. Buying ammunition legally in New York was out of the question. Chapman told wife Gloria that he was going to New York City to clear his head and with $5,000 in cash borrowed from his father-in-law made his first flight to the Big Apple on October 29, 1980. Over the next few days, he cased the Dakota attempting to become friends with the doormen and glean information as to Lennon's movements. The doormen, trained not to discuss the building's celebrity tenants, were cordial, but non-committal. Fans and autograph seekers were permitted to wait for Lennon and other star tenants (Gilda Radner, Leonard Bernstein, Mia Farrow, Lauren Bacall), but not to block the sidewalk or cause a disruption. Unable to legally purchase ammo, the 25 year old visited an old friend, a sheriff's deputy in Henry County, Georgia, in the Atlanta area on November 5. Chapman spent the day with his unsuspecting friend shooting at targets in the woods. The sheriff's deputy demonstrated a combat stance employing a two-handed grip to steady the weapon for a more accurate shot. Chapman explained his situation. He brought a gun with him from Hawaii for protection in New York City, but now could not purchase ammunition. Unwittingly, his friend gave him five .38-caliber Smith & Wesson Plus P hollow-points designed to fragment on impact. Chapman returned to the city and continued to stalk the Dakota for days without glimpsing Lennon. After being moved by the film *Ordinary People*, he called Gloria and tearfully informed her that he had planned to murder the phony rock star, but not now. Her love had redeemed him although he had proven to himself that he possessed the power to kill Lennon whenever he chose.

Chapman returned to Hawaii on November 12, 1980 a dangerously sick man. He terrorized Gloria, pushing her against a wall and spitting on her if she deigned to disagree with him. He phoned in a bomb threat to a luxury hotel and placed anonymous harassing phone calls to people in authority like his former landlord and a doctor at Castle Memorial Hospital. On the street, he confronted Hare Krishnas until someone told him they could get violent if provoked. On Saturday, December 6, 1980, Mark David Chapman made his final trip to New York City. Landing at La Guardia Airport, he took a cab to the Dakota, cased the building, and checked into a $16.50 a night room at the West Side YMCA, a ten minute walk from Lennon's residence. On the morning of Sunday, December 7, Chapman bought a copy of Lennon's recently released album, *Double Fantasy*, at a record store near the Dakota and relocated to Room 2730 at the upscale Sheraton Centre at Seventh Avenue and 52nd Street. For the next three hours, the assassin stood clutching the album outside the gate of the Dakota in the company of other fans waiting to see the rock star. Tiring, he visited a bookshop and purchased a copy of the January 1, 1981, issue of *Playboy* fea-

turing an in-depth interview with Lennon and a photograph of "Dorothy" and the "Cowardly Lion" in *The Wizard of Oz*. Back in his room at the Sheraton, Chapman called an escort service, but when the hooker arrived he told her he was not interested in sex. He just wanted to give her a soothing massage. She left hours later with $190 for engaging in mutual masturbation. Afterwards, he phoned wife Gloria collect and informed her of his need to get Christ back in his life. Ringing off, Chapman picked up the room copy of *The Bible*, turned to the Book of John and wrote in pen "Lennon" after the words *The Gospel According to John*.

The assassin woke early on the morning of Monday, December 8, and before leaving his room carefully arranged a tableau on the dresser for the authorities to find after he murdered John Lennon. In a semicircle arrangement, he placed his passport, an eight-track tape of Todd Rundgren tunes, *The Bible* opened to the amended *The Gospel According to John* ("Lennon"), a letter of commendation from his YMCA supervisor at Fort Chaffee, and photographs of himself surrounded by smiling Vietnamese children. He put the recently purchased photo of "Dorothy" and the "Cowardly Lion" in pride of place in the center of the arrangement. Returning to the bookstore, Chapman bought another copy of *The Catcher in the Rye* and a black Bic pen. On the inside cover of the book he wrote his twisted explanation for the heinous act he was about to commit — "*This is my statement. Holden Caulfield, The Catcher in the Rye.*" Walking to the Dakota with his copy of *Double Fantasy* under his arm, Chapman milled around with other fans. Remarkably, he missed Lennon step out of a cab and enter the building earlier in the day. Later, he briefly interacted on the street with Helen Seaman, Sean Lennon's nanny, and her charge, the rock star's five-year-old son. Chapman made a point to shake Sean Lennon's hand. Around 5:00 P.M., Lennon and Yoko Ono emerged from the Dakota in the midst of their entourage to take a limousine to the Record Plant, a recording studio on West 44th Street. Free lance photographer Paul Goresh caught the eerie image on film of Lennon graciously signing a copy of *Double Fantasy* for the man who would kill him six hours later. The photographer left around 8:00 P.M. leaving Chapman to await the rock star's return with José Perdomo, the Dakota doorman stationed at the sentry booth. Around 10:50 P.M., the limousine carrying

Lennon and Yoko pulled up to the Dakota. Yoko got out first and walked up the driveway under the archway toward the steps. Lennon followed carrying a tape recorder and some loose cassettes and walked by Chapman. The rock star was a few steps inside the archway when the assassin pulled the .38-caliber pistol from his coat pocket, dropped into a two-handed combat stance and pumped five shots at Lennon's back. The first two hollow-points struck the former Beatle in the back, spinning him to face his killer as two of the next three bullets slammed into his shoulder, and exploded in his body wreaking deadly havoc in his chest cavity and severing his windpipe. Lennon staggered up the five stairs to an interior guard office and fell face-down on the floor. Chapman let Perdomo shake the gun out of his hand and was intermittently sitting on his coat and pacing up and down on the sidewalk reading his copy of *The Catcher in the Rye* when police arrived minutes later. Taken into custody, he begged officers not to hurt him. Police carried the mortally wounded rock star to their patrol car and sped him to Roosevelt General Hospital. In the emergency room, a team of seven doctors worked furiously to save Lennon, but he had lost 80 percent of the total volume of blood in his body. Lennon, to many the voice of his generation, was pronounced dead at 11:07 P.M. At the police station, his 25-year-old killer signed a handwritten confession and told psychiatrists that the book he signed was his only statement. Lennon's remains were cremated on December 10, 1980 at a crematorium in Hartsdale, New York, and the ashes given to Yoko Ono. On December 14, 1980, the unprecedented outpouring of grief at Lennon's senseless murder was shared by millions of his fans. At 2:00 P.M. EST all stood united in a ten-minute silent vigil observed world-wide in memory of the martyred rock star.

Chapman was charged with second-degree murder and ruled competent to stand trial after being examined by psychiatrists at Bellevue Hospital. Fearful that outraged fans would storm the hospital and lynch Lennon's killer, authorities moved him to Rikers Island. At a hearing in January 1981, Chapman pleaded "not guilty by reason of insanity." In his solitary cell at Rikers the troubled assassin experienced a "revelation." He killed Lennon to promote the reading of *The Catcher in the Rye*. Chapman had boxes of the novel brought to his cell so he could inscribe them with his name (adding under it, "The Catcher in the Rye").

Lennon had to die so he (Chapman) could be the "Catcher in the Rye" for his generation. Chapman later gave up his insanity defense in June 1981 after the Lord "spoke to his heart" and instructed him to plead guilty. He later regretted doing so. Chapman's murder plea was accepted on August 24, 1981 and he was sentenced to a prison term of 20 years to life. Currently incarcerated in a protective custody unit in Attica to prevent his certain killing were he to be placed in general population, Chapman has been denied parole five times since October 2000 although he insists he is "ashamed" of the murder and is no longer a threat to the community. The 55-year-old killer is scheduled to be interviewed by a three-member parole board panel during the week of August 9, 2010. Yoko Ono, as she has done since the murder, opposes Chapman's release. Given his erratic mental state and the fact he killed one of the most beloved and recognizable people of the twentieth century it seems highly unlikely that "The Catcher in the Rye" will ever be released.

Further Reading

Bresler, Fenton S. *Who Killed John Lennon?* New York: St. Martin's, 1989.

Fawcett, Anthony. *John Lennon: One Day at a Time: A Personal Biography of the Seventies.* New York: Grove, 1976.

Goldman, Albert Harry. *The Lives of John Lennon.* New York: W. Morrow, 1988.

Jones, Jack. *Let Me Take You Down: Inside the Mind of Mark David Chapman, the Man Who Killed John Lennon.* New York: Villard, 1992.

Lennon, Cynthia. *John.* New York: Crown, 2005.

Norman, Philip. *John Lennon: The Life.* New York: Ecco, 2008.

Seaman, Fred. *The Last Days of John Lennon: A Personal Memoir.* Seacaucus, NJ: Carol, 1991.

Leonard, Harry (M-S)

For three years 55-year-old film character actor Harry Leonard (*Ramona*, 1916) longed to marry Anneska Frolik, 24. Shortly after dusk on August 31, 1917, Frolik's 24th birthday, Leonard arrived at her home at 1115 South El Molino Street in Los Angeles carrying two packages. While waiting for the young woman to return home, Leonard spoke amiably with her sister-in-law and mother. Opening one of the packages to reveal a pile of unpublished screenplays tied with a red ribbon, Leonard declared that they would be valuable properties after the war. The women's patronizing smiles elicited a strange comment from the aging actor, "Ah, you laugh. Tragedy follows in the wake of laughter." Leonard fell into a dejected silence for the rest of the evening until Frolik returned at 9:00 P.M. The women left them alone to talk.

Whispers in the parlor were interrupted by three pistol shots in quick succession. Rushing into the room, Frolik's family saw her (bleeding from two shots to the chest and one in the stomach) grappling with the actor. Leonard produced a pint bottle of steaming sulfuric acid from his coat, tossed it in Frolik's eyes, and in the general direction of the horrified pair, before taking another bottle filled with carbolic acid from his pocket and drinking it. The actor staggered out of the house brandishing the automatic weapon.

Leonard was found shortly afterward and returned to Frolik's home. Shortly before passing out from the pain, the actor indicated two typewritten letters addressed to the girl's father lying near the manuscripts. Both Anneska Frolik and her aged suitor later died. One of the letters, addressed "Not to be opened under any circumstances while I am in existence," willed the packaged screenplays to Frolik's father. The other, also written to the man, intimated that while the young woman once promised to marry him, she experienced a change of heart. Leonard concluded, "I must show you I cannot live with her in this hell and I will try my best to live with her in Heaven, if there is one. I will take her with me through my act and I hope that you will forgive me. I hope we all will meet over there."

Further Reading

"Two Dying in Love Tragedy — Aged Suitor Shoots Beauty." *Los Angeles Examiner*, September 1, 1917, sec. I, p. 1.

Leopold, Joseph Walter (V)

A member of the American Society of Composers, Authors and Publishers (ASCAP) since 1942, Leopold was a veteran novelty songwriter ("Oh! How She Can Dance," 1919) who, as piano accompanist to his wife, singer Emma Carus, toured vaudeville for many years. In the 1950s, the songwriter changed professions to work as a collection investigator for loan and credit companies. On December 28, 1956, the 66 year old was paying for his groceries in a Hollywood market at 1921 N. Cahuenga Avenue when an armed gunman burst into the store and demanded money from the counter attendant. The robber scooped $50.00 out of the register and was fleeing the scene when Leopold tossed a can of enchilada sauce at the gunman striking him in the shoulder. The man whirled, fired a single shot from a .38-caliber pistol, and ran to the parking lot where an accomplice waited in a light green sedan. Leopold,

struck in the left temple, died a few minutes after being ambulanced to Hollywood Receiving Hospital. Shooter Charles F. Neely, 26, and wheelman Norman Golland, 30, were arrested the next day. Both pleaded guilty to the murder and were sentenced to terms of life imprisonment.

Further Reading

"Store Bandit Kills Man Who Hurled Can at Him." *Los Angeles Times*, December 29, 1956, p. 7.

Lindsey, Darnell Quincy *see* Icewood, Blade

Longet, Claudine (M)

Best known today as the subject of a devastating *Saturday Night Live* parody in which she accidentally shoots a downhill skier numerous times, Claudine Longet was a successful singer as well as the one-time wife of crooner Andy Williams before the tragic incident that transformed her into a near recluse. Born in Paris on January 29, 1942, Longet began performing in the Las Vegas production of the Folies Bergère at 19 eventually becoming the show's premier dancer. In Vegas she caught the eye of "Moon River" singing sensation Andy Williams whose popular television variety show had made him a household name in America. Fourteen years her senior, Williams had first noticed Longet as a beautiful nine-year-old child roller-skating in Paris. Their paths crossed again in 1961 when Williams helped Longet with a car problem after one of her lounge shows. Married that same year, Longet took time out of her career to bear the singer the first of their three children. By 1964, however, Longet was ready to return to work landing (with Williams' undoubted help) guest shots on several television shows including *Combat!*, *Hogan's Heroes*, and *12 O'Clock High*. Regular appearances on *The Andy Williams Show* led to a recording contract with A&M in 1966 and the release the next year of her first album, *Claudine*. Longet's heavily accented breathy voice appeared regularly on A&M albums throughout the late 1960s (*The Look of Love*, 1967; *Colors*, 1968; *Love Is Blue*, 1968) and beginning in 1969 on Williams' own Barnaby imprint with *We've Only Just Begun* and *Let's Spend the Night Together* (1972). In motion pictures, Longet's most enduring role was as a French ingénue opposite Peter Sellers in *The Party* (1968).

Although Longet and her three children continued to appear as the "happy family" on Andy

Williams' highly rated annual holiday shows, the couple separated in 1970 and divorced in 1976 after fourteen years of marriage. Longet, however, had "moved on" long before the final split relocating with her children to the ritzy Rocky Mountain ski resort town of Aspen, Colorado. By 1972 she was romantically involved with Vladimir "Spider" Sabich, a top downhill skier who won back-to-back pro skiing championships in 1970–1971. Sabich, semi-retired since suffering a serious accident in the final race of the 1973 season, was a popular local celebrity and a darling of Aspen society. In 1974, Longet with children in tow, moved into Sabich's $250,000 chalet in the exclusive Starwood subdivision of the mountain ski resort. Life for Longet was idyllic as she related to a reporter two months before her divorce from Andy Williams in 1976 — "I am a fortunate woman. I have a husband. I have my children and I also have my man. There is no reason two people can't live as Andy and I do."

Two years into the living arrangement, however, Sabich was seemingly ready to redefine his cooling relationship with Longet and her three children (ranging in ages from 6 to 12). In early 1976, he asked her to find separate living arrangements and set April 1 as the deadline for her to move out. On the evening of March 21, 1976, Sabich was in the bedroom of his chalet packing to leave for a ski show in Las Vegas the next day. Clad only in blue thermal underwear, the champion skier was in the bathroom preparing to shower when Longet approached him with a .22-caliber pistol he had purchased months before for home protection. According to Longet, the gun accidentally discharged while Sabich was instructing her on how to safely use it. Struck in the left side of the abdomen, he fell to the bathroom floor and was rapidly bleeding out in Longet's arms when her three children appeared on the scene. She frantically called the ambulance and was with her lover as he died en route to the hospital.

The skier's death rocked the closely knit town of Aspen with popular opinion decidedly against Longet, an "outsider" in the ski community. Weeks later on April 7, 1976, Longet was arraigned in an Aspen courtroom on a felony manslaughter charge and, if convicted, faced a possible 10 year prison sentence. As he did throughout all his ex-wife's subsequent legal proceedings, Andy Williams was in the courtroom lending her moral (and most likely financial) support. Armed with Longet's personal diary found in a police search

of the couple's bedroom, District Attorney Frank Tucker, a longtime friend of the dead man, felt he had a compelling case for a felony conviction. The diary chronicled the couple's deteriorating relationship, a fact supported by interviews with friends who told of increasing friction between the singer and the skier. Blood tests rumored to show Longet had used cocaine prior to the shooting further bolstered the prosecution's case. Under advice of co-counsels Charles Weedman from Los Angeles and Aspen attorney Ronald Austin, Longet pleaded "not guilty" to the charge on June 10, 1976. The couple was deeply in love, her lawyers argued, and the shooting was accidental and under the law was criminally negligent homicide, a misdemeanor. Legal wrangling over the potentially damaging evidence continued until December 1976 when the Colorado Supreme Court dealt the prosecution a near lethal blow. In a unanimous ruling the court held the police should have requested a search warrant prior to searching the bedroom for evidence. Longet's diary, found in the bedroom dresser hidden under a pile of clothing, was ruled inadmissible as was the blood test reportedly showing drugs in her system.

Jury selection in January 1977 revealed the depth of anti–Longet sentiment in the community. One potential juror, the town's mayor, was excused because he had already told a number of his constituents that the singer-actress was guilty. Five days and 62 juror interviews later, five women and seven men (with a median age in the mid–40s) were impaneled to hear the case against Longet. In the courtroom lending his support, often seated next to the ubiquitous Andy Williams, was Aspen regular Jack Nicholson. The trial began on January 9, 1977, with prosecutor Frank Tucker arguing that while the shooting was accidental Claudine Longet's reckless actions caused the German Luger knockoff to discharge. Andy Williams, surely among the most supportive ex-husbands in the history of show business, was called to the stand to emphatically refute the testimony of an Aspen restaurateur who reportedly overheard the singer refer to Longet as "a crazy chick" who "likes to ski fast and drive fast." The doe-eyed entertainer took the stand and tearfully related the tragic events of March 21, 1976. Admitting Sabich had given her a "mutually" acceptable move-out deadline, Longet maintained that they still remained a devoted couple. The gun accidentally discharged while Sabich was showing her how to use it to protect herself and the children during his absence on a business trip to Las Vegas. She attempted to administer mouth-to-mouth resuscitation, but the mortally wounded skier died in the ambulance en route to the hospital. Longet's "slippery finger" story was supported by the defense's firearms expert who testified that not only was the gun's safety broken (a point conceded by the prosecution), but also a "greasy residue" on the weapon's internal workings might have caused the fatal misfire.

The case went to the jury on January 14, 1977, with Longet facing a maximum of 10 years in prison and a $30,000 fine if convicted of felony reckless manslaughter. Three hours and forty minutes later the singer sat expressionless as the verdict was announced — acquittal on the felony charge, but guilty of misdemeanor negligent homicide. Outside the courtroom Longet told reporters, "There is not really very much to say. Only that I have too much respect for living things to do that. I'm not guilty." Co-counsel Charles Weedman blamed Aspen for the verdict. "The evil in this town was the gossip about Spider and Claudine. For all of this, there should be some shame in this community." On January 30, 1977, Longet was sentenced to 30 days in jail and placed on two years probation, an unusually light judgment considering the maximum sentence could have been two years in prison and a $5,000 fine. Angered the judge would not let her set her own dates of confinement around the care of her children, Longet lashed out at District Attorney Frank Tucker, an individual she characterized as "more concerned with his own ambitions than with justice." In her defense, Tucker was found guilty in January 1978 of two counts of felony embezzlement of public funds and forced to leave office in disgrace. By the time the convictions were overturned, the former district attorney was out of the legal profession. In March 2000 Frank Tucker reportedly owned a mortuary business in the Aspen area.

If Longet thought the legal system was through with her after she served her month in a 14' by 16' cell in Aspen's Pritkin County Jail she was naive. In May 1977 the parents of her dead lover filed a $1.3 million lawsuit against Longet alleging she acted with "malice, insult and a wanton and reckless disregard of Sabich's rights." The case was settled in September 1979 for an undisclosed sum of money. At the time, Longet signed a confidentiality agreement and to date has not spoken publicly

of the tragic killing of Spider Sabich. The woman who before March 21, 1976, was most famous for being the ex-wife of Andy "Moon River" Williams married Ron Austin, the Aspen-based attorney who co-defended her, and lives quietly in the ski resort town. Sabich has achieved an immortality of sorts in Aspen's Hard Rock Café where his skis and medals are offered in a framed display.

Further Reading

"Andy Stands by Claudine." *Los Angeles Times*, March 22, 1976, sec. A, p. 1.
"Claudine Charged in Slaying." *Los Angeles Times*, April 8, 1976, sec. A, p. 1.
"Miss Longet Is Guilty on Lesser Count of Homicide." *The New York Times*, January 15, 1977, p. 16.

Los Padrinos de la Sierra *see* Appendix 1

Loucks, David G. (V)

On March 8, 1995, Loucks was found dead in the control room of his recording studio, Alternative Productions, at 4033 Aurora Avenue North in Seattle, Washington. The 34-year-old studio owner was struck on the head and hogtied with duct tape. He died of asphyxiation after being unable to breathe through the tape over his mouth and nose. Missing were five digital recording machines valued at $30,000. A separate investigation conducted by the victim's father, attorney Allan Loucks, linked the theft with a series of audio equipment robberies going back over six months in Washington state. According to the studio owner's scheduling book, a man using the name "Paul Waller" made an appointment to record for 7:00 P.M. on the evening of March 7. The name turned out to be fictitious, but led to two arrests in November 1996 following the stolen equipment leads. Under police questioning, Shawn Daniel Swenson, 25, confessed to being "Paul Waller" and admitted being at the recording studio on the night Loucks was killed. Swenson's admission further led to a charge of first-degree murder against Joseph Adam Gardner, 23, already serving time in Walla Walla State Penitentiary on unrelated felony and drug offenses. In June 1997, Gardner pleaded guilty and agreed to testify against Swenson in a bid to escape a statutory maximum penalty of life imprisonment. According to Gardner, he was recruited by Swenson to steal recording equipment from Alternative Productions. When they arrived, Swenson distracted Loucks by pretending to record a rap song. Gardner grabbed Loucks from behind placing him in a chokehold while Swenson dazed the man with multiple zaps from a stun gun. The pair hogtied Loucks with tape "accidentally" suffocating him in the process. Over the next several days they pawned and sold the man's equipment in Spokane and California. On August 6, 1997, Swenson was found guilty of first-degree murder and sentenced to over 20 years. Gardner was subsequently sentenced to nearly 29 years in prison, four more years than his attorney expected for his client's cooperation. In June 1999, Allan Loucks was awarded $4,360 by the city of Seattle in support of a claim that after the murder trial police wrongly returned audio equipment stolen from his son's business to a Spokane couple who had purchased the hot property from a pawnshop.

Further Reading

Santana, Arthur. "Guilty Verdict in Murder at Recording Studio." *Seattle Times*, August 7, 1997, sec. B, p. 3.

Love, Melissa *see* **Januskevicius,** Melissa A.

Lyde, Leval *see* **Cavlar**

Mac Dre (V)

Born Andre Hicks in Vallejo, California, on July 5, 1970, gangsta rapper Mac Dre became recognized as one of the pioneers of Bay Area rap and is, arguably, "V-Town's" most famous contribution to the genre. While still a student in Peoples High School, Mac Dre's first song, "Too Hard for the Radio," was nevertheless played on local airwaves. In the rap, he mentioned the Romper Room Gang, a reference Vallejo police used as probable cause to investigate him and other members of the real-life gang. Ironically, Mac Dre had recently released the single "Punk Police," a rap slamming V-Town cops for letting criminals rob them blind, when he was arrested with five other gang members in Fresno, California in April 1992 on charges of conspiracy and attempted bank robbery. While in jail awaiting sentencing, the rapper reportedly recorded the single "Back N da Hood" using the facility's telephone. In the rap, Mac Dre again taunted the police this time mentioning several officers by name. Released from prison in February 1996, Mac Dre hit the streets ready to rap. His "street cred" buttressed by his prison stretch and cemented by two 1992 records, *What's Really Going On* and *Young Black Brotha*, the gangsta rapper signed with the Romp label in 1996 and released the albums *Mac*

Dre Presents the Rompalation, Vol. 1 and *Stupid Doo Doo Dumb* in 1998. In 2000, he moved from Vallejo to Sacramento with an eye toward putting the thug life behind him. He started his own label, Thizz Entertainment, and planned to hire and mentor at-risk teens. The rapper funded children's programs, gave free concerts, and at Thanksgiving handed out free turkeys to underprivileged families. Authorities, however, remained skeptical. To them, Mac Dre would be forever associated with the Romper Room Gang, the criminal group linked to a string of some forty Northern California credit union and bank robberies from 1995 to 1997 which had netted more than $1.5 million.

Bay Area rappers are incredibly popular in Kansas City, Missouri where Mac Dre, 34, was brought in to perform a show at the National Guard Armory on Friday, October 29, 2004. On Sunday, October 31, the rapper showed up at a private VIP party where he was prominently mentioned in flyers for the event, but did not perform. Around 3:30 A.M. on Monday, November 1, Mac Dre was a passenger in a van northbound on U.S. 71, the four-lane highway cutting through the heart of downtown Kansas City, when a car drove up alongside the driver's side of the diesel van, sprayed the vehicle with gunfire, and forced it across the median. The rapper, seated in the backseat of the van behind tinted windows, died instantly from a wound to the back of his neck. Although the van was riddled with dozens of bullet holes, Mac Dre was the only casualty. Acting upon an anonymous tip, police recovered an abandoned black 2003 Infiniti G36 with no license plates stolen months earlier from the Kansas City area. Investigators rapidly uncovered a possible motive linked to the heavily promoted VIP party. A local promoter had rented out the private club, the Atlantic Star, and charged ticket prices of $15 and $20 (collecting around $3,000) to see Mac Dre perform. The only problem, however, was that the rapper had not been informed that he was expected to do a show. Mac Dre arrived at the club, learned of the promoter's plan, and left the scene at 10:30 P.M. after staying less than half an hour. Several angry clubgoers demanded their money back. Five hours later, Mac Dre was shot to death on a highway in Kansas City. Not surprisingly, the rapper's entourage refused to cooperate with local authorities.

On November 9, 2004, Mac Dre's body lay in state at the Mount Calvary Baptist Church in Fairfield, California, in an open platinum-plated steel casket outfitted with cardinal red crush velvet interior as the rapper's music blared from hundreds of cars outside in the parking lot. More than sixty law enforcement officers from Vallejo, Vacaville, and the Solano County Sheriff's Department watched during the five hour visitation as thousands of fans filed past the dead celebrity's coffin. The specially designed clear fiberglass shield placed over his face to prevent mourners from touching and kissing the rapper was removed for the family's last moments with their murdered loved one prior to his burial in Mountain View Cemetery in Oakland, California. In July 2005, some two hundred young people gathered at "Mac Dre Day" in Vallejo to hear speakers address the need for the community to curb violence, drugs, and alcohol. Billed as a "peaceful salute" to the martyred rapper, the ceremony featured a talent show in which pre-teens did the "thizzle dance" to Mac Dre's music. Reportedly coined by the gangsta rapper, the term "thizzle" refers to the state of being high on the drug Ecstasy.

Despite the best intentions of V-Town, however, the violence continued. On November 1, 2005, the one year anniversary of Mac Dre's murder, Michael Clint Banks, 21, was shot to death while attending a memorial for the slain rapper in North Vallejo. Months earlier in what police characterized as payback for Mac Dre's assassination, Kansas City rapper Anthony "Fat Tone" Watkins, 24, and Jermaine "Cowboy" Akins, 22, were found shot to death in Las Vegas on May 23, 2005. After eluding police for ten months, Mac Dre's friend and fellow-rapper, Mac Minister (Andre Dow), was arrested in San Francisco in March 2006 following the profiling of Dre's case on the television program, *America's Most Wanted*. Dow and accomplice Jason "Corleone" Mathison were both convicted in March 2006 on two counts of first-degree murder and sentenced to life imprisonment without the possibility of parole. Mac Dre's grave marker in Oakland's Mountain View Cemetery was stolen in August 2006 and when a $10,000 reward offered by the dead man's friend and fellow-rapper, AP.9, failed to secure its return, another was subsequently installed.

Further Reading

Arnold, Eric K. "Requiem for a Mac: Mac Dre's Embodiment of the Tupac Thug Lifestyle Ended the Only Way It Could." *East Bay Express*, November 10, 2004. www.mac-dre.info.

Mac, the Camoflage Assassin (M)

As gangsta rapper Mac, the Camouflage Assassin, McKinley "Mac" Phipps, Jr., released his first CD, *Shell Shocked*, in July 1998 on Priority, a branch label of No Limit Records, the New Orleans–based recording company owned by rap mogul Master P (Percy Miller). The 22 track CD contained raps like "Murda, Murda, Kill, Kill," "Soldier Party," as well as collaborations with other No Limit rappers like Soulja Slim ("Can I Ball") and C-Murder ("Tank Dogs," "Memories"). Both No Limit rappers would be touched by violence. C-Murder (see entry) was convicted of murder in September 2003, while Soulja Slim (see entry) was shot to death in New Orleans on November 26, 2003. Mac, despite his hard-edged, militant street persona, never logged a single arrest. His second CD, *World War III*, released on Priority in September 1999, again featured raps with C-Murder ("Just Another Thug"), as well as tracks like "We Deadly," "Bloody," and "Assassin Nation."

On the night of February 20, 2000, Mac, 22, headlined a rap show billed as "World War Party on the Northshore" at the Club Mercedes, a second-rate nightspot located at 2294 U.S. 190 West in Slidell, Louisiana. Since opening three months earlier, the club had been the scene of numerous fights and gunfire. At 1:22 A.M. the following morning, a fight erupted on the dance floor between club-goer Desmond Parker, and members of the rapper's posse (identifiable by the "Mac" tee shirts they wore). The incident was evidently sparked by a run-in Parker had a week earlier with the group in a bar in Brown's Village near Alton, Louisiana. Barron C. Victor, Jr., a 19-year-old high school basketball standout, jumped into the melee to help his friend Parker, who was on the floor being repeatedly kicked by Mac's bodyguards. According to an eyewitness, Mac pulled a .38-caliber semiautomatic pistol, pressed the barrel into Victor's left shoulder, and fired a round that passed through the teen's lung and heart. In the ensuing chaos as more than two hundred terrified club patrons fled for the exits, Mac was hustled out of the nightspot by his entourage before the arrival of authorities. A short time after the shooting, Victor was pronounced dead at Slidell Memorial Hospital. Mac and another man, Larnell Warren, Jr., 29, were arrested a few hours later at the rapper's apartment at 17935 Glen Park Drive in Baton Rouge. Police confiscated four guns from his residence, but none turned out to be the murder weapon. The rapper, initially denying that he was in the club at the time of the shooting, was booked on a charge of first-degree murder. Warren, his companion, was held on a charge of obstruction of justice.

In March 2000, as Mac faced a grand jury that reduced the charge against him to second-degree murder, St. Tammany Parish officials revoked the liquor license of the Club Mercedes (closed since the slaying) blocking the site from reopening as a bar. The nightclub made news the next month after one of its owners, 29-year-old Dwight Guyot, was arrested on a federal drug charge. The government maintained that Guyot was the leader of the largest cocaine distribution ring in the history of St. Tammany Parish racking up monthly sales of more than a half million dollars.

Meanwhile, the prosecution's case against Mac, the Camoflage Assassin hit a snag. Witnesses to the shooting reported receiving phone calls threatening death if they testified against the rapper. Not surprisingly, many who received the calls welcomed possible jail time for contempt of court over the prospect of being murdered. In September 2001, the second-degree murder proceedings against Mac in Covington, Louisiana abruptly ended in a mistrial after the judge agreed with defense attorneys that the prosecution had unfairly exploited the rapper's stage name. In their opening argument, the prosecution had accused the rapper of using his vicious image as the "Assassin" to frighten and intimidate witnesses (a crime for which he had not been charged). The defense had argued that Mac's violent stage image was purely for entertainment purposes. However, five days after the mistrial, an Appeals Court judge reversed the trial judge's ruling without comment after apparently being swayed by the prosecution's claim that the rapper's intimidation had not risen to the level of a crime.

The star witness for the prosecution, Nathaniel "Jay" Tillis, related how he and his cousin, Barron Victor, were in the Club Mercedes in the early morning hours of February 21, 2000. Tillis was on the dance floor when he saw one of the rapper's entourage knock Desmond Parker down while other posse members started kicking him. Victor pushed his way through the crowd to help his friend when, Tillis testified, "Mac come from the side and shot him ... I looked dead in his eyes." The defense, however, had their own murder suspect waiting in the wings, Thomas Williams. The 36-year-old husband of Mac's mother's sister worked security for the rapper and confessed to shooting Victor shortly after the murder. Police videotaped their interview with Williams, but discounted him as a suspect after his account of shooting a bottle-wielding Victor from ten feet away did not fit the forensic evidence (the deadly contact wound on the victim's body). Further, Williams could neither describe nor produce the murder weapon. In a pre-emptive strike to undermine the defense, the prosecution introduced the videotape of Williams' confession, pointed out these inconsistencies, concluding that Mac's in-law was trying to take the rap for the rapper. The defense never called Williams to the stand. On September 21, 2001, a jury deliberated seven hours before voting 10–2 to convict Mac on the lesser charge of manslaughter. Outraged by the verdict, defense attorney Jason Williams vowed to appeal. "There's a kid who has never done anything wrong in his life, never violated a law, who was convicted of a crime he didn't commit," Williams told the press. "And there wasn't one piece of evidence linking him to the crime or a reason or a motive. And he cried like a kid (after the verdict) — a little kid." Sentenced to thirty years in prison, Mac, the Camoflage Assassin (as of July 2005) is serving time at the Winn Correctional Center in Winnfield, Louisiana. The rapper's earliest possible parole date is 2010.

Further Reading

"Rapper Convicted of Manslaughter in Nightclub Slaying." *The Advocate* (Baton Rouge, LA), September 25, 2001, p. 5.
"Rapper Identified as Killer at Concert." *The Times-Picayune* (New Orleans), September 19, 2001, p. 1.

Madingoane, Tebogo (V)

The composer-rapper with female lead singer Nhlanhla Sibongile Mafu and songwriter-singer Theo Kgosinkwe comprised the popular South African group Mafikizolo. A leading exponent of *kwaito*, a local style of hip-hop deeply rooted in South Africa's sprawling black townships, the group released its first album, *Mafikizolo*, for Sony Music in 1997. Other albums followed (*Music Revolution*, 1999; *Gate Crashers*, 2000) including *Sibongile* (Zulu for "Thank you God") which sold over 300,000 copies upon its release in 2002. In April 2003, Mafikizolo won recognition as the Best Duo or Group and for Best Afro Pop Album at the South African Music Awards in Sun City. Dynamic live performers, the group toured throughout South Africa, and in neighboring countries like Mozambique, Lesotho, Botswana, Swaziland, and Zimbabwe. Mafikizolo also played London, other gigs in the United Kingdom, and appeared in the United States at an international music conference in Miami.

In the early morning of February 14, 2004, Madingoane, 32, and his girlfriend were driving in the township of Soweto south of Johannesburg, when another car barreled through a red light nearly colliding with the singer's Volkswagen. Madingoane caught up with the driver at an intersection and heated words were exchanged before the man drove off. The *kwaito* star angrily pursued the driver pulling in behind him at a garage along the Soweto highway. Madingoane approached the other car to continue the argument with its driver, Lazarus Baloyi, and was shot once in the chest by the 32-year-old Soweto resident. The singer was pronounced dead on arrival at the Chris-Hani Baragwanath Hospital. Baloyi, who had a license for the 9mm handgun, reported the shooting to police and was arrested at the scene. By August 2004, Baloyi had been in custody for six months awaiting trial for murder when the Johannesburg High Court, at the request of the Prosecutor Advocate, dramatically withdrew all charges against him over the stunned objections of Madingoane's family and legion of fans. According to the state prosecutor, an inquest conducted at a lower court was needed to determine whether the road rage shooting rose to the level of "criminal liability." Baloyi, frightened for his life, immediately went into hiding upon his release. To date, he has not been tried for Madingoane's death.

Further Reading

www.mafikizolo.co.za.

Maloney, Robert N. (M-S)

Unemployed for a month since last performing his magician act in Hancock, Maryland, Maloney (a.k.a. Willard the Wizard) with wife Othello and their one-year-old daughter, Frances, moved to Cincinnati, Ohio, in November 1913. In the Queen City, the 27-year-old magician stayed on a month-long drinking binge, often consuming a quart of whiskey a day. In the early hours of December 29, 1913, a drunken Maloney returned to his room at the Hotel Walton and loudly accused his wife of being unfaithful. During the ensuing argument (according to Maloney's police state-

ment), he saw the "devil" in Othello's eyes and in the sacred pictures on the walls of the hotel room. The crazed magician produced a gun and rapidly fired three shots into his wife, striking her in the stomach, right temple, and both ankles. Seeing similar devils in his child's eyes, Maloney shot Frances in the back of the head, and crushed the infant's fingers with the butt of the pistol. "I beat them like you'd beat meat and potatoes," he told sickened detectives. Maloney was apprehended one hour later running through the streets in his underwear. A court-ordered psychiatric evaluation of the double-murderer concluded: "Insanity due to excessive drink, taking the form of delusions of infidelity on the part of his wife." Awaiting trial on two counts of first-degree murder in the Central Station Jail on June 21, 1914, Maloney climbed to the second-floor tier of cells and shouting, "I said I was going to do it, and I'm going to!" dove headfirst to his death on the concrete courtyard forty feet below.

Further Reading

"Devils Seen by Slayer." *Cincinnati Enquirer*, December 30, 1913, p. 9.
"Murderer of Wife and Baby Leaps to His Death in County Jail." *Cincinnati Enquirer*, June 22, 1914, p. 12.

Mansfield, Edward (M-S)

Elsie Orr, 24, and sister, Helen Stolte, were known theatrically in the Bath Beach section of Brooklyn, New York, as the Carr Sisters. Expert swimmers and divers since the age of 12, the pair was members of a water carnival show managed by Edward Mansfield, and following a two year run, were together again in the chorus of *Very Good, Eddie*. Mansfield became obsessed with Helen Stolte, recently separated from her husband, but was opposed by Orr who warned her sister against having any involvement with him. Orr was married less than three weeks to Edward Orr, a member of the Canadian Flying Corps, when Mansfield invited Stolte to Metuchen, New Jersey to pick up a car there he had promised to give her. Suspicious of his intentions, Orr accompanied her sister to Metuchen on June 15, 1918. Mansfield told the pair that the car was in a forest outside the town and drove them to a remote area near a rubber factory. Stolte waited in the car while Elsie Orr walked into the woods with the theatrical manager to retrieve the vehicle. Fifteen minutes later, Stolte heard moans coming from the woods. Investigating, she found the theatrical manager standing beside a stream holding a bloody pen knife, his throat gashed, and drinking from a bottle. Asked by Stolte where her sister was, Mansfield ominously replied, "Where she will never go on the road again." Stolte fled the scene, returning minutes later with police. Mansfield lay unconscious on the ground from a near fatal dose of paris green while, nearby, Orr was found in a clump of bushes with her throat cut. Mansfield expired from the overdose later that night in Metuchen's St. Peter's Hospital.

Further Reading

"Murders Actress; Commits Suicide." *The New York Times,* June 18, 1918, p. 24.

McCall, Roger (V)

Known "on air" as Unkle Rog, the 52-year-old African-American disc jockey had been employed at Rochester, New York radio station WCMF-FM since 1974. McCall worked the overnight shift and on Sunday nights hosted a show spotlighting local area bands. On the evening of December 12, 2003, McCall was shot to death during a robbery attempt while collecting a rent payment on a house he owned on Madison Street in Rochester. Despite a $5,000 reward, no arrests have to date been made.

Further Reading

"Radio Host Shot to Death in Attempted Robbery." Associated Press, December 14, 2003.

McDonald, Jessica Lyn Schwartzbauer *see* Schwartzbauer, Jessica Lyn

McMullen, Tara Correa (V)

McMullen made her big screen debut in 2005 at the age of 15 in *Rebound* starring Martin Lawrence, but was best-known for playing a former gang member, "Graciela," on the CBS television series *Judging Amy*. Like her fictional television counterpart, McMullen endured a troubled childhood and would die as the result of gang violence. After scoring in the film and series, the actress got her own apartment in early 2005, and started dating an older street gang member. Encouraged by friends and family to finish school, McMullen instead preferred to live the "street life," and recently began hanging out with a "bad crowd." Her behavior on *Judging Amy* became so erratic that the young star's talent agency dispatched a driver to make sure she arrived on the set. After missing an audition, the agency dropped her as a client.

The 16-year-old actress was standing with two male friends outside an apartment complex at 605 E. Plymouth Street in Inglewood, California on October 21, 2005, when she was shot to death in what police characterized as a probable gang-related shooting. The two men sustained wounds, but survived the attack. At the funeral service in Forest Lawn Memorial Park–Hollywood Hills, McMullen was remembered by her parents as a person who "made friends with everyone at every level" be they a "grip or a caterer." On March 1, 2006, 20-year-old Damien Watts, already in custody on a separate shooting case, was charged with McMullen's murder and with two counts of attempted murder. The day before the deadly attack on the actress, Watts and friend Joseph Wayne Jones were suspected of shooting to death Thomas Sanders, 31, as the man loaded laundry in his car on South Halldale Avenue. That same day, the gunmen fired shots at three other men working on a car. Watts explained to authorities that he just wanted to shoot up rival gang territory. On January 23, 2009, Watts, 23, was convicted on two counts of first-degree murder (McMullen and Sanders) with special circumstances (allegations of gang membership, multiple murders) and subsequently sentenced to two consecutive life terms in prison without the possibility of parole. His co-defendant, Joseph Wayne Jones, awaits trial as of January 2010.

Further Reading

"Slain 'Judging Amy' Actress Remembered at LA Funeral." Associated Press, October 29, 2005.

McNelley, Robert E. (M-S)

A founding member of the Dayton, Ohio–based country-rock group McGuffey Lane, whose song "Long Time Lovin' You" reached Number 85 on the *Billboard* Top 100 chart in 1981, "Bobby Gene" McNelley, 36, left the group in 1984 to pursue a songwriting career (with little success) in Nashville, Tennessee. The musician was living with his 25-year-old girlfriend, Linda Sue Green, in a rented house at 5330 Linworth Road in Sharon Township near Columbus, Ohio, when, on January 7, 1987, a series of domestic arguments culminated in murder when McNelley shotgunned his lover in the head. Six hours later, he turned the gun on himself.

Further Reading

Steiden, Bill. "Ex-Band Member, Woman Found Slain." *Columbus Dispatch,* January 8, 1987, sec. D, pp. 1–2.

Meek, Joe (M-S)

Called the "Phil Spector of Britain," Meek (born April 25 1929 in Newent, Gloucestershire) became that country's premier independent record producer of the 1960s after beginning his career in 1954 as an engineer with the IBC, the leading independent recording studio of the period. At the IBC, Meek worked with Lonnie Donegan, Frankie Vaughn, and Humphrey Lyttelton, and wrote "Put a Ring on Her Finger" for singer Tommy Steele in 1958. Meek went independent in 1960, ultimately setting up a studio-apartment above a leather-goods shop at 307 Holloway Road in North London. It was in these cramped surroundings he dubbed "the bathroom" that the innovative producer pioneered the unusual sounds (ranging from electronic instruments to flushing toilets) that characterized much of his work.

In 1961, Meek founded The Tornados, an instrumental group he used as a house band at the Holloway Road studio to back solo performers like Billy Fury, John Leyton, and Don Charles. By 1962, their space aged instrumental, "Telstar," had sold four million copies, and became the first British rock record to reach Number 1 on the American charts. Co-written and produced by Meek, the tune's success established him as the top British independent producer of the era. In the mid–1960s, the move toward more melodic music spearheaded by the Beatles made Meek's music seem gimmicky. To accommodate the new trend, the producer countered in 1964 with The Honeycombs' Top 5 hit "Have I the Right?" The single proved to be Meek's last success, and following a string of musical flops he found himself largely unemployable and drowning in debt.

Ever a violent personality, Meek's erratic behavior (fueled by amphetamine use and fear that he would be publicly exposed as a homosexual) alienated many of his longtime friends. As Meeks sank deeper into drug abuse and mental illness, he became convinced that his studio-living quarters were bugged and that unseen forces were trying to steal ideas directly from his mind. To thwart them, the 35-year-old burned all his notes and private documents except one that read, "I'm going now." An ardent spiritualist, Meek told friends that the spirit of British occultist Aleister Crowley was keeping him up all night by walking up and down the staircase outside his apartment. Meek's tenuous grasp on reality further frayed in January 1967, when the mutilated corpse of Bernard Oliver, a 17-year-old warehouseman from Muswell Hill, was found packed into two suitcases behind a hedgerow by a tractor driver working in a field in the Suffolk village of Tattingstone. Meek, who was arrested in November 1963 for soliciting sex in a men's restroom, knew Oliver as a sex partner and was certain to be among those questioned by police.

On February 3, 1967, Meek was informed by his landlady, 54-year-old Violet Shenton, wife of the downstairs shopkeeper, that he would have to find another place to live since they were selling their business and the building. As she was leaving the upstairs apartment, Meek fired a 12-gauge shotgun blast into her back, which knocked her down the stairs. Shenton died en route to nearby Royal Northern Hospital. Meek reloaded, and ten seconds later shot himself in the head. The murder-suicide occurred on the eighth anniversary of Buddy Holly's death in 1959, a rock 'n' roll star Meek idolized.

Further Reading

Repsch, John. *The Legendary Joe Meek: The Telstar Man*. London: Woodford House, 1989.
Williams, Richard. "Roots: Joe Meek." *Melody Maker*, June 17, 1972, pp. 24, 50.

Melrose, Percy C. (M-S)

Melrose, 57, a former circus performer in a bicycle act, made a small fortune in the teens manufacturing patent medicine in the area of Columbus, Ohio. Married with two children, Melrose started an affair with his neighbor's wife, Eva Tootle, the 27-year-old mother of a small child. The affair ended in tragedy on May 16, 1918, with the discovery of the bullet-riddled bodies in the front seat of Melrose's car parked on a road near Lockbourne, just south of Columbus. A passing motorist found the pair after noticing that the windshield of the car was covered over with newspapers and its curtains were drawn. Ballistics and a note found on the car's rear seat told the story of a murder-suicide. According to authorities, Melrose shot Tootle three times in the head during a struggle (as evidenced by defensive wounds on the woman's hands) then fired one bullet into his head just behind the right ear. The note read, in part: "Facts: A ruined home and a ruined life, all because my wife was so extravagant. We have not loved each other for three or four years. I love little Eva because she is so pure. God have mercy on my soul and grant that my wife will rear my two children in the right way."

Further Reading

"Percy C. Melrose Shoots Woman; Then Kills Self." *Columbus Evening Dispatch*, May 17, 1918, p. 3.

Menson, Michael (V)

This disturbing hate crime exposed incompetence, corruption, and racial prejudice within London's Metropolitan Police. Menson, the seventh of eleven children born in 1966 to a Ghanaian diplomat and his wife stationed in Moscow, was raised since age two in North London. As a child, his involvement in church choir led to a few years stint with the English National Opera then touring England in a production of *Der Rosenklavier*. By the mid–1980s Menson was studying at Barnet College on the edge of North London just miles from where the city's club scene was exploding. Menson was drawn to the dance clubs and became a regular at the Electric Ballroom in Camden. With friends from school, the 18 year old started working as a DJ on the club circuit, and later formed Double Trouble and the Rebel MC. Described by group members as not so much a band as "an organization of producers, mixers, and DJs," Double Trouble featured a danceable mix of drum rhythms, mixing, and sampling. In 1989, "Street Tuff," the group's first thumping reggae beat single, peaked at Number 11 on the British charts. Double Trouble released a few other charting singles, toured Europe, and appeared on the television show *Top of the Pops*, before changing musical tastes in the early 1990s spelled an end to the group's popularity. In 1993, Double Trouble as a performing entity ended in personal bitterness among its members. Menson, however, still put in 18 hour days working to keep the group's studio afloat by remixing the tracks of other bands and producing radio jingles. That same year, he suffered the first of several nervous breakdowns precipitated by the loss of his career and the inevitable failure of the recording business. Menson, a diagnosed schizophrenic, spent the next few years in and out of hospitals for depression, and living, heavily medicated, in various halfway houses in the North London district.

In the early hours of January 28, 1997, motorists on the North Circular Road in Edmonton, North London, encountered a horrific sight — a black man, naked except for a pair of socks, standing dazed in the street still smoldering where flames had seared his back, thighs, and buttocks. A grisly trail of burnt clothes and charred flesh some 350 yards long pointed to where Michael Menson, 30, had wandered. Constable Johanna Walsh, the first officer on the scene, reported that Menson appeared to be "in a trance." She asked him three times who had done this to him without receiving a response. Asked a fourth time, Menson replied, "Lee." Believing the man had set himself ablaze in a suicide attempt, Constable Walsh failed to treat the area as a crime scene and did not cordon off the site. Menson, suffering third-degree burns over 25 percent of his body, was initially transported to nearby North Middlesex Hospital, but was soon transferred to the regional burns unit at Billericay Hospital, Essex. At hospital, Menson told his brother Kwesi that he had been attacked by four white youths who doused him with a flammable liquid and set him ablaze when he was trying to return by bus to the North Middlesex Hospital where he was staying. Twelve hours after the incident, Kwesi alerted authorities that his brother was the victim of a hate crime. Police opened an investigation, but during the intervening twelve hour delay valuable forensic evidence and potential witnesses had been lost. Aware of Menson's well-documented history of mental health problems, the authorities remained convinced he had harmed himself, and so were in no hurry to question the burn victim. On January 31, police finally paid a call on Menson, but finding the man sedated after the first of several painful skin grafts, decided he was medically unfit to interview. Unbelievably, no detectives returned to the hospital to question Menson who had sufficiently recovered from his injuries to be able to read and work crossword puzzles. Kwesi and the Menson family continued to beg police to investigate the incident, but in the absence of official interest, the dedicated brother began writing down the injured man's bedside statements concerning the attack. On February 3, 1997, the comatose Menson died of multiple organ failure after developing septicaemia and suffering two heart attacks. In the 16 days between the attack and his death, the musician had described the incident in detail to nine different people.

Outraged over the lack of Metropolitan Police interest in the case, Menson's family publicly maintained that the department's unwillingness to seriously investigate the incident demonstrated their fundamental failure to recognize race as a factor in the crime. Such charges of "color blindness" were not unknown to the Metropolitan Police. In 1993, Stephen Lawrence, a black teenager, was stabbed to death by racists in London. The subsequent government inquiry led to a vigorous condemnation of "institutional racism" in British police forces. The reputation of the Metropolitan Police took another devastating hit at the Menson inquest conducted at Hornsey's Coroner's Court in September 1998. Authorities reiterated their initial position that they were unsure whether Menson had committed suicide or was murdered. Earlier, police admitted in a letter to the dead man's family that serious mistakes were made in the early stages of the inquiry, but insisted they had not affected the ongoing investigation. An internal Scotland Yard review of the four officers involved resulted in three of them retiring or being permitted to retire thus making them immune to disciplinary action. A fourth was "given advice" and allowed to continue working. The letter, however, failed to apologize to the Mensons for the shoddy police work. Psychiatric testimony established that while Menson was a registered schizophrenic who suffered from bouts of psychosis and delusional hallucinations, it was highly unlikely that he would commit suicide. This assessment was reinforced by forensic scientists and pathologists who maintained that the nature of the burns, largely restricted to Menson's back, made it almost "inconceivable" that he had set himself alight. Though police had since spoken to nearly three hundred people and taken up to two hundred statements, not one person had been able to provide a useful fact. On September 17, 1998, the inquest jury ruled that Menson had been "unlawfully killed."

Bolstered by the inquest's findings, the Menson family continued their media campaign against the Metropolitan Police and their flawed handling of the case. Not only had the police failed to consider race as a possible motive in the crime, they had compounded the problem by adopting a defensive attitude towards the dead man's family. The campaign worked. The Menson case was referred to the Police Complaints Authority with the Cambridgeshire constabulary conducting an inquiry on their behalf to determine what went wrong in the initial investigation. Meanwhile, the Menson family met with Home Secretary Jack Straw in November 1998 to discuss the case and the police response. On December 1, 1998, the Metropolitan Police officially apologized to the Menson family for the numerous mistakes made in the racist murder of Michael Menson. The investigation was reopened with Scotland Yard's Racial and Violent Crimes Task Force directly in-

volved in following up 43 lines of investigation. In a move widely hailed as "inspired," the Task Force posted leaflets to the homes of suspects and witnesses to ensure they watched the 150th edition of BBC's *Crimewatch* in which Menson's family issued an emotional appeal to viewers on the anniversary of Michael's death. Days after the broadcast the Task Force caught its first break. Acting on a tip generated by the show, bugging devices were installed in suspect Charalambous "Harry" Constantinou's flat. In a series of chilling conversations recorded during February–March 1999 between the suspect and his friend, Husseyin "Chris" Abdullah, the 26-year-old Edmonton man incriminated himself along with cronies Mario Pereira, 26, and Ozyguy "Ossie" Cevat, 24. Constantinou told Abdullah, 50, that "Mario was just saying things about him, saying, 'He's a nigger, he's a black, let's burn him.' I persuaded them not to, but then Mario started again. Ozzie got out of the car and tried to light his jacket but it didn't work so they went back to Mario's house, got some fuel, spirit or something, went back to him." After the murder Pereira reportedly boasted to a friend, "It was a joke that had gone wrong ... so what, he was black."

In March 1999, officers from the Racial and Violent Crimes Task Force arrested Constantinou and Pereira for Menson's murder and Abdullah on a charge of conspiracy to pervert the course of justice by obstructing a police investigation. Pereira and Constantinou's accomplice in the murder, Ozyguy Cevat, a 24-year-old Briton of Turkish-Cypriot origin, was arrested in Northern Cyprus in July 1999. Days after the assault, Cevat had fled Briton to escape prosecution for the crime. As London had no extradition treaty with the break-away republic, Cevat was tried in Northern Cyprus and on November 25, 1999 found guilty of the lesser charge of "causing the death" (manslaughter) of Michael Menson. Cevat was sentenced to 14 years in prison, but the sentence was not immediately announced so as to avoid prejudicing the legal proceedings against his co-conspirators in London. That same month, Pereira and Constantinou were tried on first-degree murder charges in the Old Bailey while Abdullah faced a charge of conspiracy to cover up the crime. Linden Niaken, a friend of Pereira's, testified that the defendant told him that he, Cevat, and Constantinou attacked Menson because Pereira thought the black had "stressed out" his girlfriend. Pereira admitted to several other acquaintances that the attack was meant to be a "joke." The three men were driving in Edmonton when they observed Menson wandering on the street as though lost. Shouting racial epithets, they robbed the musician of his portable stereo and Cevat tried to light Menson's parka on fire. When it failed to catch, the men drove a short distance, picked up white spirit or gas, and drove back to the scene where Pereira doused Menson's parka with the flammable substance. Pereira claimed to have said, "Ossie lit a match and threw it at him. He burst into flames. He did not seem to notice. He had a bag with him and we shared things out," adding, "We didn't think he would go up in flames like that." On December 21, 1999, Mario Pereira was found guilty of murder and subsequently sentenced to life imprisonment. His accomplice, Charalambous "Harry" Constantinou, was given a ten year sentence for manslaughter plus two years to run consecutively for impeding a police investigation. Husseyin Abdullah, Pereira's confidante on the police tape, was sentenced to 21 month for perverting justice. Remarkably, Mr. Justice Gage pronounced the motive for the attack as "unclear," although he was positive that Pereira had made the "so what, he was black" remark. After the verdict, Metropolitan Police Deputy Assistant Commissioner John Grieve praised the Menson family. "What they have done is really quite remarkable. Their behavior is the stuff of legends. Their utterly steadfast campaign was really pivotal and can be seen as a model of how to keep a murder investigation in the public mind and reminding witnesses and those with information to do their public duty."

In May 2003, the Crown Prosecution Service announced the findings of its two year inquiry into the bungled murder investigation. The scathing seven hundred page report, completed at a taxpayer cost of more than £1 million, concluded the conduct of the Metropolitan Police immediately following the attack on Menson was "unprofessional, uncoordinated, in part negligent, and at best inept." It further found police had altered witness statements before they were logged so as not to contradict their initial suicide theory. One detective was quoted as saying to a colleague, "I don't know why they are worried — this only concerns a black schizophrenic." Despite the damning report, the CPS decided against prosecuting any of the 18 officers involved as the "obvious" failings in the investigations were not considered to be "sufficiently willful or grave as to justify criminal proceedings." Prior to the issuance of the report, ten senior officers were permitted to retire with the remaining eight almost certainly guaranteed they would escape any form of disciplinary action.

Further Reading

Gentleman, Amanda. "No Justice, No Apology." *The Guardian* (London), September 17, 1998, p. 1.

Rayner, Jay. "Who Killed Michael Menson? Racist Youths Get Away with Murder." *The Observer*, November 1, 1998, p. 15.

Merker, Jack Ronald (V)

Merker enjoyed a long and distinguished career in San Diego, California, radio as an executive producer at KNSD/Channel 39, program director at both KOGO/AM 600 and KSDO/AM 1130, and as an on-air broadcast news personality. Colleagues credited him with making radio news in the area more lively and competitive as well as for launching the talk show host career of Michael Reagan, son of former President Ronald Reagan. In 1996, the openly gay Merker produced a radio show about AIDS that was honored with the New York International Radio Award. He served as the county's director of media and public relations for two years until ill health in 1999 prompted him to retire to the desert community of Palm Springs, California. The 63-year-old former radio executive was staying at the home of a friend in Palm Springs when he was last seen leaving a local bar on November 28 or 29, 2001, with a man later identified as Erik Levaughan Wright, a 22-year-old resident of nearby Rancho Mirage. Days later on December 1, a real estate agent showing the home of Merker's friend to a prospective buyer discovered the radio man's body tossed into a laundry room. Merker, bound and gagged, had died of "compression of the neck." Prime suspect Erik Wright proved easy for Palm Springs authorities to find. The day prior to the shocking discovery of Merker's body, Wright had been arrested by local police for the recent robbing and repeated stabbing of a motorist who had given him a ride. At trial, Wright admitted choking Merker, but only to disable him after the elderly man became violent during their sexual encounter. The prosecution maintained Wright deliberately killed Merker to get money for drugs. Found guilty of second-degree murder on January 6, 2004, Wright was subsequently sentenced to a prison term of 15 years to life.

Further Reading

Chacon, Daniel J. "Slain Man was Former San Diego Media Executive and On-Air Personality." Copley News Service, December 5, 2001.

Merrige-Abrams, Salwa (M-S)

Throughout her 19-year marriage to James Abrams, a 45-year-old National Airlines pilot, Merrige-Abrams tailored her opera career around him and their children, Jack, 14, and Melissa Ann, 10. A talented mezzo soprano, the 43-year-old singer refused national roles in order to perform cameos in the Miami, Florida, area with the Greater Miami Opera Guild, the Civic Opera of the Palm Beaches, and the Miami Beach Symphony. Following the couple's separation in 1971, Merrige-Abrams underwent psychiatric counseling. On the afternoon of July 14, 1973, one day after their divorce became final, the singer phoned her ex-husband to come over to the home they once shared at 5450 SW Sixtieth Court in Miami to remove the remainder of his possessions. "I got a real surprise for you," she promised. James Abrams, now living at a nearby residence with another woman, disregarded his attorney's advice to send a mover for his remaining property and returned to the house. There, Merrige-Abrams repeatedly shot the man with a .38-caliber revolver before reloading. Systematically moving to other parts of the house, she killed her two children. Apparently unable at the last minute to shoot herself, the singer downed several tranquilizers and barbiturates. She was found unconscious in the dining room near a piano covered with photos from her career and a handwritten will. With three unserved first-degree murder warrants still facing her, Merrige-Abrams died at the South Miami Hospital at 1:15 A.M. on July 19, 1973.

Further Reading

Buchanan, Edna. "Miami Singer Kills Mate, Two Children, Police Say." *Miami Herald*, July 15, 1973, sec. 1, p. 1.

Miller, Corey *see* C-Murder

Miller, Lyndl (V) (M-S)

Miller (married name Gorosch), principal viola player for the sixty member Las Vegas Symphony, also played the violin in backing orchestras for major showroom acts like Neil Sedaka in casinos including Caesars Palace and Bally's. On the afternoon of March 17, 1991, the 46 year old performed as a soloist at a concert given by the Nevada Chamber Orchestra broadcast live on radio station KNPR-FM. After the hour-long performance, Miller returned to the home she shared with husband Bent Gorosch, 48, at 1106 Orange Circle in northwest Las Vegas. Gorosch, a native of Sweden in the U.S. since 1977, owned a floral shop in the city and was seemingly depressed over large gambling losses. Police theorized that sometime during the night, the couple argued and Gorosch shot his wife once in the head with a .357-caliber Magnum in the master bedroom of their home then turned the gun on himself. According to friends of the dead man, the florist never psychologically recovered from the childhood memory of his parents' suicide in Sweden in the wake of World War II.

Further Reading

Burbank, Jeff. "Deaths Called Murder-Suicide." *Las Vegas Review-Journal*, March 20, 1991, sec. A, p. 1.

Miller, Seagram (V)

The Oakland, California, gangsta rapper best-known for his 1995 album *Reality Check* was caught in a hail of gunfire on July 31, 1996, as he exited a van in the 1900 block of 24th Avenue in "the Twamps," an area in East Oakland known for violence and drug trafficking. Miller died an hour later at Highland Hospital. The 26-year-old rapper's unnamed companion (identified on some websites as rapper Gangsta P) was shot in the head, but survived. In 1993, Miller survived unscathed an assassination attempt allegedly ordered by Emanuel Lacy, a drug kingpin. It was widely believed that a song written by Miller about a rival gang had greatly angered the drug trafficker. Police refused to speculate whether the attacks were related. To date, no arrests have been made.

Further Reading

Glover, Malcolm. "Oakland Rapper Dies in Gunfire." *San Francisco Examiner*, August 2, 1996, sec. A, p. 10.

Milocevic, Milos (M-S)

Milocevic, an aspiring Yugoslavian actor known professionally as Milos Milos, worked in Paris as Alain Delon's stand-in before a marriage to a Chicago socialite living in Los Angeles followed by a quickie divorce granted him U.S. citizenship. In Hollywood, Delon introduced the young actor to Mickey Rooney and his fifth wife, Barbara Ann Thomason, then in midst of marital difficulties brought on by the diminutive actor's drug abuse, overwork, and philandering. Milocevic, 24, and Thomason, 29, began an affair in 1965 while

Rooney was in Beirut filming *24 Hours to Kill*, co-starring Walter Slezak (a suicide in 1983). The affair deepened as Rooney, in serious tax trouble, was constantly on the road to generate income. While Rooney was in the Philippines shooting *Ambush Bay*, Thomason spent two weeks with her lover on location in Fort Bragg, California, where he had a small part as a submarine crewman in director Norman Jewison's *The Russians Are Coming! The Russians Are Coming!* When shooting wrapped, Milocevic spent nights with Thomason and her four children in Rooney's $200,000 Brentwood home at 13030 Evanston Street. Rooney, returning from the Philippines with a debilitating blood infection, was informed by Thomason that she wanted him out of the house. The couple officially separated on December 23, 1965.

A seasoned veteran of divorce court, the 44-year-old actor took the offensive. On January 24, 1966, he filed papers charging Thomason as an "unfit mother" and demanding sole custody of their children. Milocevic reacted by phoning Thomason's friends and threatening them not to testify in Rooney's behalf. When one friend refused, Milocevic allegedly said, "If Barbara even looks at another man I'll shoot her and myself in the bedroom or bathroom. It'll be like a film. We'll be sleeping like two lovers together. It'll be great. We'll be in the headlines." Terrified of losing her children, Thomason visited Rooney in St. John's Hospital in Santa Monica on January 30, 1966. Unknown to the actor, she wore a wire that transmitted their conversation to a private detective parked outside the hospital who was taping the interview. During their talk, Thomason got Rooney to admit that she was not an unfit mother. Rooney offered to retract the statement in the press after they reconciled. As she was leaving, Thomason reassured him, "If it makes you unhappy for me to see Milos, then I won't even see him as a friend." That same evening, Thomason played the tape at home for Milocevic, her private detective, and two friends who were staying in the guest house on the property. After hearing the tape, an apparently calm Milocevic asked to speak with his lover in the master bedroom around 8:30 P.M. Everyone else, except three of the four Rooney children who were asleep in the house at the time, left for the evening. The fourth child was staying with Rooney's mother. The next afternoon, house guest Wilma Catania became alarmed when a maid informed her that

neither Milocevic nor Thomason had been seen that day. Catania secured a key and entered the bedroom. She found Thomason dead on the bathroom floor with the lifeless Milocevic sprawled atop her. A chrome-plated .38-caliber automatic registered to Rooney lay beside them. Police speculated that Thomason's statement about not seeing her lover again prompted Milocevic to shoot her once in the lower part of the jaw before firing a fatal shot into his temple.

Further Reading

Rooney, Mickey. *Life Is Too Short*. New York: Villard, 1991.

Mineo, Sal (V)

The son of a Sicilian immigrant father and a first generation Italian-American mother, Sal(vatore) Mineo, Jr. (born January 10, 1939, in East Harlem, Bronx, New York) was a star at 16, a has-

The darkly handsome Sal Mineo was a talented actor who was unfortunately typecast as the troubled teen in films including *The Blackboard Jungle* (1954) and *Rebel Without a Cause* (1955). Despite Oscar and Emmy nominations, Mineo was unable to sustain stardom as he aged into adult roles. Following a career-ending turn as a psychopathic rapist in *Who Killed Teddy Bear?* (1965), Mineo openly acknowledged his homosexuality and directed a couple of gay-themed plays (*Fortune and Men's Eyes* and *The Children's Mass*) before his murder in West Hollywood on February 12, 1976.

been by thirty, and a murder victim at 37. As a child, Mineo played Christ in a Catholic grade school production prior to being expelled from the institution as a troublemaker. A beautiful, exotic looking youth with dark curly hair and sultry eyes, the youngster enrolled in dance school and appeared on local television on *The Ted Steele Show*. Mineo's first theatrical break came in 1950 after a Broadway producer chose the 11-year-old to appear as "Salvatore" in the Tennessee Williams play, *The Rose Tattoo*, starring Eli Wallach and Maureen Stapleton. The play debuted on Broadway on February 3, 1951, with the 12-year-old Mineo earning $65 a week. In August 1952, the young actor played "Prince Chulalongkorn" opposite Yul Brynner in the smash Broadway musical *The King and I*. On the strength of his nearly 900 performances in the part during 1952–1953, Mineo landed television work in the *Hallmark Hall of Fame* production of "A Woman for the Ages" (May 5, 1952), *Omnibus*, *Philco Playhouse*, and *Big Town*.

In 1955, Mineo appeared in his first film, *Six Bridges to Cross*. The movie was shot in Boston, and while in Hollywood to do sound looping for the film the 15-year-old was signed by Universal-International to appear opposite Charlton Heston in *The Private War of Major Benjamin*. That same year, Mineo landed the role that would make him a star while also hopelessly typecasting him as the "troubled youth." Evan Hunter's popular and shocking 1954 novel of juvenile delinquency, *The Blackboard Jungle*, was optioned by MGM and released to big box office as a Glenn Ford film in March 1955. In addition to being one of the first movies to convincingly portray rebel youth, *The Blackboard Jungle* also featured an early appearance of rock 'n' roll; Bill Haley & His Comets doing the classic "Rock Around the Clock." Anxious to carve out a chunk of the lucrative teen film market, Warner Bros. signed Nicholas Ray to direct James Dean, Natalie Wood, and Sal Mineo in *Rebel Without a Cause*. As the sexually ambiguous teen "Plato," Mineo's role would later be heralded by critics as the first appearance of a gay teen in American cinema. Dean, 24, died in a car crash four weeks before *Rebel* opened to huge business in late October 1955. Mineo, a slight 5'5", 120-pound, 16-year-old, received an Oscar nomination as Best Supporting Actor, but lost the award to Jack Lemmon as "Ensign Pulver" in *Mr. Roberts*. His acting kudos continued, however, with an Emmy nomination for Best Actor as the title character in "Dino" in a June 2, 1956, installment of *Studio One*. Mineo again lost the award, but in 1957 appeared in the film version of *Dino* to good reviews.

Earning two acting nominations in two mediums within two years of setting foot in Hollywood, the diminutive, but darkly handsome Mineo was officially a "hot property" based almost exclusively on his convincing portrayals of "troubled youth." Studios, never particularly known for a willingness to take chances, continued to cast the actor in juvenile delinquent roles in films like the 1956 *Crime in the Streets* in which Mineo earned the lasting nickname, "The Switchblade Kid." After appearing in the 1957 rock 'n' roll opus *Rock Pretty Baby* for Universal-International, Mineo recorded the single "Start Movin'" for Epic. The record stayed on the *Billboard* chart for 19 weeks, peaking at Number 9, and selling 1.2 million units. The actor released three other singles on the label through January 1958 with the most successful, "Lasting Love," peaking at Number 27 in late 1957. In the late 1950s, Mineo feared that he was rapidly becoming typecast as the brooding juvenile delinquent. As a change of pace, he appeared as the Indian "White Bull" in the 1959 Disney film *Tonka*. Oddly enough, in 1964 Mineo would be cast as another Indian over director John Ford's objections in *Cheyenne Autumn*. In 1959, the actor scored his first adult film role as the title character in *The Gene Krupa Story*, the screen bio of the big band drummer. It was, however, in 1960 that the 21-year-old star scored his biggest acting triumph as "Dov Landau," the concentration camp survivor, in director Otto Preminger's epic *Exodus*. Mineo won the Golden Globe for his performance, but yet again lost the Best Supporting Actor Oscar, this time to Peter Ustinov in *Spartacus*. Bitterly disappointed by the loss, Mineo was at a critical juncture in his career. Too old to continue playing juvenile roles, the actor was physically changing from a baby-faced heartthrob into a man with the looks of a character actor. Mineo's ill-considered decision to appear as a psychopathic rapist and murderer in the 1965 bomb *Who Killed Teddy Bear?* ended any chance he had of continuing as a name actor in Hollywood. The film, while a favorite of the gay subculture because of Mineo's muscular physique, succeeded in placing the actor on what he later called "the weirdo list" among Hollywood movie producers. Essentially *persona non grata* as a lead in motion pictures, the actor turned to television series guest shots from the mid–1960s to late–1970s.

The death of Mineo's movie career, however, did yield an important personal, and later, career benefit. Freed from the need to hide his sexuality from filmgoers, Mineo openly embraced the homosexual lifestyle. Although the actor first experienced clandestine gay sex in 1961 at the age of 22, any indiscreet homosexual liaison then would have spelt career suicide. Romantically linked to *Exodus* co-star Jill Haworth in the early 1960s, Mineo no longer felt the need to sustain the heterosexual fiction as the doors of Hollywood closed to him in the mid–1960s. A regular at gay nightclubs in West Hollywood, Mineo increasingly turned to casual sex with many partners and increased drug use as the decade drew to a close. The one-time teen star was almost broke and living on a $25 a week allowance doled out by his business manager when he was signed to direct the gay-themed prison drama *Fortune and Men's Eyes* in an Off-Broadway production in 1969. The play, which features a brutal homosexual rape, was savaged by the New York critics with Clive Barnes unkindly referring to director Mineo as "a minor Hollywood player." Later that year, *Fortune* was transplanted to Los Angeles where, in addition to directing, Mineo played the character "Rocky" to favorable reviews, especially in the city's burgeoning gay press. Now officially "out of the closet," Mineo tried to revive his film career, but with little success. Actor and friend Roddy McDowell used his influence to get Mineo his last film role in the 1971 science fiction movie *Escape from the Planet of the Apes*. The twice Oscar nominated actor played the chimp scientist "Dr. Milo." Seemingly barred from "traditional entertainment," Mineo turned to the gay-themed play, *The Children's Mass*, which quickly appeared then disappeared Off-Broadway in a blizzard of bad reviews.

In 1976, however, the actor's long run of bad luck appeared to be ending when he was cast in the San Francisco production of *P.S. Your Cat Is Dead* at the Montgomery Playhouse in North Beach. Mineo received strong reviews as "Vito," the bisexual hustler-burglar, and at 37 must have felt he was finally on the comeback trail. It was with a renewed sense of career optimism that the actor received the news that the show was moving to the Westwood Playhouse in Los Angeles. Mineo was renting a $75 a month one-bedroom, two-story apartment at 8563 Holloway Drive just below the Sunset Strip in the heart of gay West

Hollywood while rehearsing the play with co-star Keir Dullea. On the evening of February 12, 1976, the actor drove home from a rehearsal at the Westwood Playhouse arriving around 9:30 P.M. Moments later, a neighbor heard someone yell, "Oh, no! Oh, my God. No! Help me, please." The neighbor, looking out the rear window of his apartment, saw a "white man" running away. Sal Mineo was found lying on the pavement in the rear carport area behind his apartment dead from a single knife wound in the chest. An autopsy determined the actor was killed with a hunting knife that perforated the heart causing a massive hemorrhage. Mineo's wallet was found at the scene thereby initially ruling out robbery as a motive to sheriff's detectives investigating the murder. Once inside the actor's apartment, however, investigators quickly formed another theory of the case. Nude photographs of muscular men adorned the walls and gay pornography was found stacked in piles in the actor's bedroom. Combined with Mineo's reputation for recreational drug use, authorities operated on the dual assumptions that the killing was either a "fag murder" (a lover's quarrel), or, the result of a drug deal gone wrong. Some 250 attendees, including *Exodus* co-star Jill Haworth, friend Desi Arnaz, Jr., *Rebel* director Nicholas Ray, and curiosity seekers, joined Mineo's family in mourning the dead actor on February 17, 1976, at a funeral mass at Holy Trinity Roman Catholic Church in Mamaroneck, New York. The actor was buried in Gate of Heaven Cemetery in Valhalla.

The case stagnated for 15 months until May 1977 when the L.A. Sheriff's Department was contacted by Theresa Williams, the disgruntled wife of Lionel Raymond Williams, a one-time pizza delivery man with a history of violence. The woman told investigators that on the night of Mineo's murder, Williams came home with blood on his shirt explaining that he just stabbed someone. When local television news flashed a photo of the actor, Williams allegedly told his wife, "That's the dude I killed." Theresa Williams also told authorities that her husband used a hunting knife (recently purchased for $5.28) in Mineo's murder and in several other robberies committed in the area. Lionel Raymond Williams, a 21-year-old light-skinned black, was currently serving time in Michigan for passing a bad check. The convict allegedly bragged to a cellmate in the Calhoun County Jail that he had killed Sal Mineo a "while back." Other victims of robberies committed in West Los Angeles around the time of Mineo's murder picked Williams out of a photo array. Tried in Los Angeles during January–February 1979, Williams was found guilty of second-degree murder, but innocent of the charge of attempted robbery in the Mineo case thus sparing the killer the death penalty. Williams was further convicted on nine counts of first-degree robbery and on one count of second-degree robbery for the holdups committed in the two-month period in 1976 that included the night the actor was killed. On March 15, 1979, Superior Court Judge Bonnie Lee Martin imposed consecutive sentences of five years to life for Mineo's murder and nine of the robberies, recommending, "The defendant should be committed to state prison for as long as the law allows." The sentences totaled 51 years to life, but under California's set-term law Williams made parole in the early 1990s after serving roughly 14 years. He quickly reoffended and ended up back in prison. In August 1991 Carlos Gonzalez commemorated the tragic life of the actor in a one-man show, *Sal*, at San Francisco's Climate Theatre. Commenting on the one-time star's untapped potential, Gonzalez concluded, "I think Sal Mineo would have been like Dean Stockwell, Dennis Hopper. These were his peers. As he got older there came a time when he stopped picking his roles. They picked him. He died before the Dustin Hoffmans came along. Now leading men come in all shapes and sizes."

Further Reading

Jeffers, H. Paul. *Sal Mineo: His Life, Murder, and Mystery*. New York: Carroll and Graf, 2000.
www.salmineo.com.

Minor, Charlie (V)

The quintessential Top 40 promo man, "Good Time" Charlie Minor was credited by Sting, Bryan Adams, Amy Grant, and other major recording industry stars as helping to establish their careers by aggressively marketing their music to radio stations. Born in Marietta, Georgia, Minor unofficially entered the music business in the late 1960s while attending the University of Georgia. As social chairman for Kappa Sigma, he booked bands for weekend football parties and the fraternity's other social events. By the time Minor graduated with a business degree in 1971, he was booking every band that played in Athens for a percentage of their appearance fee. Briefly working for local publisher Lowery Music pro-

moting the records of fading 1960s bands, Minor was hired by A&M Records in 1971 to handle their regional promotion in Atlanta. He proved so tireless and energetic in convincing Atlanta radio stations to play singles by A&M artists like Cat Stevens, Peter Frampton, and Styx, that the company transferred him to Los Angeles in 1973 to do national sales promotion.

In L.A. he threw himself into learning all aspects of record promotion developing contacts with radio program directors and industry executives across the country. Good looking, charming, and charismatic, the fast-talking "good-ol-boy" from Georgia possessed the unique ability to make everyone feel they enjoyed a close personal relationship with him. In a typical day, Minor was on the phone early talking to dozens of radio stations cajoling deejays into playing singles from his client list that included Kenny Rogers, the Carpenters, Supertramp, Janet Jackson, and many others. Sting praised the promoter for making hits out of the Police singles "Don't Stand So Close to Me" and "Every Little Thing She Does is Magic." Herb Alpert, co-founder of A&M, nicknamed his top promo man "Jaws" in tribute to Minor's ability to juggle five different conversations on five different phones at one time. At night, Minor drove his black Rolls Royce convertible to L.A.'s top nightspots outfitted in $2,000 designer suits by Armani, Donna Karan, and Versace. More often than not, the man universally recognized as the "king of record promoters" was accompanied by one of his stable of seemingly interchangeable beautiful, busty blondes. According to friends, Minor drew his woman of preference from the ranks of industry groupies, stewardesses, second-tier models, and wannabe performers. A typical Minor relationship lasted two intense months before he moved on to the next blonde of choice.

By the late 1980s and early 1990s Minor's hard partying lifestyle of sex, drugs, booze, and rock 'n' roll had left him with a bad liver and a major substance abuse problem. In early 1989, then-wife Danica Bujic and several of the promoter's friends organized an intervention designed to save his life. Minor agreed to be assessed at the Scripps Clinic in La Jolla, California, then checked himself into the ultra-chic La Costa Resort and Spa in Carlsbad to detox. Though ultimately achieving sobriety, Minor continued to be a regular on the L.A. club scene leading one program director to call him an "'80s man who cleaned up his act but ... still maintained that fun-spirited image." In

1990, Minor was the senior vice president of promotion at A&M when he was passed over for the presidency of the company. Deeply hurt and disappointed, the industry's top promo man cashed out $3,284,000 in A&M stock and left the company after 17 years. In early 1991, Minor's nine year marriage to actress-swimsuit model Danica Bujic ended in a bitter divorce and costly custody battle over their only child. Career-wise, Minor rebounded in March 1991 and accepted a $500,000 a year job as president of newly formed Giant Records. Lacking any major acts to promote, however, the company foundered and was losing money when, in September 1992, Minor became the focus of rumors that he engaged in sexual misconduct with a woman in his office. Giant Records parent company Time Warner announced an in-house investigation into allegations that Minor had used his office to receive oral sex and/or had sex on his desk. Though the results of the investigation were never made public, the executive resigned six months later. Forced out of Giant by scandal, the promoter announced in March 1993 the formation of his own company, Minor Promotion and Marketing. Concurrently, Minor was hired by *Hits Magazine*, a Sherman Oaks–based weekly trade publication, as president of its new business division.

Since his divorce in 1991, the fun-loving Minor had played the field, "dating" sexy blondes for a couple months before moving on to his next star-struck conquest. In mid–1994, the 46-year-old record promoter met Suzette Melina McClure, 27, a stripper performing under the name "Mindy" at Bailey's Twenty/20, an upscale club he often frequented in Century City near the Los Angeles International Airport. McClure did not fit the stripper stereotype. In 1990 she earned a B.S. in math and science from the California Polytechnic University in Pomona and landed a job as a computer programmer in the finance department at Hughes Aircraft in Long Beach. The ambitious professional took night classes in computer programming to strengthen her resumé. McClure's future in the aerospace industry looked secure until Hughes announced in July 1993 that it was downsizing. The attractive 5'2", 100-pound computer programmer was laid off and forced to find another way to pay the mortgage on her one bedroom condo at 1518 Yale Street in Santa Monica. In January 1994, McClure started dancing three or four nights a week at Bailey's Twenty/20 and earned as much as $600 a shift in tips from the professional men in the music industry who patronized the club. Ashamed of being a stripper, however, she told her parents she was waitressing in a sports bar. Minor, a regular at the club, began casually dating McClure in mid–1994. McClure occasionally came over for weekend sex in Minor's Malibu beachhouse and attended his industry parties there three or four times a week. Later, many of the promoter's friends claimed never to have met the woman. A close business associate discounted the stripper as "someone Charlie had a physical relationship with a few times, maybe six or seven times."

By late December 1994–early January 1995 Minor tired of McClure and severed their relationship. Casual sex with the stripper and others was replaced by a monogamous bi-coastal love affair with Dara Sowell, a strikingly beautiful blonde New York socialite. McClure, reeling from the split, received another shock when Bailey's Twenty/20 lost its lease and abruptly closed its doors on February 3, 1995. She quickly found employment at Fantasy Island, a second-tier strip club on West Pico Boulevard where $20 lap dances were offered to a mixed crowd of record industry personnel and college students. Depressed and possibly anorexic, McClure was fired from the club on March 17, 1995, for losing too much weight. Shortly after 8:00 A.M. on Sunday, March 19, 1995, McClure phoned Minor at his two-story Malibu beachhouse at 9624 Heather Road and asked to come over. Minor, who had refused to speak with his ex-lover for the past week, was lounging in bed with his new love, Dara Sowell. He instructed her not to and hung up. Around 11:22 A.M. the record promoter was making love to Sowell in the upstairs master bedroom when McClure, who had crept into the house through an unlocked door, appeared in the doorway. An angry Minor shouted at her to leave and McClure reluctantly did so, or so the couple thought. Forty minutes had passed since McClure's intrusion when Dara Sowell went downstairs for a glass of water. Sowell encountered an agitated McClure coming back up the stairs. The stripper had spent the intervening time cowering on all fours in a closet until discovered by a housemaid. Sowell let McClure pass and she went downstairs to the kitchen to give the couple time to resolve the uneasy situation. "I didn't want to embarrass Charlie," Sowell remembered. "He'd probably had a little fling with her, and he didn't need me standing around while they spoke. I thought she wanted to confront him about what he wanted to do with her." Sowell was in the kitchen for about 1½ minutes when she heard a commotion and gunshots. Upstairs on the landing outside the master bedroom an argument between the couple culminated in McClure pulling a .25-caliber semiautomatic handgun and pumping six or nine shots (accounts vary) into her former lover's head, neck, back and right arm. According to McClure's later police statement, Minor simply said "Ouch" before falling over dead. Sowell ran next door for help as a dazed McClure drove back to her condo in Santa Monica. On the landing next to Minor's body police found McClure's black vinyl fanny pack containing her driver's license and credit cards. McClure, appearing "quiet and calm," was quickly arrested at her Yale Street condo where police turned up the murder weapon lying in plain sight on the living room floor.

On March 22, 1995, in Hollywood, 1,600 friends and business associates attended a memorial service for the slain promo man held under a giant tent on a sound stage of A&M Records on La Brea Avenue. An estimated 2,000 people had to be turned away from paying their respects or from just gawking at the celebrity crowd. Letters from Minor's past clients including Sting, Janet Jackson, and Amy Grant were read during the service. For many, Canadian rocker Bryan Adams' letter summarized the sentiments of the assembled company. "Goodbye, Charlie," he wrote, "I hope that the records up there are as much fun to get played and that the girls take good care of you." As friends paid their last respects to Minor, McClure's court-appointed attorney, Deputy Public Defender Verah Bradford, portrayed her client as the "other victim" in the case. "Record promotion depends on the use of strippers and prostitutes, who are used as objects of pleasure and commercial bargaining chips," Bradford maintained. "We will prove that Suzette was a victim of the way wealthy men use women — and in the process, we'll blow the lid off the music industry." A defense psychologist characterized McClure as "the one bullet in a deadly game of Russian roulette" adding that the way Minor used women "any one of them could have snapped." Despite the pre-trial rhetoric, McClure cut a deal with the district attorney's office on May 15, 1997, agreeing to plead guilty to second-degree murder in exchange for a 19 year to life prison sentence and a $10,000 fine. Under the terms of the agreement, she must serve a minimum 85 percent of the sentence. The D.A.'s office offered the deal in October 1995 after a judge dismissed a special allegation of "lying in wait" (premeditation) as unproven that would have made McClure eligible for first-degree murder and the death penalty if convicted. At the formal sentencing in June 1997, the courtroom was filled with Minor's friends, among them several beautiful blondes, wearing photo buttons of the dead man. McClure quietly told the court, "I wish I'd known Charlie longer or maybe known him better and that I hadn't been misguided about where we were going." In a footnote to the case, Minor's family filed a "wrongful death" suit against Westec Security alleging that an improperly maintained security system allowed McClure entry into house. In May 1998 the company settled out of court for $150,000.

Further Reading

Wilkinson, Peter. "Death of a Salesman." *Rolling Stone*, 715 (August 24, 1995):58–60, 62–65.

Mintiks, Helen Hagnes *see* **Hagnes**, Helen

Mr. Cee (V)

A preacher's son who grew up on Ingalis Street just south of the Hunters Point housing projects in San Francisco, California, Hubert ("Kyle") Church, III, was just a boy when his father abandoned the family leaving him to be raised by a devoted extended family. His relatives were so religious that his friends from the projects nicknamed him "Church Boy." By three the youngster was playing drums and within two years was a fixture in the choir of his grandfather's church. In 1990, Church (street name Mr. Cee) started rapping with Chris (Black C) Matthews, a lifelong resident of the Hunters Point project who had recently lost an eye in a drive-by shooting. Calling themselves RBL Posse (Ruthless by Law), their first album, *Lesson to Be Learned*, was released in 1992 through local independent label In-A-Minute Records. With lyrics shaped by the dangerous futility of life in the ghetto, the album sold a phenomenal 229,000 copies. Friction, however, soon developed within the group after Douglas ("Boobie") Stepney, a childhood friend of Matthews' who appeared on the album cover and helped promote the record, was asked to leave the "posse." According to Stepney (who later formed his own music company, Big Block Productions), "They got some money and said they didn't want us around." The rap duo's second album released in October 1994 on In-A-Minute Records, *Ruthless By Law*, sustained their growing popularity racking up another 200,000 in sales for the independent label. RBL Posse was on the verge of signing a $1.5 million contract with national label Atlantic when Hunters Point reached out and claimed Mr. Cee.

Shortly after 5:00 P.M. on New Year's Day 1996, the 22-year-old rapper was talking with a friend on Harbor Road near the projects when an assailant wearing a hooded sweatshirt ran up to him, and squeezed off nine rounds from a black 9mm semiautomatic pistol into his body continuing to fire even as the fatally wounded man fell to the ground. Though many believed the rapper was targeted because of a turf war between rival gangs in the neighborhoods of Bayview and Hunters Point, or, as the result of a drug deal gone bad, Tony Jackson, RBL's manager concluded, "It was another case of being in the wrong place at the wrong time." In September 1997, Chris (Black C) Matthews, the remaining partner in RBL Posse, replaced Mr. Cee with Hitman for the RBL Atlantic debut album, *An Eye for an Eye*, featuring the track "Gone Away," a "requiem rap" for Mr. Cee. The album sold a disappointing 88,000 units nationwide. To date, the Mr. Cee murder remains unsolved.

Further Reading

Sward, Susan. "The Killing Streets." *San Francisco Chronicle*, December 16, 2001, sec. A, p. 1.

Mr. Livewire (V)

An aspiring local rapper and rock show promoter known professionally as Mr. Livewire, Dante R. Johnson was shot on December 17, 2003, as he and a passenger in his 1988 Chevy Blazer were driving onto an I-70 onramp in Denver. Johnson, hit three times with gunfire, lost control of the SUV and smashed into a guardrail shattering several bones in his passenger's body. Johnson died at Denver Health Medical Center on December 18, 1993, his 21st birthday, leaving a wife and three children under the age of two. A motive for the shooting was not determined.

Further Reading

Gutierrez, Hector. "Man Shot While Driving Dies." *Rocky Mountain News*, December 19, 2003, sec. A, p. 13.

Mitchell Brothers (M-V)

"The Potentates of Porn," brothers Jim and Artie Mitchell revolutionized the adult entertainment industry from the 1960s to the 1980s, with the 1969 opening of the infamous O'Farrell Theatre in San Francisco's notorious Tenderloin district, and later with their production of the erotic film classic *Behind the Green Door* in 1972. The Mitchells, a pair of true fun-loving eccentrics infamous for thumbing their noses at society, have achieved iconic status in the City by the Bay. The porn pioneers were the first to make sexually liberated films that couples could attend without embarrassment featuring attractive "girl-next-door" types like their discovery Marilyn Chambers. The sons of a professional gambler from Oklahoma and a school teacher from Arkansas, James Lowell Mitchell (born November 30, 1943 in Stockton, California) and Artie Jay Mitchell (born December 12, 1945 in Lodi, California) grew up in the blue-collar mill town of Antioch, 45 miles east of San Francisco. Jim joined the Army after graduating high school in 1961 largely to avoid becoming a drone in Antioch's steel and chemical industries. After his discharge in the mid–1960s, he took advantage of the G.I. Bill and enrolled at Diablo Valley College in Pleasant Valley, California, later transferring to San Francisco State. Though a political science major, Jim became more attracted to his minor in film studies, and was a devotee of French New Wave Cinema. As a doorman at the New Follies, an old-time burlesque house converted to show nudie films, Jim recognized an opportunity to realize his twin dreams of making money and films. Armed with a still camera and an overabundance of chutzpah, he began offering $10 each to San Francisco hippie girls in exchange for letting him take their pictures topless. The photos found a ready market among horny Bay area sailors set to go to sea on maneuvers.

The real money, however, was to be made in supplying nudie films to theatres like the New Follies and Roxie where the demand for fresh bodies was insatiable. Jim Mitchell took a 16mm camera to the Haight district and, in the sexually liberated atmosphere of late 1960s San Francisco, found several attractive "flower children" willing to earn $25 for "starring" in a ten-minute film showing and fondling their breasts. Not only was Jim paid $100 for each "loop," the contracting theatre also supplied the raw film and covered its processing fee. By the time Artie mustered out of the military and joined his successful brother in San Francisco in 1969, the Sexual Revolution had evolved to the point that Jim was no longer shooting tame nudies, but rather "beaver" films, so-called because they featured almost clinically gynecologic close-up shots of female genitalia. With lessening social and legal restrictions, the Mitchell brothers soon evolved into producing their own hard-core sex films to exhibit in their new business venture, the O'Farrell Theatre.

Located in the Tenderloin on the corner of Polk and O'Farrell Streets, the O'Farrell opened on July 4, 1969, and has since become a cultural landmark in San Francisco as well as a symbol of the sexual revolution in America. Spotlessly clean with plush seats and state of the art sound and lighting, the sex club was at the forefront of presenting what was permissible in adult entertainment, be it lap dancing or live sex. As such, the O'Farrell was constantly busted by local police on charges ranging from obscenity to prostitution, and the brothers took great relish in legally challenging, and winning, cases that essentially changed and expanded the legal definition of what constituted legal adult entertainment. In one memorable obscenity bust instigated by future San Francisco mayor Dianne Feinstein, then a porn crusader on the city's Board of Supervisors, the police shut down a live sex show at the O'Farrell. Typical of their anarchic sense of humor, the Mitchells displayed Feinstein's home phone number on the O'Farrell billboard with the instruction to call her "for show times." In another celebrated bust, porn star Marilyn Chambers was arrested at the theatre on February 2, 1985, while performing her "Feel the Magic" show after local officers allegedly witnessed members of the audience digitally penetrate the dancer and fondle her breasts. The case was later dismissed.

Jim and Artie ran their empire (at its height 11 porn palaces and 2 X-rated movie theatres) from the upstairs mezzanine office at the O'Farrell. Over the years, the office with its full-size pool table and bank of video monitors overseeing various parts of the club, became *the* gathering place for such countercultural types as gonzo journalist Hunter S. Thompson and Black Panther leader Huey Newton. It was in that office in 1971 that the brothers, at Jim's insistence, planned *Behind the Green Door*, a full-length feature film designed to play the O'Farrell. Marilyn Briggs, a fresh faced 19-year-old who had recently posed for an Ivory Snow box cover holding an infant, was signed for the sextravaganza and renamed Marilyn Chambers. Made on a budget of $60,000, the ambitious movie was shot on 16mm by former film studies

student Jim and directed (with a lot of input from his brother) by Artie. Premiered at the O'Farrell in 1972, *Behind the Green Door* ran 72 minutes, boasted higher production values than the usual porno feature, and seemingly expressed the sexual revolution of the 1960s. The film made Marilyn Chambers a superstar in the adult entertainment industry and grosses ($60 million by some estimates) went through the roof after the brothers disclosed its star was the innocent faced mother on the Ivory Snow box cover. Procter & Gamble quickly removed the box from store shelves replacing the "offensive" image of the porn star holding child with a stylized drawing of a mother holding her infant. *Behind the Green Door* made the Mitchell Brothers key players in the adult film industry packing theatres across the country and even playing at the Cannes Film Festival. Subsequent films by the brothers like *Resurrection of Eve* (1973), the pretentious *Sodom and Gomorrah: The Last Seven Days* (1975), and the commercially disastrous "safe sex" feature *Behind the Green Door— The Sequel* (1986) failed to realize the success of their landmark 1972 film that at least one critic has dubbed the "*Citizen Kane*" of porn movies.

While both Mitchells lived the bohemian lifestyle, Jim was universally recognized as the more serious and responsible of the brothers. As the 1980s progressed, "Party Artie," the perpetual adolescent, degenerated into a dangerously volatile substance abuser. A full-blown alcoholic, the drunk by noon Artie spent most of his time in the upstairs office at the O'Farrell indulging in a variety of drugs including coke, LSD, Ecstasy, and psychedelic mushrooms. Under the combined abuse of various substances, his behavior once seen as playfully humorous deteriorated into boorishness. No O'Farrell dancer was safe from Artie's drug-fuelled groping, and friends were routinely insulted and threatened. Jim, in the perpetual role of his brother's keeper, realized by 1990 that Artie needed professional help. Not surprisingly, Artie refused to enter rehab even as his behavior became more dangerous to himself and others. In one memorable episode, an enraged Artie shot up a poster in the second-floor office at the O'Farrell, earning an immediate banishment from the theatre by his older brother. By early 1991, Jim tried a new tactic to scare Artie into rehab. While, according to his attorney, Jim never meant to break up their 22 year partnership, he began pressuring Artie to divest his part of their business holdings. Jim, no longer interested in making movies, wanted to devote more of his time and money to the publication of *War News*, an anti–Gulf War newspaper, that he viewed as perhaps his last chance to do something worthwhile. Artie, already feeling intense pressure from a bitter custody battle with his third wife, reacted badly to Jim's ruse to buy him out of their partnership. In January 1991, Artie provided an impromptu middle of the afternoon floor show at Maye's Original Oyster House on Polk Street when he drunkenly lurched into the restaurant brandishing a loaded .38-caliber pistol.

Artie Mitchell, 45, spent the final day of his life, February 27, 1991, making a series of threatening phone calls. In the early afternoon, he phoned Jim, 47, and angrily berated his older brother for hiding behind an attorney to end their partnership rather than confronting him face-to-face. Around 6:30 P.M., Artie called his mother, Georgia Mae, to complain about Jim, screaming "I'd like to take my gun, put it between his eyes, and pull the trigger." After Artie rang off, Georgia Mae was so concerned she immediately called a hospital in Sacramento to inquire about having her son committed for drug and alcohol problems. Artie, however, saved his most threatening phone call for Jim and his live-in lover, Lisa Adams, a former dancer turned secretary at the O'Farrell. Later that evening, Jim and Adams returned to their home near San Francisco's Ocean Beach to find a slurred message from Artie on the answering machine: "Hey Mr. Perfect. It's your brother, Mr. Perfect. You're so bad I had to call Mother about you. You promised your girlfriend you were going to quit smoking but you haven't. Those cigarettes are going to take twenty years off your life. But don't worry, I'm going to kill you first, motherfucker!" Concerned Artie had access to guns, Jim decided over Adams' objections to drive over to his brother's house in Corte Madera to confiscate them. Before doing so, he armed himself with a .22-caliber rifle, and strapped on a shoulder holster containing a .38 Smith & Wesson Chief's Special. His plan — have Rocky Davidson, a cousin and custodian at the O'Farrell, and Dr. Skip Dossett, a physician at an alcohol treatment facility in downtown San Francisco, meet him at Artie's to help him handle the drug addict.

Shortly after 10:00 P.M., Jim met with Davidson on the street near Artie's modest three-bedroom home at 23 Mohawk Drive. Deciding not to wait for Dr. Dossett, Jim first punctured the tires on Artie's car (ostensibly to keep his brother from driving away), then entered the house to "scare" him. According to Julie Bajo, Artie's live-in lover, they were in bed together when they heard gunshots in the living room. Artie picked up a makeshift weapon, a Heineken bottle, and went into the darkened living room to investigate while Bajo dialed 911 from inside a closet. The former O'Farrell dancer was on the line when she heard more gunshots. Police responded shortly after 10:18 P.M. and without incident arrested Jim Mitchell "walking away awkwardly" down Mohawk Avenue, the 22-caliber rifle stuffed down a pant leg. According to the arresting officer, Jim had the most desperate look he had ever seen on a human face. Inside the house, police found seven .22-caliber shell casings on the floor and Artie's body in the bathroom. "Party Hearty Artie" had been shot once in the abdomen, once in the shoulder, with the fatal shot entering through his eye into the brain. A coroner's report determined that while Artie had no drugs in his system at the time of his death, his blood alcohol level was .25, more than three times the legal limit to drive in California.

People familiar with the Mitchells were shocked by news of Artie's death at the hands of his brother. The pair had always been close and, in March 1990, Jim had literally saved Artie from drowning in a surfing accident at Ocean Beach in San Francisco. Everyone had watched helplessly as Artie's spiral into alcohol and drugs angered and embarrassed his brother who had done all he could to try and help. Marilyn Chambers, the star they had created in *Behind the Green Door*, put the latter day Cain and Abel story into sharp perspective — "Artie lived on the screaming edge of insanity, and that can never last for long." At trial in January 1992 in the Marin County Superior Court Jim Mitchell faced a 30 years to life sentence if convicted of first-degree murder. Mitchell's attorney, Michael Kennedy, never disputed Jim fired the fatal shots that killed Artie. The distinction, Kennedy insisted, was between "killing" (which Jim did) and "murder" (which Jim did not do). Legally, the distinction meant the difference between a murder rap with serious prison time or manslaughter with a greatly reduced sentence. Kennedy characterized the shooting as an "intervention gone awry" with Jim on a mission "to save Artie from himself." Testimony from numerous witnesses, including the brothers' mother, chronicled in minute detail Artie's degeneration from a fun-loving party animal to a weirdly belligerent out-of-control drunk. An O'Farrell employee testified that less than one month before the shooting, Artie had viciously kicked his lover, Julie Bajo, in her surgically repaired knee. Witnesses were unanimous in declaring none had seen Artie sober in over a year. Lisa Adams, Jim's girlfriend, related to the court that Artie viewed her as the source of the trouble between the brothers, and had repeatedly threatened to "blow her brains out."

Arguing that Jim killed his brother "in cold blood ... with malice aforethought," the prosecution averred that the number of weapons Jim took with him (rifle, pistol, knife, bullets) proved he was ready to "go to war." Utilizing a computer-generated animation to re-enact the crime (a first in a criminal trial) in conjunction with the audiotape of Bajo's 911 call to police, the district attorney pointed to a 28 second gap (demonstrating premeditation) before Jim fired the final, fatal shot to Artie's eye. The motive? Jim was tired of his brother's drug-induced antics and sought to profit by Artie's death by being named as a co-trustee of the dead man's estate. Five weeks into the trial, Jim Mitchell testified that the only reason he went to his brother's house that night was to calm him down and to take away his guns. Jim remembered firing a single shot into the ceiling after seeing Artie approach him in the darkness with what appeared to be a gun (the Heineken bottle), but could remember nothing else until being stopped by police on the street outside the house. The temporary memory loss, termed "psychogenic amnesia" by mental health professionals, often occurs as the result of an unexpected traumatic event. The high point of Jim's testimony, however, was undoubtedly when he quietly told the packed courtroom that he would willingly trade places with his brother. In his closing argument, defense attorney Michael Kennedy eloquently restated his thesis that the killing was not a murder, but a voluntary manslaughter (defined in California law as a willful killing done in the heat of passion). The jury of 9 men, 3 women deliberated just two days before returning on February 19, 1992, with a verdict agreeing with Kennedy's interpretation of the case — voluntary manslaughter committed in the "heat of passion" without premeditation. Despite receiving letters asking for leniency from top San Francisco politicos (Mayor Frank Jordan, Police Chief Richard Hongisto, Supervisor Terrence Hallinan, Sheriff Michael Hennessey), Marin County Superior Court Judge Richard

Breiner sentenced Jim Mitchell to 6 years on April 24, 1992. "I can not make my decision in this case as if this were a popularity contest." Breiner ruled. "The gravity of the crime itself— killing a human being — compels me to impose a prison sentence." Mitchell managed to remain free on bail for 3 years while appealing his sentence on a procedural consideration, but ultimately was sent to San Quentin on October 26, 1994. According to a San Quentin spokesperson, Inmate J388838 distinguished himself as a "discipline-free, conforming inmate" who "did what he needed to do." Mitchell was released on October 3, 1997, but placed on parole for the next three years during which time he was ordered to meet with a parole officer, submit to drug testing, not drink alcohol, and to see a therapist. In a brazen example of Hollywood gimmickry, the tragic story of the Mitchell Brothers was the subject of the 2000 motion picture *Rated X* directed by and starring Emilio Estevez, along with his real life brother Charlie Sheen. Sheen, at the time a tabloid poster-child for drug use and an illicit sex-charged lifestyle, played Artie opposite his brother's portrayal of Jim. On July 12, 2007, Jim Mitchell, 63, died of a heart attack at his ranch near Petaluma, California, in western Sonoma County. He was buried next to Artie at Cherokee Memorial Park in Lodi, California.

Further Reading

English, J. T. "Cain and Abel in the Skin Trade." *Esquire*, 115(6) (June 1991):33, 35, 126–28.
Hubner, John. *Bottom Feeders: From Free Love to Hard Core: The Rise and Fall of Counter-Culture Gurus Jim and Artie Mitchell.* New York: Doubleday, 1993.
Martin, Douglas. "Jim Mitchell, 63, Filmmaker; Made 'Behind the Green Door.'" *The New York Times*, July 19, 2007, sec. B, p. 7.
McCumber, David. *X-Rated: The Mitchell Brothers: A True Story of Sex, Money, and Death.* New York: Simon & Schuster, 1992.

Mizell, Jason William *see* **Jam Master Jay**

Monday, Jerry (M-S)

A twenty year veteran of radio, 15 at Gospel-formatted 1450 WLAF-AM in LaFollette, Tennessee, the popular deejay hosted the 5:00–9:00 A.M. weekday morning call-in show, "The World's Famous Trading Post," featuring items listeners wanted to buy, sell, or give away. Monday also served as weatherman on Channel 4, WLAF's cable access television station. Friends knew that Monday and Esties, his wife of four years, were experiencing marital problems so they were concerned when he failed to show up for work at the station on December 5, 2003. Campbell County authorities entered the couple's home on Wildwood Circle in LaFollette that morning to discover that Monday had first shot his wife then turned the gun on himself in a classic murder-suicide scenario.

Further Reading

"Deejay, Wife Dead in Murder-Suicide." *Knoxville News-Sentinel*, December 8, 2003, sec. B, p. 7.

Monroe, Marilyn (V-suspected)

Accident, suicide, or murder? Nearly a half century after the death of the Hollywood star speculation continues unabated regarding the events surrounding her untimely, if not tragically predictable, passing at 36 on August 5, 1962. Depressed, lonely, and addicted to barbiturates, Marilyn Monroe was at a career crossroads. Fired by 20th Century–Fox days before her death, the emotionally fragile star also faced an uncertain personal future. According to numerous biographies written by champions of the "murder conspiracy theory," Monroe was conducting simultaneous affairs with President John F. Kennedy and his younger brother, Attorney General Robert F. Kennedy. As rumors of the illicit relationships spread and Monroe became a potentially explosive political liability, the Kennedys severed their connection with the star. Allegedly, the spurned Monroe planned to publicly announce the affairs as a form of retribution against the powerful brothers. Most of the conspiracies positing her murder by various governmental agencies (C.I.A., FBI) or outside contractors (the Mafia) all share in common the notion Monroe had to be silenced before she could harm the Kennedys. More traditional biographers simply see in the star's death a woman too tired and emotionally damaged by the industry and those around her to sustain the will necessary to continue living. Whatever may be the case (accidental death, suicide, murder) Marilyn Monroe remains the instantly recognizable iconic face of Hollywood throughout the world.

The future film goddess was born Norma Jeane Mortenson in Los Angeles on June 1, 1926, the illegitimate daughter of Gladys Pearl Monroe Mortenson and an unidentified man. While the identity of her father has never been positively established, Monroe believed it was the manager at the Consolidated Film Laboratories where her mother worked as a negative cutter. The Mortenson family had a history of mental illness. Monroe's grandmother died in a mental asylum in 1927. In January 1934 her mother, Gladys Mortenson (née Baker) was diagnosed as a paranoid schizophrenic and institutionalized for the remainder of her daughter's life. Her mother's institutionalization signaled the beginning of lifelong feelings of insecurity and self-doubt for the eight-year-old child. Monroe was made a ward of the County of Los Angeles and placed with a series of foster parents who were given a stipend of $20 a month for her care. At one facility, she was molested by an elderly man who afterward gave her a nickel "not to tell." The child was not believed when she reported the incident.

Largely to avoid placement with yet another set of foster parents, the 16-year-old Van Nuys High School student married James Edward Dougherty, a 21-year-old metal worker at Lockheed Aircraft in Westwood on June 19, 1942. The couple had little in common and rarely spoke. Norma Jeane Dougherty dropped out of school and, after her husband joined the U.S. Merchant Marines in early 1944, took a $20 a week job as a parachute inspector at a defense plant in the San Fernando Valley. David Conover, an Army photographer assigned to shoot a feature on the women of the war for *Yank* magazine "discovered" the alluring 18 year old working on the assembly line. Conover's photos of the teenager captured a sensually innocent young woman with a lush physique perfectly at ease in front of a camera. After Norma Jeane confided to Conover she longed to be a model, the photographer shot some studies of her in the Mojave Desert for her portfolio. Soon after the photos were seen, she quit her job at the defense plant and signed a contract with the Blue Book Model Agency in Hollywood. Under the direction of Emmeline Snively, head of the agency, she became a full-time model and began making cover appearances on second-tier magazines like *Click*, *See*, and *Laff*.

Through Snively's contacts in the motion picture business, Norma Jeane Dougherty came to the attention of studio casting executive Ben Lyon. Impressed by the curvaceous teen, Lyon signed her to a $75 a week stock contract with 20th Century–Fox in September 1946. Lyon instantly changed the new contract player's name to the more glamorous sounding Marilyn Monroe. On October 2, 1946, just weeks after gaining financial independence with her Fox contract, Monroe divorced James Dougherty while he was overseas. She continued to pose for cheesecake photographers while taking acting and diction lessons at the studio.

In 1948, the actress made her first film appearance in a microscopic part in *Scudda Hoo! Scudda Hay!* Later in the year she was cast as a waitress in the juvenile delinquency exploitation drama *Dangerous Years*. Also in 1948 she met the first of several powerful older men who helped her career. Joe Schenck, co-founder with Darryl F. Zanuck of 20th Century–Fox, was an executive producer in his seventies when he saw the sexy young Monroe walking on the studio lot. He invited her to the regular Sunday afternoon brunches at his home where she became a welcome fixture. Whether Monroe's relationship with the septuagenarian producer was sexual or platonic has long been debated. Schenck did use his considerable influence to get her signed with Columbia Pictures on March 9, 1948, after Fox dropped her contract. Monroe appeared in only one Columbia film, the ingénue lead in the 1948 musical *Ladies of the Chorus*, before the studio dropped her option six months later on September 8, 1948. According to Hollywood legend, the actress was let go after refusing to sleep with studio head Harry Cohn. However, a comparable Hollywood legend maintains that she did. Monroe fared a little better in a sexy walk-on role in the 1949 Marx Brothers romp *Love Happy*, but still could not find steady film work.

In the summer of 1949, following her dismissal from Columbia, Monroe was unemployed and desperate for money. Sporting long, curly reddish-brown hair, the out-of-work actress posed in a swimsuit for a Pabst Blue Ribbon billboard ad shot by photographer Tom Kelley. Initially declining his offer to pose naked, Monroe returned a few days later and agreed to pose lying on red velvet because she needed the $50 fee to pay her rent. Kelley sold the color shots and complete reproduction rights to a lithographer who featured the nude Monroe on a calendar. Chicago-based publisher Hugh Hefner later featured the nude shot in the inaugural issue of *Playboy* in 1953. An upcoming star at the time of the provocative photo's publication, Monroe was not adversely affected by its publication. Her explanation, "I was hungry," silenced the critics.

Around October 1949, the 22-year-old actress was discovered by Johnny Hyde, executive vice

president of the William Morris Agency, who was taken with her cameo in *Love Happy*. The 53-year-old talent agent responsible for directing the careers of cinema sex queens Rita Hayworth and Veronica Lake fell madly in love with Monroe. Hyde, suffering from heart disease, left his wife and family to devote his entire energy to building his young lover's career. The smitten agent transformed Monroe into "the Blonde" icon known throughout the world. Under his direction, she learned how to dress and had plastic surgery done on her nose and jaw. In 1950 Hyde landed Monroe the second female lead in the Mickey Rooney film *The Fireball*. That same year Hyde convinced his client, director John Huston, to cast his protégé as the secretary-mistress to Louis Calhern's shady lawyer in MGM's crime drama *The Asphalt Jungle*. On the strength of Monroe's sizzling portrayal in the film, Hyde negotiated a seven year contract for her with 20th Century–Fox in December 1950. Weeks after closing the deal, Hyde suffered a fatal heart attack on December 17, 1950, the day Monroe began filming *As Young as You Feel* (1951). Many in Hollywood felt Hyde had literally worked himself to death promoting Monroe's career. Despite a request by Hyde's family not to attend the funeral service at Forest Lawn, a distraught Monroe did so and threw herself screaming across his casket. In his 1984 biography *Legend: The Life and Death of Marilyn Monroe*, Fred Lawrence Guiles reports that shortly after the funeral the young star attempted suicide while staying at the home of her friend and drama coach Natasha Lytess. Returning early from a day of shopping, Lytess found a note pinned to Monroe's bedroom door that read, "Don't let Barbara [Lytess' four-year-old daughter] in." The drama coach found the actress unconscious in bed, her mouth filled with a purplish paste — some thirty half-dissolved Nembutal tablets.

In 1950, Monroe appeared in a small but memorable role as "Miss Caswell," the aspiring actress-girlfriend of theatre critic "Addison DeWitt" (George Sanders) in *All About Eve*. Throughout the early 1950s the studio carefully increased Monroe's acting duties including appearances in five movies in 1952: *Clash by Night*, *We're Not Married*, *Don't Bother to Knock*, *Monkey Business*, and *O. Henry's Full House*. In 1953, Monroe appeared in *Niagra*, the film that made her a star and cemented her image as the screen's quintessential sex goddess. Cast as an adulterous wife with murderous intent, Monroe stole the picture undulating in a skintight red satin dress. *The New York Times* reviewer noted, "The producers are making full use of both the grandeur of the Falls and its adjacent areas as well as the grandeur that is Marilyn Monroe," adding, "The Falls and Miss Monroe are something to see." The star's two 1953 follow-up movies, the hugely successful *Gentlemen Prefer Blondes* and *How to Marry a Millionaire*, typecast her as filmdom's "dumb blonde," a persona that rankled the actress and was at odds with her off-screen attempts to better herself through the study of literature.

During her suspension at Fox for refusing to star in the film *Heller in Pink Tights*, Monroe married retired New York Yankees baseball legend Joe DiMaggio in a civil ceremony in San Francisco on January 14, 1954. "The Yankee Clipper," then arguably the most famous baseball player in the world, was 12 years older than Monroe and insanely jealous of the star. Following a brief honeymoon in Paso Robles, the couple traveled to Japan where DiMaggio was regarded as a national idol. Cheering crowds at the airport, however, barely noticed the man on the arm of Marilyn Monroe. Angered over the slight, DiMaggio argued with his wife about her commitment to entertain U.S. Army troops stationed in Korea. As the baseball great fumed alone in Tokyo, Monroe was onstage in Korea provocatively performing in front of 100,000 screaming soldiers. Their marriage was already on the rocks when she agreed to do the Billy Wilder–directed comedy *The Seven Year Itch* (1955). An intensely private man, DiMaggio despised the show biz crowd and, in his unwillingness to accommodate Monroe's career in any fashion, wanted her to be his wife full-time.

The situation reached its crisis during location shooting in New York City in September 1954. In order to shoot the film's most famous scene, Monroe standing over a Times Square subway grating, Wilder started shooting at 2:30 A.M. and closed down an entire city block around Lexington Avenue and 51st Street. Even at that hour, a thousand raucous spectators had to be restrained behind police barricades. Blowers were installed under the grating to simulate the breeze generated by a passing subway train. Unknown to the cast and crew, DiMaggio arrived unannounced from the coast to watch the filming. As the scene was shot, he watched in silent rage as his wife's pleated sundress was blown up around her waist to reveal a pair of scant ivory colored panties. The marriage was over nine months after it began. Shortly after the film wrapped, Monroe entered Cedars of Lebanon Hospital for gynecological surgery (some sources say to abort DiMaggio's child). On October 3, 1954, she filed for divorce from the baseball legend citing mental cruelty. At the hearing Monroe told the judge, "I was allowed to have no visitors: maybe three times in the nine months we were married. Once when I was sick he did allow someone to come and see me. The relationship was one of coldness and indifference." Monroe was granted an interlocutory divorce decree on October 27, 1954, although she and DiMaggio remained close friends.

Dating from this period, Monroe started seeing a psychiatrist five times a week until her death in 1962. In January 1955, the popular actress walked out on Fox, defiantly resisting the studio's attempt to stereotype her in fluff like *The Revolt of Mamie Stover*, *How to Be Very, Very Popular*, and *The Girl in the Red Velvet Swing*. She went to New York, formed Marilyn Monroe Productions, and began to seriously study acting under Lee and Paula Strasberg at the Actors Studio. While mingling with the intellectual New York City set she became playwright Arthur Miller's unlikely lover. In January 1956, Monroe returned to Hollywood and signed a lucrative seven year non-exclusive, multi-picture deal with 20th Century–Fox. Under the terms of the contract, the actress was paid $100,000 a picture and given director, script, cameraman, and make-up man approval. In 1956, Monroe received good reviews for her sensitive performance in Joshua Logan's film version of *Bus Stop*, a play by William Inge. On June 29, 1956, shortly before leaving for England to star opposite Laurence Olivier in *The Prince and the Showgirl*, the actress married Arthur Miller after converting to Judaism.

The Olivier-directed film was intended to expand Monroe's range as an actress. Instead, it proved to be a career and personal debacle. The classically trained Olivier was unsympathetic to the hours Monroe spent on-camera burning film searching for her character's "motivation." At other times, production stalled while cast and crew were forced to await the arrival of the chronically late box office star. Olivier considered the popular American actress as little more than a "troublesome bitch." Monroe, at odds with Olivier, turned to Miller for support. The playwright, however, was also disenchanted with the manner in which she interacted with Olivier and by her lack of professionalism on the set. Monroe went over the edge after discovering a secret diary Miller was keeping about their marriage. In it, he denigrated his wife and accused her of making "love a drudgery." Monroe suffered a nervous breakdown near the end of filming that necessitated her psychiatrist to be flown from New York to London so she could complete the film. Miller returned alone to New York. Frustrated, Monroe sharply increased her intake of champagne and sleeping pills to combat chronic insomnia. Not surprisingly, given the conditions under which it was made, *The Prince and the Showgirl* received bad reviews. More strain was put on the faltering marriage after the actress suffered a miscarriage on August 1, 1957.

In July 1958, Monroe again teamed with Billy Wilder to begin shooting *Some Like It Hot* (1959) with Tony Curtis and Jack Lemmon. Unfailingly late to the set and usually unprepared once she got there, Monroe alienated everyone on the film. Tony Curtis, disgusted by his buxom co-star's demands for multiple retakes, later said making love to her was like "kissing Hitler." Interviewed years later about Monroe, Curtis said that the sexy star created so much tension on the set that "nobody wanted to talk to her." Five days before filming wrapped on November 6, 1958, the 32-year-old actress collapsed on the set. Rushed to hospital, she was informed she had once again miscarried.

Trouble in the Monroe-Miller became even more pronounced while the star was shooting *Let's Make Love* (1960) with French star Yves Montand, husband of actress Simone Signoret. Monroe, deeply in love with Montand, began an affair with the actor during the film's production. Convinced he would leave Signoret, Monroe was crushed when Montand refused to do so and further dismissed her affections for him as a "school-girl crush." Montand later ungallantly told the press that his co-star was a "sick lady" who "threw herself at me." Seventeen days after *Let's Make Love* wrapped, Monroe reported for work in Reno, Nevada, to begin filming Arthur Miller's *The Misfits*. Directed by John Huston and starring Monroe's idol, Clark Gable, the film was destined to be the final screen appearance for both megastars. Temperatures in the desert where most of the film was shot soared to more than 100 degrees daily and physically punished the cast and crew. By mutual agreement, Miller and Monroe decided to postpone their divorce until after the film was com-

pleted. Still, Monroe openly argued with Miller over the script, which he refused to change to accommodate the subtleties of her character. During the shooting, the actress was hospitalized for an overdose of sleeping pills and exhaustion. On November 16, 1960, 12 days before the end of shooting, Clark Gable, 61, died of a heart attack brought on by the physical demands of the film. She divorced Miller in Cindad Juárez, Mexico, on January 20, 1961, one week before the film's opening.

Depressed, totally exhausted, and dangerously abusing alcohol and sedatives, Monroe required institutionalization less than one month after the film's premiere. Believing her psychiatrist was only going to check her into a rest home, Monroe was floored when she was admitted under the name "Faye Miller" into New York's Payne-Whitney Hospital, a psychiatric facility for highly disturbed mental patients. In the hospital's atmosphere of locked down wards and padded walls, Monroe descended into hysteria and begged to be released. It took three days, but ex-husband Joe DiMaggio stepped in and had her transferred to a private room in the Neurological Institute, a unit of Columbia-Presbyterian Hospital. Monroe remained there for three weeks resting and withdrawing from pills. Shortly after being released, the actress was recuperating in her New York City apartment at East 57th Street when she became suicidal after reading a newspaper interview with Clark Gable's widow. Kay Gable claimed Monroe's erratic behavior on the set prolonged *The Misfits* for weeks, thereby contributing to her husband's death. Guilt-ridden, Monroe reportedly opened the window in her apartment and was seriously considering jumping when, at the last moment, she recognized someone on the street below she thought she knew. Friends hurriedly moved her out of the apartment and back to Hollywood where she purchased a one-story hacienda-style bungalow at 12305 Fifth Helena Drive in Brentwood. Monroe's psychiatrist, Dr. Ralph Greenson, hired live-in housekeeper Eunice Murray to monitor his patient's condition.

In early April 1962 Fox scheduled Monroe to start work on *Something's Got to Give* co-starring Dean Martin. Unhappy with the script, she delayed production until April 23, 1962. Claiming physical illness, the actress had spent only six partial days on the set by May 1962. Against studio orders, Monroe flew to New York City to appear at President John F. Kennedy's birthday party at Madison Square Garden on May 19, 1962. The pair met in November 1961 at a private dinner at the beach house of actor Peter Lawford, husband of Pat Kennedy, John's sister. Lawford, a member of the Rat Pack led by Monroe's one-time lover, Frank Sinatra, acted as the couple's "pimp" arranging trysts for them at his home. Monroe fell deeply in love with the president and naively hoped he would one day divorce wife Jacqueline and marry her. At Kennedy's celebration, Monroe (dressed in a tight fitting sequined gown that left little to the imagination) wowed the crowd with a breathy rendition of "Happy Birthday, Mr. President." After the Madison Square Garden event, rumors ran rampant that the president and the movie star were having an affair. Monroe's frequent calls to the White House and to President Kennedy's private number at the Justice Department made her a distinct security risk. The actress was already on the FBI grid because of her association with Sinatra and his connections with the Chicago Mafia which, many believe, manipulated the vote in Cook County to give Kennedy the win in the 1960 presidential election. The actress was ordered not to contact the president and, according to which writer one reads, Robert Kennedy was charged with explaining the situation to Monroe. According to various writers, Attorney General Robert Kennedy was either already sexually involved with the actress, or, became so during the process of disentangling his brother from the politically disastrous relationship. In any event, Monroe was devastated when she learned her association with the Kennedys was at an end. Again, accounts differ wildly, but Monroe allegedly intimated to friends (including Peter Lawford) she planned to announce at an upcoming press conference her amorous connection to the Kennedys. Conspiracy theorists point to the spurned star's threatened act of retribution as one of the catalysts for her murder by elements within the government (C.I.A., FBI), or, contracted by the government to an outside contractor (the Mafia) seeking to eliminate the source of a threat to the president and his brother. Murder theories ranging from the possible (various permutations of the Kennedys' involvement) to the fantastic (the killing was part of the government's cover-up of the alien landings in Roswell, New Mexico) are summarized in Adam Victor's *The Marilyn Encyclopedia* (1999), and British author Paul Donnelley briefly lists eleven theories in his primer, *Marilyn Monroe* (2000).

Rebuffed by the president, Monroe returned to Hollywood and the set of *Something's Got to Give* where she celebrated her 36th birthday on June 1, 1962. Still complaining of illness, the star managed to film a nude pool scene but little else. Fox executives pulled the plug on the production and fired Marilyn Monroe on June 7, 1962 citing "willful violation of contract." The actress continued to suffer from insomnia, deepening depression, and was meeting daily with her psychiatrist, Dr. Ralph Greenson. Depending upon which of the three hundred plus biographies one reads, the actress was also frantic to reestablish contact with President Kennedy and his brother, Robert. The final 24 hours of Monroe's life have, and will continue to be, the source of endless speculation. Again, numerous theories running the gamut from murder to accidental death (overdose by her psychiatrist) to suicide have been advanced to explain the death of the 36-year-old movie queen. Sloppy police work, discrepancies in the autopsy and toxicology reports, and the passage of time have conspired to render the true nature of Monroe's death unknowable at this point.

On August 4, 1962, Monroe spent the day at her Brentwood home speaking to friends on the phone. Dr. Ralph Greenson left at 7:00 P.M. after heavily tranquilizing the star. Around 8:00 P.M. Peter Lawford phoned to convince her to spend the evening with him and his wife, Pat. According to Lawford, the actress was despondent and tired, and her speech was slurred. As Monroe's voice became less and less audible, Lawford started shouting in an attempt to revive her. Monroe finally told him, "Say good-bye to Pat, say good-bye to Jack [President Kennedy], and say good-bye to yourself because you're a nice guy," and hung up. Around midnight companion-housekeeper Eunice Murray noticed a light under Monroe's bedroom door. Murray, however, became alarmed when the light was still on at 3:00 A.M. and a phone cord from Monroe's private line now led under the closed door of the room. Murray listened, heard nothing, and banged on Monroe's door. Unable to rouse the star, she went outside to look in through the bedroom window. She saw the nude Monroe lying motionless in the bed clutching a phone receiver. Hurrying inside, Murray phoned Dr. Greenson. When Greenson arrived around 3:30 A.M., he broke the bedroom window with a fireplace poker and entered the room. He notified Monroe's physician, Dr. Hyman Engelberg, who arrived around 3:50 A.M. to confirm the star was dead. Police were not notified until around 4:30 A.M. Fifteen bottles of medication, including an empty bottle of prescription Nembutal, were found on a bedside table near the body, but no glass with which to wash them down. Death was officially pronounced at 3:45 A.M. on August 5, 1962. Conspiracists accuse the LAPD of involvement in a cover-up noting Monroe's phone records were confiscated suggesting authorities either sought to protect Robert Kennedy (said to have visited Monroe on August 4) or to use as potential fodder for blackmail.

Deputy Medical Examiner Dr. Thomas Noguchi conducted the Monroe autopsy, which was characterized by numerous discrepancies. Although there was a high concentration of barbiturates in her bloodstream, the equivalent of between forty to fifty pills, her small intestine where the pills would be dissolved was not tested due to "lack of facilities." No pill residue was found in her stomach or any other internal organs suggesting the pills had not been ingested orally. Murder theorists suggest the lethal overdose of barbiturates was injected, pointing to a bruise low down on Monroe's back as a possible injection site. Noguchi, however, failed to make any note of needle marks in his initial report only remembering the suspicious bruise in 1985. Another theory posits the fatal dose of barbiturates was administered by enema. The autopsy revealed the colon had "marked congestion and purplish discoloration." Monroe's death was recorded as a "probable suicide." Joe DiMaggio took charge of his ex-wife's funeral at the Westwood Village Funeral Chapel on August 9, 1962. Per his instructions, her show business friends (Sinatra *et al.*) were barred from the small private service. Actors Studio head Lee Strasberg delivered the eulogy, calling the star "a symbol of the eternal feminine." *The Los Angeles Herald-Examiner* reported that the funeral "ended with fans playing their usual roles of desecration as they stormed the vault after the mourners had departed to ruthlessly rip to pieces the floral offerings for 'souvenirs.'" The world's greatest star was interred in a wall crypt in Westwood Memorial Park, Corridor of Memories, #24. A bronze identification plate reads simply, "Marilyn Monroe — 1926–1962."

Further Reading

Donnelley, Paul. *Marilyn Monroe*. Harpenden: Pocket Essentials, 2000.
Guiles, Fred Lawrence. *Legend: The Life and Death of Marilyn Monroe*. New York: Stein and Day, 1984.
_____. *Norma Jean: The Life of Marilyn Monroe*. New York: McGraw-Hill, 1969.
Mailer, Norman. *Marilyn, a Biography*. New York: Grosset and Dunlap, 1973.
Monroe, Marilyn. *My Story*. New York: Stein and Day, 1974.
Shevey, Saundra. *The Marilyn Scandal: Her True Life Revealed by Those Who Knew Her*. New York: W. Morrow, 1987.
Spoto, Donald. *Marilyn Monroe: The Biography*. New York: HarperCollins, 1993.
Summers, Anthony. *Goddess: The Secret Lives of Marilyn Monroe*. New York: Macmillan, 1985.
Victor, Adam. *The Marilyn Encyclopedia*. Woodstock, NY: Overlook, 1999.

Morelle, Denise (V)

The popular Canadian actress (born in Montreal in 1927) was a versatile performer equally at home in films (*Don't Let It Kill You*, 1967; *Once Upon a Time in the East*, 1974; *L'Amour blesse*, 1975; *The Late Blossom*, 1977) and theatrical productions (*Bonjour, là, Bonjour*; *L'Impromptu d'Outremont*). It was, however, as the hysterical opera diva "Dame Plume" on the late 1960s children's afternoon television show, *La Ribouldingue*, that Morelle became an instantly recognizable and beloved figure in Quebec. As a member of the National Arts Centre's French ensemble under director André Brassard, she was scheduled to appear in the premiere of *Albertine, en cinqs temps* in a role Michel Tremblay had written specially for her, when a tragic confluence of random coincidences resulted in Morelle's brutal death.

On July 17, 1984, the 59-year-old actress visited a ground-floor flat she was considering renting on Sanguinet Street in central Montreal. The landlord, unable to meet Morelle at the apartment, gave her permission to view the unlocked residence alone. The next day, friends reported the actress missing to police after she failed to appear for her stage performance in *Ste. Adele*. Authorities found Morelle's body in the empty flat savagely beaten with an iron bar which had shattered her nose, jaw, and skull. The killer had heated the bar on a gas stove and sadistically burned her before raping then strangling her to death with a rope. Montreal police collected liquids from the scene and sent the specimens to a DNA bank in Ottawa where they failed to match any samples on file from known criminals. Meanwhile, more than 1,000 friends, family, and mourners gathered at St. Clement's Roman Catholic Church in Montreal's east-end for a memorial service for the beloved actress.

The Morelle murder remained unsolved, but not forgotten, by Montreal police for 23 years until the department's collaboration in April 2007 with the producers of a French language television network documentary on the case aired and finally yielded the tip authorities needed to make an arrest in August 2007. Using advancements in DNA, cold case detectives matched the sample taken at the Morelle crime scene in 1984 with a specimen collected in 2006 from a "solved" rape. In both instances, the perpetrator was Gaétan Bissonnette, a 49-year-old lifelong junkie whose criminal career between 1976 and 2006 was comprised of an unbroken record of 19 convictions for offenses like theft and breaking and entering. Two months after the discovery of Morelle's savaged body, Bissonnette was convicted of breaking into a woman's apartment and raping her at knifepoint over a seven-hour period. Remarkably, the career criminal received only a three year sentence, but the DNA sample from this case led to Bissonnette being charged for first-degree murder in the Morelle homicide.

Confronted with the irrefutable DNA evidence, Bissonnette accepted the Crown's offer to allow him to escape trial in exchange for a guilty plea to second-degree murder with its mandatory life sentence, but with the possibility of parole. As Bissonnette supplied details of his deadly 1984 encounter with the actress it became painfully aware to everyone that the murder had sprung from pure coincidence, a simple matter of a person having been in the wrong place at the wrong time. Bissonnette, 26 at the time, was squatting in the vacant unlocked apartment when Morelle entered the flat to view it for possible rental. While the Crown and Bissonnette's lawyer had previously agreed on the life sentence with no eligibility of parole for at least 14 years, Justice James Brunton took just twenty minutes to overturn the joint sentencing suggestion observing that it was not "harsh enough" given the seriousness of the crime. In a later proceeding, Bissonnette was ordered to serve 20 years before the possibility of being declared parole eligible in 2027.

Further Reading

Montgomery, Sue. "Justice After 23 Years." *Montreal Gazette,* November 17, 2007, sec. A, p. 8.

Morgan, (Edward) Lee (V)

Incredibly prolific during a 33-year life marred by drug addiction, Morgan is universally recognized as among hard bop's greatest jazz trumpeters. Born in Philadelphia on July 10, 1938, Morgan formed his own group with bassist James "Spanky" DeBrest and both attended weekday workshops at the Music City club where he met jazz trumpeters like Clifford Brown and Miles Davis. After graduating high school, Morgan and DeBrest filled in for a couple of missing players in Art Blakey's Jazz Messengers with the bassist agreeing to stay on in the group. Unwilling to sign a contract, Morgan joined Dizzy Gillespie's big band for two years (1957–1958) prior to reuniting with Blakey's Jazz Messengers from 1958–1961. Hooked on heroin, the trumpeter drifted for a couple of years surfacing in New York City in the summer of 1963 to record his most commercial record, *The Sidewinder*, the title track of which was used in Chrysler ads during the 1965 World Series. Briefly rejoining Blakey (1964–1965), Morgan left in 1965 to front his own bands seeking to recapture the success of *The Sidewinder*. In all, the influential trumpeter recorded over twenty albums for Blue Note from 1956 to 1971.

Morgan, a full-blown heroin addict in New York City during the early 1960s, met a woman in a club there in 1967 named Helen Moore (some sources say "More"). Some 14 years his senior, Moore knew all the local drug dealers (though not herself a user at the time) and empathized with the strung-out trumpeter. They soon moved in together in an apartment at 940 Grand Concourse in the Bronx where Moore undertook the arduous task of rebuilding Morgan's tattered reputation among downtown club owners fed up with his unreliability. Helen Morgan (she took his name as his "common-law" wife) placed the musician into a methadone program that enabled him to begin working again on a regular basis. As his *de facto* secretary and manager from 1965 to 1970, Helen was able to schedule him gigs and recording sessions. As Morgan became healthier, however, he sought to distance himself from all associations with his past life including Helen. The relationship was well on its way to ending when Morgan was booked into a week-long engagement at Slug's, a jazz club on Manhattan's Lower East Side, in February 1972. Around 2:45 A.M. on February 19, 1972, Morgan, 33, was at the club's bar when Helen, 47, approached him to return a set of keys. The couple started arguing when Morgan's girlfriend approached prompting him to unceremoniously toss his common-law wife out on the street without her coat. The trumpeter was on his way to the stage to do his final set of the evening when Helen Morgan re-entered the club, took a .32-caliber Harrington & Richardson pistol from her handbag, and shot the trumpeter once in the heart. Morgan was pronounced dead on arrival in the emergency room of Bellevue Hospital. Tried in August 1973, Helen Morgan pleaded guilty to manslaughter, served her time, and was released around 1978 (details are vague due to a missing police file). She died of congestive heart failure in Wilmington, North Carolina, on March 9, 1996.

Further Reading

Huey, Steve. "Lee Morgan." www.billboard.com.
McMillan, Jeffrey S. *Delightfulee: The Life and Music of Lee Morgan.* Ann Arbor: University of Michigan Press, 2008.
Perchard, Tom. *Lee Morgan: His Life, Music and Culture.* London: Equinox, 2006.
Thomas, Larry Reni. "The Lady Who Shot Lee Morgan." http://carolinajazzconnectionwithlarrythomas.blogspot.com/.

Moss, Al (V)

The area of South Florida is a hotbed of pirate radio activity with a hundred or more reggae, hip-hop, Latino, and other type music stations competing for limited frequency space. As fast as the Federal Communications Commission (FCC) confiscates equipment and levies fines against the operators, new stations emerge seeking to carve out a portion of the lucrative revenues to be made from running nightclub ads. In the world of fast buck pirate radio operators, deejay Uncle Al Moss was a class act. A mainstay of Miami's hip-hop scene, Moss (a.k.a. Uncle Peace) first gained local prominence as a guest DJ on WEDR radio working with rapper Luther Campbell of 2 Live Crew fame. Over the years, Moss mixed hundreds of original songs, produced numerous albums from the Miami scene, mixed at area underground radio stations and clubs, and contributed to the soundtracks of two locally produced films, *Dirty South* and *Luke Freak Fest 2000*. Perhaps more importantly, Uncle Al was a hero to Miami's African-American community where he was revered for blocking off streets and throwing free music parties for disadvantaged neighborhood kids.

On the afternoon of September 10, 2001, three men reportedly from a Broward-based pirate reggae station, knocked on the front door of Moss' North Miami duplex. Moss, 31, split the duplex with another pirate radio jockey known as "Joe" who was operating station 98.7 FM from his apartment. There were several incidents of signal interference between the two stations, threats were made, and the trio was there to confront Joe about who "owned" the 98.7 dial spot. According to witnesses, Moss, 31, answered the door and was

telling the men, "I think you're looking for the guy in the back," when all three opened fire hitting the deejay in the hip, arm, and side. Moss died in surgery later that day at Jackson Memorial Hospital. To date, no one has been arrested in connection with Moss' murder. The Miami community continues to remember Uncle Al with an annual "Peace in the Hood Festival" conducted in his honor.

Further Reading

Sokol, Brett. "You Coulda Called Him Al: Pirate Radio Terrorism Claims Its First Victim." *Miami New Times*, September 27, 2001.

Munro, Viola Gordon (M–S)

Viola, 55, a former stage actress, and husband Alfred, 75, a one-time theatrical representative of the Schubert organization in Boston, occupied a modest apartment over a two-car garage in Norfolk, Connecticut. On the morning of June 21, 1949, their downstairs neighbor noticed blood dripping from the ceiling as he went to get his car out of the garage. Police entered the Munro's apartment and found the former theatrical manager dead in bed from a gunshot wound to the head inflicted by his wife, who had then fired a fatal shot through her right ear. The destitute pair had been unemployed for several months and was facing imminent eviction.

Further Reading

"Poverty Seen as Factor in Munro Deaths." *Hartford Courant*, June 22, 1949, p. 2.

Myles, Raymond Anthony, Sr. (V)

Called "the Little Richard of gospel music," Myles made his singing debut at five with his mother, Christine, at the New Hope Baptist Church in New Orleans. The flamboyant teenager was already a local legend when he scored a regional hit with the single, "Prayer from a 12-Year-Old Boy," in which he called for an end to the Vietnam War. In addition to opening for such artists as Harry Connick, Jr., Al Green, and Aretha Franklin, the singer and his choir the RAMS (Raymond Anthony Myles Singers) toured extensively in the South and Europe. In 1997, Myles released a live gospel album, *Heaven Is the Place*, and music industry executives predicted mainstream stardom for the singer after he announced his intention to record his first R&B tracks.

On October 11, 1998, the 41-year-old gospel

singer was found dumped on his back at the corner of Elysian Fields Avenue and Chartres Street in New Orleans dead from a gunshot wound to the heart and two in the thigh. His bloodstained white 1998 Lincoln Navigator was found abandoned nearly two miles from the murder site. A couple of days later a fisherman found the singer's driver's license and other personal papers discarded near the area's Industrial Canal. As police searched for clues to the apparent carjacking, Myles was laid to rest in a public ceremony attended by more than 4,000 mourners at the Greater St. Stephen Full Gospel Baptist Church. His tomb, steps away from that of gospel great Mahalia Jackson, was inscribed with his nickname, "Maestro." On December 15, 1998, a phone tip to Crimestoppers, a nonprofit organization where citizens can report information on crimes, led to the arrest of Rodrick Natteel, a 21-year-old career criminal with a history of felony convictions dating back to 1995. At a pre-trial hearing in 1999, the prosecution introduced evidence that the accused used Myles' cell phone less than one hour after the killing and pawned a miniature television set taken from the abandoned $40,000 Navigator. Natteel allegedly told his girlfriend that Myles picked him up in the French Quarter and solicited him for oral sex. She told authorities that while Natteel never admitted to shooting Myles, he did claim responsibility for moving the car and pawning some of its contents. On August 16, 2001, Natteel cut a deal in which he pleaded guilty to being an accessory after the fact to first-degree murder and of possession of stolen property. A substantial reduction over the charge of first-degree murder filed against Natteel nearly three years earlier, the repeat offender was sentenced to a total of 20 years with two years credited for time served. Another man suspected by police of being the triggerman in the Myles murder was supposedly killed during the commission of a crime three months after the singer's death.

Further Reading

Clendenning, Alan. "Raymond Myles Found Shot Dead on New Orleans Street Corner." Associated Press, October 12, 1998.

Nance, Jack (V)

The iconic wild-haired "Henry Spencer" in the 1977 David Lynch directed cult classic *Eraserhead*, Nance led a darkly tortured life more troubled than any of the offbeat film characters he played during a career spanning over 25 years. Born Marvin John Nance in Boston, Massachusetts on December 21, 1943, he majored in journalism at North Texas State University, but dropped out after he discovered acting. Nance began his acting career with Paul Baker, founder of the Dallas Theater Center, but at 20 impetuously relocated to Los Angeles to perform at the prestigious Pasadena Community Playhouse. Surprised to discover that the Playhouse was no longer in operation, Nance moved north to San Francisco and took up residence as a "guest artist" at San Francisco State University. At SFSU, he met his future wife, acting student Catherine E. Coulson, while both performed in a stage adaptation of Franz Kafka's *Amerika*. In the late 1960s, director David Lindemann cast Nance in the title role of the radical stage play *Tom Paine*. The show was a hit on the San Francisco stage and Nance turned down some potentially lucrative television commercials and series guest shots in Hollywood to travel with the production. After the show's run, however, the actor returned to Los Angeles to discover casting directors were no longer interested. Unable to find work, Nance drew unemployment and joined the Do-Da Gang, an ensemble of struggling fellow-actors. The troupe of performance artists staged various skits to draw attention to their acting skills with Nance once lying motionless in a coffin for three days. In 1971, the actor made his film debut in the forgettable racing picture *Jump*.

Nance's career was going nowhere fast when David Lindemann, the director of *Tom Paine*, recommended to David Lynch, a fellow-student at the American Film Institute's Center for Advanced Film Studies, that he talk to the actor about appearing in his student film, *Eraserhead*. At their initial meeting in 1972, Nance was unimpressed with Lynch's script and not interested in taking the perceived backward career step of appearing in a student film. Lynch then showed him a 35-minute, 16mm animation-live-action short called *The Grandmother* that he had made with a $5,000 AFI grant. In the film about a kid who plants a seed that grows into his grandmother, Nance would later tell interviewers that he recognized in Lynch a "mad little genius at work." When principal photography began on *Eraserhead* in May 1972 Lynch informed Nance that the shoot would last only "six weeks." Instead, production on the film dragged on for nearly five years. At one point, both men supported themselves by delivering the *Wall Street Journal* around West Los Angeles. *Eraserhead*, Lynch's directorial debut, premiered at a midnight showing on March 19, 1977. Although the mainstream press almost universally panned the surreal film that featured Nance as the weird haired zombie-like misfit "Henry Spencer," the underground embraced the movie as a cult classic. Lynch achieved mainstream status in 1980 with his next film, *The Elephant Man*, but was unsuccessful in convincing the film's producers to cast his friend. Nance, however, became an inseparable part of Lynch's subsequent career appearing in four of his films (*Dune*, 1985; *Blue Velvet*, 1986; *Wild at Heart*, 1990; *Lost Highway*, 1997) as well as in Lynch's short-lived cult television hit, *Twin Peaks* (1990–1991), as the semi-regular character "Pete Martell."

A lifelong drinker, Nance's alcoholism adversely affected his career. Lynch reported that during the shooting of *Eraserhead* the actor was often unable to make his set calls. At times the actor was so drunk that he passed out and woke up in vacant lots. Unmotivated, Nance had to be sought out by directors before he would work. Francis Ford Coppola, a friend from the San Francisco days, got Nance a small role in director Wim Wenders' *Hammett* (1982). After Nance appeared in bit parts in *Johnny Dangerously* (1984), *City Heat* (1984), and *Ghoulies* (1985), he was contacted by Lynch in 1986 for a role in *Blue Velvet* starring Dennis Hopper as the sadistic drug dealer "Frank Booth." During shooting, Nance told Hopper (no stranger to substance abuse problems) that if he did not help him stop drinking he would commit suicide. Hopper took Nance to Studio 12, a rehab clinic in Los Angeles, where the actor eventually got sober. The lifesaving action forged a bond between the two men and, whenever possible, Hopper used Nance in the films he directed (*Colors*, 1988; *The Hot Spot*, 1990). While at the facility, Nance met Kelly Jean Van Dyke, the junkie daughter of Jerry Van Dyke, brother of Dick, and co-star of the popular television series *Coach*. Sober and with his career on the upswing, Nance (since divorced from first wife Coulson), married Van Dyke in May 1991. The marriage quickly soured, however, when Van Dyke started using drugs again and began performing in the porn industry under the name "Nancee Kellee." Nance tried desperately to support his wife, but fearful that her drug-fueled lifestyle would endanger his own sobriety, wanted out of the marriage in less than a year.

On November 17, 1991, the actor was filming a rare leading role in *Meatballs 4* on a remote location in Madera County, California, near Yosemite when he phoned Van Dyke at her apartment in North Hollywood to inform her that her abuse problems were driving him away. Van Dyke pleaded with her husband not to leave her, warning him that "If you hang up on me, I'm going to kill myself." As if on cue, an electrical storm in Madera County knocked out the connection disabling all the phones in the camp. A concerned Nance drove to a nearby police station where the duty officer called the Los Angeles Police Department. Minutes later, Nance was informed by authorities that Van Dyke, 33, had committed suicide by hanging herself from a rope plant hanger in the bedroom of their apartment. The actor never forgave himself for his wife's death, but managed to stay sober for another two years before giving up the struggle. In 1993, Nance phoned a friend to announce, "It's funny, I woke up and I knew I had to drink again. And there was no stopping me." Dennis Hopper again tried to intervene, but Nance told him not to bother, there was nothing he could do. The actor continued to drink through two strokes and bit parts in increasingly weaker films (*Voodoo*, 1995; *The Secret Agent Club*, 1996). The producer of *Joyride* (unreleased at the time of the actor's death) observed that Nance was so drunk when he picked him up at 11:00 A.M. that the actor could not fasten his seat belt. Nance would not live to see his final performance in old friend David Lynch's *Lost Highway* released in 1997.

By late 1996, the 53-year-old actor was living in a modest home in South Pasadena and when not working, which was most of the time, stayed drunk. Around 5:00 A.M. on Sunday, December 29, 1996, Nance left his house and walked to nearby Winchell's Doughnut House at 424 S. Fair Oaks Avenue. As he was walking across the parking lot of the doughnut place he was brushed into by two young Hispanic men walking in the opposite direction. Friends of the irascible actor were well aware of his ill-advised habit of "popping off" to young people in the street whose appearance or attitude did not meet with his approval. Nance evidently said something to the men like, "Why don't you two change out of those baggy clothes and go get a job?" prompting one of them to punch him in the face knocking the actor to the pavement. Nance stumbled back to his home and later recounted the incident over lunch to friends, actress Catherine Case and screenwriter Leo Bulgarini. The actor, pointing to a black eye, admitted that "I mouthed off and got what I deserved," then possibly embellished the story by adding that during the altercation he wrestled one of the men to the ground. Bulgarini, doubtful of the frail alcoholic's account of the tussle, talked to people at the doughnut shop, but none had witnessed the incident. The next day, Bulgarini returned to Nance's home to help him with his laundry and found his friend dead on the bathroom floor. An autopsy ruled that Nance died from an acute subdural hematoma caused by blunt force trauma consistent with his story of being punched. The actor's blood alcohol was an astounding .24 percent and the autopsy revealed his liver to be in an advanced state of cirrhosis. Although the Los Angeles County Coroner's office officially ruled the death a homicide, given the lack of eyewitnesses and the victim's lifestyle investigators could not rule out that Nance's death might have resulted from a drunken fall. At the time of his death, the actor was working on an autobiographical screenplay, *A Derelict on All Fours*, suggested by his Chihuahua dog, Daisy. In 2001, Nance was the subject of the film documentary, *I Don't Know Jack*, directed by Chris Leavens. Perhaps fittingly, around Halloween 2001 Nance was posthumously recognized by Filmfest Kansas City with a best actor award for his work in the documentary. To date, Nance's homicide remains open with little real hope that it will ever be solved.

Further Reading

I Don't Know Jack [DVD]. Directed by Chris Leavens. 91 minutes. [California?]: Next Step Studios Had to Be Made Films, 2004.
Potter, Maximillian. "Erased." *Premiere*, 10(12) (August 1997): 92–95, 106–7.
www.jacknance.com.

Neal, Jackie (V)

Daughter of internationally renowned Baton Rouge blues man Raful Neal, "Jazzy Jackie" was born on July 7, 1967, the eighth of ten children. A hairdresser and owner of Jazzy Jackie's Beauty Salon in Baton Rouge, Neal released four CDs on small independent labels (*The Blues Won't Let You Go*, 1995; *Lookin' for a Sweet Thang*, 2000; *Money Can't Buy Me Love*, 2002; *Down in da Club*, 2005) all characterized by an eclectic blend of soul, pop, funk, and blues. Since the mid–1990s, Neal's career was steadily building in the Southeast thanks

to airplay on black radio stations in cities such as Mobile, Birmingham, and Baton Rouge. In support of songs like "Nooky Thang," "Right Thang, Wrong Man," and "Twurk It," Neal crisscrossed the region by bus often playing weekend gigs. In early–2003, Neal met James Haskell White at her concert in Baton Rouge. White wooed the singer with flowers and for a time drove her tour bus until his increasing jealousy over her access to fans prompted the entertainer to end their relationship in December 2004. Unwilling to accept the breakup, the 39-year-old threatened to kill Neal and in early March 2005 punched the windows out of her car in the parking lot of a nightclub.

On March 10, 2005, Neal, 37, was getting a manicure at T'Nails and Hair Salon on 4369 Florida Boulevard in Baton Rouge prior to a weekend tour in Alabama. At 6:00 P.M. White entered the crowded shop and calmly talked to Neal before leaving without incident. He returned ten minutes later, however, fired a shot from a .45-caliber revolver into the ceiling, and yelled "Get the fuck out of here." During the mass exodus out the front door, White shot customer Angela Myers, who survived the attack. Neal, now alone with White in the shop, was not so fortunate. The singer's estranged lover shot her three times, laid on her body, then shot himself in the chest. Neal was pronounced dead at the scene while White, briefly hospitalized under police guard, survived and was charged with first-degree murder (Neal) and attempted murder (Myers).

As the killer recuperated in hospital with a cop posted outside the door of his room, Baton Rouge said goodbye to a performer many felt was just beginning to be recognized as a major talent. Nearly 3,000 mourners thronged Neal's funeral service in the Great Hall at the Bellemont where the singer, her lips and eyelids painted red and her hair close-cropped on the sides and spiked on top, lay in state for hours. The massive turnout led one family member to comment, "I just wish they could have turned up for her like that while she was living. If she could have had this much love when she was living, how great would that be?" Neal was buried in Roselawn Memorial Park and Mausoleum.

Found mentally competent to stand trial in December 2005, White was advised by counsel to accept the D.A.'s offer of life imprisonment rather than risk a proceeding where death by lethal injection loomed as a probable outcome. In January 2006, Neal's family (who approved the plea offer) was in a Baton Rouge courtroom where they expected White to accept the generous deal. At the last minute, however, he stunned everyone by insisting that he go to trial. White's attorneys were busy preparing for a pre-trial hearing in February 2006 when he informed them that he was now ready to accept the deal. Later that month, White pleaded guilty to the original charges and was sentenced to a prison term of life plus 50 years.

Further Reading

Noel, Josh. "Overflow Crowd Turns Out for Jackie Neal's Funeral." *The Advocate*, March 16, 2005, sec. B, pp. 1–2.

Neal, Tom (M)

Neal, a dependable actor in some 180 films from 1938 to 1953, is nevertheless fated to be remembered in Hollywood lore for two acts of violence committed 14 years apart. Born in Evanston, Illinois, on January 28, 1914, Neal enjoyed a privileged life as the son of a banker. Excelling at sports at Northwestern University, Neal became a Golden Gloves boxing champ ... a skill he would later use to deleterious effect in Tinseltown. Briefly flirting with a Broadway stage career in the early 1930s, he earned a law degree from Harvard University in 1938, but never practiced. That same year, Neal arrived in Hollywood and appeared in his first screen role as a bit player in MGM's *Out West with the Hardys*. The good-looking, muscular actor worked almost nonstop from the late 1940s until his final film, *The Great Jesse James Raid*, in 1953. Often cast as the tough guy or suave leading man in grade B motion pictures, Neal's film credits include *6,000 Enemies* (1939), *Flying Tigers* (1942), *Behind the Rising Sun* (1943), *Thoroughbreds* (1944), *Crime, Inc.*, (1945), *The Brute Man* (1946), *Call of the Klondike* (1950), and *Danger Zone* (1951). In 1946, Neal starred as the Fate-stricken character, "Al Roberts," in the Edgar G. Ulmer directed film *Detour* for Poverty Row production company PRC (Producers Releasing Corporation). Shot in six days on the microscopic budget of $30,000, *Detour* has since become a darling of critics who laud it as a major example of *film noir*. The movie was remade in 1992 starring Tom Neal, Jr., the actor's son.

No doubt Neal would have continued his undistinguished, but solid acting career in B movies if not for his disastrous involvement in an ill-fated love triangle. Barbara Payton, a sexy blonde "star" of such forgettable early 1950s films as *Kiss Tomorrow Goodbye* (1950) and *Drums in the Deep South* (1951), was better at garnering headlines than acting. Though only 25, Payton was very publicly engaged to the 45-year-old actor, Franchot Tone, the patrician-looking ex-husband of Joan Crawford. The press followed the couple's every movement and, shark-like, smelled blood in the water when the buxom star broke off her engagement with Tone in July 1951. The reason? Payton "knew in a minute" that she "loved" Tom Neal after spying the muscular 37-year-old actor in swim trunks poised on a diving board at a mutual friend's pool party in Hollywood. The pair generated headlines of their own when the mercurial Payton decided to renew her friendship with Franchot Tone. On September 14, 1951, two days before Payton was set to marry Neal, the young star and Tone spent the evening dining and dancing at Ciro's. Neal was waiting for the couple at Payton's Hollywood home at 1802 Courtney Avenue when they arrived from their "date" around 1:30 A.M. the next morning. The fickle bombshell ordered Neal to leave and, when he refused, instructed Tone to make him. Tone, nine years older and twenty pounds lighter, invited the 5'10", 180-pound former Golden Gloves boxing champion (who, incidentally, spent his spare time lifting weights) out on the front patio to settle the dispute. Not surprisingly, Neal beat Tone senseless, breaking the actor's nose and fracturing his cheek. Tone woke up in California Hospital 18 hours later suffering from a cerebral concussion. He later underwent two hours of facial surgery to save his distinguished good looks. Tone never landed a punch.

As Tone slowly recovered, Payton informed the press that her engagement to Neal was off. The star of *Bride of the Gorilla* (1951) now intended to wed Franchot Tone as soon as he was sufficiently recovered. Neal, left to twist in the legal wind while awaiting Tone's decision whether to file felony assault charges against him, told his side of the "parlor man" versus the "athlete" story in a September 17, 1951 *Los Angeles Times* article bearing his by-line. Maintaining his love for Payton, Neal said she instigated the confrontation with Tone over a period of months by playing the two men off against one another. Of the altercation:

> Barbara came out and asked Franchot when he was going to get rid of me and then threw her arms around him and kissed him. That's what touched it off. Tone said, "Let's go." He threw a right and I threw a right and mine got in faster. I struck him several more times and it was all over. I saw them

Tom Neal, seen above with Ann Savage in the 1946 *film noir* classic *Detour*, made some 180 films before a one-sided fistfight in September 1951 with actor Franchot Tone over sex bomb Barbara Payton ended his motion picture career in 1953. Retired from acting and living in Palm Springs, California, with third wife Gail, the 51-year-old landscaper was arrested and charged with murder after she was found dead in their home on April 2, 1965. Convicted of manslaughter, Neal served seven years in prison before dying of a heart attack at 58 on August 6, 1972.

carry him into the house.... It was one of those things, where I had to defend myself and where the sight of the girl I love kissing another man just made me see red. I mean, when you're fighting for a girl — well, you just lose your head a little, I guess. I have nothing against Tone whatever. I'm sorry he's in the hospital and I'm ready to do anything I can do to help him. And I hope he and Barbara will be happy.

On September 27, 1951, Tone announced that he would not file charges against Neal for their one-sided fistfight. The next day, Payton and Tone married in the sexy star's hometown of Cloquet, Minnesota. The couple separated after 53 days of marriage amid rumors Payton was still in love with Tom Neal. Tone divorced the fickle ac-

tress on May 19, 1952, citing "extreme mental cruelty." The court papers did not mention his former rival, but Payton had resumed a torrid relationship with the actor that eventually fizzled after they appeared together in Neal's final film, *The Great Jesse James Raid*, in 1953. Rendered unemployable by the scandal, Neal was forced to leave Hollywood for Palm Springs where the broke former B-movie actor was reduced to working as a gardener. Still, he fared better than Barbara Payton, who was also made *persona non grata* in the film capital by the scandal and her subsequent bizarre behavior. After making her last movie in 1955, *Murder Is My Beat*, Payton descended into a nightmare world of alcoholism, check kiting, homelessness, and prostitution. The sexy woman movie stars once fought over died on May 8, 1967, at the age of 39 from heart and liver failure in San Diego.

By 1965, the 51-year-old former actor had seemingly pieced his life back together. Married since June 1961 to third wife Gail, a 29-year-old receptionist at the upscale Palm Springs Tennis Club, Neal operated a modest, but successful, landscaping business in the desert town. Long forgotten by movie fans, Neal once again became press fodder by committing another violent act … this time with fatal consequences. At 6:30 A.M. on Friday, April 2, 1965, Palm Springs police received a phone call from Neal's Beverly Hills attorney, James P. Cantillon, requesting that they meet him and his client at an intersection one block from Neal's house. Neal led the group to his home at 2481 Cardillo Road where authorities discovered Gail peacefully stretched out on the living room sofa, partially covered by a blanket, dead from a single .45-caliber bullet wound behind her right ear. The bullet exited Gail's left temple and was recovered from a sofa pillow beneath her head. A spent cartridge was found four feet from the woman's body. The gun was never found. Neal was cooperative with authorities, but under the advice of Cantillon refused to make a statement. An autopsy fixed the time of Gail's death between 2:30 P.M. on April 1 and 2:30 A.M. on April 2. As the former actor sat in the Riverside County Jail in Indio without bond, detectives worked to fix his movements during that time frame. The outlook for Neal looked bleak after investigators questioned Robert L. Balzer, the Buddhist monk owner of the Tyrol Restaurant in Idyllwild, a mountain resort in the San Jacinto Mountains behind Palm Springs. Balzer, a friend of the Neals, told police that the former actor showed up alone at the restaurant early in the evening of April 1. Neal looked a "little disturbed," and in the course of their conversation told him Gail was his "whole life and he could not live without her." Neal concluded the frank discussion with the admission that he had shot his wife "in the head" with a .45-caliber pistol. He was subsequently charged with first-degree murder and remained in jail pending trial steadfastly maintaining his innocence.

Following jury selection (three men, nine women), the Neal trial opened in Indio on October 19, 1965. The prosecution's case against the former actor looked solid. The motive — Neal shot his wife while she slept because she was in-

volved with other men and planned to divorce him. Adding to Neal's "confession" to Balzer, a local real estate broker testified that on April 1 he had gone to the Neal house to deliver a letter of recommendation to Gail who intended to divorce her husband of four years and relocate to Los Angeles to seek employment. The realtor was surprised to find Neal in the home since the couple was separated since January 1965 and the one-time actor had been living in Chicago. Embarrassed, the real estate broker quickly left the home on Cardillo Road. He was the last person except for Neal to see Gail alive. Nine days later after calling only eight witnesses, the D.A.'s office rested its case against Neal. Seemingly outgunned by the prosecution, Neal was forced to take the stand in his own defense. He told the packed courtroom the shooting was accidental. As he argued with his wife about the other men in her life, Gail suddenly became angry, produced a .45-caliber automatic, and threatened to kill him. The gun discharged accidentally as he attempted to disarm the hysterical woman. As a rebuttal witness, the prosecution called Dr. Armand Dollinger, the pathologist who performed the autopsy on the dead woman. According to Dollinger, Neal's account of the shooting was "unlikely" based upon the direction of the wound. Three of Gail's co-workers at the Palm Springs Tennis Club testified that she planned to leave town after learning her husband was returning from Chicago. Gail was terrified Neal would kill her when he learned she had filed for divorce on March 11, 1955, citing physical cruelty as the grounds. In the divorce papers, the 29-year-old receptionist accused Neal of threatening her with a .45-caliber automatic. Present in the courtroom for at least one day was Neal's old flame, Barbara Payton. The two exchanged glances, but did not speak. Remarkably to most observers, jurors needed only ten hours after a six-week trial to find Neal guilty of the lesser charge of involuntary manslaughter on November 18, 1965. While awaiting sentencing, the star of *Detour* remained free on $2,750 bail. Describing Neal as a "cold, deliberate" killer, Superior Court Judge Hilton H. McCabe imposed the maximum prison sentence of one to 15 years on the angry ex-actor on December 10, 1965. There would be no probation. Neal called the sentence a "railroad job" as he was hustled off to begin serving his time. He was paroled from the California Institution for Men at Chino on December 6, 1971, after serving seven years. Neal's freedom, however, was short-lived. On August 6, 1972, the 58-year-old complained of heartburn prior to retiring to bed in his North Hollywood home. The next day, Neal's 15-year-old son, Patrick, discovered his father's body. The man with the violent past was pronounced dead from "natural causes" (congestive heart failure) by a fire department ambulance crew summoned to the scene.

Further Reading

Gilmore, John. *L.A. Despair: A Landscape of Crimes and Bad Times*. Los Angeles: Amok, 2005.
Neal, Tom. "Neal Relates His Version of Brawl." *Los Angeles Times*, September 17, 1951, p. 2.
www.palmspringslife.co/whisper/neal.html.

Newt, Ronnie (V)

The 16-year-old lead singer of the rap group The Newtrons was shot to death by a convenience store clerk in San Bernadino, California, on May 1, 1991. According to eyewitness testimony, Newt, 19-year-old Eric Daniel Howard, and two other youths allegedly pistol-whipped the store owner, Jong Soo Yoo, and took cash and food stamps. As the four assailants were leaving the store, Yoo grabbed a gun from under the counter and fatally wounded Newt and Howard. The two other youths fled the scene. MCA released the group's unheralded debut album, *The Newtrons*, on March 20, 1990.

Further Reading

"Store Owner Kills Rapper During Holdup." *Washington Times*, May 6, 1991, sec. A, p. 6.

Ngor, Haing S. (V)

In a twist of Fate almost too cruel to be believed, Dr. Haing S. Ngor survived the killing fields of Cambodia only to become a victim of Los Angeles street crime. The son of a Khmer mother and ethnic Chinese father born in Samrong Yong, Cambodia on March 22, 1940, Ngor became a doctor specializing in obstetrics and gynecology. After medical school, he set up his own clinic in the capital city of Phnom Penh while serving as a medical officer in the Cambodian army. In 1975, the Khmer Rouge, Maoist guerillas led by the dictator Pol Pot, assumed power in Cambodia. Dedicated to a radical Communist ideology intent upon ridding Cambodia of all Western cultural influences, the Khmer Rouge "evacuated" millions of people from the towns and cities to perform manual labor in the countryside. Concurrently, the group unleashed a wave

of cultural genocide targeted at the intelligentsia, i.e. any person with the slightest degree of education, or, even those who wore eyeglasses. Until the Pol Pot regime collapsed in May 1979, the Khmer Rouge was estimated to have murdered two million Cambodians either through forced labor, starvation, or execution. As a bespectacled doctor, Ngor was at the top of the Khmer Rouge's hitlist. Hiding his glasses, he was imprisoned and tortured repeatedly on suspicion of being a physician. Somehow he managed to convince his captors that he was an illiterate taxicab driver. In June 1978, Ngor was forced to standby helplessly while his beloved wife (in actuality, his fiancée), Chang My Huoy, died in childbirth. As a trained gynecologist, Ngor could have saved her, but would have been instantly killed as a member of the outlawed intellectual class. Before his flight with a niece across the Cambodian border to Thailand in 1979, Ngor had lost both parents, two sisters, and two of three brothers to the Khmer Rouge. Besides the clothes on his back, the only other possession the one-time doctor owned was a treasured photograph of Huoy. Ngor wrote movingly of his harrowing experiences in his 1987 autobiography, *A Cambodian Odyssey*, co-written with journalist Roger Warner.

For the next 18 months, Ngor worked as a doctor in refugee camps along the Thai-Cambodian border while awaiting permission to immigrate to either Australia or the United States. In October 1980, he was admitted to the U.S. arriving in Los Angeles with $4.00 in his pocket. Barred from practicing medicine in the States (the American Medical Association refused to recognize his French credentials), Ngor landed a job as a night security guard for a company near the outskirts of Chinatown. In November 1980 the former doctor became a counselor for the Chinatown Service Center, an organization dedicated to helping Cambodian refugees find jobs in their new country. If Ngor had done nothing other than serve as a caseworker at the CSC he would have fulfilled his commitment to helping those displaced by the Khmer Rouge. However, in March 1982 the he became involved in a project that would forever place a human face, his, on the Cambodian Holocaust. Friends had to convince Ngor to audition for a part in film director Roland Joffe's *The Killing Fields*, the true-life story of the relationship between *New York Times* columnist Sydney H. Schanberg, posted to Cambodia from 1972 to 1975 during the Khmer Rouge's toppling of the government, and his translator and assistant, Dith Pran. The motion picture told the story of Dith Pran's imprisonment by the Khmer Rouge and his escape from the war-torn country; in essence, an almost mirror image of Haing Ngor's experiences. Ngor was on location in Thailand when he was told he was cast to play the co-lead as Dith Pran opposite Sam Waterston. Viewing the role as a chance to honor his deathbed commitment to Huoy to inform the world about the horror in Cambodia, Ngor was riveting in the film. In 1984, he was given the Academy Award as Best Supporting Actor, the first time since *The Best Years of Our Lives* (1946) that another non-professional, Harold Russell, was so honored with the Oscar. Other films in which Ngor appeared include *The Iron Triangle* (1989), *Vietnam, Texas* (1990), *Ambition* (1991), director Oliver Stone's *Heaven & Earth* (1993), *Fortunes of War* (1993), and *The Dragon Gate* (1994). On series television, he did guest shots on *Miami Vice* (1984), *Highway to Heaven* (1984), *China Beach* (1988), and *Hotel* (1990).

Acting, however, was only the means for Ngor to realize a twofold purpose: focus world-wide attention on the plight of Cambodian refugees and to generate income for his human rights concerns. By 1996, the Academy Award winner had organized at least two international aid organizations targeted at alleviating the suffering of refugees in camps near the Thai-Cambodian border — the Aides aux Personnes Déplacées (Aid to Displaced Persons) based in Brussels, and the Paris-based Les Enfants d'Angkor. Dr. Ngor also served as an advisor to the Campaign to Oppose the Return of the Khmer Rouge (CORKR). In addition to establishing a medical training center on the Cambodian border, the human rights activist was also involved in numerous business dealings (operating hotels, exporting rice, timber harvesting) in his former country.

On the evening of February 25, 1996, Ngor (after delivering a lecture on Cambodia) pulled his late-model Mercedes-Benz into the carport of his modest two-bedroom apartment building near the Chinatown district of Los Angeles. As he was getting out of the car, three young gang members high on crack ordered him to hand over his valuables. Ngor, 55, was willing to give them his wallet and the $6,000 Rolex on his wrist, but categorically refused to part with the gold chain and locket around his neck containing the photograph of wife Huoy he had smuggled out of Cambodia.

If the doped up gang members thought they could intimidate a man who had been systematically tortured by the Khmer Rouge over a period of years, they were mistaken. First, the hoods beat him to the pavement with a baseball bat, and when Ngor still refused to part with the locket, one tough shot him in the leg. Still, Ngor refused to surrender the beloved object. Gang members shot the award winning actor once in the heart and took the locket off his corpse. In their haste to flee the scene, the thieves overlooked a wallet in Ngor's jacket pocket containing nearly $3,000 in cash.

Initial speculation that the human rights activist was murdered in retaliation for his crusade to bring Pol Pot and others responsible for the Cambodian Holocaust to the bar of international justice was quickly discounted after police charged three members of the L.A. street gang Oriental Lazy Boyz (OLB) with the crime in April 1996. Suspects Jason "Cloudy" Chan, 18, and Indra "Solo" Lim, 19, were already in custody on unrelated robbery charges when police arrested their 19-year-old accomplice, Tak Sun "Rambo" Tan. The Oriental Lazy Boyz, a Chinatown gang notorious for "follow-home" assaults, specialized in carjacking and home invasions to finance crack buys, not in terrorist activities aimed at eliminating political dissenters. According to prosecutor Craig Hum, "Dr. Ngor ... died on the cold pavement of a carport in Chinatown gunned down by these men for a few lousy rocks of cocaine." Sadly, like the victim, parents of two of the accused killers had also escaped Pol Pot's reign of terror.

Tried for first-degree murder under the special circumstance of killing a person during the commission of a robbery, the three gang members faced a possible death sentence as their trial opened in Los Angeles in February 1998. While the three men were tried simultaneously in the same courtroom, three different juries (each designated a specific color-coded badge) were impanelled to hear the case. Prosecutor Hum eloquently argued that Ngor was murdered because he refused to give up the gold chain and locket containing the photo of his martyred love, Huoy. The three OLB members pleaded innocent to the crime, but did admit they were high on crack when they "found" Ngor's Rolex and heart shaped locket. They were too stoned, however, to remember where they sold the items. On April 16, 1998, all three were convicted of first-degree murder and second-degree robbery following a nearly two month trial. Ironically, the verdict was announced one day after Pol Pot's death from a reported heart attack. The D.A.'s office breathed a sigh of relief. The defendants had all changed their stories on the stand, and potential witnesses had refused to testify out of the very real fear of gang reprisal. The case against the men had been built almost entirely on tape recordings of police interviews with gang members who fingered the defendants fleeing the scene of Ngor's murder. Still maintaining their innocence, the OLB members were sentenced on May 19, 1998: Indra Lim, 26 years to life; Tak Sun Tan, 56 years to life; and Jason Chan, life without the possibility of parole (the longer sentence meted out because of his lengthy list of prior offenses dating back to when he was 13).

Then on April 26, 2004, the unthinkable happened when a federal judge gave final approval to a magistrate's November 2003 decision to overturn the conviction of Tak Sun "Rambo" Tan. The magistrate found that prosecutor Craig Hum unfairly played upon the jury's sympathies when describing in moving detail the horrors Ngor suffered in Cambodia. The prosecutor further muddied the legal waters (i.e. arguing facts not in evidence) by maintaining Ngor struggled to retain the gold locket because it contained the only surviving photo of his dead wife, Huoy. In reality, Ngor had another photo in his bedroom as well as the negative for the locket photograph. Should the ruling stand, "Rambo" Tan must either be given a new trial or released. On July 7, 2005, however, a federal appeals court in San Francisco reinstated the life terms and convictions for all three defendants ruling the evidence against them was "overwhelming." Dr. Ngor is buried in Rose Hills Memorial Park in Whittier, California under a flat burial marker bearing a smiling photograph of him holding the Oscar for *The Killing Fields* above the inscription in Cambodian letters, and in English, "Haing S. Ngor — Beloved Brother & Uncle — March 22, 1940–February 25, 1996."

Further Reading

Ngor, Haing S., and Roger Warner. *A Cambodian Odyssey.* New York: Macmillan, 1987.

Niquette, Richard (V)

Niquette (born January 28, 1951) appeared on several French language television shows in Quebec including the highly rated mid–1980s hockey soap opera *Lance et compte* (*He Shoots, He Scores*).

At the time of his murder, the 44-year-old actor last worked as host on the program *Meurtre et mystère* (*Murder and Mystery*) broadcast on an interactive television channel. At 4:30 A.M. on February 19, 1995, Montreal Urban Community police responding to a 911 call found Niquette's naked blood-soaked body slumped against a parked car in the east-end Hochelaga-Maisonneuve district. Death resulted from numerous stab wounds through the heart. The blood spoor led from the murder scene across Cuvelier Street to a basement apartment in a nearby building. Authorities questioned the apartment's tenant, 22-year-old Sylvain Jomphe, later arresting him and accomplice, Patrick Gendron, 19. Niquette apparently left a gay bar and ended up in Jomphe's apartment where he was robbed of more than $300 and stabbed repeatedly before stumbling naked into the street where he died. A spokesman for the Committee for Lesbians and Gays Against Violence decried the murder as a "hate crime" committed by a killer who stalked gay bars looking for victims. The killing, the nineteenth in four years committed against homosexuals in the so-called "Gay Village" area of Montreal, underscored what the organization cited as the pressing need for the Canadian government to enact legislation identifying murder based on sexual orientation as a hate crime. On December 20, 1995, Jomphe pleaded guilty to a charge of second-degree murder and was sentenced to life in prison with no chance of parole for ten years. Jomphe's accomplice, Patrick Gendron, was found guilty of conspiracy to assault with a weapon and received a suspended sentence with three years probation.

Further Reading

Noel, Albert. "Actor's Slaying was Hate Crime Against Gays, Activists." *The Gazette* (Montreal), March 1, 1995, sec. A, p. 3.

Nixon-Nirdlinger, Fred G. (V)

The son of Samuel F. (Nirdlinger) Nixon, a successful entrepreneur and partner in the theatrical firm of Nixon & Zimmerman, Nixon-Nirdlinger (born 1877) established himself as the top theatre chain owner in Philadelphia. The manager of that city's Park and People's Theatres, he also owned the Erlanger Theatre and the Academy of Music. In 1920, Nixon-Nirdlinger was part of a group that purchased Philadelphia's Metropolitan Opera House. Shortly after doing so, the theatre magnate announced the venue was changing its focus from grand opera to "popular" entertainment. Throughout the 1920s Nixon-Nirdlinger's personal life fought for newspaper headlines with his business successes. Married four times (twice to the same woman), the theatre owner had a history of allowing his marriages to be broken up by wannabe actresses who he then tried to promote. Nixon-Nirdlinger was 45 and married to Laura McKenna, a promising actress who had broken up his first marriage, when he spied Charlotte Isabel Nash competing at the Atlantic City beauty contest in 1923. The 18-year-old "Miss St. Louis" was a strikingly beautiful, curvaceous, blue-eyed blonde with deep dimples (the theatre magnate later insured them for $100,000). Charlotte finished second in the pageant, but won the heart of the millionaire who was old enough to be her father. Though still married to McKenna, Nixon-Nirdlinger married his "child bride" in Hagerstown, Maryland, in 1924. The next year, McKenna divorced her errant husband in Paris on the easily proven grounds of infidelity and desertion claiming a healthy financial settlement in the bargain.

Nixon-Nirdlinger was obsessed with fashioning Charlotte into a wife who could seamlessly fit in with his globe-trotting lifestyle. He sent her to an exclusive finishing school where the Missouri-born beauty was taught to ride, play the piano, sing, proper elocution, and all the other social amenities the theatre owner felt necessary. Quoted in a *Los Angeles Evening Herald* post-murder article dated March 13, 1931, Nixon-Nirdlinger had allegedly vowed, "I will make her more desired than Cleopatra. I will make her mind as gorgeous as her body. I will do with a living woman what painters and sculptors seek to do with paint and clay." Finally deemed fit to represent him in polite society, Charlotte escorted the millionaire on a honeymoon to Paris in 1925. There the theatre owner accused her of flirting with other men, they quarreled over his jealous rages, and Charlotte temporarily left him. The cycle repeated endlessly until the couple divorced in 1926. Charlotte charged that Nixon-Nirdlinger was cruel and violent while the eccentric millionaire claimed his beautiful young wife was "cold" and refused to return home. A judge ruled they were both equally to blame. Nevertheless, the couple remarried in Paris in 1928 and spent the next few years traveling and throwing lavish parties in Switzerland, New York, and on the French Riviera. To

friends the May–December union looked healthy with both Nixon-Nirdlinger and Charlotte devoted to their two children (ages 3 years and 18 months). The reality, however, was quite different. The aging theatre magnate continued to be insanely jealous of his beautiful wife and railed against her whenever she danced with men in the jazz nightclubs they frequented. In early 1931, the 26-year-old former beauty queen purchased a small caliber hammerless handgun after Nixon-Nirdlinger, 54, threatened in a jealous rage to shoot her with his own Browning pistol. His outbursts became so routine that she kept the gun in a nightstand by the bed.

At 10:30 P.M. on March 11, 1931, the marital discord between the two ended in tragedy in their apartment on the Promenade des Anglais in Nice, France. In a statement to police taken immediately after the tragedy, Charlotte described the scene: "We dined together at the usual hour. My husband drank wine and whiskey at dinner. After the meal I went to my room to change into pajamas. On rejoining my husband in the drawing room.... He seemed restless and preoccupied. I picked up an Italian newspaper. This action seemed to annoy him and he insinuated that if I wanted to learn Italian it was because I had an Italian lover. The incident started a quarrel and my husband said he would alter his will and disinherit our children. He then went into the kitchen, where he took some more whiskey, while I retired to my bedroom." Fearful that her drunken husband might turn violent, Charlotte removed her small caliber revolver from the nightstand and put it within ready reach under her pillow. "My husband came into the bedroom and began to undress," she continued. "Suddenly he flew into another rage and was more violent than I had ever seen him before. He shouted he would kill me rather than see me have an Italian lover. I told him he had nothing to fear on that account and begged him to be quiet. Then he rushed at me and seized me by the throat and I only wrenched myself away with difficulty. He was advancing to attack me again as I was standing near the bed. I snatched the revolver from beneath the pillow and fired at him without realizing what I was doing. He let go my throat and staggered from the bedroom into a little boudoir. I swooned and it was only when I came to that I rushed down to the porter's lodge for assistance. It had to be done. If I had not killed him he would have killed me."

In the days that followed, Charlotte languished in a French jail while her children were cared for by the couple's Swedish nurse, Irma Stolt. Medical and forensic evidence supported the young woman's story. Bruises and red marks were still visible on her throat and the trajectory of the bullets was consistent with being fired from the position described by the distraught widow. An autopsy ruled that Nixon-Nirdlinger died as a result of two bullet wounds: one shot entered under the left eye lodging in the base of the skull, the other traversing his left side and ripping open a lung. Irma Stolt told police, "Every quarrel was started by her husband. Every one was without cause. She is beautiful, and he could not stand having a man look at her, even when he was with her. They always attended cabarets and public places together, and it was seldom she left the house alone. When the police finish tracking down her movements they will find out how true this is." Sydney Chaplin, brother of comedy great Charlie, and his wife told a magistrate that while they were neighbors of the Nixon-Nirdlingers on the French Riviera the theatre man was unreasonably jealous of his young wife without the slightest provocation. Even friends of the dead man admitted that his past life with his two former wives was marked by fits of jealous rage. It was later learned that on the morning of his death Nixon-Nirdlinger had hired a private investigator to monitor his wife's activities. While awaiting trial, it was announced that under the terms of a pre-nuptial agreement made between Nixon-Nirdlinger and Charlotte after their remarriage in 1928 the former beauty queen was to receive one third of her husband's estate, roughly $240,000.

Warmly embraced by the French public, Charlotte faced a reduced charge of "murder with excuse of provocation" as her trial began on May 20, 1931, at the Criminal Court of the Alpes Maritimes in Nice. If convicted, she faced a two to five year prison sentence. Hundreds jammed the courtroom while police contained thousands more of her supporters in the streets. Aware of the weaknesses in its case and the strong public support for the widow, the prosecution produced no witnesses. Pleading self-defense, Charlotte was portrayed as a faithful woman wronged by a brutal husband who was both mentally and physically ill. Scores of witnesses supported Charlotte who, taking the stand in her own defense, tearfully and haltingly told the court of the nightmare her life had been with the violently jealous older man.

Her defense attorney ended an eloquent summation by pointing to his client and pronouncing, "She is too beautiful to be bad." The jury (12 French men all under the age of forty with seven of them bachelors) needed only nine minutes (a record for Riviera tribunals of justice) on the opening day of the trial to find Charlotte not guilty. Sailing back home to America on the steamer *Roma*, she told reporters dockside in Villefranche, "Though I have suffered here, I can never forget the kindness, sympathy and understanding shown me by everybody. France has been kind to me." Upon arriving in the States, the former "Miss St. Louis" reportedly signed a contract to appear in vaudeville. On February 21, 1932 the Fox Film Company released the feature, *She Wanted a Millionaire*, suggested by the Nixon-Nirdlinger tragedy. Starring Joan Blondell and James Kirkwood in the principal roles, the film's first story outline was completed just sixteen days after the killing. In September 1932, Charlotte visited the Fox studio reportedly to make a screen test, but to this writer's knowledge has never appeared credited in any motion picture.

Further Reading

"Beauty Freed in Death Case." *Los Angeles Times*, May 21, 1931, p. 3.
"F. Nixon-Nirdlinger Slain; Wife Is Held." *The New York Times*, March 12, 1931, pp. 1, 4.
"Slaying Laid to Frothy Life." *Los Angeles Times*, March 13, 1931, p. 2.

Norwood, John (M)

An aspiring Scots actor, Norwood appeared in small roles in the Glasgow gang film *Small Faces* (1995), *The Acid House* (1998), and the 1997 made-for-television movie, *Bumping the Odds*. On September 22, 1996, the 20-year-old actor invited his uncle, Matthew Houston, to his second-floor flat in Glasgow. During the visit, the inebriated Houston continued to verbally abuse Norwood's mother and girlfriend both present in the apartment. In the ensuing scuffle to eject Houston from the premises, Norwood admitted his punches and kicks caused his uncle to fall off a balcony outside the flat. Although badly injured, Houston refused his nephew's pleas to obtain immediate medical attention and sent away an ambulance. Houston died three days later in hospital from internal injuries suffered in the fall. In accepting Norwood's plea of culpable homicide, the High Court in Edinburgh noted the actor's violent assault, but found Houston partially responsible for his own death by stubbornly refusing medical treatment. Norwood, who described the entire incident as a "nightmare from which he would never recover," was sentenced to three years detention.

Further Reading

McKain, Bruce. "Actor Gets Detention for Killing." *The Herald*, October 10, 1997, p. 7.

Notorious B.I.G. (V)

Forever linked in death as icons of East and West Coast rap, respectively, the Notorious B.I.G. and his former friend, Tupac Shakur, were the finest gangsta rappers ever to pick up microphones. Their unsolved murders roughly six months apart offer a sobering glimpse into lives lived on mean streets and the glittering, but violent world of hip-hop. The rapper destined to become internationally known as the Notorious B.I.G. was born Christopher George Latore Wallace on May 21, 1972, in the Clinton Hill section of Brooklyn to mother Voletta, a Jamaican who became a naturalized American citizen, and George Latore, a Jamaican born businessman who left the family before the child turned two. The child only saw the man once again when he was six and was raised by a single mother who worked two jobs to support the family. Voletta Wallace moved into a nice third-floor apartment on 226 St. James Place in Clinton Hill just a ten minute walk to Bedford-Stuyvesant, the most dangerous and drug-infested section of Brooklyn. Nicknamed "Big" as a kid because of his intimidating size, he inherited Voletta's work ethic and by 11 was bagging groceries at a local food market. "Biggie" realized early the overarching importance money played in escaping the ghetto and saw rapping as the ultimate vehicle by which he could earn lots of it in a hurry. While telling everyone within earshot that he was one day going to be a rap star, the teen began selling $5 and $10 bags of pot on the streets of Clinton Hill and Bed-Stuy. In a series of personal contradictions which would only add to Biggie's mystique, the young pusher was an excellent student at a private Catholic high school as well as a Big Brother volunteer, but dropped out after his junior year to make instant money on the streets. Shortly after leaving school, the 17 year old was arrested for selling crack while visiting friends in North Carolina and served nine months (accounts vary to as little as three days) in jail waiting to make bail.

Biggie, already known in parts of Brooklyn for rapping his own rhymes of hard-scrabble times on inner city streets, began taking his music seriously upon his release. Gifted with a husky voice and an imposing physical presence (standing 6' 3" and weighing 390 pounds), he began recording his gangsta raps in a friend's home studio under the name of Quest in early 1992, and performed with local acts OGB (Old Gold Brothers) and the Techniques. The homemade four-track tapes, circulated on the streets of Brooklyn and sold in area record shops, made the rapper a celebrity in the 'hood and brought him to the attention of Mr. Cee, a local DJ. Mr. Cee (unrelated to the San Francisco rapper in this book) knew talent when he heard it, and gave the tapes to *The Source*, a hip-hop magazine which featured a column on new unsigned artists. A favorable review of the tape and a photo of Biggie appeared in the March 1992 issue where it was seen by Sean "Puff Daddy" Combs, an ambitious young producer at Uptown Records who was always on the lookout for fresh talent. According to hip-hop legend, Combs tracked Biggie down on the streets of Brooklyn and told the rapper that he could make him rich, just the words Biggie wanted to hear. (At the time of his death, the rapper earned $65,000 a show). Combs signed his new find to Uptown Records and immediately dropped the monicker Quest in favor of "Biggie Smalls," a name based on a character in the 1974 film *Uptown Saturday Night* starring Sidney Poitier and Bill Cosby. Later, they dropped Biggie Smalls in favor of Notorious B.I.G. to avoid confusion with another rapper of the same name in California. A shrewd promoter of image and talent, Combs decided to capitalize on his new acquisition's rough appearance by marketing him as gangsta rap's first "mob don" and often outfitted Biggie in striped tailored suits and brimmed "playa" hats. Combs had nearly completed work on Biggie's first album when he was fired from Uptown Records by its CEO, Andre Harrell, over a dispute. Unwisely, Uptown also let go of Biggie. The sacking proved a blessing for both men. Combs scored a $15 million distribution deal with Arista Records that allowed the creative entrepreneur to take the label Uptown had started for him, Bad Boy Records, to the next level.

On September 13, 1994, the Notorious B.I.G.'s debut album, *Ready to Die*, was released to universal acclaim. Generally credited with reinventing East Coast gangsta rap, Biggie emerged as a powerful storyteller whose tales of life on the streets instantly connected with listeners. The album yielded two number one double platinum singles ("Big Poppa" and "One More Chance") and sold over four million copies. "One More Chance" was selected as *Billboard*'s Rap Single of the Year and Biggie was also honored by the organization as Best Rap Artist of the Year. *Ready to Die* made Biggie a rap superstar and Sean "Puff Daddy" Combs' Bad Boy Entertainment a key player in a field once almost exclusively dominated by Marion "Suge" Knight, the mercurial CEO of Death Row Records who would soon sign his own rap superstar, Tupac Shakur (see entry). Biggie opened for 2Pac when the West Coast rapper performed in New York City and the men respected and liked one another. This was destined to change, however, on November 30, 1994 in the lobby of Quad Recording Studios in downtown Manhattan. 2Pac was shot several times during a robbery and suspected that Combs, Biggie, and Andre Harrell, all upstairs in the recording studio at the time of the shooting, had set him up (an allegation all denied). This suspicion festered during the time 2Pac was in prison on a sex abuse conviction and was fully articulated after Knight posted a $1.4 million bond to free the rapper on October 12, 1995, and signed him to Death Row Records.

As Biggie's reputation in the violent drug-fueled world of gangsta rap grew so did his rap sheet. In June 1995, the rapper was arrested and charged with robbery and assault after his entourage beat down Nathaniel Banks, a 31-year-old music promoter, in Camden, New Jersey. Biggie became enraged with Banks after trying to collect the balance of a performance fee for a cancelled show and allegedly broke the man's jaw. The rapper was cleared of the robbery charge, but in January 1997 a jury in a Camden, New Jersey civil trial ordered him to pay Banks $41,700 in damages and medical bills. Around 4:30 A.M. on March 23, 1996, two fans approached Biggie for an autograph outside the Palladium nightclub in Manhattan. Words were exchanged and the two men drove off in a cab with the rapper and his friend Damien Butler, 23, in hot pursuit. When the cab stopped for a light at Union Square West and 16th Street, Biggie and Butler jumped out of their car and smashed in the taxi's windows with baseball bats. Both men were arrested for assault, but after pleading out to criminal mischief and fourth-degree harassment were only ordered to

perform one hundred hours of community service. On July 23, 1996, Biggie was arrested on weapons and drug charges after police raided his condo in Teaneck, New Jersey and found a Tec-9 pistol with one thirty-round clip, two guns with laser-targeting devices, hollow point bullets, and nearly fifty grams of marijuana. The serial numbers on the guns had been abraded, a common practice employed in the sale and purchase of illegal firearms. In all, the raid netted seven members of Biggie's rap group, the Junior M.A.F.I.A., all of whom were charged with possession of marijuana. Biggie posted bond and was given a court date. Finally, on September 15, 1996 an anonymous tip led to the arrest of Biggie and two associates caught smoking marijuana in his parked luxury car in Brooklyn. The trio was charged with drug possession and each released on their own recognizance. Biggie, however, would be dead before the case came to trial.

In the midst of his swirl of arrests and court dates, the then 20-year-old fathered a daughter (T'Yanna) with a young woman from his old Clinton Hill neighborhood, but elected not to marry her. On August 31, 1995, he met fellow-label mate and singer Faith Evans during a midtown Manhattan photo shoot for Bad Boy Entertainment. The attraction was instant and they married eight days later on September 8, 1995. The troubled union produced one son (Christopher Jordan), and they separated 18 months later. During their ongoing estrangement, Biggie was linked with several women and made no attempt to hide his relationship with Lil' Kim, a member of his group the Junior M.A.F.I.A. With 2Pac now out of prison thanks to Death Row Records and still fuming over his belief Combs and Biggie were behind his near murder, the rapper ratcheted up the tensions between the East Coast (Bad Boy Entertainment) and the West Coast (Death Row Records). In his June 1996 single "Hit 'Em Up," 2Pac bragged about having had sex with Faith Evans and threatened his former friend. Biggie responded in kind in his single, "Who Shot Ya," by suggesting that 2Pac accidentally and ineptly shot himself during the robbery with the gun he kept in his waistband. The tension between the posses of Biggie and 2Pac escalated throughout 1996 and 1997 in various awards shows (see entry on Tupac Shakur) culminating in what many observers of the so-called "rap war" believe was the sanctioned hit of 2Pac in Las Vegas on September 7, 1996. 2Pac died six days later on September 13,

1996. Both Biggie and Sean Combs denied any involvement in the murder, but acknowledged tensions between the two camps were at an all time high. In numerous interviews Biggie expressed concern for his safety not only due to possible retaliation for 2Pac's killing, but also because he was a high profile celebrity.

During February 1997, Biggie and Combs stayed in Los Angeles to take advantage of the city's superior production facilities in order to film videos for the rapper's long anticipated second album, *Life After Death*, set for release on March 25, 1997. In a radio interview conducted three days before his death, the rapper told listeners that he loved California and wanted no trouble with anyone in the city. On the evening of March 7, 1997, Biggie was a presenter at the eleventh annual *Soul Train* Music Awards at L.A.'s Shrine Auditorium and Expo Center. Onstage, his voice was drowned out by boos from a hostile group of Bloods who flashed West Coast gang signs from their position in the upper balcony. The rapper put up a brave front, but left the show immediately and watched the remainder of it on television in the safety of his suite in the Westwood Marquis. The next night, March 8, Biggie and Combs attended the by invitation only post-awards party thrown by *Vibe* (a popular hip-hop magazine) at the Petersen Automotive Museum at 6060 Wilshire Boulevard near Hollywood. They arrived with their entourage in rented Chevy Suburbans around 9:00 P.M., too late to find parking in the garage, and were forced to park on Fairfax Avenue one block from the facility. The party, attended by some 2,000 industry insiders and hip-hop royalty, was shut down by fire marshalls due to over capacity at 12:35 A.M. Biggie and Combs discussed going to another party as they walked back to their parked cars on Fairfax. Biggie piled into the green Suburban's front passenger seat next to his driver-bodyguard with Lil' Ceasar, Damien Butler, and Groovy Luv sitting in the back. They fell in behind Combs' white Suburban containing his driver and three bodyguards. A black Chevy Blazer filled with off-duty officers from the Inglewood Police Department brought up the rear. As the motorcade stopped for a light on Fairfax some one hundred yards from the driveway entrance to the Petersen Automotive Museum, a dark sedan (possibly a Chevrolet Impala Super Sport) pulled up along the passenger side of the SUV carrying Biggie. The car's driver, a black man in his early twenties wearing a dress shirt and bow tie, pulled a 9mm handgun and sprayed the vehicle with bullets. Of the five individuals in the Suburban, only the rapper was hit clearly marking him as the target of a professional hit. The dark sedan sped off chased by the Chevy Blazer containing the off-duty police bodyguards hired for the occasion. The hitman, however, quickly lost the pursuit car and the trained police officers were unable to even record a partial plate leading to some speculate as to their possible involvement in the hit. Combs jumped out of his white Suburban lead car and rushed back to his friend. The Notorious B.I.G. was slumped against the dashboard bleeding through his jacket from seven shots to this massive chest. Unable to extricate Biggie from the car because of his size, Combs and his driver, Kenneth Story, jumped in the car and floorboarded it to the Cedars-Sinai Medical Center some two miles away. At the hospital's emergency entrance, it took six people to place the nearly 400 pound rapper onto a gurney. As Combs and the rest of Biggie's entourage fell to their knees and prayed, the Notorious B.I.G. was pronounced dead at 1:15 A.M.

In the aftermath of the deadly attack speculation was rampant that the hit was payback for the murder of 2Pac, a form of perverse "tit for tat" engineered by Death Row CEO Marion "Suge" Knight against Bad Boy mogul Sean "Puff Daddy" Combs. Knight vehemently denied the charge and it was never proven that anyone connected with Death Row was in any way involved in Biggie's execution. Like 2Pac's murder, as well as most other killings in the world of rap, the official investigation was hampered by the unwillingness of potential witnesses to step forward and share their information with police. The murders of rap's two biggest stars, however, did accomplish a *rapprochement* of sorts between factions of the East and West Coast. Days after Biggie's death, representatives of the East and West coast including Snoop Doggy Dogg and Chuck D. met in Chicago at a rap summit sponsored by the Nation of Islam's Louis Farrakhan. Both sides pledged support for a unity pact that would include a joint peace tour and an album.

On March 12, 1997, Biggie's body was flown from Los Angeles to New York in preparation for a memorial and motorcade through his beloved neighborhood of Clinton Hill which he had steadfastly supported through charitable contributions since first tasting success. On the morning of March 18, nine days after the murder, the rapper lay in state in an open oversized $15,000 mahogany casket at the Frank E. Campbell Funeral Chapel on New York City's Upper Eastside. True to his "rap don" image, Biggie was laid out in a color-coordinated white double-breasted suit, silk shirt and tie, and derbylike "playa" hat. The hour-long service was attended by 350 invited guests among them fellow-rap stars Dr. Dre, Busta Rhymes, Foxy Brown, Mary J. Blige, and Lil' Kim and fellow Junior M.A.F.I.A. members. Mother Voletta Wallace read biblical scriptures and estranged wife Faith Evans sang "Walk with Me, Lord." Sean "Puff Daddy" Combs performed the eulogy. Following the emotional service, a motorcade of twenty black stretch limos led by the hearse containing the rapper and two flower cars slowly rolled past police in riot gear and thousands of fans lining the streets of Brooklyn chanting "B-I-G Forever." The rapper's music blared from car radios, ghetto blasters, and storefront loudspeakers, while on the doorstep outside his former home at 226 St. James Place in Clinton Hill neighbors and fans had erected makeshift shrines comprised of photos, flowers, dollar bills, and booze bottles. The procession was remarkably peaceful until it moved past the residence and a scuffle broke out between police and mourners. In the ensuing confrontation, ten were arrested and four police officers and two civilians were briefly hospitalized for pepper spray burns. Biggie's body was taken to the Fresh Ponds Cemetery in Middle Village, Queens, where it was cremated and the ashes given to his mother. Although the rapper signed divorce papers ending his ill-conceived marriage to Faith Evans, the document was never filed and by default she was left the lion's share of his considerable estate. To her credit, Evans voluntarily split the estate with Voletta Wallace in recognition of Biggie's devotion to his mother who continues to press authorities to find the person(s) responsible for her only child's murder. To date, no arrests have been made.

Seventeen days after being gunned down on the streets of Los Angeles at the age of 24, Biggie's second album, a two-disc set entitled *Life After Death*, was released on March 25, 1997 and immediately soldout. An ambitious combination of gangsta rap and pop songs heavily influenced by its producer Sean Combs, the 24 track album featured Biggie on its cover leaning against a hearse. The album yielded three hit singles ("Mo Money Mo Problems," "Hypnotize," "Sky's the Limit")

and sold eight million units. On December 7, 1999, nearly three years after his death, the album *Born Again* was released featuring unreleased rhymes rapped by Biggie supported by guest performers including Busta Rhymes, Method Man, Ice Cube, and Snoop Dogg. Produced by Combs, the "outro" consists of a touching reminiscence of her son by Voletta Wallace. To date, Biggie has been the subject of two films of note—a documentary and a theatrical motion picture. Director Nick Broomfield's 2002 documentary, *Biggie and Tupac*, is based on Randall Sullivan's book *LAbyrinth* and suggests that corrupt LAPD officers involved with "Suge" Knight's Death Row Records were responsible for the rapper's murder. In the well reviewed 2009 film *Notorious*, Biggie was played by Jamaal Woolard (better known as the rapper Gravy).

Further Reading

Brown, Jake. *Ready to Die: The Story of Biggie Smalls, Notorious B.I.G., King of the World and New York City: Fast Money, Puff Daddy, Faith and Life After Death: The Unauthorized Biography*. Phoenix: Colossus, 2004.
Coker, Cheo Hodari. *Unbelievable: The Life, Death, and Afterlife of the Notorious B.I.G.* New York: Three Rivers, 2003.
Scott, Cathy. *The Murder of Biggie Smalls*. New York: St. Martin's, 2000.
Sullivan, Randall. *LAbyrinth: A Detective Investigates the Murders of Tupac Shakur and Biggie Smalls, the Implication of Death Row Records' Suge Knight, and the Origins of the Los Angeles Police Scandal*. New York: Atlantic Monthly, 2002.

Novarro, Ramón (V)

One of filmdom's earliest Latin stars, the Mexican-born Novarro established himself in the 1920s and early 1930s among MGM's top male actors based on his career-making role as "Judah Ben-Hur" in the 1925 blockbuster *Ben-Hur*. Today, however, the silent film star is destined to be unfairly remembered almost exclusively as an alcoholic, closeted homosexual who was tortured and murdered by two hustler brothers in his Hollywood home on October 30, 1968. The future heartthrob was born José Ramón Gil Samaniego in Durango, Mexico on February 6, 1899. His father was a respected and well-to-do dentist who, with his devoted wife, brought up twelve children (another child was stillborn) in the Roman Catholic faith. Doted on by his mother, the child was taught to play piano at age six, was performing puppet shows by eight, and as a teen took singing and dancing lessons. In September 1916, the political unrest in Mexico prompted his parents to send the 17-year-old Ramón and his younger brother to live with relatives in El Paso,

One of the silent screen's greatest "Latin lovers," Ramón Novarro achieved superstardom after MGM cast him in the coveted title role of *Ben-Hur* opposite May McAvoy in 1925. However, due to the studio's mismanagement of his career and concerns over the Mexican-born actor's ability to transition into sound films, MGM dropped him in 1935. Although Novarro made a few more films, he was relegated to television guest shots during the 1960s. A closeted homosexual who paid hustlers for sex, the 69-year-old actor was tortured and beaten to death in his Hollywood Hills home by two brothers on October 30, 1968.

Texas. The pair eventually made it to Los Angeles on Thanksgiving Day 1916 where Ramón was determined to make it big in the movies. In 1917, Ramón Samaniego snagged an uncredited bit part as a Mexican bandit in *The Jaguar's Claws*, a Famous Players-Lasky release. While occasionally appearing as an extra in the movies, Samaniego supported himself with a variety of odd jobs (grocery clerk, busboy, piano tuner) including a stint as a nude model at the J. Francis Smith School of Illustration and Painting. The young actor's most meaningful work, however, was as a combination usher-bit player at the Majestic Theatre in downtown Los Angeles. The dual job not only allowed the 18-year-old to rub shoulders with celebrities and talent scouts, it also afforded him a virtual apprenticeship in the theatrical stock company. In the summer of 1918, choreographer Marion Morgan saw the 5'6" actor onstage at the Majestic and, impressed by his physique, delicate features, and refined manners, selected him to dance in the ballet *Attila and the Huns* set to tour on the Orpheum Circuit in the northern United States and Canada. In June 1919, the 20-year-old dancer dropped out of the company after it returned to Los Angeles and re-dedicated himself to becoming a motion picture actor.

Samaniego's dancing talent led to extra work in movies like the 1921 hit *The Four Horsemen of the Apocalypse* starring screen sensation Rudolph Valentino and Alice Terry, wife of the film's director, Rex Ingram. In the movie, he dances in the background during Valentino's famous tango scene. He also appeared in stylized dancing sequences in two 1921 films (*Man—Woman—Marriage*; *A Small Town Idol*) before landing *Mr. Barnes of New York* in 1922, his first billed appearance as Ramón Samaniego. Committed to further developing his craft, the actor joined the Hollywood Community Theatre in the fall of 1921. While the theatre did not pay its performers, it did offer a venue where young actors could get noticed while established stars could demonstrate their versatility with challenging roles. Director Rex Ingram saw the 22-year-old actor perform there and also in an unreleased 1921 film, *The Rubiyat* (ultimately released in 1925 as *A Lover's Oath*) and hired him to play a small, but important role, in *The Prisoner of Zenda* for Metro. The film was a hit and a friendship developed between the young actor, Ingram, and especially his wife, Alice Terry. Over the next two years, Ingram featured Samaniego in *Trifling Women* (1922), *Where the Pavement Ends* (1923; Novarro's first starring role), *Scaramouche* (1923; the film that made him a star), and *The Arab* (1924). During the production of *Trifling Women*, the actor was rechristened Ramón Novarro because studio execs found Samaniego too difficult to pronounce. As Novarro's popularity increased at Metro, the studio's publicity department began a press blitz aimed at deflecting rumors that their rising star preferred the sexual company of men. Photos of Novarro engaged in the "manly" activities of tennis, jogging, and rowing were salted in fan magazines and his name was romantically linked with numerous actresses including Elsie Janis, Edith Allen, Greta Garbo, and Barbara La Marr. Not surprisingly, one of Novarro's longest-lasting homosexual relationships was with his publicist, Herbert Howe, who in the early to late 1920s helped guide the star's career by touting the studio myth of Novarro as the "Latin Lover" in articles appearing in the fan magazines.

In 1925, Novarro starred in his greatest screen role as "Judah Ben-Hur" in the epic *Ben-Hur*. Taken away from director Rex Ingram and given to Fred Niblo by MGM brass, *Ben-Hur* was a huge success with the physically slight Novarro garnering rave reviews as "manly, handsome, (and) heroic." Along with John Gilbert, an alcoholic whose career ended with the advent of talking pictures, Novarro was MGM's top male star earning a reported $5,000 a week. The studio's lack of focus in managing the career of one its biggest as-

sets, however, severely hampered and ultimately destroyed Novarro as a top box office draw. Outside of a couple films like the 1927 feature *The Student Prince in Old Heidelberg* directed by the noted Ernst Lubitsch, Novarro would be wasted in trifles like *A Certain Young Man* (1928) and *Forbidden Hours* (1928). Dissatisfied with his career, the star seriously considered joining a Catholic religious order, but was turned down. Studio concerns that Novarro's Mexican accent could hurt him in talking pictures proved unfounded when the star's first sound film, *Devil-May-Care* (1929), did excellent box office despite lukewarm reviews. Today, Novarro's only sound film that is still remembered is the 1931 MGM production *Mata Hari* and that because it starred Greta Garbo in the title role. By 1933, the actor was sinking into the second-tier of screen stardom, his good looks dissipated by years of binge drinking and late night cruising in gay bars accompanied by a "beard" like friend Alice Terry. After three box office losers in a row (*Cat and the Fiddle*, 1934; *Laughing Boy*, 1934; *The Night is Young*; 1935) totalling a loss of nearly a quarter of a million dollars, MGM released its 36-year-old star in January 1935 with a $19,000 severance check. In his nearly 11 years with the studio, Novarro's 22 films generated more than $31,000,000 in profits, second only to Joan Crawford. Novarro's subsequent career continued sporadically with roles in legitimate theatre, vocal concerts, the occasional movie (the last being *Heller in Pink Tights*, 1960), and some interesting television guest shots in 1960s series like *Combat!*, *Rawhide*, *Thriller*, *Dr. Kildare*, *Bonanza*, and *The High Chaparral*.

Novarro's lack of professional activity did not seriously threaten his Hollywood lifestyle thanks to astute real estate investments in the San Fernando Valley and his home country of Mexico. When not engaged in acting projects, the aging actor increasingly turned to alcohol to fill the slack in his career. Beginning in 1938, reports of Novarro's alcohol-related car accidents were frequently reported in the newspaper. In May 1960, the actor's uncontrolled drinking resulted in two arrests for drunkenness within a 48 hour period. In February 1962, he was arrested for drunkenness, paid a fine, and served a day in jail. Physically, alcohol was taking its toll on Novarro's liver bloating his once chiseled body and face. No longer the "idol of millions," Novarro started discreetly paying for companionship and sex through male escort services in Hollywood. In the summer and fall of 1968, the drunken actor wrote nearly 140 checks in the $25.00 to $40.00 range to euphemistically named "gardeners" and "masseuses" operating out of a gay hustler escort service, "Masseurs — The Best" on Fountain Avenue in Hollywood. Often too drunk to perform, Novarro fondled his companion or simply walked around naked. Well-liked by the hustlers because he was a good tipper, the actor promised a few prostitutes to get them in the movies although his time of being able to do anyone a favor at a studio had long since passed.

On the afternoon of October 30, 1968, Novarro, 69, received a phone call from a man he had never met offering sex for money. The caller, 22-year-old Paul Robert Ferguson, was an unemployed house painter-handyman only a few months in Los Angeles from the Chicago area. Ferguson, arrested as a youth for beating up an elderly man, had been married four times and, the week prior to calling Novarro, had been left by his current wife. Complicating matters was the arrival in L.A. of his 17-year-old brother, Thomas Scott Ferguson, a runaway from the Chicago Youth Authority. Desperate for money, Paul Ferguson did some nude modelling and was earning around $25.00 a trick hustling gay men. Victor Nichols, a friend of the elder Ferguson, told the hustler that Novarro was a "soft touch" and gave him the actor's number recommending that he tell the faded star that it had been supplied by Larry Ortega, another homosexual hustler who was a personal friend of Novarro's. A family affair, Ortega was married to Ferguson's sister. Intrigued by Paul Ferguson's description of himself, Novarro invited the hustler and his younger brother, Tom, over to his sprawling Spanish-style mansion at 3110 Laurel Canyon Boulevard in the Hollywood Hills for drinks around 5:30 P.M. At 6:30 P.M. Novarro phoned his friend Leonard Shannon, a film publicist for United Artists. Shannon had yet to return home from the studio, so Novarro spoke to the man's wife launching into a bizarre and effusive description of Paul Ferguson as a tall, good-looking young man who possessed "star quality." Ringing off, the actor suggested that the three men lunch "at the studio" later in the week. It was the last phone call Ramón Novarro ever made.

At 8:30 A.M. the next day, Halloween, Edward Weber, the actor's personal secretary for nearly a decade, arrived at the mansion for work. Letting himself in with a key through the kitchen door

as usual, Weber found signs of a struggle in the living room, den, and the master bedroom. Opening the blinds in the bedroom, he found Novarro's bloody nude body face-up on the disarranged bed. The police investigation determined the aging actor's hands were tied behind his back with electrical cord also binding his ankles. On the right side of his neck the initial "Z" or "N" was carved. In his right hand an unused condom was recovered from between two fingers. Novarro's head, neck, chest, left arm, penis, and knees were a bloody mass of lacerations and bruises. A broken silver-tipped cane with an ivory handle, a memento from one of the former star's films, was on top of his right thigh. The name "Larry" was scribbled in ink on the bedsheet, the ball-point pen found under his body. "Larry" was also scrawled four times on a notepad near the living room phone. The smudged message, "Us Girls are better than fagits (sic)," was written across the bedroom mirror. Bloody fingerprints were everywhere and, outside near a fence enclosing the property, police recovered a pile of bloody clothing. Robbery as a motive was ruled out — there were no signs of a break-in and nothing had been stolen. The autopsy determined that Novarro slowly suffocated to death on the blood flowing into his air passages from his fractured nose and the numerous lacerations on his mouth. The actor's blood alcohol level was a whopping .23.

A police investigation into Novarro's bank accounts revealed the faded star often used a male escort agency employing one Larry Ortega. A county jail inmate stepped forward to offer information that he and Ortega often hustled together adding that the man's brother-in-law, Paul Ferguson, was also a male prostitute known for his incendiary temper. A dump of Novarro's phone records showed that on the day of his death a 48-minute call from the mansion to Chicago was placed. On November 5, 1968, Ortega and his sister, Mari Ortega Ferguson, were questioned by detectives. Mari Ferguson described her troubled relationship with Paul and mentioned that his younger brother, Tom, was staying at an apartment in the L.A. suburb of Gardena. Larry Ortega admitted Novarro called him on the day of his death to ask him about "Paul." Not making the connection with his brother-in-law, Paul Ferguson, Ortega told his client-friend he did not know anyone by that name. The case, however, ultimately came together when detectives learned the call placed from Novarro's home to Chicago was to Tom Ferguson's girlfriend. The bloody fingerprints retrieved at the death scene matched the Fergusons (on file from their numerous infractions with the law). On November 6, 1968, both brothers were arrested without incident in the L.A. suburb of Bell Gardens.

On July 28, 1969, the brothers were tried individually with separate counsel in the same courtroom in the Los Angeles Superior Court. Paul Ferguson faced a possible death sentence if convicted of first-degree murder. Tom Ferguson, 17 at the time of the killing and too young under the law to be executed, was tried as an adult and faced life in prison. Deputy District Attorney James M. Ideman played down Novarro's homosexual lifestyle while portraying the brothers as opportunistic hustlers who tortured then murdered the actor after he refused to tell them where he had hidden $5,000 in cash in his home. Novarro, it was later learned, never kept that much cash on hand. Not surprisingly, both brothers insisted the other man committed the murder. Tom Ferguson, who earlier bragged to fellow-inmates that he killed the "old faggot," now testified that his family had convinced him to accept blame for the crime since as a minor he would escape the death penalty while his older brother could not. According to Tom Ferguson, he was passed out drunk on the sofa while older brother Paul was in Novarro's bedroom having sex with the man. He entered the room to find Paul Ferguson covered in blood, a stunned, badly beaten Novarro sitting on the edge of the bed insisting he had no money in the house. Tom Ferguson told the court he decided to tell the truth about Paul killing the actor when he learned Novarro had been bludgeoned with a cane. At one point, an exasperated Paul Ferguson threw a ball-point pen at his brother and angrily shouted, "Oh, you punk liar ... you son of a bitch." Both, however, admitted to drinking heavily then overturning the furniture and planting evidence (like the condom) to make police believe the murder had been the result of a robbery attempt. In his closing argument, Ideman cautioned the jury not to put Novarro on trial because of his homosexuality. "He has paid for whatever he did and now it is the Fergusons' turn to pay for whatever they may have done."

On September 17, 1969, just eight hours after receiving the case, the jury found both brothers guilty of first-degree murder. During the penalty phase of the trial, Superior Court Judge Mark Brandler sentenced each man to life imprisonment with a strong recommendation that both never be given parole. In 1975, however, Tom Ferguson was placed on probation. While on a work furlough program in 1976, he violated probation, and was returned to prison. Remarkably, he was again paroled on June 15, 1977. In June 1986, Tom Ferguson, 34, was arrested in a Chico, California motel and charged with raping a 54-year-old woman. In January 1987, he pleaded guilty to sexual assault and was given the maximum eight year prison sentence. Paroled in 1990, Ferguson was again sent to prison in 1997 for failing to register as a sex offender within the state of California. He was last reported serving six years for the crime at the California Medical Facility in Vacaville. Older brother Paul used his time in San Quentin to better himself earning an associate of arts degree in epistemology. After winning a fiction prize from the P.E.N. Prison Writing Committee, he taught creative writing courses to fellow-inmates. Paroled on July 17, 1978, a scant nine years served for murdering Novarro, Ferguson was discharged in 1981. Variously employed as a steeplejack, builder, and nightclub owner, Paul Ferguson was arrested in March 1989 for first-degree rape and sodomy, and subsequently sentenced to a 30 year prison term. The international heartthrob of millions of women during the 1920s and early 1930s who died a brutal, lonely death that exposed his carefully concealed sexual secret was buried in Calvary Cemetery, Los Angeles, beneath a simple, flat ground marker bearing a crucifix and the inscription, "Beloved Brother — Ramón Novarro — 1899–1968."

Further Reading

Ellenberger, Allan R. *Ramon Novarro: A Biography of the Silent Idol, 1899–1968: With a Filmography.* Jefferson, NC: McFarland, 1999.

Harrison, Joel L. *Bloody Wednesday.* Canoga Park, CA: Major, 1978.

Soares, Andre. *Beyond Paradise: The Life of Ramon Novarro.* New York: St. Martin's, 2002.

Olsson, Tony (M)

The 26-year-old Swede was serving a six-year sentence for plotting to murder a mother of five when he was allowed out of jail to rehearse and perform in a play, *7:3*, at Sweden's National Theatre in mid–1999. The title referred to the section of Sweden's penal code that deals with escape-prone repeat offenders and the drama focused on prisoners with violent neo–Nazi beliefs. Olsson returned to prison following the evening performance on May 27, 1999, and left the next morning on a weekend furlough. Later that day, Olsson and two confederates robbed a bank in the southern Swedish city of Kisa fleeing the scene in a stolen Saab. Two police officers were killed in the ensuing escape. Murder is a rare crime in Sweden where only thirty police officers in the past century had lost their lives in the line of duty. Suspect Andreas Axelsson, 28, was arrested on the day of the robbery after being injured in the police roadblock shoot-out which claimed the lives of two additional officers. Fellow-suspect Jackie Arkloev, a black 26-year-old former mercenary convicted of war crimes in Bosnia, was shot in the chest and arrested in Stockholm on June 1, 1999 just days after the robbery. Olsson, with Axelsson and Arkloev a member of the National Socialist Front, Sweden's largest extreme-right group, was arrested without incident on June 5, 1999 in Alajuela, Costa Rica where he was staying with his mother who traveled to the Central American country to convince her son to surrender to authorities. In the wake of the armed robbery and police killings, the artistic director and chief producer for Sweden's National Dramatic Theatre were forced to resign. At trial in January 2000, Olsson and Axelsson were convicted of robbery and murder and sentenced to life in prison. Tried separately after a psychiatric evaluation ruled him mentally competent, Jackie Arkloev was found guilty of murder, attempted murder, armed robbery, and also given a life term. In June 2000, an appeals court upheld the sentences ruling that all three men were equally guilty of the killings even if it could not be determined who actually fired the fatal shots.

Further Reading

"Nazi 'Terror' Trial Shocks Sweden." *The Observer*, November 25, 1999, p. 25.

Omer, Danielle (V)

On the morning of June 28, 1999, Salt Lake City firemen responded to a blaze at the two-story home of popular local actress Danielle Omer at 4912 S. Bitter Root Drive (3300 West) in Taylorsville, Utah. Separate fires raging upstairs and in the downstairs bedroom suggested arson, later confirmed when an accelerant was discovered at the scene. After the fire was extinguished, authorities found the body of a woman (later identified as the 45-year-old actress) on the floor of the downstairs bedroom. Omer was gagged and her hands bound behind her back. An autopsy revealed the actress was stabbed to death before the house was torched. Two days earlier, a 27-year-old woman in the same Taylorsville neighborhood had been attacked in her home at knifepoint, bound in a similar manner to Omer, and raped as her young children slept in a nearby bedroom. She survived the ordeal to provide authorities with a description of her assailant.

The grisly rape-murder shocked the Utah capital where Omer, the mother of four daughters, was recognized by the Salt Lake theatre community as one of its top actresses. Fellow-thespian Beth Bruner stated that patrons often called the Desert Star Playhouse box office to be sure the local celebrity was in a show before buying tickets. Omer appeared in major roles in community theatre productions of *White Christmas, Elvis in Viva Salt Lake: Eat My Rust, Less Misérables, or a Whole Lot Less Miserable, Dracula, the Vampire, or He Loved in Vein, Beverly Hillbillies 90210, Space Wars: A 2002 Space Oddity of Olympic Proportions, Calamity Jane or All's Riot on the Western Front,* and her most recent role parodying a fading film star in *Miracle on 42nd Street* during the winter season of 1998.

In July 1999, a suspect was arrested based on the composite sketch, but freed by DNA evidence. Working off DNA and a second composite sketch supplied by the surviving rape victim, Salt Lake County sheriff's deputies arrested Robert Lee Overstreet, 34, on August 1, 1999 as he slept in his car in a campground parking lot in Springville Canyon, south of Provo. Overstreet, a.k.a. "Robert Hagelman," was paroled from prison 18 months earlier after serving five years to life on a prior aggravated rape charge. First arrested at 17 for setting fire to an Ogden youth corrections facility, Overstreet served three stints totaling twelve years at the Utah State Prison for crimes including rape, burglary, and assault. In custody, the career criminal matter-of-factly confessed to the rapes and Omer's murder stating that things "snowballed" when he discovered the actress home during his daytime burglary of her residence. Found mentally competent to stand trial, Overstreet pleaded guilty in February 2001 to four felony charges in the non-fatal rape and was sentenced to three consecutive life terms. In August 2002, he avoided the death penalty in Omer's rape-murder by agreeing to spend the rest of his life in prison without the possibility of parole. The D.A.

offered the plea bargain deal after the U.S. Supreme Court ruled the execution of mentally retarded people unconstitutional because it represented cruel and unusual punishment. Overstreet had dropped out of school after the fifth grade and intelligence tests placed his IQ in the 69–71 range (results below 70 are considered to denote retardation).

Further Reading

Hunt, Stephen. "Detective's Testimony Details Actress's Murder." *Salt Lake Tribune*, November 24, 1999, sec. C, p. 2.

Ott, Paul Alan (M)

On the afternoon of January 19, 2004, a scantily clad barefoot woman with duct tape hanging from her wrists and ankles pounded on the door of a house in the 13900 block of Sherman Way in Van Nuys, California, frantically screaming, "He's going to kill me, he's going to kill me." According to police who responded to the homeowner's 911 call, the hysterical woman said she was kidnapped by a white man in the Rampart area of Los Angeles, forced to help him load a dead body into an SUV, driven to an apartment in Van Nuys, and forced to commit oral sodomy on him. Left alone when her attacker went to buy beer, she escaped her bounds and fled the scene. Police located the plastic-wrapped corpse of Edith I. Mejia, a 42-year-old mother of ten, in a Ford Explorer parked in the carport of a Van Nuys apartment building in the 7100 block of Costello Avenue. The parking space was registered to Paul Alan Ott, a 35-year-old Hollywood grip on films including *The Breaks* (1999), *Michael Jordan: An American Hero* (1999—made-for-television-movie), *The Puzzle in the Air* (1999), *Brother* (2000), and *Sueño* (2003). Ott matched the victim's physical description of her attacker (bald, 5'9", 170 pounds, heavily tattooed, white) and police sought him for questioning. The man with a devil's head and the word "Otter" tattooed on his upper body remained at-large until the early morning of January 22, 2004 when detectives assisted by the FBI arrested the unarmed film grip after he jumped from the second-floor window of an apartment building at 7130 Hollywood Boulevard. Ott was charged with the knife murder of Mejia, the rape of the escaped woman, as well as the sexual assault of another woman on January 15, 2004, who stepped forward after seeing the laborer's photo on television.

At trial in May 2004, Ott insisted he acted in self-defense when Mejia, a casual friend, lunged at him with a knife. Jurors discounted the idea in favor of the prosecution's characterization of Ott as murderer acting under a week long "drug-induced" rampage. On May 11, 2006, the 38-year-old grip was found guilty of second-degree murder in Mejia's death and of the sexual assault of his escaped captive. The earlier sexual assault case was dropped before trial. He was sentenced to a combined prison term of 61 years to life (31 years for murder, 30 years for forcible oral copulation). "It was one of the sickest cases I have known," Deputy District Attorney Shellie Samuels, prosecutor in the Robert Blake (see entry) murder trial said. "It's a sad case for everyone involved because [Ott] has two little girls, but I'm happy with the sentence." In July, 2007 a state appellate court panel upheld Ott's conviction.

Further Reading

Abram, Susan. "30-Year Prison Term in Murder." *The Daily News of Los Angeles* (Valley ed.), June 28, 2006, p. 4.

Palmer, Pearl (V) (M-S)

Throughout their two year engagement, Palmer, a 23-year-old prima donna best known for her role in Victor Herbert's opera *Princess Pat*, delayed marrying Herbert Heckler, a 27-year-old opera singer from Chicago, in order to pursue a career. On September 26, 1915, Palmer was in her studio at the Conservatory Building at No. 240 West 72nd Street in New York City when a depressed Heckler arrived for a visit. Palmer complained she was ill and dispatched her beau to a pharmacy for medication. A friend who accompanied Heckler later told authorities that the singer burst into tears when discussing his suspicion that Palmer no longer loved him. Returning to her studio, Heckler entered the room alone. Moments later, the sounds of a violent argument were heard followed by four gunshots in quick succession. When police forced the door they discovered Palmer unconscious, a bullet lodged in her head and two in her body. The prima donna died shortly afterward in the Polyclinic Hospital. Heckler, the spurned suitor, lay dead in the center of the room, a gaping gunshot wound in his forehead.

Further Reading

"Shoots Girl Opera Star—Kills Self." *New York American*, September 27, 1915, p. 1.

Panou, Akis (M)

One of Greece's best-known folk musicians and

composers, Panou (born 1933) rose to fame with such songs as "I Don't Want Anyone's Compassion" and "My Life Is Just One Cigarette that I Don't Like, but Drag Away At." Panou retired from performing in the late 1970s after a falling out with his record company and relocated from Athens to Xanthi. On August 1, 1987, the 64-year-old composer committed a "crime of honor" when he shot his daughter's married lover, Sotiri Yialamas, point-blank in the face at Panou's home in the village of Lefki. Describing the truck driver at trial as a "druggie," "thug," and a "gangster," Panou insisted honor demanded that he kill the man who had humiliated him by making his 20-year-old daughter pregnant. A jury disagreed and in March, 1998, a remorseless Panou was sentenced to the maximum term of life imprisonment. The 66-year-old died of cancer on April 7, 2000.

Further Reading

"Folk Singer Receives Life for Murder of Daughter's Boyfriend." Associated Press, March 23, 1998.

Pappalardi, Felix (V)

One of the most talented and respected rock producers and bass guitarists of the late 1960s and early 1970s, Pappalardi (born December 30, 1939, in the Bronx, New York) received classical music training at the University of Michigan with an eye to becoming a choral conductor. While at Michigan Pappalardi conducted the Opera Association and for 2½ years conducted opera in Detroit. Leaving school at 22 in the early 1960s, the musician sought work as a conductor in New York City, but mostly hung out in Greenwich Village attracted by the area's exploding folk music scene. Pappalardi began as a solo artist playing guitar and singing, but was soon backing performers like Tom Rush and Tom Paxton. Exposure on the Greenwich Village folk circuit led to tours with the Canadian duo Ian & Sylvia. By the mid–1960s, Pappalardi established himself in New York as a first-class arranger and studio musician working for record labels Elektra and Vanguard. The transition to record producer came easily for the classically trained musician who began to introduce electric instruments into many of the artists he produced like Tim Hardin, Richard and Mimi Farina, and the Youngbloods for whom he produced the 1967 (re-released 1969) hit "Get Together." After forming the production company Windfall with Bud Prager, Pappalardi started

haunting the halls of Atlantic Records hoping to find work with big name acts. Lightning struck in 1967 when he was selected to produce *Disraeli Gears*, the second album of all-star British supergroup Cream. The power trio (bassist Jack Bruce; drummer Ginger Baker; guitarist Eric Clapton) raised psychedelic blues-rock to another level and Pappalardi was, in essence, the unheralded fourth member of the group. With wife Gail Collins and Eric Clapton, he co-wrote the album's song, "Strange Brew," and produced the group's subsequent albums *Wheels of Fire* (1967) and *Goodbye* (1969). Pappalardi played viola on the hit song "White Room" and piano on the group's last single, "Badge." After Cream disbanded in 1969, Pappalardi produced bassist Jack Bruce's solo album, *Songs for a Tailor*, but longed to fill the musical vacuum left by the super group. In the mid–1960s, the now internationally known producer had worked at Vanguard with a Long Island, New York band called the Vagrants which featured a phenomenally talented 300 pound plus lead guitarist named Leslie West. When the Vagrants disbanded in 1968, Pappalardi produced West's solo album, *Mountain*, released in September 1969 on Bell. In addition to production chores, Pappalardi co-wrote eight of the album's 11 songs including four with wife Collins ("Blood of the Sun," "Better Watch Out," "Blind Man," "Baby, I'm Down"). The album's favorable reception prompted Pappalardi to form the hard rock band Mountain around West on July 2, 1969. With Pappalardi playing bass and sharing vocals with West the original group consisted of drummer Norman D. Smart and keyboardist Steve Knight. Mountain had only played three gigs when they were paid $5,000 to perform at Woodstock in August 1969. Drummer Smart was replaced by the metronomic Canadian Corky Laing prior to the group entering the studio in 1970 to record the Windfall-Bell album *Mountain Climbing!* The LP included the smash single "Mississippi Queen" which has since become the band's signature song. Pappalardi also produced and performed on the Mountain albums *Nantucket Sleighride* (1971), *Flowers of Evil* (1972), *Mountain Live— The Road Goes on Forever* (1972), and after a two year hiatus from the group, his final studio collaboration, *Avalanche* (1974). This incarnation of Mountain formally disbanded in 1975 and Pappalardi, partially deafened by his years in the high volume group, retired from live performing and returned to the recording studio. In 1976, he produced the album *Felix Pappalardi & Creation* for A&M. Creation, a Japanese hard rock band, had opened for Mountain on its tours in that country. He recorded his final album, the solo work *Don't Worry Mum?* for A&M in 1979.

Asked in a 1973 interview to explain wife Gail Collins' influence on his work, Pappalardi answered, "She's a very important part (of my work). All the lyrics that I've *ever* set to music are hers." Besides co-writing the Cream songs "Disraeli Gears" and "World of Pain," Collins was seemingly a major contributor to Mountain. She is credited with co-writing four songs on Leslie West's 1969 solo album, *Mountain*, and with Pappalardi contributed greatly to Mountain's success with songs like "Nantucket Sleighride," "Boys in the Band," "Crossroader," "Don't Look Around," and "Never in My Life." In addition, Collins did the album art on all the original Mountain albums and designed the exotic clothing Pappalardi wore on stage. For years Pappalardi and Collins, 43, enjoyed an "open" marriage with women and men often joining the couple for strictly recreational three-way sex and drug parties. However, in 1982 the 43-year-old musician began an 11-month love affair with Valerie Merians, a 27-year-old blonde aspiring singer. Pappalardi, according to Merians, had spoken to her of marriage and presented her with a wedding band engraved with "*Je t'aime—Felix*" and a gold watch engraved "I love you—Felix." One of his last compositions was a love song, "*Je t'aime*" ("I love you") dedicated to Merians and recorded in France by French-Algerian singer Enrico Marcias. Collins, 43, knew of the affair, but unlike his other sexual partners may possibly have felt threatened by its intensity and exclusivity.

While questions still surround the death of Pappalardi in the early morning hours of April 17, 1983, the following details are known: The producer-arranger returned to the fifth-floor luxury apartment he shared with Collins at 30 Waterside Plaza on Manhattan's East Side late on April 16 after spending the evening with Valerie Merians. Shortly before 6:00 A.M., a tearful Collins phoned police and let them into the apartment. Pappalardi, clad only in underwear, was found lying in bed with his legs crossed fatally wounded from a single gunshot to his neck. A .38-caliber two-shot Derringer with one shot fired was found nearby. Pappalardi was pronounced dead at the scene. Collins was initially charged with second-degree murder, criminal possession of a weapon, and held without bail for psychiatric tests.

At her trial in a Manhattan courtroom in September 1983, two very different portraits of Gail Collins and her marriage to her rock star husband emerged. Collins testified that her well-documented open marriage to Pappalardi defused the prosecution's claim that she shot her husband in a jealous rage over his relationship with Merians. "I was the one who urged him to see her because she had a calming effect on him," Collins told the court. Rather, Pappalardi was accidentally shot by her when he was showing her how to properly handle the Derringer during a pre-dawn lesson in gun safety. Collins insisted that she was terrified of guns and, when presented with the murder weapon in court, recoiled and sobbed, "I can't touch that gun, I can't, I can't touch that." The prosecution presented Frances Laing, wife of Mountain drummer Corky Laing, to counter Collins' contention that she was not jealous and extremely fearful of firearms. Laing testified that in August 1975 she and Pappalardi were sitting alone in a car outside of a restaurant in Nantucket when an angry Collins arrived at the window and pointed the .38-caliber Derringer in her face. Collins was "quite proud" when Pappalardi bought her the gun and often joined the Laings for shooting practice in a Nantucket sandpit. Pappalardi's 72-year-old father also testified that in a phone call with Collins four months prior to the fatal shooting she intimated that her marriage to her rock star husband was failing. Most observers of the case were stunned when on September 21, 1983, a six man, six woman jury rejected the D.A.'s charges of murder and manslaughter to instead find Collins guilty of criminally negligent homicide, the lowest possible charge for the killing. Instead of the sentence of 25 years to life for murder, negligent homicide carried only a four year maximum prison term. On October 12, 1983, Collins' attorney addressed the court prior to his client's sentencing to argue that it was only right that she be sentenced to the five months she had already spent in confinement awaiting trial. Gail Collins had "suffered enough." Supreme Court Justice James Leff rejected the plea and sentenced Collins to the maximum of 16 months to four years in prison, adding, "All the clemency, all the sympathy, all the mercy due Mrs. Pappalardi was given by the jury. She is not due one further bit of leniency." Collins served four years in the penitentiary and since her release has remained out of the public eye.

Further Reading

Loder, Kurt. "Felix Pappalardi: 1939–1983." *Rolling Stone*, 396 (May 26, 1983):55.
Scoppa, Bud. *The Rock People*. New York: Scholastic, 1973.
West, Leslie, and Corky Laing. *Nantucket Sleighride and Other Mountain On-The-Road Stories*. Wembley: SAF, 2003.
www.mountaintheband.com.
www.pappalardi.com.

Parks, Wole (M-not charged)

On January 22, 2006, 25-year-old graduate student Hannah Engle was crossing a street in the company of her sister and friends in Manhattan around 1:30 A.M. when she was struck by a car at 14th Street and Second Avenue. The driver stopped his 2001 Hyundai, got out, gave his license to a police officer, and wandered away on foot. Four hours later, Wole Parks, 23, turned himself in at the 94th Precinct station house in Greenpoint, Brooklyn. By the time Parks, an African-American actor who played "Brett" in the sixth season of MTV's soap opera *Undressed* was charged with multiple vehicular-related offenses (driving while intoxicated, leaving the scene of an accident, driving with a suspended license), Engle was pronounced dead at Bellevue Hospital Center. The officer at the scene reported Parks exhibited "watery, bloodshot eyes" and had alcohol on his breath. Inside the car was an open can of beer. However, when Parks was tested (five hours after the hit-and-run) his blood still showed signs of containing alcohol, but was under the legal limit. No stranger to drinking and operating a motor vehicle, Parks temporarily lost his license in July 2005 after being convicted of driving while impaired on the upper West Side. His license was reinstated in October after the completion of a court ordered drunk driving program, but he lost it again in December for failing to pay a fine.

Parks pleaded "not guilty" to a laundry list of charges and, over time, the felony count of leaving a scene of an accident was reduced to a misdemeanor, while the other counts of driving while intoxicated and without a license were dropped. Under a plea deal agreed upon by the assistant district attorney in June 2006, Parks pleaded guilty to the misdemeanor count of leaving the scene of an accident after causing physical injury and was promised a sentence of one year probation, 250 hours of community service, and counseling that included an alcoholism program. Reacting to public outrage over the apparent leniency of the sentence, the district attorney's office maintained the misdemeanor plea was appropriate because evidence indicated Parks had done nothing wrong in the crash—he had the green light and was not speeding. Despite the assessment of the cop at the accident scene, Parks had shown no signs of intoxication. The actor maintained that he drank *after* the accident which explained the presence of alcohol in his blood. As the test administered to Parks many hours after the accident failed to identify him as legally drunk it was deemed impossible to win a felony conviction against him.

Further Reading

Peterson, Helen. "Actor Suspected in Fatal Hit-Run had Lost License in DWI Rap, Victim's Loved Ones 'In a State of Shock.'" *New York Daily News*, January 24, 2006, p. 4.

Parnell, Wallace R. (M-S)

The son of Fred Russell, a brilliant ventriloquist on the London variety stage of the teens, Parnell briefly followed in his father's footsteps before turning to theatrical promotion. After mounting several revues like *Beauty on Parade* in the 1920s and 1930s, he suffered a nervous breakdown in 1934 and was in and out of British bankruptcy courts for the next few years. Following a family dispute, Parnell went to America and distinguished himself as an advertising wonder boy. Returning to England, yet another family fracas forced him away this time to Australia where his tireless efforts as a theatrical producer made him an important figure in that country's entertainment industry. In 1942, Parnell immigrated to America with his sights set upon a theatrical producing career in Hollywood. His one success, *The Beaustone Affair*, played for a record setting eleven weeks at the Las Palmas Theatre in 1951. Four weeks into the show's run, the press revealed the play's author, "L. Len Rap," was in fact, Parnell (with his name spelled in reverse). In the mid–1940s, the theatrical producer resuscitated his advertising career and founded a highly profitable direct mail business, Canterbury Press. He was also the president of Karseal, Inc., a wax polish firm sharing offices with his advertising business at 915 N. Highland Avenue in Hollywood.

Known by friends and business associates to be prone to spells of moodiness, Parnell also suffered from a dangerous physical condition in which any bruise he sustained could result in a life-threatening blood clot. These maladies combined with the recent tumult in his business life, perhaps, offer an insight into the deadly rampage that was to come. Early in 1954, Parnell became convinced that Beryl Erickson, his executive secretary at Canterbury Press, was responsible for the loss of several big accounts. Despite being close friends with the 35-year-old divorced mother of three young children, Parnell hired a private investigator to monitor Erickson's activities. Concurrent with the investigation, the 59-year-old businessman's house was twice burgled. At Parnell's request, the P.I. purchased his employer a .38-caliber pistol ostensibly for home protection. The situation apparently improved on April 7, 1954 when Parnell sold a controlling interest in Canterbury to Erickson and instructed his operative to destroy all documents pertaining to the investigation. He seemed in a good mood and told everyone he was taking his third wife on a trip to Australia before settling down in his home country of England.

Prior to opening hours on May 19, 1954, the janitor in the Highland Avenue building housing Canterbury Press and Karseal, Inc. made a gruesome discovery. Beryl Erickson lay face-down on the floor beside her desk dead from a single gunshot wound inflicted at close range to the left side of her face, below the temple. Parnell's briefcase was beside the body and among the documents found in it was a detective magazine with a front page article entitled, "She Was His Woman and He Was Ready to Kill to Keep Her!" The businessman's body was found in a nearby executive washroom where he had shot himself in the right temple. Attempts to explain Parnell's murder of Erickson and his suicide as motivated by any romantic interest between them were discounted by everyone who knew the close friends.

Further Reading

"Stage Producer and Woman Ex-Secretary Found Slain." *Los Angeles Times*, May 20, 1954, p. 2.

Parsa, Nasrat (V)

Born in Kabul on February 22, 1969, Parsa was first noticed as a six-year-old after performing two songs by his idol, Ahmad Zahir, during a New Year's celebration broadcast live on Radio Kabul. Zahir was so impressed by the young singer that he mentored Parsa and opened the door for him to study classical music under Ostaad Mohammaed Houssein Sarahang. Forced to flee Afghanistan with his family at age 12, Parsa moved to Pakistan, then India, finally settling in Frankfurt, Germany. In 1989, he released his first album,

Lanaai-e-Eshq, followed over the next dozen or so years by nine records filled with both traditional Afghan songs as well as danceable pop tunes. By 2005, based largely on nonstop touring in countries like Australia, Britain, Germany, and the Netherlands, Parsa was universally recognized as one of Afghanistan's top recording stars.

On Saturday, May 7, 2005, the 34-year-old singer was in Vancouver, British Columbia on the last stop of a Canadian tour to promote his latest album, *Dil.* Billed as a Mother's Day concert, Parsa's soldout show at the Queen Elizabeth Theatre was attended by nearly five hundred people, mostly Afghani families. Throughout the concert, audience members jumped onstage to dance with the visibly distracted performer and handed him song requests. At one point, a raucous group down front loudly interrupted Parsa and one drunken man hopped onstage to demand that he perform faster music. The Afghani superstar politely explained that being a Mother's Day concert, not a wedding, he could not respectfully comply with the request. Around 1:30 A.M. the next morning, Parsa and brothers Ehsan and Najeeb were carrying luggage out of the lobby of the Days Inn hotel to load their car for a drive to a cousin's home in Coquitlam when they were approached by three men. According to Ehsan, the brothers recognized the men as the concert-goers whose requests for livelier music had been denied by the singer. Parsa, carrying luggage in one hand, extended the other to offer a friendly handshake when one of the men grabbed his wrist and sucker punched him once in the side of the head. The singer fell awkwardly down a set of four steps and struck his head on the concrete pavement. He would die from massive brain injuries some eight hours later at Vancouver General Hospital. Police, who happened to be near the hotel at the time of the assault, saw the men flee and used a tracking dog to quickly locate one of the suspects hiding in an alley a couple of blocks away. Another man found nearby was also taken into custody. At a memorial service conducted in Farsi for the slain singer attended by 150 family, fans, and band members at the British Columbia Muslim Association in Richmond, one mourner put the entire tragedy into crystalline perspective—"A guest comes all the way from Germany, leaves his own mother to come and sing for our mothers on Mother's Day ... and then we return his dead body to his mother."

Charged with manslaughter in the attack was

19-year-old high school student Ahmad Seiar Froogh of Burnaby, B.C., who moved to Canada from Afghanistan in 2002. In May 2008, Froogh was found guilty in New West Minster Supreme Court after his claim that the incident was just an accident that occurred while he was attempting to obtain an autograph from Parsa was discounted. On February 20, 2009, the Afghani immigrant was sentenced to 2 years of house arrest, 3 years probation, and banned from using a firearm for 10 years.

Further Reading

Ankeny, Jason. "Nasrat Parsa." www.allmusic.com.
Badelt, Brad, and Doris Sun. "City Mourns Slain Afghan Singer." *Vancouver Sun*, May 12, 2005, sec. B, p. 1. www.nasratparsamusic.com.

Pasolini, Pier Paolo (V)

One of Italy's most important post-war filmmakers, Pasolini was a radical Marxist intellectual whose murder in November 1975 is still the subject of intense debate and conjecture. Born March 5, 1922, in Bologna, Italy the son of an army officer, Pasolini left the University of Bologna in 1943 upon being conscripted into the military. The 21-year-old published poet had been in the army only a week when the Italian military surrendered to German forces. Pasolini fled the prison camps and took refuge in Casara, a small town in the Friulian section of northeastern Italy near the border of Austria and Yugoslavia where his family had connections. In Friuli, Pasolini wrote poetry in the language of the district and became a strong supporter of the peasant struggle against the war lords in the area. In 1944, he and some friends founded L'Academiuta di lenga furlana (Friulian Language Academy) to help foster the publication of works in Friulian. Always sympathetic to the plight of the poor and downtrodden, Pasolini became the secretary of a Communist Party cell in Casarsa in 1947, but soon lost the post and his party affiliation amid scandal. By 1949, Pasolini's increasingly overt homosexuality and radical politics had made him an easy blackmail target. A priest with an opposing party affiliation demanded the poet either give up his political life or risk having his teaching career at a secondary school ruined by being identified as a homosexual. In late 1949, Pasolini was arrested for committing homosexual offences (mutual masturbation) against a 16-year-old and two younger boys. The intellectual acknowledged his sexual participation with the minors, but posited the creative defense that their actions were merely a literary experiment in the manner of André Gide. At trial, Pasolini was convicted of committing lewd acts against minors. Although an appeals court in April 1952 would absolve him of the crime based on insufficient evidence, the immediate consequences of the conviction resulted in Pasolini's dismissal from his teaching position and expulsion from the Italian Communist party on the grounds of "moral and political unworthiness."

Leaving the district for Rome in 1949, Pasolini entered a period of intense creative effort writing poetry and publishing his controversial first novel, *Ragazzi di vita/The Ragazzi* in 1955. The book's subject matter, the sordid lives of sub-proletariat teenagers in Rome's impoverished shantytowns, was condemned by the church and prosecuted for obscenity. Pasolini's next novel, *Una Vita violenta/A Violent Life*, again objectively examined the desperate lives of young teens in Rome's slums. The 1959 book was rejected out of hand by the judges of the Strega Prize, Italy's most prestigious literary award, for obscenity, but did win a rival prize called the Cortone. Throughout his life, Pasolini continued to write novels, poetry, essays, and film criticism, but it was as a filmmaker that he was destined to leave his enduring mark on the arts. In 1954, the 22-year-old entered films as a screenwriter first for director Mario Soldati (*La Donna del Fiume*) and later for Federico Fellini (*Le Notti di Cabiria/The Nights of Cabiria*, 1956) and Mario Bolognini (*La Notte Brava*, 1959; *Il Bell'Antonio*, 1960). In 1961, Pasolini began his career as director with *Accattone!*, a feature film based on his novel *Una Vita violenta*. His next film, *Mama Roma* (1962) continued his fascination with Rome's violent lower classes and featured Anna Magnani as a prostitute attempting to better her position in society. Pasolini's most important works, however, were a series of films dealing with both religious (*Il Vangelo Secondo Matteo/The Gospel According to Saint Matthew*, 1964) and literary themes (*Oedipus Rex*, 1967; *The Decameron*, 1971; *The Canterbury Tales*, 1972; *Arabian Nights*, 1974). Although an avowed atheist, *The Gospel According to Saint Matthew* and his *Teorema* (1969) were honored by various Catholic organizations. *The Decameron*, while one of Italy's biggest moneymakers of all time, was condemned by the church for its graphic depiction of sexuality as was his final film, *Salo, or 120 Days of Sodom* (1975) based on the Marquis de Sade's work, but updated and presented as a stinging indictment of the sadistic Fascist rule of Benito Mussolini during 1943–1945. *Salo* and *The Canterbury Tales* were both declared obscene by the Italian courts and their releases in that country were delayed by months. In fact, during the course of his nearly 25 year directing career Pasolini endured some thirty legal trials.

By 1975, Pier Paolo Pasolini was universally acknowledged as one of Italy's top, if not most controversial, directors. He had won numerous international film awards, among them the 1972 Golden Bear at Berlin for *The Canterbury Tales* and the Grand Prize of the Jury at Cannes in 1974 for *Arabian Nights*. Openly homosexual, radically Marxist, the left wing intellectual's weekly column in the Milan newspaper *Corriere della Sera* had unfailingly attacked Italy's conservative ruling Christian Democratic party. *Salo*, scheduled to premiere in Paris on November 23, 1975, had already generated death threats against the director from neo–Fascist groups. Against this backdrop, the deadly events of November 2, 1975 can either be viewed as the logical, if tragic, outcome of Pasolini's sexual interest in the so-called sub-proletariat of the Roman slums, or, as a political assassination perpetrated by neo–Fascist thugs. According to the "official" version of events, on the evening of Saturday, November 1, 1975, the 53-year-old director picked up Giuseppe Pelosi, a skinny 17-year-old street hustler, outside Rome's main railway station and offered him 20,000 Lire for sex. Known as "Pino the Frog" to friends, Pelosi had a criminal record for juvenile delinquency and auto theft. Pasolini drove Pelosi in his metallic grey Giulia 2000 Alfa Romeo GT to a cheap restaurant near the Basilica of St. Paul and after eating headed to the beach resort of Ostia, a financially depressed Roman suburb. The couple arrived at a secluded seaplane basin on the beach near a muddy soccer field around 1:00 A.M. on Sunday, November 2. Pelosi testified at his trial that Pasolini performed oral sex on him before making him get out of the car. Pasolini allegedly tried to pull down the youth's pants from behind, but met with opposition became enraged, picked up a fence stake, and tried to jam it into the teenager's rectum. The pair briefly struggled and Pasolini struck the youth over his head and various parts of his body with the stake. Pelosi managed to grab a wooden fence stake and break it over the director's head and kick him in the testicles before running to the parked Alfa Romeo. In his haste to flee the scene, Pelosi inadvertently ran

over Pasolini's body. A few minutes later, "Pino the Frog" was pulled over for speeding by local police and quickly tied to the deadly assault. He later confessed to the encounter. At dawn that day, Pasolini's horribly battered and bloodied corpse was found by a carpenter on his way to work. An autopsy determined the famed director had still been alive when the car rolled over him. Death was officially attributed to internal hemorrhaging and heart rupture.

From the outset, the Pasolini murder investigation was marred by unanswered questions and sloppy police work. Although in his early fifties, Pasolini was an athlete and it seemed highly unlikely to those who knew him that a skinny 17-year-old street hustler could have alone overpowered the physically fit director. Despite a furious struggle on a wet soccer field Pelosi's clothes were only lightly mudstained. Photos of Pasolini's battered and bloodstained face (almost unrecognizable with one of his ears nearly torn away) gave testament to a savage beating hardly ascribable to fists and a sodden wooden board. Yet, no bloodstains found on Pelosi's clothing. More disturbingly, the police collection of evidence was incompetent, if not downright criminal. No fingerprint checks were taken in the area around the body and authorities chose to ignore a bloodstain found on the roof of the car on the passenger's side suggesting that either Pelosi or someone else had driven the car. A green sweater, belonging to neither Pasolini nor Pelosi, was found in the back seat of the vehicle which had not been there when the director's cousin had thoroughly cleaned the Alfa Romeo the day prior to the murder. Remarkably, the car was left unsecured by police and any possible fingerprint evidence that could have been lifted from the bodywork was lost when the vehicle was left out in the rain. In the crowning touch of official incompetence, the police wrecked the car (rendering worthless any remaining forensic evidence) en route to an investigating magistrate who had requested to view it. As the police investigation stumbled along, journalists learned through their underworld contacts that a motorbike had followed Pasolini's car after he picked Pelosi up outside the train station and that their stop at the restaurant (at the youth's request) was made to allow their pursuers a chance to catch up with them. On April 26, 1976, the self-confessed killer was convicted in juvenile court of homicide in "collusion with others" and sentenced to a prison term of nearly 10 years. Without explanation, a Roman higher court almost immediately amended the juvenile court's ruling eliminating the reference to "unknown others" effectively making Pelosi the sole murderer.

Pasolini's violent death, however, refused to be relegated to the forgotten pages of Italian history. Family and friends of the director, certain Pelosi had acted in concert with others, kept alive several rumors that offered possible explanations to the motives behind Pasolini's murder. Many believed Pelosi was pressured to cop to the killing because as a minor he was nearly guaranteed a more lenient prison sentence. Others viewed Pasolini's murder as a political assassination carried out by Fascist thugs within the ruling Christian Democratic party fed up by Pasolini's overt homosexuality and left wing Marxist attacks published in his weekly column in the Milan newspaper *Corriere della Sera*. All pointed to death threats from neo–Fascist groups received by Pasolini in the weeks prior to his death in reaction to his current motion picture, *Salo, or 120 Days of Sodom*. In 1995, the release of director Marco Tullio Giordama's docu-drama, *Pasolini, un delitto italiano* (*Pasolini: An Italian Crime*), continued to keep the case alive in the Italian popular imagination. Inspired by Enzo Siciliano's 1982 book, *Pasolini: A Biography*, the film's central thesis suggested that the "official" version of the case was a cover-up. Pelosi either acted in concert with Fascists or hit-men employed by the Italian secret service. In May 2005, the case once again made news when Pino Pelosi, now 47, conducted an interview with Italian television in which he flatly recanted his confession. The street hustler was with Pasolini in Ostia on the night of the killing when three men in their forties surprised them and amid profanity-laced shouts of "dirty Communist" and "queer" beat the director to death. Pelosi confessed to the murder at the time to protect his parents from the men, but had now stepped forward, despite receiving anonymous death threats, to finally tell the truth since his parents were dead and the killers were now either also dead or too old to harm him. Based on Pelosi's admission, Pasolini's family and friends demanded that police reopen the twenty year old case.

Later that month, the city council of Rome opened their own inquiry into the case and listened with interest to the assertions of director Sergio Citti, a close friend of Pasolini, that the murder was politically-motivated. Citti, based on a source known to him, maintained Pelosi was used as bait by five men who murdered the director elsewhere, dumped his body in Ostia, then coerced the youth into the role of fall-guy. "Pelosi had to play the game played by these people," said the director, "the 'respectable' people who ordered the murder." Magistrates subsequently reopened their files on the killing, but shelved the case in November 2005 after declaring they had found no new evidence. In June 2007, Rome's left wing mayor, Walter Veltroni, echoing the sentiments of many who believed the official version of the case to be a lie, called for prosecutors to officially reopen the case. Veltroni's demand was endorsed by a petition signed by 700 intellectuals who maintained that Pier Paolo Pasolini was assassinated because he was set to reveal a complicated cover-up of corruption and murder in the international oil business. To date, the investigation has yet to be launched even though most observers of the case no longer believe Pasolini's death was due solely to homosexual misadventure.

Further Reading

Owen, Richard. "Mayor Calls for Inquiry into 1975 Murder of Pasolini." *The Times* (London), June 21, 2007, p. 42.
Siciliano, Enzo. *Pasolini: A Biography*. New York: Random House, 1982.

Pastorius, Jaco (V)

The self-proclaimed "World's Greatest Bass Player" lived up to his hype by redefining the role of the fretless electric bass in jazz and rock. With fellow-bassist Stanley Clarke, "Jaco" is considered by many jazz historians to be one of the most influential players of the 1970s based largely on three solo albums, his ground-breaking work with Weather Report, and collaborations with Joni Mitchell (*Hejira*, 1976), Ian Hunter (*All-American Alien Boy*, 1976), Al DiMeola (*Land of the Midnight Sun*, 1976), and many others. Born John Francis Anthony Pastorius, III in Norristown, Pennsylvania on December 1, 1951, he was greatly influenced by his father, Jack, a jazz drummer. Nicknamed "Jocko" (he later changed it to "Jaco"), the seven year old was already playing drums when his family moved to Fort Lauderdale, Florida, in 1958. A football injury to his wrist forced Pastorius to shift to bass guitar, and by the time he graduated high school in 1969 he was making a name for himself playing with various groups in nightclubs around South Florida. In the summer of 1972, the 20-year-old bassist joined Wayne Cochran and the C.C. ("Chittlin'

Circuit") Riders for a ten month series of grueling one-nighters throughout the South. Quitting the group in early 1973, Pastorius returned to Fort Lauderdale and became involved with a 13 piece band called Bakers Dozen prior to joining the Peter Graves Orchestra in 1974. The Peter Graves Orchestra was the house band at the Bachelors III nightclub in Fort Lauderdale and backed such visiting headliners as The Temptations, Mel Torme, Bobby Rydell, and Charo. Through his wife Tracy, a waitress at the club, Pastorius was introduced to Bobby Colomby, drummer for the popular band Blood, Sweat & Tears. Colomby, impressed with Jaco's virtuosity, introduced the bassist to Epic Records executives in New York City. Pastorious signed with Epic on September 15, 1975, and his first solo album, *Jaco Pastorius*, featuring friends and favorite musicians like David Sanborn, Wayne Shorter, and Herbie Hancock was released to strong reviews in August 1976. Jaco, however, attained superstar status only after replacing Alphonso Johnson as bassist for the jazz fusion group Weather Report on April 1, 1976. A dynamic stage performer who treated the bass as a solo instrument, Pastorius' inspired musical interplay with the band's other musicians earned him the nickname "the Catalyst." On his first record with the group, *Heavy Weather* (1977), he co-produced, and wrote the standout tunes "Teen Town" and "Havona." Pastorius re-energized Weather Report and before leaving the band near the end of 1981 had recorded three other influential studio albums — *Mr. Gone* (1978), *Night Passage* (1980), and *Weather Report* (1982).

A mercurial personality, Pastorius began drinking heavily and binging on coke while on tour with Weather Report in Japan in 1981. Venerated as a guitar god in that country, the jazz bassist was honored with Japan's Golden Disc Award for *Word of Mouth* (1982), his second solo album. During the tour, he stunned bandmates by intentionally misplaying his bass parts. After leaving Weather Report at the end of 1981 to form his own band, Word of Mouth, Pastorius exhibited a downward spiral of bizarre behavior that alienated fellow-musicians, audiences, and record executives alike. While touring with his new 20 piece band in Japan during the summer of 1982, he painted his face, stripped off his clothes, and appeared naked onstage. Once, he drove a motorcycle into a hotel lobby, passed out, and when hotel employees attempted to revive him they found a dead squid under his shirt. Wild mood swings became

commonplace with band members finding their leader either laughing hysterically or weeping uncontrollably. In 1983, Word of Mouth played the *Playboy* Jazz Festival at the Hollywood Bowl emceed by comedy great Bill Cosby. The performance began well, but quickly deteriorated after Pastorius turned up his amp and purposely began to play out of time. Amid raucous boos from the crowd, disgusted band members exited the stage one-by-one leaving Jaco alone to play and knock over equipment. A clearly embarrassed Cosby got stagehands to remove Pastorius then apologized to the disgruntled crowd. That same year, Warner Bros. dumped Pastorius after he harassed a receptionist and intimidated employees at its East Coast corporate offices. "The World's Greatest Bass Player" spent most of 1984 living on the streets of New York City often hanging out at the basketball courts in Washington Square Park. Though performing the occasional gig, Pastorius was essentially a street person by 1985, and it was common to witness him spitting and screaming obscenities at pedestrians. Arrested in September 1985 on a breaking and entering charge while visiting his father in Philadelphia, Jaco agreed to enter a hospital. Prescribed lithium to counteract his violent mood swings, Jaco went off the drug after it left him impotent and with shaking hands. In the summer of 1986, his brother convinced the musician to check into the psychiatric ward at Bellevue Hospital. During his 17 week stay in the facility, Jaco was diagnosed as a manic-depressive whose condition was exacerbated by alcohol and drugs. "Clean" when released, Pastorius soon began binging on alcohol and cocaine. Back in the Fort Lauderdale area ostensibly to get his "sound back," he logged a series of arrests for traffic violations, vagrancy, breaking and entering, and generally bizarre behavior. Untouchable by any major record label and all but unemployable, the ill-kempt bassist had been banned from several area bars and nightclubs.

On September 11, 1987, Pastorius, 35, attended a Carlos Santana concert at the Sunrise Music Theatre near Fort Lauderdale. During a solo by Santana bassist Alphonso Johnson (the musician he replaced in Weather Report in 1975) Jaco jumped up onstage, but was quickly and roughly tossed from the venue by stagehands failing to recognize him as "The World's Greatest Bass Player." Around 4:10 A.M. the next day, September 12, Pastorius attempted to enter the Midnight Bottle Club, a members-only bar located in a shopping center complex in the Fort Lauderdale suburb of Wilton Manors. The Midnight was one of the many area clubs from which he was banned because of past disruptive behavior. Refused entrance, Pastorius started kicking the door, and was confronted by Luc Havan, the club's 25-year-old bouncer. Havan, a Vietnamese immigrant whose parents owned the club, was also known as an expert in the martial arts. According to Havan, Jaco swung at him, but missed causing the bassist to swing around from the force of his own blow. The bouncer claimed he shoved the drunken bassist causing him to fall backwards and strike his head on the sidewalk. When paramedics arrived, Pastorius was lying face-down on the pavement in a deep pool of his own blood. Unconscious when admitted to the IC unit of Broward County General Medical Center, Jaco remained comatose and suffered a stroke on September 19. In the absence of brain activity, his parents gave the order to remove him from life support two days later, September 21, 1987. A subsequent medical examiner's report strongly suggested Jaco's injuries could not all have been sustained in the manner described by Luc Havan. His skull had been fractured as were numerous facial bones, and his right eye had been ruptured and knocked out of its socket. Given the extent of Jaco's injuries and his massive internal bleeding, doctors advised the bassist's family that had Pastorius survived he would most likely have been blind in his right eye and unable to use his left arm. Following a funeral service conducted at St. Clement's Catholic Church in Wilton Manors on September 25, 1987, Pastorius was buried in Our Lady Queen of Heaven Cemetery in North Lauderdale.

The death of Jaco Pastorius upgraded the initial aggravated battery charge filed against Havan to one of second-degree murder. On November 7, 1988, just days before the start of his trial on the more serious felony charge, Havan accepted the prosecution offer of manslaughter. Admitting he had repeatedly struck Jaco, the bouncer was sentenced to 21 months in prison and placed on 5 years probation. He was released on "good behavior" time after serving only 4 months. Pastorius is destined to be remembered as an influential player, composer, and arranger in jazz fusion. Perhaps, however, a graveside mourner more accurately characterized Jaco as "brilliant goods in a damaged package."

Further Reading

Benarde, Scott and Tom Moon. "Bassist Jaco Pastorius Dead at Thirty-Five." *Rolling Stone*, 513 (Nov. 19, 1987):29–30.
Milkowski, Bill. *Jaco: The Extraordinary and Tragic Life of Jaco Pastorius, "The World's Greatest Bass Player."* San Francisco: Miller-Freeman, 1995. (Includes music CD.)
www.jacopastorius.com.

Peaklica, Piseth (V)

Orphaned by the Khmer Rouge during Pol Pot's murderous reign (1975–1979), Peaklica (like fellow-countryman Haing S. Ngor, see entry) survived the killing fields of Cambodia to emerge as that country's most famous film actress, the star of movies like the 1980s melodrama *Sramol Anthaka* (*Shadow of Darkness*). A veteran dancer in the Royal Cambodian Ballet, she taught traditional ballet (all but expunged from the Cambodian national consciousness by the Khmer Rouge) to students at Phnom Penh University's School of Fine Arts. On the morning of July 9, 1999, the 34-year-old actress, accompanied by her sister, Sao Peana, and her seven-year-old niece, Saren Sereiman, shopped for a bicycle in a crowded open air market in Phnom Penh. Moments after Peaklica stepped from her car, a gunman approached her and fired five times at close range. Three bullets struck the actress while the other two wounded Sereiman in the arm and abdomen. The assailant jumped onto the back of a Honda motorcycle driven by an accomplice and sped off into traffic. Rushed to a nearby hospital, Peaklica underwent emergency surgery. Two bullets were removed, but a third lodged in her back severed the dancer's spinal cord. Doctors listed Peaklica's condition as serious, but stable, with the proviso that should she recover, the dancer would be paralyzed from the waist down. Cambodia's "People's Princess" died of her wounds on July 13, 1999, as dozens of fans crowded outside her room offering to donate blood. Hours after her death, Peaklica's body was clad in a white gown and placed in state on the grounds of the University School of Fine Arts where, through her efforts as a teacher of traditional dance, she had virtually saved the art form from cultural extinction. As police attempted to keep a semblance of order, thousands of heartbroken fans passed by the bier while Peaklica's sister quietly sat over the body shooing away mosquitoes with a handkerchief. A comment by a tearful fan placed Peaklica's murder into national perspective —"Her performances represent the entire nation and her death is like losing Angkor Wat. The person who raised his hand to kill her also killed the nation's soul." A crowd of 10,000 witnessed the ritual burning of Peaklica's body in a crematorium hastily erected in the school's courtyard.

The national press coverage given to the assassination of the beautiful 34-year-old star surpassed even that afforded to the April 1998 death of Khmer Rouge leader Pol Pot, a ruthless dictator whose regime killed an estimated 1.7 million Cambodians. The Cambodian police termed the murder a possible "contract hit" or "revenge crime," and formed a special task force to investigate. Given the notoriously corrupt nature of the Cambodian police force, however, few believed that anyone would be brought to justice. Speculation over possible motives for the murder gripped the country. Peaklica had recently undergone a very bitter and public divorce from husband Khay Prasith, a popular actor who after her death offered a huge reward for information leading to the killers' arrest and conviction. Several powerful men were also known to have proposed marriage to her. The most persistent rumor, however, was that Peaklica's killing was linked to her affair with a high ranking government official whose scorned wife hired gunmen to "hit" the beloved actress. An article published in the October 7, 1999 issue of the French magazine *L'Express*, based largely on interviews with Peaklica's family (since safely relocated outside of Cambodia), named names. The investigative piece quoted entries from Peaklica's diary in which she described a torrid affair with Cambodian Prime Minister Hun Sen, and later, a meeting with National Police Chief and Sen loyalist, Hok Lundy, in which he warned her not to continue to see Sen because it infuriated Bun Rany, the Prime Minister's wife. After the meeting, Peaklica wrote in her diary, "Bun Rany is angry and wants to take my life." The article quoted Peaklica's seven-year-old niece, Saren Sereiman, as saying that shortly after the shooting, the wounded star turned to her and whispered, "It is Mrs. Hun Sen who did this." *L'Express* also asserted that Hun Sen bought Peaklica an $180,000 house, and opened a $200,000 bank account for her. Both Hun Sen and his wife denied any involvement in Peaklica's murder crediting the numerous allegations against them to a politically motivated smear campaign orchestrated by their opponents in the government. As of this writing, the specially appointed police task force has failed to generate any substantial leads in the case, not even a description of Peaklica's

killer, despite the many witnesses who saw the attack.

Further Reading

"Hun Sen's Wife Denies Killing Actress, Vows to Sue French Magazine." Associated Press, October 13, 1999.

Peña, Zayda *see* Appendix 1

Perez, Daniela (V)

In Brazil, nightly prime time soap operas (*telenovelas*) are the most popular shows on television avidly watched by an estimated 80 million viewers. None approached the cult status of *De Corpo e Alma* (*Of Body and Soul*) an hour-long, six nights a week *telenovela* written by Glória Perez, mother of the show's beautiful star, 23-year-old Daniela Perez. On the series, the married Perez played the sexy role of "Yasmin," the object of desire of three men including the violently jealous boyfriend "Bira," acted by Guilherme de Pádua. Prior to landing his breakout role as a male stripper on Brazilian television's number one rated show, de Pádua, 23, danced on the gay theatre circuit in the erotic revue, "The Night of the Leopards." Married to 19-year-old Paula de Almeida Thomaz, de Pádua had his wife's name tattooed on his penis in mid–December 1992 while she had his etched on her inner thigh. As a further symbol of their love, each wore one half of a broken amulet on a chain around their necks. Professionally, however, de Pádua's career took a major hit when his character was written out of *De Corpo e Alma* after the plot line had Daniela Perez's character reject him. Following the shooting of his final lines on December 28, 1992, de Pádua broke down and wept on the set.

Hours later, Perez's body was found in a pool of blood in an empty lot in Rio de Janeiro's chic beach district of Barra da Tijuca. The young actress was stabbed 18 times in the throat and chest with what police believed to have been a pair of scissors. Five of the wounds punctured her heart. De Pádua was arrested the next day and confessed to killing his co-star. According to the former exotic dancer, his ongoing quarrel with Perez was rooted in his refusal to sleep with the actress because of his devotion to his pregnant wife. Other actors on the soap opera told a far different story, one in which de Pádua was in constant pursuit of Perez. Thomaz initially informed authorities that she was present in the car with her husband and Perez during the murder, but later recanted stating she was shopping at a nearby mall at the time of the incident. Police offered a simple theory of the crime — Thomaz's insane jealousy over Perez prompted the murder.

The murder of the beautiful actress generated a media frenzy in Brazil where the latest Perez-de Pádua news even took precedence over the resignation of the country's president. Protesters outside the 16th Precinct in the Barra da Tijuca beach district where de Pádua was held carried signs reading, "Guilherme: Devil in Human Form." Other outraged fans sent telegrams to the police recommending that they "torture, kill, (and) cut him in pieces." In 1993, de Pádua made an initial statement to a judge that, under Brazilian law, took the place of a formal plea allowing the case to proceed to trial. "I killed her. I killed Daniela," confessed de Pádua while insisting that his wife was not present at the murder. Weeks later, however, the actor recanted his confession and stated that Thomaz alone carried out the killing in a fit of jealous rage. The couple divorced while awaiting trial.

In January 1997, more than five years after the brutal murder of Daniela Perez, de Pádua finally went on trial in what was called the Brazilian equivalent of the O.J. Simpson (see entry) case. The proceedings were carried on live television and national radio, and spectators turned away from the packed courtroom flooded the streets outside the courthouse in Rio. De Pádua, now 27, admitted having an affair with Perez because it was in his best career "interests" to do so. After all, the star's mother, Glória, scripted *De Corpo e Alma* and he wanted to stay on her good side. De Pádua testified that he watched while his insanely jealous wife repeatedly stabbed the soap star with a pair of scissors as she lay unconscious on the ground. A five man, two woman jury took only 1½ hours to convict de Pádua of pre-meditated murder on January 26, 1997. In the absence of a death penalty or life sentence in Brazilian law, de Pádua faced a prison term of between 12–30 years. The judge split the difference sentencing the actor to 19 years. Thomaz, now 23, pleaded "not guilty" at her murder trial in May 1997 and maintained she was at a shopping mall when the crime took place. Unable to produce any purchase receipts or alibi witnesses, Thomaz was convicted and sentenced to 18 years and six months (less time than de Pádua because she was under 21 years of age at the time of the murder). Remarkably, under Brazil's notoriously lenient penal code, both con-

victed killers became eligible for parole in early 1998. In Brazil, first time offenders are required to serve only ⅓ of their sentence and are eligible for work-release after serving ⅙ of their prison term. With time awaiting trial counted as time served, de Pádua was paroled in October 1999 after spending only seven years in prison for a premeditated murder. Thomaz was paroled the next month leading the prosecutor in both cases to comment, "Unfortunately, life has no value in Brazil."

Further Reading

"Slaying of Soap Opera Star Dominates News in Brazil: Case Demonstrates Public Fascination with Nightly 'Telenovelas.'" *Dallas Morning News*, February 7, 1993, sec. A, p. 29.

Pitts, Karnail Paul *see* **Bugz**

Potts, Juston Michael *see* **Kanyva**

Poulain, Jean-Paul (V)

A familiar figure in the community of Augusta, Maine, Poulain, 62, used his Franco-American heritage to fashion a career as a singer of French songs. He regularly worked in local radio and accompanied himself on guitar at La Festival de la Bastille, an annual event he founded in Augusta sponsored by the town's Franco-American club, Le Club Calumet. During the mid–1990s however, Poulain's life took a downward turn which he attributed to mental illness. The depressed performer became estranged from his family and in 2005 was arrested for stealing firearms and sentenced to sixteen months in a federal prison and three years probation. Released in October 2006 with credit for time served, Poulain tried unsuccessfully to rebuild a performing career stalled by incarceration.

On April 24, 2007, Mathiew Loisel, 21, and Cory Swift, 18, went to Poulain's apartment at 21 School Street with the intention of forcing the cabaret singer to transfer money out of Swiss bank accounts from an ATM. During the robbery, Loisel discharged a round from a Llama 9mm handgun into Poulain's chest later claiming, "it was like my finger moved without my mind thinking." As the singer bled out on the floor, the pair fled the scene stashing the gun under a nearby shed where it was later recovered by police. Poulain died in an ambulance en route to the Augusta State Airport where he was to have been airlifted by helicopter to a major trauma center. He lived long enough, however, to name Loisel as the gunman. Loisel, arrested with Swift the next day, claimed to shoot Poulain because the 62 year old took sexual advantage of him months earlier. Ordered to undergo a four day evaluation in the forensic unit of the Riverview Psychiatric Center in Augusta, Loisel attempted to slash his wrists with a piece of plastic and hang himself with a noose fashioned out of a towel. Though judged mentally competent to stand trial for Poulain's murder, the self-confessed gunman was later transferred out of the Kennebec County jail to the Maine State Prison in order to protect corrections officers and fellow-inmates. Loisel routinely bit his arms until they needed stitches, ripped the stitches out with his teeth, and indiscriminately assaulted both jail staff and prisoners. Accomplice Cory Swift pleaded guilty to the lesser crime of felony murder in January 2008 and was sentenced to ten years in prison. In February 2008, the mentally troubled Loisel pleaded guilty to murder and was sentenced to 30 years, a prison term supported by the murdered singer's family.

Further Reading

"Two Charged with Murder." Associated Press, April 25, 2007.

Priceless Game (V)

As a black teenager from a ghetto in Seattle, Washington, Phillip Tyrone Griffin tallied an impressive series of arrests on charges ranging from possession of dangerous weapons, theft, reckless endangerment, and robbery. As an adult, he logged assault charges and a 1999 conviction for possession of a firearm that led to prison time in 2000. In 2002, the 23-year-old felon finally found a socially acceptable outlet for his anger — rap music. Under the name Priceless Game (P.G.), Griffin was one track from completing a debut collection of raps like "How Much Pain," and "H is for Homicide" when his violent past reached out and claimed his life. In the early hours of August 13, 2002, Griffin was seen walking with a small group of men in the 800 block of South Jackson Street, beneath an overpass in Seattle's International District. One of the men pulled a pistol and fired a shot into the rapper's chest at point-blank range. Griffin stumbled across the street to a parking lot, collapsed, and died. Tony Pharr, 29, a fellow-inmate Griffin had argued with during his incarceration at the Washington Corrections Center in 2000, was subsequently arrested and convicted of second-degree murder on

October 1, 2002. At the sentencing hearing, Priceless Game's cousin pointed to the rapper's potential snuffed out by the murder and angrily told Pharr, "The most success you'll ever have is making my license plate." Pharr was sentenced to slightly more than 20 years in prison, the middle range under state guidelines.

Further Reading

"Man Sentenced to 20 years for Fatal Shooting Beneath Overpass." Associated Press, October 10, 2003.

Pringle, Kevin (V)

Making his singing debut at five in the children's choir of Cornerstone Baptist Church, Pringle became a staple of the gospel scene in Philadelphia. An accomplished tenor and songwriter ("It is You"), he went on to sing with area gospel groups like the Philadelphia Youth Mass Choir, the Louise Williams Community Choir, and the West District/Voice for Christ. In the 1980s, the self-taught musician founded the small gospel group Kevin Pringle and Company from which sprung the highly regarded the Children of Israel Chorale in 1992. Pringle, as choral director, handpicked the 40 member all age, all denominational choir. The Children of Israel toured extensively on the East Coast, and in 1998 appeared in a huge stadium show with Sean "Puff Daddy" Combs in which they performed a gospel rendition of "I'll Be Missing You," the rapper's tribute song to his murdered friend and fellow-rapper, Notorious B.I.G. (see entry). To supplement his gospel income, Pringle worked a variety of jobs: customer service at an insurance company, record store clerk, free lance photographer, and hairstylist.

On June 2, 2003, the godson of Arthur Stanley, III, dropped by the West Philadelphia row house which his 44-year-old godfather, an alto in the Children of Israel Chorale, shared with Pringle, 42. He found Pringle in the dining room slumped in a chair in front of a computer dead from a single gunshot wound to the head. Upstairs, Arthur Stanley's body was discovered lying in bed, executed in the same manner as Pringle. Police estimated the pair had been dead a week. In the absence of any signs of forced entry, authorities conjectured that they probably knew their killer. With robbery ruled out as a motive, the homosexuality of the men became an issue. As a photographer-videographer for male strip clubs, Pringle was known to take nude pictures of men and later show them to friends. Someone was perhaps unknowingly photographed, found out about the compromising images, and murdered Pringle, then Stanley. A friend of the two men alleged that both dated outwardly heterosexual men, and believed they could seduce straight guys with oral sex. When the friend pointed out to Pringle that this behavior was incongruous with his love of the church and gospel, the musician told him, "The Bible says these are the last and evil days. Get it while you can." To date, no arrests have been made in the double homicide.

Further Reading

Gregory, Kia. "The Day the Music Died." *Philadelphia Weekly*, August 20, 2003 (www.philadelphiaweekly.com).

Pringle, Val (V)

The American actor appeared in minor roles in five films (*Shoot It Black, Shoot It Blue*, 1974; *The Last Remake of Beau Geste*, 1977; *The Strange Case of the End of Civilization as We Know It*, 1977; *Ragtime*, 1981; *Brittania Hospital*, 1982), and as the character "Lead" in an episode of the cult British sci fi ITV television series, *Sapphire & Steel*, produced between 1978–1982. As a singer, Pringle appeared with Eartha Kitt, Miriam Makeba, and Hugh Masekala. He also wrote songs, including "Louise" recorded by calypso king Harry Belafonte. In the 1980s, Pringle moved to the southern African kingdom of Lesotho after appearing there on a cultural exchange tour sponsored by the United States Information Service. He married Dutch-born Thea van Maastricht, and became a successful businessman operating a nightspot and the Lancer's Inn, a popular hotel and restaurant in the capital city of Maseru.

On the evening of December 13, 1999, Pringle, 63, and his wife were in their mansion situated on a plateau outside of Maseru when they heard intruders attempting to break into the residence. The former entertainer instructed his wife to lock herself in a room, armed himself with a 7.65mm pistol, and set off to confront the burglars. The terrified van Maastricht heard gunshots, and three minutes later emerged from her hiding place to find her husband slumped in a pool of blood in the driveway dead from 13 stab wounds. The killers took Pringle's pistol and gold watch making their escape in the dead man's BMW. The car was later found with bloodstains in the seat prompting investigators to speculate that Pringle may have shot one of his assailants. Ironically, in 1997

Pringle's brother, Carl, died from complications after being shot during a carjacking.

Eight days later, police announced the arrest of two of the three men believed to be responsible for Pringle's murder. At a memorial service for the dead entertainer held in Thuathe three days before Christmas, Tom Thbane, Lesotho's Minister of Foreign Affairs, praised Pringle as a "great black American" and sternly called for the hanging of the assassins. In a statement issued following his friend's death, Harry Belafonte was less vengeful: "He was a very, very gifted human being. It is hard to envision someone of his strength and compassion passing away under violent circumstances. Those of us fortunate enough to have worked with him, remember him not only for his humor and humility, but also for his great artistry." As of this writing, the fate of Pringle's killers remains unknown.

Further Reading

"American Entertainer Slain in Lesotho; Two Men Arrested." Associated Press, December 20, 1999.

Professor Backwards (V)

James Everett Edmondson, better known in the entertainment world as Professor Backwards, attributed his unique ability to rapidly talk, sing, and spell *backwards* to a dream he had when he was 12 years old. In the dream, everyone moved and spoke in reverse. When the youngster awoke, so could he. Prior to entering show business, Edmondson used his amazing talent working around a linotype in a Jacksonville, Florida, newspaper. As printing on a linotype is reversed, he was able to read the type quicker than any of his co-workers. It was, however, as Professor Backwards that Edmondson achieved minor nightclub and television fame in the 1950s and 1960s. Garbed in the traditional cap and gown of the academic, the Professor stood at a blackboard while audience members shouted out multi-syllable words designed to confound his efforts to write them backwards without an error. Likewise, the performer was able to immediately sing and speak backwards any word in the English language with an unerring facility. At one time, the Professor held the record for most appearances on *The Ed Sullivan Show* and also appeared on British and Australian television.

The 65-year-old show biz veteran was retired and living in a modest ranch-style home at 4185 Herschel Road in College Park, a suburb of

Atlanta, when he became the victim of a brutal robbery-murder. On the evening of January 28, 1976, three men forced their way into his home and demanded money. Edmondson's 25-year-old live-in housekeeper, Michelle Ruth Sipp, was allegedly raped by two of the men while the Professor was forced to write a check for $300 and held hostage overnight until his bank opened in the morning. The next afternoon, an Atlanta sanitation worker found the retired performer's body face-down on an isolated dirt road outside the city. Edmondson, estimated to have been dead less than an hour when discovered, was shot once in the forehead at close range and twice, execution-style, behind the left ear. His wallet was missing. Investigators were still on the scene when Michelle Sipp called the College Park police station to report the Professor's abduction and her rape. She waited four hours to make the call under threat by the assailants that they would come back and kill her.

Under questioning, Sipp's account of the three black men who forced their way into Edmondson's home began to trigger warning bells in case hardened detectives. Ultimately, the housekeeper admitted knowing one of the suspects, Michael Gantt, 22, while they were both patients a year earlier in a local mental hospital. Since that time, the pair had remained sporadic lovers. More tellingly, earlier on the day of the home invasion Sipp had been arrested for public drunkenness on a complaint filed by Edmondson. The Professor brought his employee's purse to the station and she paid the fine herself and returned to his residence. Hours later, the men arrived to rob the Professor. Sipp was subsequently charged with armed robbery and murder. Gantt was picked up and quickly fingered his accomplices — Roy Anthony (Brown) Ellerbee, 20, and Willie Edgar Bell, 17. The murder weapon, a .32-caliber pistol, was recovered in Bell's residence. At trial in Fulton County in May 1976, Sipp escaped all charges by cutting a deal with the prosecution to testify against the others. Ellerbee and Bell identified Gantt as the triggerman. Gantt, the only defendant to take the stand, claimed he only shot the Professor after hearing voices say, "Kill him, kill him, kill him." A jury deliberated only 3½ hours to find all three men guilty of first-degree murder (life imprisonment) and robbery (20 years) with sentences to run concurrently. An appeal by Gantt and Ellerbee in May 1977 was rejected.

Further Reading

Devon, Richard. "Puzzle for Atlanta Homicide Probers: Who Killed 'Professor Backwards.'" *True Detective*, 106(3) (December 1976):22–25, 58+.
Smith, Ronald L. *Who's Who in Comedy: Comedians, Comics from Vaudeville to Today's Stand-Ups*. New York: Facts on File, 1992.

Proof (V)

The MC known as Proof (born DeShaun DuPree Holton in Detroit on October 2, 1973) is credited with bringing the Motor City's rap scene to national prominence through his hosting of "battle-rap" competitions at club's like the Hip-Hop Shop and the Fight Club. Friends with Eminem (Marshall Mathers) since they were teenagers, Proof's backing of the white rapper helped legitimize the artist in Detroit's hip-hop community. In the late 1990s, Proof assembled the best of the city's talent in one super-group, D12, featuring himself, Eminem, Swift, Kon Artis, Bizarre, and Kaniva. During his tenure with the group, Proof recorded two full-length albums (*Devil's Night*, 2001; *D12 World*, 2004) ultimately forming his own label, Iron Fist Records, to record his solo album, *Searching for Jerry Garcia*, released in 2005 on the tenth anniversary of the death of the famed guitarist of the Grateful Dead. Although a talented artist in his own right (recipient of both the 1998 Inner City Entertainment's Flava of the Year Award and *The Source*'s Unsigned Hype Award in 1999), Proof will be most remembered as Eminem's best friend and right-hand rapper onstage. In the 2002 Eminem film *8 Mile*, named after the famed street dividing Detroit's economically depressed urban south from the prosperous suburban north, Proof was fictionalized as "David 'Future' Porter" and played by Mekhi Phifer. Proof appeared in a cameo role in the movie as "Lil Tic."

On April 11, 2006, Proof, 32, was in C.C.C., a nightclub along the 8 Mile featured in the film and described by a security guard employee as a "death trap." During the last decade, Detroit police responded 18 times to disturbances in the club ranging from fights to after hour liquor violations. Around 4:30 A.M. the rapper began arguing with another man over a pool game. By law, the after-hours club was barred from selling alcohol after 2:00 A.M., but continued serving to the 15–25 people still inside. Although not a participant in the disputed pool game, Keith Bender, Jr., an Army veteran of Operation Desert Storm, was in the club celebrating that he no longer needed to be on a defibrillator for the heart condition which ended his military service. According to witnesses, a verbal argument between Proof and Bender, 35, escalated into a fistfight before the rapper secured a pistol, slapped him with it, and shot the veteran in the face. Mario Etheridge, 28, the club's bouncer and a cousin of the wounded man, responded by pumping three bullets into Proof's head and chest. Proof was pronounced dead at a local area hospital. Bender died one week later. Etheridge surrendered to police one day after the shooting and was preliminarily charged with two gun felonies (carrying a concealed weapon and discharging a firearm inside an occupied building) while detectives sought to build a murder case against a man with no prior criminal history. Etheridge was released two days later after pleading "not guilty" to the gun charges and posting a $7,000 bond.

On April 19, 2006, an overflow crowd of more than 2,000 mourners packed the Fellowship Chapel on Detroit's west side to say farewell to Proof, the MC who put the city on the hip-hop map. Among the hip-hop royalty in attendance were 50 Cent, Dr. Dre, Xzibit, Lloyd Banks, and Eminem who eulogized Proof as his "best friend." Many of the speakers called for an end to the senseless violence plaguing the hip-hop community, words contradicted by Proof's raps and criminal record. In November 2002, Dearborn police confiscated a 10mm pistol and ammo found by a maid in his room at the Ritz-Carlton. Ten months later, Proof was cuffed after he swung at an officer investigating a complaint about a disruptive drunk. He was subsequently sentenced to two years probation and fined $1,260 for being a disorderly person. A February 2004 fight at a T.G.I. Friday's restaurant in Dearborn resulted in the rapper pleading no contest to misdemeanor assault and battery, and subsequently sentenced to 20 days on a work program, six months probation, and a fine of $1,620. All this was forgotten, however, as mourners viewed the open gold-toned casket containing Proof outfitted in a beige athletic suit, Kangol cap, and draped in a Chauncey Billups jersey signed by many of the Detroit Pistons. After the nearly three hour service, the casket was placed in a horsedrawn carriage to begin its journey to a mausoleum in Woodlawn Cemetery near 8 Mile. In the processional behind the slowly moving carriage were some dozen stretch limos, Hummers, and hundreds of cars that shut traffic down in the area for more than

two hours. In the cemetery, Proof's body was interred in the Rosa L. Parks Freedom Chapel just a few yards from the final resting place of the civil rights icon. In the days that followed, many questioned the thinking behind the placement of a rapper who had lived and died violently so close to the interment site of a woman who devoted her life to non-violent confrontation.

In May 2006, Wayne County prosecutor Kym Worthy announced that as Mario Etheridge had acted in self-defense in Proof's shooting the bouncer would only face trial on gun charges. At trial in September 2006, Worthy maintained that the fistfight between Proof and Bender escalated into a fatal shooting when Etheridge fired three warning shots in the ceiling of the club. Proof then secured a gun, shot Bender, thus prompting the security guard to shoot him. Etheridge was found guilty on one count of carrying a concealed weapon and on one count of firing a weapon inside an occupied building. Facing a possible five-year maximum prison term, the bouncer was sentenced to time already served (the two days he had spent in jail awaiting bond) and fined $2,000.

Further Reading

Hunt, Amber. "Violence Not New at Club: Employee Calls Detroit Night Spot a Death Trap." *Detroit Free Press*, April 12, 2006, sec. A, p. 1.
Krisher, Tom. "Eminem Pays Tribute to 'Best Friend' Proof." Associated Press, April 14, 2006.

Radin, Roy (V)

The son of "Broadway Al" Radin, a popular Manhattan nightclub owner and show biz insider during the 1930s–1950s, and Renee, an ex-showgirl, Roy Alexander Radin (born November 13, 1949) began booking rock bands into clubs in Long Island while still a teenager. It was not until he hit upon the scheme in the early 1970s of packaging has-been entertainers into a traveling road show that he became a multimillionaire. "Roy Radin's Tribute to Vaudeville" featured emcees like George Jessel and Joey Bishop announcing acts including Tiny Tim, comedian Jackie Vernon, singer Alan Jones, the Harmonica Rascals, and a French vaudeville act called Pierre Du Pont and his Wonder Dog Sparky. The tour played 36 performances in six weeks traveling by bus to do 90 minute shows in Masonic temples and high school auditoriums in towns across Ohio, Pennsylvania, Indiana, West Virginia, Virginia, and Delaware. Radin contacted local police departments to sponsor his revue and offered them 25 percent of the profits of the gate and the revenue generated by his aggressive courting of area businesses to place ads in each show's program. By 1978, the impresario made enough money to purchase Ocean Castle, a 72-room mansion in exclusive Southampton, Long Island, he shared with second wife, Toni Fillet. Despite his millions, however, legitimate theatre producers looked upon Radin as little more than a P.T. Barnum-style huckster lacking in taste and personal class. Radin, a flamboyant personality who tipped the scales at 300 pounds, dressed and acted the part of the successful theatrical producer always on the lookout to expand his business empire into Broadway plays and Hollywood films. In the late 1970s–early 1980s he became a regular at Manhattan's trendy Studio 54 where he took business meetings and snorted outsized quantities of cocaine in a private back room.

Still, the president of Roy Radin Enterprises was known only as a big spending "schlock-meister" in the insular world of show business producers until the events of April 11, 1980 splayed his name across the front pages of the tabloids. The day before, Robert McKeage, a management consultant from New Jersey, brought date, Melonie Haller, 23, to Ocean Castle for a dinner engagement with his friend Radin and a few others. Haller, a gorgeous model who had appeared in *Playboy*, acted in several episodes of *Welcome Back, Kotter*, the television series that launched John Travolta's career. After dinner, McKeage and Haller, both high on cocaine, changed into provocative leather outfits accessorized with dog collars and chains, donned Nazi caps, and visited Radin's bedroom where they commenced whipping one another. Haller quarreled with McKeage later that night, and returned to Radin's room where the coked out model began thrashing around, breaking the lens on a video camera positioned atop a tripod and aimed at his bed. Dawn the next day found Haller, bruised and bleeding from several cuts, running around the mansion screaming incoherently. McKeage was summoned, and disgustedly responded to his date by throwing Haller to the floor and viciously kicking her. He then took her to the Southampton station and unceremoniously dumped her on a train. Discovered by a conductor slumped over a seat, Haller was taken to hospital where she informed Suffolk County authorities she was beaten and raped at Ocean Front. Upon learning the woman had spoken to police, Radin ordered his home "sanitized," the drugs flushed, his sheets washed, the house hastily cleaned. Questioned at Ocean Front concerning the incident, Radin was arrested and charged with the illegal possession of a firearm after police found an unlicensed pistol in the walk-in closet of his bedroom. The charge against Radin was ultimately dropped and McKeage did only thirty days in jail after pleading guilty to beating Haller.

The negative publicity created by the case caused the producer to worry that his career, heavily dependent on the good will of law enforcement agencies across the Midwest and Northeast, was in danger of being ruined. Radin's fear was justified. In the wake of the Haller incident, his $6 million a year business shrank to almost nothing although he continued to tour his vaudeville-style show with first Joey Bishop then Jackie Vernon as emcee. Paranoid, consumed by irrational fears, and convinced that wife Toni was being serially unfaithful Radin continued taking large quantities of cocaine as his marriage disintegrated into divorce. To recoup business losses, he put his beloved Ocean Front up for sale in the fall of 1982, and looked to relocate to Los Angeles where he imagined his notoriety was not as well known. Armed with a stack of motion picture screenplays sent to him by prospective clients over the years, Radin went to the Tinseltown in mid–October 1982 and rented an apartment in the Regency Hotel. He moved there permanently in January 1983 after Ocean Front sold for $8 million. Staked by the sale of the mansion, Roy Radin aggressively pursued his desire to become a Hollywood player shopping around town a musical based on the famed Cotton Club and other projects like *I Love My Wife* and *Hallelujah Baby*. He pitched a television series at Paramount, *Miss Lonelyhearts*, about a male reporter who dressed up like a woman to get a job on a newspaper, and was elated when the studio expressed mild interest in the project.

In January 1983, Radin, 33, met thirtyish Karen DeLayne Jacobs at a party in Benedict Canyon. "Laney," as she was known, had parlayed looks and brains with a pragmatic willingness to have sex with men of ever increasing importance in the Miami drug scene, into a cocaine distributorship for Florida drugs in Los Angeles. Jacobs received the monthly coke shipments on credit, sold the product through dealers in the Southland, and sent the cash (minus her cut) to San Francisco. Like many who come to Hollywood, however, Jacobs dreamed of making it big in the entertainment industry. The narcotics dealer with delusions of becoming a motion picture producer was ecstatic when a driver who worked for Ascot Limousine, a business partially owned by film producer Robert Evans, told her he could arrange a meeting with the man who had produced such classics as *The Godfather* (1972), *Chinatown* (1974), and *The Marathon Man* (1976). A former executive vice president in charge of production at Paramount, Evans had fallen on hard times in the film community due to a series of flops including *Players* (1979) and *Popeye* (1980), and a 1980 conviction on federal drug charges in New York for possessing five ounces of cocaine. The legendary producer escaped prison time by producing a one-hour long television special, *Get High on Yourself*, targeted to youths. Despite the court-ordered special, Evans still regularly used cocaine and, as a pariah in Hollywood, was unable to secure financing for his film projects through conventional avenues, but was always on the lookout for independent investors. Enter Laney Jacobs wannabe motion picture producer. At their initial meeting, Jacobs informed Evans that she had $5 million of her own to invest and access to as much as $50 million more from her connections in Miami. According to Jacobs, she told the producer the money came from the sale of drugs, a claim Evans has since vehemently denied and, to date, has never been proven.

Roy Radin and Laney Jacobs immediately liked one another based largely on his need for cocaine and her ready access to the product. Within days she became his sole supplier in L.A. selling the impresario the drug at cost. During one of their binges, Jacobs confided to Radin her dream of becoming a movie producer, and mentioned that she was helping Robert Evans raise money for several projects. Radin, who thought Jacobs was in L.A. just to sell drugs, readily accepted his newfound friend's invitation to set up a meeting with the producer. At a meeting with Radin and Jacobs at the end of March 1983, Evans set forth his plan to make three films back-to-back: *The Two Jakes*, *The Sicilian*, and *The Cotton Club*. Radin was excited about the projects especially *The Cotton Club*, an idea he had nurtured for years as a musical, not the drama envisioned by Evans to be directed by *The Godfather* alum Francis Ford Coppola. Evans, who had not made a film in three years, tried for some time to get financing for the film, but Hollywood's traditional money men

were frightened off by stories of his drug use. For Radin's part, he was anxious to do business with the producer of *The Godfather*, but looked upon Laney Jacobs as nothing more than a broker in the deal, not as a potential partner. Shortly after the trio met, one of the drug dealer's employees, Tally Rogers, ripped off $270,000 in cash and cocaine with a street value of over $1 million from Jacobs' home. Laney Jacobs either had to find the product, make good the loss out of her own pocket, or face retribution from her Miami boss. She immediately suspected Radin was somehow involved in the theft since Rogers lived near him in the Regency Hotel. She angrily called Radin, accused him of complicity in the crime, and was met with a strong rebuff. Unconvinced by his protestations of innocence, Jacobs got in touch with some muscle — William Molony Mentzer, a 38-year-old bodybuilder and bodyguard for Larry Flynt of *Hustler* magazine, and his friend, Alex Lamota Marti, 22, a fellow-bodybuilder and one-time Flynt bodyguard who also happened to be a rabid Nazi sympathizer and Jew hater. Jacobs soon became sexually involved with Mentzer, a pattern of seduction the narcotics distributor had followed since her earliest days in the business.

Although his relationship with Jacobs had soured, Radin pushed forward with his negotiations with Evans pitching a plan whereby they could form a partnership and finance the three films in conjunction with a Puerto Rican banker with ties to that country's government. Each of the producers would have a 45 percent share with the banker receiving 10 percent of the $35 million already promised by the island nation. Radin and Evans, both wired on cocaine, tried for days to hammer out a mutually agreeable partnership, but Evans, who had a proven (if spotty) film production track record, understandably wanted a controlling voice in the enterprise. Further complications arose when Evans told Laney Jacobs of his negotiations with Radin. The drug dealer angrily called Radin demanding a percentage of the company, was flatly refused, and fumed as he offered her only a $50,000 finder's fee for the introduction to Evans. Their antagonism increased after Radin's nose began to bleed and he stopped payment on a $4,000 check to Jacobs claiming the coke was "bad." Behind the scenes, however, Jacobs was exerting influence on Evans (with whom she was now allegedly having sex), and the producer was concerned that the Haller affair marked Radin as some sort of notorious character. Besides,

Jacobs convinced Evans that she could set up financing for the films with associates at American Express and totally cut Radin out of the picture. At his next meeting with the impresario, Evans informed Radin that Jacobs wanted a percentage of the company and suggested that he give her half of his 45 percent stake. Radin flew into a rage and called off the entire deal. A few days later, Radin received a telephone death threat that should have signaled the end of his time in Los Angeles, but the binge cocaine user refused to see the danger signals.

Laney Jacobs called Radin and set up one last meeting on May 13, 1983, to determine if they could settle their differences regarding the Evans matter. She would pick him up at the Regency Hotel in a black limousine and they would dine at the fashionable La Scala restaurant in Beverly Hills. Advised by associates not to see Jacobs, Radin devised a plan to guarantee his safety. He engaged Demond Wilson, the cocaine addicted *Sanford and Son* actor he once managed, to wait in a car and follow the limo to the restaurant. Jacobs, however, had her own plan which involved Mentzer and Marti following in a car behind the limo driven by their confederate Robert Ulmer Lowe posing as a chauffeur. Around 9:30 P.M., Radin left with Jacobs in the limo and it took less than five minutes for Demond Wilson in the tail car to lose them in traffic. Minutes later, Lowe pulled the limo over and Mentzer and Marti, following in another car, entered the vehicle on either side of the terrified Radin. Jacobs left in their car to begin setting up her alibi. Questioned later by authorities in Radin's disappearance, Jabobs gave conflicting accounts of an argument between them which ended in one version with Radin getting out of the car on Sunset Boulevard, and another, in which she exited the vehicle en route to the restaurant. In reality, Mentzer and Marti roughed up Radin in the limo in an unsuccessful attempt to have him cop to the drug theft (he was never involved) as Lowe drove to a secluded desert location 65 miles northeast of Los Angeles near the town of Gorman. At the end of a narrow canyon road in a dry riverbed, Radin was removed from the car and shot 27 times in the head with a .22-caliber pistol. Marti, the self-confessed anti–Semite, fired the majority of the shots. Radin's body was found 28 days later on June 10, 1983 by an apiarist looking for a remote storage location for his beehives.

In the ensuing police investigation, both Rob-

ert Evans (who denied he ever had a production deal with Radin) and Laney Jacobs (despite her conflicting accounts of her final meeting with the aspiring producer) were questioned, but not charged. Radin's family hired a private investigator, ex–L.A. police detective John O'Grady, who developed leads strongly implicating Jacobs and handed them over to authorities. As the case officially languished, Laney Jacobs left Los Angeles and her dream of becoming a movie producer, and returned to Florida where she married "retired" drug dealer Larry Greenberger in September 1984. She allegedly told Greenberger about the Radin contract killing stating that it was motivated both by her desire to remove the overweight impresario from contract negotiations with Evans over *The Cotton Club* and as payback for his suspected involvement in the massive cash and drugs ripoff perpetrated by Tally Rogers. Radin's murder would have remained just another unsolved L.A. homicide, albeit a high profile one, if not for the inability of the steroid-popping contract killers, William Mentzer and Alex Marti, to keep their mouths shut. Both men bragged to their one-time boss, William Rider, former chief security officer for *Hustler* magazine publisher Larry Flynt, about the execution. Marti, the Nazi sympathizer, proudly admitted to Rider that he "enjoyed shooting the big fat Jew." Both men proved their connection to the case by bringing their former boss a newspaper clipping about the discovery of Radin's body at the exact location outside of Gorman, California, where the men used to go practice their marksmanship. Rider contacted police resulting in arrests and murder charges filed against Jacobs, Mentzer, Marti, and Lowe in October 1988.

"The Cotton Club Murder," as dubbed by the tabloid press, contained all the elements of a Hollywood movie — drugs, sex, and violent death. At a pre-trial hearing in May 1989, producer Robert Evans, represented by attorney Robert Shapiro (see O.J. Simpson entry), won the right to invoke the Fifth Amendment against self-incrimination. On the witness stand, Robert Evans refused even to admit he knew Roy Radin. At a later preliminary hearing, however, star witness William Rider testified that both Mentzer and Marti told him that Evans was involved in Radin's killing. All four defendants faced first-degree murder charges as the trial opened on October 31, 1990, nearly eight years after the impresario's brutal killing. Arguing that the motive for Radin's murder was two-fold (payback for a suspected drug theft and his removal as a rival producer in the financing of *The Cotton Club*), the prosecution relied heavily on the testimony of William Rider. A highlight of the ten month trial was the testimony of Laney Jacobs-Greenberger, the now 43-year-old wannabe producer accused of ordering the hit on Radin. According to Jacobs-Greenberger, she and Radin were in the back of the limo discussing her role in the production of the film when Mentzer, charged by a Miami narcotics kingpin with determining Radin's involvement in the $1 million drug ripoff, ordered her out of the car and sped away with the vaudeville revival producer. She did not learn of the murder until told of it by Mentzer early the next morning. Producer Robert Evans was not called as a witness in the trial. On July 22, 1991, a jury of ten men and two women deliberating over the course of eight days found all the defendants guilty. Triggermen Mentzer and Marti, convicted of first-degree murder and kidnapping, were later sentenced to life in prison without the possibility of parole. Limo driver Robert Ulmer Lowe, found guilty of second-degree murder and kidnapping, received a similar sentence. Karen DeLayne "Laney" Jacobs-Greenberger, the mastermind of the entire operation, was convicted of second-degree murder and kidnapping and sentenced on February 7, 1992, to life imprisonment without the possibility of parole. *The Cotton Club*, marred during its production by infighting between Robert Evans and director Francis Ford Coppola, was released on December 14, 1984, and quickly bombed at the box office.

Further Reading

Prial, Frank J. "Roy Radin: Life and Death in the Show-Business Demimonde." *The New York Times*, July 20, 1983. sec. C, p. 15.

Wick, Steve. *Bad Company: Drugs, Hollywood, and the Cotton Club Murder*. New York: St. Martin's, 1991.

Ramirez, Israel (V)

A well-known and respected security man, Ramirez (born February 7, 1977) protected rap stars for over a decade and was a bouncer at several trendy Manhattan nightspots like Exit. At 6'1", 250 pounds, the black belt in karate seldom carried a weapon or wore a protective vest. In December 1999, Ramirez made the news after Sean "Puff Daddy" (a.k.a. "Diddy") Combs and then girlfriend Jennifer Lopez were in the midtown Club New York when a shooting left three people wounded. Ramirez, a security guard at the club, testified at Combs' 2001 gun trial that the hip-hop superstar was not armed when the shots were fired. Combs was acquitted.

On February 5, 2006, just days short of his 30th birthday, Ramirez was working security and holding "bling" for hip-hop giant Busta Rhymes (Trevor Tahiem Smith, Jr.). Rhymes, his posse, and fellow-rappers and hip-hop stars including DMX, Mary J. Blige, 50 Cent, Missy Elliott, and Lloyd Banks were assembled at the Kiss the Cactus studio on 259 Green Street in the Greenpoint section of Brooklyn for an all-star music video shoot for Rhymes' "Touch It (Remix)." Throughout the day and into the evening fans, the entourages of the various celebs, and rubberneckers swelled the excited crowd to an estimated several hundred outside the converted warehouse where the video was being shot. Inside the makeshift studio, while various stars awaited their cameos, nearly one hundred people jammed the area near the stage. According to anonymous sources, tensions began to run high after members of 50 Cent's posse, G-Unit, became involved in a heated argument with Rhymes' producer Swizz Beatz. G-Unit members Tony Yayo and Lloyd Banks became enraged with Beatz when they felt the producer gave their tracks to rapper Cassidy. Banks, scheduled to be filmed for a cameo in the video, loudly refused to take the stage while Beatz was in the area. Another man clad in a G-Unit jacket when asked to leave the 9th floor set responded angrily, "Who the fuck are you to tell me to be quiet? I'm on parole, motherfucker!" Around 11:30 P.M., Yayo and Banks stormed out of the building prompting Busta Rhymes to reassure Beatz, "Yo, man, I got no problem with you, we're cool." Forty-five minutes later, a man approached bodyguard Ramirez in the hall and said, "Yo, so-and-so's on his way over here, and some shit might go down."

Ramirez was in his security position outside on Green Street in a milling crowd of around 75 people when Rhymes walked Beatz out of the building towards the rapper's car. The bodyguard was standing near Rhymes when eight shots rang out, one striking him in the chest. Some believe that Ramirez grabbed the gun trying to protect Rhymes, a possible target. In the ensuing panic, the shooter escaped. Police found dozens of shell casings around Ramirez's body, and hours later, recovered a muddy .45-caliber handgun tossed into a construction site near the scene. Ramirez, the father of three sons (ages one to ten), was pronounced dead on arrival at the Woodhull Medical and Mental Health Center. Despite seeing the entire incident unfold, Rhymes and others refused to cooperate with police. One investigator summarized the "code" of the hip-hop industry as follows: "You don't talk to cops. If you do, your career tanks." Rhymes did, however, offer a version of the shooting to Ramirez's family at the wake. The rapper was standing next to Ramirez and another bodyguard when the shooter supposedly yelled out, "It has nothing to do with you, just get out of the way!" then fired at someone behind the trio accidentally killing Ramirez. Though widely criticized by the family and others for not showing enough "respect" to the man who probably saved his life, Busta Rhymes paid all funeral costs and promised to provide for the education of Ramirez's three children. At the time of publication for this book, however, the rapper's vow to dispense his own brand of "justice" to the unidentified killer has yet to materialize. To date, no arrests have been made in the murder of Israel Ramirez.

Further Reading

Celona, Larry. "Busta's Gem Guard Slain in Video Shoot." *New York Post*, February 6, 2006, p. 5.

Raver, Harry Rush (V)

A leading film distributor in the teens, Raver was among the first to hold press previews for films. In 1914, he previewed the Italian film *Cabiria* in the Gold Room of New York City's Astor Hotel. Crippled by arthritis, Raver retired from show business and operated an antiques store before going blind. On September 5, 1941, a burglar broke into the 62-year-old man's home at 1366 N. St. Andrews Place in Los Angeles. Ignoring Raver's pleas not to hurt him because he was blind, the robber took $39 and beat him severely. "If I verify the fact you are blind," Raver quoted the bandit, "I'll send your money back." Raver died of his injuries on September 14, 1941. A nightclub entertainer appearing before a Coroner's jury stated that for the last 1½ years Raver wrote the scripts for *Busy Blind*, a radio program featuring sightless talent.

Further Reading

"Blind Man Treated in Bandit Assault." *Los Angeles Times*, September 6, 1941, p. 13.

Reeves, George (V-suspected)

The career of George "Superman" Reeves is Hollywood's most graphic example of an actor talented enough to perform in stronger material, but tragically typecast in a role from which the public would not let him escape. Whether the actor was driven to suicide by career frustrations or, as some have suggested, murdered as a direct result of his one-time involvement with the wife of a powerful studio executive, one essential fact remains — George Reeves will only be remembered in popular culture because he played the "Man of Steel" on television. Conceived out-of-wedlock, the future actor was born George Keefer Brewer in Woodstock, Iowa, on January 15, 1914. To prevent her child's illegitimacy, mother Helen Lescher browbeat the father, Don C. Brewer, into marrying her. They divorced soon after the child's birth with Helen taking her infant son to live with her parents in Ashland, Kentucky. Mother and son moved to Pasadena, California, where she married Frank Joseph Bessolo. In 1927, the 13-year-old was adopted by his stepfather and legally given the man's surname. The marriage, however, lasted only eight years. Frank Bessolo later fired a bullet into his brain. By all accounts, Helen Bessolo was an ultra-possessive mother who emotionally suffocated her son. Over her objections, George excelled in boxing at Pasadena Junior College. He also received acting training at the Pasadena Community Playhouse with fellow-players Victor Mature and Robert Preston.

Suicide or murder? George Reeves was on track for a solid film career after earning strong reviews in *So Proudly We Hail!* (1943), but was unable to regain momentum following service in World War II. Desperate, the actor turned to television and played the Man of Steel in the 1950s syndicated kiddie show *The Adventures of Superman*. He was unhappily typecast as Superman, and his career was foundering when he died under mysterious circumstances on June 16, 1959.

In 1939, Warner Bros. studio head Jack Warner signed George Bessolo to a contract with plans to develop him as a B-unit player. Warner changed the fledgling actor's name to the more box office friendly, less ethnic sounding George Reeves and cast him in three 1939 shorts: *Pony Express Days*, *The Monroe Doctrine*, and *Ride, Cowboy, Ride*. That same year, Reeves made his full-length motion picture debut as "Stuart Tarleton," one of "Scarlett O'Hara's" suitors in the MGM Civil War epic *Gone with the Wind*. On September 22, 1940, Reeves married actress Eleanor Needles, his girlfriend of two years. The couple quietly divorced in 1949. After the box office success of *Gone with the Wind*, Reeves worked steadily in supporting roles in quality films like *Torrid Zone* (1940), *The Strawberry Blonde* (1941), *Blood and Sand* (1941), and *Lydia* (1941). In 1943, the actor scored a solid hit as the lead opposite Claudette Colbert in Paramount's World War II film *So Proudly We Hail!* Director Mark Sandrich was so impressed by Reeves's standout performance that he promised to make him a star when the war ended. Reeves, secure in the knowledge he had a powerful ally in Hollywood, entered the Air Force Special Services shortly after the film was released. Unfortunately for the actor, Sandrich died in 1945.

After the war, Reeves struggled to restart his career and was briefly forced to work in radio in New York City. Relocating to Hollywood, the actor landed a bit part in *Variety Girl* (1947) before starring in two low-budget jungle films in 1948 — *Jungle Goddess* and *Jungle Jim* featuring Johnny "Tarzan" Weissmuller in the title role. In 1949, the fading actor reached the nadir of his film career when he starred as the title character in *Adventures of Sir Galahad*, a second-rate Columbia serial. With his career in motion pictures essentially ended, Reeves turned to television in 1950 as a last resort. The frustrated actor, suspecting his jump to the small screen would in all likelihood signal the death knell to any future film opportunities, gambled few in the industry would see his television performances. In 1950, he was chosen from among 200 other actors to star in the syndicated kiddie television show *The Adventures of Superman*. No one, least of all Reeves, felt the half-hour program would last longer than a few months. However, when the show debuted in July 1951 (backstopped by the low-budget film *Superman and the Mole Men*) it was an instant hit and continued to run until November 1957. At the height of its popularity, the show was watched by

91 percent of all households with children under the age of 12. Reeves ultimately earned $2,500 a week playing the "Man of Steel," but called acting in the series "the bottom of the barrel." Though he continued to work in films (*Rancho Notorious*, 1952; *The Blue Gardenia*, 1953), his association with the Superman character proved detrimental. The actor had a sizable supporting role in director Fred Zinneman's 1953 classic *From Here to Eternity*, but was all but edited out of the film after a preview audience started laughing and shouting "Superman!" when he appeared on screen. In his last film appearance, Walt Disney's 1956 *Westward Ho the Wagons!*, Reeves was forced to appear in whiskers and a broad-brimmed hat. The unhappy actor stalked the set telling anyone who would listen, "Here I am, wasting my life."

Shortly after divorcing Eleanor Needles in 1949, Reeves began a long affair with Toni Mannix, wife of Eddie Mannix, a powerful vice president at MGM who served as "eyes and ears" for studio head Louis B. Mayer. Mannix, the studio "fixer," specialized in cleaning up scandals like the suicide (possibly murder) of producer Paul Bern (see entry) in 1932. Nicknamed the "Bulldog," he reportedly helped circulate the vicious (and many contend untrue) rumor that Bern, sex bomb Jean Harlow's husband at the time of his death, was impotent and possessor of a microphallus. Bern's suicide was sold to the public as the only way he could atone for his "sin" against MGM's popular screen goddess. Mannix suffered from heart trouble, knew of his wife's infidelity with Reeves, and sanctioned it. Mannix had a Japanese mistress and they would often go out to dinner with Reeves and Toni. As Catholics, however, divorce was out of the question. Eleven years older than Reeves when they met, 46-year-old Toni Mannix, like his mother, was an incredibly jealous and possessive woman. Toni called him "the Boy" while Reeves referred to her as "Mom." Mannix set her lover up in a house at 1579 Benedict Canyon and lavishly furnished it to "the Boy's" taste. Always a big drinker, Reeves alcohol consumption escalated as his television show continued to gain in popularity. By the mid–1950s booze had bloated "Superman" to the point where he was forced to wear a corset under his cape. Concerned that he might not have an acting career after the series ended, Reeves convinced the producers to let him direct three episodes during the show's final season in 1957. After seven years, 104 episodes, and one full-length movie, *The Adventures of Superman* wrapped on November 27, 1957, amid speculation that the show might be picked up in 1958.

In the fall of 1958 Reeves was in New York City on a promotional tour for the series when he met and fell hard for Leonore (some sources cite Lenore) Lemmon, a sometime torch singer. Lemmon, 35, twice married and 18 years younger than Toni Mannix, had a hard-earned reputation as a shady character with a history of writing bad checks. In the early 1940s she was barred from the Stork Club for brawling. Reeves unceremoniously dumped Mannix and installed Lemmon in his house on Benedict Canyon Drive. Toni Mannix, devastated and still paying the bills on the home, became obsessed with the couple. Reeves alerted police the jilted woman was stalking him and making harassing phone calls. By mid–June 1959, the 45-year-old actor had not worked in two years and was living off residuals from the *Superman* series. Plans to set up a series of boxing exhibitions with prizefighter Archie Moore were cancelled due to poor ticket sales. Through it all, Reeves continued to wrack up a $600 a month booze bill. One week before his death, however, he signed to do another season of *Superman* in which he would be allowed to direct several episodes. Additionally, he announced plans to marry Leonore Lemmon, 35, in Mexico on June 19, 1959 (disputed by friends close to the actor).

What exactly occurred during the early morning hours of June 16, 1959, in the star's house at 1579 Benedict Canyon Drive remains a matter of contention. Many believe Reeves, depressed over his stalled career and not looking forward to playing "Superman" in another 26 television episodes, simply committed suicide. Others (most notably Sam Kashner in his 1996 study of the case, *Hollywood Kryptonite*) maintain Reeves was murdered on the order of Eddie Mannix who either acted at the behest of his jilted wife or without her knowledge in order to put an end to the affair that was emotionally devastating his wife and embarrassing him. E.J. Fleming in *The Fixers: Eddie Mannix, Howard Strickling and the MGM Publicity Machine* (2005) opts for a theory in which Leonore Lemmon shot Reeves during an argument (perhaps over a broken engagement). Eddie Mannix, in touch with police for many years as a studio "fixer," quickly learned of Reeves' death and engineered the suicide theory to head off embarrassing press reports linking his wife to the dead actor. Lemmon and the rest of the guests in the death house were only too happy to play along with the fiction.

In the official version of the case, Reeves retired to his upstairs bedroom early on the evening of June 15, 1959, leaving Lemmon alone downstairs with house guest Robert Condon, a writer doing a biographical piece on the actor. Sometime after midnight on June 16th, friends William Bliss and Carol Van Ronkel dropped by the house for a drink. Those familiar with the habits of the couple understood that a glowing porch light meant drinks were still being served while a switched off light signaled they did not want to be disturbed. That night, Lemmon inadvertently left the porch light on. Lemmon, Condon, Bliss, and Van Ronkel were enjoying themselves when Reeves emerged from his upstairs bedroom clad in a dressing gown. The actor, angry at being disturbed, yelled at the new arrivals for calling so late and strongly told them in no uncertain terms that he was in no mood for a party. After threatening to physically toss Bliss out of the house, Reeves was chastised by Lemmon, apologized, had a quick drink, and went back upstairs to bed.

According to published reports, Lemmon then "narrated" the events leading up to her lover's death. As she heard Reeves settling into his room over the garage, Lemmon announced, "That's George, he's going to shoot himself." As the sound of a drawer was heard opening she said, "See he's opening the drawer to get the gun out." Seconds later as a shot rang out Lemmon shouted, "See there, I told you; he's shot himself." Bliss rushed up the stairs to find Reeves' nude body sprawled across the bed bleeding profusely from a gunshot wound through the right temple. The .30-caliber bullet tore through the actor's left temple and lodged in the ceiling. The weapon, a 9mm German Luger, was on the floor a few feet away. The heavily oiled gun surprisingly yielded no fingerprints or smudges. An autopsy determined that Reeves' alcohol level was .27 percent. The legal level of intoxication in California in 1959 was .15. Lemmon later told police she was only "kidding" when she foretold Reeves' death. In support of the coroner's suicide finding, Lemmon added: "George couldn't exist in this kind of world. That's why he killed himself. He died of a broken heart. From being Superman he couldn't get a job. He had been Superman on TELEVISION for eight years. A year and a half ago they stopped making them. George hadn't had a job since. His dignity was shattered. He was typed, and it was

'Sorry, George. We think you're great, but we can't use you.' He had been depressed for months, but he hid it. He was full of chuckles...."

Supporters of the murder theories point to numerous failings in the subsequent police investigation and inconsistencies in the autopsies. Helen Bessolo immediately arrived in Hollywood and hired celebrity attorney Jerry Giesler (see Cheryl Crane) and the Nick Davis Detective Agency to investigate the death of her son. Private investigators quickly found key evidence overlooked by the LAPD. Besides the bullet hole in the ceiling caused by the fatal shot when it exited, two other bullet holes were found in the floor of the murder room covered by a rug. Leonore Lemmon, prior to being permitted to leave Los Angeles by police within two days of the violent death of her lover, later "remembered" she had once playfully fired the gun off in the room to hear what it would sound like. Detectives blindly accepted the guests' contention that the shooting was a suicide and did not photograph the body or the crime scene. The autopsies revealed no powder burns to Reeves' temple suggesting the fatal shot was fired at a distance of at least 18" (more likely farther) suggesting the actor could not have pulled the trigger. Also, bruises were found on the actor's forehead, left temple, and right shoulder. Remarkably, the initial autopsy failed to test for gunpowder residue on the actor's hand. Giesler stayed with the grieving mother for a while (pocketing a hefty $50,000 fee), but finally quit after informing Bessolo dangerous people were involved in the case and she would be well-advised to walk away as well. Meanwhile, Reeves left his entire estate (the house, car, and $25,000) to Toni Mannix freezing out so-called fiancée Leonore Lemmon and his mother. Helen Bessolo had her son's body cremated and, after her death in 1964, the cremains were placed in the Mountain View Cemetery in Altadena, California. The urn reads: "My Beloved Son 'Superman'—George Bessolo Reeves—Jan. 6, 1934–June 16, 1959." In 2006, the film *Hollywoodland* refocused attention on the controversy surrounding the death of the 45-year-old actor convincingly played by Ben Affleck. Other principals in the George Reeves' sage were portrayed by Diane Lane (Toni Mannix), Bob Hoskins (Eddie Mannix), and Robin Tunney (Leonore Lemmon). In 1983, Toni Mannix (a recluse since "the Boy's" death) died at 77 of Alzheimer's related complications in Beverly Hills. Leonore Lemmon, the younger woman who stole Reeves away from her, died in New York City on January 1, 1990, reportedly an alcoholic and occasional prostitute. Much like the cases of Marilyn Monroe (see entry) and Thelma Todd (see entry), the mysterious death of George Reeves will continue to generate speculation among those who refuse to accept "Superman" would ever have committed suicide.

Further Reading

Fleming, E.J. *The Fixers: Eddie Mannix, Howard Strickling and the MGM Publicity Machine.* Jefferson, NC: McFarland, 2005.
Henderson, Jan Alan. *George Reeves: The Man, the Myth, the Mystery.* Hollywood: Cult Movies, 1995.
_____. *Speeding Bullet: The Life and Bizarre Death of George Reeves.* Grand Rapids, MI: M. Bifulco, 1999.
Kashner, Sam, and Nancy Schoenburger. *Hollywood Kryptonite: The Bulldog, the Lady, and the Death of Superman.* New York: St. Martin's, 1996.

Reid-Thomas, Elliott (V)

Ghetto Concept, rappers Kwajo Boateng and partner L. "Dolo" Frazer, came out of the Rexdale community of Toronto, Ontario, in the early 1990s, and in 1994 won a Juno Award for their independently released single "Certified Dope." In 1998, the hip-hop duo released a highly regarded debut album, *Ghetto Concept*, on their own 7 Bills Entertainment label. The album graphically portrayed life in the disadvantaged Rexford district of inner city Toronto; a theme expanded upon in 2001 with the release of their single, "Rest in Peace," Ghetto Concept's eulogy for 16 of their friends killed in street violence in Rexdale. Kwajo and Dolo were in Los Angeles cutting a new album and music video when they learned that their longtime manager and unofficial third member of Ghetto Concept, Elliott "Blacks" Reid-Thomas, was yet another victim of violent death.

Around 4:45 A.M. on February 21, 2004, Reid-Thomas, 29, was leaving the rear exit of an after-hours club at Toronto's Vaughan Road and Oakwood Avenue with friends when a man stepped up behind him and shot him once point-blank in the back of the head. Some of the crowd of nearly one hundred described the shooter as a 25-year-old dark-skinned man with silver colored caps on his teeth wearing a white tee shirt, blue jeans, a blue cap, and a white bandanna. He was last seen driving from the scene in a late model Honda. A friend of the murdered manager told the press, "They couldn't even look him in the face. They had to shoot him in the back of the head. It's jealousy in the neighborhood they grew up in." While jealousy over the success of Reid-Thomas may have been a motive, earlier in the evening the manager had intervened when a young woman was being harassed by a group of men outside the club. With limited cooperation from witnesses, however, Toronto police have to date been unable to solve the murder.

Further Reading

Bradley, Kim. "Dead for Rap Success? Manager of Ghetto Concept One of 3 People Killed in Area in 2 Days." *Toronto Sun*, February 23, 2004, p. 4.

Reilly, Catherine (M-S)

Reilly, a fashion model-actress who played the "little blue nun" in television commercials for Blue Nun wine, shot her 34-year-old lover, New York City transit cop Michael Condon, then turned the gun on herself, ending a loud quarrel in her Manhattan apartment at 315 East 54th Street on July 7, 1982. Condon, separated from his wife and occasionally living with the 28-year-old actress, was shot once in the chest with his own .38-caliber revolver before Reilly fired a round into her mouth. The fully clothed pair was found sprawled together in the living room with the murder weapon and Condon's unfired 9mm pistol lying nearby. Reilly appeared in off Broadway plays, television soap operas, and in small roles in the films *Annie Hall* (1977) and *Superman* (1978).

Further Reading

"Model Kills Officer and Then Herself." Associated Press, July 8, 1992.

Renaudin, Lester (M-S)

Renaudin, a 21-year-old emcee at the Club Plantation in New Orleans, was married to his childhood sweetheart, Mary Lee Roberts, a 19-year-old dancer at the Club Avalon in Metairie Ridge, Louisiana, for two years when their recent estrangement exploded into a murder-suicide on January 26, 1933. Shortly before midnight, Renaudin waited in his car outside the Club Avalon for Roberts to report to work. When she arrived, he invited her into the car to talk. Minutes later, Renaudin pulled out a revolver, shot her through the heart, and fired a bullet into his brain. Roberts continued to scream, "Please don't let me die," until expiring (with her husband) en route to the hospital. A letter addressed to his father found on the dead emcee read, "I can't possibly live without Mary Lee and can do anything living with her.

She is the only girl that could ever enter my life. I suppose I am crazy — I must be to do a thing like this. I would have gone crazy before the day was over. I never was happy in my life, so don't worry, my poor, good, sweet family. I loved you more than I ever could express. I would write more, but you know how I feel. Your down-hearted son, Lester."

Further Reading

"Night Club Floor Manager Kills Wife, Takes Own Life." *New Orleans Times-Picayune*, January 27, 1933, pp. 1, 3.

Ritchie, Adele (M-S)

Once known as the "Dresden china doll of the musical comedy stage," Ritchie was born in Philadelphia in 1877. In 1893, she made her first public appearance in the light opera *The Algerian*. Leading roles in other operas ensued, followed by a stint in vaudeville. On November 3, 1916, the recently divorced actress married stage actor Guy Bates Post in Toronto shortly before his matinee performance as the lead in *Omar the Tentmaker*. After the marriage, Ritchie all but retired from the theatre although she did aid America's World War I recruiting effort by singing patriotic songs in vaudeville in 1917. The couple divorced in 1929 and the 52-year-old actress relocated to the exclusive artist colony of Laguna Beach, California, where she directed plays for the Community Playhouse. There, Ritchie became close friends with Doris Murray Palmer, dubbed the "most beautiful woman in Laguna Beach," a wealthy divorcee some twenty years her junior. The pair was inseparable companions until Palmer's popularity in the community's closely knit social circle began to eclipse Ritchie's. A past collaborator with Ritchie in the Community Playhouse, Palmer had designed all the stage settings and scenery for the theatre's latest offering, *The Lady from Memphis*, and was set to direct alone.

The pair's relationship reached a crisis on April 24, 1930, at Palmer's hillside bungalow at 2337 Glenneyre Street in Laguna Beach. Ritchie was visiting her friend when she learned that Palmer had been invited to a luncheon and she had not. Ritchie insisted on attending, but Palmer was equally adamant that she was not invited, and angrily turning her back on the former actress, walked down a hallway leading to the garage. Ritchie pulled a nickel plated, pearl-handled .32-caliber revolver from her purse and shot the 35-year-old woman once in the back (the bullet entering under the left shoulder blade and piercing the heart) and once at close range in the back of the head. According to the police reconstruction of the crime, Ritchie then spent the next two hours driving around the community trying to decide upon a course of action. Finally, she returned to the crime scene and moved Palmer's body to a room adjoining the living room. Ritchie carefully arranged her friend's body: folded her arms across her chest, straightened out her clothes, combed her hair, placed a pillow beneath the head, then applied rouge, lipstick, and powder to Palmer's face. She then retired to the adjoining living room and, after first firing a shot at her head

By the late 1920s, Adele Ritchie, the formerly popular actress-singer in comedy and light opera roles, was retired and enjoying her status as the doyen of the Laguna Beach, California, arts community. Ritchie and Doris Murray Palmer, the "most beautiful woman in Laguna Beach," enjoyed an intense friendship until the retired star felt the younger woman's popularity was eclipsing her own. Following an argument with Palmer on April 24, 1930, the 52-year-old actress murdered her friend and took her own life.

that missed, reclined on the sofa, placed the gun to her right ear, and pulled the trigger. In the throes of her death agony, the actress rolled to the floor. Their bodies were later discovered by a mutual friend who stopped by the bungalow to return Palmer's lost dog. Guy Bates Post, informed of his former wife's murder-suicide before a performance of *The Play's the Thing* in Hawaii, said, "We lived together fourteen years, but frankly I never felt I knew her. She was very proud."

Further Reading

"Guy Bates Post Goes on with Play." *Los Angeles Times*, April 26, 1930, pt. 1, p. 1.

Rogers, Derek (V)

A 22-year veteran stationed at Upland Air Force Base near Ottawa, Rogers, 47, played trombone for the Canadian Central Command Band and was active in the Salvation Army. Rogers and his wife of twenty years, Faith, took annual vacations to Old Orchard Beach, Maine, where the couple rented a cottage. The couple was there several weeks when Faith left to return to work leaving her husband alone to enjoy the beach. Unable to sleep, Rogers took a walk in the early morning hours of July 31, 2002. Sometime between 2:15 and 2:30 A.M. the trombonist was attacked on the boardwalk in the town's Ocean Park area. Vacationers reported hearing one or more women and at least two men loudly arguing at the time of the assault. The group departed in a light-colored sedan. A fisherman discovered the musician's body lying face-up amid a litter of beer cans and a Subway drink container bearing the name "Kelly" near the entrance to the boardwalk at 3:30 A.M. Beaten about the face until unrecognizable, his nose and mouth stuffed with sand, Rogers died of asphyxiation. Positive identification was made through dental records. Police traced the cup back to Angela Kelly Humphrey who initially cut a deal with authorities to testify against her brother and his girlfriend. In August 2002, Benjamin Humphrey, 29, and his lover, 23-year-old Aimee Pelletier, were arrested in a shopping mall in Rapid City, South Dakota and extradited back to Maine to face a murder charge.

According to Kelly Humphrey's account of the fatal incident, she, brother Ben, Aimee Pelletier, and a teenaged friend were on the beach when Rogers introduced himself and bought beer for the group. The group started talking about Canada and Rogers asked the Humphreys about being "Native American." Despite attempts by the brother and sister to steer the conversation away from the topic, Rogers persisted until he allegedly referred to Kelly Humphrey as a "squaw," a term some Indians equate roughly with "whore." Kelly Humphrey was unable to stop her brother from attacking Rogers and stuffing handfuls of sand into his mouth to stifle any screams for help. The account, decidedly out of character for the soft-spoken Rogers, was disputed by the dead man's family. On the brink of trial for murder in July 2003, Benjamin Humphrey cut a deal with the district attorney allowing him to plead guilty to the lesser charge of manslaughter in return for testifying against his sister, Kelly. As part of the plea agreement, Humphrey was sentenced to 20 years in prison, with all but five years suspended. Charged with murder and perjury, Kelly Humphrey awaited her day in court while serving time at the Maine Correctional Facility in Windham for violating parole on an unrelated conviction. In November 2003, the 29-year-old woman admitted her role in the killing in exchange for a ten-year sentence on the reduced charge of manslaughter and perjury. Both deals, according to the prosecutor, were made because the state feared that by pointing the finger at one another the Humphreys might find a jury that would acquit one of them on the ground of reasonable doubt. Charges against Humphrey's girlfriend, Aimee Pelletier, were dropped when investigators determined she had not been at the scene.

Further Reading

Staples, Sarah, and Jen Fish. "Ottawa Musician's Killer Gets 5 Years in Plea Bargain." *National Post* (Toronto), July 17, 2003, sec. A, p. 9.

Rose, George (V)

Born the son of a butcher on February 19, 1920 in Bicester, England, Rose trained as a musician prior to enrolling at the Central School of Speech and Drama where his performances in various Shakespearean comedy roles attracted the attention of British acting giants John Gielgud and Laurence Olivier. In 1944, Gielgud directed Rose in the role of "Dogberry" in the Bard's *Much Ado About Nothing* at the Old Vic. Two years later, the versatile actor made his Broadway debut to strong notices in *Henry IV*. In the 1961 production of *A Man for All Seasons* Rose gained national attention for his portrayal of the "Common Man,"

a demanding role in which he assumed eight different guises. Rose moved permanently to New York City in 1961 purchasing a loft in Greenwich Village. On Broadway, the actor distinguished himself over a forty year stage career in both dramas and musical comedies including *Coco* (1969, Tony nomination), 1968 and 1972 revivals of *My Fair Lady* ("Alfred P. Doolittle"), *My Fat Friend* (Tony and Drama Desk Award nominations), a 1979 revival of *Peter Pan* ("Captain Hook"), and as "Maj. Gen. Stanley" in a 1981 run of the Gilbert & Sullivan operetta, *The Pirates of Penzance*. A two-time Tony Award winner (*My Fair Lady*, 1976; *The Mystery of Edwin Drood*, 1986), Rose also appeared in more than thirty films including *A Night to Remember* (1958), *Hawaii* (1966), and *A New Leaf* (1971), and on television.

In 1984, the 64-year-old thespian began thinking about life after acting and purchased a three-bedroom beachfront home in the small town of Sosua, one hundred miles northwest of Santo Domingo, capital of the Dominican Republic. Two years later, Rose adopted Juan Ralfe Vazquez, then a 16-year-old he had met two years earlier. The pair lived together as homosexual lovers and, according to the terms of the older man's will, Vazquez stood to inherit upon Rose's death the actor's $2 million estate. Rose, as the "master of ceremonies" in the Joseph Papp produced stage production of *The Mystery of Edwin Drood*, considered his Tony Award winning performance to be the capstone of a brilliant theatrical career. He agreed to the time-consuming, but lucrative cross-country tour of the show on the stipulation he could periodically take time off to visit his retirement retreat in the Dominican Republic. When *Drood* concluded its Washington, D.C., run in the first weekend of May 1988, Rose took advantage of a three week hiatus to fly down to Sosua. Landing on May 2, Rose returned to a domestic situation fraught with drama. Earlier, he was forced to fire a couple of household servants and not long afterwards found his pet parrot with its head severed. Likewise, a beloved cat was hacked into quarters and its parts nailed to a tree in what most likely represented a voodoo ritual. Friends warned him that the island culture was just too foreign and dangerous for a 68-year-old Britisher turned American transplant to live in retirement.

At 6:30 A.M. on May 5, 1988, a passerby found a car flipped upside down in a roadside ditch one mile from Rose's home in Sosua. The actor's body was found by the side of the car a victim of what police first suspected was a high speed traffic accident possibly caused by either falling asleep at the wheel or a heart attack. Besides a passport and $4.14 in Dominican and U.S. currency recovered from Rose's person, authorities were interested in a bag of white powder (later identified as cocaine) inside the car. An initial autopsy ruled the two gashes on Rose's forehead were caused when the car overturned. An official verdict of "no foul play" was returned. Friends of the actor, unwilling to believe the man they knew who hated to drive would be killed in a car accident on a straight road he knew intimately, pressed the U.S. Embassy to become involved in the case. Acting under pressure from the embassy, a second autopsy revealed Rose had, in fact, been savagely beaten about the head and arms prior to being placed in a car that was overturned to make the scene look like a fatal traffic accident. A small trace amount of cocaine derivative was found in the actor's body, but it could not be determined when it was taken.

On May 12, 1988, a police spokesman announced at a news conference three men had been arrested for the murder while a fourth suspect, Luis Manuel Boribio, was still at-large. In custody were Rose's adopted son-lover Juan Ralfe Vazquez, 18, his natural father, Juan Antonio Vazquez Padilla, and his uncle, Maximo Vazquez Padilla. At the conference, the teen's father confessed he and his son planned the killing because they were jealous and fearful that Rose's attraction to a 14-year-old boy, Juli, might result in an adoption by the actor which would disinherit Juan. The "outraged" father also spoke of taking revenge on the actor whose homosexual activities had prostituted his son since the age of 13 and threatened to do so to other area youths. Father, son, and uncle paid Boribio $2,000 to take Rose to an isolated location and murder him. On May 4, Rose was driving his adopted son Juan to Santiago when three men by the side of the road forced the car to stop. The men got in, leaving Juan by the side of the road, and drove to a secluded farm house where they held the actor for eight hours prior to torturing and bludgeoning him to death with a club. They split the man's money, placed the body in the car, and flipped it into a ditch. In, what apparently is not unusual in the annals of Dominican Republic jurisprudence, all four men were held for a year without trial. Juan Vazquez, the adopted son, was released on bail and claiming police coercion retracted much of his original statement. His birth father, Vazquez Padilla, also changed his statement claiming Rose's death was accidental. To date, none of the men have been put on trial or sentenced. Juan cut a deal with the alternative beneficiary of Rose's will, a small church in Bucknell, England, in which he was able to claim the house in Sosua in exchange for a cash settlement. Juan has since sold Rose's retirement home for $250,000 and spent seven years in America before resettling in a small village near Sosua. In March 1997, the three men in custody were released and almost certainly will never see the inside of a Dominican courtroom. As for George Rose, he is buried in an unmarked grave in a rundown cemetery outside Sosua.

Further Reading

Ryder, Bill. "Murder of the Beloved Actor," in *Celebrity Murders*, ed. by Art Crockett. New York: Windsor, 1990.

Rosolino, Frank (M–S)

Rosolino (born August 20, 1926, in Detroit, Michigan) was a premier jazz trombonist who performed with Gene Krupa, Stan Kenton, Dexter Gordon, and Quincy Jones. A staff musician in the early 1960s on *The Steve Allen Show*, "Mr. West Coast Trombone" was also a talented comedian and scat singer. In a fit of depression on November 26, 1978, the 52-year-old musician shot his two sons (ages 11 and 7) with a .38-caliber pistol as they lay asleep in separate bunk beds at their home on Nordhoff Street in Sepulveda, California. Rosolino was found fatally wounded on the living room floor. A note detailing his despondency was found at the scene. Seven-year-old Jason Rosolino survived. Of the bebop trombonist, renowned alto saxophonist and bandleader Benny Carter said, "He was a fantastic musician, but behind that cut-up personality was a troubled man. He was like Pagliacci."

Further Reading

Feather, Leonard. "Rosolino Death Shocks Musicians." *Los Angeles Times*, November 28, 1978, sec. IV, p. 7.

Ross, Nat (V)

Ross (born in San Francisco, California, on June 13, 1902) directed several silent pictures for Universal Studios in the 1920s (*Ridin' Wild*, 1922; *Pure Grit*, 1923; *The Slanderers*, 1924; *College Love*, 1929) before turning to producing in the 1930s with films like *The Man from Guntown* (1935), *The Outlaw Deputy* (1935), and *Crash Donovan* (1936). The one-time assistant to producer Irving

Thalberg was out of the movie business by 1941 and was the co-owner-night foreman at a rag factory on S. Broadway in midtown Los Angeles. On the night of February 24, 1941, Ross was informed by a co-worker that Maurice (M.) L. Briggs, 25, was outside waiting to speak with him. A few weeks earlier, Ross fired the man, an ex-convict who served three years in a South Carolina prison for bank robbery. Less than two weeks earlier an intoxicated Briggs had turned up at the factory and threatened Ross with a pocket knife. Complicating the situation was the ex-con's 21-year-old estranged wife, Betty Susan Briggs, a worker at the rag factory supervised by the 38-year-old former film director. After only two weeks of marriage, the woman left Briggs in December 1940. Convinced that Ross was "chasing around" with his wife, the jealous ex-con decided to confront him. When Ross went outside to meet the disgruntled former-employee, Briggs fired two rounds from a .25 to .35-caliber rifle into the man's chest killing him instantly. Twenty-five horrified employees witnessed the murder and saw the assailant flee the scene on foot. Briggs was arrested a few minutes later after he was observed tossing the rifle on a lawn. Stopped by a pedestrian and asked why he was discarding the gun, Briggs reportedly said, "Oh, I just killed a guy. Better call the cops." In custody, Briggs told police he would have killed Ross ten days earlier, but had to wait for his unemployment check before purchasing the weapon for $8.00. "Am I sorry I shot him?," Briggs allegedly told detectives, "Yes — I'm sorry I can't do it again." A distraught Betty Briggs denied ever having a relationship with the murdered man. Following months of bragging about the murder, Briggs pleaded "not guilty by reason of insanity" when told that he faced the death penalty if convicted of capital murder. At trial in July 1941, Briggs testified he was driven into a deep depression by the breakup of his marriage and suspicions Ross was "chasing around" after his unhappy wife. The situation reached its crisis, according to Briggs, when he allegedly learned the woman had obtained an abortion, perhaps funded by Ross. Briggs bought the gun with the intention of killing himself at the rag factory, not Ross. To no one's surprise, a jury found Briggs to be both sane and guilty of first-degree murder on July 21, 1941. His appeal for executive clemency rejected by the governor, Briggs was executed in the gas chamber in San Quentin on August 7, 1942.

Further Reading

"Ex-Convict Tells Jury How He Killed Rag Factory Head." *Los Angeles Times*, July 19, 1941, sec. A, p. 3.

Rothenberg, Paul E. (V)

On July 5, 1973, vice cops arrested Rothenberg and six others at Triple A Film Company and Arro Laboratories, the "legitimate" business he owned and managed in Lower Manhattan. In the raid, police seized 9,000 reels of pornographic movies estimated to be worth $500,000. No stranger to law enforcement, the 42-year-old film distributor was arrested in 1965 for promoting obscene material, convicted, but skated on appeal because of a faulty search warrant. Since that time, authorities had identified Rothenberg as a major national distributor of porno films despite his insistence he was only a "self-employed photo finisher." Rothenberg was facing a trial on a first-degree felony count of promoting obscenity when authorities believe that the Carlo Gambino crime family acted decisively to prevent the distributor from talking to police about pornography in the Times Square district. Approximately three weeks after the bust, Rothenberg's body was discovered around 10:50 A.M. on July 29, 1973, sprawled in an alley off Northern Boulevard in the Long Island village of Flower Hill. He was shot twice execution-style in the back of the head. Police found $500 in cash, a gold wristwatch, and the keys to Rothenberg's Cadillac on the body, ruling out robbery as a motive. No arrests were ever made in the case. (See entry William H. Door.)

Further Reading

Weisman, Steven R. "Reputed National Distributor of Smut Is Shot to Death Near Home in Nassau." *The New York Times*, July 30, 1973, p. 23.

Rountree, Roderick ("Khalil") (V)

A 20-year music industry veteran, Rountree worked in various managerial and support staff capacities with Harold Melvin and the Blue Notes, the Manhattans, and the Gap Band prior to becoming the tour manager for Motown R&B supergroup Boyz II Men. The group, appearing in Chicago on the same bill with M.C. Hammer on the performer's Too Legit to Quit Tour, was moved by Rountree from a motel in outlying Rosemont to the Guest Quarters Suite Hotel at 198 E. Delaware in Chicago's Gold Coast. At 5:00 A.M. on May 25, 1992, the morning after the concert, Qadree El-Amin, Rountree's assistant, heard his boss scream his name. Emerging from his room on the hotel's 26th floor, El-Amin saw Rountree in the elevator with three black men. Rountree excitedly told El-Amin that the trio attempted to break in his room and he was taking them downstairs to security. Suddenly, the men started lashing out and one fired his weapon hitting El-Amin in the knee and fatally striking Rountree in the head and chest. A gun was found in the dead man's pocket. A few days later, El-Amin picked three 22-year-old South Side men out of a line-up—alleged shooter, Christopher Babbington, Christopher Foley, and Kenneth Copeland. Police later found the murder weapon hidden in a VCR in one of the suspect's homes. According to the suspects' attorney, the three men were on the 26th floor of the hotel looking for "females and liquor" when they "knocked on the wrong person's door at the wrong time, and a man as big as the three of them combined (Rountree weighed 330 pounds) took a very aggressive attitude, pursued them into an elevator, (and) hit them." At the three defendants' simultaneous bench trial in May 1994, Babbington maintained he shot Rountree in "absolute desperation" to end an unjustified pistol-whipping inflicted by a man the defendant's attorney characterized as "an extremely large thug." Foley and Copeland were released after Criminal Court Judge Bertina E. Lampkin ruled there was insufficient evidence to hold them accountable for Babbington's actions. Babbington was found guilty of second-degree murder and sentenced to 14 years in prison.

Further Reading

O'Donnell, Maureen. "3 Charged in Slaying of Boyz II Men Manager." *Chicago Sun-Times*, May 29, 1992, p. 3.

Rovig, Melita Powell (M–S)

During the years 1910–1912 Rovig sang with the New York Metropolitan Opera Company under the stage name "Horatia Powell." Relocating to Los Angeles, the retired singer started manufacturing an exclusive line of cosmetics targeted at an upscale clientele. In 1935, she married Charles Rovig, a 53-year-old sales manager for a liquor house. On the night of January 13, 1936, the pair was enjoying a quiet evening in their apartment at 706 South Mariposa Avenue when Rovig, 44, jealously accused her husband of numerous marital indiscretions. A loud argument ensued in which Melita Rovig, brandishing a revolver, threatened to kill him. The liquor salesman disarmed the hysterical woman, hid the gun

in a bureau drawer, and retired to bed. Shortly after daybreak, Rovig shot the sleeping man in the stomach and chest, and turned the gun on herself. He survived long enough to notify police and give a dying declaration. In a note addressed to a sister, Rovig wrote she was contemplating suicide because she feared her husband planned to leave their marriage.

Further Reading

"Ex-Songbird Slays Mate." *Los Angeles Times*, January 14, 1936, pt. II, p. 5.

Rudebeck, John W. (V)

Guitarist Rudebeck and bass player, Brian Smith, formed the St. Louis–based blue-eyed soul band Mind Over Soul (a.k.a. Mindoversoul), in mid–1995. The band mixed original compositions with covers and released one CD, *'00*. On the evening of January 24, 2000, Rudebeck, 26, was clerking at the Sunshine Daydream shop at 6604a Delmar Boulevard in the University City Loop section of metropolitan St. Louis when he was fatally shot in the neck and robbed of approximately $100. Police arrested 25-year-old James A. Needy III in Texas County, about 140 miles southwest of St. Louis, after receiving a tip the man talked about the killing. Needy, hospitalized numerous times since the age of 13 for psychiatric disorders, gave a detailed confession to authorities which led to the recovery of the murder weapon, a .22-caliber pistol. Although psychiatric evaluations found him to be suffering from mental illness, Needy repeatedly told the judge, "I believe I am OK, and I know what I am doing here." Judged competent to stand trial, Needy pleaded guilty to first-degree murder over the objections of his public defender and was automatically sentenced to life in prison without parole on February 13, 2002.

Further Reading

Lhotka, William C. "Man Pleads Guilty of Murder in Killing of Clerk." *St. Louis Post-Dispatch*, February 14, 2002, sec. B, p. 3.

St. Louis, Keith Cedric (M)

In 1994, St. Louis was brought from the West Indies to the Portsmouth, Virginia, area by the Portsmouth Community Development Corporation to teach local children and adults how to play Trinidadian pan music. A former police officer in Trinidad, St. Louis was a member of the island band the Trinidad and Tobago Pan Professionals.

By 2001, the man described as having the "patience of Job" had taught the art of steel drumming to more than nine hundred students privately and through the Urban Arts Center in Portsmouth. On May 21, 2001, Arthur Stephen Hinton, Sr., 42, dropped by his ex-wife's apartment in the 100 block of Dahlgren Avenue in Portsmouth. A struggle between St. Louis, now married to the woman, and Hinton ended when the musician fatally plunged a butcher knife into the man's heart. St. Louis, 52, was convicted of second-degree murder on October 23, 2001, and subsequently sentenced to 12 years in prison, less than half of the 27 year sentence asked for by the jury. Upon release, the musician is to be placed on supervised probation.

Further Reading

"Killing Wife's Ex-Husband Brings 12 Years." *The Virginian-Pilot*, December 12, 2001, sec. B, p. 3.

Salanti, Theodore ("Rocky") (V)

Following the advice of his doctor, the Pittsburgh native relocated to San Diego in a bid to find relief from an acute sinus condition. A draftsman by trade, Salanti apparently gave up the profession in San Diego and, as a member of the Screen Actors Guild, briefly pursued a career in the early 1990s appearing in bit parts on the television shows *Silk Stalkings* (filmed in the city) and *Renegade*. By 2005, the 57 year old was allegedly a drug user who dealt methamphetamines. On September 30, 2005, a friend (unable to reach Salanti after repeated phone calls) drove to the former actor's condominium in the San Diego suburb of Santee. Confronted at the door by an overwhelmingly foul odor and suspecting the worst, the man immediately called 911. Paramedics forced their way into the residence and were overcome by what one called "the smell of death" emanating from a large green suitcase covered in a blanket by the front door. The place had been ransacked, blood was everywhere, the carpet torn up in several areas, and holes punched in the wall. Drag marks on the bloody floor from the suitcase led from a back room to the front door. The case was opened to reveal a badly decomposed Salanti, bound and gagged with duct tape, stuffed inside. Amid obvious signs of a struggle inside the condominium, several items appeared to missing including Salanti's car. An autopsy confirmed Salanti had been dead for several days with death attributed to "homicidal violence including asphyxiation." Simply stated, the duct tape over Salanti's face caused him to suffocate as his assailant searched the residence for items to steal.

On October 12, 2005, police arrested Amy Heather Davis, 25, an "escort" Salanti had met two years earlier in an internet chat room. Addicted to meth, Davis once stole $30,000 from Salanti, but he forgave her despite being warned by friends to terminate the relationship. In custody, Davis told authorities she was standing outside Salanti's condominium smoking a cigarette on September 23, 2005, when two men approached and forced her at knifepoint to help them rob the former actor. She did so under duress and the influence of her drug addiction. At trial in San Diego on March 12, 2007, Davis faced a first-degree murder charge with special circumstances (murder committed during a burglary and robbery). If convicted, she would receive an automatic sentence of life imprisonment without the possibility of parole. Rather than an unwilling participant in the crime, Davis was painted by the prosecution as a woman who betrayed Salanti's friendship for the opportunity to rob him of drugs and cash. She knew the combination to Salanti's safe, and more damningly, her fingerprints were found on the duct tape used to bind the former actor. Three days into the proceedings, a mistrial was declared after the evidence of a polygraph test administered to Davis was inadvertently entered into the trial record. A new jury was quickly impaneled and after deliberating for three days found Davis guilty of first-degree murder with special circumstances on April 11, 2007.

Further Reading

Hughes, Joe. "Woman Is Arrested in Death of Local Actor." *San Diego Union-Tribune*, October 14, 2005, sec. B, p. 1.

Salmi, Albert (M-S)

Salmi (born March 11, 1928, in the Coney Island section of Brooklyn, New York) took up acting following military service in World War II. From 1948 to 1954, the actor studied in New York with the Dramatic Workshop of the American Theatre Wing and the Actors Studio. Salmi appeared in several plays before achieving critical recognition as "Bo Decker," the Montana Romeo, in the 1955 Broadway production of *Bus Stop*. He turned down the role in the film version because, like other actors in Lee Strasberg's Actors Studio, he did not want to be thought of as a "Hollywood sell-out." In 1956, Salmi (with Paul Newman and George Peppard) appeared on the early dramatic television program *The U.S. Steel Hour* in a highly regarded adaptation of "Bang the Drum Slowly." In 1958, Salmi overcame his feelings toward Hollywood and appeared as "Smerdyakov" in *The Brothers Karamazov*, director Richard Brooks' adaptation for MGM of the Dostoyevsky novel. Many film Westerns followed (*The Bravados*, 1958; *The Unforgiven*, 1960; *Hour of the Gun*, 1967), but Salmi is probably best remembered for his 150-plus television credits on shows like *Rawhide*, *Bonanza*, *Wagon Train*, *The Big Valley*, and *The High Chaparral*. The beefy actor was also a regular on two series: the character "Yadkin" from 1964 to 1965 in the NBC program *Daniel Boone* starring Fess Parker, and "Pete Ritter" in *Petrocelli*, the NBC series from 1974 t0 1976 starring Barry Newman in the title role. In recognition of his realistic portrayal of cowboys on the small screen, Salmi was given the Western Heritage Award from the National Cowboy Hall of Fame.

The 62-year-old veteran of some twenty films was unemployed and living in Spokane, Washington, with his second wife, Roberta, when marital difficulties brought on by Salmi's drinking and physical abuse forced them to separate in February 1990. Salmi continued his abuse, this time by leaving her notes that read, "War of the Roses. You're a stupid girl. You're living out your fantasy.... We had a good thing going, too bad you tripped in the final straightaway." Fearful for her life after filing for divorce, the 55-year-old woman hired a private detective as a bodyguard, but dismissed him after family members convinced her she was being foolish. On April 23, 1990, a neighbor dropped by the Salmi house to check on Roberta after not seeing her for two days. When no one answered the door, she peered through the kitchen window and saw her friend lying in a pool of blood on the floor. Police entered the home and found Roberta Salmi shot to death with a .25-caliber handgun. In an upstairs den, Salmi had fired a fatal .45-caliber pistol shot into his chest. Authorities estimated that the pair had been dead for less than 24 hours.

Further Reading

Folkart, Burt A. "Actor Albert Salmi, Wife Found Shot to Death." *Los Angeles Times*, April 25, 1990, pt. A, p. 16.

Grabman, Sandra. *Spotlights & Shadows: The Albert Salmi Story*. Boalsburg, PA: BearManor, 2004.

Rovin, Jeff. *TV Babylon II*. New York: Penguin, 1991.

Sampih (V)

The most famous traditional dancer of his day, Sampih was a boy living in the small village of Sayan in southeast Bali when Canadian composer Colin McPhee, residing in the area to study its music, adopted him. Under McPhee's tutelage, the youngster trained under the finest Balinese dancers and within a year was a nationally recognized prodigy. Later, British impresario John Coast showcased Sampih in a "Dancers from Bali" troupe that performed to sold out venues across the United States from September 1952 through January 1953. The ambitious undertaking marked the first time in a generation the outside world was permitted to see Balinese performers dancing to a traditional Gamelang orchestra using xylophones, gongs, drums, and cymbals. Although Sampih served as the chief artistic adviser to Coast and was paid the same $75 weekly salary as the other dancers, he was the acknowledged star of the troupe. The dancer's popularity and financial success, however, led some in the company and his home country to feel he had somehow changed and now considered himself to be better than others. In Bali's rigid social system, Sampih belonged to the lowest caste and his purchase of a modest motorbike, and the fact that prominent people in higher castes now recognized him, made many of his fellow-countrymen angry and jealous. Evidently oblivious to the undercurrent of hostility around him, Sampih continued to ride his motorbike around his home village of Sayan where he lived with his wife and small child.

While on an official trip to Bali on February 28, 1954, President Sukarno of the Indonesian Republic requested that Sampih dance for him later that evening at a festival near the town of Sayan. When the 28-year-old dancer failed to appear, messengers were dispatched to his home and were informed by Sampih's wife that he left on his motorbike earlier that afternoon. Either that afternoon or three days later (accounts vary), the dancer's body was found floating in the Lauh River that flows past Sayan. Sampih had been strangled and his face beaten almost beyond the point of recognition. His motorbike, the apparent symbol of the dancer's sin against Balinese society, was smashed and buried nearby. Sampih's murder remains unsolved.

Further Reading

Bowers, Faubion. "Letter from Bali." *New Yorker*, 31(7) (October 29, 1955):114, 116–26.

McPhee, Colin. *A House in Bali*. Singapore; New York: Oxford University Press, 1979.

Sampson, John E. (V) (M-S)

Employed at Desilu Studios as a film editor on the ABC television doctor drama, *Ben Casey*, Sampson, 50, was at the center of a troubled homelife. For two years the editor and his wife, Jeane Sampson, 40, had violently quarreled in front of their ten-year-old child, Terry, in their home at 1103 Eilinita Avenue in the Verdugo Hills section of Glendale, California. On the afternoon of May 6, 1962, the distraught woman phoned her parents vacationing in Palm Springs and threatened to end it all. They begged her to do nothing until they arrived and hastily left to return to Glendale. During the evening, however, Jeane called her daughter into the bathroom and locked the door. The child screamed when she saw her mother clutching Sampson's .38-caliber pistol. Sampson came to the door and, ignoring his daughter's plea, "Go away, Daddy, or you'll get hurt," broke into the bathroom. During the struggle with his wife the film editor was shot point-blank in the abdomen. He died hours later during emergency surgery in the Glendale Memorial Hospital. Jeane could not explain why she locked herself in the bathroom with her child, but told authorities she meant the child no harm. She intended to kill herself, not Sampson, because "I ... got tired of being used as a punching bag." While awaiting trial, Jeane Sampson was found dead from an overdose of barbiturates at her home in Glendale on the weekend of August 11–12, 1962.

Further Reading

"Wife Held for Murder in Film Editor's Death." *Los Angeles Times*, May 8, 1962, p. 28.

Sanchez, Chalino *see* Appendix 1

Sanders, Scott (M-S)

According to his friends, the 26-year-old drummer of the heavy metal band Castleblak went "psychotic" after Jennifer Lee Lilly, 23, ended their two-year relationship. Around 2:00 A.M. on April 4, 1991, Sanders tracked down a car Lilly and a group of her friends were driving in near Webster and Hayes streets in San Francisco. Shouting that he was "going to end this once and for all," the obsessed drummer forced Lilly into his car and sped away. Shortly afterward, the kidnapped woman phoned her roommate from an unknown location to report Sanders had a gun.

When asked her location, the phone went dead. Authorities found Lilly's bullet-riddled body at 3:20 A.M. near a Bay Area Rapid Transit station in Lafayette, California. Three hours later, a motorist on State Road 29 near the Napa River watched as Sanders fired a round from a .38-caliber revolver into his chest and the car he was in plunge down a hundred-foot embankment.

Further Reading

Sonenshine, Ron. "Drummer, Ex-Girlfriend Dead in an Apparent Murder-Suicide." *San Francisco Chronicle*, April 5, 1991, sec. A, p. 6.

Santana, Merlin (V)

Born March 14, 1976, in New York City to parents from the Dominican Republic, Santana was encouraged to perform by his mother who saw it as a way to save him from the mean city streets. He did a fast food commercial at three, and his first big screen appearance (uncredited) was as an extra in the 1985 Woody Allen film, *The Purple Rose of Cairo*. In Hollywood, the good-looking young actor snagged recurring TV roles in *The Cosby Show* (late 1991–early 1992 as "Stanley"), *Moesha* (1996 as "Ohagi"), and as "Romeo" on *The Steve Harvey Show* (1996). Santana's likable performance in the latter series earned him nominations for the National Association for the Advancement of Colored People Image Awards and Alma Awards, which honor Hispanic performers. Selected by *Ebony* magazine as one of its Top 29 Bachelors of 2001, he also appeared in 2001 in the Eddie Murphy and Robert De Niro film, *Showtime*.

A promising career was brutally cut short in the early hours of November 9, 2002, in the Crenshaw District of south Los Angeles. Unknown to police at the time of the tragedy, days before Santana, 26, had met Monique King (a.k.a. "LaDawn Taylor," "Mercedes Brown"), a 15-year-old repeat foster care facility runaway, and her female friend outside a Chinese restaurant. Santana and one of his friends partied with the pair, and the actor later called King to set up another meeting. The morning of the tragedy, Santana and two male friends met with King in a house on Victoria Avenue in south L.A. Santana and one of his friends left the house and were sitting outside in a parked car when King apparently phoned her girlfriend to report Santana had "made some sort of physical advance on her." King later admitted to police she had fabricated the entire story. The girlfriend informed Damien Andre Gates, 20, and Brandon Douglas Bynes, 23, about the alleged rape. The enraged men secured weapons and located Santana and his friend parked on the street outside the house. Gates, armed with a rifle, and Bynes, carrying a handgun, walked up to the car and fired at Santana who was sitting in the passenger seat. The driver, unhurt in the attack, managed to speed away and flag down a police prowl car at Crenshaw and Exposition boulevards. Santana was pronounced dead at the scene from a head wound.

King, whose name was not released until a court ruled that she was "unfit to be tried as a juvenile," was arrested two days later. Gates and Bynes, both armed, were picked up by police on November 21, 2002. Each was held on $2 million bail as cases against them were readied. Jury selection was already under way in January 2004 for the first-degree murder trial against Damien Gates when his accomplice, Brandon Bynes, pleaded guilty to charges of voluntary manslaughter and attempted murder (the man with Santana). Bynes was sentenced to a 23 year prison term. The next month, a jury needed only one day to convict Andre Gates on separate counts of attempted and first-degree murder. Sentenced to three consecutive life terms, plus seventy years, Gates most likely will never again see the outside of a prison. Monique King, the teenager whose "rape lie" resulted in the murder of Merlin Santana, was tried in adult court in March 2004, but caught a huge break. Early in the trial, attorneys for both sides and the judge agreed to dismiss the jury and sentence her as a juvenile. Superior Court Judge Larry Fidler found King, 17, guilty of second-degree murder and attempted murder, and ordered her confined to the California Youth Authority prison until she turns 25 in 2012.

Further Reading

"Three Sentenced in Shooting Death of TV Actor Merlin Santana." *Jet* 105(43) (May 10, 2004):18.

Schaeffer, Rebecca (V)

The untimely shooting death of the 21-year-old actress at the hands of an obsessed fan in 1989 focused national attention on the increasing threat and price celebrities pay for their fame, and more importantly, led to laws designed to protect them. Schaeffer, born November 6, 1967, in Eugene, Oregon, was raised in Portland and knew from an early age what she wanted to do in life. She

began modeling at 14 two years later left high school in her junior year to relocate to New York City. In between modeling assignments Schaeffer earned her high school diploma at the Professional Children's School in New York. In 1984, the attractive curly haired 17 year old added to her professional resume by modeling in commercials and on magazine covers in Japan. Returning to New York in 1985, Schaeffer was cast as "Annie Barnes" in the perennially popular ABC soap opera *One Life to Live*. Schaeffer was 19 when she landed a co-starring role opposite Pam Dawber on the CBS comedy series *My Sister Sam*. The actress briefly lived with Dawber during the show's run from October 1986–April 1988. Her exposure on the short-lived series led to film work in Woody Allen's *Radio Days* (1987), *Scenes from the Class Struggle in Beverly Hills* (1989), *The End of Innocence* (1990), and the 1990 made-for-television movie *Voyage of Terror: The Achille Lauro Affair*. On the day of her murder, July 18, 1989, the 21-year-old actress was scheduled to meet with director Francis Ford Coppola to discuss a role in his upcoming film *The Godfather: Part III*.

As Schaeffer's life and career flourished in Hollywood, her self-proclaimed "biggest fan," Robert John Bardo, 19, was struggling in Tucson, Arizona, with an untreated mental illness. Bardo, the seventh child of an alcoholic father and a reputedly schizophrenic mother, started manifesting obsessive behavior while still in his teens. In 1983, the 14-year-old became fixated on Samantha Smith, an 11-year-old who gained international attention when she spent two weeks in the U.S.S.R. at the invitation of Soviet leader Yuri Andropov. Smith became an international symbol of peace and her celebrity fired Bardo's imagination. In December 1983, Bardo ran away from home and was arrested by alert police in Manchester, Maine, two blocks from Smith's house. Returned to his family in Tucson, the teenager attempted suicide by repeatedly stabbing himself in the arm with a ball-point pen. Bardo's odd behavior brought him to the attention of high school officials in 1984. He told one school counselor, "Who cares about punishment? The only punishment is my home. I'm going to be the next Hitler." Alarmed, the school referred Bardo to Child Protective Services. The troubled teen told his counselor there that the "people at the school did a good job stopping me from killing myself (but) they made a mistake cause now the Devil must kill." In January 1984, Smith became obsessed with a female teacher who apparently made the mistake of being nice to him. He wrote to her voluminously, attempted to get her phone number, and became threatening when he felt she had made an unkind comment about him. In February 1984, the school referred Bardo to the Palos Verdes Hospital for psychiatric help. While at the facility, he compared himself to John Hinckley, the would-be assassin of President Ronald Reagan, and spoke openly of his murderous compulsions. In April 1984, the principal of the high school met with Bardo's parents to discuss their troubled son. Both refused to accept that Bardo was mentally ill and immediately withdrew him from school and any further forced contact with Child Protective Services. In the summer of 1985, Bardo was briefly treated in a mental facility, but dropped out after his parents refused to fill his prescriptions or take him to counseling. Samantha Smith, the earlier object of Bardo's obsession, was killed in a plane crash at 13 with her father near Auburn, Maine on August 25, 1985.

In August 1986, Bardo found a new object for his obsession after seeing Rebecca Schaeffer on a promotional ad for her new television series *My Sister Sam*. He wrote her a fan letter and Schaeffer responded by sending him an autographed studio photo and a brief handwritten postcard reply. Bardo interpreted her response as interest in him and showered her with letters. Collecting every photo and article he could find of the young celebrity, the fixated teen videotaped every episode of the series and watched them endlessly alone in his room. In June 1987, Bardo took time off his occasional job as a janitor at a local Jack-in-the-Box, to travel by bus to Los Angeles to meet the object of his obsession. Security guards at the Burbank studios where *My Sister Sam* was shot were leery of the young man who showed up at the gate carrying a 5' teddy bear and a bouquet of flowers demanding to see Rebecca Schaeffer. Bardo was brought to the office of the studio's security chief, John Egger, 62, and told by the former Beverly Hills police captain he would not be permitted to see the star. Egger drove the cooperative Bardo back to the rundown Hollywood motel where the teen was staying and left without feeling suspicious about the incident. At Bardo's trial, Egger described the meeting: "I thought he was just lovesick, which I think he was. He was terribly insistent on being let in. 'Rebecca Schaeffer' was every other word. 'I gotta see her. I love her. If I could just see her for a minute.' He seemed to be

an intelligent kid, no raving lunatic, no dumbbell, but something was definitely wrong, mentally. There was something haywire going on, but I didn't perceive it as potentially violent." The next day, Bardo called Egger to thank him for his kindness and to inform the security chief he was returning by bus to Tucson. According to noted forensic psychiatrist Park Elliott Dietz (later hired by Bardo's public defender to assess his client's mental state at the time of the killing), the teenager's outward calm at being rebuffed by Egger masked a volcanic inner turmoil. After being dropped off by the security chief, Bardo bought a bottle of over the counter sleeping pills, took the entire bottle, and laid on the bed next to the teddy bear waiting to die. Instead, he awoke sick and in a foul mood. Bardo went to Hollywood Boulevard and bought a copy of the book about the Beatles, *The Love You Make*, featuring a chapter on John Lennon's killer Mark David Chapman, a person with whom he strongly identified (see entry John Lennon).

The cancellation of *My Sister Sam* in April 1988 did nothing to lessen Bardo's obsession with its pretty young star. When Schaeffer no longer answered any of his many letters and her agent refused to let him speak to her on the phone, Bardo was determined to profess his love in person. In June 1989, he paid a Tucson private detective $300 to locate Schaeffer's home address in Los Angeles. The private eye spoke to a contact in Los Angeles who for $5 was able to obtain the young star's address from the city's Department of Motor Vehicles. Around the same time, the under-aged 19-year-old had his older brother buy him a .357 Magnum pistol on the pretext that it would afford him protection during his frequent trips to Los Angeles to meet movie stars. Days after learning the 21-year-old Schaeffer was living in an apartment at 120 North Sweetzer Avenue in the Fairfax district of West Hollywood, Bardo left Tucson on a bus bound for Los Angeles.

By 6:30 A.M. on July 18, 1989, Bardo was in Schaeffer's neighborhood showing her photo to people on the street to determine if they knew where she lived. The white plastic shopping bag (termed an "assassin's kit" by the deputy district attorney) he carried contained the .357 Magnum, extra bullets, the personalized postcard Schaeffer had sent in reply to his first fan letter, a copy of J.D. Salinger's book *The Catcher in the Rye*, a CD of the U2 album *Joshua Tree*, and a love letter he had written to the star. Around 9:30 A.M. Bardo worked up enough courage to ring the buzzer under Schaeffer's name by the security door in the front of the building. He was startled when she arrived in person at the front door rather than asking who it was through the speaker. Dressed in jeans with her hair pulled back, Schaeffer talked briefly with Bardo about the postcard she had sent, smiled at him, and said, "Please take care," and shook his hand as he left. As he was walking away, he remembered he had forgotten to give her his love letter and the U2 CD. Around 10:15 A.M. Bardo returned to the apartment and rang the doorbell. According to the videotaped interview he gave in the L.A. Men's Central Jail in September 1991, Bardo stated this time Schaeffer answered the door in a bathrobe and did not seem happy to see him. Bardo: "She said, 'You came to my door again.' It was like I was bothering her again. 'Hurry up, I don't have much time.' I thought this was a callous thing to say to a fan." In response, Bardo pulled the gun from the bag and shot Schaeffer once in the chest. Neighbors reported hearing the young actress scream twice, "Why, why?" A tenant in Schaeffer's four-unit apartment complex, Lynne Marte, disputed Bardo's claim he spoke with the actress on his second visit. She told authorities she could have heard if any words were exchanged even though she was in her apartment. The gunshot was almost instantaneous between the time the doorbell rang and Schaeffer answered it. After the shooting, Bardo fled the scene and caught a bus back to Tucson. Schaeffer was pronounced dead on arrival at Cedars-Sinai Medical Center.

Hours after arriving home, Bardo was arrested by police on July 19, 1989, after they received a report that a man in a disoriented state was apparently attempting to commit suicide by running in front of cars on an exit ramp off Interstate 10 in downtown Tucson. Hearing of Schaeffer's murder, Bardo's father had immediately called police to finger his son as the killer and to warn them he may be armed. In custody, the 19-year-old began to cry, admitted he had shot someone, and asked to be arrested. As the legal machinery ground on to extradite the confessed killer to Los Angeles, Schaeffer was buried on July 23, 1989, at the Ahavoi Shalom Cemetery in Portland, Oregon. Among the 250 in attendance was her co-star, Pam Dawber, accompanied by her husband, actor Mark Harmon. Leaflets of the young star's writings tied with ribbon were circulated among family members and the presiding rabbi likened her death to that of Anne Frank saying both had been "snuffed out by a senseless society." On August 10, 1989, the Los Angeles County district attorney's office caught a break when Bardo's public defender challenged the extradition in the wrong court. Within hours of the mistake, Bardo was on a plane to Los Angeles thus averting months of legal wrangling over the killer's mental competency.

In July 1991, Bardo agreed to be tried without a jury in exchange for the state taking the death penalty off the table. Superior Court Judge Dino Fulgoni, an acknowledged expert in psychiatric matters, presided over the case while eleven year veteran Deputy District Attorney Marcia Clark, later to become a household name for her unsuccessful prosecution of O.J. Simpson (see entry), represented the people. Public defender Steve Galindo appeared for Bardo. As testimony began on September 25, 1991, Bardo sat motionless in court, his head hung down, the courtroom filled with both his and Schaeffer's relatives. If convicted of first-degree murder under the law's special circumstance statute of lying in wait to commit the crime the 19 year old would automatically be sentenced to spend the rest of his life in prison without the possibility of parole. Galindo, basing his defense on the doctrine of diminished capacity, argued that while Bardo was not insane, he did not possess the mental capacity to plan and commit the crime. As such, he was not lying in wait to kill Schaeffer, but only formed the intent to kill her at the time of his second visit after he perceived her to be "arrogant." Marcia Clark argued Bardo planned to kill Schaeffer before arriving in Los Angeles. He was the classic stalker interested in the fame his crime would confer on him.

Forensic psychiatrist Park Elliott Dietz, the star witness for the defense, characterized Bardo as a deeply troubled youth whose mental illness was largely untreated due to the refusal of his parents to acknowledge his problems. Three weeks into testimony, Dietz played a tape of the U2 song "Exit" from the band's *Joshua Tree* album eliciting Bardo's first visible display of emotion in the trial. The young killer rocked back and forth in his chair, drumming his hands on his legs, mouthing the words to the song. One lyric Dietz maintained held a special meaning to Bardo who interpreted it as giving him the idea for his "mission" to shoot Schaeffer. Bardo felt this would be the feeling he experienced the first time he met the star. According to the psychiatrist, Bardo had a history of being drawn to people like Schaeffer who seemed "accessible and non-threatening." However, his intense emotion of adoration could change in an instant (like a "toggle switch") to feelings of resentment if he sensed the person was aloof or did not like him. Bardo told Dietz his initial meeting with Schaeffer "calmed" him, but sensed she was annoyed with him for disturbing her a second time. He told Dietz, "I love you (Schaeffer) but if you're going to be some arrogant kind of person you're no good anyway." Dietz concluded Bardo was too emotionally disturbed to plan Schaeffer's murder, but rather killed her without forethought when he perceived the actress was annoyed with him.

Clark pointed out two years earlier Bardo had written a list referring to the gun, its bullets, and had taken the time to scratch the serial number off the gun. Like fellow-assassin Mark David Chapman, the man who murdered ex–Beatle John Lennon in New York City in December 1980, Bardo craved the publicity he would gain after killing a celebrity. Bardo, in fact, visited New York's Dakota apartment building where Lennon was gunned down, and like Chapman, also carried a copy of *The Catcher in the Rye* at the time of the murder. As further proof of premeditation, Clark introduced a letter written by Bardo to his sister in which he stated, "If I can't have her (Schaeffer) nobody will." On October 29, 1991, Superior Court Judge Dino Fulgoni found Bardo guilty of first-degree murder. "The defendant is not a normal person," Fulgoni ruled. "The defendant may even have schizophrenia of some sort. But ... schizophrenics can lie in wait and can premeditate and can have intent to kill." Bardo, the prototypical celebrity stalker, was sentenced to life imprisonment without the possibility of parole on December 20, 1991. At the sentencing, the killer angrily refuted Clark's claim he murdered the actress for publicity. "The idea that I killed Rebecca Schaeffer for fame is totally preposterous," Bardo railed. "I do realize the difference between right and wrong, and I realize what I did was wrong. If you're going to sentence me to life in prison, go ahead and do it, but there's no need to compound the case against me with all these lies." Schaeffer's murder, however, did result in legislation making other celebrities somewhat safer. In 1990, California became the first state to pass an anti-stalking bill. That same year, the Los Angeles Police Department created the country's first

unit solely assigned to investigate stalking cases. California legislators have since greatly restricted public access to motor-vehicle records, the means by which Bardo was so easily able to find then kill Rebecca Schaeffer.

Further Reading

CA v. Bardo. New York: Courtroom Television Network, 1993. (Videorecording, 110 min.).

Kolson, Ann. "Obsessed with Stars: Study Estimates 200,000 Fans in U.S. Harbor Celebrity Fixations." *Austin American-Statesman*, October 23, 1989, sec. C, p. 1.

Kuklenski, Valerie. "Bardo Re-Enacts Shooting Actress." United Press International, October 21, 1991.

Rovin, Jeff. *TV Babylon II*. New York: Penguin, 1991.

Schuster, Roy Edgar (M)

A former vaudeville dancer, Schuster, 26, took a job as a dance instructor for theatrical producer Ned Wayburn in New York City to support his one-time actress wife, Amy, and their four-year-old daughter. The four-year marriage crumbled in mid–1930. Schuster was living alone and struggling to pay a court ordered alimony settlement of $40 a week while attempting to reconcile with his wife when he lost his job in January 1931. On the morning of May 2, 1931, the dancer showed up at the fourteenth-floor office of his wife's attorney, Israel Siegel, at 49-51 Chambers Street to make one last attempt at reconciliation. Schuster argued with his estranged wife in an outer office of the law firm and became even more irate when Siegel told him to stay put while he conferred alone with his client in a private office. Schuster drew a .32-caliber revolver and shot his wife twice in the head killing her instantly. Before the crazed dancer fled past dazed office workers he emptied his gun leaving Siegel with two flesh wounds in the arm. On May 28, 1931, the former dancer was arrested in Little Rock, Arkansas, where he was living under the name "Anderson" and writing a book on dancing. While awaiting extradition to New York on a murder charge, Schuster insisted he only went to the law office with the intention of killing himself if the reconciliation failed. "I guess I'll get the electric chair," he told authorities, "for no jury will listen to my story. But the killing was accidental ... I went to the door and I supposed Siegel was trying to dissuade my wife from coming back to me. I pulled out a gun to end it all. But Siegel thought I was going to shoot him and he rushed toward me. We grappled and the gun went off several times as we scuffled. When I regained my senses my wife was dead and Siegel was gone." Schuster was found guilty of second-degree murder on October 22, 1931 and sentenced to 25 years to life in prison. At the state penitentiary in Ossining, New York, Schuster was a member of the Sing Sing Minstrels, a group of talented prisoners who put on public shows with proceeds earmarked for a relief fund for families of inmates.

Further Reading

"Arrest Roy Schuster, Fugitive Wife Slayer." *The New York Times*, May 29, 1931, p. 11.

Schwartzbauer, Jessica Lyn (V) (M-S)

Schwartzbauer (born October 16, 1970) was the popular lead singer of the GooneyBirds, a rock 'n' roll band that achieved near institutional status in Minneapolis, Minnesota, during the late 1980s and 1990s. The band, named after the mythological bird that used to ride on the top wing of biplanes in World War I, was formed by the vocalist and high school classmates. Following studies at the prestigious MacPhail Center for Music in Minneapolis, Schwartzbauer moved to San Francisco in the mid–1980s and met her husband, William "Ric" McDonald. The marriage lasted six years and produced two children (ages six and three) before McDonald's alcoholism and abuse forced the 32-year-old singer to file for divorce on May 19, 2003, in Great Falls, Montana. Fearful for her safety and that of her children, Schwartzbauer sought a restraining order against her 44-year-old husband citing in court papers the impending divorce could incite him to "physical violence." On June 3, the day before a hearing to make the restraining order final, the couple filed an agreement allowing McDonald to return home. However, less than one month later on July 1, 2003, police entered the McDonald home in Great Falls to discover a scene of domestic horror. Schwartzbauer, shot in the head as she slept, was found dead in her bed, as was the couples' six-year-old son in his. Anika, their 3-year-old daughter, was shot to death in her crib. McDonald's body and a 9mm handgun were found on the floor near one of the bodies. A musical foundation established in Schwartzbauer's name annually awards a $1,000 scholarship to a "talented vocal music performer" at MacPhail.

Further Reading

"Police Say Husband Responsible for Triple-Murder Suicide." Associated Press, state and local wire, July 3, 2003.

Scott, Linda (V)

Scott, not to be confused with the popular 1960s singer of the same name who recorded the single "I Told Every Little Star," was born in Sunflower, Kansas, and achieved modest success as a country and western singer under the name "Charlee." Her 1976 single "Keep Them Pillows Soft and Warm" sold 100,000 copies, but failed to chart. A recent unreleased album recorded in Nashville, Tennessee, *Standing in Your Shoes*, was dedicated to her two children from a previous marriage and her fiancé, attorney and business manager George Osserman. On November 10, 1978, the body of the 28-year-old singer was found by her two daughters in an upstairs bedroom of her $200,000 Tudor-style mansion in New Rochelle, New York. Scott was lying facedown on a blood-spattered bed and had several blood-encrusted head wounds. No weapon was found, but suitcases used by the singer during a six week concert tour which ended the day before were found lying half-unpacked near her body. On that same day, the divorced Scott had announced her engagement to George Osserman who lived with her and the children in the house on 134 Elk Avenue. With no signs of a forced entry or theft police focused their investigation on the house's staff. Four days after the fatal bludgeoning, Scott's 21-year-old chauffeur-handyman-stagehand, Michael D. Spearman, was arraigned on a charge of second-degree murder. Spearman, employed by the singer since October 1977 and living in the New Rochelle house, admitted killing the singer with a baseball bat as she slept in her bed. The murder was apparently the culmination of an ongoing argument between employer and employee over the extent of his work duties. On May 24, 1979, Spearman was found guilty of second-degree murder and sentenced to a maximum prison term of 25 years to life.

Further Reading

McNamara, Joseph. "Show Business Beauty Hammered to Death," in *Celebrity Murders*, ed. Art Crockett. New York: Pinnacle, 1990, pp. 274–86.

Scott, Walter (V)

Born Walter Simon Notheis, Jr., on February 7, 1943, in St. Louis, the future lead singer of the one hit wonder group, Bob Kuban and the In-Men, joined the band the Royaltones while still in high school. By the summer of 1963, the good-looking Notheis was drawing local raves with his deep, black sounding raspy singing voice. Approached by local band leader-drummer Bob Kuban in the summer of 1963, Notheis renamed himself "Little Walter Scott" and became the lead singer of the eight-member Bob Kuban and the In-Men. A solid local success by 1965, the group achieved national prominence in early 1966 with the release of their one and only hit single, "The Cheater," on local record label Musicland, U.S.A. The classic track written by In-Men bassist, Mike Krenski, debuted on January 29, 1966, reached Number 12 on the *Billboard* chart, and sold over 500,000 copies. Riding the tune's popularity, Bob Kuban and the In-Men did a brief tour of Los Angeles playing in that city's famed Whiskey-a-Go-Go and the Peppermint Lounge. An album for Musicland, *Look Out for the Cheater*, released in April 1966 stayed on the charts for only five weeks peaking at a disappointing 129. A scant three months later, the band disintegrated in a feud over money. Scott, with the core of the In-Men, reformed as Walter Scott and the Guise. The band's 1966 album for Musicland, *Great Scott*, failed to chart and the group broke up in the summer of 1967. The talented lead singer joined the St. Louis group, the Kommotions, ultimately breaking up the band to front Walter Scott and the Cheaters in October 1969. For many years, the group enjoyed regional fame in the Midwest and up and down the East Coast.

Scott's modest success, however, had cost him personally. Serially unfaithful to his first wife, Sharon, he walked away from her and their two children in 1969 shortly after forming his new band. That December, he married JoAnn Marie Calcaterra, a woman he had met at a gig four years earlier. Despite his oft-stated claim that he wanted no more children, JoAnn gave birth to twins on August 11, 1972. The marriage was in deep trouble by October 1982 when electrical contractor James Howard Williams, Sr., 43, arrived at the Scott home at #30 Pershing Lake Drive in Park Charles South, a subdivision in St. Charles County, to fix some wiring. Constant touring had made Scott an absentee father and husband. When JoAnn, 36, discovered Scott was having an affair with a dancer in his show, she asked for a divorce. Scott refused. Williams and JoAnn began their own affair hiding it from his wife, Sharon. On October 19, 1983, Sharon Williams was found near death in her 1982 Cadillac. The car was nose down in an embankment near a one-lane bridge in St.

Charles County. A passerby told authorities that he extinguished a small fire by the driver's side of the car and turned off its ignition. The car smelled strongly of gas although its tank had not been ruptured. Remarkably, no one questioned why Sharon Williams was saturated with gasoline, or, why the placement of her body (wedged under the dashboard on the passenger side of the car with her head resting on the transmission hump) was inconsistent with the wreck. The next day, James Williams gave doctors the authority to disconnect his wife of 25 years from life support. Sharon Williams was buried (without an autopsy), her husband collected $210,000 in life insurance, and later bought JoAnn a new Chrysler Laser.

On December 27, 1983, a little more than two months after the death of Sharon Williams, Walter Scott disappeared while (according to his wife) driving to a nearby service garage to buy a battery. The next day, JoAnn reported him missing to police and suggested they check the parking lot at Lambert Field in St. Louis. Authorities found his snow-covered Lincoln there on the top parking deck, but no Scott. In August 1984, JoAnn filed for divorce against her missing husband claiming adultery, emotional abuse, abandonment, and requesting alimony and child support for their twins, age 12. On April 6, 1986, JoAnn and James Williams married and moved into his home at 5647 Gutermuth Road in St. Charles County, Missouri. Although authorities strongly suspected JoAnn and Williams of involvement in Scott's disappearance, the case languished until early 1987 when Dr. Mary Case, recently appointed Chief Medical Examiner for St. Charles County, decided to reexamine the death of Sharon Williams. For Case, the head injuries that caused Williams' death could not have been caused by the car accident, but rather pointed to multiple blunt trauma impacts. On April 1, 1987, the body of Sharon Williams was exhumed from its resting place in the Fountain Cemetery near her birthplace in Marion, Illinois. Dr. Case's examination confirmed the woman died as the result of homicide inflicted by blows from a blunt, linear instrument, possibly a lead pipe or crowbar. The murder of Sharon Williams and the subsequent disappearance of Walter Scott raised a red flag with authorities.

Days later, sheriff's deputies working on the cases interviewed the dead woman's son, James ("Jimi") Williams, Jr., in his cell in the Monroe County Jail in Key West, Florida. During the interview, Williams mentioned the existence of a cistern in his father's backyard that the man had covered with a flower box. Armed with a search warrant, sheriff's deputies converged on the house of James Howard Williams, Sr. on Gutermuth Road on April 10, 1987, and laboriously removed the cistern's 800 pound concrete lid. Inside, they found the bloated body of Walter Scott dressed in a blue-and-white jogging suit floating on top of the water about two feet below the top of the cistern. The singer's hands were crossed in front and tied with a yellow rope that circled each wrist then dropped to hogtie his knees and ankles. Draining the cistern, authorities discovered several large concrete blocks (possibly used to weigh the body down), three spent .410 shells, and a bag containing the victim's credit cards and driver's license. An autopsy determined Scott died from a gunshot wound to his upper left chest that scattered bone fragments into his heart. Williams was arrested on charges of murdering his first wife, Sharon, and Walter Scott. Soon afterwards, JoAnn was arrested for her husband's murder. The pair remained free on combined bonds of over $1 million paid by various neighbors and friends who had pledged their property as a show of support. Finally, after an endless series of motions and counter-motions, James Williams, Sr., 53, was brought to trial on November 2, 1992 in the St. Charles County Circuit Court in St. Louis on two counts of capital murder. The wheels of justice had ground slowly. Nine years had passed since the murders during which time the pair had enjoyed 2,032 days of freedom since their initial arrests. Testimony showed Williams had solicited information from one of his former employees about hiring a hitman, and had also stalked Williams for weeks before the man's disappearance. The case went to the 6 man, 6 woman jury on November 16, 1992 and they needed only 4 hours to find Williams guilty in the deaths of Sharon Williams and Walter Scott. In a separate phase of the trial, Williams escaped the death penalty, but was sentenced to life in prison with no possibility of parole for 50 years. JoAnn Marie Williams fared much better. In a plea agreement on February 1, 1993, the 46-year-old woman was allowed to plead guilty to a reduced charge of hindering prosecution, and sentenced to a maximum prison term of 5 years and a $5,000 fine. The dead man's son from his first marriage, Scott Notheis, 26, spoke for many when he said, "She got off easy. She played all her cards just right. It ain't fair."

JoAnn Williams was released from prison in October 1994 after serving just 18 months.

Further Reading

Priesmeyer, Scottie. *The Cheaters: The Walter Scott Murder*. St. Louis: Tula, 1996.
Riley, Marianna. "Stalking of Scott Alleged, Prosecutor Begins Case in Williams Murder Trial." *St. Louis Post-Dispatch*, November 10, 1992, sec. A, p. 3.

Selena (V)

Described as the "Tex-Mex Madonna," the Tejano singing sensation became an icon in the Hispanic community paving the way for future Latina stars like Jennifer Lopez who would play her in a 1997 biopic. Born Selena Quintanilla (some sources cite as Quintanilla-Pérez) in Lake Jackson, Texas, on April 16, 1971, the future star's major influence was her father, Abraham Quintanilla, Jr. A member of the doo-wop group Los Dinos ("the boys") when he was a teen, Quintanilla quit the band in 1969 to devote his energies to his three children — Suzette, Abraham ("AB"), and Selena. Recognizing his children, especially Selena, possessed musical talent, Quintanilla organized them into a garage band with "AB" on bass, Suzette on drums, and six-year-old Selena fronting the band as singer. By 8, Selena was already winning area talent shows and performing with her siblings at birthdays, weddings, and parties. In 1980, Quintanilla opened a family Tex-Mex restaurant in Lake Jackson, Papa Gayo, as a venue where his children could perform. The business failed in early 1981, but not before the family band, Selena y Los Dinos, became well-known in South Texas and generated interest among record labels in Corpus Christi where the family settled. For the next several years, Quintanilla kept the band (now with additional members) on the road performing Tejano music (a lively blend of Texas and Mexican rhythms) in the area all the while releasing albums on regional labels. Though forced to drop out of school in the eighth grade to maintain the grueling schedule, Selena earned her high school equivalency degree through correspondence courses.

In 1986, the 15-year-old performer scored two regional hits with the songs "Dame Un Beso" and "A Million to One." Bolstered by regional radio play and a nonstop touring schedule, Selena won the best female vocalist and performer of the year at the Tejano Music Awards in 1997. Although unable to speak Spanish, Selena learned the lyrics phonetically to the songs principally written by her brother, AB. In 1989, her cover of "La Bamba" again led to recognition at the Tejano Music Awards and she was honored as female entertainer and vocalist of the year. In 1990, Selena signed with Capitol EMI Latin Records and released her debut album, *Ven Commigo*, again with songs mainly written by AB. The album and Selena's memorable stage shows in which the sexy, but wholesome, soprano wore jeweled bustiers, skin-tight leather pants and a bare midriff made her a sensation in the Latino community. Her 1994 album, *Amor Prohibido*, showcased various musical styles (reggae, mariachi bolero) and spawned three hit singles ("Bidi Bidi Bom Bom," "No Me Queda Más," "Techno Cumbria"). The Grammy nominated album sold 600,000 units in the United States, and the hit, "Bidi Bidi Bom Bom," won song of the year at the Tejano Music Awards in 1995. Remarkably, at the same show Selena won 5 of the 15 awards presented. Her *Selena Live* album released in 1994 sold two million records and was awarded a Grammy in the Best Mexican American Performance of the year. Also in 1994, the versatile performer made her feature film debut as a singer in *Don Juan DeMarco* starring Johnny Depp and Marlon Brando. Recognizing Selena's potential crossover appeal, SBK Records signed the artist to an English language album deal in early 1994 and teamed her with top producer K.C. Porter. The album, *Dreaming of You*, would be designed to introduce English speaking audiences to what Latino's had known for years — Selena's phenomenal singing voice, beauty, and unlimited show business potential.

At 4'9", the frumpy Yolanda Saldivar was the physical opposite of her idol, Selena. For years the registered nurse had attended all of the performer's concerts in top San Antonio clubs like Tejano Rose and Tejano Rodeo screaming like a teen (she was then in her late twenties) throughout Selena's sets. Since the mid–1980s Saldivar had pestered Abraham Quintanilla by phone in an attempt to infiltrate the superstar's world by offering to form and operate a Selena fan club in San Antonio. Worn down by Saldivar's stubborn persistence and obvious devotion to his daughter, Quintanilla caved in and gave her the go ahead in 1991 to set up the fan club. Not only would the non-profit organization donate a portion of its proceeds to Selena's favorite charities, it would also publicize his daughter's career and sell her clothing line. Inspired by the sequined stretch pants, spiked heels, and bejeweled bustiers that she fa-vored onstage, the singer had opened her own clothing line and boutique, Selena, Etc., in Corpus Christi and San Antonio in the early 1990s. Selena hired fashion designer Martín Gómez in 1993 to design a line of clothing targeted to the youthful Hispanic women who idolized her. Selena, Etc., was envisioned as a one-stop boutique and beauty salon where women could receive make-overs and leave wearing Selena's signature clothes. As Saldivar became increasingly useful to the singing sensation and her family, she was given a larger role in Selena's business dealings.

Unknown to Abraham Quintanilla and Selena, however, Saldivar was the last person who should have been given access to any sort of business. In 1984, Aetna Casualty and Surety Company took civil action against Saldivar after a San Antonio dermatologist accused her of "manipulating account books" to the tune of $9,200. The case was dismissed after the litigants settled out of court. In the early 1980s, Saldivar left her job as a nurse's aide at San Antonio's University Hospital under mysterious circumstances administrators refused to discuss. After earning a nursing degree in December 1990, a law firm in Austin, Texas actively continued to try to collect a $5,361 student loan. Though renewing her nursing license in October 1992, Saldivar spent the early part of the decade making herself indispensable to Selena. Under the woman's singleminded stewardship, the Selena fan club grew to an impressive 5,000 members, but more importantly for Saldivar, gave her unlimited access to the object of her obsession. Soon she was a permanent fixture on the band's bus and her continual praise of Selena as her *mija* ("daughter") ultimately earned her the role of the singer's "personal assistant."

In mid–1994, Saldivar's infiltration of Selena's world became total after the singer fired the manager of Selena, Etc. and chose her "personal assistant" to manage the boutiques in Corpus Christi and San Antonio. Problems began almost immediately. Newly installed fan club president Irene Herrera informed Abraham Quintanilla that several new members reported not receiving their promised tee shirts, cassettes, and membership packets. Quintanilla's review of the fan club books uncovered gross accounting irregularities. Saldivar had written a $3,000 check to herself on the fan club bank account and instructed fans to make out their checks to her not the club. Digging deeper, Selena's father learned Saldivar had deposited checks written from the fan club account to herself under fictitious names in at least four different San Antonio banks. Nor did Selena, Etc. escape Saldivar's financial mismanagement. Head designer Martín Gómez quit claiming he could not work with the mean and manipulative Saldivar and warned Selena problems lay ahead if she kept the woman in the top position. Medical insurance for boutique workers and clerks went unpaid. Employees complained that hair care products were not being restocked, and models and hairdressers for a December 1994 fashion show went unpaid. The New York vendors who supplied the disastrous show lost a collective $20,000.

Abraham Quintanilla, seeing his starmaking work of 15 years undone by Saldivar, forcefully confronted the woman in a March 9, 1995 meeting. He laid out the various discrepancies in the fan club and Selena, Etc., and demanded her resignation. Saldivar remained composed and fended off the allegations of disgruntled fan club members as made by malcontents who wanted free Selena merchandise. Allegedly frightened of Quintanilla, the 34-year-old Saldivar purchased a Brazilian-made .38-caliber Taurus revolver the next day for "protection." Finally convinced by her father that Saldivar was ruining her business reputation and stealing from her, Selena agreed to fire the woman. On the morning of March 30, 1995, the 23-year-old singer phoned Saldivar in Monterrey, Mexico where she was overseeing the proposed opening of another Selena, Etc. store. Saldivar drove back to Corpus Christi that day, later phoning Selena to report her car had been stolen and she had been kidnapped and raped. Concerned, Selena took the distraught woman to a local hospital where she ultimately retracted her story after doctors could find no evidence of a sexual attack. Selena checked Saldivar into Room 158 of the Days Inn Motel off Interstate 37 on the city's northside promising to come see her alone later that evening to pick up all the business records for the fan club and boutiques. Instead, she brought husband Christopher Pérez (the bass player in her band she wed in 1992) and informed Saldivar that she was no longer her personal manager. Saldivar handed over the bank records, but it was determined later that evening not the ones documenting October–December 1994, a crucial time of her suspected malfeasance. Saldivar called Selena later that evening to report she had the missing records and could give them to her tomorrow morning. Selena phoned her father to inform him she would be at the family's recording studio at 10:00 A.M. the next day to continue to lay down tracks for her crossover album after picking up the business records.

On March 31, 1995, Selena and Saldivar were concluding a contentious meeting when the older woman pulled a gun and shot the singer in the back of the right shoulder (bullet exited the chest) as she was leaving the room around 11:50 A.M. Mortally wounded, Selena stumbled to the nearby manager's office and uttered, "Yolanda—158," before collapsing. The 23-year-old Latina performer with the unlimited future was later pronounced dead on arrival from massive blood loss at Memorial Medical Center at 1:05 P.M. Saldivar left the room and for 9½ hours sat in a red 1994 GMC pickup in the Days Inn parking lot periodically threatening suicide with the murder weapon pressed to her temple while Corpus Christi police negotiators tried to talk her out of the vehicle with a cell phone they provided. During the audiotaped marathon negotiation, Saldivar accused Abraham Quintanilla of raping her a month-and-a-half ago and further violating her with a stick. According to the woman, Quintanilla threatened to kill both her and her family if she spoke of the attack. Saldivar only bought the gun to protect herself and them from Quintanilla. No proof of the attack was ever offered nor did Saldivar report the alleged incident to authorities. Learning of Selena's death over the radio, Saldivar expressed a desire to kill herself and inferred that the gun discharged when she was attempting to do so following the devastating meeting with her beloved friend. Saldivar finally surrendered to authorities after they convinced her she would not be shot by them after relinquishing the weapon.

As Saldivar sat in jail awaiting trial for the first-degree murder of her friend and former employer, the Hispanic community honored the martyred singer in scenes reminiscent of the outpouring of grief and love accorded ex–Beatle John Lennon (see entry). Celebrities including Julio Iglesias, Madonna, Gloria Estefan *et al.* sent condolences while thousands of bouquets, rosaries, and votives were sent to the Quintanilla family. A vigil for the singing star at the Bayfront Plaza and Convention Center drew 1,500 mourners. The star's funeral, held at Corpus Christi's Memorial Coliseum where she had recorded the smash album *Selena Live*, was attended by 10,000 mourners who filed past her coffin. Likewise, memorial services were held in Tejano music strongholds like Los Angeles and in separates sites in San Antonio. Immediately after Selena's death, sales of her existing cassettes and CDs sharply spiked. *Dreaming of You*, her highly anticipated English language crossover album released posthumously in the summer of 1994, became the first Tejano album to reach Number One in America and, on the strength of the hit single "I Could Fall in Love," went double platinum by the end of the year. Amid the sadness, loss, and unprecedented record sales the Quintanilla family announced that during the five-month period between September 1994 and January 1995, Saldivar had embezzled $30,700 from the singer's businesses.

Yolanda Saldivar's defense team faced an uphill battle representing a suspected embezzler who had signed a murder confession in police custody hours after the shooting of a beloved rising star. Following a change of venue from Corpus Christi to Houston, a six man, six woman jury was impaneled in the Harris County Criminal Courthouse in October 1995 to hear the first-degree murder case against Yolanda Saldivar. Maintaining the shooting was accidental, Saldivar's attorneys characterized the fatal incident as accidentally occurring when the older woman waved the weapon around during an attempt to take her own life. The prosecution painted a simpler case — Selena was shot at the height of an argument over Saldivar's criminal mismanagement of the star's business affairs. The testimony of three hotel employees who witnessed the aftermath of the shooting bolstered this theory of the case. After hearing a loud "pop," they saw Saldivar pointing the gun at the singer's back as she painfully escaped. Afterwards, the woman lowered the revolver and calmly went back into Room 158. One witness reported that the business manager called Selena "bitch" after shooting her. Jurors listened to six hours of the standoff tape in which Saldivar first accused Quintanilla of raping her then expressed a desire to commit suicide after learning Selena had died. A weapons expert testified the .38-caliber revolver was not defective, as the defense claimed, but rather the trigger had to be pulled in order to make the gun discharge. On October 23, 1995, the jury finally received the case and left the courtroom to deliberate Saldivar's fate. The accused murderer seemed unconcerned and honored dozens of requests from media and spectators to autograph their courtroom passes. Two hours and twenty minutes later the jury returned and announced Yolanda Saldivar was guilty of murdering Selena. In the penalty phase of the trial Saldivar

was given a life sentence with the stipulation she must serve 30 years in prison before she can be considered eligible for parole consideration in 2025. In August 1999, a Texas Court of Appeals declined to consider Saldivar's request for a new trial based upon a claim that her confession had been coerced. Two years earlier, another Latina performer of incredible promise, Jennifer Lopez, realized the widespread stardom denied to the young singer by Saldivar's murderous act, by portraying the Tejano sensation in director Gregory Nava's motion picture, *Selena*, co-starring Edward James Olmos as Abraham Quintanilla.

Further Reading

Arraras, Maria Celeste. *Selena's Secret: The Revealing Story Behind Her Tragic Death*. New York: Simon and Schuster, 1997.
Patoski, Joe Nick. *Selena: Como la Flor*. Boston: Little, Brown, 1996.
Richmond, Clint. *Selena!: The Phenomenal Life and Tragic Death of the Tejano Music Queen*. New York: Pocket, 1995.

Sepúlveda, Jorge Antonio *see* Appendix 1

Shabalala, Headman (V)

Founded by Shabalala's brother, Joseph, in Ladysmith, South Africa in the early 1970s, Ladysmith Black Mambazo became the world's most popular Zulu acapella singing group especially after being featured on Paul Simon's 1986 landmark album *Graceland*. In 1987, Headman Shabalala and his vocal group released their U.S.–U.K. debut album *Shaka Zulu*. Produced by Simon, the album blended traditional Zulu sounds with Christian-influenced choral music and enjoyed strong reviews and sales. The group just completed its 27th album when a "roadside disturbance" with a white security guard on the night of December 10, 1991, in the east coast city of Pintetown, Durban, South Africa, claimed the life of the 44-year-old singer. Paul Simon called for an immediate inquiry into his friend's death and was outraged when Sean Clyde Nicholas, 26, the alleged killer, was released on a small cash bail pending trial. The American musician pledged an undisclosed amount of money and performed a charity concert amid anti-apartheid unrest in Durban to fund a music academy in Shabalala's name. At trial in November 1992, Nicholas testified he pulled over the car driven by Shabalala on suspicion that the driver was drunk. Nicholas allegedly approached the car with gun drawn and the singer was shot when he tried to pull it from the security guard's hand. The court rejected

Nicholas' assertion and found him guilty of culpable homicide. Remarkably, Nicholas was sentenced to only three years in prison prompting Simon to deem the verdict "a miscarriage of justice" with "race" as the cause.

Further Reading

Maclean, William. "Singer Paul Simon Slams 'Graceland' Case Sentence." *Reuters News*, November 19, 1992.

Shakur, Tupac (V)

Shortly after 25-year-old gangsta rapper Tupac Shakur was shot multiple times on September 7, 1996, Sgt. Chuck Cassell of the Las Vegas Metro Police Department's gang unit commented, "In my opinion, it was a black gang-related and probably a Blood-Crips thing. Look at [Shakur's] tattoos and album covers — that's not the Jackson 5 … it looks like a case of live by the sword, die by the sword." Shakur's death six days later marked the inevitably violent conclusion to an all-too brief life filled with contradictions and almost unlimited promise. Tupac Shakur was born into revolution. His mother, Afeni, was 22 when she joined the New York Black Panther party in September 1968. With then husband Lumumba Abdul Shakur and 19 other New York Panthers, Afeni was arrested in April 1969 and charged with multiple felonies including conspiracy to bomb public places in New York City. While out on bail she began dating two men: Billy Garland, a fellow-member of the Panthers, and "Legs," a local low-level gangster. Afeni's bail was revoked in February 1971 and the now-pregnant revolutionary was placed in the Women's House of Detention in Greenwich Village to await trial along with the other "New York Panther 21." In May 1971, the Panthers were acquitted of all charges. Afeni gave birth to a young son of undetermined parentage on June 16, 1971 in New York University Hospital. Named Tupac Amaru ("shining serpent") after an Inca chief, and surnamed Shakur (Arabic for "thankful to God"), the future rap star (with mother Afeni and younger half-sister Sekyiwa) spent the first 12 years of his life shuttled between homeless shelters and the residences of friends and relatives in the Bronx and Harlem. Billy Garland, generally believed to be Tupac's biological father, saw his son occasionally until the boy turned five. The two would not be reunited until 1992 after Garland recognized Tupac in the poster for the film, *Juice*.

In 1983, Legs began living with the Shakur family and quickly got Afeni addicted to crack. The woman spent much of the 1980s dealing with her addiction while attempting to raise two young children. Tupac, longing for the stabilizing influence of a man in the family, assumed the drug dealer was his father and later bragged the "thug" in him came from Legs. The man was imprisoned for credit card fraud in the mid–1980s and died of a crack-induced heart attack. In September 1983, Afeni enrolled her 12-year-old son in the 127th Street Ensemble, a Harlem theatre group. Tupac earned a role in the play, *A Raisin in the Sun*, and the experience instinctively taught the youngster that a world existed outside the ghetto that he was talented enough to one day enter. In September 1986, the Shakur family moved to Baltimore, an experience that fundamentally changed Tupac's life. The 15 year old was accepted into the Baltimore School for the Arts where he flourished in an intellectual and creative environment that gave free vent to his creativity. Tupac excelled in ballet, acting, and began writing poetry and rapping. In later life, the rapper pointed to his time at the school as his salvation just as he identified being forced to leave this nurturing environment as the beginning of his trouble with the law. Tupac was 17 when his family moved to Marin City, California in June 1988. Instead of being exposed to the arts, he argued with his mother, dropped out of Talmapais High School, left home, and was on the streets peddling crack and crashing with friends. Although living the "thug life," Tupac continued to write poetry about the things he knew best — hustling and the feelings of misery and desperation which are a day-to-day fact of ghetto life. In 1989, Tupac's professional music career began when he was introduced to Shock-G (Greg Jacobs), leader of the Bay Area rap group Digital Underground. The next year, he toured with the group as a combination roadie and secondary rapper-dancer and debuted on the 1990 DU collection, *This Is an EP Release*, and the album, *Sons of the P* (1991). While on tour, Tupac worked on his own material and was devastated to learn his mother was once again abusing crack cocaine.

On November 12, 1991, Shakur released his debut album on Interscope, *2Pacalypse Now*, containing the hit single "Brenda's Got a Baby." At 20, 2Pac was already an angry young man and the album's uncompromising lyrics about ghetto life soon came to the attention of moral watchdogs like Vice President Dan Quayle, who singled out the album during a re-election year as an example of the breakdown of family values in the recording industry. Interscope ignored Quayle's demand that the album be removed from store shelves. On the heels of 2Pac's gold album, his movie debut, *Juice*, was released on January 17, 1992. Directed by Ernest Dickerson, the film attempted to display violent hip-hop culture and featured the rapper as the gangsta "Bishop." As 2Pac's public profile increased so did his numerous brushes with the law that in the world of gangsta rap translated directly into "street cred." In November 1991, he filed a $10 million suit against Oakland police for allegedly roughing him up following an arrest for jaywalking. The following April, 2Pac again made headlines when the attorney for 19-year-old Ronald Hay Howard, claimed his client was incited to kill a Texas State Trooper after listening to the violent lyrics in *2Pacalypse Now*. The trooper's widow filed a multimillion dollar suit against the rapper, Interscope, and then-parent company Time Warner claiming the lyrics influenced the killer. 2Pac's claim to notoriety, however, stemmed directly from the tragedy that occurred on August 22, 1992 in Marin City, California, during a 50th anniversary celebration of the city's ghetto area, the Jungle. An altercation between 2Pac's crew and old acquaintances resulted in an exchange of gunfire that left a six-year-old boy dead. The fatal bullet was traced back to a gun owned by the rapper's half-brother, Maurice "Mopreme" Harding, who was arrested, but later released due to lack of evidence. No charges were filed in the incident, but a civil suit filed by the dead boy's family against 2Pac and Interscope was settled out of court for an estimated $500,000.

2Pac's second album, *Strictly 4 My N.I.G.G.A.Z.*, released on February 1, 1993, went platinum largely on the strength of the single and video for "Keep Ya Head Up," his tribute to black women. Chided by relatives for being "pretty" as a child, the adult 2Pac was at 5'8", 150 pounds a charismatic figure whose good looks, intelligence, and sensitivity many women found irresistible. However, the gangsta rapper continued to demonstrate a disturbingly violent aspect to his personality. In March 1993, 2Pac was arrested in Hollywood for fighting a limo driver who accused him of doing drugs in the car. The charges were dropped. On April 5, 1993, he was arrested in Lansing, Michigan, for swinging a baseball bat at a local rapper. He served ten days in jail, but was out in time for the July 23, 1993, release of his second film, director John Singleton's *Poetic Justice* starring Janet Jackson. The movie bombed, and is memorable only for the controversy caused during its production when the pop diva demanded 2Pac take an HIV test prior to the filming of their kissing scenes.

On November 18, 1993, 2Pac and three of his crew were arrested in New York City and charged with the sodomy and sexual abuse of a 19-year-old woman he had picked up four days earlier at Nell's, a jumping nightspot in downtown's Chelsea district. Released on bond, 2Pac was in the studio working on tracks for his third album, when an earlier beat-down of director Allan Hughes precipitated by the filmmaker's dropping of the rapper from his film, *Menace II Society*, netted him 15 days in an L.A. jail beginning on March 10, 1994. Meanwhile, the negative publicity generated by his arrest on sex charges forced director John Singleton to bow to pressure from Columbia Pictures to drop the rapper from his next film, *Higher Learning*. Less than two weeks later, 2Pac's third film was released, *Above the Rim*, in which he played the role of "Birdie," a troubled drug dealer. Shortly after midnight on November 30, 1994, one day after a jury began deliberations in his sexual abuse trial, the 23-year-old rapper was shot five times while attempting to resist a robbery in the lobby of the building housing Quad Recording Studios in downtown Manhattan. 2Pac, in the company of his manager Freddie Moore and friend Randy "Big Stretch" Walker (see entry Big Stretch), refused the gunmen's demands to give up his jewelry and in the ensuing scuffle the rapper was shot in the hand, head, and groin. Moore was also wounded, but Big Stretch Walker was unhurt in the attack. The gunmen escaped with 2Pac's large diamond ring and gold chains valued at $45,000. 2Pac, despite a police report finding the crime was random, believed he had been the target of a planned attack engineered by people he refused to identify to police. The rapper underwent emergency surgery at Bellevue Hospital and, fearful the hired gunmen would finish the job, checked out of the facility against medical advice three hours later. 2Pac narrowly missed being killed and lost a testicle in the attack. Days later, 2Pac was not in the courtroom as he and another defendant, were found guilty on three counts of sexual abuse, i.e. they had groped and touched the woman without her consent. At his sentencing on February 7, 1995, the rapper wept and apologized to the woman and to the youth of America "for falsely representing them." He was sentenced to a maximum prison term of four years of which he had to serve only 18 months before being considered for parole. In the penitentiary, he renounced the "Thug Life" stating that others must now carry the torch for the gangsta lifestyle.

Me Against the World, released on April 1, 1995, while 2Pac was in prison, presented the rapper at his most introspective and many critics cite the album which contained the hit single, "Dear Mama," as the foundation of his cult-like veneration in the hip-hop community. The LP went double platinum in seven months fueled by the street cred generated by his numerous prosecutions. As the album topped the charts, 2Pac unexpectedly married his longtime girlfriend Keisha Morris in a ceremony in New York's Clinton Correctional Facility (the marriage was annulled shortly after he signed with Death Row Records). Not long afterward, the rapper was confined to his cell for two months after guards smelled marijuana and he failed a drug test. In a prison interview, 2Pac broke his silence about who he believed was behind the near fatal ambush in the lobby of the Quad Recording Studios fingering Sean "Puff Daddy" Combs, CEO of Bad Boy Entertainment, and his top rapper Notorious B.I.G. (see entry), and Andre Harrell, CEO of Uptown Records, all present upstairs in the recording studio when the robbery occurred. Also implicated by 2Pac was his close friend and fellow-rapper, Randy (Big Stretch) Walker, who was unharmed in the attack. All the men vehemently denied any involvement in the incident. During 2Pac's incarceration in the New York state correctional system, his attorneys worked tirelessly to secure his freedom on bond pending appeal of his sex abuse conviction. On October 12, 1995, eight months into his sentence, 2Pac was released from the Clinton State Prison in Dannemora after Marion "Suge" Knight, the 30-year-old CEO of L.A.–based Death Row Records, posted a $1.4 million bond. By the evening of the same day, the rapper had flown to L.A., signed a contract with Death Row (home of Dr. Dre and Snoop Doggy Dogg), and began recording his next album, *All Eyez on Me*.

Backed by the premier standing of Death Row Records within the world of gangsta rap, 2Pac's allegations against the East Coast faction of the industry (Sean "Puff Daddy" Combs" and the Notorious B.I.G.) were voiced in inflammatory

interviews, rap songs, and music videos. The escalating accusations and counter-accusations flying between the two armed camps fanned the flames of the so-called "East Coast–West Coast" rap war that would leave a trail of bodies in its wake. Among the first to die was 2Pac's former friend, Randy (Big Stretch) Walker. On November 30, 1995, one year and five minutes to the day of the attack on 2Pac, Big Stretch was gunned down in a drive-by execution in Queens. As of 2007, a suspect in prison on another murder has since been implicated in Walker's death. If the man's story is proven true at trial, the rapper's murder was a remarkably coincidental case of mistaken identity that would clear 2Pac of any involvement. At the time of Walker's murder, 2Pac had "no comment." The war of words between 2Pac and rap's East Coast faction escalated in 1996. In his single "Hit 'Em Up," 2Pac raps he slept with the Notorious B.I.G.'s wife, Faith Evans, with whom he worked on his single, "Wonder Why They Call U Bitch." Evans denied the claim. On February 13, 1996, 2Pac released his first Death Row album, *All Eyez on Me*, which debuted at Number 1 on the *Billboard* Top 200 chart and went quintuple platinum. Rap's first double CD of all original material, the 23 songs ("California Love," "How Do U Want It," "2 of Amerikaz Most Wanted") were a declaration of the gangsta lifestyle which 2Pac had repudiated from his prison cell in early 1995. As MTV kept the East Coast–West Coast feud on the front burner with heavy rotation play of videos featuring 2Pac (with Snoop Dogg) and the Notorious B.I.G. in a dueling war of words, behind the scenes tensions were rising between the two camps. On March 29, 1996, an angry exchange of words between Bad Boy and Death Row personnel led to drawn guns after the *Soul Train* award show in Los Angeles. At the MTV Video Music Awards show at New York City's Radio City Music Hall on September 4, 1996, 2Pac and his entourage scuffled backstage with six other men.

Three days after the incident, September 7, 1996, 2Pac and "Suge" Knight, 31, were ringside at the Mike Tyson–Bruce Selden heavyweight fight at the MGM Grand Hotel in Las Vegas. The fight lasted 109 seconds with "Iron Mike" destroying the hapless Selden. Around 8:39 P.M. as 2Pac was leaving the event with his Death Row entourage, he got into an argument with Orlando "Lando" Anderson, a 22-year-old known member of the

Crips L.A. street gang, which quickly escalated into a fight. An MGM Grand security camera captured images of 2Pac and his bodyguards knocking Anderson to the floor and kicking him. The altercation was broken up by casino security and 2Pac and Knight left the facility at around 8:55 P.M. After a brief stop at the Luxor Hotel for an unknown reason, 2Pac and Knight drove to the home of the Death Row Records executive in southeast Las Vegas to change clothes. Ironically given 2Pac's recent past, he was scheduled to attend a highly publicized anti-gang youth event sponsored by the Las Vegas Metropolitan Police Department at Club 662, a nightspot owned by Knight located at 1700 E. Flamingo Road. On a telephone key pad, the club's name "662" spells out "MOB," reputedly standing for "Members of Bloods," a street gang to which "Suge" Knight was allegedly affiliated. Knight, with 2Pac in the passenger seat next to him, was at the lead of a ten car convoy of Death Row employees and friends en route to the club when he stopped his black BMW 750 at a red light on East Flamingo Road in front of the Maxim Hotel about 11:15 P.M. According to witnesses, a white, four-door late model Cadillac with California plates containing four people pulled up to the passenger side of the BMW. One man pulled a Glock and sprayed the car with an estimated 13 shots. 2Pac, uncustomarily not wearing a bulletproof vest, was struck twice in the chest, and once in the hand and leg. Bullet fragments grazed the top of Knight's head. The Cadillac sped off as Knight instinctively U-turned against oncoming traffic away from the scene of the attack. Police, responding to the sound of gunshots, stopped Knight's bullet-riddled car at the intersection of Las Vegas Boulevard and Harmon Avenue. An ambulance transported Knight and the badly wounded rapper to the University of Nevada Medical Center where he was listed in critical condition. Knight, sustaining only a minor head wound, was treated and immediately released. Over the next couple of days, the 25-year-old underwent two operations, one of which removed his lung, to stop the internal bleeding. In a bid to relieve the pressure on his struggling constitution, doctors induced a medical coma and placed 2Pac on a respirator. Four days after the attempt on 2Pac's life, a suspected member of the Southside Crips street gang was shot to death in his car in Los Angeles reportedly as payback. On September 13, 1996, six days after the deadly attack, 2Pac passed away at approximately

4:03 P.M. from what doctors listed as respiratory failure and cardiopulmonary arrest. In accordance with his family's wishes, the rapper's body was cremated and private services were conducted the next day in Las Vegas. In early November 1997, Yafeu "Yak" Fula, known as Kadafi in 2Pac's backup group The Outlawz, was shot execution-style in a housing project in Irvington, New Jersey, and died in a hospital in Orange. At the time of 2Pac's shooting, the 19-year-old was in a car behind the rapper's and was the only witness to tell police he could possibly identify the gunman. 2Pac's album, *The Don Killuminati: The 7 Day Theory*, was released eight weeks after his death under his pseudonym of Makaveli. Amid claims of crass exploitation, the Death Row production sold 600,000 copies in its first week. Also posthumously released in 1997 were three motion pictures the rapper had completed at the time of his death: *Bullet, Gridlock'd,* and *Gang Related*. The Notorious B.I.G. was shot to death in an eerily similar drive-by shooting in Los Angeles on March 9, 1997, roughly six months after 2Pac's murder. Speculation continues as to whether the hit on Biggie was in retaliation for 2Pac's murder. To date, no arrests have been made in either homicide while both martyred men have since achieved iconic status in the world of gangsta rap.

Further Reading

Alexander, Frank, and Heidi Siegmund Cuda. *Got Your Back: The Life of a Bodyguard in the Hardcore World of Gangsta Rap*. New York: St. Martin's, 1998.

Bastfield, Darrin Keith. *Back in the Day: My Life and Times with Tupac Shakur*. New York: Ballantine, 2002.

Scott, Cathy. *The Killing of Tupac Shakur*. Las Vegas, NV: Huntington, 1997.

Sullivan, Randall. *LAbyrinth: A Detective Investigates the Murders of Tupac Shakur and Biggie Smalls, the Implications of Death Row Records' Suge Knight, and the Origins of the Los Angeles Police Scandal*. New York: Atlantic Monthly, 2002.

Vibe, eds. *Tupac Amaru Shakur, 1971–1996*. New York: Crown, 1997.

White, Armond. *Rebel for the Hell of It: The Life of Tupac Shakur*. New York: Thunder's Mouth, 1997.

Shibley, Nassib Abdullah (M–S)

For months, the Syrian-born attorney and manager of Hungarian gypsy violinist Janczy Rigo had become increasingly jealous of the influence the performer's wife, Katherine Emerson Rigo, exercised over his own wife, Leonore. Though husband and wife continually argued about the intensely emotional relationship existing between the women, Leonore continued to see Mrs. Rigo. On the night of November 3, 1908, some three weeks after Leonore consulted an attorney regarding a divorce, Shibley fatally chloroformed his wife in the bedroom of their spacious apartment at 508 W. 122nd Street in New York City. The young attorney placed her body in bed, and spent the next few hours writing letters. Shibley waited until a servant fed their two-year-old son and left the apartment to take the child for a walk before re-entering the bedroom. There, he laid next to his dead wife, slit an artery in his left arm above the elbow with a razor blade, stabbed himself near the throat, and covered their bodies with a sheet.

A handwritten letter to Leonore's sister found on the dining room table read: "Better this than her life as exampled by the past few months. Take care of the baby. I could not take him. You see why I took it all in and said nothing." In another letter, unaddressed, Shibley issued a warning to American men:

> Maybe I am insane; maybe not. I have loved my wife with a love that passeth human understanding. Let the men of America get out of their lives the artificial life — the restaurant life — smoking, drinking, especially among women, and such things as this will never be. Breed in your little girls the love of home so that they may see, and breed their children when women. I am happy. No temptation can now reach my loved wife. No stage, no restaurant, no automobile that I cannot provide, but peace — Goodbye, mother and brothers. By death I wipe out the sins of life. We prefer to be cremated or in one grave. This is only a parting. If men would only bring their wives to live within their means, and modestly, America would be a Paradise and each woman could not set another an example. Oh, my people — I am, the first of you, a murderer and a suicide! How the words do burn! Forgive me!

In a statement to *The New York American* published on November 5, 1908, Leonore's sister blamed Mrs. Rigo for the tragedy: "I feel convinced that my sister's death must be laid at the door of Mrs. Rigo. The violinist's wife seemed to exercise a strange fascination over my sister. The luxurious manner in which Rigo's wife lived undoubtedly had an effect on Mrs. Shibley. She had been perfectly happy at first in marrying a man who was devoted to her, but after she met Mrs. Rigo she at once began to show a distaste for domestic duties. Mrs. Rigo initiated her into all the hollow enjoyments of suppers at midnight restaurants and automobile rides to out-of-town inns. All that was out of keeping with her home environment." While Mrs. Rigo denied that any "unusual relationship" existed between them, she did admit she "seemed to exercise a fascination" over Leonore, adding, "But if she wished to admire me, why should I object?" Mrs. Rigo also maintained Nassib Abdullah Shibley was "insanely infatuated" with her, but "met with no response."

Further Reading

"Nassib Shibley, Noted Lawyer, Poisons Wife, Slays Self." *The New York American*, November 4, 1908, pp. 9–10.

Silva, Fernando Ramos da (V)

One of a family of ten children raised by his widowed mother in the slums of São Paulo, Brazil, Silva (born November 29, 1967) was 11 when director Héctor Babenco selected him from more than 1,300 boys to play the title role in *Pixote* in a 1980 film about Brazilian street children. The motion picture was an international critical success and focused much needed attention on the plight of that country's downtrodden, and largely forgotten urban youth. Overnight, Silva (who was paid less than $1,000 for the role) was made into an international star while in his home country he became the poster child for a class of disenfranchised slum children more likely to die at the hands of police than live to become adults. The youngster appeared on Brazilian television promoting Christmas cards for the United Nations Children's Fund. TV Globo, Brazil's major television network, gave Silva a one year contract to appear as a juvenile delinquent on a soap opera, but unable to read his lines, he quit showing up for work and was fired after six months. Similarly, the mayor of Duque de Caxias, an impoverished suburb of São Paulo, awarded the young star a scholarship to an acting school, but Silva quit after two days preferring instead to hang out at neighborhood theatres to watch *Pixote*. After appearing briefly in the role of an errand boy in *Gabriela, Cravo e Canela*, a 1983 film by Bruno Barreto, Silva returned to the slums of São Paulo and logged a series of arrests for theft.

In May 1984, Silva, 16, was arrested for the fifth time since *Pixote* for what police inspector João Paulo de Quieroz called, "doing in real life what he was portrayed as doing in the film." Arrested in São Paulo where he lived with his mother and nine brothers and sisters, the former child star admitted stealing a television set, stereo equipment, and clothes from the home of a luncheonette owner. Silva escaped from jail three months later. It all ended on August 25, 1987, in Diadema, an industrial suburb of São Paulo. Silva, 19, and two others were shot to death while fleeing from a botched robbery attempt. Police maintained the one-time actor was armed with a .32-caliber Smith & Wesson and was gunned down resisting arrest. Silva's family disputed the official version of his death maintaining he was murdered by a police force well-known throughout the world for its roaming death squads who kept peace by eliminating suspected petty criminals. According to family reports, Silva had become more settled after the birth of his daughter two years earlier. He even returned to acting having recently returned home from northeastern Brazil where he appeared as a hired assassin in a play called *Atalipa My Love*. Silva, who felt trapped by his association with *Pixote*, was targeted and harassed by police who thought he *was* the role that he had played. The family's contention was bolstered one day after the shooting when an unidentified woman appeared on TV Globo and gave a radically different account of Silva's last moments than the official police version. She was in her home when Silva rushed in and tried to hide under a bed. When confronted by police, Silva shouted, "Don't kill me, I have a family!" "Pixote" was shot eight times even though the woman insisted he was unarmed. A forensic report confirmed the man was prone on the floor and shot from above when he died. In September 1987, three state troopers were arrested and dismissed from the force after they allegedly attempted to falsify reports and tamper with evidence in the case.

Further Reading

"Three State Troopers Expelled in Actor's Death." Associated Press, September 2, 1987.

Simmons, Kadamba (V)

Born in London in May 1974, Kadamba (Hindi for "flower of enlightenment") Simmons was better known for her nonstop partying lifestyle than her career as a model and film actress. Dropping out of school and leaving home, the 16-year-old rented a flat in Notting Hill, West London, and soon became a regular on the club scene. Strikingly beautiful, the sultry wannabe attracted the attention of a string of celebrity lovers including Bros singer Matt Goss, record producer Nellee Hooper, rock star Liam Gallagher of Oasis, and by age 21, champion boxer Prince Naseem Hamed. Although some reports stated Simmons converted to Islam to be "spiritually closer" to the boxer, Hamed broke off the relationship seemingly

alarmed by her flamboyant lifestyle characterized by heavy drinking and drug abuse. Professionally, Simmons modeled in ads for Martini, Pantene shampoo, and appeared in small roles in the films *Mary Reilly* (1996), *Cash in Hand* (1998), *Breeders* (1998), and *The Wonderland Experience* (2000).

By 1997, however, Simmons had become increasingly disenchanted with the endless cycle of work and all-night parties. According to family members, she stopped being the "London party girl," began reading D. H. Lawrence, watched classic films, and gradually transformed into "a daytime girl." Seeking spiritual fulfillment, Simmons traveled with her sister, Kumari, to India for a six-week holiday in the spring of 1998. While vacationing in Goa, a former Portuguese colony on the country's west coast, the 24-year-old actress was approached by Yaniv Malka, a 22-year-old former Israeli soldier. Living in a rented shack, the near penniless Malka was barely surviving on a small pension from the Israeli army. Infatuated with Malka, Simmons moved in with him the day after they met. Obsessed by his lover's beauty, Malka picked fresh flowers for her every morning, and placed them with candlewax formed into the shapes of hearts around her pillow before she woke. When sister Kumari returned to London, Simmons and Malka left India for Berlin where they eked out a living working in a fruit juice stall. According to Kumari, one month in Germany alone with Malka convinced the actress she had made a terrible mistake. Malka was too reliant on her, she said, and things had deteriorated to the point where they stayed in different rooms all day and did not speak.

In June 1998, Simmons managed to disengage herself from her lover and returned alone to London. After receiving several hysterical calls from Malka in which he threatened to kill himself, Simmons agreed to see him. The night before their fateful meeting, she told her father, "He is a loser. I don't want to end up with a loser." On June 13, 1998, Malka arrived in London and, after spending the day with Simmons, went with her to a friend's borrowed flat in Islington, North London. The next day, Simmons' naked body was found in the blood-smeared apartment hanging in the shower suspended from a leather strap. Later that morning, police spent ninety minutes coaxing a sobbing Malka off the fifth-floor ledge of a residential block at University College, Central London. In custody, the former soldier denied strangling his lover to death in anger over her desire to end their relationship. Instead, he claimed her death was the culmination of a suicide pact they had forged in Germany. After making love in the apartment, she asked him to strangle her. Unable to do so with his hands, Malka used a ligature fashioned from a luggage strap to hang her in the shower. Afterwards, he repeatedly slashed his wrists, arms, and neck with a knife in an unsuccessful attempt to complete the pact. None of the injuries were remotely life-threatening. He was still allegedly trying to keep his side of the bargain when police foiled his suicide attempt. At trial in London's Old Bailey in March 1999, the prosecution discounted the suicide pact theory maintaining Simmons was manually strangled to death by a jealous lover then placed in the shower with a noose around her neck. The subsequent faked "suicide" attempt was made to bolster Malka's claim of a mutual death pact. Displaying no emotion, Malka was sentenced to life imprisonment on March 29, 1999. In February, 2000, an Appeals Court upheld the killer's conviction.

Further Reading

Lee, Adrian, and Richard Duce. "Rejected Lover Guilty of Model's Murder — Trial." *The Times* (London), March 30, 1999, p. 1.

Simpson, O.J. (M–acquitted)

In what can be described as an American tragedy, O.J. Simpson's stunning fall from grace surpassed even that of Roscoe "Fatty" Arbuckle (see entry), the silent screen comic who was acquitted after three trials of causing Virginia Rappe's death in the aftermath of a wild booze party in 1921. The public grudgingly accepted Arbuckle's exoneration and allowed him after a decade spent working under aliases to resume his career under his own name. At the time of his death from a heart attack in 1933 "Fatty" was mounting a comeback that held at least the possibility that the comic could regain some of his lost stature in the motion picture industry. Simpson, a brilliant running back who parlayed collegiate and professional football glory into a post-sports career in commercials and acting, apparently "had it all" when he was accused of murdering ex-wife Nicole Brown Simpson and her friend, Ronald Lyle Goldman in 1994. The "Trial of the Century" received unprecedented media coverage and Simpson's subsequent acquittal due largely to prosecutorial incompetence and a successful defense strategy focused on race and the suggestion of corrupt policing revealed a vast and ugly racial divide within the United States. O.J., though winning a questionable acquittal, found his acting career ruined and unlike Arbuckle, there would be no chance at redemption. The former football great's 2008 conviction on charges of armed robbery and kidnapping stemming from an incident in a Las Vegas hotel-casino involving the ill-conceived retrieval of allegedly stolen sports memorabilia marked a sad, albeit satisfying to many, end to a storybook American success story.

The future football and media star was born Orenthal James Simpson in San Francisco on July 7, 1947, the third of four children, to James and Eunice. The obscure origin of the nickname "O.J." according to family lore was contributed by an aunt. Simpson's father, James, was an intermittent and disturbing figure in the young boy's life. O.J. was deeply embarrassed by his father's admission in later life that he was a homosexual and the man died of AIDS in 1985. Like many black families, mother Eunice was the breadwinner and worked nights as an orderly and then a technician in the psychiatric ward of San Francisco General Hospital. A member of the Persian Warriors, a street gang in his neighborhood of Potrero Hill, Simpson vandalized and shoplifted, but was saved from the inevitable life of crime that claimed many of his friends by his outstanding athletic ability. While O.J. was still in high school, a concerned adult arranged for Willie Mays, the All-Star centerfielder for the hometown San Francisco Giants, to speak with the troubled teenager. The "Say Hey Kid" spent a day with O.J., but instead of trying to intimidate him with a hard-sell "scared straight" diatribe, the baseball legend took Simpson to his luxurious house in Forest Hill and showed him the type of life that could be achieved by excelling at sports. The visit profoundly impacted O.J. After high school, Simpson spent two years at the City College of San Francisco, a local junior college, running track and playing football. His average of ten yards a carry quickly put him on the radar of top four-year schools and he became one of the most recruited players in the country. The University of Southern California, however, provided the pageantry and media exposure Simpson knew could take him to the ultimate promised land of the National Football League. As a USC Trojan, O.J. Simpson established himself as the premier running back in the vaunted football school's history.

In 1967, the junior's final play touchdown run in the Rose Bowl earned the Trojans a dramatic victory over Indiana University. O.J. was named player of the game and led the Trojans to a national championship although he was denied the Heisman Trophy in a close vote to UCLA senior quarterback, Gary Beban. As a senior, Simpson won the Heisman in a landslide vote. USC accorded the running back its highest honor by retiring his jersey number, 32. In the late 1960s, however, the concept of "student athlete" did not hold the same sense of mutual responsibility between student and school as it does today. Before the National Collegiate Athletic Association began monitoring more closely the recruitment and education of its athletes it was a routine practice for top football schools to offer scholarships to individuals who were barely literate. By his own admission, Simpson considered his two-year stop at USC as merely a high media profile apprenticeship for the NFL. To say he received virtually no education at USC may be overstated (he did attend some home economics courses), but as his later written notes to Nicole Brown Simpson and others attest he could barely write a coherent, grammatical sentence.

In the 1969 NFL draft, the Buffalo Bills had the first overall pick and they selected O.J. ("Juice") Simpson. With the Bills from 1969–1977 the 6'1", 212 pound running back established team rushing records and spent his final season in 1978–1979 reunited with his hometown team the San Francisco 49ers. During his 11 seasons Simpson put up staggering numbers rushing for 11,236 yards, gaining another 2,142 yards on 203 pass receptions, while returning 33 kickoffs for 990 yards (a 30 yard average). In total, "Juice" amassed 14,368 combined net yards and scored 456 points on 76 touchdowns. In 1973 (arguably his finest year), Simpson became the first back to rush for over 2,000 yards racking up 2003 for a 14 game season. He led the league in rushing in 1972, 1973, 1975, and 1976 in addition to being named All-AFC and All-Pro five straight years from 1972 through 1976. Simpson played in six Pro Bowls earning Player of the Game in the 1973 contest. In 1985, "Number 32" was enshrined in the Pro Football Hall of Fame in Canton, Ohio.

While starring on the gridiron, Simpson had also begun work on his post-football career by acting small roles in television programs (*Dragnet 1967*, 1968; *It Takes a Thief*, 1968; *Ironside*, 1968; *Medical Center*, 1969; *Cade's County*, 1972) and movies (*The Klansman*, 1972; *The Towering Inferno*, 1974; *Killer Force*, 1976; *The Cassandra Crossing*, 1976). Handsome, likable, and affable, O.J. cultivated an approachable image that Jim Brown, the Hall of Fame Cleveland Browns running back and among the first black athletes to translate sports glory into a successful motion picture career, had never attempted. Jim Brown was viewed by white America as a dangerous and threatening revolutionary figure largely because the political and social causes he embraced were targeted at improving the lot of black people. Conversely, Simpson never had a "black agenda" once telling an interviewer, "I'm not black, I'm O.J." While Jim Brown was pictured in the media standing shoulder-to-shoulder with African-American revolutionaries, O.J. Simpson was seen in national television commercials for Hertz Rent-A-Cars running through airports and jumping over benches on his way to catch a plane or rent a vehicle. As a television personality, O.J. reached millions of people a week as a football analyst for NBC then ABC, but his post-football popularity reached its zenith as the character "Officer Nordberg," the partner and best friend of "Sgt. Frank Drebin" (Leslie Nielsen) in the lucrative *Naked Gun* series of comedy films (*The Naked Gun: From the Files of Police Squad*, 1988; *The Naked Gun 2½*, 1991; *Naked Gun 33⅓*, 1994).

On the personal front, O.J. married Marguerite Whitley, a black woman he started dating while still in high school, in 1968 shortly before the birth of their first child, Arnelle. The marriage by all accounts was a sham with Simpson carrying on an uninterrupted series of affairs even during the birth of his son, Jason. The couple was separated and O.J.'s football career was winding down when he purchased the house on 360 North Rockingham in upscale Brentwood for $650,000 on February 23, 1977. Shortly after moving into the gated and brick walled mansion situated on a desirable corner lot, Simpson, nearly 30, began dating Nicole Brown, a beautiful white 18-year-old blonde, he met while she worked briefly as a waitress. The end of the Marguerite and O.J. Simpson relationship coincided with his retirement from football in 1979, but any good memories they may have shared during their 11 year marriage were overshadowed later that year when their 23-month-old daughter, Aaren, died in a swimming-pool accident at the North Rockingham address. An emotionally broken Marguerite was awaiting word on the child's condition outside the hospital's intensive-care unit when Simpson arrived on scene screaming, "She murdered my child! She murdered my child!" According to observers, the football great had to be restrained from physically accosting his ex-wife. By the time the couple divorced in 1979, Nicole was already installed in the Rockingham house. Nicole and O.J.'s marriage in 1985 (the year of his Hall of Fame induction) was followed eight months later by the birth of their daughter, Sydney, and in 1988 a son, Justin, was added to the Simpson family.

As during his marriage to Marguerite, however, O.J. continued to be a serial adulterer while expecting and demanding Nicole to observe the roles of dutifully faithful wife and devoted mother. Unknown to his legion of fans who saw only the likable public face of the former football star turned product pitchman and movie star, O.J. Simpson had a documented history of domestic violence with Nicole extending back to 1977. In the fall of 1985, Mark Fuhrman, then a young uniformed LAPD officer, answered a domestic disturbance call at the Rockingham house. Arriving, Fuhrman saw an agitated Simpson pacing up and down the driveway while Nicole sat on a Mercedes-Benz crying. Simpson, angered by something Nicole had done, had taken a baseball bat and broken out the windshield of the car. Nicole refused to press charges. On January 1, 1989, a 911 call was received at 3:58 A.M. by the LAPD placed from a phone traced to 360 North Rockingham. The sounds of a woman screaming and slaps were heard before the connection was abruptly terminated. Police quickly responded to the scene and were met at the front door by a housekeeper who assured them nothing was wrong. Insisting to speak with the woman who placed the 911 call, the officers were startled to see Nicole Brown Simpson stagger out from behind the bushes near the gate wearing only a bra and a pair of soiled sweatpants. "He's going to kill me!" screamed Nicole identifying O.J. as her assailant. The woman's lip was cut and bleeding, her left eye black-and-blue, her forehead bruised, and the imprint of a hand was still visible around her neck. Nicole related how her husband had slapped, punched, and pulled her by the hair. She agreed to sign a crime report against O.J., but told the officer in disgust, "You guys never do anything.... You come out. You've been out here eight times. And you never do anything." O.J., wearing only a bathrobe, screamed at the cop that he no longer wanted Nicole in his bed or house to which the

policeman explained he was going to be placed under arrest for beating his wife. Incredulous, O.J. argued that what had occurred was a "family matter" and he had never been arrested on any of the eight previous occasions police had responded to calls at his home. Simpson went back inside to change, but instead of accompanying officers to the station, he took off in his Bentley out of another gate on the property. Police gave pursuit, but could not locate the fugitive. Nicole explained to the officers that the incident arose out of her displeasure with two women O.J. had staying with them. Earlier in the day, she discovered her husband had sex with one of the women. Although Nicole later refused to press charges, the matter was referred to prosecutors. After several adjournments and much negotiation by his attorney Howard Weitzman, Simpson agreed to plead "no contest" to a misdemeanor charge. On May 24, 1989, O.J. was given a 24-month suspended sentence, fined $470, ordered to perform 120 hours of community service, and compelled to receive counseling twice a week. Additionally, O.J. was instructed to pay "restitution" of $500 to the Sojourn Counseling Center, an abused women's shelter in Santa Monica.

The couple divorced without trial on October 15, 1992 and under the terms of a pre-nuptial agreement O.J. kept the house on North Rockingham, and agreed to pay $10,000 a month in child support for Sydney and Justin, and a one-time payout of $433,750 from which Nicole was expected to purchase her own residence. She initially bought a residence at 325 Gretna Green Way, before ultimately settling in a condo at 875 South Bundy Drive in a less prestigious section of Brentwood only a five minute drive from the home she once shared with O.J. On the night of October 25, 1993, Nicole placed a frantic 13½ minute 911 call from Gretna Green Way. While her children slept upstairs, the distraught woman begged police to rescue her from her infuriated ex-husband. During the entirety of the tape, Simpson (who broke the back door of the condo to gain access) could be heard screaming abuse while a terrified Nicole pleaded for police to hurry because, "He's going to beat the shit out of me." Much later in the tape the dispatcher asked Nicole if this sort of thing had happened before to which she replied, "Many times." The incident was allegedly precipitated by an occurrence in 1992 in which O.J. caught Nicole in a sexual encounter with another man identified as Keith Zlomsowitch.

Although Simpson was currently dating model Paula Barbieri, his continued intrusion into his ex-wife's life betrayed an obsession with the woman and an unwillingness to relinquish control. More tellingly, five days before her murder Nicole contacted the Sojourn Counseling Center (the public battered women's shelter to which O.J. was ordered to donate $500 as a condition of his 1989 "no contest" plea) to report that her ex-husband, O.J. Simpson, was stalking her.

On the evening of Sunday, June 12, 1994, the couple's eight-year-old daughter, Sydney, performed in a dance recital at her school attended by Nicole and her family. Simpson, who had been told earlier in the day by Barbieri that she was ending the relationship, arrived late carrying a bouquet of flowers for Sydney and was greeted by the entire Brown family except for Nicole. Simpson, no longer considered a part of his ex-wife's family, sat alone at the recital and reportedly stared angrily at Nicole. After the program, the Brown family decided to eat at the Mezzaluna, an Italian trattoria in Brentwood at 11750 San Vicente Boulevard, and as they left for the restaurant it became apparent to Simpson that he was not invited. Nicole and the children arrived back at her condo on 875 South Bundy Drive around 9:40 P.M. and moments later received a phone call from her mother, Juditha Brown, to report she had dropped her glasses on the sidewalk outside the restaurant. Nicole called the Mezzaluna and asked that her friend, Ronald Lyle Goldman, a waiter there, drop them by the house. According to later testimony, Goldman left for Nicole's around 9:50 P.M. Around 10:15 P.M. neighbors in the vicinity of Nicole's condo began to hear the uninterrupted howling of a dog. Neighbor Steven Schwab had a weekend ritual of walking his own dog right at 10:30 P.M. after the conclusion of his favorite television program. Passing the alley behind Nicole's condo on Bundy Drive around 10:55 P.M. Schwab noticed a white Akita barking at a house. Schwab, concerned the dog might be abandoned, made contact with the frightened animal. After examining the dog's expensive collar for owner information (there was none), the man noticed blood on all four of the animal's paws. Schwab returned home with the dog in tow arriving back at his residence shortly after 11:00 P.M. As the man and his wife considered what to do with the agitated Akita, Schwab's neighbor, Sukru Boztepe, and his wife, Bettina Rasmussen, arrived home around 11:40 P.M. Boztepe and his wife agreed to keep the

dog overnight, but the animal was so overwrought inside their apartment that the couple decided to take the Akita for a walk. Outside, they let the dog lead the way and it dragged them back to the front gate of 875 South Bundy Drive. Boztepe looked down the darkened pathway behind the gate and saw a woman's body lying in a pool of blood. The Akita, named "Kato" by the children after their father's "gofer," Brian ("Kato") Kaelin, and later renamed "Satchmo," had been the sole witness to a double homicide destined to become one of the most sensational criminal cases in the history of American jurisprudence.

LAPD patrolman Robert Riske and his partner arrived at the South Bundy address around 12:09 A.M. on Monday, June 13. Shining a flashlight down the walkway, Riske saw the body of Nicole Brown Simpson lying in a halo of blood at the base of four stairs leading up to a landing and the front door. Next to her corpse was a bloody heel print, but no shoe prints leading down the tiled walkway out the front gate on Bundy Drive. To the right of Nicole lay the body of a young man, Ron Goldman, with his shirt pulled up over his head. Goldman was slumped against the metal fence separating No. 875 from the next door property. Near the dead man's feet, police found a black knit stocking cap, a white bloodstained envelope, and a single leather glove. Riske shined his flashlight down the walkway (which extended 120' along the northern length of the property ending in a rear gate and an alley shared by other neighbors) and discovered a single set of bloody shoe prints leading away from the double homicide. To the left of the bloody shoe prints were fresh drops of blood suggesting the killer may have been bleeding from the left hand as he walked away. Officer Riske, careful not to step in any of the blood, entered the residence through the open front door. There were no signs of struggle or theft and lighted candles in the master bedroom and a bathtub filled with water suggested Nicole was preparing to bathe. Sydney and Justin were asleep in separate bedrooms blessedly unaware of the slaughter that had claimed their mother and her friend. On a front hall table, Riske noticed a letter with a return address from O.J. Simpson. A poster of the football star adorned a wall and he was featured prominently in many of the family portraits scattered throughout the home. Leery of broadcasting news of a double homicide involving a celebrity over a walkie-talkie that could be monitored by reporters listening to the police band,

Riske phoned the station to report the murders. While awaiting arrival of detectives, Riske and his partner secured the crime scene with yellow tape blocking off access to South Bundy Drive and to the back alley. The children were taken to the West L.A. police station.

At 2:10 A.M. the on-call homicide detective, Mark Fuhrman, a 19 year veteran, arrived at a crime scene already teeming with 16 police officers. To avoid contaminating the bloody walkway, Fuhrman and other detectives walked around to the back alley entrance where another detective pointed out a blood smudge on the rear gate. Fuhrman with other detectives entered the residence through the garage and out to the front door landing where Nicole's body lay in a bloody heap at the base of the stairs. At 2:40 A.M., Fuhrman was notified his tenure as lead detective was at an end. The case promised to be so high profile that it was being kicked to the prestigious Robbery-Homicide Division. To avoid a potential crush of unwanted publicity, those detectives would notify O.J. Simpson of the grisly death of his ex-wife Nicole. At 4:05 A.M., Philip Vannatter of Robbery-Homicide arrived at South Bundy Drive with instructions from his superiors to locate O.J. as soon as possible so as to spare him the anguish of hearing about the murder through the media. Vannatter first, however, wanted to carefully review the crime scene. While doing so, he was joined 25 minutes later by his longtime partner, Tom Lange. Vannatter decided that given the high profile of the case and the fact that Simpson's children would have to be collected from the station, he would have detectives Lange, Fuhrman, and Ron Phillips, accompany him to Simpson's home on Rockingham Drive. Around 5:00 A.M. the four detectives made the two mile (five minute) trip from South Bundy to North Rockingham after first determining the address off a license plate on a car in Nicole's garage. Fuhrman commented that he was vaguely aware of the address from having answered a domestic disturbance call there several years before. Approaching the gated house on Rockingham surrounded by a 6' high brick wall, Vannatter noticed a white Ford Bronco by the curb. The car, situated directly in front of number 360, was slightly askew at the curb suggesting it may have been hurriedly parked.

A couple lights were on in the mansion, but there was no answer when Vannatter repeatedly rang the buzzer by the iron gate, although there were two cars in the driveway. A sign posted at the gate announced the home was protected by Westec, a top security firm in Los Angeles, and detectives were ready to place a call to the agency when a Westec vehicle drove by. Vannatter persuaded the guard to give them Simpson's phone number, but his repeated calls were picked up by an answering machine. While his three colleagues attempted to contact someone in the house, Mark Fuhrman went alone to investigate the Bronco. Shining his flashlight into the backseat of the vehicle, the detective saw papers addressed to O.J. and noticed a small red stain just above the door handle on the driver's side. Several more red stripes were visible near the bottom of the door. Fuhrman reported the find to Vannatter. The car's plates were run and it came back as owned by the Hertz Corporation, the company Simpson repped as a pitchman. A criminalist was called to examine the car in more detail. A decision now faced lead detective Philip Vannatter. Faced with a double homicide at Bundy Drive involving Simpson's ex-wife, O.J.'s lighted house at Rockingham where no one answered, and possible bloodstains on a car most likely connected to O.J., Vannatter later testified that he feared there may be other victims in the house. He made the determination to go onto the property. Fuhrman, the youngest and best conditioned of the detectives, was hoisted over the wall into the Rockingham compound and opened the gate. Vannatter knocked on the front door. There was no answer. On the rear of the property was a row of three connected guest houses each with its own entrance. Detective Phillips knocked on one of the doors and it was opened by a sleepy man with shaggy hair, Kato Kaelin, O.J.'s handyman who lived on the grounds rent-free in exchange for performing odd jobs. Kaelin did not know if O.J. was home, but suggested knocking on the door of the adjacent guest house where Simpson's daughter, Arnelle, lived. Fuhrman remained alone with Kaelin while the other three detectives went to contact the woman. Fuhrman quickly examined Kaelin's room then asked if anything out of the ordinary had occurred the previous night. Kaelin reported that around 10:45 P.M. he had heard three loud thumps on his bedroom wall near the air conditioner which he initially interpreted as the onset of an earthquake. Fuhrman led the man to the other guest house where his fellow-detectives were questioning Arnelle Simpson then left to follow-up on what Kaelin had reported. In a narrow passage between the back of the guest houses and a cyclone fence the detective saw a black glove on the leaf covered path. The glove, similar in appearance to the one at the crime scene on Bundy, appeared moist and sticky. Meanwhile, Arnelle had let the other detectives into the main house. Arnelle called O.J.'s secretary who informed Phillips that her employer had taken the redeye flight to Chicago the previous night and was staying at the Chicago O'Hare Plaza near the airport. Phillips called Simpson around 6:05 A.M. and notified the football star that his ex-wife had been killed. A distraught Simpson asked about his children and told the detective he would fly back to L.A. on the next available flight. Surprisingly, to the detective, O.J. never asked how or when Nicole had been killed, questions that are routinely asked by individuals informed of the death of someone close to them.

Detectives quickly put together a preliminary theory of the case aided by Vannatter's discovery of blood drops leading from the North Rockingham gate to the front door of the residence. Vannatter applied for a search warrant after first touching base with the District Attorney's office. Marcia Clark, an assistant district attorney who had never even heard of O.J. Simpson, answered the call, took Vannatter's affidavit, and secured a warrant. Armed with the document, Vannatter entered the house on Rockingham around noon on June 13 (roughly the time O.J.'s plane touched down in Los Angeles). Unlike most police investigations, the O.J. case presented a mountain of forensic evidence. In addition to the blood drops leading to the house, Vannatter found similar blood drops behind the door in the foyer. Fuhrman returned to Rockingham to report the right hand glove found behind the guest house was a match to the left hand glove found at the murder scene on South Bundy Drive. Forensics would later determine the glove at Rockingham contained elements of the blood of both victims. A presumptive blood test done by criminalist Dennis Fung on the stains on the exterior of the Bronco suggested they were human blood (later determined to be a DNA match to O.J. Simpson). Likewise, blood found on the inside driver's side panel and on the vehicle's console between the two front seats was also a DNA match to Simpson with one spot showing a mixture of blood from O.J., Nicole, and Ron Goldman. Upstairs in O.J.'s room, detectives found a pair of socks later determined to contain Nicole's blood. Meanwhile,

O.J. had arrived from Chicago where he had traveled the previous night to play golf that day in the Hertz Invitational in Northbrook. Simpson, enjoying a $500,000 year salary from Hertz as its corporate pitchman, played annual regional tournaments where the company's top customers could meet and shoot a round of golf with the football legend. Upon touching down in Los Angeles, O.J. immediately contacted Howard Weitzman, the criminal attorney who had gotten him off with a slap on the wrist for the New Year's Day 1989 domestic violence incident. O.J. arrived at his home on Rockingham (now surrounded by media trucks) as police were processing the residence. A patrolman led the confused ex-athlete to a secluded area of the yard and briefly cuffed him in a scene caught by an enterprising photographer. Vannatter removed the restraints when he arrived on scene, but in doing so noticed a bandage on the middle finger of Simpson's left hand (possibly the source of the blood drops to the left side of the bloody shoe prints leading away from the bodies on Bundy Drive). Simpson instantly agreed to accompany Vannatter downtown to be questioned.

Remarkably, O.J. agreed not to have Howard Weitzman present during questioning a decision the attorney inexplicably signed off on. During the 32 minute taped interview Simpson was never specifically asked about his whereabouts during the interim period after the recital and his departure for the airport. This failure, as noted by Jeffrey Toobin in his definitive 1996 book on the case, *The Run of His Life: The People v. O.J. Simpson,* allowed O.J.'s defense team to variously claim that their client was sleeping, showering, or chipping golf balls on the lawn in the dark. Simpson initially explained his cut finger as occurring when he broke a glass in Chicago after being informed of Nicole's death. Later in the interview when told of the blood in his house and in the Bronco he remembered that he may have cut himself while hurriedly getting ready before the car service came to drive him to the airport. As a golfer, he added, his hands were always getting nicked up. Detectives, much too deferential to a man they now had to consider a prime suspect in a double homicide, never pressed O.J. to describe or produce the clothing he was wearing the night of the murders. As incriminating evidence against Simpson mounted (especially the damning DNA findings at South Bundy and North Rockingham), the former athlete fired Howard Weitzman who had stupidly allowed police to interview O.J. without being present to advise and shield his client. His replacement, Robert Shapiro, began his tenure as lead counsel on shaky ground by permitting O.J. to take a lie detector test which he failed miserably. The well-known attorney cut a deal with authorities that in the event O.J. was charged with the murders Shapiro would arrange for his client to surrender at any time the detectives specified. On Friday, June 17, 1994, an arrest warrant was issued charging O.J. with double homicide, a "special circumstance" that eliminated any possibility of bail. Shapiro agreed to produce Simpson at 11:00 A.M. at the Parker Center, but as time passed it was apparent something was wrong. Simpson had spent the night before his surrender at the Encino home of his longtime friend and attorney Robert Kardashian and was experiencing difficulty meeting the designated time. Tired of waiting, Gil Garcetti, L.A.'s District Attorney, dispatched detectives to Encino to arrest Simpson. The police arrived at the Kardashian residence around noon to discover that Simpson had fled the scene in a 1993 white Ford Bronco driven by his close friend Al Cowlings. Back at Parker Center Garcetti declared in a widely televised news conference that O.J. Simpson was officially a fugitive from justice and an all-points bulletin had been issued for Al Cowlings. Robert Shapiro, his credibility with police badly damaged by O.J.'s flight, called a press conference imploring his client to turn himself in immediately. Shapiro then introduced Robert Kardashian who read a rambling two page letter handwritten by Simpson two days earlier. In the barely literate "suicide" note, Simpson maintained his innocence, described his up-and-down relationship with Nicole, thanked several friends, and begged his readers to "Please think of the real O.J. and not this lost person." Meanwhile, around 6:00 P.M. the white Bronco had been spotted on the I-5 freeway setting off a low speed car chase that was watched on television by an estimated 95 million television viewers, 5 million more than viewed the Super Bowl that year. As various law enforcement agencies shut down on-ramps onto the numerous roadways traveled by the Bronco, police formed an armada of escort vehicles behind the fugitives. Driver Cowlings kept in touch with a 911 operator by cell phone as O.J. crouched in the backseat with a gun pressed to his own head. As it became clear the pair was returning to O.J.'s home at 360 North Rockingham media helicopters and camera crews on the ground captured throngs of pedestrians along the route watching the bizarre chase. In what should have been a tip-off to prosecutors, streetside spectators in black areas of the city cheered O.J. as the Bronco passed. At Rockingham 25 SWAT specialists awaited the arrival of the fugitives while detectives kept company inside the house with Robert Kardashian and O.J.'s son, Jason. When the Bronco finally arrived Simpson stayed crouched in the backseat of the car for an hour while he spoke with a police crisis negotiator inside the house. Finally, O.J. gave up. Inside the Bronco, SWAT team members recovered a travel bag containing O.J.'s passport, a fake goatee and mustache, and a bottle of make-up adhesive remover. Simpson later claimed that he carried the fake hair so he could walk with his children at zoos and amusement parks unmolested by fans. Also found in the car was a loaded Smith & Wesson pistol purchased for Simpson by a policeman who once worked security for the sports great. At the station, Cowlings was found to be carrying $8,750 in cash. Both men stated they had just wanted to visit Nicole's grave one last time before O.J. turned himself in, but could not get near the cemetery because of the media.

Once Simpson was in police custody and formally declared himself "not guilty" of the murders at his arraignment on June 24, 1994, the media circus that became the O.J. Simpson case swung into high gear. Robert Shapiro, an attorney skilled at cutting deals, had never taken a murder case to trial. Backed by his millionaire client's seemingly bottomless pockets, Shapiro began assembling what the press dubbed "The Dream Team" comprised of a battery of high price attorneys each a specialist in areas of the law deemed germane to the Simpson defense. Johnnie Cochran, an eloquent African-American attorney who made his name and considerable fortune taking on cases of LAPD corruption, had once represented Michael Jackson (see entry) on a child-abuse charge. Cochran's central theme in the majority of his successful defenses was unchanging — the white police establishment was corrupt and entered into conspiracies to deny rights to ethnic defendants. In racially divided Los Angeles, Cochran's assertions carried much weight. Numerous instances of insensitivity by the LAPD including their handling of the Watts riot in 1965 and several documented cases of brutality directed against blacks had understandably made the African-American community distrustful of their city's police force.

The flashpoint, however, occurred on April 29, 1992, when four LAPD officers caught on video-tape in 1991 viciously beating Rodney King, an unarmed black motorist, were acquitted by an all-white jury in Simi Valley. The unpopular and un-just verdict triggered a riot in African-American sections of the city. Shapiro's friend, legal heavy-weight F. Lee Bailey, was added to the team for his skill in preparation while Barry Scheck and Peter Neufeld came on board as experts in DNA. Attorneys Gerald Uelman, dean of Santa Clara University law school, and Harvard professor Alan Dershowitz, an expert at filing legal motions who had once aided Shapiro in his defense of Christian Brando (see entry), rounded out the team. Shapiro was the acknowledged leader of "The Dream Team" until suggesting to his shocked colleagues that his review of the case left room for O.J. to cut a deal for manslaughter. Afterwards, Simpson chose Johnnie Cochran, the silver-tongued litigator who understood black people, to replace Shapiro, the deal maker, as leader of his defense.

From the outset of the proceedings, the prose-cution and the defense approached the case from fundamentally different perspectives. Marcia Clark and co-counsel Christopher Darden viewed O.J.'s murder of Nicole Brown Simpson as the tragic conclusion of an ongoing drama of domes-tic violence. Ron Goldman, the Good Samaritan, just happened to be in the wrong place at the wrong time. Johnnie Cochran, confronted by an avalanche of incriminating forensic evidence that on its surface strongly suggested his client was guilty, posited a vast police conspiracy having at its center Mark Fuhrman, a detective with a shaky past who (at this early date) was most likely a racist like many of his fellow-officers on the LAPD. Simpson, although he routinely invited police over to his home and never evinced much interest in black causes or in having black friends, was now presented as the victim of a police frame-up because he was an African American. If a con-spiracy existed then the physical evidence (the glove, the knit cap, the blood and hair) could be explained as police plants. Even if they could not, it could perhaps be demonstrated that the collec-tion of the DNA evidence was so incompetent as to rule it unreliable and therefore useless. To de-termine how their respective theories of the case might play out in front of a jury, both the defense and prosecution conducted test focus groups. This procedure took on crucial importance in lieu of

Gil Garcetti's decision to try the case downtown where the jury pool would contain more blacks (based on the county's African-American popu-lation) rather than in the predominantly white county of Santa Monica where the courtroom had been damaged by the Northridge earthquake. The mock juries were instructive and boded well for the prosecution. Blacks as a whole felt O.J. was innocent, while black women were three times less likely than their male counterparts to think him guilty. Conversely, black women took a strong dislike to Marcia Clark who they found overbearing and described in questionnaires as a "bitch." Nor did the black mock jurors find the prosecution's domestic violence argument to be particularly compelling. Forty percent of the black women polled accepted as "normal" the use of some type of physical force in a marriage. If O.J. did occasionally beat his wife it did not necessarily mean that he killed her. Cochran and his defense team used the data gathered from the mock juries to seat jurors sympathetic to O.J. Simpson while Marcia Clark chose to ignore the results. Accord-ing to the defense's jury consultant, the perfect O.J. juror would be black, female, young, less ed-ucated, blue collar, and from a lower income group. Ultimately, the 24 member jury (12 jurors, 12 alternates) impaneled on November 3, 1994 was composed of 15 blacks, 6 whites, and 3 His-panics. In a county where just 11 percent of the population was black, this jury would seem to have been an ideal one for the defense.

Following lengthy pre-trial hearings that ruled on several issues including just how much the jury could hear regarding O.J.'s past history of domestic violence, opening arguments in the so-called "Trial of the Century" began in the Crim-inal Courts Building on January 24, 1995. Pre-siding Judge Lance Ito allowed one lone camera in the courtroom to broadcast the proceedings live to a plethora of media outlets. Court TV (fol-lowed closely by CNN) offered gavel-to-gavel coverage of the proceedings and everyone con-nected with the trial enjoyed at least some degree of momentary celebrity. As stated, the defense theory of the case was simple. O.J. was the classic domestic violence abuser and murdered Nicole out of an obsessive jealousy, a contention some-what hurt by Judge Ito's exclusion as hearsay of a detailed diary kept by Nicole chronicling ex-amples of his ongoing abusive behavior which in addition to beatings included stalking and verbal humiliation. Johnnie Cochran's opening statement for the defense was more direct and played to the racial make-up of the jury. Sprinkling his oration with references to Martin Luther King and Abraham Lincoln, Cochran presented the case as part of the continuing black struggle to realize equal rights. "This case is about a rush to judgment," Cochran maintained, "an obsession to win at any cost and by any means necessary." To do so, certain nefarious and racist elements within the LAPD engaged in a conspiracy to frame O.J. for the double murders. Unmentioned was the fact that prior to the crime O.J. had a great relationship with the police department as evidenced by the numerous times they had smoothed over his domestic violence beefs. O.J. threw parties for cops at the Rockingham address, let groups of them swim in his pool, and made yearly guest appearances at their Christmas parties where he happily signed footballs. Subtly expanding on his racial theme, Cochran played on a crucial bit of information revealed during the mock jury tests. Black women, as a group, held little or no sympathy for Nicole Brown Simpson, a white woman perceived as having "got" O.J., the iconic black man. Nicole, according to Cochran, had a well-documented catalog of sexual exploits including sex on a couch with Keith Zlomsowitch while her children slept upstairs, an affair with football running back Marcus Allen, and others. More damningly, Nicole chose to number among her best friends Faye Resnick, a known drug abuser who had been forced by her husband to enter a drug rehabilitation facility. Cochran hinted that the truth behind the murders lay in the world of drugs in which Faye Resnick and by extension Nicole Brown Simpson moved.

Christopher Darden, charged with developing the domestic violence thesis, opened the prosecution's case by playing the infamous 13½ minute 911 call Nicole made to police on October 25, 1993. Denise Brown, called to provide firsthand knowledge of her younger sister's abusive relationship with O.J., so obviously despised the defendant and felt him guilty that instead of helping the defense, she alienated the jury. Moreover, Darden blundered by showing a photograph allegedly taken of Nicole's bruised face following one of the domestic violence incidents without being able to tie it to a single identifiable date involving O.J. By and large, the defense chose to ignore the domestic violence angle already having learned from mock juries that it was a non-issue with most jurors. The case was about murder, not

domestic violence, and the defense chose to focus its energies on proving that not only did O.J. lack the time to commit the murders, but was a victim of a racist police force.

Marcia Clark, lead counsel for the prosecution largely by virtue of the fact that circumstances within the D.A.'s office had made it politically disadvantageous for Gil Garcetti to replace her, outlined the prosecution's murder case against O.J. Simpson. Clark set the timeline for the murders at 10:15 P.M. based on the reports of the so-called "dog witnesses" at Bundy Drive. The defense, needing the murders to happen later to show O.J. did not have time to commit the acts, maintained the crimes occurred at 10:35 P.M. or thereafter. According to the prosecution's timeline, O.J. had no alibi for the time between 9:40 P.M. (when he was last seen by Kato Kaelin during their drive to McDonald's for food) and 10:55 P.M. (when Allan Park, a limo driver, saw him going into the house on Rockingham). Mark Fuhrman took the stand on March 9, 1995 and expertly testified about the events at Bundy and Rockingham. Fuhrman, however, had a dubious past that made him a tailor-made target for a racially based defense. In the endless months leading up to the trial, Cochran *et al.* had appeared on every available talk show, magazine, and newspaper floating the racist cop angle in the O.J. case. On July 19, 1994, Kathleen Bell wrote to Johnnie Cochran, the loudest pro–O.J. media voice, regarding her knowledge of Mark Fuhrman, the "good guy" cop who had discovered the bloody glove at Rockingham. According to Bell, during 1985–1986 she was employed as a real estate agent in Redondo Beach, California and occupied an office above a Marine recruiting station where Fuhrman sometimes visited friends. She remembered him distinctly because of his imposing height (6' 3") and muscular build. Bell informed Cochran that Fuhrman used to regale the soldiers with stories of "niggers" and how we would pull them over on some pretext if he saw them driving in cars with white women. Going further, the LAPD cop allegedly said he would like to see all "niggers" herded together in one place and bombed to extinction. Beyond Bell's claim that the officer displayed signs of hateful racism (the prosecution was already aware of her assertions) Fuhrman had a contentious history within his own department. In August 1983, he filed suit against the City of Los Angeles Fire and Police Pension Fund in an attempt to claim a stress-related disability. In his own documentation supplied to the court, Fuhrman emerged as a dangerously unbalanced man who probably should not remain a police officer. The city countered that Fuhrman was a competent officer who was involved in an elaborate ruse to win a pension. The city won the case and Fuhrman remained on the force. F. Lee Bailey, until then a minor player in the case most known for his feud with "Dream Team" colleague Robert Shapiro, cross-examined Fuhrman, but was unable to damage his testimony concerning his actions on the night of the murders. The next day, Bailey grilled the detective about his use of the word "nigger" battering the racist term into the minds of the jury by its relentless repetition. Asked by Bailey if he had used the epithet "nigger" within the last 10 years, Fuhrman unconvincingly responded that he could not recall.

If there was one witness in the entire O.J. Simpson saga whose integrity was unimpeachable it was Allan Park, the limo driver. Park had not discussed the case with the media and had refused thousands of dollars from gossip rags and tell-all TV shows to spill his story. More importantly, the limo driver had cell phone records to back up his testimony. Park was scheduled to pick up O.J. at his Rockingham address at 10:45 P.M. to take him to the airport for the football star's 11:45 P.M. flight to Chicago, but arrived twenty minutes early to be certain of making the trip on time. At 10:25 P.M. when Park arrived outside the locked gate the white Bronco was not there. He rang the bell at the gate at 10:40 P.M. and receiving no answer drove to another gate to repeat the process. Still, no Bronco was in evidence. Beginning to panic, Park placed calls on the limo's cell phone to his boss and even his mother. The Simpson house was dark except for a single light upstairs. At 10:52 P.M. Park's employer called back and as they were trying to figure out what to do the driver noticed a couple of minutes later some movement up near the house. Kaelin emerged from the shadows near the back of the house. Then, a person Park described as a 6' tall, 200 pound black individual walked into the front door of the house from the outside. Park buzzed the residence again and the downstairs lights came on. O.J. answered the intercom, opened the gate, and told the relieved driver that he overslept and had just got out of the shower. Simpson would later embellish his story by adding that he was also outside during this time chipping golf balls in the dark. During the next five minutes Simpson collected a few bags

which Park and Kaelin loaded into the limousine. O.J. insisted that only he touch a small black duffel bag. The prosecution later maintained this bag contained the clothes Simpson wore during the murders. Shortly after 11:00 P.M., Park drove the car out of the North Rockingham gate now noticing the white Bronco parked at the curb. At the airport, skycap James Williams checked in Simpson's bag and testified Simpson stood next to a big trash can on the sidewalk near the parked limo. The black duffel bag mysteriously disappeared and did not make the trip to Chicago. Johnnie Cochran was unable to shake Park's testimony.

More compelling, however, than Park's unimpeachable testimony which in essence fit the prosecution's timeline by establishing that O.J. was not at home when he claimed to be, was the unbroken mountain of DNA evidence leading from the murder scene on South Bundy to his upstairs bedroom at Rockingham. The blood drops to the left of the bloody footprints leading down the walkway at South Bundy to the back gate matched O.J.'s DNA. The knitted sock hat found at Bundy contained hairs consistent with Simpson's as did a hair found on Ron Goldman's shirt. The bloody smudge discovered on the back gate at Bundy was a DNA match to Simpson. Statistically, there was only a 1 in 170 billion probability that the blood belonged to anyone but O.J. At the time, there were only five billion people on Earth. Simpson had a cut on the middle finger of his left hand which he was unable to convincingly explain. In addition to the evidence of the bloody gloves and blood drops at Rockingham were the 20 bloodstains found on Simpson's socks which had DNA characteristics matched by only 1 person in 6.8 billion. Defense lawyers Barry Scheck and Peter Neufeld, blood experts whose pioneering work with the Innocence Project had used DNA to free many innocent prisoners on Death Row, faced the daunting task of arguing away an overwhelming amount of evidence that led inexorably to an inescapable conclusion — O.J. Simpson was a murderer. Scheck built upon the foundation of police corruption and conspiracy established by Cochran adding the element of incompetence to the mix. Not only were the police racist and involved in a massive conspiracy against O.J. the evidence technicians on the force were also incompetent. Unable to argue away the science of DNA that statistically made it astronomically improbable that anyone but Simpson committed the murders, Scheck attacked the evidence from the standpoint of its collection based on a simple theorem — garbage in, garbage out. Criminalist Dennis Fung aided by Andrea Mazzola had collected evidence from both Bundy and Rockingham on the morning after the murders. The Simpson case was only the third crime scene Mazzola had ever processed. In earlier statements, Fung maintained he had collected the bulk of the forensic evidence, but under Scheck's intense questioning was forced to admit that the inexperienced Mazzola had processed much of the scenes. Moreover, Fung's collection techniques were sloppy and did not adhere to departmental procedures. In many instances, the criminalist had failed to use gloves during collection leaving open the possibility of evidence contamination. Scheck pointed out inconsistencies in Fung's work noting he had not collected the blood on the back gate at South Bundy until nearly three weeks *after* the murders. While the DNA collected on the walkway at Bundy on the day following the murders had degraded the blood on the back gate collected later had not and appeared to contain preservatives. This contention dovetailed with Cochran's earlier assertions that the police (most notably Mark Fuhrman) had planted the blood on the gate, in the Bronco, and on O.J.'s socks. Fung had further erred in leaving collected blood evidence in the back of his un-air-conditioned car for hours allowing the DNA to degrade in the heat. Scheck's nine-day grilling of Fung was so devastating that O.J. shook the criminalist's hand as he left the stand. Although more conclusive DNA evidence had been presented in the Simpson case than in any other trial in American history ultimately the overwhelming statistical probabilities pointing to O.J.'s guilt were neutralized by Fung's shaky testimony. Based on Fung's courtroom performance, it was also beyond the bounds of belief that someone so inept could ever be an important cog in a vast police conspiracy.

Against the backdrop of Scheck and Neufeld's masterful neutralizing of the damaging DNA evidence based on the perceived incompetence of its collection, the prosecution presented what it had to believe were two pieces of slam-dunk evidence, the gloves and shoes tying O.J. to the murders. The gloves (the left retrieved at Bundy and its right hand mate found at Rockingham) were a rare type made by Aris. Using credit card receipts, police determined Nicole had purchased two pairs of the extra large size gloves at Bloom-

ingdale's in New York City on December 18, 1990. Only 200 pairs of the Aris Light model had been sold and numerous photographs and videos revealed Simpson wearing identical gloves. Richard Rubin, general manager of the Aris Isotoner business in the early 1990s, was brought in by the prosecution as an expert witness to present background on the gloves. Remarkably, Christopher Darden never spoke with Rubin prior to putting him on the witness stand. This particular model of leather glove was designed to fit tight like a racing glove and stretched to fit the hand when worn. Since their recovery at the crime scenes, the blood soaked gloves had undergone numerous DNA tests and had swatches removed for testing. Marcia Clark specifically instructed Darden not to risk a demonstration of the gloves in open court especially as Simpson would have to wear latex gloves under the evidence gloves that would inhibit a comfortable fit. Darden, however, goaded by a jibe from F. Lee Bailey, unexpectedly decided without consulting his team to have O.J. try on the gloves in front of the jury. In what many courtroom observers would later claim was his most convincing performance since his turn in the *Naked Gun* movies, Simpson theatrically struggled to pull the leather gloves over the latex gloves he was wearing for the experiment. Darden's disastrous decision gave Johnnie Cochran his most famous soundbite, "If it doesn't fit, you must acquit." The prosecution next turned to the bloody shoe prints leading away from the bodies on Bundy Drive. An FBI forensics expert identified the prints as having been made by a pair of Bruno Magli, a rare and expensive Italian shoe sold in only forty locations across the United States including Bloomingdale's where Simpson regularly shopped. Impressions found on Nicole's back matched O.J.'s size 12 shoe prints and suggested how she may have been killed. The killer planted his foot on the unconscious woman's back, grabbed her hair in his left hand, and cut her throat with the knife in his right hand. Defense attorneys argued that O.J. did not own a pair of Bruno Magli shoes and claimed that the photo submitted by the defense clearly showing him wearing a pair had been doctored. The defense's implication that a second killer was at the scene based on their interpretation of the shoe evidence was quickly discredited. On July 6, 1995, following 92 days of testimony, 58 witnesses, 488 exhibits, and over 34,500 pages of transcript, the prosecution rested its case against Orenthal James Simpson.

In his defense of Simpson, Cochran continued to hammer away at the familiar themes of police racism and conspiracy while attacking the blood evidence as either incompetently collected or planted. Robert Huizenga, a Beverly Hills internist, testified that the cumulative injuries sustained by O.J. during his years of playing football made it physically impossible for him to commit the murders. The doctor's credibility was somewhat damaged when the prosecution produced video clips of Simpson hawking an arthritis relief product called Juice Plus and bragging that the product gave him an extra ten yards on his golf drives. Similarly, raw film footage taken from the former football star's soon-to-be released exercise video, *O.J. Simpson Minimum Maintenance for Men*, showed an apparently healthy O.J. working out. The footage was shot just two weeks prior to the murders and seemingly disproved the defense's claim that Simpson did not possess a physical range of motion sufficient to have committed the murders. On July 7, 1995, "The Dream Team" received a call from Laura Hart McKinny that proved to be the proverbial "gift from God." McKinny was an aspiring screenwriter working on a film script about female police officers at the time she met Officer Mark Fuhrman in February 1985. During twelve hours of taped interviews conducted by the screenwriter, Fuhrman related harrowing tales of his involvement in the beating of suspects and betrayed a marked dislike for blacks as evidenced by his repeated use of the word "nigger" on the tapes. Cochran subpoenaed the tapes and following legal maneuvering in and out of the courtroom (the attorney managed to leak the tapes to the media) Judge Ito ruled the jury could hear the testimony of Laura Hart McKinny and excerpts from the tapes. On the stand, McKinny testified that during their taped interviews Fuhrman had used the "N" word 41 times, a claim corroborated for the jury by Fuhrman's own voice on the tape. His previous testimony denying the use of the "N" word for the last decade now totally discredited, Fuhrman under defense questioning was reduced to invoking the Fifth Amendment privilege against self-incrimination. If Fuhrman had lied about being a racist cop by extension could he be trusted not to have planted evidence incriminating a black suspect? Marcia Clark in her summation was forced to admit that while Fuhrman was clearly a bad racist cop it did not necessarily follow that the prosecution had failed to prove Simpson

guilty of murder. Darden concluded by providing the jury with a chronological listing of O.J.'s history of domestic violence painting the former football star and actor as a "burning fuse" whose final act of jealousy and control was the murder of his wife and her friend who just unfortunately happened upon the scene. Cochran, in his summation, downplayed the domestic violence angle and while admitting that O.J. was not perfect, his treatment of Nicole did not add up to murder. The case was after all not about O.J., but rather the racist LAPD and Mark Fuhrman as its poster boy. The incriminating blood containing the statistically damning DNA was planted by Fuhrman who Cochran in a moment of unrestrained oratory likened to Adolf Hitler. Even if it were not, the LAPD's collection of the blood evidence was so slipshod and incompetent that all incriminating results suggested by it had to be summarily dismissed. Finally, Cochran argued, the glove just did not fit.

On Friday, September 29, 1995, a jury that had been sequestered like prisoners in a hotel under the watchful eyes of sheriff's deputies for the duration of the nearly nine month trial was finally given the case. The jury, now composed of nine blacks, one Hispanic, and two whites (both women), cast an initial vote that broke along the lines of race for an acquittal with only the two white women casting guilty votes. The jury asked to see the transcript of Allan Park's testimony the morally unimpeachable limo driver whose courtroom appearance was seemingly so damning to Simpson's case. After deliberating for a total of four hours following nine months of grueling testimony highlighted by complex scientific evidence, the jury notified Judge Ito that it had reached a verdict. The verdict would be announced after various attorneys in the case could be reassembled. That night, a juror leaked the "not guilty" decision to a deputy guarding them who in turn told a sheriff's deputy at the L.A. County Jail. The deputy informed Simpson that he would soon be a free man. An estimated television audience of 95 million viewers tuned in on October 3, 1995 as the verdict was read acquitting O.J. Simpson of killing Nicole Brown Simpson and Ronald Lyle Goldman. Reaction to the decision depended largely upon one's race with a large percentage of the African-American population thrilled that O.J. had beaten the rap while stunned whites reacted with a mixture of disbelief and disgust. Clearly, the predominantly black jury had accepted the defense's contention that the LAPD was a racist organization fully willing to frame a black man. Neither did the domestic violence argument resonate with the jury who found it to be irrelevant. The lone African-American male juror raised his fist in a black power salute as he left the jury box. One juror, a 72-year-old black woman when asked about the overwhelming scientific evidence presented in the case, said, "I didn't understand the DNA stuff at all. To me, it was just a waste of time. It was way out there and carried absolutely no weight with me." Robert Shapiro, the original architect of "The Dream Team" and an attorney whose presence in the spotlight had waned as Johnnie Cochran's had waxed, acknowledged in an interview with Barbara Walters that the defense team had played the "race card" (and) "dealt it from the bottom of the deck." Simpson beat the murder rap, but now found himself a pariah in the predominantly white world he had always chosen to inhabit. Gone were offers of movie roles, the Hertz contract, or any chance of attracting new commercial endorsers. Also, he still had to face a proceeding in civil court stemming from the murders of which he had been acquitted.

Both the Brown and Goldman families were devastated by the acquittal and in September 1996 united in the so-called "Sequel of the Century," a "wrongful death" suit against Simpson in which the burden of proof was much less great than in the criminal trial. In order to find O.J. liable for the deaths of Nicole Brown Simpson and Ronald Lyle Goldman and assign financial damages only 9 out of 12 jurors needed to be convinced that a preponderance of evidence (50.1 percent) pointed to him as their killer. In this trial, the jury was taken from the West side of Los Angeles and included jurors drawn from the higher income areas of Brentwood and Santa Monica. Unlike media friendly Judge Lance Ito, Los Angeles Superior Court Judge Hiroshi Fujisaki banned cameras from the courtroom and imposed a strict gag order. Nor would the proceedings be bogged down by endless motions like those filed by "Dream Team" member Alan Dershowitz in the first trial. Judge Fujisaki refused to read any motion over five pages long. A controversial new law in California permitting statements of crime victims as admissible opened the door for Nicole's diary containing instances of O.J.'s abuse to be introduced into the court record. Predictably, O.J.'s attorney Robert C. Baker portrayed Nicole as a heavy drinking drug abusing party animal who enjoyed many lovers and once had an abortion. Following the divorce, Nicole continued to cling to her ex-husband who, rather than being a jealous obsessive, was in reality her confidant and supporter as she sought to begin a life without him. In the civil trial, Simpson was compelled to take the stand and under relentless questioning by Goldman family attorney Daniel Petrocelli offered up a testimony rife with inconsistencies, memory lapses (he could not recall taking a polygraph test), and statements directly contradicted by numerous witnesses, Nicole's diary, and the official police account. Petrocelli forcefully observed that in order for O.J. Simpson's account of his non-involvement in the murders to be truthful everyone else except him would have to be lying. In February 1997, Simpson was found guilty of causing the deaths of Nicole and Goldman by a unanimous jury vote and ordered to pay a total of $33.5 million to various parties in the suit. Over the years, Simpson has paid only a pittance of the settlement due, in small part, to their being listed tenth on a list of creditors behind lawyers and mortgage companies. In any event, "Juice" moved to Florida in order to take advantage of a state law allowing him to earn a set amount of money that could not be touched by creditors including his $25,000 a month pension from the NFL along with money earned by signing autographs. The man depicted by attorneys in his criminal trial as too arthritic to commit the murders played golf six days a week in the "Sunshine State."

Simpson stayed out of the public eye except for the occasional lover's quarrel and an acquittal in 2001 on a charge of assault and battery stemming from a road rage incident in Florida until early 2007 when it was reported that he had signed an $880,000 deal with HarperCollins/ReganBooks to write *If I Did It* in which he offered a fictional tell-all account of how he might have committed the murders. Furor over the tastelessness of the "quasi-confession" forced cancellation of the deal, but the book was published in 2007 by Beaufort Books after financial considerations were made to the family of Ronald Goldman. Later that year in what some might call a case of divine justice, Simpson, 60, was arrested in Las Vegas, Nevada for his role in an armed robbery of sports memorabilia from a $35-a-night room in the Palace Station Hotel-Casino. On September 13, 2007, Simpson and five other men (two armed with guns) burst into the room of Alfred Beardsley, a sports memorabilia dealer from Glendale, California, and left with armfuls of football-related material including his own Hall of Fame certificate, photos and books signed by the sports star, lithographs of San Francisco 49ers quarterback Joe Montana, and Beardsley's cell phone. Simpson had come to Las Vegas on a tip supplied by Tom Riccio, an auction house owner, that memorabilia allegedly stolen from the football star was in Beardsley's possession. Riccio, who arranged the confrontation, was carrying a tape recorder when the group invaded Beardsley's room and the incriminating dialogue captured on the tape did not help Simpson at his trial in Las Vegas in October 2008. Simpson maintained he was only attempting to retrieve articles stolen from him, but this contention was undercut by four of his cronies in the raid who cut plea deals with the prosecution in exchange for their testimony. One of the gunmen testified O.J. not only knew weapons would be involved in the raid, but asked him to bring a gun. On October 3, 2008, 13 years after his controversial acquittal, Simpson was convicted by an all-white jury on 12 felony counts, including armed robbery and kidnapping, along with co-defendant, Clarence Stewart. O.J. was later sentenced to a minimum of nine years in state prison and a maximum of 33 years, a generous sentence when the Parole and Probation Division had recommended an 18-year minimum. Clarence Stewart was given a minimum 7½ year sentence. Addressing the court, a humbled O.J. Simpson apologized, but continued to insist that he did not think at the time he had done anything illegal. Many have interpreted the guilty verdict in Nevada as long-delayed "payback" for the football star's acquittal in the double homicide in Brentwood in 1994. While pleased with Simpson's conviction, Fred Goldman, Ron's long-suffering father, told reporters on the courthouse steps, "There's never closure; Ron is always gone. What we have is satisfaction that this monster is where he belongs, behind bars." As of 2009, Simpson is incarcerated at the Lovelock Correctional Center, a facility housing just under 1,500 inmates in two-bed cells, about 90 miles northeast of Reno. O.J.'s attorney vowed an appeal based largely on the racial argument that the jury pool was manipulated by the district attorney to produce a panel with no African-Americans. In October 2010 the Nevada Supreme Court rejected O.J.'s appeal.

Further Reading

Barbieri, Paula. *The Other Woman—My Years with O.J. Simpson: A Story of Love, Trust, and Betrayal.* Boston: Little, Brown, 1997.

Bugliosi, Vincent. *Outrage: The Five Reasons O.J. Got Away with Murder.* New York: W.W. Norton, 1996.

Clark, Marcia, and Teresa Carpenter. *Without a Doubt.* New York: Viking, 1997.

Cochran, Johnnie L., and Tim Rutten. *Journey to Justice.* New York: Ballantine, 1996.

Darden, Christopher A., and Jess Walter. *In Contempt.* New York: ReganBooks, 1996.

Dershowitz, Alan M. *Reasonable Doubts: The O.J. Simpson Case and the Criminal Justice System.* New York: Simon and Schuster, 1996.

Eliot, Marc. *Kato Kaelin: The Whole Truth, the Real Story of O.J., Nicole, and Kato from the Actual Tapes.* New York: Harper, 1995.

Fuhrman, Mark. *Murder in Brentwood.* Washington, DC: Regnery, 1997.

Lange, Tom, Dan E. Molden, and Philip Vannatter. *Evidence Dismissed: The Inside Story of the Police Investigation of O.J. Simpson.* New York: Pocket, 1997.

Petrocelli, Daniel, and Peter Knobler. *Triumph of Justice: The Final Judgment on the Simpson Saga.* New York: Crown, 1998.

Resnick, Faye D., and Mike Walker. *Nicole Brown Simpson: The Private Diary of a Life Interrupted.* Beverly Hills, CA: Dove, 1994.

Riccio, Thomas J. *Busted! The Inside Story of the World of Sports Memorabilia, O.J. Simpson, and the Vegas Arrests.* Beverly Hills, CA: Phoenix, 2008.

Schiller, Lawrence, and James Willwerth. *American Tragedy: The Uncensored Story of the Simpson Defense.* New York: Random House, 1996.

Shapiro, Robert L., and Larkin Warren. *The Search for Justice: A Defense Attorney's Brief on the O.J. Simpson Case.* New York: Warner, 1996.

Simpson, O.J. *I Want to Tell You: My Response to Your Letters, Your Messages, Your Questions.* Boston: Little, Brown, 1995.

_____. *If I Did It: Confessions of the Killer.* New York: Beaufort, 2007.

Spence, Gerry. *O.J., the Last Word.* New York: St. Martin's, 1997.

Toobin, Jeffrey. *The Run of His Life: The People v. O.J. Simpson.* New York: Random House, 1996.

Weller, Sheila. *Raging Heart: The Intimate Story of the Tragic Marriage of O.J. Simpson and Nicole Brown Simpson.* New York: Pocket, 1995.

Smith, Allen (M-S)

Smith, a 28-year-old unemployed theatrical press agent formerly with the Paramount–Newark Theatre, pumped two rounds into his girlfriend, Mrs. Lois Duffy, then turned the .32-caliber gun on himself as the pair sat in a car on a lonely road outside the Mount Pleasant Cemetery in Newark, New Jersey, on April 18, 1937. Though Duffy, a 32-year-old telephone operator, was long estranged from her husband, she refused to divorce and marry Smith because of her devout Catholic upbringing. Duffy was found slumped over the steering wheel with a bullet in her right temple and another in her right breast. On the seat beside her, Smith still held the gun in his right hand, dead from a shot to the temple.

Further Reading

"Woman Shot Dead; Suitor Ends Life." *The New York Times*, April 19, 1937, p. 22.

Smith, Jay R. (V)

Smith (born August 29, 1915) was ten years old when he joined the cast of the Our Gang comedies in mid–1925. Paid $5 a week by producer Hal Roach, the heavily freckled youngster helped support his parents during the Depression playing the minor, but recurring roles of "Freckles" and Specks in three dozen silent two-reelers made between 1925 and 1929. These include *Boys Will Be Boys* (1925, debut), *Buried Treasure* (1926, as Jay R. "Specks" Smith), *Shivering Spooks* (1926), *Bring Home the Turkey* (1927), *Heebee Jeebees* (1927), *Playin' Hookey* (1928), *Crazy House* (1928, as the prissy "Percy"), and his final short in the series, *Election Day* (1929). Smith never again worked on a major film production. After serving in the Army during World War II, Smith settled in Hawaii and opened a paint store where he specialized in crafting custom picture frames.

In the early 1990s, the former child actor retired to an upscale gated mobile home complex in Las Vegas, Nevada, with his wife of 46 years, Florine. Following her death in February 2002, the 87-year-old briefly moved in with his stepdaughter, Janine Henry, but feeling cramped left after a week to return to his mobile home. "Pinky" (as he was affectionately known to family and friends because of his fair-skinned complexion) stunned friends when he announced six months later that he was allowing a homeless man named "Wayne" to live in the spacious tool shed behind his home in exchange for doing odd jobs around the house. At Smith's insistence, "Wayne" cut his hair and trimmed his beard. The pair appeared to be friendly to the extent that the homeless man accompanied Freckles on one of his many trips to sign autographs at Our Gang/Little Rascals conventions. As late as August 2002, people warned the elderly man that it was dangerous to associate with a homeless person, but Smith angrily dismissed them. By September 17, however, his feelings had changed to the point that he told a friend, "He's cramping my style, so I think I'm going to get rid of him."

Jay R. "Freckles" Smith was last seen alive by a family member on October 1, 2002. Four days later, a badly decomposed body was found wrapped in a sheet in the desert near Apex, Nevada, about 15 miles northeast of Las Vegas near

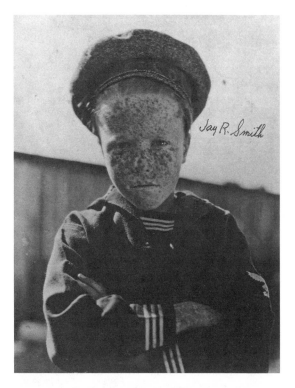

Jay R. Smith, "Freckles" in some three dozen Our Gang silent two-reelers from 1925 to 1929, never appeared in another major film production and owned a specialty paint store in Hawaii until retiring in the early 1990s to a gated mobile home community in Las Vegas. Against the advice of family and friends, the former child actor took in a homeless person as a handyman. Smith's body was found dumped in the Nevada desert on October 5, 2002. Tragedy seems to follow in the wake of the popular series; fellow Our Gang/Little Rascals alumni Carl ("Alfalfa") Switzer was murdered and Robert ("Mickey") Blake was acquitted of murder.

Interstate 15. An autopsy determined that death was due to multiple stab wounds and bludgeoning. Five days later, on October 10, 2002, Smith's stepdaughter, Janine Henry, phoned the Clark County coroner's office to inquire about the "John Doe" found in the desert whose reported description sounded remarkably similar to her missing stepfather. Henry described Smith to an unidentified employee adding the details that her stepfather had been wearing a necklace from which hung two gold rings (his and his dead wife's), each inscribed with the words "Kuippo," Hawaiian for "sweetheart." Also, her stepfather was missing part of two fingers. While the necklace containing the rings was found around the "John Doe's" neck, the employee did not mention this to Henry and compounded the error by failing to identify the body as Smith's because the corpse was only missing part of *one* finger. The body remained unidentified in the coroner's office until October 17 when Las Vegas police received a missing-persons report on Smith and checked the morgue. Clark County coroner Ron Flud later admitted that the office mishandled two calls from Henry allowing precious time to be wasted in pursuing Smith's killer. In a public statement apologizing for the error, Flud stated, "It should not have happened. And if I have anything to say about it, it never will again." The body identified, Las Vegas police began looking for their prime suspect, the homeless handyman known only as "Wayne."

During the thirteen day interval between the time the body was found in the desert and its belated identification, the killer systematically drained Smith's bank account of nearly $3,300 using the dead man's ATM debit card. Graydon Brooker, 46, a homeless man known to residents in the mobile home complex, was initially picked up, questioned, and cleared. On October 24, 2002, Charles "Wayne" Crombie, 52, was arrested in the Palms Hotel-Casino food court. Jay Smith's 1998 Buick was recovered in the parking lot of the Palms. Less than a week later, Crombie confessed to stabbing Smith three times in the stomach and beating him to death in the bedroom of his benefactor's home. He wrapped the former actor's body in a sheet and drove the Buick to a remote desert area outside of Las Vegas to dump the remains. During his subsequent days of freedom made largely possible by the incompetence of the Clark County coroner's office, Crombie used Smith's debit card for fun activities like gambling and movies, and even pawned the dead man's television and VCR for $20. In February 2005, Crombie pleaded the equivalent of "no contest" to the murder and other charges. Prior to sentencing, the man who had fatally abused Smith's kindness submitted an eloquently written statement to the judge — "An incident occurred; a death was the result. I now have blood on my hands that shall never wash clean; a remorse that time will never ease; a self-loathing of which only God's forgiveness has allowed me to partially overcome." Crombie was sentenced to two life terms (forty years to life) and is eligible for parole after serving 40 years. (See also entries Robert Blake and Carl Dean ["Alfalfa"] Switzer.)

Further Reading

Curreri, Frank. "Slaying Victim Once 'Little Rascals' Actor." *Las Vegas Review-Journal*, October 22, 2002, sec. B, p. 3.
Maltin, Leonard, and Richard W. Benn. *The Little Rascals: The Life and Times of Our Gang.* Updated ed. New York: Crown, 1992.

Smith, Robert McAdam (V)

Aspiring to be an actor since the age of nine, Smith worked as an office temp and restaurant cashier while attending Fordham University and New York's prestigious Acting Studio, Inc. from which he graduated in 1991. Impressed by the 21-year-old actor's seriousness and facility while at the Acting Studio, Vivian Matalon, the Tony Award–winning director of *Another Time,* cast Smith in a major role in the Dallas Theater Center production of the play. Also cast as the older version of Smith's lead character was 60-year-old Perry MacDonald Tutchings (stage name Pirie MacDonald). The veteran character actor was no stranger to the Dallas, Texas theatrical scene having played opposite Eva Le Gallienne in the national tour of *Elizabeth the Queen* in the early 1960s. In addition to multiple stage credits, Tutchings (MacDonald) also appeared in films (*Network*, 1976; *Wall Street*, 1987; *Talk Radio, 1988*) and television (*Law & Order*).

On December 10, 1992, the two New York actors had been in Dallas only four days when shortly after parking their car around 6:20 P.M. outside their Oak Lawn apartment in the 3600 block of Travis Street they were approached by a group of four men. Forced at gunpoint to hand over their valuables, Tutchings heard one of the robbers say, "I'm going to shoot them." The gunman shot both men in the head, killing Smith who was on his knees with his hands locked behind his head, and severely wounding the older actor who managed to phone authorities. Tutchings miraculously survived the murder attempt, but lost an eye. Dallas police linked the fatal attack to at least five robberies spread over two days scattered from North Dallas to Oak Cliff. During the increasingly violent spree, the robbers had stolen two cars, threatened the kidnap of a child, shot the two actors, and struck another man on the head with a gun butt. Days after the killing, police had four teenagers, the oldest 17-year-old Freddie Leon Rudd, in custody with Rudd and two of the juvenile gang identifying a 14-year-old in the group as the triggerman. As debate raged over the issue of proceeding against the juveniles as adults on a charge of capital murder, over one hundred friends of the murdered actor pressed Dallas authorities to vigorously prosecute the case to the full extent of the law. Three of gang (Rudd, Corey Drake, 16, and Deprece Pratt, 17) were certified as adults, but the 14 year old identified by the others as the shooter was found to be mentally retarded and was committed in early 1993 to a Texas mental health and mental retardation facility. Pratt was convicted of capital murder in October 1993 and given a mandatory life sentence. He will be ineligible for parole until he is at least 52. Freddie Rudd's trial in February 1994 on a charge of capital murder ended in a hung jury after the jury remained split 9–3 in favor of conviction. Retried in July 1994, Rudd was found guilty of Smith's murder and sentenced to life imprisonment. He must serve a minimum of 35 years. Corey Drake, who testified against Pratt, pleaded guilty to aggravated robbery and received four concurrent life terms. He will serve at least 15 years before being parole eligible.

Family and friends of the murdered actor, however, continued to press for action against the mentally retarded killer who escaped trial to a mental health facility. In March 1995, Smith's parents presented Texas Governor George W. Bush with a petition signed by thousands seeking punishment for the youth. The petition drive was started after the Smiths learned the detainee had briefly returned to Dallas during a leave from the State School in Mexia. They also expressed concern that under Texas state law the youth will be released from the school with no chance of prosecution when he is 18 years old. Their petition helped create a law passed by the Texas legislature in 1995 allowing the state to prosecute people who avoided trials as juveniles because of mental disabilities, if they are later deemed competent to stand trial. In August 1997, the youth (identified in the press as 18-year-old Cary Houston) failed to return from a furlough from the Mexia State School. Houston remained at-large for six months until January 1998 when his family brought him back to the facility after an award was offered for his capture. Remarkably, Houston, 22, was released from the state school in December 2000 and returned to Dallas to live with his parents.

Further Reading

Copilevitz, Todd. "Three Held in Spree of Holdups: Actors Among Victims of Group, Police Say." *Dallas Morning News*, December 12, 1992, sec. A, p. 1.

Sorrells, Robert (M)

Born in 1930, Sorrells was a bit player in films, especially Westerns, from the early to late 1960s. His films include *All Fall Down* (1962), *Morituri* (1965), *Gunfight in Abilene* (1967), *The Last Challenge* (1967), *The Ride to Hangman's Tree* (1967), *Death of a Gunfighter* (1969), *Bound for Glory* (1976, as Woody Guthrie's father), *Bad News Bears Go to Japan* (1978), *Fletch* (1985), and *Nowhere to Run* (1989). Sorrells also landed small parts in three made-for-television movies (*San Francisco International*, 1970, NBC; *Female Artillery*, 1973, ABC; *Gus Brown and Midnight Brewster*, 1985, NBC), and was seen in the early 1960s to mid–1970's on a variety of Western television series (*Gunsmoke, Bonanza, Rawhide, Lancer, Cimarron Strip*).

The 74-year-old actor was retired and living in a low income senior citizens complex in Simi Valley, California, when an argument in a bar on July 24, 2004, turned deadly. The night before, Sorrells drank until closing at the Regency Lounge, a seedy downtown bar located on Los Angeles Avenue and Galt Street about twenty miles northwest of L.A. The next morning, he revisited the tavern to inquire about a lost credit card, returning later in the afternoon to resume drinking. Sorrells harassed a female bartender to the extent Arthur DeLong, a 45-year-old painting contractor who was drinking at the tavern, escorted the elderly man outside. Sorrells drove his Volkswagon minibus back to his apartment in Heywood Gardens, retrieved a semiautomatic pistol, and returned to the Regency Lounge around 5:00 P.M. What next transpired was captured on silent videotape from a surveillance camera mounted in the ceiling above the bar. Sorrells, a silver-haired man with a Col. Sanders–type goatee, walked into the bar, held the gun to DeLong's back, fired, and shot another round at the man as he lay dead on the barroom floor. The former Western actor then turned the gun on another patron seated at the bar, Edward Sanchez, 40, shooting him in the face and back. Sanchez survived the attack. Stunned patrons recalled prior to exiting the bar, Sorrells shouted, "Does anybody else want to fuck with the cowboy?" Simi Valley police apprehended the retired actor in his van minutes later three blocks from the shootout, and booked him in the Ventura County Jail on suspicion of murder and attempted murder. A detective later testified that five hours after the shooting Sorrells' blood-alcohol level was still more than twice the legal limit.

Interviewed by detectives, the former actor's friends painted a sad picture of a man in emotional decline. Friendly and outgoing, Sorrells was a practicing vegetarian who kept a small shrine to an Eastern god in his apartment. Proud of his former screen accomplishments, he often showed friends residual checks from the Screen Actors Guild. The death of his mother and poodle in 2003, however, radically changed Sorrells' personality. He cut himself off from others, and resumed drinking. Paramedics once called to his apartment described Sorrells in their report as a "babbling drunk." A friend who spent the last ten years performing with Sorrells (a talented guitarist) in a weekly jam session reported how after the deaths the elderly man began acting "weird." Sorrells started calling the man to complain of how he felt he ruined his life by "pickling his brain" with alcohol and drugs. Later, he received a threatening phone call from Sorrells announcing their friendship was over. "I don't like you," the actor said. "I have a gun and will come after you." The music group banned the aging actor, a self-professed celibate yogi with the email username "yogibob," after he propositioned one of its female members. A woman in Heywood Gardens sadly commented, "He was my friend, but he was a wacko, no doubt about it. My intuitive reaction is that he's nuts.... It's so heartbreaking."

The damning videotape recorded by the surveillance camera in the Regency Lounge was played at a preliminary hearing in October 2004 to determine a trial date. The prosecutor likened Sorrells to a "gunslinger" in one of his 1960s Westerns. The trial date set, Sorrells later pleaded guilty to first-degree murder and attempted murder in May 2005 after a psychiatric examination determined he was sane at the time of the shooting. On July 13, 2005, Sorrells was sentenced to 25 years to life in prison.

Further Reading

Bartholomew, Dana. "'Cowboy' Arrested in Barroom Killing." *Los Angeles Daily News*, July 27, 2004, sec. Valley, p. 1.

Soulja Slim (V)

James A'Darryl Tapp, known as Soulja Slim in the world of gangsta rap, was poised on the brink of national prominence when he was gunned down in his hometown of New Orleans on November 26, 2003. Growing up in the city's violent Magnolia public housing project, Tapp attended Booker T. Washington High School and, as Magnolia Slim, started rapping at open air bounce parties in "the circle," the project's courtyard. The next year he allied himself with local Hype Enough Records and began guesting on local rap albums. "Street cred," the essence of believability so important to the reputation of a gangsta rapper, was never a problem for Tapp. An abuser of heroin and cocaine, the teenager carried a gun to ripoff drug dealers. By the time Tapp was through with the justice system, he logged more than five years prison time on charges including armed robbery, auto theft, battery, drug possession, and parole and probation violations. Like badges of honor or harbingers of Fate, bullet wounds from two separate attacks on the rapper in the Magnolia project within a four month period around late 1996–early 1997 left scars on Soulja Slim's arms, chest, and leg. No arrests were made in either shooting. Rappers, however, turn the violence of ghetto life into rhymes and Tapp's profanity-laced songs overflowing with images of gang life, drugs, and drive-by shootings reflected his experience. In the exploding New Orleans rap scene, Soulja Slim became a hero on the streets primarily because (as his producer KLC noted) there was "nothing studio in him."

In 1998, Tapp renamed himself Soulja Slim and released his debut solo album, *Give It 2 'Em Raw*, on No Limit, the New Orleans–based label owned by childhood friend and rap mogul Master P. Ironically, another No Limit rapper, C-Murder (see entry), younger brother of Master P, was convicted of murder in September 2003. The cover of *Give It 2 'Em Raw* embodied Soulja Slim as the ghetto street warrior and featured the rapper dressed in camouflage surrounded by flames and exploding tanks. The album sold nearly 500,000 units and would have earned a gold record had Tapp been able to tour in its promotion instead of doing time in prison on a parole violation. No Limit, now a nationally known rap label, released Soulja Slim's second album, *The Streets Made Me*, in July 2001. The album sold 200,000 copies, but sales were again hampered by Tapp's incarceration for yet another parole violation. Released from the penitentiary in 2001, Tapp's career suffered another setback when an argument with Master P over finances led the rapper to angrily leave No Limit in 2002. Asked by a magazine interviewer at the time whether he planned to sue the label, Tapp replied, "I got some paperwork where I could try to go to war, but I ain't no nigga to go to court.... You heard me? I get it in blood, nigga."

In December 2002, Soulja Slim independently released the album *Years After* on his own label, Cut Throat Committy. With no national distribution outlets, the album sold an astonishing 30,000 units by word of mouth alone, and brought the rapper to the attention of national label Koch Records. Months before Tapp's death, Koch signed the rapper and released *Years Later ... A Few Months Later* (an updated version of his independent record) in August 2003. Backed by Koch, the "Tupac of the South" (as he was called by many), was ready to break nationally. Soulja Slim had the rap, the street cred, the gangsta attitude, and the look: numerous tattoos, prison cross between his eyes, gold-capped teeth, and a diamond encrusted Rolex. In November 2003, Tapp shot a music video in support of the album set to air on MTV and BET. Still, the rapper was unable or unwilling to tone down the violence in his personal life. Weeks prior to his murder, Soulja Slim had punch ups in clubs in Florida, Mississippi, and Louisiana. According to a source quoted on the website allhiphop.com who witnessed the New Orleans incident: "Slim was wildin' out, he was on X (Ecstasy) hard. He was out at a club on the West Bank. Someone said something like fuck Magnolia (the Magnolia projects in New Orleans) then all of Magnolia busted 'em up. The dude that got jumped has been walking around with a vest on all week, looking for Slim."

On November 26, 2003, the 25-year-old rapper spent the afternoon in the upstairs apartment-music studio he maintained in his mother's two-story duplex at 4618 Lafaye Street in New Orleans viewing a copy of the music video Koch Records was planning to launch his new album. Years earlier in 1998, Tapp used money earned from rapping to move his mother out of the dangerous Magnolia housing project and buy her a home in the more sedate Gentilly neighborhood. Around 4:30 P.M., Soulja Slim left the house to run some errands in his fully loaded grey Cadillac Escalade tricked out with the Throat logo engraved on every seat. Returning an hour and fifteen minutes later, the rapper was walking across the lawn to the front door of the house when a gunman wearing dark clothes pumped at least three shots into his face and one into his chest. Police arrived and found Tapp dead on the front lawn with the driver's side door of the SUV open and his gun still inside the vehicle. Garelle Smith, 22, was arrested on December 30, 2003 and charged with Tapp's murder after a ballistics test on the murder weapon, a .40-caliber Glock semiautomatic allegedly stolen by Smith from a New Orleans police officer's home, tied him to the execution-style killing. According to police, Smith was paid $10,000 for the hit that had something to do with the record industry and a rival record company. Hip-hop insiders, however, largely discounted the killing was linked to bad blood between Soulja Slim's old and new record labels pointing to the deep friendship between C-Murder (Master P's younger brother) and the dead rapper.

Tapp's family was blindsided in March 2004 when the New Orleans district attorney's office refused the charge against Garelle Smith citing the evidence was insufficient to prove the crime. Still reeling from the release of the prime suspect, the family was again floored when police announced their investigation into Soulja Slim's murder uncovered evidence implicating the murdered rapper in the shooting death of truck driver Robert Lee Paige, Jr., in September 2003. Paige's body was found weighted down with cinder blocks in the New Orlean's City Park lagoon. Tapp's manager, Anthony "Antman" Murray, ripped the police for making Soulja Slim a posthumous suspect, charging, "That's just their way of closing their books. Nothin' on the street was serious enough for him to bother with like that. Nothing that crucial.... He wasn't on that type of time. He was on artist-type time." As to Soulja Slim's killing, KLC, the dead rapper's producer, spoke the final word, "It could have been jealousy, it could have been a lot of things. You hear so much, you don't know what to believe. But the streets talk, and with the following that Slim had, the truth is going to come out." Garelle Smith, still considered by authorities as the prime suspect in Soulja's alleged contract killing, has as of 2009 walked free on three other suspected murders.

Further Reading

Perlstein, Michael. "DA's Decision Shocks Family of Slain Rapper; Charges Refused Against Suspect." *New Orleans Times-Picayune*, March 22, 2004, p. 1.
www.allhiphop.com.
www.rapnewsdirect.com.
www.sohh.com.

Spector, Phil (M)

Though just 5'5" and tipping the scales at 130 pounds, producer Phil Spector was a giant in the music industry during the late 1950s to mid–1960s and created a trademark "Wall of Sound," an innovative multiple track production technique that layered instruments and voices into a dense, echoing orchestration not previously heard in pop music. Had he produced only classic "teenage symphonies" like "I Love How You Love Me," "He's a Rebel," "Be My Baby," or the timeless Righteous Brothers classic, "You've Lost That Lovin' Feelin'," the most played record in the history of American radio, his place in rock history would have been assured. In 1970, however, years after the British pop invasion spearheaded by the Beatles had forever changed musical styles making Spector's mid–1960s work passé, John Lennon (see entry) enlisted the producer for the "Fab Four's" final album, *Let It Be* (1970). Afterwards, Lennon called upon Spector to produce his anthemic single "Imagine" (and the 1971 album of the same title) while he also produced George Harrison's *All Things Must Pass* in late 1970. Perhaps more importantly in the history of pop music, Spector turned on its head the notion that the performer was the single most important component behind a successful record as well as the entrenched notion that the producer's role was to serve him. In the studio, Spector reigned supreme and as he produced hit after hit with his "Wall of Sound" technique, the performer became almost extraneous. During Spector's golden era of the early 1960s only the Righteous Brothers emerged from his shadow and many would argue not to their ultimate advantage. By the early 1970s Spector would enter a period of professional self-exile marked by increasingly bizarre and dangerous behavior, principally towards women, that would tragically, if not inevitably, end in his mansion in Alhambra, California in the early morning hours of February 3, 2003.

Harvey Philip Spector was born of Ukrainian-Jewish ancestry on December 26, 1939 in the Bronx, New York. For reasons unclear, Spector would later add another "l" to his birth name, Philip. A small, sickly, overweight child, Spector was doted upon by his mother, Bertha, but idolized father Ben, an iron worker. Not surprisingly, an undersized intellectually active Jewish kid who had trouble making friends was constantly bullied at school. Spector was forced to spend most of his time at home in the company of his older sister, Shirley, and his overprotective mother. On April 20, 1949, the nine-year-old boy's life was irrevocably changed when his beloved father was found asphyxiated in the front seat of the family car, a rubber hose leading from its muffler into the vehicle's interior. Fatefully, the legend on Ben Spector's gravestone read "To Know Him Was to Love Him." The truth of his father's death was kept from Spector for some time, and even after he learned it was a suicide he often hid the fact from others. In 1953, the Spector family moved to Los Angeles to start a new life settling in the city's predominantly Jewish Fairfax district. The City of Angels was not a good fit for the teenager who did not like the weather or the laid back vibe. Unathletic and not particularly good looking, "Phillip" (as he now insisted he be called) spent most of his time in his bedroom listening to pop music on the radio. Music had always been in the Spector family home and the teen played French horn in the school orchestra. A quick study with the ability to sight read and improvise, Spector earned pocket money playing accordion at weddings and bar mitzvahs. Mother Bertha encouraged her socially awkward son's interest in music and on his thirteenth birthday bought him a guitar as a bar mitzvah present. Spector embraced the instrument spending every non-school moment in his room listening on the radio to the burgeoning sounds of mid–1950s rock 'n' roll and copying it on his instrument. The guitar became Spector's entrée into school society with classmates impressed by his ability to mimic the rock performers of the day. Marshall Lieb, a handsome and popular teen at Spector's school, befriended Spector and both began taking guitar lessons.

The musical life of Phil Spector, however, can be said to have begun on his fifteenth birthday when his mother took him to see Ella Fitzgerald in concert in Hollywood. In the jazz great's group that night was Barney Kessel, a highly respected and in demand L.A. session guitarist, who floored the teenager. Spector collected every record Kessel appeared on and idolized the guitarist to the point he wrote *Down Beat* a letter praising the musician. Spector's sister, Shirley, contacted Kessel, informed him her brother had written the laudatory letter to the jazz magazine, and set up a meeting between them in November 1956. The awe-struck teen hung on Kessel's every word especially his career advice to get in on the ground floor of rock 'n' roll as a songwriter or producer, both professions that had longer shelf lives than performing. Kessel took the 16 year old under his wing teaching the already accomplished Spector even more about the instrument. At school, Spector and Lieb joined the social club and with others formed a doo-wop group that played frat parties and was good enough to win a talent competition sponsored by television station KTLA. Spector graduated high school in 1957, but never forgot or forgave the imagined or real indignities he suffered there. A decade later (and now the most successful record producer in America), Spector attended his high school reunion accompanied by two bodyguards with instructions not to let anyone approach him.

Certain that his career lay in music, Spector nevertheless gave into his mother's demand that he have a fall back career as a court stenographer. Marshall Lieb and Spector enrolled in Los Angeles City College in the fall of 1957, but neither man took their respective studies seriously. In the fall of 1958, Spector took some songs he had written in to Gold Star, a small recording studio in West Hollywood where Eddie Cochran had laid down his rock 'n' roll masterpiece, "Summertime Blues." Spector, with Lieb and friend Annette Kleinbard, pulled together $40 for a two-hour recording session and as the Teddy Bears (a name inspired by the Elvis Presley hit) began laying down tracks good enough to get them a contract with a small independent label, Era Records, in July 1958. Under the terms of the contract, the Teddy Bears divided one cent between them for every copy sold with Spector earning slightly more as the songwriter and copyright holder. In the cramped Gold Star studio Spector was in his element alternately arranging material, placing microphone stands, and explaining to Lieb and Kleinbard exactly the sound he wanted. Originally intended as a "B-side" to "Don't You Worry Little Pet," Spector's composition "To Know Him Is to Love Him" was cut in one hour for $100 in mid–July 1958. Unknown to his group-mates in the Teddy Bears the song was inspired by the epitaph on his father's tombstone. By the final week of September 1958, the song was stuck at Number 88 on the *Billboard* chart until Lew Bedell, owner of Era Records, called his friend Dick Clark, the former Philadelphia disc jockey turned popular host of the teen dance television show, *American Bandstand*. Regularly played by Clark on the show, "To Know Him Is to Love Him" shot up the charts reaching Number 4 in late October 1958. On November 22, 1958, the Teddy Bears performed their hit single on *American Bandstand* launching the tune to the top of the chart, a spot it would occupy for three weeks. In Britain (a country, perhaps, more

appreciative of Spector's talents than America), the single climbed to Number 2. Before dropping off the charts four months later, "To Know Him Is to Love Him" sold nearly 1.4 million copies and forever ended any future career Spector might have had as a court stenographer.

Success changed Spector. Already a high energy combination of insecurities, overwhelming confidence, charisma, and Napoleonic ego, the 17-year-old now took firm control of the group and his future. He immediately dropped his old label for a better contract and royalty rates (3 cents a single) at Imperial Records, an L.A.–based R&B company that boasted a roster of talent that included Fats Domino and Ricky Nelson. Under relentless pressure from his mother, Bertha, Spector reluctantly agreed in January 1959 to let his sister Shirley manage the Teddy Bears. It was on a tour of one nighters and sock hops in towns along the Eastern seaboard that an incident allegedly occurred that became a pillar in the Phil Spector mythology. After a performance one evening, thugs followed the diminutive guitarist-singer into the men's room where they held him down and urinated on him. Though perhaps apocryphal, the incident would explain Spector's almost obsessive need for bodyguards later in his life. On the road, Spector and Shirley argued constantly with most of the woman's venomous attacks directed at Teddy Bears singer Anne Kleinbard. After a single and a 1959 LP, *The Teddy Bears Sing*, flopped Lieb and Kleinbard refused to sign a contract that formally named Shirley Spector as the manager of the Teddy Bears. The group died, leaving Spector an open field to pursue his dream of producing hit rock 'n' roll records.

In spring 1959, Lester Sill, sales manager of L.A. R&B label, Modern Records, contracted the 20 year old as a songwriter and producer. Sill, the man credited with discovering songwriting greats Jerry Leiber and Mike Stoller, had observed Spector in the studio producing the Teddy Bears and liked what he saw. Over the next months, Sill became Spector's mentor even allowing the aspiring producer to move in with his family to escape the withering arguments with mother Bertha. Lynn Castle, Spector's girlfriend at the time, later reported that Spector's mother disliked any woman who tried to get close to her son. More ominously, Castle experienced with the young Spector a dysfunctional pattern with women he repeatedly played out in later relationships. Overly possessive and controlling to the point of near stalking,

Spector's obsessive behavior prompted Castle to call it quits and walk away. In the spring of 1960, Spector convinced Sill to send him to New York, then the capital of the pop music industry, to learn the business from Leiber and Stoller whose songwriting collaborations for Atlantic Records had yielded such hits as "Hound Dog," "There Goes My Baby," "Charlie Brown," as well as many other hits for groups like the Coasters and the Drifters. Although the songwriters regarded the new arrival as "strange," both were impressed by the 20 year old's obvious talent and signed him to a two-year deal with their company, Trio Music. Spector used his apprenticeship under Leiber and Stoller to absorb standard recording techniques and make powerful connections within the pop music industry. He produced the Ray Peterson song "Corinna, Corinna" which peaked at Number 9 on the charts in November 1960, and followed up his success by writing "Spanish Harlem" with Leiber and Stoller for former Drifters front man Ben E. King. The track peaked at Number 10 in January 1961.

Near the end of 1960, Spector met Ahmet Ertegun, co-founder of Atlantic Records, who was so impressed with the 21 year old that he offered him a job as his personal assistant and staff producer at the R&B label. Leiber and Stoller felt understandably betrayed by Spector's lack of loyalty to them, but were unable to block his departure when informed by the producer that his contract with Trio Music was invalid — he was underaged when he signed it. The brash producer was unliked by colleagues at Atlantic and his brief tenure there failed to produce any hits. The Atlantic experience, however, did provide Spector with the opportunity to further develop his signature sound by the use of echo and the radical placement of microphones in the studio. Of note, Spector began seeing a psychiatrist in 1960 and continued to do so for the rest of his life. Realizing he was not a great songwriter and needed strong material to perform his magic in the studio, Spector sought out Don Kirshner, president of New York City–based Aldon Music, and a man renowned in the industry as possessing an ear that could immediately determine if a song had hit potential. Although Kirshner found the dictatorial producer odd, he recognized talent when he saw it. Underwritten by Kirshner and given access to the company's songwriters, Spector entered the studio in mid–1961 with the Paris Sisters and produced the heavily string laden hit, "I Love How

You Love Me." The single entered the charts in October 1961 and shot to Number 5. The Kirshner-Spector relationship was already finished, however, hastened by the producer's unwillingness to recognize any authority but his own. Spector needed to be his own boss to fully realize his vision in the studio and when the opportunity to be independent presented itself in early 1961 he was ready to make a bold career move.

As partners, Phil Spector and Lester Sill formed Philles ("Phil" and "Les") Records, a label that gave the producer complete artistic control over his music. Spector, already acknowledged in the industry as the king of the girl group, stole The Crystals away from another label and in late 1962 had them in Gold Star studio recording the Gene Pitney composition, "He's a Rebel." Among the first records to feature Spector's "Wall of Sound," the 23-year-old employed two guitarists, two bass players, and numerous other "shadow" instruments playing the same lines hour after hour in the studio until the sound was just right. The single charted Number 1 in November 1962. Suspicious that his partner was holding out on royalties, Spector bought out Sill for $60,000 in the summer of 1962. Spector now had total control over the label and its master recordings. Assembling a core of 25 musicians known as the "Wrecking Crew," Spector continued to refine his signature recording style grounded in the idea that multiple instruments played in unison when combined with the creative placement of microphones in the studio would create a "Wall of Sound" ideal for the "teen symphonies" he was creating with acts like Bob B Soxx and the Blue Jeans, and Darlene Love. In 1963, back-to-back hits with The Crystals ("Da Doo Ron Ron" and "Then He Kissed Me") solidified Spector's position as the most successful rock 'n' roll producer in the United States. The records also made him a multimillionaire.

On February 18, 1963, Spector married high school friend Annette Merar in New York City, but the marriage was doomed from the outset. A workaholic, Spector flew back to Los Angeles the day after the wedding to persuade an all-girl black trio, The Ronettes, to sign with Philles Records. The group signed in March 1963 and by late July 1963 Spector had them in the studio recording "Be My Baby," a song he had co-written. The attraction between producer and Veronica ("Ronnie") Bennett, the curvaceous lead singer for The Ronettes, was immediate and reciprocal. Spector liked being seen with the sexy singer while Ronnie, at some level, undoubtedly saw the influential producer as a way to further a solo career. "Be My Baby" rocketed to Number 2 on the charts, but in spite of his obsession with his new lover, Spector was unable to produce another Top Ten hit with the group. In January 1964, he traveled to Britain to finalize a deal with Decca to release his Philles product. The Beatles were in the process of revolutionizing rock music and, with Bob Dylan, would herald in a new musical era in which performers able to write their own music would replace professional songwriters and redefine the producer's role in the studio from that of autocrat to collaborator. During his stay in Britain, Spector spent time with the Beatles while The Ronettes toured with the Rolling Stones. John Lennon venerated Spector's music and the two men became close friends. The producer was on the Pan Am flight from Heathrow with the Beatles that touched down at JFK Airport in New York on February 7, 1964, a date that signaled the "official" launching of the "British Invasion" in American rock 'n' roll.

Back in America, Spector attempted unsuccessfully to reconcile with neglected wife Annette Merar (fuming over his affair with Ronnie Bennett) while trying to produce a record that could challenge the Beatles' monumental single "I Want to Hold Your Hand." In October 1964, Spector went into Gold Star studio with the Righteous Brothers, baritone Bill Medley and tenor Bobby Hatfield, to record the single, "You've Lost That Lovin' Feelin'." The duo offered the producer a way to break loose of the girl group rut of The Crystals and The Ronettes while presenting two white men who would be easier to market on radio and television. Spector gave the song (which featured Medley's near solo performance) the complete "Wall of Sound" treatment letting the emotion grow over the song's "official" label time of three minutes and sixteen seconds (it is longer) rather than limiting himself to the industry standard pop tune length of 2:30. Considered by most critics to be the pinnacle of Spector's career as a producer, "You've Lost That Lovin' Feelin'" was released in December 1964 and was Number 1 by Christmas. To date, it remains the most played song in the history of American radio. Spector produced two other Top Ten Hits for the blue-eyed soul duo ("Just Once in My Life" and "Unchained Melody") before an acrimonious breakup sent Medley and Hatfield to MGM. Heralded as

the "Tycoon of Teen," Spector was nevertheless musically living on borrowed time ... and he knew it. *Rubber Soul*, the Beatles December 1965 album, ushered in the rise of the LP over the single while the L.A. music scene was being dominated by performing bands like the Byrds who either covered Dylan songs or wrote their own socially conscious material. As 1965 was ending, Merar divorced her wandering husband, who responded by purchasing a 21 room mansion at 1200 La Collina Drive in the heart of Beverly Hills and setting up house with Ronnie Bennett.

Painfully aware of the forces of change within the music industry he felt were marginalizing his hard won importance, the 26-year-old record company owner looked to prove his relevancy with a work of undeniable brilliance that would reaffirm his premier standing. In the autumn of 1965, Spector saw Ike and Tina Turner perform and was mesmerized by the woman's incredible voice and feral sexuality. In late 1965, Spector presented the Turners with a simple proposition — he would give them a Number 1 record, but only if Ike was in no way involved in the production. Ike Turner willingly agreed, but only after ensuring his name would appear on the record. During the first weeks of 1966, Spector and Tina Turner entered the studio to create the producer's magnum opus, the single "River Deep–Mountain High," over a marathon five sessions that cost $22,000 to complete. The overproduced single was released on May 14, 1966, stalled at Number 88, and was gone from the charts in five weeks. In Britain, however, the song was a hit peaking at Number 2. Feeling betrayed by the American public, Spector took out ads in the trades which read, "Benedict Arnold Was Right." He closed Philles Records in 1967 and after appearing in a small role as a drug dealer in *Easy Rider* (1968) retreated behind the walls of his Beverly Hills mansion to live in near seclusion with his bodyguards, servants, and Ronnie Bennett.

On April 14, 1968, Phil Spector married Ronnie in a small ceremony in Beverly Hills City Hall. According to Ronnie in her book, *Be My Baby*, living with the troubled record producer was sheer hell. Spector slept all day and spent nights alone in his locked study, or, in endlessly watching the film, *Citizen Kane*. Ronnie soon felt like a prisoner in the mansion with her every moved monitored by intercoms her husband had installed in every room. Four months after the wedding, she filed for divorce but withdrew the petition. Bored, frustrated, and no longer performing, Mrs. Spector began drinking more heavily and took to hiding booze in the house. After watching a television program on adoption, Ronnie decided to adopt a child she named Donte Phillip Spector. Husband Phil was initially a doting father, but soon lost interest. In February 1969, he tossed Ronnie a professional bone and recorded the single "You Came, You Saw, You Conquered," released under the name of The Ronettes, Featuring the Voice of Veronica. When the single tanked Ronnie's depression deepened and she drank more. Terrified by the Manson Family murders in August 1969 (see entry Sharon Tate), Spector became even more security conscious and ordered the installation of barbed wire fences and attack dogs on the mansion property. Ronnie, in her perpetually drunken state, viewed her husband's safety precautions as just another expression of control over her not much different than ordering her to hide upstairs out of sight whenever company visited. In an ill-conceived ploy to bind Ronnie even more closely to him, Spector adopted two six-year-old twins, Gary and Louis, without bothering to inform his wife. As Ronnie descended into alcoholism, even welcoming her weekly Alcoholics Anonymous meetings as a way to escape the mansion if only for an afternoon, Spector's own out of control drinking resulted in bizarre and embarrassing public incidents. In January 1972, Spector was arrested at a club in L.A. for pointing a gun at a woman. He was cited for "conspicuous carelessness," fined $200, placed on one year probation, and ordered not to possess any dangerous weapons. Following a brutal physical confrontation in the mansion with her drunken husband, Ronnie filed for divorce on June 12, 1972. The marriage was dissolved in 1974 with Ronnie walking away with only $50,000 in community property, no interests in any of Spector's businesses, and $2,500 a month spousal support for three years. Spector was awarded sole custody of the three children.

During the years his marriage to Ronnie was tortuously unravelling Spector periodically tried to revive his career as a major record producer. In January 1969, John Lennon invited him to London to take over production of a rough collection of Beatles songs tentatively titled "Get Back" that would become the group's final album, *Let It Be*. Lennon and McCartney were in the middle of a bitter band-killing feud and could agree on nothing. Lennon and Harrison, both huge fans of

Spector and the "Wall of Sound," were pro–Spector while McCartney disliked the producer and his music. Ringo was willing to support anyone who could finish the album and get him out of the studio. Although McCartney was furious over Spector's flowery arrangement of his composition "The Long and Winding Road," the critically panned song (the Beatles' last single) sold 1.2 million units in two days. *Let It Be* was awarded a Grammy. Impressed by Spector's work on the album, George Harrison asked him to produce his first solo album, the two record *All Things Must Pass*. At the sessions from May to August 1970, Spector filled the Abbey Road studio with three drummers (including James Beck Gordon, see entry), four pianos, and four guitars in an attempt to recreate the "Wall of Sound." Harrison, weary of the endless takes, quickly angered Spector by showing signs of boredom with the production. The producer began drinking and his behavior fluctuated wildly between kindness and anger. Often drunk in the control room, Spector left England in August 1970 after laying down the basic tracks. Released in November 1970, *All Things Must Pass* was hailed as a critical masterpiece rising to Number 4 in Britain and spending seven weeks at Number 1 in America. The Spector-produced single "My Sweet Lord" charted Number 1 in both countries, the first single by an ex–Beatle to earn that distinction.

In December 1970, Spector signed with close friend John Lennon and his wife, Yoko Ono, to produce their album, *John Lennon — Plastic Ono Band*. Largely on the strength of the hit single "Instant Karma," the LP rose to Number 6 on the *Billboard* chart. In mid–1971, Spector produced Lennon's classic *Imagine* album and the anthemic single of the same title. "Imagine" shot to Number 3 on the U.S. chart and is universally acknowledged as the masterpiece of John Lennon's post-Beatles career. Spector and Lennon reunited in 1973 to produce an album of rock standards designed to get the ex–Beatle back to some semblance of financial solvency. Separated from Yoko Ono and living a life of drunken dissolution in Los Angeles, John Lennon was on the verge of a nervous breakdown. While in the studio recording the album *Rock 'n' Roll* the mood quickly turned sour. Both men were binge drinkers and the tension in the sessions as hour after unproductive hour passed was palpable. Spector took to wearing a shoulder holster and once accidentally fired his gun while waving it in Lennon's direction to make a point. The record and their friendship ended bitterly when Spector, who had paid for the sessions, left with the master tapes and refused to return them to Lennon or the record company. Ultimately, federal marshalls were called in to retrieve the hostage tapes. Released in 1975, the album was unmemorable. Spector's only other musical collaborations of note were with Canadian poet-songwriter Leonard Cohen in 1978 (*Death of a Ladies' Man*) and with the New York punk rock band The Ramones in 1979–1980 (*End of the Century*). While recording with Cohen, the drunken producer pressed a gun into the singer's neck and threatened to pull the trigger. The Ramones, worn out by Spector's endless retakes, never again worked with him.

The murder of John Lennon on December 8, 1990, deeply affected Phil Spector. He briefly stopped drinking and married girlfriend Janis Zavala in 1982 after she gave birth to twins. A devoted husband and family man, Spector was living comfortably on the income generated by the selective licensing of his classic catalog to motion pictures. In 1986, he moved out of the mansion in Beverly Hills and into another heavily fortified estate in Pasadena. Three years later, he was inducted into the Rock and Roll Hall of Fame in the "nonperformer" category. At the induction ceremony in New York City, Spector was so drunk he could barely ramble through an incoherent acceptance speech prior to being ushered off-stage. On December 25, 1991, Phil Spector suffered an emotional shock from which he never fully recovered. The death by leukemia of his nine-year-old son with Zavala, Phillip, Jr., effectively curtailed the 52-year-old's public life. Zavala and Spector had separated shortly before the boy's death leaving the former producer who had not made a record in over a decade alone in the mansion with only alcohol, prescription antidepressants, servants, and a bodyguard as company. The next decade was spent in momentary involvements in projects that never reached fruition, drinking, and being periodically honored by an industry who while recognizing his status as a legend, nevertheless now viewed him as an out-of-step eccentric who liked to wave guns around.

Lana Jean Clarkson, born in Long Beach, California, on April 5, 1962, was only six months old when Spector produced the Number 1 hit "He's a Rebel" for the Ronettes. An excellent athlete, Clarkson played basketball in high school and soon after the family moved to the San Fernando Valley area of Los Angeles the beautiful 6' blonde and buxom 16 year old was booking modeling shoots in Japan, Switzerland, France, and Mexico. Small parts in several television shows (*CHiPs, Laverne and Shirley, Hill Street Blues, Fantasy Island*) led to her first speaking role in director Cameron Crowe's 1981 teenage comedy, *Fast Times at Ridgemont High*. The 18 year old played the improbably beautiful wife of "Mr. Vargas," the school's nerdy science teacher, and spoke one line, "Hi." In *Brainstorm*, the 1983 science fiction movie that marked Natalie Wood's last screen appearance, Clarkson played the uncredited "Food Fantasy Girl." That same year the beautiful Hollywood newcomer also appeared in the Al Pacino vehicle, *Scarface*, as one of the dancers in the Babylon Club. Clarkson's movie career, however, did not ignite until 1985 when B-movie director Roger Corman (impressed by her in a small role in his 1983 film, *Deathstalker*) cast her as the lead, "Amathea," in his 1985 sword-and-sorcery epic, *Barbarian Queen*. The low-budget campy film allowed Clarkson to display her athleticism as well as her semi-nude body splayed across a rack in the film's memorable torture scene. The movie, said to have inspired the Lucy Lawless television series, *Xena: The Warrior Princess*, made Clarkson a "star" in the insular fan world of the genre and a staple at fantasy film conventions and comic book shows. Following an appearance as the stacked alien, "Alpha Beta," in *Amazon Women on the Moon* (1987), Clarkson returned to the genre which had made her famous with two 1989 featured roles as a scantily clad swordswoman in *Barbarian Queen II: The Empress Strikes Back* ("Amathea") and *Wizards of the Lost Kingdom II* ("Athalia"). The 1990 exploitation film, *The Haunting of Morella*, in which Clarkson portrayed an evil governess with lesbian overtones, marked the downward arc of her acting career. Over the next decade, the beautiful, but aging, actress appeared on several television shows (*Silk Stalkings, Land's End*), worked as a print and commercial model for Mercedes-Benz, Kmart, Playtex, and had roles in the motion pictures *Love in Paris* (1997), *Vice Girls* (2000), and the 2001 independent film, *March*. In December 2002, the 40-year-old actress needed a job that would help both pay the rent and keep her at least nominally in the eye of key Hollywood players. Around Christmas, Clarkson became the hostess in the Foundation (VIP) Room at the House of Blues on Sunset Boulevard across from the Chateau Marmont hotel. Membership in the VIP lounge cost $1,000 a year and the venue was recognized as a favored watering hole for music and film industry bigwigs.

Phil Spector, a member of the Foundation Room, entered the VIP lounge with friend, Kathy Sullivan, at 1:30 A.M. on February 3, 2003. The 63-year-old record producer with Sullivan in tow had spent the early part of the evening drinking at places like Trader Vic's and Dan Tana's restaurant. By the time Spector arrived at the Foundation Room it was estimated he had imbibed four daiquiris and two Navy Grogs all containing liberal shots of rum. According to a later statement made by his limousine driver, Adriano De Souza, Spector was already slurring his words as he walked in the House of Blues. At the lounge, Spector ordered a straight shot of rum and became incensed when Sullivan opted for water. Spector called hostess Lana Clarkson over to the table and ordered her to take Sullivan to the limousine with instructions for De Souza to drive the woman home then return for him. The record producer and the actress spoke together for some time while waiting for the limo driver to return without Kathy Sullivan. Clarkson clocked out at 2:21 A.M. and escorted the producer to the waiting 1965 Rolls-Royce Silver Cloud after he left a $450 tip for an $8.50 rum and a $5 water. Spector asked Clarkson to go home with him, she refused, but did accept his invitation to drive her to her car. En route, he repeatedly pressed the invitation until the worn down actress agreed to accompany him to the 33-room mansion he had purchased in 1998, the Pyrenees Castle, atop a hill in suburban Alhambra, a working class neighborhood east of Los Angeles. The limo arrived at the heavily fortified mansion at around 3:45 A.M. De Souza let the couple out at the bottom of the hill and together they walked up a flight of stone steps to the castle's front door while he drove the car up the hill and parked it in the roundabout near the back door. De Souza was waiting in the Rolls to return Clarkson to her car in Hollywood when Spector emerged from the back door 15 minutes later and retrieved a DVD player from the backseat of the vehicle. Sometime before 5:00 A.M., De Souza heard a gunshot (he told police "a popping noise") and exited the limo to investigate. Spector emerged from the mansion's back door carrying a revolver with a blood smear across the back of his hand. "I think I killed somebody," the dazed producer told De Souza. Looking past Spec-

tor into the hallway, De Souza could see the blonde actress slumped in a chair, her face awash with blood. Shaken, the driver tried to call 911 on his cell phone, but failing, left the message, "You have to come here. I think Mr. Spector killed somebody," on the answering machine of Michelle Blaine, the producer's personal assistant.

Shortly after 5:00 A.M., police responded to De Souza's repeated 911 call, forced open the iron gates at 1700 Grandview, and cautiously approached the Pyrenees Castle. Spector let the officers into the house, but after refusing their numerous requests to remove his hands from his pockets, was Tasered at least three times (none of shocks appeared to work). The 5'5" record producer was wrestled to the floor and handcuffed. Clarkson, dead from a single gunshot wound to the face, was slumped in a chair, her broken teeth scattered across the foyer. A blood spattered unregistered .38-caliber Colt six-shot revolver with one spent cartridge was found under the woman's left leg. In a conversation taped at the scene, Spector told officers "the gun went off accidentally" and that he was "just gonna go to sleep." A search of the mansion yielded an additional 13 guns and ammunition identical to that in the gun which had killed the actress. Lana Clarkson was pronounced dead at 6:24 A.M. A toxicology test by the coroner's office revealed her blood alcohol level was .12 percent and she had "therapeutic levels" of Vicodin in her system. A verbally abusive and seemingly inebriated Phil Spector was booked into the Alhambra police station around 6:28 A.M. A urine test taken 13 hours after the shooting registered his blood alcohol level at .08 percent, the legal floor for intoxication in California. During his subsequent interrogation, Spector told detectives Clarkson had taken the gun in her hand, put it to her head, and pulled the trigger. At 7:00 P.M. that day, Spector's attorney, Robert Shapiro (see O.J. Simpson entry), freed his client on $1 million bail. As Shapiro assembled a forensics dream team to prove Clarkson had committed suicide, Spector (no doubt on the advice of counsel) went on the offensive to argue his innocence in the media. First in *Esquire* (July 2003) and then in *Vanity Fair*, the producer maintained that a drunken Clarkson produced a firearm and "kissed the gun" before firing the fatal shot into her mouth. Seven-and-a-half months after the shooting, the Los Angeles County Coroner ruled Clarkson's death a homicide, and Spector was formally charged with her murder on November 20, 2003. If convicted of murder with the use of a firearm (a sentence enhancement), Spector faced the possibility of spending a minimum 15 years in a California penitentiary. In January 2004, the producer fired Robert Shapiro claiming that under the guise of friendship the attorney lined his pockets with over $1 million in non-returnable fees. Shortly afterwards, he hired celebrity attorney Leslie Abramson, a woman well-known for her aggressive cross-examination and powers of persuasion. Abramson lasted less than eight months before abruptly resigning. Bruce Cutler, best known for his successful defenses of Mafia crime boss, John Gotti, was her replacement. In 2005 as a trial date was still in the distant future, Spector met Rachelle ("Chelle") Short, a songwriter-entertainer 40 years his junior, and the couple married in a ceremony conducted in September 2006 in the foyer where Clarkson was killed.

On April 25, 2007, more than four years after the death of Lana Clarkson, Phil Spector went on trial resplendent in a revolving wardrobe of Edwardian suits and a parade of outlandish wigs. Cutler, whose role in the defense dwindled over the course of the trial, attacked the English language skills of Brazilian-born driver Adriano De Souza maintaining Spector had not told the man he had "killed somebody." Describing De Souza as an illegal alien who was "taking a siesta" at the time of Clarkson's suicide, the defense team questioned the meaning of the driver's statements to police. More difficult to overcome, however, were statements made by five women who all testified they had endured physically intimidating "gun dates" with Spector. With each, the producer had brandished a gun at them when they asked to leave his company. Spector's high power and expensive forensics team headed by Drs. Henry Lee and Michael Baden argued the blood spray and dispersal of teeth fragments in the mansion's foyer was consistent with a self-inflicted gunshot wound, not a murder. In a bid to portray the struggling actress as a self-deluded hanger-on in Hollywood, the defense played "Lana Unleashed," a portfolio videotape Clarkson had made to showcase her talents to would-be employers. The argument fell flat. Witness after witness stepped forward to insist Clarkson was not depressed at the time of her death, but looked forward to the future. As the evidentiary phase of the trial wound down, Bruce Cutler announced in September 2007 that he was leaving the defense team. Remarkably, a mistrial was declared on September 26, 2007, after

the jury hopelessly deadlocked on a 10–2 vote to convict the record producer of second-degree murder.

On October 29, 2008, the 69-year-old Spector again found himself in a Los Angeles courtroom to be judged by a six-man, six-woman jury. Gone were his team of five lawyers from the first trial and in their stead was attorney Doron Weinberg. Also largely absent in the early days of the proceedings was the mainstream media that had turned the first trial into a circus. Weinberg faced the unenviable task of discounting the damning testimony of the five women who stepped forward to describe in excruciating detail their "gun dates" with the eccentric musical genius. In the end, all he could do was attack De Souza's English, try to raise doubt as to the interpretation and validity of the forensic evidence, and to assassinate the character of the victim as a failed actress who chose to take her own life in a stranger's mansion in a moment of drunkenness. Deputy District Attorney Alan Jackson derided Spector's defense experts as "hired guns" whose testimony had cost $419,000 all in an attempt to prove a depressed Clarkson committed suicide. On the morning of the day before she died, the actress purchased eight pairs of shoes and responded, "I can't wait," to a party invitation. More compelling, perhaps, was Deputy District Attorney Truc Do's assessment of Phil Spector's pattern of behavior with women as devastatingly portrayed by the earlier testimony. Ultimately, Do argued, "This case is about a man who has had a history of playing Russian roulette with the lives of women. Five women got the empty chamber. Lana got the sixth bullet." Six years and two months after Clarkson's death, the jury deliberated 30 hours prior to finding Spector guilty on April 13, 2003, of second-degree murder with the use of a firearm. On May 29, 2009, the 69-year-old Rock and Roll Hall of Famer received a mandatory life sentence of which he must serve 19 years before becoming eligible for parole. His bail application denied, Spector was taken immediately into custody as Doron Weinberg vowed an appeal based largely on his contention that the testimony of his client's five "gun dates" should never have been admitted into evidence. The record producer still faces a "wrongful death" civil suit filed in January 2005 by Donna Clarkson, mother of the slain actress. At the time of this book's publication, Phil Spector is housed in the "sensitive-needs yard" at the California Substance Abuse Treatment Facility and State Prison in

Corcoran. Wife Rachelle Spector, 29, manages the producer's vast catalog and steadfastly maintains her husband's innocence.

Further Reading

Brown, Mick. *Tearing Down the Wall of Sound: The Rise and Fall of Phil Spector.* New York: Knopf, 2007.

Ribowsky, Mark. *He's a Rebel: Phil Spector—Rock and Roll's Legendary Producer.* New ed. Cambridge, MA: Da Capo, 2006.

Smith, Carlton. *Reckless: Millionaire Record Producer Phil Spector and the Violent Death of Lana Clarkson.* New York: St. Martin's, 2004.

Spector, Ronnie. *Be My Baby: How I Survived Mascara, Miniskirts, and Madness, or My Life as a Fabulous Ronette.* New York: Harmony, 1990.

Thompson, Dave. *Wall of Pain: The Biography of Phil Spector.* London: Sanctuary, 2003.

Stahl, Jennifer (V)

The daughter of affluent parents in Titusville, New Jersey, the vivacious, blue-eyed blonde had what friends called a "rebellious" streak. In the mid–1980s, Stahl was settled in New York City studying ballet and trying to break into movies. She appeared in a small part in the forgettable 1986 film *Necropolis* and worked occasionally at strip clubs in New Jersey. While awaiting her big break, Stahl sold pot to make ends meet. That break appeared to come in 1987 when producers of the film *Dirty Dancing* were scouting for good-looking kids that could dance and work for cheap. Stahl fit the bill on both counts. The young hopeful was cast as a "dirty dancer" to provide background action behind the gyrations of stars Patrick Swayze and Jennifer Grey. The film was a smash, but Stahl managed only to capitalize on its success by briefly teaching a "How to Dirty Dance" class in 1988 in Rockland County. Dreams of a movie career ended with minuscule parts in *Firehouse* (1987) and *I'm Your Man* (1992).

Divorced, estranged from her parents, and no longer a member of Actors' Equity, Stahl shifted her career focus to singing. She converted a room in her apartment five stories above the Carnegie Delicatessen in Midtown Manhattan into a soundproof recording studio and cut a CD as "Calamity Jen" that sold poorly in Japan. As her singing career tanked, Stahl expanded her pot dealing. Claiming to work for an R&B record company, the former dirty dancer sold high grade marijuana to a select clientele out of her apartment in a Donald Trump owned building at 854 Seventh Avenue. Inside her front door, a cardboard sign listed prices for a half-dozen types of exotic grass selling from $300 to $600 an ounce.

Stahl's motto to her handpicked customers: "Buy more, come less." Though never busted in New York City, Stahl was on a watchlist of possible drug dealers coming in and out of Puerto Rico and Barbados.

On the evening of May 10, 2001, as tourists ate at the popular Carnegie Delicatessen, Stahl, 39, was relaxing in her sixth-floor apartment with some friends (not connected with her drug business). Anthony Veader, 37, a hair stylist who had worked on the sets of movies (*Men in Black*, 1997; *8mm*, 1999) was cutting Stahl's hair as she drank wine with Rosemond Dane and musician Charles Helliwell, III, both 36, who had arrived that day from the Virgin Islands to attend a wedding in New Jersey. Also present was Stephen King, 32, an accomplished trombonist from Michigan who planned to record in Stahl's apartment sound studio. At 7:27 P.M. two men wearing bandanas (caught on the building's surveillance camera) climbed the stairs to the drug dealer's apartment. According to a surviving witness, Stahl opened the door to them, called one of them "Sean," and was forced by the man into the adjacent recording studio. The man's companion ordered Veader and King to the floor and used duct tape to bind King's hands and feet. From the recording room, Stahl could be heard saying, "Take the money, take the money. Take the drugs. Don't hurt anybody." A single shot was fired. Dane and Helliwell emerged from a third room and were forced to the ground by the gunman. Helliwell's hands and feet were bound then Veader heard the sounds of multiple gunshots including one that grazed his head. The assailants fled the scene with a book bag filled with about $1,000 in cash and a dozen one-fourth ounce bags of pot. In all they had been in the building five minutes and forty seconds. The wounded Veader called 911 and police quickly arrived at the scene as diners at the delicatessen below wondered what all the fuss was about. Helliwell and King died instantly from execution-style gunshot wounds to the back of the head. Stahl expired in the Weill Cornell Medical Center a few hours later from a pistol shot to her forehead. Dane and Veader survived with head wounds lucky, according to one investigator, that the shootings had been a "rush job." On the street below, one observer called the scene "like something out of *Law & Order*. It was pandemonium. There were police cars backing down Seventh Avenue, police horses in full gallop."

Evidence at the scene linked Joseph Sean Salley,

29, and Andre S. Smith, 31, to the carnage in Apartment 9. Salley, a one-time production worker for musician George Clinton and the P-Funk All-Stars, had a rap sheet covered with charges for assault, robbery, and weapons possessions in three states. According to police, Salley's music industry connection linked him to Stahl through her home recording studio. Smith, Salley's suspected confederate, was on parole for a violent robbery committed in 1993 when the so-called Carnegie Deli murders occurred. In fact, the convicted felon should never have been on the street. Arrested in New Jersey in February 2001 (three months prior to the murders) on charges of possessing 311 grams of marijuana near an Irvington public school, Smith should have been immediately jailed for the parole violation, but was not due to an oversight by New Jersey state officials. On May 22, 2001, Smith was arrested by New York authorities after he confessed to taking part in the robbery and tying up the victims. According to Smith, his partner Salley was the triggerman. "I saw Sean walk over calmly to each person and shoot each one once in the back of their necks," Smith wrote in his statement. Salley allegedly told him that he knew of a woman drug dealer who "(sold) weed to the high-class music industry people." The plan, as it was presented to Smith, was to strong-arm Stahl into handing over the drugs and money. Salley remained at-large for over two months before a segment featuring his case on the television show *America's Most Wanted* led to his arrest in Miami, Florida, on July 15, 2001. Salley admitted accidentally shooting Stahl with a gun given to him by Smith, but insisted his accomplice shot the other four people so they could not later identify him. Due to their conflicting confessions, prosecutors did not have enough evidence to charge Smith and Salley with the capital crime of first-degree murder. Instead, both defendants were charged with second-degree murder and tried simultaneously in the same New York City courtroom, but with different juries in May 2002. Seven weeks later on June 18, 2002, Joseph Sean Salley was found guilty of three counts of second-degree murder and two robbery counts. Andre S. Smith was also found guilty on murder counts even though prosecutors maintained Salley alone shot all the victims. Both subsequently received the maximum 120 year to life prison term and are eligible for parole after serving 116 years.

Further Reading

Barry, Dan. "A Fading Actress, a Pile of Drugs and 3 Slayings." *The New York Times*, May 12, 2001, sec. A, p. 6.

Saulny, Susan. "Survivors Recount Details of Killings Above Carnegie Deli for 2 Juries." *The New York Times*, June 5, 2002, sec. B, p. 1.

Stiles, Grady F., Jr. (V)

Born in Pittsburgh, Pennsylvania, on July 18, 1937 with ectrodactyly, a genetic defect commonly known as lobster-claw syndrome, Stiles was seven or eight when he joined his similarly afflicted father in a side show attraction billed as the "Lobster Family." Stiles, a fixture on the carnival circuit for many years, exhibited his pincer-like hands-feet and stunted body as "Lobster Boy" before retiring from performing to become an independent side show operator. Recognized by his peers as a shrewd businessman who turned a devastating congenital deformity into a marketable asset, Stiles was widely respected by the carnival community as a man who cared for his family and often took in workers who had no place to stay. To his family, however, "Lobster Boy" was a violent alcoholic who, in 1978, murdered his oldest daughter's boyfriend with a shotgun in Pennsylvania. He was convicted of third-degree murder, but sentenced to only 15 years probation due largely to the fact the Pennsylvania prison system was not set up to accommodate a prisoner with his disability.

On Sunday, November 29, 1992, Stiles, 55, was in the trailer at 11117 Inglewood Drive in Gibsonton, Florida, he shared with his wife, Mary Teresa Stiles, 54, and her son by another marriage, 18-year-old Harry Glenn Newman, III. In 1973, Mary Stiles divorced "Lobster Boy" and married Harry Glenn Newman, a midget billed on the carnival circuit as the "World's Smallest Man." She remarried Stiles in 1988 bringing her son by Newman with her to be raised by the carnival performer. Gibsonton, an unincorporated area south of Tampa known as Showton, was a popular rest site for weary carnival and circus performers during the winter months when touring was traditionally suspended. On the night of the tragedy, Grady Stiles was alone in the living room of the trailer seated in a recliner in his underwear drinking heavily, smoking Pall Malls, and watching the video *Monkey Boy*. Mary Stiles and Newman were visiting a nearby relative when around 11:30 P.M. a gunman entered the trailer through an unlocked door and pumped three shots into the back of the man's head. Twenty-four hours later, police arrested

Mary Stiles and Harry Newman who confessed paying $1,500 to 17-year-old neighbor turned hitman, Christopher Wyant. Dennis John Cowell, 18, was also arrested for attempted murder after leading authorities to a wood where he buried the murder weapon, a Colt .32-caliber automatic. Police suspected Cowell of helping Wyant purchase the gun in exchange for some of the money paid to the contract killer.

In custody, Mary Stiles painted a horrific picture of life with "Lobster Boy," one in which she was regularly beaten, head butted, choked, and sexually abused by the deformed one-time side show attraction. Eventually, everyone related to Stiles told their own stories of his alcoholic rages, violent beatings, and nearly continuous threats to kill them all. In June 1993, a Hillsborough Circuit judge ruled the woman and her son could plead the battered spouse and syndrome defense, the first time such a defense was ever permitted in a murder-for-hire case in the state of Florida. Challenged by the prosecution, the ruling was working its way through the state appeals process when teen hitman Christopher Wyant was convicted on January 19, 2004, on the lesser count of second-degree murder and conspiracy to commit murder. Wyant was sentenced to 27 years on each count with the sentences to be served concurrently. Dennis Cowell, the teen who helped buy the gun then bury it, pleaded guilty to being an accessory after the fact in May 1994 and received a prison term of 3½ years.

At trial in Tampa, defense attorney Arnold Levine argued Mary Stiles acted in self-defense when she and her son set up the murder-for-hire scheme. "In spite of his deformities, he was a powerful, powerful man," Levine said. "When he was drunk and wanted to take it out on you — he did." Unable to leave because of the man's threats to kill them, the entire family was held hostage by his cruelty. Even Stiles' own birth son (also afflicted with electrodactyly as was his sister and her child) felt a sense of relief at his father's murder telling authorities "now we don't have to worry about the yelling, the beatings and threats." While the prosecution sympathized with the victimized woman, it was argued she had other alternatives besides murder to escape the physical and psychological terror of life with "Lobster Boy." On July 28, 1994, Mary Stiles escaped a first-degree murder conviction when she was found guilty of the lesser charge of manslaughter with a firearm and conspiracy to commit murder. She was sub-

sequently sentenced to 12 years in prison tearfully telling the sympathetic judge, "I am sorry. But my family is safe now." In a separate trial, Harry Glenn Newman, III, known on the side show circuit as the "Human Blockhead" for his ability to hammer nails into his nose, was found guilty of first-degree murder and conspiracy to commit first-degree murder. He was sentenced to life in prison without the possibility of parole for 25 years. Grady Stiles, Jr., the infamous "Lobster Boy," is buried in the International Independent Showmen Garden of Memorials in Thonotosassa, Florida.

Further Reading

McIver, Stuart. *Murder in the Tropics*. Sarasota, FL: Pineapple, 1995.
Rosen, Fred. *Lobster Boy*. New York: Kensington, 1995.

Stohn, Carl, Jr. (V)

With Tony DeSantis, Stohn helped establish the Drury Lane Theatre South in Chicago in 1953. In addition to producing several plays at the theatre in Evergreen Park, he was also active with the Pheasant Run Playhouse in St. Charles, Illinois from its opening in 1964 until leaving in 1978 over a disagreement with the administration over their abandonment of the star system approach for the dinner theatre. Though just beginning a job with Chicago's John Waggoner Art Gallery in 1980, Stohn was actively exploring options on how to return to theatrical production. In the meantime, he had a small role in the James Caan film *Thief* being filmed on location in the Windy City.

On August 21, 1980, the 58-year-old producer left the movie set around 1:45 A.M. and was on his way to pick up his dog at a friend's house when he was confronted on the street by some black men. After a brief argument, Stohn was shot once in the forehead in front of 950 N. La Salle Street across from the Henrotin Hospital on the city's Near North Side. Stohn's empty wallet was found at the scene, but in their haste to leave the robbers had no time to search his clothing. On September 16, 1980, what would have been the producer's 59th birthday, two dozen of Stohn's closest friends including comedienne Phyllis Diller and *Sun-Times* columnist Irv Kupcinet (whose daughter, Karyn Kupcinet (see entry) was also a murder victim) remembered him at a tribute held at the Drury Lane Theatre. Announced at the event was the establishment of a memorial fund in Stohn's name to benefit off–Loop theatres in the Chicago area.

In November 1980, two men were charged with Stohn's murder after unrelated arrests made by the Gang Crimes unit of the Chicago Police Department led to their being implicated. Melvin Burnett, 25, identified as the leader of the South Street Disciples currently on probation for a robbery conviction, admitted shooting Stohn and fingered 20-year-old accomplice Billy Martin then in the Cook County Jail for robbery. Under questioning, the pair described the producer's murder as a random robbery that escalated to murder when Stohn refused to give Martin his wallet, and in the ensuing struggle was shot by Burnett. In January 1982, a judge citing Melvin Burnett's diminished mental capacity ignored the district attorney's request for the death penalty and sentenced the gang leader to a ninety year prison term. Burnett will be eligible for parole at the age of 71. Accomplice Martin received a 75 year sentence.

Further Reading

McCabe, Michael. "Theater Producer Carl Stohn Is Slain." *Chicago Tribune*, August 22, 1980, p. 2.

Stratten, Dorothy (V) (M–S)

In the nearly half century since Hugh M. Hefner founded *Playboy* magazine and its subsequent Hydra-headed expansion into various avenues of popular entertainment (casinos, television, films) one prize has been beyond the Empire's reach — not one of its Playmates has ever been recognized as a legitimate star. Claudia Jennings enjoyed a film career of sorts before dying in a car crash on October 3, 1979, but it was in low-budget exploitation films like *Unholy Rollers* (1972), *The Single Girls* (1973), and *Moonshine County Express* (1977). Likewise, blonde bombshell Anna Nicole Smith, a one-time stripper turned Guess Jeans model, did similar films (*To the Limit*, 1995; *Skyscraper*, 1997; *Wasabi Tuna*, 2003) prior to deteriorating into self-parody on her television reality program, *The Anna Nicole Show* (2002–2004). By the time Smith died of an accidental drug overdose on February 11, 2007, she had long been dismissed as an entertainment joke. Dorothy Stratten, however, was different. From the time Dorothy R. Hoogstraten first traveled from her home in Vancouver, British Columbia to Los Angeles in August 1978, until she was renamed as Dorothy Stratten and met her

mind-numbingly tragic death in August 1980, hers was a life and career moving towards personal happiness and professional legitimacy. Remarkably unaffected, undeniably beautiful, and eagerly willing to work to develop her talent, Dorothy Stratten held the potential to become a legitimate actress if only she could have escaped her past.

Born Dorothy Ruth Hoogstraten in Vancouver, British Columbia on February 28, 1960, her father deserted the family in 1963 leaving her to be raised with a brother (and later a sister, Louise) by her mother. In June 1974, the 14-year-old took a job at the counter of a local Dairy Queen and was still there working her way through high school when Paul Leslie Snider, 25, entered the restaurant in October 1977. Snider was immediately impressed by the tall blonde 17-year-old and reportedly confided to a friend, "That girl could make me a lot money." Eight years older than Dorothy, Snider had been forced to grow up quickly on the mean streets of Vancouver's East End. Following his parents' divorce, Snider dropped out of school in the 7th grade, briefly cut leather in his father's shop, but was ultimately more interested in what he could learn on the streets from white and black pimps. The "Jewish pimp," Snider's nickname, became a regular on the Vancouver club scene where women were attracted to his slick good looks, dark hair, black mustache, and flashy clothes. A small time promoter of automobile and motorcycle shows at the Pacific National Exhibition in 1978, Snider hustled drugs and women to supplement his legitimate income. Real underworld types in the city, however, considered the black corvette driving mink coat wearing "Jewish pimp" to be a wannabe hood who was little more than a clown. In 1978, Snider found out what it meant to play with real gangsters. Unable to pay off a loan shark, the collector held Snider by the ankles out of the window of a 30-story office building. Through his tears, Snider talked his way out of being dropped, but hastily left Vancouver for Los Angeles. In the City of the Angels he acquired a limousine and briefly pimped women on the fringes of Beverly Hills. Unable to realize his dream of becoming a big time talent producer, however, Snider returned to Vancouver.

By February 1978, naïve 18-year-old Dorothy Hoogstraten had been won over by her older lover's charm. Impressed by the clothes and jewels Snider bought her, his luxurious pad, his compliments on her ripening body, and his professional plans for her future, Dorothy was still reticent about his insistence she pose nude for *Playboy* magazine. In 1974, Snider had tried unsuccessfully to promote a stripper for Playmate consideration, but suspected Dorothy's combination of girl next door beauty and native innocence would be a winning combination. After months of skilled cajoling, Snider convinced the technically under-aged Dorothy to pose for nude test shots in August 1978. Forging the signature of Dorothy's mother (still unaware of his intent) on the consent form, Snider contacted Ken Honey, a Vancouver photographer with a track record of selling shots to *Playboy*, to shoot the frightened teenager at the "Jewish pimp's" apartment. Despite Snider's insistence that all the top stars now posed for the magazine, Dorothy reportedly cried throughout the photo session. *Playboy* flipped when they received the photos and immediately summoned Dorothy, without "manager" Snider, to Los Angeles for a series of test shots and a meeting at the mansion with "Hef." Based on the *Playboy* shots, Dorothy (her last name later changed by the magazine to the non-ethnic sounding "Stratten") was immediately placed in contention with 16 other beauties for the 25th Anniversary Playmate. Stratten lost out to Candy Loving, but was announced as the Playmate of the Month for August 1979. In order to legally keep the Canadian-born Stratten in the States, *Playboy* hired the former Dairy Queen counter girl as a bunny at the Century City Playboy Club.

Fearful of losing his well-cultivated meal ticket, Snider arrived in Los Angeles in October 1978 and set up housekeeping with Dorothy in a small apartment in Westwood. Stratten was instantly placed in an untenable position. Beholden to Snider for her shot with *Playboy*, she was aware that Hefner and everyone connected with the magazine recognized her lover for what he was — a badly dressed, small-time opportunist seeking to cash in on her burgeoning celebrity. While *Playboy* steered Stratten into small acting roles on television shows including *Buck Rogers* and *Fantasy Island*, Snider found work on the fringes of show business promoting exotic male dancers and staging wet underwear and tee shirt contests in the San Fernando Valley. As the date for Stratten's August 1979 centerfold approached, Snider escalated his demands they marry, a move that would give him some legal control over her career as her manager. Stratten, out of a sense of obligation, married Snider in Las Vegas on June 1, 1979. The

"Jewish pimp" celebrated the union by finding them a new apartment in West Los Angeles and purchasing himself a black Mercedes-Benz with vanity plates "Star-80." He could now afford both. As the husband-manager of a rising star he was entitled to 50 percent of her income and could remain in the U.S. as long as she did.

Stratten had done a few small movie roles (*Autumn Born*, 1979; *Skatetown, U.S.A.*, 1979; *Americathon*, 1979) prior to being officially "introduced" in the 1980 sci-fi comedy *Galaxina*. That same year Peter Bogdanovich, the celebrated 40-year-old director of *The Last Picture Show* (1971), offered the 19-year-old actress her first serious role in a major motion picture, *They All Laughed*, opposite actors John Ritter, Ben Gazzarra, and Audrey Hepburn. The pair first met at the *Playboy* mansion in October 1978, and again in October 1979, but fell deeply in love during the shooting of *They All Laughed* in New York City during March–July 1980. While back in L.A. Snider continued to supplement his cut of Stratten's earnings with the meager proceeds of wet tee shirt contests, Stratten and Bogdanovich were living together in the director's suite in the Plaza Hotel. Snider, suspecting an affair, hired a private detective, but quickly realized there was little he could do to prevent Dorothy from being with Bogdanovich. Still, he was heartened when Stratten agreed to meet him for a lunch date in Los Angeles on August 8, 1980, to discuss their situation. At the meeting, she informed Snider that she loved Bogdanovich, and would make financial arrangements that would take care of him after the divorce. One week after their disappointing reunion, Snider purchased a 12-gauge Mossberg pump shotgun for about $200.

On August 14, 1980, Stratten, unknown to Bogdanovich, agreed to meet Snider one last time to hammer out a financial settlement at the apartment they had formerly shared at 10881 Clarkson Avenue in Westwood. The 20-year-old actress arrived between noon and 1:00 P.M. Their bodies were not discovered until shortly after 7:00 P.M. The police reconstruction of the crime had Snider forcing Stratten into the bedroom and taping her into a bondage machine he had designed and was marketing for sale. Snider raped and sodomized his wife, untied her, and placing the shotgun against the left side of her face over her eye, pulled the trigger. Bloody handprints on Stratten's buttocks and left shoulder suggest that Snider moved the body to the bed where he possibly violated the corpse prior to kneeling and shooting himself in the right side of the head. Stratten's naked body was found with her knees on the floor, her upper body spread across the lower corner of the bed. Snider, also nude, fell face-down on top of the gun (his hands still clutched) parallel to the foot of the bed. In Stratten's purse was found a note in Snider's handwriting explaining his pressing need for money and a rejection of her flat buyout of $7,500. Assessing the tragedy, a shaken Hugh Hefner commented, "A very sick guy saw his meal ticket and his connection to power, whatever, slipping away. And it was that that made him kill her." Dorothy Stratten was buried in Westwood Memorial Park in Los Angeles beneath a grave-marker listing her birth and death dates and bearing an inscription about courage taken from Ernest Hemingway's novel *A Farewell to Arms*.

In August 1984, the publication of Bogdanovich's best selling book, *The Killing of the Unicorn: Dorothy Stratten (1960–1980)*, ignited a firestorm of controversy. Part loving reminiscence and part feminist screed, *Unicorn* accused "Hef" of seducing the Playmate and derided the *Playboy* empire as responsible for Stratten's murder. Hefner denied the allegations and pointed out the director's hypocrisy in "attacking behavior which he himself has done." On March 6, 1985, the 59-year-old *Playboy* publisher suffered a mild stroke which he attributed to the stress generated by the director's "pathological book." Unrelenting, Bogdanovich responded in a statement, "Confronting Hugh Hefner with the reality of his life and in particular what he and his magazine do to women apparently is something he can't face. I'm sorry if making him face it had something to do with making him sick. I feel a lot worse for the human cost paid by all the women who don't issue press releases." Seven months after the publication of the damning book, Hefner took the offensive in a news conference in April 1985 in which he aired the hour-long *Playboy*-produced documentary, *A Portrait of Dorothy Stratten*. Cobbled together from interviews and behind the scenes footage taken of the Playmate, the documentary demonstrated, according to Hefner, that Stratten's last two years were "the happiest, most fulfilling and rewarding of her life because of *Playboy*." Hefner, backed up by Burl Eldridge (Stratten's stepfather for nine months), stated Bogdanovich had not only "seduced" Louise B. Hoogstraten (13 at the time of her 20-year-old sister's murder), but also her mother, Nelly Schaap. It was further alleged

the director had paid for Louise Hoogstraten to undergo cosmetic surgery in a bid to make her look more like Dorothy. On April 8, 1985, Hoogstraten, 17, filed a $5 million libel suit against Eldridge and *Playboy* claiming slander, invasion of privacy, and intentional infliction of emotional distress. Hoogstraten dropped the case in late August 1985 (ostensibly so she could lead a normal life) and signed releases dismissing all claims against Hefner and *Playboy*. Hefner's attorney, Michael Glassman, issued a "conciliatory" statement, "Our investigation demonstrated that Mr. Bogdanovich relied on substantial misinformation in making unfounded charges against me that appear in his book. In all probability Mr. Bogdanovich's emotional state following the death of Dorothy Stratten caused him to accept as true, information that has no basis in fact." Bogdanovich, 49, married 20-year-old Louise Hoogstraten (a.k.a. L.B. Stratten) on December 30, 1988. The couple divorced after 12 years of marriage in 2001. The short and tragically truncated life of Dorothy Stratten has been the subject of a made-for-television movie (*Death of a Centerfold*, 1981, starring Jamie Lee Curtis) and a theatrical film (*Star 80*, 1983, featuring Mariel Hemingway).

Further Reading

Bogdanovich, Peter. *The Killing of the Unicorn: Dorothy Stratten (1960–1980)*. New York: W. Morrow, 1984.
Carpenter, Teresa. "Death of a Playmate," *Village Voice*, 25(45) (November 5–11, 1980):1, 12–14, 16–17.

Stringbean *see* **Akeman**, David ("Stringbean")

Stromberg, Larry (M)

For the past five years the 30-year-old struggling actor worked as a fitness trainer at the Riverside Racquet and Fitness Club in the Philadelphia suburb of Bala Cynwyd. Stromberg appeared in minuscule parts in two films partially shot in Philadelphia (*12 Monkeys*, 1995; *Up Close & Personal*, 1996), and most recently in the 1997 B horror-comedy *Blades*. The actor was writing a script about a serial killer when his troubled three year marriage to Stefan Stromberg, 30, finally disintegrated amid his wife's alleged infidelity and subsequent abortion. In mid–April 1996, the woman obtained a protection-from-abuse order against her husband citing his threats and violence. On April 28, 1996, eleven days after the decree was filed, Paula Rathgeb, Stefan Stromberg's mother, was helping her daughter move out of the married couple's apartment in the Germantown section of Philadelphia. Larry Stromberg slashed and stabbed both women to death and fled into the woods in suburban Montgomery County. He surrendered to police a few days later and was charged with one count of first-degree murder (his wife) and one count of second-degree murder (his mother-in-law). At trial in May 1997, Stromberg pleaded "not guilty" by reason of insanity. Arguing his client was psychotic on the day of the killing, defense attorney Nino V. Tinari maintained Stromberg was the product of a mentally ill mother and a domineering father who had been molested as a child by babysitters and his mother's boyfriends. "He couldn't interact with women," Tinari said. "At age 30, he still played with dolls given to him at age 10." When Stromberg learned of his wife's affair, pregnancy, and abortion, he became irrational and fatally inflicted a total of 34 wounds on his two victims. Prosecutors presented a simpler case — the actor killed his wife and mother-in-law out of rage. Stromberg was found guilty on both murder counts on June 6, 1997, and sentenced to two consecutive life sentences (plus 10 and 20 years) after a jury deadlocked over imposing the death sentence on the double killer.

Further Reading

"Horror Movie-Maker Sought for Two Murders." United Press International, April 30, 1996.

Struebing, Kurt Alan (M)

Struebing with some high school friends in Federal Way, a community 22 miles south of Seattle, Washington, formed the black metal band, N.M.E. (pronounced "enemy") in 1985 from the remains of a group called Night Prowler. The heavy metal band released two albums in 1985 (*Machine of War* and *Satan's Revenge*) prior to recording in less than four hours the genre's well-regarded *Unholy Death* for $400 in late 1985. Released on January 28, 1986 on Dutch East India's Pentagram Records (later LSR), the album featured tracks like "Evil Dead," "Acid Reign," "Speed Kilz," and "Louder Than Hell." Struebing, the guitarist and acknowledged driving force behind N.M.E. (a.k.a. "New Messiah Emerging"), designed the album's cover and insert. By mid–1986, however, the 20-year-old guitarist was acting strange even by black metal standards. Though friends and bandmates denied Struebing abused drugs, he inexplicably cut off his waist-length hair and, on April 6, 1986, drank a bottle

of rug shampoo to "clean himself out." Repeatedly vomiting, the guitarist stripped off his clothes and drove to his adoptive mother's home.

The next morning, Struebing phoned the Seattle 911 number to report he had just killed his mother, Darlee K. Struebing, a 53-year-old data processor for Pacific Northwest Bell. The guitarist was naked and waiting in a parking lot outside the residence when the patrol car arrived minutes later. "I killed my mother and then I killed myself," he told the officer. Inside on the floor of the master bedroom layed the body of the partially-clothed woman, her head caved in by repeated blows from a bloodstained hatchet found next to a bloody pair of scissors on a chest of drawers in the room. Darlee Struebing was repeatedly stabbed in her left breast and neck, while both arms bore bloody testament to her futile attempt to fend off the scissors attack. The victim's night clothes, pulled up over her hips, suggested rape (later confirmed by the autopsy). According to the police report partially cited in Pamela Des Barres' book, *Rock Bottom*, authorities recovered photos of Kurt Struebing in "staged death scenes" and several books on "the occult and Satan" at the scene. En route to the police station, Struebing offered a confused explanation of why he butchered his mother. "I just got caught up in everything," said the black metal musician. "I couldn't cry. I learned too late that I could be whatever I want to be." Though his parents were divorced, the guitarist seemingly loved and respected his mother. A psychiatric evaluation (partially cited by Des Barres) revealed the depth of Struebing's paranoia. Believing all people were robots, he was unable to sleep and endured periods of hyperactivity. Fearful his friends were going to kill him, Struebing once bludgeoned one with a baseball bat. He was convinced he was a robot placed on Earth in order to build up the planet for some other conquering force. The examining psychiatrist concluded, "Apparently he felt that if he killed himself and his mother, he would be killing robots who would be replaced by the other force.... (The murder) was an experiment for him to determine whether or not they were actually robots."

While undergoing a court-mandated psychiatric exam at the Western State Hospital, Struebing tried to kill himself by jumping off his bed and landing headfirst on the cement floor. After several psychiatrists ruled he was psychotic at the time of the slaying, the prosecution and defense agreed the musician should be shown leniency. In April 1986, the district attorney accepted the guitarist's plea of second-degree murder and recommended an eight-year prison sentence. King County Superior Court Judge Susan Agid, however, failed to concur and sentenced the guitarist to 12 years in the mentally-ill offenders unit of the Monroe Reformatory. Struebing was given early release in April 1994 and returned to the Seattle area where he slowly rebuilt his life. He reformed N.M.E., became a co-owner of Reprographics, a graphic arts firm in Seattle, even married and fathered a son to whom he was utterly devoted. Active in the Seattle music scene, Struebing used Reprographics to produce fliers for up and coming area metal bands. As recently as October 2004, N.M.E. was doing gigs in Tacoma and Seattle. Though at the time he refused to discuss the murder and his imprisonment, the guitarist had apparently turned his life around and was well-liked and respected. On March 9, 2005, the 39-year-old musician and family man inexplicably died in what was either a dramatic suicide or tragic accident. Just before 1:00 P.M. Struebing drove his Volkswagen Jetta out of a line of stopped traffic, past several waiting cars, and through both a wooden arm warning gate and a metal barrier on Spokane Street just as the span opened on the lower West Seattle Swing Bridge for a tugboat on the Duwamish Waterway. The car plunged more than fifty feet to the pavement landing on its roof. Struebing was pronounced dead at the scene. Aerial shots of the bridge revealing skid marks leading to the edge of the draw span tended to support the claims of the dead man's friends and family that his death was just a terrible accident. An impromptu benefit concert was held at The Olde Shipwreck tavern in Tacoma for his wife and five-year-old son.

Further Reading

Castro, Hector. "Driver Off Bridge Had Dark Past; After Murder Sentence, However, He Turned His Life to Family and Music." *Seattle Post-Intelligencer*, March 11, 2005, sec. B, p. 1.
Des Barres, Pamela. *Rock Bottom: Dark Moments in Music Babylon*. New York: St. Martin's, 1996.
www.nme666.com.

Switzer, Carl Dean ("Alfalfa") (V)

One of the most beloved of the popular Our Gang/Little Rascals characters, Carl ("Alfalfa") Switzer was a success at seven and a has-been by 13. His storybook rise and tragic fall is the classic Hollywood cautionary tale of the talented child star unable to make the transition into adult roles. Born in Paris, Illinois, on August 8, 1927, Carl and older brother, Harold, made a name for themselves singing at local auctions and fairs. During a trip to Hollywood in 1935 to visit their grandmother, the boys tried to audition at the Hal Roach Studio, the production company for the hit Our Gang comedy series, but were turned away at the gate. Undiscouraged, they walked across the street to the public Our Gang Cafe where several studio people ate lunch and waited. They were entertaining the diners with impromptu songs when studio head Hal Roach entered, saw their potential, and put them under contract. In a nod to the farmboys' rural heritage, Roach dubbed Carl "Alfalfa" while brother Harold was nicknamed "Slim" and "Deadpan." Roach immediately cast the boys in the two-reeler, *Beginner's Luck*, released on February 23, 1935 by MGM. In the short, they are seen as "Tom and Jerry, the Arizona Nightingales" and do a winning rendition of "She'll Be Comin' Round the Mountain." In an eerie presentiment of the violent death awaiting Switzer, his first film assignment featured two individuals who later committed suicide. In August, 1940, Gus Meins, the veteran director of *Beginner's Luck*, chose carbon monoxide poisoning as the vehicle by which to escape charges of committing immoral acts with six boys ranging in age from 10 to 15. Likewise, Switzer's Little Rascals castmate Scotty Beckett, unable to make the transition from child star to adult actor, ended his life with barbiturates on May 10, 1968, in a room at the Royal Palms Hotel in Los Angeles.

Over the next six years and 61 Our Gang shows Switzer perfected the winning screen persona of Alfalfa, the unpredictably breaking voiced, bug-eyed boy whose waxed cowlick stood straight up from the top of his head. The actor's squeaky voiced solos and duets became a staple in several of the best Our Gang two-reelers. After nearly six years of stardom as one of the Gang's most endearing characters, Switzer last appeared as Alfalfa in the short *Kiddie Kure* released by MGM on November 23, 1940. Though perhaps considered too old at 13 to be part of a kid troupe, Switzer was thought by many to be difficult to work with and was known to cause trouble on the set. Switzer's post–Our Gang career followed a pattern of decline now all too predictable for former child movie stars hoping to continue as adult actors. After sizable roles in *Reg'lar Fellers* (1941, based on the long-running cartoon strip of the same name) and the short-lived "Gas House Kids" film series (*Gas House Kids*, 1946; *Gas House Kids Go West*, 1947; *The Gas House Kids in Hollywood*, 1947) Switzer was cast in smaller and smaller parts in forgettable films like *House by the River* (1950), *The WAC from Walla Walla* (1952), and *Francis in the Navy* (1955) among numerous others. Still, he managed to hold on in Hollywood occasionally turning up in bit parts in "A" productions like *Going My Way* (1944), *It's a Wonderful Life* (1946), *State of the Union* (1948), *Pat and Mike* (1952), and *The Ten Commandments* (1956, as a slave).

Bitterly frustrated by the downward spiral of his career, Switzer started drinking more heavily. In between increasingly infrequent acting assignments he supported himself by tending bar part-time at Wolf's Den in Studio City and renting himself out as a hunting guide to celebrity clients like Henry Fonda and Roy Rogers. On May 22, 1954, Switzer married Kansas heiress Diane Collingwood in a ceremony in Las Vegas. The marriage ended after less than four months with Collingwood charging Switzer with cruelty and requesting in court papers he return her property. In April 1955, Interstate Television Corporation packaged the Our Gang shorts into a half-hour syndicated series titled *Little Rascals*. The series played in 46 markets easily dominating its time slot against popular performers like Arthur Godfrey. As the television series pre-dated the now routine contractual clause of residuals, Switzer and his fellow-actors never made a dime off the endless reruns. Bad luck continued. On January 26, 1958, the 30-year-old was shot in the upper right arm by a sniper in Studio City as he was getting into his car. He escaped further injury by running into a nearby bar. Four days later, Eugene Earl Butler, 30, was arrested for the sniper ambush on Switzer. Butler denied shooting the actor, but did admit he believed Switzer was seeing his estranged wife. Butler was later released for lack of evidence. In October 1958, Switzer appeared in his final film, director Stanley Kramer's racial drama, *The Defiant Ones*, starring Sidney Poitier and Tony Curtis. The motion picture was well received and Switzer may have thought that 1959 was the year he would make his big comeback. If so, that dream ended on the night of January 21, 1959.

For weeks the 31-year-old actor had brooded over an incident involving his friend, Moses S. ("Bud") Stiltz, 37, a welder in Sepulveda. Switzer had borrowed a dog from Stiltz, lost it on a hunting trip near Lake Shasta, and when confronted by the angry welder over its loss, posted a $35 reward for the animal's return. The finder returned the dog to the bar where Switzer was working, claimed the reward, and left after downing $15 in free drinks. Switzer felt Stiltz should reimburse him the $50 he was out of pocket for the lost dog, but his irate friend felt no obligation to pay for his own dog that he was not responsible for having lost in the first place. The evening of the tragedy, Switzer drank three beers and a martini in a bar in the company of a friend, studio still photographer Jack Piott, 37. The more the frustrated actor drank, the angrier he became. Finally, the pair decided to confront Stiltz at the home he shared in the San Fernando Valley area of Dennis Park with Rita Corrigan, the estranged wife of Western film star Ray "Crash" Corrigan, and her children. Accounts vary as to how the men entered the house (whether Switzer pretended to be a Western Union man, or, if he flashed a fake policeman's badge provided by Piott), but once inside the enraged actor demanded his $50 from Stiltz. According to Stiltz, when he refused Switzer picked up a heavy clock and struck him over the right eye with it. The welder managed to produce a .38-caliber pistol from a closet and shoot Switzer once in the stomach as the actor brandished an open pocket knife. Switzer, the beloved Alfalfa of Our Gang/Little Rascals fame, died en route to nearby Valley Emergency Hospital. Stiltz was treated and released from the facility for a badly cut right eye. The murder charge against Stiltz was dismissed after a coroner's jury returned a verdict of "justifiable homicide." Rumors persist that Switzer never carried a knife and that the one found *under* his body was not even open. Carl "Alfalfa" Switzer was buried with little fanfare in Hollywood Memorial Park (renamed Hollywood Forever) under a gravestone bearing, ironically, the image of a dog. Our Gang fans insist it is "Pete the Pup," the group's mascot, but it is more likely a hunting dog reflecting Switzer's love of the sport. (See also entries Robert Blake and Jay R. Smith.)

Further Reading

"Alfalfa of 'Our Gang' Films Slain Collecting $50 Debt." *Los Angeles Times*, January 22, 1959, pp. 2, 13.

Maltin, Leonard, and Richard W. Bann. *The Little Rascals: The Life and Times of Our Gang*. Updated ed. New York: Crown, 1992.

Talkov, Igor (V)

The 35-year-old Russian pop singer-songwriter was so well-known for his far right political views he was suspected of helping to finance the radio broadcasts of the ultra-nationalist Pamyat organization, a "patriotic" group characterized by the sitting Russian government as harshly anti–Semitic. On October 6, 1991, Talkov was fatally shot in the chest at point-blank range during a performance of social protest songs in the Yubileiny Sport Palace in St. Petersburg. The assailant escaped during the subsequent melee, but ten days later Igor Malakhov, reportedly the lover and bodyguard of rival pop singer Aziza, turned himself in to police. Malakhov denied being the shooter, but admitted packing a gun at the concert. According to Malakhov, he was twice invited by Talkov's entourage to speak with them before they began beating him up. When Malakhov regained consciousness, his weapon was missing. Unhappy with the official police investigation, Pamyat launched their own inquiry quickly asserting Malakhov's innocence and offering "proof" that a plan to assassinate Talkov was made as early as June 1, 1991, after the singer performed patriotic songs at the presentation of the group's newspaper. By April 1992, police had determined the murder weapon used to kill the singer belonged to Malakhov, but it had fallen out of his hands during a backstage struggle with Talkov's bodyguards. A childhood friend of Malakhov's then picked up the weapon and used it to murder Talkov. After the crime, the gunman (identified as Vadim Shlyakhman although some sources cite as Valery Shlyafman), fled the scene for Israel, a country lacking extradition or legal cooperation treaties with Russia. To date, Shlyakhman, an Israeli citizen, has successfully avoided formal meetings with either Russian or Israeli law enforcement officials.

Further Reading

Kislinkova, Larisa. "Russia Seeks Extradition of Singer's Murderer from Israel." TASS, June 6, 1995.

Tamim, Suzanne (V)

Known for her striking green eyes and luxuriant mane of flowing brown hair, Tamim rose to fame in 1996 after winning the television talent show *Studio al-Fann*, the Lebanese equivalent of the wildly popular *American Idol*. Soon afterwards, the beautiful singer became fodder for the international gossip raps after divorcing her husband Ali Musannar then marrying Lebanese impresario Adel Maatouk who became her producer. The couple quickly divorced and Tamim fled her home

in Beirut for Egypt reportedly to escape a series of lawsuits filed by the disgruntled Maatouk. In 2004, he accused his ex-wife of backing an attempt on his life. Professionally, Tamim's career was winding down after a fast start fueled by her 1996 television show win. Backed by Rotana, the Arab world's largest entertainment group, the sultry singer released her last album in 2002, and her final song, "Lovers," in 2006 was dedicated to the memory of assassinated Lebanese Prime Minister Rafik Hariri. It was the beauty's personal life, however, that held the most interest for the Arab public.

Sometime in 2005, Tamim became secretly involved with Egyptian tycoon Hisham Talaat Mustafa, the head of the multi-billion dollar real estate conglomerate, the Talaat Mustafa Group. A close personal friend of Egyptian President Hosni Mubarak's powerful son, Gamal, Mustafa was the top man in the ruling National Democratic Party and a member of the Shura Council, Egypt's upper house of Parliament. In 2006, Mustafa asked Tamim to marry him, but the billionaire withdrew the proposal after his mother disapproved of the union. Although already married, Mustafa was permitted other wives under Islamic law. In early 2006, Tamim severed the relationship and relocated to Dubai. Bitter over the breakup, Mustafa tried unsuccessfully in a Geneva court to sue his ex-lover for the return of the estimated $12 million in cash and gifts he had given her during the course of their affair. In 2007, Tamim married Riyad al-Azzawi, an Iraqi kickboxing champion she met while living in London. According to Azzawi, the jilted billionaire continued to pursue Tamim first offering her $50 million to return then, when she refused, threatening to have her killed for $1 million. In London, the married couple was routinely followed and received harassing phone calls over an 18-month period. In one, a contract killer warned Azzawi that he was coming to London to kill him if he did not hand over the woman. The boxer produced tape recordings of the harassing calls to British police, but was informed that since Mustafa was such a high ranking government official in Egypt all they could do was install a panic alarm in the couple's flat.

On July 28, 2008, the 30-year-old Lebanese singer was found dead in her luxury apartment in the Dubai Marina complex in the upscale neighborhood of Al-Jumeira. Tamim was stabbed repeatedly over most of her body and her attacker had disfigured her face while she was still alive prior to inflicting an eight inch slash across her neck which nearly decapitated the pop diva. Dubai police quickly solved the vicious crime. The inept killer was clearly seen on the lobby security camera posing as a workman sent by the building's superintendent. Once Tamim buzzed him up, the assailant attacked the singer as soon as she opened the door to her apartment. Investigators found bloody overalls and a cap in a trash can outside the complex. Based on a wealth of evidence (DNA at the scene, bloodstained clothes, a Swiss Army knife, video footage, credit card receipts, a bloody footprint), Dubai police notified their Egyptian counterparts resulting in the arrest of Moshen al-Sukkary one hour after he landed in Cairo on the day of the murder. Sukkary, a retired Egyptian State Security Officer, worked as a security contractor for several companies including the Four Seasons Hotel in the Red Sea resort of Sharm el-Sheik owned by Hisham Talaat Mustafa. Under questioning, Sukkary told authorities the Egyptian billionaire offered to pay him $2 million for the hit and helped facilitate visas and tickets for him to stalk the singer first in London then Dubai. The clumsy hitman supplied police with tapes of his conversations with Mustafa in which the tycoon talked about the payoff and urged the killer to get on with the job.

As rumors circulated in the Egyptian media concerning the billionaire's possible role in the beautiful pop singer's grisly murder, few familiar with that country's political scene believed a man as powerful and connected as Mustafa would ever be charged. Taking the offensive, he denied any involvement and complained on television the baseless allegations were hurting the national economy. The Egyptian government finally banned press reports on the murder effectively informing the media Mustafa was off-limits. Still, the taped telephone conversations between the hitman Sukkary and Mustafa were too compelling to be ignored. On September 2, 2008, the 49-year-old billionaire became possibly the wealthiest man in history to be charged with contracting a murder, but then only after the government first stripped him of his parliamentary immunity. The November 2008 trial, conducted in Cairo because Egyptian law does not allow its citizens to be extradited to other countries, became a symbol of the decadence of big business and its ties to government. Inside the packed courtroom, both Sukkary and Mustafa denied any involvement in

the killing, while in the streets surrounding the courthouse riot police fought to maintain order. In a controversial move reportedly instigated by the publication of a book proclaiming his innocence written by Mustafa and published by his defense team, the presiding judge limited media access to the trial. Under the ban, reporters were permitted in the courtroom but prohibited from taking notes. Only previous court decisions, adjournments, and sentences could be publicized. In the face of overwhelming physical evidence, both men claimed the items recovered at the crime scene (bloody clothes and a knife) could have been planted or tampered with by United Arab Emirates authorities and should be dismissed. The prosecution's theory of the case was simple and direct. Mustafa hired Sukkary to murder Suzanne Tamim out of revenge for breaking up with him. Of note, the officer who arrested Sukkary testified that during interrogation the hitman said Mustafa requested the pop singer's severed head be delivered to him prior to paying for the murder. Following a nearly seven month trial, both men were found guilty on May 21, 2009 and sentenced to be hanged. After conferring with the grand mufti, Egypt's highest religious authority, the sentences were upheld by a higher court on June 25, 2009. Under Egyptian law, death sentences automatically go to an appeal and both men were awaiting new trials as of late 2010.

Further Reading

Leppard, David. "'Marry Me for $50m – or You're Dead.'" *The Sunday Times* (London), September 7, 2008, sec. Home News, p. 7.

Tanin, Ihor (M-S)

Tanin, described as a fixture in the Milwaukee music scene, repaired equipment at his store, the Rock 'n Roll Hospital, for bands like the Violent Femmes and Streetlife. Known as "E" (a nickname for the pronunciation of his first name), the 45-year-old electronics wizard began in the industry in the 1970s with Gary Tanin in the band Otto & the Elevators, and in the Skunks. On November 15, 2003, in what friends of the dead woman called Tanin's "ultimate act of control" over her, the music equipment repairman repeatedly shot Kristy-Jo Szentes, 35, before turning the gun on himself in the townhouse the couple shared in the 1200 block of Balmoral Court in Brookfield, Wisconsin. The bodies were found by Tanin's teenage daughter whom Szentes had raised as her own for several years. Szentes, a 2003 graduate of Lakeland College with a degree in medical administration, worked at Zablocki Veterans Affairs Medical Center. The Szentes family had given Tanin his start in the music business 25 years earlier by letting him repair equipment in the back room of their store, Uncle Bob's Music Center, in West Allis.

Further Reading

Seibel, Jacqueline. "Rock Figure, Girlfriend Are Shot; Brookfield Police Label Couple's Deaths at Home as Murder and Suicide." *Milwaukee Journal Sentinel*, November 18, 2003, sec. B, p. 1.

Tate, Sharon (V)

The gruesome murder of Sharon Tate and her friends in August 1969 by drug-crazed counterculture types acting under the influence and direction of career criminal and cult guru Charles Manson is arguably the most important celebrity crime in show business history. The killings have achieved iconic status and, with the disastrous Rolling Stones concert at Altamont Speedway in December 1969, are often cited as marking the violent end of the "Peace and Love" decade of the 1960s. Perhaps only in such a time as the 1960s and place like Los Angeles could the paths of two such dissimilar individuals, the beautiful actress and the small-time hoodlum turned cult leader, ever cross with such deadly and historically important consequences. Born in Dallas, Texas, on January 24, 1943, Sharon Marie Tate was the product of parents who were a study in polar opposites. Paul Tate, a career Army man, was a quietly reserved disciplinarian while wife Doris was an affectionately outgoing woman who doted on her daughter. Convinced Sharon could be a star, Doris entered the six-month-old child in the "Miss Tiny Tot of Dallas Pageant" and was not surprised when she won. Unlike her mother, Sharon was naturally shy and the transient nature of her father's military service only served to exacerbate the condition. By the age of 16, she had attended schools in Texas, California, and Washington. In the late 1950s, the Tate family was posted outside Seattle, Washington where the stunningly beautiful teenager was a popular, but reserved high school student. At 16, Sharon set the goal of competing in the "Miss Washington State Pageant" and tuned up for the main event by entering and winning a series of beauty titles including "Miss Richland, Washington" and "Miss Autorama" at a local car show. Perhaps flat-

tered that a military publication was impressed by his daughter's beauty, the usually strict disciplinarian Captain Tate permitted Sharon to be photographed for the cover of *Stars and Stripes* sitting astride a missile wearing a swim suit, boots, and a cowboy hat. Her dream of state pageant glory, however, was abruptly ended in 1959 when intelligence officer Tate was transferred to a military base outside of Verona, Italy. At the Vicenza American High School Sharon was a head-turningly popular student who became a cheerleader and was voted homecoming queen. Although largely forbidden by her father to date and then only under a strict curfew, the 17-year-old Sharon was raped during a date with a soldier in 1960. Ashamed and fearful that news of the attack would somehow dishonor her father, she never reported the sex crime to military authorities.

That same year, Sharon and school friends on tour in the hills around Verona encountered an American film crew shooting the Paul Newman vehicle, *Adventures of a Young Man*, based on the writings of Ernest Hemingway. The group of teenagers was asked to fill out a crowd scene and afterwards, actor Richard Beymer invited the beautiful young woman to dine with him and the rest of the cast. The pair dated and Beymer gave the now aspiring actress contact information for his agent in Hollywood. In the spring of 1961, Sharon introduced herself to popular American singer Pat Boone while he was in Verona filming an ABC television special. Boone and wife Shirley discussed with the teen at great length the obstacles facing an acting career and offered sound practical advice on where to stay in Hollywood after adding a personal note of caution about the toll a career can take on personal relationships. Following the meeting, Sharon let it be known at the Army base, a contact point for film companies shooting in the area, that she was interested in extra work in and around Verona. Later that spring, her big chance came when she landed a small non-speaking part in *Barabbas*, a biblical picture starring Anthony Quinn in the title role supported by veteran actor Jack Palance. While on set, Sharon spoke to Palance about a career in movies and the smitten actor arranged for her, accompanied by mother Doris, to go to Rome for a screen test. Understandably, Tate's father was not pleased with the older man's interest in his 18-year-old daughter and opposed the plan, but Doris was determined that Sharon have a career. Had he known, Captain Tate would have been furious over Sharon's next move. After Richard Beymer returned to Hollywood upon completion of *Adventures of a Young Man*, he had remained in touch with the beautiful teenager. Anxious to be reunited with her lover, Sharon told her parents she wanted to go to Los Angeles to investigate colleges. Upon arrival in Tinseltown she quickly wrote her folks that she intended to pursue a career in motion pictures. The separation from her beloved daughter proved too much for Doris Tate. She suffered a nervous breakdown necessitating Sharon's hasty return to Italy. In February 1962, however, Captain Tate was transferred to Fort McCarthy outside San Francisco, California, a manageable distance from Hollywood for an aspiring actress.

Once back in the Golden State, Sharon Tate resumed her love affair with Beymer who introduced the leggy 5'5" blonde to his agent, Hal Gefsky, vice president of the Agency for the Performing Arts. The veteran agent was floored by Tate's beauty and immediately found her work in a television commercial for Chevrolet. In 1963, the 22 year old came to the attention of Martin Ransohoff, chief executive of Filmways, Inc., a television production company responsible for some of the most popular sitcoms of the day (*Mr. Ed*, *The Beverly Hillbillies*). Ransohoff was no stranger to shaping the careers of beautiful actresses having orchestrated the star build-ups of Ann-Margaret and Tuesday Weld. The television executive signed Tate to an exclusive seven year contract with Filmways that paid her $750 a month while she attended classes in acting, speech, singing, and body-building. Instructors were unanimous in their assessment of Tate — she was heart-stoppingly beautiful, but lacked self-confidence. Ransohoff brought the young actress along slowly first having her do a couple of un-billed walk-ons in late 1963 episodes of *Mr. Ed*, then a recurring role as a bank secretary (wearing a black wig) in 13 episodes of *The Beverly Hillbillies* from 1963 to 1965. In the fall of 1963, Ransohoff enrolled his protégé in the prestigious Actors Studio in New York City. She moved in with current lover, 23-year-old French actor Philippe Forquet, whom she had met while he was shooting *Take Her, She's Mine* with James Stewart and Sandra Dee. Hopelessly intimidated by the intense acting experience, Tate dropped out after a few weeks and returned to Hollywood. Adding to her professional crisis, Forquet asked the actress to marry him over the objections of both her parents and Martin Ransohoff who did not relish seeing his $100,000 investment in Tate's career sidetracked by marriage to a struggling foreign actor. Their opposition caused an unbreachable rift in the couple's relationship that culminated in a violent argument that sent Tate to an emergency room and Forquet back to France.

A beautiful woman, however, is never alone for long. On November 25, 1964, Tate met 24-year-old Jay Sebring (real name Thomas John Kummer), a celebrity hairstylist who served as the basis of the character played by his friend Warren Beatty in the 1975 film, *Shampoo*. Handsome and likable, Sebring boasted a client list of Hollywood heavyweights including Kirk Douglas, Paul Newman, Steve McQueen, and George Peppard. He was among the first top hairstylists to franchise his shops, Sebring International, and quickly became a multimillionaire. Sebring introduced Tate into a Hollywood club scene awash in drugs like marijuana, mescaline, and LSD. Unknown to Tate's parents, who heartily approved of their daughter's new suitor, Sebring was also a well-known drug contact for his celebrity pals. Although still married (he would divorce in March 1965), Sebring proposed to Tate who, at the time, was more interested in furthering her career than entering into another heavy relationship. In the fall of 1965, the hairstylist accompanied Tate to London where she was signed to appear in *Eye of the Devil*, a horror thriller starring David Niven and Deborah Kerr. Tate, who played a witch in the film and received seventh billing, remained in London after the completion of shooting for post-production work. Prior to returning to Los Angeles, Sebring introduced Tate to Victor Lownes, head of Playboy Enterprises in the United Kingdom, and asked his friend to introduce her to London society.

In early 1965, Sharon Tate briefly met Polish director Roman Polanski, 33, at a luncheon in London given by Victor Lownes. Polanski, basking in the warm glow of international acclaim for his brilliant 1962 Polish language film *Knife in the Water*, was equally famous for his unbridled sexual appetite. Though only 5'5", Polanski's slight frame supported a difficult and all-consuming ego which demanded unquestioning subservience to his will. Martin Ransohoff, in London to negotiate a Filmways distribution deal for Polanski's motion picture *Cul-de-Sac*, signed the director to write and direct the horror genre spoof, *The Fearless Vampire Killers*, with the strong suggestion that he cast Sharon Tate as its romantic lead. Polanski, favoring Jill St. John for the role, resisted Ransohoff's pressure until presented with an ultimatum — either use Tate or there would be no film. During the shooting of *Fearless* in the Italian ski resort town of Ortisei, the attraction between Polanski and Tate became apparent even while he forced the nervous actress to do endless retakes. They made love during the film's production and upon returning to London in April 1967 lived together in the director's house. Tate informed Jay Sebring of her new status and, after he met with Polanksi, the hairstylist told his ex-lover that he liked the new man in her life. According to friends, however, Sebring continued to love Tate and there is strong reason to believe they would have eventually reunited had they not been murdered. In the swinging London mod scene of the mid–1960s, Polanski and Tate became *the* couple to have at a party. Both consumed copious amounts of drugs and Tate soon painfully realized that if she expected fidelity from her philandering husband she would be serially disappointed.

In late 1966–early 1967, the offer of a comedic role in the Tony Curtis vehicle, *Don't Make Waves*, necessitated Tate's return to Los Angeles. Polanski, signed to direct *Rosemary's Baby*, accompanied her to Hollywood where the couple set up house and became fixtures in the trendy clubs on Hollywood's Sunset Strip. Professionally, 1967 offered great promise for Sharon Tate. She was prominently featured in the media ads for *Don't Make Waves*, but her role as "Malibu, Queen of the Surfers" was received with mixed critical reviews. In March 1967, Tate appeared in a *Playboy* pictorial hawking the upcoming release of Polanski's *The Fearless Vampire Killers*, but even her nudity could not save the film when it was released in November 1967. Under the terms of his contract with Polanski, Ransohoff retained the rights to the film's final cut and, upon release, the end product had been so badly butchered by the film executive that the director tried unsuccessfully to have his name removed from the credits. Not surprisingly, *Fearless* sunk like a stone at the box office. *Eye of the Devil*, completed two years earlier, was finally released and bombed. Most disappointing of all, however, was Tate's involvement in director Mark Robson's production of *Valley of the Dolls* for 20th Century–Fox based on the best selling book by Jacqueline Susann. The actress received fifth billing for her role of "Jennifer," an actress short on talent, but long on beauty who

commits suicide with pills upon learning she has breast cancer. Released in mid–December 1967, the film meant to launch Tate's career as a serious actress was instead universally condemned as an embarrassment to the film industry. Stung by the film's reception and possibly seeing disturbing resonances of herself in the character of "Jennifer," the 24-year-old actress approached Ransohoff and asked to be let out of the remaining three years of her Filmways contract. She told the executive she planned to retire from acting to devote herself to starting a family with the film director. To his credit, Polanski had always been bluntly honest with Tate when it came to their relationship. He did not wish to marry or have children, but if they did wed he would continue to see other women. She had agreed to his terms early in their affair, but in the face of ongoing career disappointments a commitment to him may have seemed like her only alternative. Ransohoff let her out of the contract on condition that she actually retire from acting. Soon, the famous director and his alluring lover became international jetsetters equally at home with the "beautiful people" in Hollywood and on the Continent.

Remarkably, Polanski married Tate on January 20, 1968, in a media circus-like atmosphere in London. Afterwards, the newlyweds attended a star-studded reception hosted by Victor Lownes at his Playboy club. Tate was naïve if she thought marriage would tame Polanski. Though initially intrigued by the novelty of his new state, the director quickly reverted to form and bedded a string of both past and present girlfriends. Tate accepted Polanski's serial adultery as a "European thing," but even her faith in the marriage was shaken to its foundations when she found a videotape of her husband having sex with another woman in their bed. She confided her frustration to Jay Sebring, who was still in love with Tate and only too willing to offer a sympathetic ear and Platonic companionship. Under the terms of her original contract with Filmways, Tate was still committed to appear in *The Wrecking Crew*, an entry in Dean Martin's lucrative "Matt Helm" series of spy spoofs. Released in early 1969, *The Wrecking Crew* brought Tate largely positive reviews and revealed her talent for light comedic roles. While in Los Angeles, Polanski and Tate were temporarily living in a house on Summit Drive owned by Patty Duke, her *Valley of the Dolls* co-star. Duke informed the couple that she needed the house back, and on February 12, 1969, they signed a one year lease on a two bedroom house at 10050 Cielo Drive in the Benedict Canyon section of Los Angeles. Both Tate and Polanski had previously attended parties in the home once occupied by music producer Terry Melcher and his then girlfriend Candice Bergen. The $1,200 a month house featured a three-car garage, the services of a caretaker living in a separate residence on the grounds, and landscaping service, all in a secluded hillside setting within an easy drive of downtown Hollywood. Within one month of signing the lease on the house on Cielo Drive, Tate and Polanski traveled together to Europe to work on separate films leaving the director's friend, Wojiciech ("Voytek") Frykowski, 32, and his girlfriend, Abigail ("Libby") Folger, the heiress to the Folger coffee fortune, to house sit. Frykowski, a heavy drug user and pusher, regularly entertained in the home and the Cielo Drive address quickly became known to the seedier underground element in Los Angeles.

The Polanskis arrived in London on March 24, 1969. Now convinced Roman was incapable of being faithful, Tate sought to resurrect her career. She agreed to appear in the Italian-French production of *Thirteen Chairs* for her biggest fee to date, $125,000. Unknown to Polanski, however, Tate learned prior to leaving for London that she was pregnant. Terrified that her husband who had repeatedly told her he did not want a child would demand she have an abortion, Tate decided not to tell Polanski until the baby was too far along to abort. She, of course, confided the pregnancy to Jay Sebring. Ultimately, the time came when she could no longer hide her pregnancy from Polanski. Predictably, the director was initially furious over the idea that the child would restrict his freedom and lessen his control over the marital relationship, but for a while warmed to the idea of fatherhood. Tate finished shooting *Thirteen Chairs*, the semi-nude scenes shot early in her pregnancy, and was eight months along when she left London alone on the *Queen Elizabeth II* bound for the United States while Polanski remained alone and unfettered in London to continue work on the script for *The Day of the Dolphin*. Back in Los Angeles, the 26-year-old actress busily began making plans to redecorate the house on Cielo Drive in anticipation of the baby's due date on August 18 (also Roman Polanski's birthday). Although Tate remained uneasy about the continued presence in the house of Folger and Frykowski (who routinely had drugs delivered to

the address), Polanski insisted his friend remain on-site as protection. As the mother-to-be prepared for the birth of her child, Polanski continued his unrestrained partying and adultery in London. For Tate, the ultimate humiliation came when she learned her close friend, Michelle Phillips of the singing group The Mamas and the Papas, had a drunken affair with her husband in England. Crushed by the news, she reportedly confided to her inseparable companion, Jay Sebring, her plan to divorce Polanski after the child's birth if his philandering did not end. For now, however, Sharon Tate passed the days in the house on 10050 Cielo Drive quietly awaiting her husband's return in the company of friends like Frykowski, Folger, and Sebring.

Born "No Name Maddox" to a 16-year-old prostitute in Cincinnati, Ohio, on November 12, 1934, Manson never met his father. Taking his surname from a man his mother briefly married, the young child spent his early life shuffled between relatives and foster homes. In 1939 Manson's mother was convicted of armed robbery and during her imprisonment the five year old was sent to live with a strict, religious aunt and her violent husband. To "toughen up" the youngster, the man forced Manson to wear a dress to school on the first day of class. Released from the penitentiary after serving 5 years, Manson's alcoholic mother reclaimed the boy but soon tired of having him underfoot. Once in a drunken stupor, she reportedly "gave" him to a barmaid in payment for a drink. In 1947 at the age of 12, Manson was placed in the first of many institutions, the Gibault School for Boys in Terre Haute, Indiana. Ten months later he fled, supporting himself on the streets by stealing. During the next several years, Manson received his early instruction in criminal behavior at a variety of institutions including Father Flanagan's Boy's Town and the reform school at Plainfield, Indiana. In his 1986 book, *Manson in His Own Words*, the convicted killer graphically described his hellish three-year stay at Plainfield where, if he is to be believed, the diminutive delinquent was routinely raped and beaten by larger inmates. Escaping from Plainfield in February 1951, Manson was recaptured and spent most of the 1950s and 1960s in and out of state and federal lockups for crimes including homosexual assault, car theft, forging and cashing stolen U.S. Treasury checks, and pimping and transporting prostitutes across state lines.

On March 21, 1967, Manson was paroled from

Terminal Island Prison in San Pedro, California, after serving a long term at the federal prison McNeil Island in the state of Washington for car theft and pimping. Instinctively, the 32-year-old Manson realized that the 19 years he had spent behind bars had rendered him ill-equipped to adapt to the outside world and he begged authorities to permit him to remain in the penitentiary. They refused and with $35 in his pocket Manson drifted north to San Francisco, then ground zero of the Hippie movement. Thoroughly schooled in the art of the "jail house con," the charismatic Manson soon realized that there was a place for him in the Haight-Ashbury district. A budding musician-songwriter (Alvin "Creepy" Karpis of the Ma Barker gang had taught him to play guitar in prison), Manson used his music combined with an addled messianic philosophy buttressed with marijuana and mind-altering drugs to seduce a coterie of young middle-class white women who had renounced their parents' values to find "Truth" and "God." Manson used his groupies to attract to his self-styled "Family" disaffected males who possessed the skills he needed to make his cult self-sufficient; a handiness with weapons and automobile mechanics. With his Family in tow, Manson relocated to the Los Angeles area and settled his commune at Spahn Ranch, an old film set and horse ranch in Simi Valley near Chatsworth. In exchange for care and sex from Manson's women, George Spahn, the 80-year-old owner, allowed the Family to stay there free. Manson used the ranch as a base from which to sell drugs and to convert stolen cars into dune buggies.

At Spahn Ranch, Manson solidified his total control over the 30 or so members of his cult. Feeding them a steady stream of his twisted philosophy laced with marijuana and LSD, the guru orchestrated sexual orgies calculated to rid his followers of any of their "hang-ups." Calling himself "Jesus Christ" and "God," the 5'2" ex-convict preached his version of the upcoming Apocalypse which combined his bizarre interpretation of the biblical book of *Revelation* with the imagined depths of meaning he found in the Beatles' *White Album*, more specifically the song "Helter Skelter." According to Manson's paranoid reasoning the coming race war between the blacks and the whites was inevitable. In the ensuing struggle, the blacks would emerge victorious but lack the intelligence to rule the world. At this point, Manson and his followers would emerge from their "Bot-

tomless Pit," a place of safety in California's Death Valley to which they had fled to avoid the carnage, and take over the planet. Tired of waiting for "Helter Skelter," the day of the Apocalypse, Manson decided to instigate the event by sending out four of his most devoted disciples to kill prominent members of the white Establishment, then plant evidence implicating black revolutionaries. Terry Melcher, the record producer son of Doris Day and boyfriend of actress Candice Bergen, was targeted as a victim because he had earlier refused to sign Manson to a recording contract. The couple had been living at 10050 Cielo Drive in the Benedict Canyon section of West Los Angeles, but had vacated and the house was being let by Roman Polanski and his wife Sharon Tate. In early August 1969, the eight-and-a-half month pregnant actress was living in the home and waiting for her husband to return from England where he was writing the script for a proposed film, *The Day of the Dolphin*. For protection, the director had asked his longtime friend, Voytek Frykowski, a 32-year-old Polish émigré drug dealer, and his lover Libby Folger, 25-year-old heiress to the Folger's coffee fortune, to live with Tate until he returned.

The opening salvo in "Helter Skelter" was the brutal murder of Gary Hinman, a 34-year-old Hippie music teacher who had befriended Manson and Family members Robert ("Bobby") Kenneth Beausoleil, a 22-year-old wannabe musician, and Susan Denise ("Sadie Mae Glutz") Atkins, a 21-year-old topless dancer. Manson, desperate for money, learned that Hinman had recently come into an inheritance and on Friday, July 25, 1969, dispatched Beausoleil (a.k.a. "Cupid"), Atkins, and Mary Theresa Brunner, a 25 year old who held the dubious distinction of being the first member of the Family, to the music teacher's home in Malibu to rob him. Beausoleil, informed by Hinman that he had no money, began the torture session by pistol-whipping the man, but to no avail. Frustrated, Cupid called Manson who arrived at the musician's home with 26-year-old Family member Bruce McGregor Davis. Manson responded to Hinman's pleas for mercy by hacking off part of the bound man's ear with a sword then giving him an ultimatum — sign over everything he owned or die. After Hinman signed over the pink slips to two automobiles Manson and Davis left the scene. Beausoleil continued to cut and stab the bound man finally murdering him on Sunday, July 27, 1969. Prior to leaving Hinman's home, Beausoleil wrote "Political Piggie" on the living room wall in the victim's blood and left a bloody palm print, to incriminate the Black Panthers whose symbol was a paw print, thereby hoping to spark the race war Manson prophesied. The wealth of physical evidence left at the scene as well as Beausoleil's own stupidity (he retained the knife and was driving one of Hinman's cars) led police directly to him and Cupid was booked on suspicion of murder on August 6, 1969. Remarkably, law enforcement agencies initially failed to see any similarities between the bloody counterculture themed writings left on the wall of Hinman's home and those similar inscriptions left at the upcoming Tate-LaBianca killings.

On the night of Friday, August 8, 1969, Manson assembled his drug-addled "hit team" instructing its appointed leader, Charles ("Tex") Denton Watson, a 23-year-old one-time "A" student and high school football star, that "You're going out on the Devil's business tonight" and to "kill everyone inside" the house. Accompanying Watson were Susan ("Sexy Sadie") Denise Atkins, Patricia ("Katie") Krenwinkel, the 21-year-old daughter of a middle-class insurance salesman, and Linda Kasabian, the group's 20-year-old driver and lookout who had left her Midwest home in a drug-fuelled search to find God. Shortly after midnight, in the early morning hours of Saturday, August 9, Watson and the three women invaded the grounds of Sharon Tate's home on Cielo Drive. First to die was Steven Earl Parent, 18, who was simply in the wrong place at the wrong time. Parent dropped by the property to visit William Garretson, a caretaker who lived in a cottage on the grounds who was lucky enough to remain undetected in the impending horror. Tex Watson shot Parent four times at close range with a .22-caliber pistol as the teenager sat in his parked car in the driveway. Entering the house (Kasabian waited outside) Watson accompanied by Atkins and Krenwinkel ultimately herded the terrified occupants into the living room. Visiting the 26-year-old actress that night were Voytek Frykowski, his lover Abigail Folger, and Jay Sebring, 35, Sharon Tate's devoted former lover and confidant. In the ensuing slaughter, Frykowski was stabbed 51 times, shot twice, and pistol-whipped by Watson with such force that the handle of the gun broke off. His body was found on the front yard of the estate where Watson ran him to ground as he fled from the house. Abigail Folger was stabbed 28 times with a bayonet by

Krenwinkel and Watson before dying on the lawn near her lover. Jay Sebring was shot once in the chest and stabbed seven times. Last to die was Sharon Tate who, after pleading for the life of her unborn baby (a son), was told by "Sexy Sadie" Atkins, "Look bitch ... I don't care if you're going to have a baby.... You're going to die and I don't feel anything about it." The group stabbed the actress 16 times. Per Manson's instructions, Watson tossed a rope over an exposed ceiling beam and wrapped the ends around the necks of Tate and Sebring. Atkins, who actually tasted Tate's blood, wanted to cut out the woman's fetus and take it to Manson for ritualistic purposes, but was told by Watson that it was time to leave. Before doing so, however, Atkins daubed a towel in Tate's blood and scrawled the word "PIG" on the front door.

On the night of the same day, Saturday, August 9, Manson accompanied in a car by Watson, Atkins, Krenwinkel, Kasabian, Steve ("Clem") Grogan, and Leslie ("Lulu") Sue Van Houten, 19, randomly cruised the city looking for suitably Establishment-type victims to kill. They settled on a neighborhood in the Los Feliz section of Los Angeles 15 miles from the site of the Tate massacre. Manson, armed with a gun, entered the home of Leno and Rosemary LaBianca at 3301 Waverly Drive. He tied up the 44-year-old supermarket tycoon and his 38-year-old wife assuring them both as he left that they would not be harmed. Returning to the car with the couple's money, Manson ordered Watson to kill the bound pair. Tex, Krenwinkel, and Van Houten entered the home as Manson and the rest of his group drove away. Inside, they separated the bound couple taking Rosemary into a bedroom and leaving husband Leno in the living room. Watson placed a pillow case over the woman's head and tied it with the cord of a lamp. They did the same with Leno LaBianca then went into the kitchen to find knives. Tex began repeatedly stabbing Leno with the bayonet he brought until called by Van Houten and Krenwinkel who were having difficulty slaughtering the terrified Rosemary in the next room. The former high school athlete left the dying man to deliver a few bayonet thrusts into the man's dying wife. Once subdued, Krenwinkel and Van Houten began furiously stabbing the defenseless woman. An autopsy later determined Rosemary LaBianca had been stabbed 41 times, all but six of the wounds would have been sufficient to kill her. Watson returned to stabbing

Leno LaBianca and in his frenzy broke off the blade of a steak knife he left protruding from the 44 year old's throat. Krenwinkel joined in the stabbing and carved the word "WAR" into the man's stomach. When found, LaBianca had been stabbed 26 times and in addition to the knife left in his throat, Krenwinkel had left a two-pronged ivory-handled carving fork stuck in his stomach. To mimic the Tate killings, Manson had ordered that graffiti be left at the scene to further ignite "Helter Skelter." Loyal Family member Katie Krenwinkel daubed paper in Leno's blood and scrawled "Rise" and "Death to Pigs" on the living room wall moving to the door of the refrigerator to add "Healter (sic) Skelter." All ate snacks and took a shower before leaving the LaBianca residence to hitchhike back to Spahn Ranch. Acting on Manson's instructions, the killers dropped the wallet of one of their victims in a black neighborhood hoping someone in the area would be caught by police using a stolen credit card thereby leading authorities to conclude the murders had been racially motivated.

As public horror mounted over the back-to-back massacres and celebrities like Frank Sinatra and Jerry Lewis either left town or went into guarded seclusion, a shattered Roman Polanksi returned to Los Angeles to bury his wife and unborn son (Paul Richard). In the press, speculation raged around inhospitable rumors that the dark nature of the director's work had somehow precipitated the killings. Angrily denying that his marriage to Sharon was ever in trouble, Polanski and several of his famous friends formed a $25,000 reward fund for information leading to the arrest and conviction of those responsible for Tate's murder. Overcome with grief, Polanski would later give away everything they had amassed during their life together and signed a waiver making her father, Paul, the executor of his daughter's estate. Meanwhile, Victor Lownes (under police escort) went to the Cielo Drive crime scene to select from the dead actress' closet the Emilio Pucci mini dress in which she would be buried. Two hundred people (among them Kirk Douglas, John and Michelle Phillips, Warren Beatty, Yul Brynner, Lee Marvin, Peter Sellers) attended the private closed-casket memorial service conducted in the chapel of the Holy Cross Memorial Cemetery at Baldwin Hills in Culver City. Afterwards, Sharon Tate, 26, and her son (wrapped in a shroud) were buried in the same silver casket in a grave close to the final resting place of actor

Bela Lugosi. The inscription on the grave marker reads:

> Our Loving Daughter &
> Beloved Wife of Roman
> Sharon Tate Polanski
> 1943–1969
> Paul Richard Polanski
> Their Baby

Later that afternoon, Jay Sebring was remembered at a memorial service at Forest Lawn Memorial Park in Glendale, California attended by many of the same celebrities. He was buried in Holy Sepulchre Cemetery in Southfield, Michigan. Abigail Folger was interred in the Main Mausoleum in the Holy Cross Catholic Cemetery in Colma, California. The body of her lover, Voytek Frykowski, was returned to his native Poland and buried in Saint Josef's Cemetery in Łódź. Fellow-Family victim Rosemary LaBianca was cremated while husband Leno was interred in the wall of an outdoor mausoleum in the Calvary Cemetery in Los Angeles.

Shortly after the Tate-LaBianca murders, Manson relocated the Family to Barker Ranch on the edge of Death Valley where in October 1969 he was arrested with 22 members of his group on unrelated charges of grand theft auto and arson. The killers were identified as suspects in the Tate-LaBianca murders after Susan Atkins, held at the Sybil Brand Institute as a suspect in the torture-murder of Gary Hinman, told a cellmate about butchering the people on Cielo Drive on "Charlie's" orders. Sexy Sadie also bragged about Manson's future plans to shake up the Establishment by murdering well-known celebrities like Tom Jones and Elizabeth Taylor among others. At a police press conference in Los Angeles on December 1, 1969, authorities announced the Tate-LaBianca cases solved. In a spectacular nine-month trial in which Linda Kasabian turned state's evidence in exchange for immunity from prosecution, assistant district attorney Vincent Bugliosi brilliantly presented the case against Manson, Atkins, Van Houten, and Krenwinkel. All were convicted of murder on March 29, 1971, and subsequently sentenced to death. Tried separately, Charles ("Tex") Watson received a similar verdict and sentence. Meanwhile, Manson, Bruce Davis, and Steve ("Clem") Grogan were found guilty in a combined trial for the murders of Gary Hinman and Donald ("Shorty") Shea, a would-be actor and hand on the Spahn Ranch. Susan Atkins pleaded guilty in Hinman's death and was given a life sentence as was Steve Grogan who was determined to have been too stupid and hopped up on drugs to be responsible for his actions. In a separate trial, Bobby Beausoleil was convicted of Hinman's murder and sentenced to death.

The murderous elements of the Family were all awaiting execution when in 1972 the California Supreme Court invalidated the state's existing capital punishment statute commuting their death sentences to life in prison. All the principals in the Manson murders have been eligible for parole since 1978, but their petitions have been consistently denied due largely to the efforts of Sharon Tate's mother, Doris, who by tirelessly attending every parole hearing to argue against the release of anyone connected with the murders has emerged as a champion for victims' rights. Leslie Van Houten was subsequently retried in 1976 because her attorney, Ronald Hughes, disappeared during the first trial. Hughes' remains were found four months later in a mountain wilderness prompting speculation he was killed by Family members because of his refusal to follow Manson's defense strategies. A second trial for Van Houten ended in a hung jury, but she was finally convicted in 1978 and sentenced to life in prison. Tex Watson, who married and fathered two children in prison during conjugal visits, found God and served as an assistant Protestant pastor at the California Men's Colony at San Luis Obispo. The women convicted in the case have undergone similar religious conversions and have since taken advanced educational degrees and counsel new female inmates.

Manson, still sporting the swastika he carved into his forehead, continues to be a figure of media fascination. Thoroughly institutionalized and realistic enough to know he will never be released from the penitentiary, Manson no longer attends his periodic parole hearings. Still, prison is a dangerous place for the man who proclaimed himself to be "God." On September 25, 1984, Manson was hanging about the hobby shop in the California Medical Facility at Vacaville when he argued with fellow-inmate Jan Holmstrom over the man's incessant recital of Hare Krishna chants. Holmstrom, a 36-year-old devotee of the sect doing life for the 1974 shotgun murder of his father, doused Manson with paint thinner and tossed a match on him. Manson survived, but was treated for second and third degree burns over his face, scalp, and hands. In 1993, the convicted killer was again thrust into the public spotlight when the Los Angeles–based mega-group Guns N' Roses featured his song, "Look at Your Game, Girl," as the 13th and final cut on their *The Spaghetti Incident* album. Though the song was not cited on the album's play list, the name "Charlie" appears in the credits and lead singer Axl Rose thanked "Chas" at the end of the song. Rose has also caught flak for wearing a tee shirt bearing the killer's likeness while performing. Manson's image was officially licensed by Zooport Riot Gear, a surf-wear company based in Newport Beach, California, which reportedly pays him 10 cents a shirt. Some writers on the case have since speculated that Manson was part of a murderous satanic organization which included "Son of Sam" killer David Berkowitz and that many of the murders he ordered were drug-related "hits." What is certain, 40 years after the Tate-LaBianca killings Charles Manson his Family have taken on iconic status to those who view them as the dark side of, and finale to, the "Peace and Love" generation of the 1960s.

Status of participants and principals in the Tate-LaBianca and Hinman-Shea killings as of August 2010:

ATKINS, SUSAN DENISE— While serving her life sentences, Atkins became a born-again Christian in 1974 and devoted herself to counseling other prison inmates. In 1977, she co-authored the book *Child of Satan, Child of God* in which she described her conversion and denied killing Sharon Tate (she only testified at trial to doing so under Manson's orders), but did admit to tasting her blood. On September 2, 1981, "Sexy Sadie," 33, married Donald Lee Laisure, a 52-year-old self-described "unemployed millionaire" from Houston, Texas, in an hour-long private ceremony in the prison chapel at the California Institution for Women in Frontera. Laisure, allegedly married 35 times before, first met Atkins in 1965 while taking pictures along a Southern California roadside, and the pair had corresponded ever since. Insisting their love would last forever, Laisure proclaimed, "Only God could possess the creativity to produce the beauty that is the ultra-beautiful, incomparable Susan "Honeybear" Atkins." The couple divorced in May 1982 because, according to the eccentric millionaire, Atkins allegedly leaked information about him to the IRS and, some sources report, attacked him during a conjugal visit. In 1988, she married Harvard-educated attorney James W. Whitehouse, 17 years her junior, who has since forcefully advocated for her release. In 2002, Whitehouse filed suit against the state of California claiming that the case's notoriety had made Atkins into a "political prisoner." The case was denied. In early 2008, the 60-year-old inmate was diagnosed with terminal brain cancer, and in July of that year was denied a "compassionate release" that would have allowed her to die outside of prison. Both Atkins' doctors and prison officials had recommended the release. At that time, it was estimated that her medical care had cost the state $1.5 million and her incarceration an additional $308,000. Whitehouse noted that if released, Atkins' condition (she had also lost a leg to cancer) would have precluded her from leaving her hospital room. On Wednesday, September 2, 2009, the terminally ill 61 year old slept through most of a four-hour parole hearing at the California Central Women's Facility at Chowchilla awaking only long enough to be led by Whitehouse, 46, through a recitation of the 23rd *Psalm*, in which she concluded in a ringing voice, "My God is an amazing God." In attendance opposing the convicted killer's release were members of the Tate and Sebring families. Atkins' appeal (her 18th) was denied. Sexy Sadie, who had long since acknowledged her role in the horrific murders, died at the facility on September 24, 2009. At the time of her death, Atkins had been in prison longer than any woman currently incarcerated in California. Her website, www.susanatkins.org, is maintained by her devoted husband, James W. Whitehouse.

BEAUSOLEIL, ROBERT—"Cupid" has spent his time in prison profitably building a recording studio and video unit through sponsorships that produce videos for at-risk children and music programs for fellow-prisoners. While incarcerated, he has written and performed the music for director Kenneth Anger's film, *Lucifer Rising*, and has remained committed to his music. He married in 1980 to enjoy the conjugal visits afforded lifers, but quickly divorced. Beausoleil married again in 1982, the same year he survived a near fatal knife attack in the Deuel Correctional Institute in Tracy, California. The couple is still together and reportedly have four children and two grandchildren. As of this writing Beausoleil (described by corrections officials as a "model prisoner") has been denied parole numerous times. He is next eligible in 2015 when he will be 68 years old. Beausoleil is currently serving life in an Oregon prison where he was moved to be closer to his family. His art and music are available through the official website (www.beausoleil.net) maintained by his wife.

BUGLIOSI, VINCENT— Following his impressive showing in the Manson trial, Bugliosi continued his career with the L.A. County district attorney's office racking up 105 out of 106 wins in felony jury trials including 21 consecutive murder convictions. A best selling author, the retired prosecutor's output in the area of "true crime" literature includes *Till Death Do Us Part* (1978), *And the Sea Will Tell* (1991), *Outrage: The Five Reasons Why O.J. Simpson Got Away with Murder* (1996), and *Reclaiming History: The Assassination of President John F. Kennedy* (2007). Bugliosi supported the parole of the terminally ill Susan Atkins (denied in September 2009) arguing that she should be allowed to die outside of prison after having spent nearly 40 years behind bars. "The mercy she was asking for is so minuscule. She's about to die," said Bugliosi. "It's not like we're going to see her down at Disneyland." Atkins succumbed to brain cancer on September 24, 2009.

KASABIAN, LINDA— Following her grant of immunity in the Tate-LaBianca killings, Kasabian dropped out of sight and reportedly lived for a while under an assumed name in New Hampshire. She surfaced in 2009 to appear on camera in full view in the two-hour History Channel docu-drama reenactment of the case, *Manson*, first aired on September 7, 2009. According to actress Elgin Kelley who portrayed her in the LIDA Project Experimental Theatre Company production, *Manson Family Values*, in Denver, Colorado in February 2003, Kasabian "likes to hang out at a local bar and tell whoever will listen, "I drove the car, man!"

KRENWINKEL, PATRICIA— A model prisoner, Krenwinkel has earned a Bachelor's degree in Human Services from the University of La Verne and has worked closely with fellow-inmates in substance abuse programs (Alcoholics Anonymous, Narcotics Anonymous) and in teaching literacy. Krenwinkel was in the first group of inmates in 2002 to participate in the Prison Pup Program, an initiative to train dogs to help the disabled. She has remained committed to the program and as of 2007 had trained seven dogs. As of this writing, Krenwinkel over the years has consistently been judged by 11 separate parole boards to pose an unacceptable risk to public safety. She is currently incarcerated at the California Institution for Women at Frontera.

MANSON, CHARLES— As of 2009, Manson, 74,

had spent 62 years of his life in some form of incarceration. Repeatedly turned down for parole, he no longer bothers to attend hearings. Like many other members of his one-time cult, Manon has entered the internet age with his own website, www.manson.direct.com, allegedly maintained by Sandra "Blue" Good, a paroled Family member who spent 1975–1984 in prison for posting threatening letters to self-identified corporate polluters. Billed as the "Official site for Charles Manson truth," the website purports to offer "the most accurate and current information available about Charles Manson." In addition to audio and video on the convicted killer, it also addresses Manson's environmental interests in the form of the acronym ATWA (Air, Trees, Water, Animals). As of 2009, Manson was serving life in the California State Prison in Corcoran shuttled (dependent upon his behavior) between the penitentiary's highly restrictive Protecting Housing Unit (PHU) and the Securing Housing Unit (SHU, or, "the Hole").

POLANSKI, ROMAN—The gifted Polish director continues to make award winning films, but is destined to be best remembered in the public mind post–Manson murders for having unlawful sex with a teenaged girl in the Hollywood home of his friend, Jack Nicholson. Polanski, 43, was on assignment to photograph teenage girls for French fashion magazine *Vogue Hommes* when he took 13-year-old Samantha Gailey (now known as Samantha Jane Geimer) to Nicholson's home at 12850 Mulholland Drive on March 10, 1977. Nicholson and then girlfriend Anjelica Huston were not at home so Polanksi spent the afternoon taking photos of the young girl in various states of undress in the Jacuzzi and poolside before ending up in bed. L.A. police arrested Polanski the next day for committing a lewd and lascivious act (sodomy) on a child under 14 and rape by use of drugs (he reportedly provided Gailey with methaqualone). Polanski's attorney got the charge reduced to unlawful sexual intercourse with a minor and the director pleaded guilty on August 9, 1977, ironically the ninth anniversary of his wife's murder. Unwilling to face a possible prison sentence, Polanski fled from America on February 1, 1978, and has since been living and working in France, a country that does not extradite its own citizens. Polanski is a French citizen. The 2008 documentary, *Roman Polanski: Wanted and Desired*, covers the case in great detail and is noteworthy for its contemporary interviews with the

victim. On September 26, 2009, the 76-year-old director was arrested at the request of U.S. authorities while in Switzerland to accept a lifetime achievement award at the Zurich Film Festival. Polanski remained in a Swiss jail for two months while a parole deal was hammered out with authorities. On December 4, 2009, the director posted $4.5 million bail and was granted house arrest at Milky Way, his three-story villa in Gstaad. On July 13, 2010, the Justice Ministry in Berne announced its decision not to extradite the director based on doubts over the legal strength of the U.S. extradition request. While Polanski is officially free, he still faces an Interpol warrant in effect in 188 countries. As of August 2010, the 77-year-old director is safe from arrest only in his home nations of France and Poland, and now, Switzerland.

TATE FAMILY—Doris Tate, Sharon's mother, became a fixture at every convicted Family member's parole hearing to argue against the release of anyone connected to the murders. By the time of her death from cancer in July 1992, she had devoted 15 years of her life to the crime victims' movement and had spent countless hours lecturing inmates confined in California institutions about the impact of crime on victims, their family members and friends. In recognition of her work on behalf of victims she had received the Governor's Community Services Award, the California Police Officer's Association Golden Eagle Award, and the Motion Picture Mothers Gold Star Humanitarian Award. Since the death of Doris Tate, her passion for victims' advocacy has been assumed by Sharon's younger sisters, Patty (until her death in 2000) and Debra, who faithfully attends each Family members parole hearings to voice her opposition. Paul Tate, Sharon's father, died at 82 of congestive heart failure on May 18, 2005.

VAN HOUTEN, LESLIE—By 2002, Van Houten, 52, had gone through alcohol and drug rehab, extensive group therapy and psychotherapy, earned a college degree in literature, and assisted in the running of drug and alcohol programs for fellow-inmates. Considered a model prisoner at the California Institution for Women in Frontera, "LuLu" (her Family monicker) also reads to illiterate inmates, records tapes for the blind, and stitched part of the national AIDS quilt. At her periodic parole hearings, Van Houten unfailingly acknowledges her active participation in the LaBianca murders and expresses remorse. If paroled, she plans to live quietly and would like to work as a literary editor. Leslie Van Houten has found an impassioned and articulate supporter in filmmaker John Waters who devotes a chapter to her in his collection of essays, *Role Models*, published by Farrar, Straus and Giroux in 2010. Waters, who supports parole for the convicted killer, greatly admires Van Houten's acceptance of her responsibility for the killings and her moral strength for not only surviving the harsh realities of prison life, but for finding a way to make meaningful contributions in that environment. On July 7, 2010, she was denied parole for the 19th time. Those familiar with the infamous Charles Manson murders still consider Leslie Van Houten to have the best, if extremely remote, chance at one day winning parole.

WATSON, CHARLES ("TEX") — In 1975, Watson became a born-again Christian (chronicled in his 1978 book, *Will You Die for Me?*) and in 1983 created Abounding Love Ministries, Inc., a prisoner outreach program. After becoming an ordained minister in 1983, Watson continued his prison ministry and in 1997 launched his ministry's website, www.aboundinglove.org, containing links to his biography, a statement of faith, as well as the full-text of his earlier book, several religious works, and *Manson's Right-Hand Man Speaks Out!*, his 2003 book written in the form of a 200 question and answer interview in which the former Family member discusses the crime and his faith. Watson married in 1978 and, through conjugal visits, has fathered three children with his wife who is an active helpmate in his ministry. As of August 2009, the 63 year old has been repeatedly turned down for parole, and is serving life in the Mule Creek State Prison in Ione, fifty miles southeast of Sacramento, California.

Further Reading

Atkins, Susan, and Bob Slosser. *Child of Satan, Child of God.* Plainfield, NJ: Logos, 1977.

Bugliosi, Vincent, and Curt Gentry. *Helter Skelter: The True Story of the Manson Murders.* New York: Norton, 1974.

Donnelley, Paul. *501 Most Notorious Crimes.* London: Bounty, 2009.

King, Greg. *Sharon Tate and the Manson Murders.* New York: Barricade, 2000.

Oney, Steve. "Manson: An Oral History." *Los Angeles* 54(7) (July 2009): 94–103, 149–154, 156, 158.

Watson, Charles ("Tex"). *Manson's Right-Hand Man Speaks Out!* Jackson, CA: Abounding Love Ministries, 2003.

_____, and Hoekstra, Ray. *Will You Die for Me?* Old Tappan, NJ: Revell, 1978.

Wells, Simon. *Charles Manson Coming Down Fast: A Chilling Biography.* London: Hodder and Stoughton, 2009.

Taylor, William Desmond (V)

Hollywood's most enduring mystery, actor-director William Desmond Taylor was murdered in his bungalow on February 2, 1922, while another subject of scandal, Roscoe "Fatty" Arbuckle (see entry), was engaged in his second trial for the manslaughter of actress Virginia Rappe as the result of a drunken Labor Day weekend party in San Francisco in 1921. Arbuckle, acquitted in record time after a third trial, lived to see his good name and career destroyed, while the deceased Taylor was blessedly saved from unjustified postmortem press reports and innuendo that branded him as everything from a narcotics peddler to a bisexual defiler of both young men and women. Like the Arbuckle scandal, the Taylor case tainted everyone it touched ultimately destroying the careers of two Hollywood stars, Mabel Normand and Mary Miles Minter, while calling into further question the integrity of the office of the Los Angeles County district attorney.

Born William Cunningham Deane-Tanner on April 26, 1872 in County Waterford, Ireland, the future film director enjoyed a privileged life on a country estate presided over by his father, Major Kearns Deane-Tanner of the British Carlow Rifles. Taylor's clashes with his authoritarian father were so numerous and intense that he ran away at 18 to join a theatrical company in Manchester, England where friends were later startled to see him billed as "Cunninham Deane" in a small role in *The Private Secretary*. Learning his son was bringing disrepute to the family name, Major Deane-Tanner in late 1889 shipped the headstrong 18 year old off to Runnymede, a dude ranch of sorts in rural Kansas where the effete sons of rich British families were toughened up through a grueling regimen of horseback riding and instruction in frontier survival skills. Taylor flourished at the ranch, particularly at riding and, when Runnymede closed due to financial problems in 1892, he spent the next several years knocking around America variously supporting himself as a day laborer, railroad man, salesman, and waiter. Tall, handsome, well-liked, and impeccably mannered, the 23 year old (now calling himself Cunninham Deane) joined the New York City–based theatrical company of actress Fanny Davenport in 1895. He spent the next three years touring with the company and was building his name as an actor when Davenport's death in 1898 forced the troupe to disband. Though largely estranged from his family, Taylor used an inheritance of £1000 realized from the death of a sister to move into an elegant apartment house in Manhattan, and open an antiques shop. In December 1901, Taylor married Ethel ("Effie") Hamilton, a 24-year-old stenographer with theatrical ambitions whom *Broadway* magazine had once called New York's prettiest chorus girl. The union produced a daughter, Ethel Daisy, in 1902 and the family moved to the upscale village of Larchmont where he reportedly chafed under the drudgery of married life. In September 1908, Taylor had finally had enough. Withdrawing $600 from the antiques store, he sent $500 to wife Effie, and hit the road with the remaining $100, under a new name, "William Desmond Taylor."

The runaway first joined the traveling company of Canadian actor-producer George Cleveland,

The British expatriate William Desmond Taylor arrived in Hollywood in 1912 and first gained industry notice as an actor in *Captain Alvarez* (1914). That same year Taylor acted in and directed *The Criminal Code* and soon rivaled Cecil B. De-Mille as the top director at Paramount. The respected director's unsolved murder on February 1, 1922, unleashed a flood of negative press, wild rumors, and salacious innuendo that sullied his reputation and destroyed the careers of Mary Miles Minter and Mabel Normand (Kenneth Anger Collection).

but in May 1909 arrived in the Yukon at the tail end of the gold rush. As timekeeper for the Yukon Gold Company in Dawson, Yukon Territory, Taylor impressed everyone with his good manners, sartorial elegance, and strong work ethic. After the gold rush, the actor continued to knock around performing roles with theatrical companies in Hawaii and San Francisco. On the advice of friends, Taylor went to Hollywood in 1912 where director Thomas Ince (see entry) of the New York Motion Picture Co. took notice of the actor's good looks and horsemanship. Ince paid Taylor $40 a week to appear in the 1913 two-reeler *The Counterfeiter* as well as several other films that year (*The Iconoclast, Bread Cast Upon the Waters, The Battle of Gettysburg*). Taylor left Ince in 1913 and moved to Vitagraph where he made several movies prior to appearing in *Captain Alvarez* in 1914 with co-star Edna Storey. The adventure film showed Taylor to his best advantage riding a horse, and performing his own dangerous stunts. *Captain Alvarez* made the industry take notice of the cultured actor and in turn, Taylor parlayed his success into convincing Balboa Amusement Producing Company to let him direct.

Dating from his first directorial effort, *The Criminal Code* (1914) in which he also appeared, William Desmond Taylor proved himself to be a highly skilled filmmaker who in addition to understanding pace, dramatic detail, and how to write screenplays, also possessed the uncanny ability to manage and motivate difficult actors and actresses. While directing Neva Gerber in this film and others (*The Judge's Wife*, 1914; *An Eye for an Eye*, 1914; *Tricks of Fate*, 1914), Taylor (divorced in 1911) fell in love with the young actress, but the relationship ended after five years when the woman's husband refused to grant her a divorce. A trend, however, seemed to be established in his relations with his leading ladies. Many of them would admit to falling effortlessly in love with the cultured, well-mannered, and strikingly handsome director. On the strength of his skill in assuming the directorial reigns of the troubled 1915 serial *The Diamond from the Sky*, Taylor became one of the most sought after filmmakers in Hollywood. Paramount signed him in 1916 for *He Fell in Love with His Wife*, the first of 16 films he would make for the studio starring actors like Jack Pickford, Dustin Farnum, and Wallace Reid that would place him prestige-wise alongside the studio's other top director, Cecil B. DeMille.

As pointed out by Charles Higham in his 2004

study of the case, *Murder in Hollywood*, World War I did interrupt Taylor's Hollywood career, but he did not (as has been generally reported) enlist in the British military in a blaze of patriotic fervor. Rather, in 1918, the 46-year-old Englishman was compelled under the terms of the British draft to enter military service. As a private in the British forces, Taylor trained in Canada and quickly impressed his superiors with his bearing and organizational skill. As a sergeant, the Hollywood director put on camp vaudeville shows and trained a black Caribbean regiment prior to being posted to England as an officer at the war's end. Triumphantly returning to Hollywood in May 1919, Taylor resumed his interrupted directing career with films like *Captain Kidd, Jr.* (1919), *Anne of Green Gables* (1919), and *Huckleberry Finn* (1920). While directing *Anne of Green Gables* starring 17-year-old Mary Miles Minter in the title role, Taylor became the unwilling focus of the young star's romantic obsession. Minter, a beautiful but unstable actress, was Paramount's choice to replace Mary Pickford, "America's Sweetheart," after she left the studio to co-found United Artists in 1919 with Charlie Chaplin, D.W. Griffith, and future husband Douglas Fairbanks. Minter's mother, Charlotte Minter Shelby, was the original "stagemother from Hell." Minter was just six years old when Shelby decided the youngster was destined to become a star, first on the New York stage then later in Hollywood movies. By 1916, Minter was busy making movies like *The Gentle Intruder* and *Her Country's Call*. Shelby, as Minter's manager, collected 30 percent of her daughter's salary, a huge amount considering the actress signed a five-year $1.3

million studio contract in 1918. Shelby, however, had her hands full protecting her investment as her teenaged daughter showed a strong liking for men that was reciprocated. At 15, Minter fell in love with 35-year-old actor James Kirkwood. One day on an outing in Santa Barbara Kirkwood convinced the naïve teen that by merely exchanging vows between one another without benefit of

Actress Mary Miles Minter was 17 and picked by Paramount to replace Mary Pickford when Taylor directed her in the title role of *Anne of Green Gables* in 1919. Minter became infatuated with the director (30 years her senior) and relentlessly pursued him while under the watchful eye of her mother and manager, Charlotte Minter Shelby. Determined to protect her investment, Shelby threatened violence against any man she felt was interested in her daughter. Following Taylor's murder in 1922, detectives found love letters from Minter and her monogrammed nightgown in the director's bungalow. The resulting scandal ended Minter's career the next year. Some researchers in the unsolved Taylor case believe Minter may have accidentally shot the director while prodding him to commit to her while many more suspect Charlotte Shelby of making good her threat (Kenneth Anger Collection).

clergy they were legally married. Not surprisingly, Minter soon became pregnant with Shelby footing the bill for an abortion, but not before threatening to kill Kirkwood should he ever attempt to see her daughter again. This episode initiated a pattern between mother and daughter. Shelby, to protect her investment, was suspicious of every man in Minter's life and was well-known for threatening violence against anyone who showed an interest in her daughter. Minter, routinely escaping the locked room in which her mother confined her at the height of their frequent arguments, looked for masculine companionship.

William Desmond Taylor, the urbane sophisticate universally respected by the Hollywood Establishment, unwittingly entered the Shelby-Minter psychodrama around 1919 while directing the teen star in *Anne of Green Gables*. Though much conjecture has centered upon the supposed relationship between the 47-year-old director and the teenager this much is certain — Minter became infatuated with Taylor. In sexually suggestive diary entries Minter wrote about waiting to give herself to the older man. Taylor, fully aware of the unstable teen's obsession with him, kept a respectful distance and did nothing to encourage her. The director's paternal attitude toward his young star did little to stop her overly protective mother from loudly accusing him on set of pursuing her daughter. Any time Minter was out late Shelby was certain she was with the director. Once (according to Taylor's secretary) when the wayward teen failed to come home at an appointed time, the incensed woman (packing a concealed .38-caliber pistol) drove to the director's bungalow at Alvarado Court in the Westlake Park district of Los Angeles and threatened to kill him if she found Minter there. Taylor calmly let Shelby search the premises to satisfy her that her daughter was not there. The director, however, continued to be the subject of arguments between the pair long after the film wrapped. Shelby accused her daughter of sleeping with the older man, Minter denied the charge, and continued to pursue the disinterested director.

Further complicating the director's personal life was his relationship with famed Mack Sennett comedienne Mabel Normand, 27 at the time they began dating in 1920. While it was unknown if the couple were ever lovers (many at the time as well as later writers on the case believe Taylor was a discreet homosexual), they did enjoy each other's company. Certainly the director stood by Normand as she tried unsuccessfully to kick a crippling addiction to cocaine repeatedly footing the bill for her expensive stints in rehab and actively policing the Paramount lot for drug dealers who made a lucrative living selling dope to industry personnel. Taylor once reportedly met secretly with United States District Attorney Thomas Green to persuade him to launch an anti-drug campaign in Hollywood. The director's virulent anti-drug stand was so well-known in the movie capital that after his death police investigated the angle that drug dealers smarting from their loss of revenue in the motion picture industry may have been responsible for his murder.

A more likely suspect, however, lay even closer to Taylor's domestic life in Bungalow 404 on Alvarado Court. In late 1919 or early 1920, the director hired Edward Sands as his combination secretary, butler, and cook. Outwardly cultured, Sands was in reality little more than a bunco artist. In eight short years he managed to be dishonorably discharged from the military, re-enlist twice only to desert each time. Sands held a position in the Paramount commissary when Taylor picked him to be his "man Friday." The director's generosity was repaid in 1921 when Sands used the opportunity of Taylor's absence in Europe to forge his employer's name on several checks. Shortly before Taylor was to return, Sands stole the man's entire wardrobe, jewelry, and his car. Enraged, the director swore out a felony warrant, but never saw Sands again. In December 1921, Taylor returned home from an evening out to find his home burgled and ransacked. A week later, Taylor received two pawn tickets in the director's birth name, "William C. Deane-Tanner," for jewelry stolen in the earlier robbery. An accompanying note signed "Jimmy Valentine" was determined by graphologists to have been written by Edward Sands.

On the day of his death, February 1, 1922, the director returned to his home between 5:30 and 6:30 P.M. after an afternoon spent editing his new film, *The Green Temptation*. His neighbors in the eight units of duplex bungalows on Alvarado Court constituted a sort of minimovie enclave numbering actors Edna Purviance, Agnes Ayres, Douglas MacLean and wife, Faith, and Paramount director Charles Maigne. Henry Peavey, the flamboyant homosexual black servant who had replaced the felonious Edward Sands, served his employer dinner around 6:30 P.M. By arrangement,

A top-flight comedienne, Mabel Normand was the star of several Mack Sennett comedies, but battled crippling addictions to alcohol and cocaine. Taylor, a close personal friend of the actress (pictured above with Russ Powell in *The Slim Princess*, 1920), paid the bills for Normand's stays in drug rehab and was wearing a locket with her picture in it at the time of his murder. She was the last person to see the director alive (other than the killer) on the day of his death. Normand, amid lingering doubts she was somehow involved in the case, saw her career tank as she continued to abuse alcohol and drugs. The 37-year-old died from tuberculosis in 1930 (Kenneth Anger Collection).

Mabel Normand arrived shortly after 7:00 P.M. to pick up a book Taylor had bought for her. Peavey left twenty minutes later with Normand leaving by chauffeured car at 7:45 P.M. Fifteen minutes later, Taylor's neighbor, Faith MacLean, heard a loud noise that sounded like a gunshot. Looking outside, she saw a man (5'9", 170 pounds) standing at the open door of Taylor's bungalow with the lamplight from the room outlining his frame in the surrounding darkness. The man unhurriedly closed the door and walked away. MacLean did not see him distinctly and thought nothing more of it until the next morning around 7:30 A.M. when a hysterical Henry Peavey awakened the entire Alvarado Court enclave with screams of "Dey've kilt Massa! Dey've kilt Massa!" Mo-

ments before, Peavey had arrived at the bungalow to fix breakfast for his employer only to discover the fully clothed 49-year-old director lying dead on his back on the living room carpet, arms at his side, head near a desk, feet under a chair, with only a bit of dried blood at the corner of one side of his mouth to suggest foul play.

In the ensuing pandemonium, neighbors crowded the crime scene destroying the integrity of valuable forensic evidence. The first call was not to police, but rather to Paramount's general manager, Charles Eyton. The studio "fixer," Eyton rushed to the scene and as neighbors gawked at Taylor's dead body, he quickly, but methodically "sanitized" the scene removing liquor bottles (it was Prohibition) and any other incriminating evidence like letters, etc. that could place Paramount at risk. A decade later a similar scenario would occur when film executive Paul Bern (see entry), husband of cinema sex goddess Jean Harlow, died in mysterious circumstances and MGM's fixer beat the cops to the death scene. Twenty minutes later, around 8:00 A.M., detectives arrived, ordered out the rubberneckers and were interviewing neighbors when a passing doctor stuck his head in the door and offered to examine the dead body. Remarkably, the doctor pronounced the cause of death to be a stomach hemorrhage. Peavey confirmed Taylor suffered from acute stomach pain, and the lead detective entered "natural causes" in his notebook. More than an hour after the discovery of Taylor's body, the coroner arrived and supervised the flipping of the corpse onto its face to conduct a more thorough examination. A bloodstain on the carpet near Taylor's back led the examiner to lift the director's jacket to discover a wound low on his left side. An autopsy revealed that Taylor died of a single .38-caliber gunshot wound that traveled low from the left side near the back, punctured the left lung, and settled in the neck. A gunpowder burn around the wound confirmed the weapon had been pressed against the director and fired while he had his arms outstretched.

As detectives attempted to piece together a motive for the murder and question those who knew the director, the press (already at a fever pitch from its ongoing coverage of the infamous Roscoe "Fatty" Arbuckle scandal), further muddied the investigative waters by printing half-truths and lies about Taylor. A nightgown with the embroidered initials "M.M.M." (sources dispute the item was monogrammed) was found in Taylor's bungalow along with a note written by Minter on her distinctive butterfly stationery in which the 19-year-old star professed her love for the 49-year-old director. The ravenous press seized on the pair's implied sexual relationship, but did not stop there. Mabel Normand was also identified as a "bedmate" after a locket was found on the dead man containing a picture of the friend he had repeatedly tried to help kick cocaine. Tales of drug abuse also became a way to sell newspapers. Rather than being a tireless champion against illicit drugs, the cultured director was portrayed by the press as having been an opium smoker who supplied drugs to movie stars. Beyond that, drugs played an important part in the libel that Taylor belonged to a "love cult" where the smoking of opium was but a prelude to ritualized homosexual activity. The film industry knew that the press accounts of Taylor, the president of the Motion Picture Directors' Association, were bold-faced lies, but an American public tired of Hollywood's excesses in the porcine form of Roscoe "Fatty" Arbuckle, the accused defiler and murderer of an innocent woman, readily believed anything was possible in Tinseltown. On February 7, 1922, blessedly unaware of the irreparable harm being done his reputation, Taylor was buried in his old military uniform in Hollywood Memorial Park Cemetery following a funeral service conducted in St. Paul's Pro-Cathedral Church on Pershing Square in downtown Los Angeles. A crowd of 10,000 jammed the streets anxious to see any movie stars who might be attending.

By present day standards, the police investigation and handling of the case by the L.A. District Attorney, Thomas Lee Woolwine, was incompetent at best and criminal at worst. The crime scene, already contaminated by a revolving door parade of "witnesses" and picked over by the studio fixer, yielded enough evidence (cigarette butts found outside Taylor's bungalow) to implicate Edward Sands as a prime suspect. Despite leads placing the embezzler in Los Angeles two days prior to the murder, Sands was never located. The drug angle was explored based on Taylor's strong stance against dope pushers lurking on the Paramount lot. Perhaps, it was speculated, the interests controlling the dope flow placed a contract hit on the director. This, too, was quickly discounted for lack of supporting evidence. More promising suspects were the women in Taylor's life, particularly Mabel Normand and Mary Miles Minter. Normand, a junkie, was known to experience dramatic mood swings and may have been angry with the director for blocking her access to drugs. Although cleared by the timeline in the case (she was being driven home by her driver at the moment of the murder) her career was destroyed by alcohol, drugs, and lingering doubts over her involvement in the case. Normand died of tuberculosis at age 37 in 1930. In the weeks and months following the murder, Mary Miles Minter continued to profess her love for Taylor in a series of press reports. At least one chronicler of the case, Charles Higham in his book, *Murder in Hollywood*, names the young actress as his accidental killer. In this scenario, Minter waited until Normand left the director's residence to arrive then pressed him for a commitment. Minter, carrying the .38-caliber pistol that she had once used in a half-hearted suicide attempt, accidentally pulled the gun's trigger as she was showing the director the gun in an attempt to convince him of the depth of her feelings. Leaving the scene, she confided the accidental killing to her mother, Charlotte Shelby, who used the time before the discovery of Taylor's body to construct various alibis. Like Normand, Minter's career was destroyed by the subsequent fallout from Taylor's murder. After appearing in *The Trail of the Lonesome Pine* in 1923, she permanently left the screen and lived as a semi-recluse off judicious real estate investments until dying from heart failure at the age of 82 on August 4, 1984. Emotionally unstable to the end, Minter supposedly made a deathbed confession to killing Taylor to her nurse who then disappeared.

Of all the principals in the Taylor murder, however, Charlotte Shelby today remains the most compelling suspect in his death. Not only had the quintessential stage mother threatened to kill several men who had shown an interest in Minter to protect her 30 percent stake in her daughter's income, Hollywood insiders knew of Minter's obsession with the director and the mother's incendiary opposition to the relationship. Some have even theorized that Shelby was attracted to Taylor. Despite the woman's well-publicized feelings toward Taylor, District Attorney Thomas Lee Woolwine, a friend of Shelby's, never asked her for a statement. Woolwine's successor in the position, Asa Keyes, questioned Shelby in 1925, but not surprisingly the intervening years since the murder had afforded sufficient time for the woman to construct a fairly tight alibi (although it did conflict with the statements of others taken at the time of the killing). Keyes was later jailed on unrelated bribery charges and his replacement, Buron Fitts, reopened the case in late 1929, but nothing came of it. Fitts committed suicide in 1973, perhaps with the gun used to kill Taylor. Hollywood's most enduring murder mystery remained out of the press until fanned into flame again by a legal suit over unpaid moneys brought by Shelby's other daughter, Margaret Shelby Fillmore, against her mother in 1937. In addition to accusing her mother of underhanded business practices, Fillmore fingered Shelby as paying a confidant, Carl Stockdale, to murder the director. Shelby denied the charges and demanded a grand jury be impaneled to either charge or clear her of Taylor's killing. After much conflicting testimony, the grand jury did neither. Shelby reportedly died in 1957. In 1982, the book *A Cast of Killers* by Sidney Kirkpatrick published director King Vidor's research into the death of William Desmond Taylor in which his industry colleague concluded that Charlotte Shelby was the director's killer. The case remains officially unsolved.

Further Reading

Giroux, Robert. *A Deed of Death: The Story Behind the Unsolved Murder of Hollywood Director William Desmond Taylor.* New York: Knopf, 1990.

Higham, Charles. *Murder in Hollywood: Solving a Silent Screen Mystery.* Madison, WI: Terrace, 2004.

Kirkpatrick, Sidney. *A Cast of Killers.* New York: Dutton, 1986.

Long, Bruce. *William Desmond Taylor: A Dossier.* Metuchen, NJ: Scarecrow Press, 1991.

Tecno Banda Fugaz *see* **Appendix 1**

Thomas, Albert *see* **Yella**

Thomas, Kid (M-V)

An obscure early blues and rock 'n' roll performer heavily influenced by Little Richard, Kid Thomas (a.k.a. Tommy Lewis/Louis) was born Louis Thomas Watts on June 20, 1934, in Sturgis, Mississippi. The family moved to Chicago when Thomas was 7 and as a teen he took harmonica lessons from Little Willie Smith, a minor bluesman in the city. By the late 1940s and early 1950s Thomas was playing harmonica at various blues clubs in Chicago sharing the stage with the likes of Bo Diddley, Muddy Waters, and Elmore James. Signed by the local King-Federal label in 1955, the harmonica playing blues singer cut two singles ("Wolf Pack" and "The Spell"), both flops. In 1956, after a stint in Wichita, Kansas, Thomas broadened his musical horizons and moved into rock 'n' roll affecting a processed pompadour in the style of Little Richard. In Los Angeles in early 1959, Thomas cut two singles for Modern Records for which he is best known today—"You are an Angel" and the aptly titled "Rockin' this Joint Tonight." The label quickly folded and the record was never promoted. Five years passed before Thomas, renamed Tommy Louis and the Rhythm Rockers, recorded two singles for Muriel—"The Hurt Is On" and "Wail Baby Wail." Again, the records failed. Throughout the mid- to late-1960s Kid Thomas performed at private parties and in clubs like the Cozy Lounge in South East L.A. One night at the Cozy Lounge, the owner of Cenco Records saw Thomas perform and brought him in the studio to record his last singles — "(You are an) Angel" and the instrumental, "Willowbrook." Like Modern Records, however, Cenco Records tanked.

Kid Thomas, the poor man's Little Richard, was operating a moderately successful lawn care service in Beverly Hills when what was left of his life forever changed. On September 3, 1969, Lou T. Watts (Kid Thomas), 35, was driving his van in the 300 block of South Doheny Drive in Beverly Hills when he accidentally struck a child riding a bicycle. Ethan Friedman, 10, died of his injuries later that afternoon. The boy's father, Eugene K. Friedman, pressed police and requested the district attorney to file manslaughter charges. Although Thomas possessed five driver's licenses (four obtained by fraudulent means), police were only able to revoke his license. In the absence of witnesses to the accident, the district attorney refused to prosecute citing insufficient evidence. Friedman hired a private investigator to tail the bluesman. On March 2, 1970, police (acting on an "anonymous" tip) arrested Thomas for driving on a revoked license. Friedman was present in court when Thomas came up on charges, but the case was postponed until April 13. That day, Eugene Friedman waited in the parking lot of the public library across the street from City Hall for the arrival of the man he blamed for the death of his only child. Immediately upon his arrival, Thomas was confronted by the distraught father. The men spoke briefly and then Friedman pulled a 9mm automatic pistol from a briefcase and fired point-blank into the bluesman. Thomas ran across the street toward the rear entrance of the police station with Friedman in pursuit still squeezing off rounds. Thomas fell to the curb, but a stray shot struck Beverly Hills Police Sgt. John Carden in the leg as he was standing at the rear door of the station. Friedman dropped his gun and was arrested without incident. Lou T. Watts, nominally well-known in certain musical circles as Kid Thomas, was pronounced dead at 9:20 A.M. at UCLA Medical Center. At his first-degree murder trial in August 1970, Friedman faced the death penalty and a charge of assault with a deadly weapon in the shooting of Officer Carden. The grieving father testified that he believed his son was standing next to him when he confronted Thomas to plead with him to stop driving. When Thomas assumed what Friedman interpreted as a menacing position the father shot him to protect his son. Following two days of deliberation, a jury

found Friedman guilty of the reduced charge of voluntary manslaughter, but acquitted him on the assault with a deadly weapon charge. Superior Court Judge Adolph Alexander subsequently placed Friedman on three years probation and ordered him to obtain psychiatric treatment, get a job, and to not use weapons or drugs. "I do not condone violence in any form," added the judge, "but if it was in my power to reduce the charge to a misdemeanor I would do it."

Further Reading

Koda, Cub. "Kid Thomas." www.allmusic.com.
Simmonds, Jeremy. *The Encyclopedia of Dead Rock Stars: Heroin, Handguns, and Ham Sandwiches.* Rev. ed. Chicago, IL: Chicago Review, 2008.
"Son Killed: Father Gets Probation in Man's Death," *Los Angeles Times*, September 26, 1970, sec. B, p. 7.

Tillis, Sanford Lewis (V)

Employed for a year as a set designer by NBC television, the 26-year-old Columbia University honor graduate left the network in May 1952 to become an assistant designer for the New Jersey–based Maplewood Theatre. During the summer of 1952 Tillis designed sets for the Grist Mill Playhouse in Andover, N.J., leaving at the end of the season to work on sets for the Brander Matthews Theatre at his alma mater. In the early hours of October 10, 1952, New York City firemen entering the set designer's burning first-floor apartment at 200 West 93rd Street at Amsterdam Avenue found his body lashed to an overturned studio couch. Tillis' hands and feet were bound behind him with electrical cord pulled from a bedroom light fixture and his face was beaten in with a charred table leg. The body was spared from total immolation when the flames of the makeshift pyre burned away from him. Investigators determined Tillis was still alive when his murderer torched the apartment. Although police ruled out robbery as the prime motive for the killing, the victim's wallet was emptied and dresser drawers were tossed. Authorities questioned thirty friends and acquaintances of the dead man, but never apprehended his killer.

Further Reading

Feinberg, Alexander. "Theatrical Set Designer Murdered, Bound to Couch Flaming as Pyre." *The New York Times*, October 11, 1952, p. 1.

Todd, Thelma (V-suspected)

In the dark history of Hollywood the suspicious death of screen star Thelma Todd in 1935 ranks with that of Jean Harlow's husband Paul Bern (see entry) in 1932 as among Tinseltown's most enduring mysteries. Born the daughter of a corrupt civil servant and an aggressive domineering mother, Alice, in Lawrence, Massachusetts, on July 29, 1906, Thelma Alice Todd was by all accounts a strikingly beautiful child. By her teens, she was already well on her way to earning her Hollywood nickname, "Hot Toddy," by dressing provocatively and "innocently" flirting with older men. After graduating high school, she enrolled in 1923 in Lowell State Normal School, one of the most prestigious teachers' colleges in the East. During the summers, Todd worked as a part-time fashion model at a local theatre where her stunning good looks attracted much attention. In 1925, Alice Todd forced her 19-year-old daughter to enter the "Miss Massachusetts" beauty pageant. Todd won and was instantly approached by a talent scout for Paramount and the Famous Players-Lasky studios. After passing a screen test, she signed a five year, $75 a week contract with Paramount, and took acting lessons at the studio in Astoria, New York.

In 1926 she made her film debut in the silent *Fascinating Youth* featuring Clara Bow. Later that year, she and her mother relocated to Hollywood where Paramount kept the actress busy in a variety of roles. By late 1928, Todd had appeared in more than a dozen films for Paramount and on loan-out to Warner Bros., First National, Columbia, and Hal Roach Studios. Though wanting to be a serious dramatic actress, Todd showed a flair for comedy unusual in such a beautiful woman. Hal Roach, after seeing her in the 1928 First National comedy *Vamping Venus*, signed her to a $75 a week deal in 1929. The king of motion picture comedy, Roach had Laurel & Hardy and Charlie Chase under contract and made the popular *Our Gang* series. While the contract with Roach permitted Todd to work (subject to his approval) for other studios, it also contained the bane of Hollywood actresses — the dreaded "potato clause." The contract option permitted the studio to unconditionally release an actress if her weight went up by more than five pounds over her original weight when she signed the contract. Todd, like many actresses of the day, was forced to self-starve and pop diet pills to fulfill her contractual obligation. The result — the beautiful young performer became addicted to amphetamines.

Under Roach and his relentless shooting schedule, Todd blossomed into a comedienne with impeccable timing. Her first film for the comedy

A rare commodity in Hollywood, a beautiful woman capable of doing comedy, Todd distinguished herself as a first-rate comedienne in films with Charlie Chase, Laurel and Hardy, ZaSu Pitts, Patsy Kelly, and the Marx Brothers. Though her death in 1935 was ruled an "accidental" case of carbon monoxide poisoning, the hard-partying actress was once married to mob figure Pasquale ("Pat") DiCicco and was the lover of notorious gangster Charles ("Lucky") Luciano. Speculation persists that "Hot Toddy" was killed by the mob after resisting Luciano's efforts to establish a casino in the restaurant she owned in the Pacific Palisades section of Los Angeles.

giant, the 1929 Laurel & Hardy talkie *Unaccustomed as We Are*, established Todd's physical look (dyed blonde hair) and screen persona (sexy, but tough). She made three other films with Stan and Ollie: *Another Fine Mess*, 1930; *Chickens Come Home*, 1931; and *Fra Diavola* (a.k.a. *The Devil's Brother*, MGM, 1933). In 1929, Todd was paired with comedian Charlie Chase in *Snappy Sneezer*. The duo clicked, on screen and off, and the actress was soon earning $500 a week appearing with Chase in comedy shorts like *Crazy Feet* (1929), *The Real McCoy* (1930), *All Teed Up* (1930), *Dollar Dizzy* (1930), *Looser Than Loose* (1930), *High C's* (1930), *The Pip from Pittsburgh* (1931), *Rough Seas* (1931), and *The Nickel Nurser* (1932).

Roach, however, wanted his studio to have a

female comedy team that rivalled his success with Laurel & Hardy. In 1931, he teamed Todd, now paid $2,000 a week, with ZaSu Pitts in *Let's Do Things*. The film's commercial success launched a series of Todd-Pitts shorts that included *Catch as Catch Can* (1931), *The Pajama Party* (1931), *War Mamas* (1931), *On the Loose* (1931), *Seal Skins* (1932), *Red Noses* (1932), *Strictly Unreliable* (1932), *The Old Bull* (1932), *Show Business* (1932), *Alum and Eve* (1932), *Sneak Easily* (1932), *Asleep at the Feet* (1933), *Maids A La Mode* (1933), *The Bargain of the Century* (1933), and *One Track Minds* (1933). Pitts left Roach in 1933 over a salary dispute and was replaced by comedienne Patsy Kelly in a series of comedy shorts directed by Gus Meins. Todd-Kelly pairings include *Beauty and the Bus*, 1933; *Back to Nature*, 1933; *Air Fright*, 1933; *Babes in the Goods*, 1934; *Soup and Fish*, 1934; *Man in Hollywood*, 1934; *I'll Be Suing You*, 1934; *Three Chumps Ahead*, 1934; *One Horse Farmers*, 1934; and *Done in Oil*, 1934. In addition to her work with Roach, Todd also appeared in two Marx Brothers movies for Paramount, *Monkey Business* (1931) and *Horse Feathers* (1932).

By the early 1930s, "Hot Toddy" was well-known in the screen capital as a hard working, hard drinking party girl who was always up for a good time. In 1931 she met Pasquale ("Pat") DiCicco, an agent with mob connections, at a studio party at the Palace Theatre. Their marriage in July 1932 was marked by DiCicco's routine physical abuse of the popular actress and his lengthy, unexplained absences. Through DiCicco, Todd met mob kingpin Charles ("Lucky") Luciano who was in Los Angeles to oversee his interests there in gambling, drugs, prostitution, and restaurant-union infiltration. By the time Todd divorced DiCicco in March 1934 on the grounds of mental cruelty, she was already deeply involved with Luciano. In August 1934, Todd and her occasional lover Roland West purchased a three-story building on Roosevelt Highway (now Pacific Coast Highway) in Pacific Palisades. West, married to fading actress Jewel Carmen, had directed Todd in the 1931 dramatic flop *Corsair* starring Chester Morris. West and Todd opened Thelma Todd's Sidewalk Café on the first-floor of the building and maintained separate apartments on the second-floor to hide their affair. The half-storied third floor was used as a storeroom. West and wife Carmen (who supplied the money for the café) lived in a house above the restaurant on Posetano Road. The couple's palatial home, Castillo del Mar, had a two car garage with an apartment above at 17531 Posetano Road situated below the house. On-foot access from the rear of the restaurant to the garage above where Todd and West kept their cars was gained by a flight of 270 cement steps snaking up the hillside.

Based on Todd's star power, the restaurant quickly became a favorite meeting place for celebrities, studio folk, and rubberneckers wishing to hobnob with the stars. As Hollywood legend goes, Luciano started putting pressure on Todd to force her to lease him the café's unused third-floor as a site for a mob controlled gambling casino catering to the Tinseltown elite. Todd resisted even though the mob boss was already supplying the restaurant's liquor, steaks, and linen service at grossly inflated prices. Despite the overflow crowd of well-heeled customers, the café never turned a profit. By December 11, 1935, Luciano's insistence that the 29-year-old comedienne lease him the third-floor space for gambling reached the point where Todd called the office of Buron Fitts, the Los Angeles district attorney, for assistance. Proven by history to have been corrupt as anyone he ever prosecuted, Fitts agreed to see Todd on December 17, 1935. In a bid to block the mobster, the actress publicly announced plans to convert the café's third-floor into a steakhouse.

Meanwhile, the Todd-West relationship had deteriorated to the point that the jealous former director had taken to imposing a 2:00 A.M. curfew on the hard partying actress. If Todd failed to return to her second-floor apartment by that hour West locked down the building. On Saturday, December 14, 1935, Todd and West argued about her plans to go alone to the Café Trocadero to attend a party for British comedian Stanley Lupino, father of film actress Ida Lupino. West sternly warned her that the building would be locked at 2:00 A.M. whether she was home or not. Todd, dressed in a blue satin, sequined evening gown and mink stole, was chauffeured to the Trocadero by driver Ernest Peters. She arrived at 8:15 P.M. Ex-husband Pat DiCicco was there with a date, but Todd spoke with Ida Lupino instead about a wonderful new man in her life who lived in San Francisco. Todd was in high spirits the entire evening, but according to party-goers her mood changed after making a phone call to an unknown person shortly after 1:45 A.M.

The actress remained at the party until around 3:00 A.M. when Peters arrived to drive her back to her apartment in Thelma Todd's Sidewalk

Café. According to the driver, Todd appeared frightened during the trip back and at her urging he pushed the car to speeds over 70 miles per hour on the Roosevelt Highway. When they arrived at the café around 3:30 or 4:00 A.M., Todd dismissed the chauffeur. As Peters drove away, he saw her walking in the direction of the cement steps leading up the hillside to the two-car garage on Posetano Road. At 10:00 A.M. on Monday, December 16, 1935, almost two days after the actress left for the party at the Trocadero, her maid, Mae Whitehead, arrived at the garage on Posetano Road to drive Todd's car to the rear of the café. Noticing the right garage door was open about six inches, Whitehead entered the garage to find her employer's body wedged between the front seat and the steering wheel of her chocolate brown 1934 Lincoln Phaeton, the apparent victim of carbon monoxide poisoning. Further examination, however, revealed bruises on her neck, a broken nose, two cracked ribs on her right side, and a chipped front tooth. The coroner explained that the neck bruising was due to "post-mortem lividity" caused by the involuntary jerking of the neck immediately before death. The bloody lip and broken bones were the result of Todd's falling into the steering wheel and door during her death throes. A blood sample revealed 70 percent carbon monoxide saturation and it was determined that the actress had been legally drunk at the time of her death.

An accidental death theory (later officially accepted as fact) was advanced that Todd, after being dropped off at her locked apartment on Sunday morning, spent the rest of the day of December 15, somewhere before choosing to sleep in her car in the early morning hours of Monday. She apparently ran the car's engine to stay warm and, inebriated, died when overcome by exhaust fumes. However, Charles Smith, the café's treasurer who lived with his wife in the apartment above the death garage, testified at the inquest that he did not hear or smell anything during the hours she was supposed to have been dying of carbon monoxide poisoning. Numerous people in different parts of Los Angeles spoke of seeing Todd at various times on Sunday in the company of a well-dressed male companion (Luciano or DiCicco?). A Christmas tree salesman in Santa Monica reported he saw the star around 11:45 P.M. that night. Alice Todd, Thelma's stage door mother, initially claimed her daughter had been murdered. Several others took her view, but ex-

perienced memory lapses when called upon to testify at the inquest. Mae Whitehead flatly told officials that anonymous men had threatened her with harm if she chose to speak about any possible mob involvement in the café. Andy Edmonds, in her provocative book, *Hot Toddy*, suggests Todd was murdered on Luciano's orders and offers a plausible chronology of events and a scenario that explains the movie star's untimely death. If nothing else, Edmonds skillfully points out the numerous investigative, forensic, and judicial inconsistencies in the official handling of the case. On December 19, 1935, thousands of friends, fans, and curiosity seekers filed past Todd's open casket at Pierce Brothers Mortuary between 9:00 A.M. and 1:00 P.M. Later that afternoon, a private funeral service attended by close friends and family was conducted at the Wee Kirk o' the Heather Chapel at Forest Lawn Cemetery in Glendale. The remains of the so-called "Ice Cream Blonde" were cremated and presented to her mother, Alice. Following Alice's death in 1969, the funeral urn containing the actress' ashes were placed in her mother's coffin and buried in the Bellevue Cemetery in Lawrence, Massachusetts.

Further Reading

Edmonds, Andy. *Hot Toddy: The True Story of Hollywood's Most Sensational Murder*. New York: William Morris, 1989.

Jacobson, Laurie, and Marc Wanamaker. *Hollywood Heartbreak: The Tragic and Mysterious Deaths of Hollywood's Most Remarkable Legends*. New York: Simon and Schuster, 1984.

Munn, Michael. *The Hollywood Murder Casebook*. New York: St. Martin's, 1987.

Torres, Angelo (V)

Bronx Zoo, a four man rock group co-founded by drummer Angelo Torres in Belleville, Illinois, in 1988, was just beginning to attract national attention. The group recorded their inaugural album, *Lustful Thinking*, in New York City in June 1990, and had opened for Blue Oyster Cult, Head East, the Romantics, and Gary Richrath, lead guitarist for REO Speedwagon. Following successful dates at L.A.'s Whisky A-Go-Go and City Lights in Dallas, the group's manager predicted Bronx Zoo was "on the very edge" of making it big. If so, the 26-year-old drummer was not fated to make the trip. Just before midnight on November 12, 1992, Torres argued with the owner of a well-known crack house in Centreville, Illinois. The drummer walked to a nearby liquor store in East St. Louis and encountered Alphonso "Capone" Fuller, a 21-year-old two-time convicted felon currently on probation from the Menard Correctional Center on a weapons charge, and three of his cronies. A heated dispute between the men over a car the drummer allegedly swapped Fuller for drugs culminated in the men beating the drummer and forcing him into the trunk of a car. Fuller and friends drove the car back to the crack house where "Capone" picked up a 9mm semi-automatic pistol. Cruising for a couple of hours, Fuller stopped the car around 3:30 A.M. in the 100 block of 80th Street in a residential section of Centreville. According to Delando Bell, 19, one of the abductors in the car who later cut a deal with prosecutors in exchange for his testimony, Fuller lifted Torres from the trunk and pointed the weapon at him. When the gun jammed, Torres turned and ran making it about 150 feet before the pursuing Fuller brought him down with two rounds. Fuller's gun jammed again, but he managed to finish the execution-style killing with a fatal chest shot delivered from less than two feet away. Torres died two hours later in St. Mary's Hospital in East St. Louis. Arrested days after the crime, Fuller was charged with first-degree murder while his three accomplices pleaded guilty to lesser charges ranging from unlawful restraint, concealing a homicide, and kidnapping, in exchange for their testimony against the triggerman. Fuller was convicted of the Torres murder in a three-day trial in July 1993 and sentenced to 60 years in prison.

Further Reading

Goodrich, Robert. "Centreville Man Found Guilty in Murder of Rock Drummer." *St. Louis Post-Dispatch*, July 16, 1993, sec. B, p. 2.

Tosh, Peter (V)

Like fellow-bandmates Carlton Barrett and Junior Brathwaite (see entries), Tosh was the third member of the legendary reggae group Bob Marley and The Wailers to meet violent death. Born Winston Hubert MacIntosh in Westmoreland, Jamaica, on October 9, 1944, the 6'6" musician co-founded The Wailers with Bob Marley in Kingston in 1964. Both men were dedicated Rastafarians, a West Indian religion advocating the return to Africa of blacks, and took seriously the use of marijuana ("ganja") as a sacrament to become closer to God ("Ja"). The Wailers became internationally recognized with their 1973 album *Catch a Fire* and as the years and records passed Bob Marley became increasingly the face of the band and reggae music particularly after the group

signed with major label Island Records. At the end of The Wailers' 1973 tour of the United Kingdom, Tosh announced he would no longer tour outside Jamaica, effectively giving notice he was out of the band. His exit became official on November 30, 1973, when he and Marley engaged in a fistfight.

Tosh's departure gave him more freedom to vent his militant political beliefs and to press his demand for the legalization of marijuana on a series of solo records like *Legalize It* (1976), *Equal Rights* (1977), and *Wanted: Dread & Alive* (1981). Resplendent in khakis and always smoking a "spliff," Tosh used live performances to spread the word of the black man's struggle in such songs as "400 Years," "Burial," and "Get Up, Stand Up." Such outspokenness, however, came at a personal price. At the One Love Peace Concert in Kingston on April 22, 1978, promoting unity and an end to the civil violence in Jamaica, Tosh preceded Marley onstage and used his set to verbally attack the government and the opposition, as well as to push for the legalization of "ganja." In the estimated crowd of 30,000, Prime Minister Michael Manley and Jamaican Labour Party leader Edward Seaga were not amused although they later joined Bob Marley onstage for an historic handshake. In the crowd, Mick Jagger was so impressed he signed Tosh to Rolling Stones Records and had the musician open for the band during its tour of the United States in 1978. In September of that year, just five months after his incendiary comments at the One Love Peace show, Tosh (smoking an omnipresent "spliff") was stopped by two Kingston police officers as he was leaving a club. In the ensuing beating Tosh suffered a severe head injury and a broken right hand.

On the evening of September, 11, 1987, the 43-year-old reggae legend was at home in his two-story bungalow on Plymouth Avenue in Barbican, a well-to-do suburb of St. Andrew, with his common-law wife, Marlene Brown, and some friends. Tosh had just returned from a promotional meeting in New York City for his latest album, *No Nuclear War*. Three armed gunman, including Dennis "Leppo" Lobban, a 32-year-old street vendor and friend of the singer who had recently quarreled with Marlene Brown, forced their way into the house. Lobban demanded money from Tosh, certain the musician had brought funds back from the States. Forcing the company to lay face-down on the floor, "Leppo" pumped two pistol shots into Tosh's forehead sparking a barrage of gunfire from his accomplices. The massacre claimed the lives of Tosh, his "herbsman" and vegetarian chef, Wilton "Doc" Brown, and Jeff "Free I" Dixon, a deejay for the state-run Jamaica Broadcasting Corporation. Injured in the massacre were Marlene Brown and three others. The body of Peter Tosh outfitted in khaki topped with a white satin brimless African cap lay in state while 12,000 mourners filed past to pay their final respects. He was buried in Bluefields, Westmoreland, Jamaica. As speculation raged over whether the musician's murder was due to drug trafficking or political revenge, Lobban surrendered to police claiming he had seen his picture on television and wished to profess his innocence. On June 19, 1978, a jury of eight women and four men needed only six minutes to find Lobban guilty of murdering Tosh, Brown, and Dixon. "Leppo" was given the death penalty, but his sentence was commuted to life imprisonment in 1995 after the Jamaican government declared an amnesty on executions.

Further Reading

Goldberg, Michael. "Reggae Great Peter Tosh Murdered." *Rolling Stone*, 511 (October 22, 1987):24, 97.
Green, Jo-Ann. "Peter Tosh." www.allmusic.com.
Steckles, Garry. *Bob Marley: A Life*. Northampton, MA: InterlinkBooks, 2009.
White, Timothy. *Catch a Fire: The Life of Bob Marley*. Rev. and enl. ed.: London: Omnibus, 2006.

Trintignant, Marie *see* **Cantat**, Bertrand

Troutman, Larry (M-S)

The Hamilton, Ohio, native with brothers Roger, Lester, and Tony, co-founded the funk band Zapp in Dayton, Ohio, in 1978. Though not performing on the band's 1980 Warner Bros. release *Zapp*, Troutman did play congas on their second album, *Zapp II*, in 1982. The first album produced the popular single "More Bounce to the Ounce" and marked Troutman's younger brother, Roger, as the band's creative force and star performer. In that 1980 hit, Roger Troutman's vocals were sung through a vocoder or talkbox, a voice distorting device that had already been used to great effect in rock music by Joe Walsh ("Rocky Mountain Way," 1973) and by Peter Frampton ("Do You Feel Like We Do," 1976). Roger Troutman continued his influential funk career throughout the 1980s and 1990s. Recording as "Roger," Troutman reached Number 3 on the *Billboard* singles chart in 1987 with "I Want to be Your Man." In the mid–1980s, older brother Larry essentially left performing to manage Zapp and

to assume the presidency of the brothers' Dayton-based company. Troutman Enterprises (formed in 1980 to train unskilled workers and to create jobs for them in Dayton) was comprised of three recording studios, real estate ventures, and contracting businesses. Nicknamed "Dollars," Larry Troutman was at the helm of the company when it filed for bankruptcy in 1992 seeking relief from a $3.8 million debt and more than $400,000 in delinquent taxes. In 1996, a judge issued a preliminary ruling that the case should be switched from bankruptcy reorganization to liquidation. As Troutman Enterprises crumbled around its president, Roger Troutman's career was resurging. In 1996, he added his vocoder sound to the Dr. Dre–produced Tupac Shakur (see entry) hit "California Love." That same year, Warner Bros. released a second greatest hits album of Zapp material under the band name Zapp & Roger. Troutman also sang back-up to rapper Nature on Dr. Dre's 1997 multi-act disc, *The Firm*, and in 1998 appeared on the track "No Man's Land" on Gerald Levert's CD *Love & Consequences*. He planned to tour in the summer of 1999.

At around 7:20 A.M. on April 25, 1999, Roger Troutman, 47, was found lying in an alley behind Catalpa Drive near the recording studio his family owned in northwest Dayton, Ohio. Four gunshot wounds, two in the front and two in the back, riddled the singer's body. He died a short time later at Good Samaritan Hospital and Health Center. A few streets away in the 2100 block of Harvard Boulevard, police found Larry Troutman's car crashed into a tree. Inside, Troutman, 54, was dead from a single self-inflicted gunshot wound to the head. A .357 Magnum pistol was found on the front seat next to his body. Ballistics proved the gun was also used to kill Roger Troutman. While none of the surviving brothers were able to supply a motive for the murder-suicide, police speculated that business problems combined with friction over Roger's desire to pursue a solo career might have prompted Larry to commit the act. On May 1, 1999, a single funeral service attended by an estimated 4,000 mourners was held for the brothers at the nondenominational Solid Rock Church in Monroe, Ohio. Rufus Troutman, III, a nephew of the brothers who had performed with Zapp, sang a variation of "Amazing Grace," using Roger's trademark vocoder. The brothers were buried in Greenwood Cemetery in their hometown of Hamilton, Ohio.

Further Reading

Grieco, Lou. "Business Dispute Between Rock-Funk Pioneers May Have Led to Deaths." *Cox News Service*, April 26, 1999.

Van Alstyne, Harold Blake (M–S)

A member of the hand balancing team of Van and Emerson, the 24-year-old acrobat became infatuated with Marian MacLaren of the vaudeville musical troupe the Five MacLarens while touring on the same circuit with them in 1922. MacLaren, 30, accepted Van Alstyne's marriage proposal, but later broke off the engagement and returned his ring. In September 1922, the acrobat turned up on the doorstep of the MacLaren home in Philadelphia demanding to speak to his former fiancée. MacLaren's father interceded informing Van Alstyne that not only would the marriage break up the family act, but their age difference was also too great. When finally allowed to see Marian MacLaren she refused to explain her reasons for cancelling the marriage although it was later reported she planned to marry another. On the night of January 12, 1923, Van Alstyne attempted to talk to MacLaren backstage at New York City's Grand Theatre where the family was performing. She again refused. The acrobat waited until after the last show and followed the four MacLarens (three sisters and a brother) to the Autodine Cafeteria on 8th Avenue. Van Alstyne walked up to their table, produced a pistol, and fired five shots instantly killing Marian and wounding her brother. He shot himself in the chest, but survived. The performer pleaded guilty to second-degree murder and was sentenced to 20 years to life imprisonment on April 13, 1923. Three days later, Van Alstyne hanged himself with a belt from his bunk in the Tombs.

Further Reading

"Slayer of Actress Ends Life in Tombs." *The New York Times*, April 17, 1923, p. 23.

Van der Walt, Deon (V)

South Africa's most famous opera star, Van der Walt (born July 28, 1958 in Cape Town) studied voice at the University of Stellenbosch making his debut as "Jaquino" in *Fidelio* while still a student. In 1981, the lyric tenor was studying abroad on scholarships when he won the International Mozart Competition in Salzburg playing "Tamino" in *The Magic Flute*. In 1985, the 27-year-old made his Covent Garden debut as "Count Almaviva" in *The Barber of Seville*. In addition to these professional accolades, he became the first South African–born singer to complete the "operatic grand slam"—performing at New York's Metropolitan Opera House, the Vienna State Opera, La Scala in Milan, and London's Covent Garden. A familiar face on the international festival circuit, Van der Walt performed in Salzburg, Vienna, Barcelona, and Zurich and was regarded as one of Mozart's most skilled interpreters. After years of almost nonstop touring, the tenor decided to spend more time in South Africa to help train young singers and oversee his winemaking business. In 1988, Van der Walt purchased property near Paarl in a valley near the Klein-Drakenstein mountains 35 miles outside of Cape Town, christened the estate Veenwouden (after the Dutch village of his ancestors), and started producing highly regarded "boutique wines" known for their excellent taste and limited production. The tenor left the management of the estate to his father, Charles, and the winemaking to his brother, Marcel, a former professional golfer. When not performing internationally, the tenor returned to Veenwouden to host intimate musical dinners in the winery's fermentation cellar.

The relationship between Van der Walt, 47, and his father had always been stormy, but it quickly deteriorated after the tenor informed the 78-year-old man of his plans to move his parents off the estate when he took up permanent residence. Around 2:00 P.M. on November 29, 2005, Van der Walt's mother, Sheila, returned to Veenwouden to find her son in his bedroom dead from two gunshot wounds to the chest. Husband Charles was found in another bedroom with a fatal bullet wound in his right temple, a .38-caliber pistol next to his body. Lore Schultz, Van der Walt's agent, said the constant bickering between father and son about the farm led directly to the murder-suicide. "It really wore Deon down," Schultz told the international press. "He may have been shot on Tuesday, but they (his family) killed him years ago. Sometimes when he told me about it I just couldn't bear to listen to the horrible stories any more."

Further Reading

Clayton, Jonathan. "Tragedy as Tenor Shot by Father." *The Australian*, December 2, 2005, p. 1.

van Gogh, Theo (V)

The great-great-great grandson of nineteenth century painter Vincent van Gogh's brother,

Theo, the director was the *l'enfant terrible* of the Dutch film industry, a tirelessly abrasive liberal gadfly known to provoke confrontations with conservative religions in the name of freedom of speech. In the wake of 9/11, fundamentalist Muslims became a particular target of choice. While conservative Muslims made up only a small part of the nearly one million followers of Islam in the Netherlands (6 percent of the national population), public opinion polls suggested Dutch citizens felt threatened by their presence. Van Gogh seemingly never missed an opportunity in the media to confront the fundamentalists often making outrageous statements like, "I'm deeply religious — I worship a pig. I call him Allah." His catchphrase for radical Islamic extremists was "goat fuckers." In his book, *Allah Knows Better*, he critiqued the Muslim clergy and the religion's militant factions as "women haters." Radical Muslims, however, took no comfort in the fact van Gogh was an equal opportunity offender when it came to religious groups. He accused novelist Leon de Winter of trading on his Jewishness to sell books, and in 1991 was fined for anti-Semitism after making the wisecrack, "Hey, it smells like caramel today — well then, they must be burning diabetic Jews."

In 2004, the 47-year-old director collaborated with Aayan Hirsi Ali, a Somali-born member of the Dutch Parliament, on a 10 minute film entitled, *Submission*. Ali, who scripted the film, fled an arranged marriage and physical abuse in her native land, and outraged many traditionalists in the Muslim community by denouncing her faith, calling the Prophet Muhammad a "pervert" and "tyrant," and criticizing the failure of Islamic families living in the Netherlands to adopt its ways and customs. Not surprisingly, Ali received death threats and was under police protection. *Submission*, a film featuring four Muslim women describing the sexual and physical abuse they endured at the hands of family members, aired on Dutch national television in August 2004 and created an immediate furor in the Muslim community. In the film, the women wore transparent robes in which their breasts were clearly visible and Koranic texts describing the physical punishments for "disobedient women" were written on their naked bodies. Van Gogh received numerous death threats from outraged Muslims who viewed the film as offensive rather than as a vehicle to force dialogue between liberal and conservative ideas.

Around 8:30 A.M. on November 2, 2004, van Gogh was bicycling on Linnaeus Street in the eastern part of Amsterdam near Oosterpark, when a young man wearing traditional Muslim garb rode up beside him and began shooting at close range. Wounded, the director fell from the bike and staggered across the street with his assailant in pursuit. As van Gogh begged for mercy, the gunman pumped another round into him and slit his throat nearly to the spinal cord with a large kitchen knife, warning a bystander, "now you know what's coming for you." Prior to fleeing the scene on foot, the killer pinned a five page note to the filmmaker's chest with another knife. Police cordoned off the park and after a brief, but intense gun battle in which the suspect fired thirty rounds, wounded an officer, and sustained a leg wound prior to being taken into custody. In his pockets was a "last will" entitled "Drenched in blood," in which he exhorted other Islamic militants to "take up the challenge." The five page typewritten manifesto pinned to the dead man's chest, "Open Letter to Hirsi Ali," threatened in Dutch and Arabic of a *jihad* against infidels everywhere. Van Gogh's assassination marked the second political killing in the Netherlands. In May 2002, the filmmaker's friend, Pim Fortuyn, an openly gay politician vocal in his criticism of open immigration and Islam, was gunned down by an environmental activist. As the filmmaker was honored as a champion of free speech at a large public memorial service and afterwards cremated, the most liberal country in Europe was polarized by the grisly killing. Attempts were made to burn mosques and the bombing of a Muslim elementary school in Eindhoven was answered by arsonists setting fire to Protestant churches in Rotterdam, Utrecht, and Amersfoort.

In custody, 26-year-old Muhammad Bouyeri, a Dutch-Moroccan national who grew up in Amsterdam, was named as the prime suspect in van Gogh's murder. Bouyeri, a one-time youth counselor in a local community center, began to embrace radical Islam following the death of his mother in 2002. Like many disaffected Moroccan youths yearning to rediscover their religion, Bouyeri visited Saudi Arabia twice, and upon returning to Amsterdam began wearing traditional Arab robes. He promptly moved out of the family home and into a one bedroom apartment that became a meeting place for young Moroccan men. As details of Bouyeri's past began to emerge, Dutch police arrested eight other suspected terrorists of North African descent thought to be members of a cell known as the Hofstad Group. All were on the radar of Dutch intelligence agencies who at any given time have at least 150 suspects on around the clock surveillance. Bouyeri, a suspected member of the group, had attended private prayer sessions with Redouan al-Issar, a Syrian spiritual leader allegedly with ties to the Hofstad Group who disappeared shortly before the van Gogh killing.

In July 2005, Bouyeri was put on trial for van Gogh's murder and charges including the attempted murder of two bystanders and eight policemen as well as the illegal possession of a firearm. The young extremist informed the three-judge panel that he had instructed his attorney not to defend him. Bouyeri freely admitted his guilt and viewed his actions as part of a holy war to replace the Dutch government with an Islamic theocracy. He told the dead director's mother, "I can't feel for you because you are a nonbeliever," and the judges, "I did it out of conviction. If I ever get free, I would do it again." On July 26, 2005, Bouyeri was sentenced to life without the possibility of parole, the first verdict of its kind to be applied under the Dutch terrorism laws enacted after 9/11. In 2006, nine Muslims including Bouyeri were convicted in Dutch court of belonging to the terrorist organization the Hofstad Group and of inciting hatred against non–Muslims. Bouyeri, already doing maximum time, received no further punishment. Nine of the convictions, including that of van Gogh's murderer, were overturned in January 2008 after an appeals court ruled the Hofstad Group could not be considered a terrorist network because its participants were not aiming, as a group, to commit or incite violent acts. The prosecution planned a possible appeal to the Supreme Court.

Further Reading

Buruma, Ian. *Murder in Amsterdam: The Death of Theo van Gogh and the Limits of Tolerance.* New York: Penguin, 2006.

van Pallandt, Frederik (V)

Dubbed the "Peter, Paul and Mary of Europe" in the early 1960s, the folk tinged singing of Nina and Frederik made the duo internationally popular. A member of Dutch royalty, Baron Frederik Jan Gustav Floris van Pallandt (born in Copenhagen on May 14, 1934) was the son of the former Ambassador of the Netherlands to Denmark. He married Nina Moller in 1954 and by Christmas 1959 Nina & Frederik had their first success in

Britain, "Mary's Boy Child," a revival of the 1957 Harry Belafonte hit. Another religious song followed, "Little Donkey," staying on the charts for ten weeks between November 1960 and February 1961, followed later in the year by the single "Sucu Sucu." In 1969, after three children and five albums, Frederik abruptly announced to Nina they were retiring. The couple separated later that year. Frederik used his career profits to live quietly on a farm in Ibiza while briefly becoming the owner of *Burke's Peerage* in 1979. Nina van Pallandt, unwilling to become a recluse like her estranged husband, continued as a solo recording artist and branched out as an actress in films like Robert Altman's *The Long Goodbye* (1973), *A Wedding* (1979), and Paul Schrader's *American Gigolo* (1980). The couple officially divorced in 1975 after 15 years of marriage. That same year, Frederik appeared in the French film *Hu-Man* with Terrence Stamp.

In 1994, the 60-year-old former folk star was living in the Philippines with his girlfriend of a decade, the thirtyish Perpetua ("Susan") Tapon, in a modest two-bedroom rental cottage on the remote Sandbar Beach Resort on Boquete Island off Puerta Galera. The couple occupied the rental for seven months while Frederik prepared to sell his luxurious speedboat. Van Pallandt and Tapon spent the early evening of May 15, 1995 entertaining a German guest. Shortly after the visitor departed, a gunman entered the home and pumped two .45-caliber slugs into van Pallandt's head. Tapon was similarly executed as she fled her attacker outside the cottage. A neighbor hearing the shots notified police and watched as the killer sped away in the dead man's speedboat. The boat was recovered the next day in Bauan in Batangas province on the Luzon mainland. Noting the cool efficiency of the execution-style murders, the lack of physical evidence, and the fact nothing was stolen from the scene, police strongly suspected a gangland killing possibly motivated by drugs. Nina van Pallandt flew to the Philippines and brought her former husband's body back to Europe. The legacy of Nina and Frederik, however, continued to endure. In October 2000, two performers with the Coventry, England–based Triangle Theatre Company formed a tribute band, "Nina and Frederik," and toured the surrounding area. The impersonation became the subject of the 2002 film, *Tribute.*

The double murder might have remained a cold case forever had not a legal fight in 2006 over the ownership of a French villa revealed a link between one of the disputants, alleged Australian drug kingpin Malcolm Gordon Field, and Frederik van Pallandt. Field, serving a seven year prison sentence in Australia for importing 34 kilograms of Ecstasy into that country, was a skilled seaman who made over a hundred drug runs by boat for Michael Hurley, the head of Australia's most infamous crime syndicate. As point man for Hurley's gang in the Philippines, Field knew all the drug traffickers in the islands. According to Australian police authorities, van Pallandt became part of the drug scene almost immediately upon settling in the Philippines in the early 1990s. The former singer teamed with a criminal named Ronald Milhench to provide transportation for Hurley's drug syndicate. By late 1993, Field reportedly owed the pair between $20 and $30 million for transporting a huge shipment of cannabis to Australia that netted the Hurley gang over $100 million. Field paid half the money to Milhench who had no intention of sharing the proceeds with van Pallandt. A furious van Pallandt flew to Australia to confront Field who had already fled the country. On the evening the couple was executed, police found a sealed note in the house written in van Pallandt's hand addressed to Tapon. It read (in part), "If something happens to me before I get payed (sic)" followed by instructions to a stash of cash and various bank accounts. Police believe Milhench, despite a passport stamp showing he was out of the country during the time of the killings, was the gunman. A suspect in six other killings, Milhench is believed to have flown back to the Philippines under a fake passport to eliminate his business partner.

Further Reading

McClymont, Kate. "Drug Tsar's Silent Fight for Villa." *Sydney Morning Herald*, December 16, 2006, p. 1.

Velez, Lilian (V)

Velez, born in Cebu City, Philippines, on March 23, 1924, was a teenager when she won a singing contest sponsored by a radio station in Manila. The prize, an all-expenses paid scholarship, allowed the dark-haired beauty to develop her voice and deepen her relationship with Joe Climaco, a radio station manager, composer, and film director. Climaco married the 18 year old in 1942 and after the war brokered a deal for Velez with LVN Pictures then grinding out a series of popular films featuring love duos. In keeping with the studio formula, Velez was paired with former child star Bernardo "Narding" Anzures in two 1947 films, *Ang Estudyante* and *Sa Kabukiran*. Shortly after their last film together, LVN decided to drop Anzures and pair Velez with rising star Jaime de la Rosa. The decision hit Anzures particularly hard as he was obsessed with the beautiful married actress. The young actor's waning popularity combined with Velez's refusal to return his affections set the stage for a deadly confrontation.

The attractive Filipino singer-actress Lilian Velez was stabbed to death in front of her daughter on June 26, 1948, by an obsessed co-star recently informed by the studio he was to be replaced by another actor in Velez's upcoming film.

Shortly before midnight on June 26, 1948, Velez, 25, her four-year-old daughter, Vivian, and her maid, Pacita, were at the actress' home in Quezon City, when Narding intruded upon the scene. The 21-year-old actor pulled a hunting knife from under his shirt and brutally stabbed Velez to death. When Pacita bravely intervened to help the actress, Anzures turned the weapon on her. The child, peeking through the crack of her bedroom door, witnessed the slaughter and was able to identify Anzures to police as the double murderer. Climaco, returning home from his job as a nightclub manager, was overcome with grief at the scene and had to be restrained by police from killing himself with a pistol. In custody, Narding told authorities, "I did it. I don't know what happened or how. I was under a spell. I do funny things sometimes and everything just goes blank." Convicted on both counts of murder, Narding contracted tuberculosis in Muntinlupa prison and died in 1949. A motion picture, *The Lilian Velez Story*, was produced in the Philippines in 1995 starring Sharon Cuneta as the tragic actress.

Further Reading

"Actress Is Slain; Leading Man Held." *The New York Times*, June 28, 1948, p. 8.

Garcia, Jessie B. *A Movie Album Quizbook*. Iloilo City, Philippines: Erewohn, 2004.

Vicious, Sid (M-suspected)

Despite releasing only one album during their short life as a band, the Sex Pistols became a cultural phenomenon in Great Britain that not only defined a musical genre, punk, but also underscored the ability of rock to offer an anarchic alternative to conventional society. In a handful of vitriolic, high energy, and invective-filled rants against the British Establishment and a wide variety of social issues, the Pistols captured the imagination of the world press for a short time in the mid–1970s before internal tensions within the group and its management led Johnny Rotten (John Lydon), the group's front man and true creative force, to walk away from the band in disgust. Today, thanks largely to the relentless marketing of his image on clothing and other items for sale Sid Vicious has become the face and symbol of the punk movement. Rock has always projected a rebel image, but past rockers like Elvis Presley in addition to defining the "look" of their generation also arguably possessed a modicum of musical talent. Sid Vicious, the spikey haired and sneering symbol of punk, could never learn to play his instrument and offered little to the band other than his well-earned outcast image that did, however, strongly connect with their fan base.

The performer destined to become the icon of punk was born Simon John Ritchie on May 10, 1957, in Lewisham Hospital in London the son of John George Ritchie, a publisher's representative, and Anne Jeannette, a psychologically troubled woman whose recreational drug use further unsettled her volatile personality. Ritchie split when Sid was two and Anne married Chris Beverley. Mother and son retained Beverley's name following his death. Desperately poor, Sid spent much of his early life with Anne moving from one squalid flat to the next in the lower class environs of the city, while she barely supported them by rolling joints. Sid took to running the streets looking for companionship and entertainment which often took the form of baiting and beating up aging hippies. The 15-year-old was already sharing his mother's syringe to shoot speed when authorities sent him to a special needs school in Stoke Newington. Sid worked briefly in a textile factory prior to enrolling in a photography course in 1973 at Hackney Technical College. At the trade school, he met another disaffected teen, John Lydon, and

the pair became fast friends based on a mutually rabid disdain for the British Establishment and similar tastes in fashion and music. Lydon and Sid began squatting together in various abandoned buildings in London and when not strolling the fashion trendy King's Road in Chelsea, worked the occasional odd job. Britain, then in the midst of one of its worst economic recessions since World War II, offered little or no hope to the working class, especially teenagers unable to find jobs. The kids were angry and as Pamela Des Barres points out in *Rock Bottom: Dark Moments in Music Babylon* (1996) the current music offered no alternative. Glam rock, expounded by fashion-conscious performers like David Bowie and Marc Bolan, was passé and heavily synthesized music ruled the airwaves.

Early on, both friends were heavily into glam rock with Sid especially known to ape Bowie's outlandish look. During their wanderings on the King's Road, the pair discovered Sex, a fetish-wear clothing store owned by Malcolm McLaren, an entrepreneur who fancied himself a poor man's Andy Warhol. The shop featured studded fetish garb, rubberwear, tee shirts bearing inflammatory slogans, and assorted accessories like dog chains, oversized safety pins and locks. McClaren had already enlisted shop regulars Steve Jones (guitar) and Paul Cook (drums) into a band with store worker Glen Matlock (bass), but needed a charismatic front man. Enter John Lydon who, although not a trained singer, possessed an authentic rage, snarling delivery, and fuck-all attitude that made the band one of the most exciting live acts in London. Lydon was renamed "Rotten" by Jones who was disgusted by the singer's obnoxious habit of picking at his rotting teeth. At the end of 1975, the band was named the Sex Pistols and essentially launched the punk movement in Great Britain. Punk, distinguished by its simplistic musical structure and incendiary lyrics attacking societal ills, struck an instant chord with Britain's disaffected youth and as promoted by McLaren became an equally potent fashion statement. Much to the shock, horror, and disgust of Establishment British society, London streets were soon awash with knotted bands of surly teens wearing studded fetish gear held together by safety pins and bandaids. In the clubs, Johnny Rotten's shouted lyrics preaching nihilism and anarchy were punctuated by his spitting into a crowd already whipped into a frenzied state by the message and the driving beat. Sid, unable to play an instrument, was the band's most ardent fan and was credited with inventing the "pogo" dance in which he rigidly jumped up and down in time with the music to better see the band in the crowded clubs. Surnamed "Vicious" by Lydon (Rotten) after the singer's pet hamster, Sid briefly played drums of a sort for Siouxsie & the Banshees, sang in a band called Flowers of Romance, but was better known in his pre–Pistols days for the mayhem he caused in clubs. At a Pistols show in June 1976, Vicious lived up to his name by whipping music journalist Nick Kent with a rusty bicycle chain at London's 100 Club. In September of that year, he hurled a beer glass at the stage and a shard reportedly struck a female audience member blinding her in one eye. Vicious was arrested for the incident, found guilty of possessing an illegal weapon (a knife), and did a short stint at an Ashford remand center.

In November 1976, the Pistols' first single, "Anarchy in the U.K.," was released to mixed reviews, but the band's subsequent profanity-laced appearances on British television and in outrageously controversial press interviews brought them to the fore of British popular culture and launched scores of punk bands. By February 1977, the tension between lyricist Johnny Rotten and bassist Glen Matlock (seemingly too fond of melody) reached a crisis. Malcolm McLaren, unwilling to anger the incendiary front man whose vision had made the Sex Pistols a controversial success, fired Matlock. Rotten immediately suggested his friend and fellow-squatter, Sid Vicious, to manager McLaren as a replacement. Who cared if the 20 year old could not play bass? He could learn (but never did) and what was more important was that Sid Vicious had the quintessential punk look. Whip thin from copious drug use, spikey black hair, snarling upper lip, and outfitted in ripped clothes from McLaren's Sex boutique held together by bondage straps and accessoried by Nazi regalia, Vicious was the embodiment of image over talent. Rotten was frankly political and his rants against the Establishment were genuine cries of anger from Britain's disadvantaged lower class. Vicious cared nothing for politics. He did, however, live to shock and McLaren saw that his "dangerous" look and persona played well in the press. Shortly after joining the Pistols, Vicious met Nancy Laura Spungen, a troubled 19-year-old American who reportedly had come to Britain for the express purpose of becoming the girlfriend of a punk star. Born cyanotic, a so-called "blue baby," the infant's

blood had to be immediately changed in an effort to stabilize her central nervous system. Later diagnosed as a schizophrenic, Spungen was unable to adjust to simple changes in routine and was frustrated by tasks as mundane as dressing or undressing. Spungen, her tenuous mental state exacerbated by an IQ of 150–160, had been in an out of mental institutions and special schools since the age of 11. Turning her younger siblings onto pot at an early age, Spungen was shooting heroin at 15. She enrolled at the University of Colorado at 16, but left after a semester and relocated to New York City to work as a go-go dancer. In the Big Apple she told anyone within earshot her dream was to become a rock star's girlfriend and bragged she had already bedded every member of Aerosmith, Bad Company, and most of the Allman Brothers. She followed the New York Dolls to London where she hooked up with Johnny Thunders & the Heartbreakers. In early 1977, repulsed by Johnny Rotten who considered her a heroin addicted slag, Spungen set her sights on Sid Vicious. The pair became inseparable especially after Spungen turned him onto heroin. The rest of the Pistols openly despised the woman to whom they referred to as "Nauseating Nancy." Spungen's omnipresence combined with the bassist's psychological dependence on her drove a wedge between Vicious and the rest of the band. Tellingly, none of the Pistols even visited Vicious during his hospitalization for hepatitis in April and May 1977.

At his first live show with the Pistols on April 4, 1977, it became instantly apparent to the band and its management that while Vicious looked the part of a punk rocker, he could not play his instrument. His sincere attempts to learn the bass were undermined by heroin addiction and drunkenness at recording sessions to the point fired former bassist Glen Matlock was hired to lay down tracks on the *Never Mind the Bollocks, Here's the Sex Pistols* album released in October 1977. As the Vicious-Spungen relationship continued to spiral uncontrollably into the depths of hopeless heroin addiction, band members and friends did their best to break up the pair and get the bassist off junk. By June 1977 when the Pistols released their hit song, "God Save the Queen," timed to coincide with the Silver Jubilee of Queen Elizabeth II, the band took the dramatic, but necessary step of often not even plugging in Vicious's instrument during live shows. For his part, Vicious posed with the instrument, sneered, and insulted the audience. Nevertheless, when *Never Mind the Bol-locks* was released it shot to Number One in the U.K. although it was banned by many national discount stores. On the strength of the album, McLaren decided to exploit the band's notoriety with an ill-conceived tour of the United States. Prior to leaving the U.K., Spungen was informed she would not be allowed on the trip.

On January 6, 1978, the Sex Pistols kicked off their U.S. tour in, of all places, Atlanta, Georgia. The audience, in fact most Americans, had little in common with the band or its politics of rage against the British Establishment. Still, reviewer John Rockwell of *The New York Times* reported the crowd enjoyed itself and described Vicious as "scrawny and scowling, but in a somehow sweet and alluring way." Peeved that Spungen, his emotional support and main source of heroin, had been banned from the tour, Vicious spent much of his time trying to score drugs in the Deep South with disastrously embarrassing results. Unreliable and acting increasingly strange, he showed up moments before a gig in Memphis with "I Wanna Fix" freshly carved in his bloody chest. As his relationship with band members, most notably Rotten, progressively deteriorated so did his onstage behavior. In Austin, Texas, he unwisely shouted at the audience, "All you cowboys are fuckin' faggots," and assaulted a photographer with his bass. Not surprisingly, he and the band were pelted with beer cans and bottles. Off-stage was worse. Road stories abound of Vicious' drug-addled escapades with groupies and rednecks. By the end of the 14-day tour in San Francisco on January 17, 1978, Rotten announced he was through and quit the band unable to stand his former mate's behavior or rein in his visceral hatred of Malcolm McLaren. The opportunistic manager was already busy collaborating with director Julien Temple on a fictionalized filmic account of the band, *The Great Rock'n'Roll Swindle*. In the movie, Vicious sang three cover songs including a disturbing rendition of Frank Sinatra's hit, "My Way."

Reunited with Nancy Spungen, the pair set up house in New York City ultimately settling in the Chelsea Hotel on West 23rd Street. A well-known residence for artists, the hotel's first few floors were little more than crash pads for junkies. Sid and Nancy lived in Apartment 100 on the ground floor. The musician briefly formed a band, managed by Spungen, called the Idols with two former members of the New York Dolls. The live album,

Sid Sings, was released in 1979. Unable to play his own instrument and hopelessly inept at writing new material, Vicious earned drug money playing Pistols tunes at local clubs. A documentary shot in London at the time, Lech Kowalski's *DOA*, featured an interview with the drug-addled pair professing their undying love while Vicious, holding a hunting knife, nods off into unconsciousness. In New York, the couple tried unsuccessfully to wean themselves from heroin dependence by enrolling at a local methadone clinic. Frequent arguments instigated largely by Spungen ended in brutal beatings dished out by her stoned lover. Mutually depressed, addicted to drugs, and psychologically co-dependent, Vicious and Spungen vowed in a quasi-suicide pact that neither would long live without the other. On the morning of October 12, 1978, Vicious, 21, awoke from a drug-induced stupor to find the dead body of his lover, Nancy Spungen, 20, in a pool of blood on the bathroom floor. Death was attributed to a single knife wound in the lower abdomen. Vicious called police and during questioning admitted he could remember little of the evening due to his drug use, but allegedly did confusedly confess to stabbing his lover of 18 months because she failed to score heroin. Vicious was arrested and held pending charges, but released days later after Malcolm McLaren persuaded Virgin Records to put up $50,000 bail.

Depressed over Spungen's death and perhaps attempting to make good on their death pact, Vicious half-heartedly attempted suicide at the Seville Hotel on October 22, 1978, by using a razor blade and a broken light bulb to slash his wrist. The cuts were minor and while Vicious did not require medical attention, he was admitted into the psychiatric ward of Bellevue Hospital for a two week period of observation. In November 1978, the bassist pleaded innocent to an indictment charging him with murder and "depraved indifference to human life" in the death of Nancy Spungen. Many friends believed Vicious when he insisted he had not killed Spungen and they offered alternative theories as to who did. The most popular (and one that Malcolm McLaren hired a team of private investigators to pursue) posited an angry young drug dealer who had killed her in a deal gone wrong. This view was lended credence by the fact that a large sum of money known to have been in Room 100 was missing after her body was discovered. However, the constant flow and type of clientele and narcotics into the Chelsea

Hotel made leads difficult to pursue. Others speculated Vicious and Spungen, both terribly depressed, had decided together that night to end it all. Spungen made good on her part of the deal while Vicious failed. Still shooting heroin, Vicious spent some of his time awaiting his upcoming trial for second-degree murder hanging out in nightclubs. On December 5, 1978, Todd Smith, brother of New York punk star Patti Smith, took a few swings at Vicious after the drunken musician propositioned and felt up his girlfriend at Hurrah's, a second-floor bar at 62nd Street and Broadway. Vicious responded by breaking a beer bottle on a table and using a shard to slash Smith across the forehead. The assault resulted in five stitches for Smith and bail revocation for Vicious who for a second time was forced to undergo the painful process of heroin detoxification while incarcerated on Rikers Island. Remarkably, bail in the amount of $60,000 was reinstated and on February 1, 1979, Vicious was released into the custody of Anne Beverley. The concerned mother traveled to America in support of son Sid during his legal and drug troubles, but also had been reportedly motivated to make the trip by the $10,000 the *New York Post* had paid her for exclusive rights to her story. Sid, accompanied by Anne and his girlfriend, 22-year-old actress Michelle Robinson, celebrated his release at a party given by the younger woman at her Greenwich Village apartment on 63 Bank Street. Shortly after midnight, Vicious shot up heroin purchased by his mother to commemorate his newfound freedom. The ex–Sex Pistol seizured, but was seemingly okay according to the guests who left the party. Anne Beverley confiscated the remainder of the heroin, but sometime around 2:00 A.M. Vicious found the junk in her purse and injected it all. Later that day, February 2, Anne and Robinson found Sid's nude and lifeless body lying face-up in his bedroom. While debate raged over whether the punk star's death had been accidental or intentional, the New York state medical examiner offered a plausible solution. Vicious, his system heroin-free thanks to the prison's detoxification program, had lost his tolerance and could no longer process the narcotic. The body of Sid Vicious was cremated on February 7, and Anne Beverley later spread her son's ashes over Spungen's grave at the King David Cemetery in Bensalem, Pennsylvania. In 1986, the couple's doomed and sordid love affair was the subject of a well-regarded feature film, *Sid and Nancy*, starring Gary Oldman and Chloe Webb. In 2006, the Sex Pistols, against the wishes of its remaining members, were inducted into the Rock and Roll Hall of Fame.

Further Reading

Butt, Malcolm. *Sid Vicious: Rock 'n' Roll Star*. Rev. and updated ed. London: Plexus, 2005.

Des Barres, Pamela. *Rock Bottom: Dark Moments in Music Babylon*. New York: St. Martin's, 1996.

Parker, Alan. *Sid Vicious: No One Is Innocent*. London: Orion, 2007.

_____. *Vicious: Too Fast to Live*. London: Creation, 2004.

Paytress, Mark. *Vicious: The Art of Dying Young*. London: Sanctuary, 2004.

Savage, Jon. *England's Dreaming: Anarchy, Sex Pistols, Punk Rock, and Beyond*. New York: St. Martin's, 1992.

Segell, Michael. "Sid Vicious Accused: A Punk Nightmare in New York." *Rolling Stone*, 279 (November 30, 1978):9, 11, 23–25.

Wagenheim, Charles (V)

Born in Trenton, New Jersey, on February 21, 1896, Wagenheim appeared briefly on the stage prior to embarking on a 36 year career in Hollywood in which he appeared in small character parts in over 120 movies including *Andy Hardy Meets Debutante* (1940), *Meet Boston Blackie* (1941), *House of Frankenstein* (1945), *The Set-Up* (1949), *A Streetcar Named Desire* (1952), *Kismet* (1955), *Cat Ballou* (1965), *The Baby Maker* (1970), and his final film, *The Missouri Breaks* (1976). The actor was also active in television from the mid–1950s (*Schlitz Playhouse of Stars*, *Science Fiction Theater*), and throughout the 1960s and 1970s turned up on *Bonanza*, *Peter Gunn*, *Surfside 6*, *Ben Casey*, and *Baretta*. Wagenheim gained his most enduring fame as a cast member on the CBS series *Gunsmoke* playing the role of "Halligan" from 1967 to 1975. The 83-year-old actor last appeared on television in the ninth season of *All in the Family* in the episode "The Return of Stephanie's Father" with veteran actor and fellow octogenarian Victor Kilian (see entry.) Twenty-eight years earlier the actors had both appeared in a 1951 MGM drama concerning the assassination of President Abraham Lincoln, *The Tall Target*, directed by Anthony Mann. Ironically, when the *All in the Family* episode aired on March 25, 1979, both men were dead, the victims of brutally senseless murders.

On the evening of March 6, 1979, Wagenheim and his invalid wife, Lillian, were in their apartment at 8078 Fareholm Drive in Los Angeles. The nurse attending Lillian, Stephanie Boone, was downstairs in the laundry room when someone

The veteran character actor Charles Wagenheim appeared in over 120 films from 1940 to 1976 but gained his most enduring popularity as "Halligan" on the CBS television series *Gunsmoke*, a role he played from 1967 to 1975. Wagenheim, 83, was beaten to death in his L.A. apartment on March 6, 1979. Five days later, fellow-actor and octogenarian Victor Kilian died under strikingly similar circumstances.

entered the apartment through a window in the bedroom where Wagenheim was resting and bludgeoned the aged actor to death. Lillian, in the living room at the time of the attack, heard nothing and was left unharmed. Five days later, Victor Kilian, 88, the infamous "Fernwood Flasher" on the sitcom *Mary Hartman, Mary Hartman*, was beaten to death in his apartment not far from the Wagenheim murder scene. No direct connection to the crimes was ever established. Nurse Boone was briefly taken into police custody, but never charged with the crime. Wagenheim's murder remains officially unsolved.

Further Reading

"Obituary: Charles Wagenheim." *The New York Times*, March 8, 1979, sec. D, p. 21.

Walker, Kenneth (V)

A hip-hop record promoter from Yonkers, New York, with a history of arrests for weapons, marijuana possession, and robbery dating back to 1989, Walker, 31, attended a 50 Cent concert on the evening of Friday, November 1, 2002. Shortly after 3:00 A.M. the next morning, police patrolling a desolate area one block from Key Skate Center, a roller skating rink and dance club in the Mott Haven section of the South Bronx, heard gunfire. They found Walker's bullet-riddled body seated behind the wheel of his parked yellow Plymouth Voyager at the corner of Rider Avenue and East 140th Street near a city housing project called the Patterson Houses. He was pronounced dead at the Lincoln Medical and Mental Health Center at 6:15 A.M. Eight spent .45-caliber shell casings were found near the van which was emblazoned with the names of several rap artists, local rap

radio stations, and Hi Rise Entertainment. Inside the vehicle were rap CDs, posters, and fliers promoting several rap performers including 50 Cent (Curtis Jackson). While Walker was known to wear an expensive piece of jewelry (missing from his body), the murder of seminal rapper Jam Master Jay (see entry) in Queens just days before led police to initially suspect the promoter's execution-style killing may have been linked rather than just a simple robbery. 50 Cent, a protégé of Jam Master Jay, had angered several in the rap world with his habit of poking fun at the gangsta style of competing rappers. Viewed in this light, the murders of Jam Master Jay and Walker could be interpreted as a harsh message to 50 Cent. The rapper cancelled a concert on the day of the murder, but refused police protection. To date, no one has been prosecuted for Walker's murder.

Further Reading

Haberman, Zach. "Hip-Hop Honcho Slain in Bronx." *New York Post*, November 3, 2002, p. 7.

Walker, Randy *see* Big Stretch

Wallace, Christopher George Latore *see* Notorious B.I.G.

Walters, Homer M. (M-S)

Walters and Lillian Tyler, both 32, played together in the orchestra at the Loew's Park Theatre in Cleveland, Ohio. During his 12-year courtship of Tyler, Walters spent $15,000 on the organist in an unsuccessful bid to marry her. In early March 1925, the musician struck the woman when he caught her entertaining a young college boy in her apartment. He was arrested for assault and battery, but released after Tyler refused to testify against him. On March 25, 1925, the frightened woman phoned authorities to report Walters had repeatedly threatened to kill her. At a joint meeting before the police prosecutor, Lillian Tyler intimated to her frustrated suitor that she "might" place him on probation and, if he behaved himself, possibly later marry him. At 5:30 P.M. on March 28, 1925, Tyler was seated alone in the front row of the Loew's Park Theatre during a non-musical interlude in the comedy film *The Burglar*. Walters, who recently quit the orchestra to become the treasurer of his father's coal company, sat down beside her. Although an estimated 200 patrons were in the theatre, no one was seated in the next ten rows behind the couple. During an action scene in the film punctuated by some fifty sound effect shots, Walters produced a revolver and pumped four rounds into Tyler's cheek, temple, neck, and eye. Afterwards, he shot himself in the head. Unaware the pistol reports they heard were not part of the movie, the audience laughed and applauded as two people lay dead in the front row. Their bodies, Tyler's slumped in her seat and Walters' splayed on the floor at her feet, were discovered by an usher ten minutes later.

Further Reading

"Kills Woman Movie Organist, Self." *Cleveland Plain Dealer*, March 29, 1925, pp. 1, 14.

Wassel, Jawed (V)

Driven from his native Afghanistan in 1979 by the Soviet invasion, Wassel came to America, learned to speak six languages, worked his way through the City College of New York, and became a U.S. citizen. Convinced the medium of film could be used to foster world peace and understanding, Wassel spent six years writing and directing *Firedancer*, an autobiographical story chronicling the pain suffered by the Afghani people under the twenty year Soviet occupation. To cut costs, the director lived with his three brothers in a rundown apartment in Chelsea, used non-professionals in the film, and exercised his considerable charm to secure financial backing for the project. Bruce Hathaway, composer for *Firedancer*, described Wassel as a "visionary" who would "promise the world" to get what he needed for the film, but disappointed many when his promises were not fulfilled. Wassel promised Nathan Chandler Powell a producer's credit and 30 percent of the gross for *Firedancer* in exchange for becoming the film's principal financial backer. On the afternoon of October 3, 2001, hours before the film's New York City premiere, the 42-year-old filmmaker showed up at Powell's Long Island City apartment in Queens in a bid to convince the investor to take a smaller percentage. The pair argued and Powell struck Wassel in the throat with a pool cue stabbing him to death as the filmmaker fought for breath. Powell dismembered Wassel's body with a hacksaw and stored the severed head in the freezer of his refrigerator. Afterwards, the producer attended the screening of *Firedancer*.

The following evening, a Nassau County police officer made a routine stop of a motorist driving a van erratically with its lights off in the area of Bethpage State Park on Long Island. "I knew I wasn't dealing with somebody going home from work," commented the officer after seeing a shovel, a pickax, and two bloody boxes stuffed with body parts in the vehicle. The van's driver, Nathan Powell, was arrested and authorities believed their murder case against the producer was air-tight after they retrieved Wassel's severed head from his freezer. In the first recorded use of the "9/11 defense," however, Powell claimed he was traumatized by the recent terrorist attack on the World Trade Center. Wassel, he claimed, told him the attack was "America's just deserts" and made similar pro–Taliban statements against his adopted country. The Afghani-American filmmaker also allegedly threatened to use his Taliban contacts to have Powell's family killed. Outraged by Wassel's anti–American remarks, the "patriotic" producer killed the traitor during a fit of temporary insanity. Powell's accusations, however, did not jibe with Wassel's actions. In the wake of 9/11, the director took to the streets to film various victims' memorials for a planned documentary entitled *New York Shrines*. Wassel had also given U.S. intelligence authorities over 80 hours of film shot in Afghanistan showing roads and mountain passes to aid in the subsequent invasion of Afghanistan. On the eve of his trial in June 2003, Powell scrapped the "9/11 defense" and pleaded guilty to the lesser charge of manslaughter. Sentenced to 20 years in prison, Powell could be out in 15 with time off for good behavior and time already served. In 2002, *Firedancer* became Afghanistan's first submission for the Best Foreign Language Film Academy Award.

Further Reading

El-Ghobashy, Tamer. "Gory Killing of Afghan Filmmaker." *New York Daily News*, October 7, 2001, p. 45.

Watts, Louis Thomas *see* Thomas, Kid

Williams, Jermaine (V)

Described by family members as an "entrepreneur," Williams had not worked as a bodyguard for rapper Busta Rhymes since being dismissed in 2000 over allegations he was ripping off drug dealers. The 35-year-old Bronx man had been missing for a day when police on May 28, 2008 noticed blood dripping from the rear of a parked Lincoln Navigator pickup on 79th Street in Ozone Park, Queens. Williams' bullet riddled body was found wrapped in a comforter in the bed of his truck. Though Williams claimed to have worked in real estate, authorities believed his murder stemmed from either a personal altercation or links to drug dealers. Williams was the second bodyguard employed by Busta Rhymes to die violently. Israel Ramirez (see entry) was fatally shot during a video shoot in Brooklyn in December 2006. On tour in Europe, Rhymes spoke of the "great loss" of his fired bodyguard in a statement released to website SOHH.com: "Jermaine Williams will be deeply missed. He has remained a dear friend, even though we have not worked together for 8 years. Our condolences and prayers go out to his family and we ask that we be allowed to mourn the loss of our friend in peace." To date, no arrests have been made.

Further Reading

"Busta Rhymes Addresses Murder of Ex-Bodyguard." World Entertainment News Network, May 31, 2008.

Wilson, Nathaniel ("Buster") (V)

Wilson (not an original member) of the Coasters was singing bass with the legendary R&B group in a lounge in Las Vegas when he disappeared from the home he was sharing with the group's manager, Patrick Cavanaugh, and the man's wife, Diana, on April 7, 1980. A decomposed body wrapped in drapes and tied with a telephone cord was found in an isolated area of rugged Del Puerto Canyon, 22 miles outside of Modesto, California on May 11, 1980. The hands and feet were sawn off the body to prevent identification and an unsuccessful attempt had been made at decapitation. Police theorized the murder (death due to multiple gunshot wounds to the head), had taken place elsewhere and the body dumped in the remote canyon. Remarkably, the victim's identity remained a mystery for nearly a year until an anonymous phone tip to Tucson, Arizona, police in April 1981 linked the 45-year-old singer's disappearance to the body. Positive identification was made through dental records. Patrick Cavanaugh, 43, the last known person to see Wilson alive, was closely questioned. The ex-manager, in custody in San Diego awaiting trial on charges of masterminding a phony check fraud scheme, denied knowing anything about his friend's disappearance or death. Cavanaugh was convicted of the check scheme in November 1981 and sentenced to nine years in prison. His wife, Diana (found to be one of four women to which

Cavanaugh was simultaneously married), also received time in the case.

The Wilson case broke in 1982 after the woman offered to testify against Cavanaugh in exchange for a reduced sentence on a lesser fraud charge. Diana Cavanaugh was the star witness against her ex-husband at his murder trial in Las Vegas in November–December 1984. She testified Cavanaugh murdered Wilson to prevent the singer from informing authorities about the massive fraud case that he had masterminded. The Coasters' manager shot Wilson in the face near Baker, California, stuffed him in the trunk of his Cadillac, and drove to Las Vegas. Finding him still alive, Cavanaugh pumped two more bullets in the man's head. According to his ex-wife, Cavanaugh showed her Wilson's hand in a bucket of acid. Cavanaugh was found guilty of first-degree murder on December 8, 1984 and sentenced to death. A tireless jailhouse lawyer, Cavanaugh used a forged medical record in November 1984 to trick a Nevada judge into overturning his conviction. According to authorities, Cavanaugh persuaded a records clerk at a Los Angeles hospital to forge a document showing he was receiving treatment at the hospital at the time (April 7, 1980) Wilson was killed in Las Vegas. In 1998, the Nevada Supreme Court subsequently upheld Cavanaugh's murder conviction. In February 1990, another member of the Coasters, Cornell Gunter (see entry), was murdered in the general vicinity of the desert gambling capital. In April 2006, Cavanaugh, 60, died in Ely State Prison of gangrene brought on by complications from diabetes. The family of the death row inmate filed suit in April 2008 against Warden E.K. McDaniel and six other prison administrators and staff charging Cavanaugh was denied adequate medical care. "Given the profound and unmistakable smell of putrefying flesh," the suit stated, "there can be no question that every medical provider and correctional officer in that infirmary was acutely aware of Mr. Cavanaugh's condition." Both sides agreed the prisoner refused all medications except aspirin, but the administrator of his family's estate was never consulted about his declining medical condition. The suit was unsettled as of January 2010.

Further Reading

"Former Manager of Coasters Found Guilty in Member's Death." Associated Press, December 8, 1984.

Wipeout *see* **Icewood**, Blade

Wizzart, Kesha (V)

A straight-A student at Parrs Wood Sixth Form College in Manchester, England, Wizzart, then 15, was also an accomplished singer who was picked from among 40,0000 hopefuls to be a finalist on the popular ITV1 television talent show, *Stars in Their Eyes: Kids*. An institution on British television, the program featured contestants dressed up to impersonate top personalities. Wizzart, impersonating R&B singer Toni Braxton, sang the star's hit "Unbreak My Heart," and although failing to win, earned unanimous praise from the judges for the quality of her voice. Though a show business career seemed a certain lock, Wizzart chose instead to pursue her dream of studying law at Manchester University. In 2007, the 18 year old was eagerly awaiting the results of her A-level exams in English Language, Law and Philosophy by visiting British universities with her father, Frederick. Though long divorced from Kesha's mother, Beverley Samuels, Frederick Wizzart remained a devoted father to Kesha and his 13-year-old son, Fred.

On July 12, 2007, Kesha's niece arrived at the three-bedroom terraced home of Beverley Samuels, a 35-year-old nurse, who lived with her son, Fred, on Thelwall Avenue in Fallowfield, Greater Manchester. Kesha, who lived with her father, decided to spend the previous night at her mother's home because she was tired from visiting universities in the area. Unable to rouse her relatives, she asked a neighbor for assistance. The obliging neighbor climbed a ladder to the first floor and looking through a bedroom window was shocked to see the walls splattered with blood. Shock and horror escalated after Manchester police entered the residence and made the grisly discovery of three horribly bludgeoned bodies. Kesha's nude body, her hands tied behind her back with her bra, was found face-down on the floor of a spare bedroom. The young woman was raped and struck at least four times in the head with a hammer. Her head was covered with her knickers after the attack. Across the landing in her mother's bedroom, Beverley Samuels was left naked and face-down on her bed covered by a brown duvet. Like Kesha, the nurse was raped and bludgeoned some seven times with a two pound steel hammer found beside her. Fred, her son, was on the floor alongside his mother. Police theorized the boy had been marched into the room and forced to kneel prior to being hammered to death. Unpublicized

in the media frenzy following in the wake of the triple murder, police had discovered a container of cocoa butter that later proved to be an unsettling clue.

Suspicion fell immediately on Pierre Williams, the 32-year-old ex-boyfriend of Beverley Samuels who had recently resurfaced in the area after being dropped by the nurse over a year before. Earlier in the evening, neighbors reported hearing a loud argument coming from the death house. A former member of Manchester's notorious Gooch Close street gang, Williams was now an unemployed fitness instructor with a history of violent sexual behavior directed at women who refused his advances. In the police description released to television stations, Williams was described as a 5'8" black man with a medium build whose right arm bore the tattoo "cream," and his chest the inscriptions "Whatever," "Down For," and "Bout It Bout." In fact, two days after the murders Williams was sitting in a bar in Birmingham watching a news report about the crime on television when he decided to turn himself in. When arrested hours later, he was carrying a Bible with passages in it referring to "special oil" boldly underlined in ball-point pen. It was thought he had mixed cocoa butter with the blood of his victims in a bizarre attempt to reflect one of the passages. Williams was sitting in a Manchester jail charged with three counts of murder when, on August 10, 2007, a thousand mourners broke into spontaneous applause as Kesha Wizzart's coffin was taken from a horse drawn hearse into the Church of the Holy Name. Following the hour-long public service, Kesha was buried in a private family ceremony in Manchester's Southern Cemetery. Perhaps more heartbreaking, six days after the funeral Kesha's A-level results were made public. The young woman who chose academia over show biz celebrity scored A's in Law and English Language, and a B in Philosophy.

At trial in Manchester's Crown Court in February 2008, the full details of what the prosecution characterized as a "sexually motivated execution" were revealed to sickened jurors. Refused sex by Beverley Samuels, Williams raped both women, and beat all three to death with a hammer. Though admitting he was at the house on Thelwall Avenue, Williams denied any involvement in the crimes maintaining he was in the back garden when a mysterious hooded figure fled the scene. He could, however, offer no explanation as to how semen mixed with the blood of all three of the victims was recovered from his underwear, or, how flecks of blood belonging to Fred Wizzart were lifted from his wallet. Emboldened by his arrest, a former girlfriend stepped forward to testify that in 2003 Williams had bound her hands and feet before twice raping her at knifepoint after she had refused to have sex with him. Found guilty of all three murders on March 6, 2008, Williams heard only the first verdict read before interrupting the proceeding with the shout, "You bastards! I'm f***ing innocent." The former gang member was promptly dragged out of the courtroom and down to the cells by several security guards. In sentencing the convicted killer to two other life sentences, Judge Mr. Christopher Pitchford told the court, "Pierre Williams is a man with a low threshold for sexual frustration. He took out his frustration by treating Beverley and her daughter with gross sexual aggression. Only he can know the terror and pain he inflicted upon them." Pierre Williams was sentenced to at least 38 years in prison. Since his conviction, three women have stepped forward to accuse the triple murderer of sexual attacks going as far back as the 1980s and 1990s when he was an active member of Manchester's Gooch Close gang.

Further Reading

"Hammer Killer Gets 38 Years." *Daily Record*, March 7, 2008, p. 7.

Wolf, Steve (V)

Wolf was in his early twenties when he joined former disc jockey and television game show host Bob Eubanks in Concert Associates, a hugely successful concert promotion business based in Southern California. Though best-known for hosting *The Newlywed Game* on ABC, Eubanks was a rock concert pioneer who promoted the Beatles show at the Hollywood Bowl in 1964. When Eubanks left Concert Associates, Wolf and fellow 24-year-old Jim Rissmiller teamed to promote some of the most notable concerts in Los Angeles including the Diana Ross and the Supremes show that soldout the 18,700 seat Forum in Inglewood, California. The pair later sold the company to Filmways and, reconstituted as Wolf & Rissmiller, became the biggest rock concert promotion firm in California, and one of the largest in the United States, promoting appearances of the Rolling Stones, Cream, and Aerosmith. Most recently in November 1977, the duo promoted the Los Angeles Philharmonic's "Star Wars Suite" at the Hollywood Bowl. Producing some 130 concerts a year, Wolf & Rissmiller grossed around $6 million annually.

At approximately 6:00 A.M. on November 21, 1977, the 34-year-old concert promoter was shot to death in the bedroom of his luxury home on Mulholland Drive above Stone Canyon Reservoir in Los Angeles. Awakened by the sound of a break in, Wolf left his bed and apparently confronted the intruders, possibly as many as four, who had entered the residence through a side door. Wolf's fiancée, 30-year-old public relations consultant Linda Grey, was also in the home, but did not witness the shooting. Stolen were two valuable cameras, a wristwatch, and diamond jewelry. Wolf died three hours later on the operating table at Riverside Hospital in North Hollywood. That night, a concert by the popular band Chicago promoted by Wolf & Rissmiller played the Forum. Two days after the murder, Jim Rissmiller offered a $50,000 reward for information leading to the identity of the killer(s). As detectives continued their investigation, Linda Grey filed a million dollar palimony suit in July 1978 claiming she and Wolf had lived as husband and wife during the eleven months they were together. According to Grey, she gave up her career as an entertainment publicist on Wolf's promise he would support her for the rest of her life.

More than a year after the concert promoter's murder, authorities caught a break when a 17-year-old in jail on an unrelated burglary charge bragged to another inmate about the killing. Police arrested the juvenile on December 27, 1978, but did not release his name to the public until after a judge ruled in 1979 that the suspect, Keith Cook, could be tried as an adult. On April 24, 1979, Cook pleaded out to second-degree murder and was sentenced to seven years. Cook admitted to being one of four men who invaded Wolf's home, but denied being the triggerman. To date, no one else has been arrested for Wolf's murder.

Further Reading

Jones, Jack. "Steve Wolf, Rock Concert Promoter, Slain." *Los Angeles Times*, November 22, 1977, sec. Orange County, p. 1.

Wyatt, Nan (V)

Wyatt (legal name Nandray Ann Walicki) was the popular co-host of KMOX radio's "Total Information A.M.," the top-rated morning drive-time news show in St. Louis, Missouri. Known for her winning personality and in-depth political analysis, the 44 year old won numerous journalism awards including the prestigious National Associated Press Award for Enterprise Reporting in 1995, and had been a regular since May 1998 on the KETC-TV Thursday night panel news show, "Donnybrook." While briefly working at Chicago radio station WBBM-AM during the mid–1990s, Wyatt met her husband, Thomas Joseph Erbland, Jr. Despite numerous attempts to fix their troubled marriage, Wyatt told friends in 2003 that she planned to divorce the 43-year-old unemployed computer consultant and petition for custody of their seven-year-old son, Drake.

On the evening of February 18, 2003, Erbland phoned police and tearfully confessed, "I've just shot my wife." He was kept on the line while officers rushed to the couple's home in the 1300 block of Woodland Oaks Drive in the St. Louis County suburb of Twin Oaks. Wyatt, shot five times with a .357 Magnum handgun, was found dead in the master bedroom. Erbland, threatening to take his own life, was arrested hours later in the parking lot of an optical store where he had agreed to meet police. Under questioning, Erbland said that while his son was in the house at the time of the murder, he dropped him off without explanation at the home of Wyatt's parents prior to calling authorities. Interviewed in jail while awaiting trial on a charge of first-degree murder, a contrite Erbland confessed that while the murder was premeditated he felt great remorse—"I stole Nan from everybody. I stole her from Drake. She loved him so much. I stole Drake from her. She didn't deserve this." According to Erbland, the murder was precipitated by his discovery of Wyatt's private journal in which she had written their marriage was irretrievably broken. In an agreement with the prosecutor's office, Erbland escaped a life sentence without the possibility of parole by pleading guilty to second-degree murder on March 13, 2004. Sentenced to two consecutive life terms in prison, he will be eligible for parole in 26 years at the age of 70.

Further Reading

McClellan, Bill. "'She Said, 'You Give Me That Gun! ... I Shot Her.'" *St. Louis Post-Dispatch*, February 21, 2003, sec. A, p. 1.

Yasuda, Yoshiaki (V)

Yasuda, president of the Japanese Theatre Association and owner of the Fuji Theatre in what the *Los Angeles Times* called the city's "Little Nippon" district, was gunned down in front of his palatial home at 241 North Dittman Street at 1:30 A.M. on June 9, 1930. The theatre owner, accompanied by his wife and their two chauffeurs, had just returned to the residence when a pair of gunmen stepped from the shadows and pumped five shots into his chest and abdomen. One assailant pitched his .38-caliber handgun in an alley about 150 feet from the site as he fled the scene. Yasuda, also the head of the Japanese Wrestling Association, recently brought a troupe of Asian actors to the city to promote a series of bouts featuring Japanese wrestlers. Police theorized the unsolved crime was the result of a long-standing feud between Yasuda and others in L.A.'s Japanese community.

Further Reading

"Slain Japanese Linked to Feud." *Los Angeles Times*, June 10, 1930, sec. A. p. 2.

Yella (V)

At 4:00 A.M. on April 5, 1997, police in New Orleans, Louisiana, found the body of Albert Thomas seated in a parked car in the 2000 block of Danneel Street. The 22-year-old rapper known as Yella in the New Orleans–based group U.N.L.V. was shot in the head at close range. U.N.L.V., the first group signed by local label Cash Money Records, was credited with pioneering a new style of hip-hop in the Big Easy beginning with their first album *6th & Baronne* released locally in 1993 (re-released in 1998). Thomas can be heard soloing on the song "Drag 'Em 'N' Tha River" on the group's 1996 *Uptown 4 Life* album. The murder remains unsolved and received national attention following as it did in the wake of the murders of fellow-rappers Tupac Shakur (see entry) and Notorious B.I.G. (see entry).

Further Reading

"Rapper Albert Thomas of New Orleans–Based Group UNLV Murdered." Associated Press, April 5, 1997.

Young, Gig (M-S)

Born Byron Ellsworth Barr in St. Cloud, Minnesota, on November 4, 1913, the future Gig Young moved to Washington, D.C., in 1932 after his family lost their canning business during the Depression. In D.C., Young worked on a used car lot by day and took acting classes at night. The classes led to his first semi-professional theatrical experience with the local Phil Hayden Players and to some screen appearances in non-union industrial films. Informing his parents that he was sharing gas expenses with a friend driving to Hollywood, the 25 year old in fact hitchhiked to the film capital in 1938. The wannabe actor pumped gas, waited tables, cut grass, and finally graduated to building scenery in order to pay his weekly tuition at the prestigious Pasadena Community Playhouse. Young acted in nine plays there from February 1939 through May 1940 before being spotted by a Warner Bros. talent scout. The studio was impressed by the newcomer's striking good looks, winning smile, easygoing manner, and obvious appeal to women, and signed him to a $75 a week long term contract on March 29, 1941. As "Byron Barr" (his real name), the fledgling actor appeared in several small parts (*The Man Who Came to Dinner*, 1941; *Sergeant York*, 1941; *Dive Bomber*, 1941; *Captains of the Clouds*, 1942) prior to landing the feature role that would simultaneously launch his career and rename him. In 1942, he played the character "Gig Young" opposite Barbara Stanwyck in *The Gay Sisters*. At studio head Jack Warner's insistence, Byron Barr was rechristened Gig Young. The Warner publicity department played up the gimmick of an actor being named after his screen character in the film's promotion. Young followed his critically acclaimed turn with another strong performance in the 1943 Bette Davis vehicle *Old Acquaintance*.

World War II halted the actor's career momentum. After his discharge from the Coast Guard in 1945, Young returned to Hollywood and a succession of weak roles in minor films (*Escape Me Never*, 1947; *The Woman in White*, 1948), which set the stage for the frustrated actor to be forever typecast as a perennial second lead, *bon vivant*, or unsuccessful suitor in a string of sophisticated comedies. Dropped by Warners in 1948, Young free lanced at various studios until signing a contract with MGM in 1951. That year he was nominated for a Supporting Actor Oscar for his true-to-life role as an alcoholic in *Come Fill the Cup* starring James Cagney. Although Young lost the Oscar to Karl Malden (*A Streetcar Named Desire*), he had every reason to believe he would be offered stronger roles. He was not. After appearing in the mediocre *Holiday for Sinners* (1952), Young performed with distinction on Broadway in *Oh Men! Oh Women!* from December 1953 through mid-June 1954. While continuing to make movies (*The Desperate Hours*, 1955), Young became the host of the ABC television show *Warner Brothers Presents* for its entire 1955–1956 run. In 1958, he received another Best Supporting Actor Academy Award nomination for his performance in the Paramount comedy *Teacher's Pet* starring Clark Gable. He lost to Burl Ives in *The Big Country*. Young was well cast as a charming con artist in the NBC television series *The Rogues* co-starring Charles Boyer, but the program only lasted the 1964–1965 season. On his third try, the aging actor won a Best Supporting Actor Oscar in 1969 for his brilliant portrayal of the Depression-era dance marathon promoter "Rocky Gravo" in *They Shoot Horses, Don't They?*

By this point in his career, however, Young's years of alcoholism and addiction to sedatives had left the actor physically and emotionally ravaged. While he continued to get supporting roles in interesting films like director Sam Peckinpah's *Bring Me the Head of Alfredo Garcia* (1974) and *The Killer Elite* (1975), Young's career was essentially over after his Oscar win. In late 1977, the actor was brought to Hong Kong to work on his 55th and final motion picture, the prophetically titled *The Game of Death*. Filming was originally suspended in 1973 after the death of its star, Kung fu master Bruce Lee, but Golden Harvest studio, attempting to cash in on the star's enduring popularity, scrapped all the scenes except Lee's and reshot a new story around them. On the set, Young met German-born Kim Schmidt, an attractive 31-year-old script girl whose lifelong dream was to marry a film star and come to America. At 63, Young had already been to the altar on four previous occasions. His first marriage to

Gig Young, a versatile actor at home in comedy or drama, was typecast as the likeable second lead in a string of romantic comedies in the 1950s and 1960s. In 1969 he won a Best Supporting Actor Oscar for his unforgettable performance as a Depression-era dance marathon promoter in director Sydney Pollack's **They Shoot Horses, Don't They?** The 63-year-old actor long battled substance abuse and was married less than a month to his fifth wife, a 31-year-old German-script assistant, when he shot her then himself in their Manhattan apartment on October 19, 1978.

actress Sheila Stapler on August 2, 1940, ended in divorce on October 6, 1949. Young married Sophie Rosenstein, a Warner Bros. drama coach six years his senior, on January 1, 1951. Deeply in love, Young remained devoted to Rosenstein until her death from cervical cancer on November 10, 1952. Marriage number three, to Elizabeth Montgomery, daughter of actor Robert Montgomery who was destined to become famous as "Samantha" on the hit television series *Bewitched*, occurred in Las Vegas on December 28, 1956. They divorced in 1963. A fourth marriage, to Beverly Hills real estate broker Elaine Whitman in 1963, produced one child and ended in a rancorous divorce in 1967.

Determined to make his marriage to Kim Schmidt work, Young moved into apartment 1BB in the Osborne at 205 West 57th Street in New York City and valiantly struggled to kick his addictions to alcohol and drugs. On October 19, 1978, between the hours of 2:30 and 3:30 P.M., the building manager heard what sounded like two gunshots issuing from the couple's apartment. He did not notify authorities, however, until becoming suspicious after groceries delivered to their apartment stood outside the door for hours. Police entered 1BB at 7:30 P.M. to find the fully clothed pair dead on the bedroom floor. Schmidt was killed instantly by a single gunshot to the base of the skull. Near her on the floor lay Young with a .38-caliber snub-nosed Smith & Wesson pistol clenched in his hand. The actor known for his sophisticated charm had placed the gun in his mouth and fired. A diary written in Young's hand and opened to September 27, 1978, was found on a desk in the sitting room. The entry read, "We Were Married Today." A search of the premises unearthed 350 rounds of ammunition and three other handguns in addition to the murder weapon. Also uncovered at the scene were explicit snapshots taken with an automatic timer of Young and his wife of three weeks engaged in various sexual positions. When the autopsy revealed no traces of alcohol or barbiturates in the actor's system, authorities offered a theory of the murder-suicide based upon available evidence. According to the police theory of the crime, Young was already acutely stressed out by money problems and his withdrawal from drugs and alcohol when the couple began arguing. Schmidt, a U.S. citizen since their marriage, may have threatened to leave him to work as a publicist for her old boyfriend. As evidenced by the existence of the sex photos

(ostensibly used to excite the dissipated actor), she may have made fun of his periodic impotence. Young's remains were cremated and interred under his real name, Byron Barr, in the Green Hills Cemetery in Waynesville, North Carolina.

Further Reading

Eells, George. *Final Gig: The Man Behind the Murder*. San Diego: Harcourt Brace Jovanovich, 1991.

Zapata, Mia (V)

Rock 'n' roll, more particularly, punk rock never forgets. Raped and murdered by an unknown assailant in 1993, the popular lyricist-singer of the Seattle-based band, The Gits, was never forgotten by the city's underground music community, or, by the police department's Cold Case squad. The daughter of media executives born on August 25, 1965, Zapata spent her formative years in Douglass Hills, an upper middle-class suburb of Louisville, Kentucky. Despite her affluent upbringing, rounded out by a parochial school education and country club tennis lessons, Zapata was a remarkably free, independent spirit, who by all accounts was totally non-judgmental. She loved her family and friends and never turned her back on them, even when later writing and singing some of the most powerful lyrics heard in punk rock up to that time. Zapata was attending Antioch College, a small liberal arts school in Yellow Springs, Ohio, when she formed the punk rock band, The Gits, in 1986 with fellow-students Steve Moriarty (drums), Matt Dresdner (bass), and Joe Spleen (a.k.a. Andy Kessler, guitar). Named after the Monty Python skit, "The Snivelling Little Rat-Faced Gits," the band shortened its name to fit on record labels. In 1989, The Gits moved west to Seattle, home of the burgeoning "grunge sound" made famous by local bands like Nirvana and Pearl Jam. Unlike these bands, however, The Gits were never really part of the city's grunge scene, preferring instead to perform their progressive punk music in underground clubs in Seattle. Fuelled by lyrics drawn from Zapata's voluminous daily journals and the singer's electric stage presence, The Gits developed a rabid local fan base, and by the early 1990s had successfully toured the U.S. and Europe without major label support. In 1992, the band released its first album, *Frenching the Bully*, on small, independent C/Z Records, and was beginning to attract national attention.

Zapata, 27, spent the night of Tuesday, July 6, 1993, drinking with friends, and fellow-musicians at The Comet, a Capitol Hill bar in Seattle on East Pike Street. The Gits recently wrapped up a two-week West Coast tour, and were scheduled to continue working on their second studio album for C/Z, *Enter: The Conquering Chicken*. The following week, the band was scheduled to play at the New Music Seminar in New York, a music convention focusing on independent and alternative record labels, and was booked for a fall European tour. Shortly after midnight, Zapata left the bar telling her drinking buddies she planned to look for a friend, then take a cab home. Minutes after 2:00 A.M., the talented singer left a friend's apartment near 11th Avenue and East Pike Street. At 3:21 A.M., a streetwalker named "Charity" discovered Zapata's body lying face-up along a sidewalk curb on the west side of 24 Avenue South at South Washington Street, next to the offices of Catholic Community Services at the Randolph Carter Center. The area, on a dead-end street near a small paved parking area, was 1.6 miles from the apartment she had left less than two hours earlier on East Pike Street. The body site was in a seedy part of the city, Central Area, known for drug buys and prostitution. Zapata was strangled to death with the cord from The Gits hooded sweatshirt she was wearing. Her body was placed face-up with arms outstretched, legs crossed at the ankles, in an attitude of crucifixion. Its battered condition led police to conjecture Zapata had a "prolonged and painful struggle" with her attacker at an unknown location, prior to the killer dumping her body on the street. Though not divulged to the press at the time, Zapata had been raped.

The singer-songwriter's murder sent a shock wave through the Seattle music scene. On July 23, 1993, local bands held a benefit concert for Zapata attended by 750 people. The show raised more than $4,000 for "Mia's Friends," a reward fund established at a local bank for information leading to an indictment of the musician's killer. On the afternoon of August 13, 1993, Seattle super-group Nirvana announced they would top a five band bill in a benefit show that night to raise money to hire a private detective to aid police in finding Zapata's killer. The show, performed at the King Performance Center (formerly the King Theatre), included local bands Hell Smells, Kill Sybil, Voodoo Gearshift, and Tad. One year after the killing, police still had no leads despite being aided in their search by Seattle-based private eye, Leigh Hearon, hired with moneys generated from the various benefit shows. Hearon interviewed hundreds of people in an attempt to reconstruct the final hour of Zapata's life. All she was able to accomplish, however, was to eliminate suspects already largely known to the police. The case was featured in a July 1995 episode of the Fox television show *America's Most Wanted*, but generated no leads. Still refusing to give up on the case or to let their friend's musical legacy die, her former bandmates formed Evil Stig (backward for "Gits Live") with new front woman Joan Jett singing Zapata's parts in mid-1995, and released the benefit album, *Evil Stig*, later that year.

By January 2003, nearly a decade after the murder, the case seemed dead. The more than $70,000 raised by concerts, donations, and album sales to pay the private detective had long been spent. Though not forgotten by family or friends, Zapata's most enduring legacy appeared to be the formation of Home Alive, a self-defense training group for women created soon after the singer's murder. The Cold Case squad of the Seattle Police Department, made up entirely of two detectives, Richard Gagnon and Greg Mixsell, continued to review the Zapata case as well as nearly three hundred other unsolved murders in the area. Established in the years prior to the use of reliable DNA tests to establish possible suspects, the Cold Case squad began systematically working through the backlog of cases in 2002 after the new DNA technology became available. Earlier in the year, the detectives had submitted a sample of saliva taken from Zapata's breast to the Washington State Patrol Crime Lab for DNA testing. At that time, no match was found when run against various national DNA databases. In December 2002, however, the DNA profile was entered into a National DNA Index system that matched a sample recently taken in Florida of convicted felon, Jesús C. Mezquia, 48. Detectives Gagnon and Mixsell travelled to the Sunshine State where on January 10, 2003, they aided the U.S. Marshall's Northwest Fugitive Apprehension Task Force in the arrest of Mezquia at his home in Marathon, in the heart of the Florida Keys. The lanky 6' 4" legal Cuban immigrant, a married father of a two-year-old daughter, supported his family as a day laborer and fisherman. Mezquia's rap sheet dated back to the early 1980s and included arrests in Florida's Dade County for attempted solicitation, resisting arrest, kidnapping, indecent exposure, false imprisonment, and carrying a concealed weapon. In Riverside County, California he logged convictions in 1986 for assault and battery and for spousal battery in 1989. Charged with robbery in 1990, Mezquia was convicted of a lesser offense, but given a suspended four year sentence and placed on probation. Less than a year later, he violated it after exposing himself. The career criminal pleaded guilty to a lesser charge, paid a fine, and was placed on misdemeanor probation. Back in Florida, he was convicted around 1998 of aggravated battery after punching his eight-month pregnant girlfriend in the face.

The Florida charge that led Seattle detectives to his door occurred in 2002 after he was convicted for the possession of burglary tools. At the time, Mezquia was required to submit a DNA sample that was then added to state's felony database. Cold Case detectives painstakingly established Mezquia had been in Seattle during the time Zapata was murdered. In 1992, the Cuban immigrant came to the city with his girlfriend later sharing an apartment with her in Leschi, a neighborhood in east central Seattle. Mezquia's neighbors described him as a superstitious character who placed garlic in the corners of his home to ward off evil spirits. When not working in a hardware store, Mezquia was always fishing. Questioned by Seattle detectives in Florida, Mezquia denied knowing Zapata when showed a photo array of women containing her picture. Unaware his DNA matched a saliva sample found on the dead singer, Mezquia would later be unable to convincingly state he had somehow transferred his DNA to the woman while she was alive. As the murder suspect fought extradition to Seattle, court papers filed against him in King County linked Mezquia to another crime committed in the city just five weeks after Zapata's murder, and close to the area where her body was dumped. A young woman walking in the 1300 block of 10th Avenue East noticed a car following her. The driver pulled up alongside of her, but quickly drove away when she saw him masturbating. The woman alertly wrote down the car's license plate number. The car was registered to Mezquia. This incident, when combined with Zapata's rape-murder, led one investigator to conclude, "He's a hunter and [Zapata] just happened to fall within his field of vision."

More than ten years after the fact, Zapata's accused killer faced a charge of first-degree murder in King County Superior Court in Seattle on March 8, 2004. Mezquia, still maintaining his innocence, wore headphones to listen to a Spanish translation of the proceedings against him. The prosecution's case was simple. Zapata and Mezquia randomly crossed paths in the early morning hours of July 7, 1993, and he killed her when she resisted his sexual advances. The DNA recovered from Zapata's body identified Mezquia as her murderer and could not have been transmitted there by casual contact, certainly not from a man who earlier denied knowing the victim. Mezquia's attorney argued the crime scene could have been contaminated by medics who tried to revive Zapata. In the end, the DNA evidence against Mezquia was just too compelling to ignore. After deliberating four days, a jury found him guilty of first-degree murder in a courtroom filled with Zapata's friends and family. Gits drummer Steve Moriarty spoke for many when he commented, "I'm just glad that he'll be rotting in prison, and that we'll be able to live a little freer lives." On April 20, 2004, Judge Sharon Armstrong sentenced Mezquia to 36⅓ years in prison noting the unusually stiff term (the state average ranges from 20 to 26 years) was due to the "particularly painful injuries" Zapata was forced to endure. With flawless logic, Judge Armstrong reasoned the killer had a decade after the crime to live his life ... all the while Mia was "in the ground." In May 2005, director Kerri O'Kane's 75 minute documentary, *The Gits*, premiered at the Seattle International Film Festival. In August 2005, a three-judge panel of the state Court of Appeals unanimously ruled that Judge Armstrong lacked the authority (under a U.S. Supreme Court ruling) to order the extra-long prison term. Remarkably, Mezquia, 54, returned to court in January 2009 and asked to have his original sentence reimposed. Judge Armstrong abided by the killer's wishes and returned him to Clallam Bay Corrections Center to serve out the remainder of his original sentence. Zapata, the woman who once told friends all she wanted in life was a cabin to live in, an old jeep to drive, and a sheep dog to ride shotgun, is buried in Cave Hill Cemetery near her former home in Louisville, Kentucky. The grave marker reads: "Mia Katherine Zapata — Aug. 25, 1965 — July 7, 1993 — Cherished Daughter — Sister — Artist — Friend — Git." In the true spirit of punk, The Gits website extends an open invitation to all to visit Zapata's final resting place — "She welcomes visitors."

Further Reading

Burkitt, Janet. "Zapata Slaying Suspect Called 'Predatory.'" *Seattle Times*, January 14, 2003, sec. A, p. 1.

Pols, Mary F. "Holding on to Mia's Magic — Singer's Killing Leaves Grief in the 2 Worlds She Lived in." *Seattle Times*, August 26, 1993, sec. A, p. 1.

www.thegits.com.

Appendix 1:
Narcocorridos

The *corrido* (ballad) has been popular in Mexico for hundreds of years and until the Mexican Revolution (1910–1920) was predominantly romantic in nature. Inspired by the ongoing struggle, however, heroic outlaws and gunmen operating along the border between Texas and Mexico became a popular subject for *corridos*. Usually instantly recognizable by its accordion-driven polka and waltz sound, *corridos* became one of the most popular types of songs among the lower classes in Mexico. With the advent of the drug cartels in the 1970s, *narcocorridos* (ballads recounting the exploits and travails of drug kingpins) became an underground phenomenon that are presently in more demand on the streets and in CD stores in Mexico than any other form of ballad. Singers of *narcocorridos* originally sold their cassettes out of the trunks of their cars and were often "adopted" by the drug traffickers whose exploits they popularized. Songs were commissioned by leaders of the drug gangs and some musicians became so intimately connected with certain narcotics strongmen that they performed at their weddings. Some law enforcement officials have speculated that traffickers have used the musical performances of their sanctioned *narcocorridos* to launder drug money. Such an association, however, presents an inherent risk to performers who repeatedly have been collateral damage in feuds between rival drug cartels in the high stakes, high profit game of international narcotics trafficking. Since the early 1990s, *narcocorridos* have become the Mexican equivalent of gangsta rap (only with an arguably higher body count and more pronounced violence).

The following chronological listing of *narcocorridos* commencing with Chalino Sanchez, the godfather of the genre and its first martyr, presents an overview of a disturbing trail of death and injury in Mexican culture that has its obvious parallel in the ongoing rap murders in America.

Sanchez, Rosalino ("Chalino") (May 15, 1992)

Raised in the small village of Sanalona twenty miles east of Culiacán in Sinaloa, a Mexican state renowned for drug trafficking, the legend of the *narcocorrido* great began early. Sanchez was a child when a local hood raped his older sister. At 15, he encountered the rapist at a local dance, walked up to man without a word, and shot him to death. The teen fled to Los Angeles where his aunt lived and soon became involved with his brother, Armando, in low-level drug and people smuggling. Armando's violent death in Tijuana is credited with Sanchez's first *corrido* written to commemorate his memory. While spending a few months in jail, Sanchez continued to write songs this time on commission for fellow-inmates in exchange for money and favors. These early recordings, like most *narcocorridos*, were quickly made and put on cassettes for easy limited distribution. Although not a particularly good singer, Sanchez had an instantly recognizable voice and delivery that when vocalizing his own sharply drawn tales of life lived on the streets made a visceral impact. Soon, local tough guys were paying Sanchez to chronicle their deeds in song. Single cassette sales to individuals soon grew into multiple copy requests for their friends. In 1986–1987, Sanchez went into a real studio for the first time and created multiple copies of cassettes that he sold out of the trunk of his car and distributed to swap dealers at meets around southern California. As his fame grew locally, Sanchez assiduously avoided any outward trappings of success and adopted an iconic style of dress that has since defined *narcocorridos*— a plain white or plaid shirt, dark pants, cowboys boot and hat, with a pistol either in a holster or jammed into a belt.

Prior to the early morning hours of January 25, 1992, Chalino Sanchez was still only a popular local singer in Sinaloa and the border region around southern California. That changed during a performance at the Plaza Los Arcos dance hall in Coachella, California, a desert town one hundred miles southeast of Los Angeles. Sanchez, 31, was performing before an enthusiastic crowd of four hundred when shortly after midnight 32-year-old Edward Alvarado Gallegos, an umemployed mechanic, approached the stage to make a song request, then pulled a gun and shot the singer in the side. Undaunted, Chalino pulled his pistol and returned fire with some reports saying he left the stage to pursue the gunman through the panic-stricken crowd. During the ensuing gun battle 20-year-old Rene Carranza was killed and at least ten others were wounded (mostly by the singer). Gallegos was disarmed by someone in the crowd and shot in the mouth with his own gun. Sanchez survived (as did Gallegos) and emerged from the hospital on his way to cult stardom. His songs, previously unplayed, started to receive radio airplay and after signing a deal with Musart, one of Mexico's biggest record and publishing companies, his album sales soared. Sanchez's popularity gave rise to *chalinitos*, or, "little Chalinos," aspiring young *narcocorridos* who sang, dressed, moved, and acted like their idol. On May 15, 1992, four months after the incident in Coachella, Sanchez performed at the Sálon Bugambilias in Culiacan. After the show, the singer left the club in a car with two of his brothers, several young women, and his cousin. Minutes later, they were pulled over by a group of armed men in a Chevy Suburban flashing state police IDs. Sanchez offered the gunmen money, which they refused, and agreed to leave with them. At dawn the next day, the godfather of *narcocorridos* was found dumped by an irrigation canal near a highway on the way out of Culiacán. Blindfolded, his wrists scarred by rope burns, Chalino Sanchez had been shot four times execution-style in the back of the head. While the case was never solved, numerous motives have been put forth for the singer's hit ranging from missing product in a drug deal, revenge over Sanchez's involvement with a drug lord's wife, and retaliation over the murder of another person associated with the Sanchez family. Chalino's son, Adam "Chalino" Sanchez, followed in his father's footsteps and became the first *banda-norteño* singer to perform at the Kodak Theatre in Hollywood. Shortly after performing at the sold out venue, the 19-year-old singer died en route to a performance in Puerto Vallarta on March 27, 2004 when the car in which he was riding with three others blew a tire and crashed on the highway between Rosario and Escuinapa in the Mexican state of Sinaloa. Sanchez was the only fatality.

Elizalde, Valentín
(November 25, 2006)

Known as "El Gallo de Oro" ("the Golden Roos-

ter"), Elizalde was renowned for singing *narcocorridos* often taken up as anthems to the Sinaloa drug cartel and its leader, Joaquín "Shorty" Guzmán. Shortly after leaving an open air festival in the Mexican border town of Reynosa across the Rio Grande River from McAllen, Texas on November 25, 2006, the van in which he was riding was strafed with more than 66 rounds from gunmen wielding AK-47s. The singer was killed along with his manager Mario Mendoza, and his driver Raymundo Ballesteros. Police investigated the link between his murder and a gruesome video posted on the internet set to one of his songs, "To My Enemies," recognized as a mockery of drug kingpin Osiel Cárdenas. To date, no arrests have been made. Although the charismatic performer's *norteño* (accordion-based) musical style albums never topped the 100,000 sales mark or were in the Top Twenty during his life, Elizalde's posthumous record, *Vencedor*, reached Number 1 on the Latin chart.

Tecno Banda Fugaz
(February 19, 2007)

Assassins with machine guns killed four members of the group in the city of Pururan in the Mexican state of Michoacan. A fifth band member survived the assassination.

Los Padrinos de la Sierra
(June 9, 2007)

Four members of the band were shot and killed in the Mexican state of Durango.

Gómez, Javier Morales
(December 2007)

The leader of the popular band Los Implacables del Norte was shot to death in a drive-by shooting at a park in Huetamo in the western Mexican state of Michoacan. Gómez performed *narcocorridos* with titles such as "Drug Tragedy" and "Death Contract."

Peña, Zayda
(December 1, 2007)

The 28-year-old lead singer of the group Zayda y los Culpables (Zayda and the Guilty Ones) was shot with two others in a hotel in Matamoros in Tamaulipas state across the border from Brownsville, Texas. Peña, with a back wound, was taken to a local hospital. The other two, a friend and the hotel manager, died at the scene. Following emergency surgery, the singer was placed in the intensive care unit. Minutes later, an assailant entered the room and shot her twice in the face at point-blank range. While most of the group's songs were romantic ballads in the style of *grupero* (rock beats blended with folky accordion melodies), one entitled "Tiro de Gracia" ("Coup de grace") was supposedly a reference to an execution-style gunshot to the brain.

Gómez, Sergio
(December 3, 2007)

On December 2, 2007, Gomez, 34, lead singer of the *Duranguense* mega-group K-Paz de la Sierra, and two music promoters were leaving the venue after the band's concert in Morelia, capital of the Mexican state of Michoacán, when the car in which they were riding was intercepted by a fleet of ten Chevrolet Suburbans. Earlier in the day, the singer chose to ignore threatening phone calls warning him not to appear at the concert. The gunmen released the promoters unharmed two hours after their abduction, but kept Gómez. The next day, the singer's body was found dumped along a rural highway exhibiting signs of a laundry list of torture including choking, severe bruising on his thorax and abdomen, and burns covering his face and legs. In 2006, the group received a *Billboard* Latin American Music Award and was the best known band in the *Pasito Duranguense* scene which featured ballads performed at an accelerated rhythm. The popular singer's body was transferred from Morelia to Ciudad Hidalgo and then to Mexico City where a mass was performed at the Metropolitan Cathedral. Gómez's body was then flown to Indianapolis, Indiana where the group's music first received regular airplay on the city's Spanish-language radio station WEDJ-FM. Gomez lived for the past few years with his wife and children in Avon, a small town west of Indianapolis. Following a closed casket service at St. Mary's Catholic Church attended by hundreds of mourners, the singer's body was cremated. Not unexpectedly, most members of K-Paz de la Sierra refused to cooperate with authorities.

Aquino, José Luis
(December 5, 2007)

A trumpeter for the band Los Condes, Aquino's body was found in a dry riverbed in the southern Mexican state of Oaxaca. The 33-year-old musician was bludgeoned about the face, his hands and feet tied, and a plastic bag secured over his head. Los Condes, formed in 1991 in the Oaxaca town of San Pedro Sultepec, recorded six albums and appeared in the Mexican film, *Mafioso pero gracioso/Funny Mobster*.

Del Fierro Lugo, Roberto
(January 9, 2008)

The former publicist and marketing manager for both the murdered *narcocorrido* star Valentín Elizalde

(see entry) and more recently the man's brother, Jesús "El Flaco" Elizalde, was shot once in the head on a street near a recording studio in the Guadalajaran suburb of Zapopan on January 8, 2009. The 47-year-old died the next day.

Sepúlveda, Jorge Antonio
(January 15, 2008)

The 20-year-old singer's bullet riddled body was found on a road near the city of Guasave in the northern Mexican state of Sinaloa. Sepúlveda's burnt out car was discovered nearby.

Alfaro (Pulido), Jesús Rey David
(February 2008)

The corpse of the singer known as "El Gallito" ("Little Rooster") was found strangled and shot in the head in Tijuana just south of the California border. The 26-year-old entertainer's body had apparently been frozen. Also recovered were the remains of two of Alfaro's staff, manager Israel Flores, and assistant José Guadalupe Topete. Both men had been tortured to death and left with written notes. Alfaro was believed to have had ties to the Arellano-Felix drug cartel.

Herederos de Sinaloa
(March 6, 2008)

Four members of the group Herederos de Sinaloa (Heirs of Sinaloa) were shot to death in downtown Culiacán by two men with automatic weapons emerging from a luxury SUV with guns blazing. Before speeding off, a gunman tossed money on the body of one of the dead men. The hit occurred directly across from the Sinaloa headquarters of newspaper publisher Organización Editorial Mexicana where a group member had just been interviewed.

Villanueva, Nicolás
(March 19, 2008)

The 38-year-old lead vocalist for the tropical musical group Brisas del Mar was shot to death when gunmen opened fire on the band as they played at a dance in the town of Quechultenango in the southern Mexican state of Guerrero. Villanueva, riddled by more than 20 bullets, died instantly, while fellow-band members Gaudencio Contreras, 21, José Santos Galeana, 17, and Alberto Nava Venegas, 13, were wounded in the attack.

Villa, Roberto
(March 23, 2009)

Villa was an original member of Conjunto Atardecer, a *Duranguense* group that placed 11 records on the *Billboard* Top Latin Album chart. The 24-year-old drummer was traveling in a van with a group of students from Escuela Normal Rural, a local secondary school in the city of Santa Maria del Oro in the Mexican state of Durango, when a car pulled up alongside their vehicle at an intersection and sprayed it with automatic gunfire. Villa and four others were killed in the attack. One unconfirmed report stated the gunmen were attempting to kidnap the drummer.

Ocaranza, Carlos (August 16, 2009)

Ocaranza, known in *narcocorrido* as "El Loco Elizalde," just left La Revancha, a bar in the western section of Guadalajara, when two gunmen ap-proached the 32-year-old and his agent, Jorge Altamirano Pelayo, and began firing. Ocaranza died instantly on the street from gunshot wounds to the head and chest while Pelayo, shot three times, expired in a hospital the next day. The gunmen escaped on a motorcycle leaving police only reluctant witnesses and 12 spent shell casings.

Further Reading

Edber, Mark Cameron. *El Narcotraficante: Narcorridos and the Construction of a Cultural Persona on the U.S.-Mexico Border*. Austin: University of Texas Press, 2004.

Quinones, Sam. *True Tales from Another Mexico: The Lynch Mob, the Popsicle Kings, Chalino, and the Bronx*. Albuquerque: University of New Mexico Press, 2001.

Wald, Elijah. *Narcocorrido: A Journey into the Music of Drugs, Guns, and Guerrillas*. New York: Rayo, 2001.

Appendix 2:
Occupations

Actors, Motion Picture, Stage, and Television

Anand, Dinesh
Arbuckle, Roscoe "Fatty"
Bacon, David G. G.
Barsi, Judith
Bennison, Louis
Benson, Lyric
Bhatt, Urmilla
Blake, Robert
Brancato, Lillo, Jr.
Brando, Christian
Cabot, Susan
Campbell, Margaret
Clary, Wilton Werbe
Cleaves, Robert Weldon
Colby, Barbara
Cooley, Spade
Crane, Bob
Crittenden, T.D.
Cunnane, Barry
Cupit, Jennifer
Davis, Myra
Del Mar, Claire
Dunne, Dominique
Echevarria, Lydia
Engels, Virginia
Ethridge, LaJean
Forsberg, Florence
Frachet, Eric
Fragson, Harry
Gelman, Eric
Gobert, Dedrick
Gomez, Audrey
Hartman, Brynn
Hedderel, Rivet
Howden, Victoria
Huffman, David Oliver
Ince, Thomas H.
Isenberg, Caroline

Ivers, Peter Scott
Jackson, Michael
Jam Master Jay
Jenkins, Ryan Alexander
Jerome, Helene
Jones, Kenneth Bruce
Kallman, Richard (Dick)
Kelly, Paul
Kilian, Victor
Knox, Robert Arthur
Kupcinet, Karyn
Laney, Barbara Jean
Lee, Anthony Dwain
Leonard, Harry
Longet, Claudine
McMullen, Tara Correa
Milocevic, Milos
Mineo, Sal
Monroe, Marilyn
Morelle, Denise
Munro, Viola Gordon
Nance, Jack
Neal, Tom
Ngor, Haing S.
Niquette, Richard
Norwood, John
Novarro, Ramón
Olsson, Tony
Omer, Danielle
Parks, Wole
Pasolini, Pier Paolo
Peaklica, Piseth
Perez, Daniela
Pringle, Val
Professor Backwards
Proof
Reeves, George
Reilly, Catherine
Ritchie, Adele
Rose, George
Salanti, Theodore (Rocky)

Salmi, Albert
Santana, Merlin
Schaeffer, Rebecca
Shakur, Tupac
Silva, Fernando Ramos da
Simmons, Kadamba
Simpson, O.J.
Smith, Jay R.
Smith, Robert McAdam
Sorrells, Robert
Stahl, Jennifer
Stratten, Dorothy
Stromberg, Larry
Switzer, Carl Dean ("Alfalfa")
Tate, Sharon
Taylor, William Desmond
Todd, Thelma
Velez, Lilian
Wagenheim, Charles
Young, Gig

Art Directors, Designers, and Make-Up Artists

Buckland, Wilfred
Landau, Jack
Tillis, Sanford Lewis

Cameramen, Editors, and Grips, Film

Gray, King David
Ott, Paul Alan
Sampson, John E.

Celebrity Spouses, Relatives, and Lovers

Brando, Christian
Crane, Cheryl

Dunne, Dominique
Hartman, Brynn

Circus and Carnival Performers and Executives

Codona, Alfredo
Jung, Paul
Mansfield, Edward
Melrose, Percy C.
Stiles, Grady F., Jr.

Composers and Songwriters

Caux, Claude
Cooke, Sam
Europe, James Reese
Foth, Steven M.
Gaye, Marvin
Jackson, Michael
Johnson, Robert
Lennon, John
Leopold, Joseph Walter
Madingoane, Tebogo
Notorious B.I.G.
Panou, Akis
Pappalardi, Felix
Pastorius, Jaco
Pringle, Kevin
Pringle, Val
Shakur, Tupac
Spector, Phil
Talkov, Igor
Tosh, Peter

Concert Promoters

Wolf, Steve

Dancers

Duarte, Pablo
Harger, (Solon) Bert
Kelly, George Augustus
Peaklica, Piseth
Sampih
Schuster, Roy Edgar
Stahl, Jennifer

Disc Jockeys

Berg, Alan
Crane, Bob
Glahn, Rebecca
Knight, Terry

McCall, Roger
Merker, Jack Ronald
Monday, Jerry
Moss, Al
Wyatt, Nan

Magicians

Maloney, Robert N.

Musicians

Chediak, Almir
Hagnes, Helen
Hill, Allan
Horner, Mark
Hull, Jay G.
Miller, Lyndl
Rogers, Derek
St. Louis, Keith Cedric
Walter, Homer S.

Musicians, Country

Akeman, David ("Stringbean")
Cooley, Spade

Musicians, Jazz

Bachemin, Johnnie
Baloi, Gito
Bornais, Claude
Bourn, Verlon
Burmeister, Christoffer
Byard, Jaki
Colwell, Timothy
Morgan, (Edward) Lee
Pastorius, Jaco
Rosolino, Frank

Orchestra Conductors and Bandleaders

Bornais, Claude
Cooley, Spade
Europe, James Reese
Walters, Homer M.

Pornography

Boham, Timothy J.
Door, William H.
Gonzalez, Israel Chappa
Holmes, John C.
King, Natel
Mitchell Brothers
Rothenberg, Paul E.

Producers and Directors, Film

Adamson, Al
Arbuckle, Roscoe "Fatty"
Bern, Paul
Dismukes, George
Ince, Thomas H.
Mitchell Brothers
Pasolini, Pier Paolo
Radin, Roy
Raver, Harry Rush
Ross, Nat
Taylor, William Desmond
van Gogh, Theo
Wassel, Jawed

Producers, Directors, and Managers, Television and Radio

Harvey, Gerald
Frodl, Helmut
Hassan, Muzzammil ("Mo")
Merker, Jack Ronald
Radin, Roy
Reeves, George
van Gogh, Theo

Producers, Directors, and Managers, Theatre

Kean, Norman
Mineo, Sal
Parnell, Wallace R.
Radin, Roy
Shibley Nassib Abdullah
Smith, Allen
Stohn, Carl, Jr.

Rappers

Behrmann, Dimitri
Bender, Christopher L.
Big L
Big Lurch
Big Stretch
Bugz
C-Murder
Camoflauge
Cavlar
Cortéz, Angel
Davis, Eric DeSean
Dolla
Freaky Tah
Howard, Malcolm

Icewood, Blade
Jam Master Jay
Kanyva
La Rock, Scott
Mac Dre
Mac, the Camoflage Assassin
Madingoane, Tebogo
Miller, Seagram
Mr. Cee
Mr. Livewire
Newt, Ronnie
Notorious B.I.G.
Priceless Game
Proof
Ramirez, Israel
Reid-Thomas, Elliott
Shakur, Tupac
Soulja Slim
Walker, Kenneth
Williams, Jermaine
Yella

Record Executives and Producers

Blackburn, Ronald
Cooke, Sam
Knight, Terry
Lawes, Henry ("Junjo")
Loucks, David G.
Meek, Joe
Minor, Charlie
Menson, Michael
Pappalardi, Felix
Pastorius, Jaco
Spector, Phil
Walker, Kenneth

Road Managers

Clarke, Rowan
Harrison, Danny
Knight, Terry
Rountree, Roderick (Khalil)

Screenwriters, Playwrights and Novelists

Ince, Thomas H.
Lees, Robert
Wassel, Jawed

Showgirls

Childs, Evelyn

Singers and Musicians, Rock, Reggae, Soul, and Folk

Abbott, Darrell ("Dimebag")
Albrecht, (Jeffrey) Carter
Arcady, John
Bany, Michael W.
Barrett, Carlton (Lloyd)
Beasts of Satan
Bourn, Verlon
Brathwaite, Junior
Burmeister, Christoffer
Cantat, Bertrand
Cooke, Sam
Davidson, Quentin (Footz)
Dorsey, Leslie
Dube, Lucky
Forrester, Rhett
Foth, Steven M.
Franklin, Melvin B.
Fuller, Bobby
Gaye, Marvin
Gordon, Jim
Gunter, Cornell
Harvey, Bryan
Haskel, Presley
Hinkley, Ineka Margaret
Jackson, Al, Jr.
Jackson, Michael
Johnson, Robert
Knight, Terry
Lawes, Henry (Junjo)
Lennon, John
Longet, Claudine
McNelley, Robert E.
Menson, Michael
Myles, Raymond Anthony, Sr.
Neal, Jackie
Panous, Akis
Pappalardi, Felix
Pastorius, Jaco
Rudebeck, John W.
Sanders, Scott
Schwartzbauer, Jessica Lyn
Scott, Walter
Selena
Shabalala, Headman
Spector, Phil
Struebing, Kurt Alan
Talkov, Igor
Tanin, Ihor
Thomas, Kid
Torres, Angelo
Tosh, Peter
Troutman, Larry
van Pallandt, Frederik

Vicious, Sid
Wilson, Nathaniel ("Buster")
Zapata, Mia

Singers, Country

Akeman, David ("Stringbean")
Cooley, Spade
Januskevicius, Melissa A.
Scott, Linda

Singers, Opera

Da Prato, Emilia
Diehl, Mary Louise
Dorsey, Leslie
Merrige-Abrams, Salwa
Palmer, Pearl
Rovig, Melita Powell
Van der Walt, Deon

Singers, Popular

Clary, Wilton Werbe
Cooke, Sam
Forsberg, Florence
Longet, Claudine
Myles, Raymond Anthony, Sr.
Parsa, Nasrat
Poulain, Jean-Paul
Pringle, Kevin
Pringle, Val
Talkov, Igor
Tamim, Suzanne
Velez, Lilian
Wizzart, Kesha

Television Personalities

Barsi, Judith
Cooley, Spade
Ivers, Peter Scott
Professor Backwards
Wizzart, Kesha

Theatre Owners, Managers, and Architects

Nixon-Nirdlinger, Fred G.
Yasuda, Yoshiaki

Vaudeville, Music Hall, and Nightclub Performers

Bennison, Louis
Elmore, Belle

Fragson, Harry
Leopold, Joseph Walter
Maloney, Robert N.

Renaudin, Lester
Schuster, Roy Edgar
Van Alstyne, Harold Blake

Notes

Abbott, Darrell ("Dimebag")

"Me and Dime planned on doing ... and that didn't include Pantera," Gary Graff, "Pantera Pair Come Up with a Dam-ageplan After Breakup," *Plain Dealer*, February 13, 2004, p. 5.

"deserves to be severely beaten," "Ex-Pantera Singer Slammed Abbot [sic] Before Death," World Entertainment News Network, December 12, 2004.

"The last thing that really matters ... I'll never see him again," "Paul: 'My Last Words to Dimebag were Van Halen,'" World Entertainment News Network, January 27, 2008.

Adamson, Al

"The industry changed ... it forced my retirement," Gordon Dillow, "Reel to Real," *Orange County Register*, August 22, 1995, sec. E, p. 1.

"Although we did a lot of horror movies... Our pictures were never this grisly," Donna Parker, "Low-Budget Filmmaker Al Adamson Had Been Missing for 5 Weeks," *The Hollywood Reporter*, August 8, 1995.

Akeman, David ("Stringbean")

"I think he's helping people...," "Man Loses Parole in 'Stringbean' Murders," Associated Press, July 15, 2003.

Arbuckle, Roscoe "Fatty"

"because ... lice ... venereal disease," Andy Edmonds, *Frame-Up!: The Untold Story of Roscoe "Fatty" Arbuckle*, p. 156.

"running abcess ... six weeks," Robert Young, *Roscoe "Fatty" Arbuckle: A Bio-Bibliography*, p. 66.

"Acquittal ... free from blame," Edmonds, pp. 247–248.

"Those who demand," David A. Yallop, *The Day the Laugh-ter Stopped: The True Story of Fatty Arbuckle*, p. 295.

Blake, Robert

"O.J. was like an MGM Grand movie. This is like a B movie from Republic Pictures," Alex Kuczynski, "Hollywood Turns Up its Surgically Correct Nose at the Blake Case," *The New York Times*, April 28, 2002, sec. 1, p. 22.

"Put the *Sorcerer* where the sun never shines. Peace & Love, Robert Blake," "Playboy Interview: Robert Blake," *Playboy*, 24(June 1977, 6):77–78, 80, 82–83, 86, 89, 92–94, 96, 98, 100–101.

"had a bullet with her name on it," Gary King, *Murder in Hollywood*, p. 48.

"If you want to know how ... I need a job," Greg Risling,

"Actor Blake Acquitted of Murdering His Wife in 2001," Associated Press, March 16, 2005.

"incredibly stupid," "District Attorney: Blake Jurors are 'In-credibly Stupid,'" Associated Press state and local wire, March 24, 2005.

"This has been going on for five years ... I have to watch my mouth," Linda Deutsch, "Christian Brando Fined for Court Behavior," Associated Press, April 26, 2006.

"probably sitting up in the room there," "Christian Brando to Appear at Blake Trial," Associated Press, April 26, 2006.

"If Robert had any money he'd be paying me," Linda Deutsch, "Appeals Court Cuts Blake Award in Half," Associated Press state and local wire, April 26, 2008.

Boham, Timothy J.

"got visited by a spirit that told me to go over and rob J.P.," Mike McPhee, "Collector's Killing Goes to Jury: The Accused Calls it Suicide, but His Mom Says He Confessed," *Denver Post*, June 6, 2009, sec. B, p. 2.

"If I get one juror to hold out ... I may get a deal for six to 10 years," Mike McPhee, "Mom Told Police Son Killed Man," *Denver Post*, June 4, 2009, sec. B, p. 3.

Brancato, Lillo, Jr.

"Don't you know who I am?," Alex Ginsberg, "Soprano's Drug-Fueled Days of Rage Led Up to Slay of Hero Cop in the Bronx," *New York Post*, December 13, 2005, p. 6.

"This kid had so much ... Zero," Bill Hutchinson, "Drugs Trashed Career & Me, Sez Jailed Lillo," *Daily News* (New York), February 20, 2009, p. 3.

Brando, Christian

"I shot him man ... in the head," "Brando Tells Police He Shot Guest, but Not on Purpose," Associated Press, May 20, 1990.

"probably sitting up in the room there," Linda Deutsch, "Christian Brando Invokes Fifth Amendment at Blake's Civil Trial," Associated Press, October 25, 2005.

"He did it... I'm taking medication for that," Linda Deutsch, "Christian Brando Fined for Court Behavior," Associated Press, May 27, 2006.

C-Murder

"You don't know who ... I don't care who you are," Joe Darby, "Witness Says Rapper Shot Teen; Argument Preceded Killing, Jury is Told," *New Orleans Times-Picayune*, September 23, 2003, p. 1.

Camoflauge

"Everyone knew it was going to happen ... with gold teeth and fancy cars," "Rapper Camoflauge Fatally Shot," Associated Press, May 21, 2003.

"You can get saved ... while you finish up a six-pack," Anne Hart, "Crowds Mourn Rapper," *Augusta Chronicle*, May 25, 2003, sec. B, p. 5.

Cantat, Bertrand

"Medically there is no more we can do ... there is no suffering, neither moral nor physical," "Hours of French Actress Said 'Numbered' After Fight with Pop-Star Lover," Agence France-Presse, July 30, 2003.

"Perhaps Marie hit her head ... and wanted to shut her up," Mary Vallis, "'She Exploded,' Rocker Tells Murder Trial," *National Post*, March 17, 2004, sec. A, p. 3.

"I want to tell you this ... I would express myself poorly," *Ibid.*

Cooley, Spade

"Ella Mae has moved out ... there isn't a chance of a reconciliation," "Spade Cooley Seeks Divorce," *Los Angeles Times*, March 24, 1961, sec. A, p. 11.

"Cold gray bars ... and you'll always be my wife," "Of Prison Bars, Love, Faith: Spade Cooley Writes Two Songs in Jail," *Los Angeles Times*, July 6, 1961, p. 21.

"I'm not worth it ... and I prayed," "Wife's Free Love Talk Led to His Attack on Her, Spade Cooley Says," *Los Angeles Times*, August 9, 1961, p. 20.

Crane, Bob

"There wasn't any proof ... not even the doctors," Eun-Kyung Kim, "Friend Acquitted in Slaying of 'Hogan's Heroes' Star," Associated Press, October 31, 1994.

"I think if my father were alive, he'd be running the site himself," Lynn Hirschberg, "First Came the Sitcom. Then Came the Murder. Then Came the Pornographic Web Site. Now Here Comes the Hollywood Biopic," *The New York Times*, September 29, 2002, sec. 6, p. 36.

Crane, Cheryl

"wouldn't let her alone for a moment," Art Ryon, "Lana's Fright at Acapulco Bared," *Los Angeles Times*, April 10, 1958, pp. 1, 25.

"In the Turner case Cheryl isn't the juvenile delinquent; Lana is," "Inquest on Johnny Stompanato," *Los Angeles Times*, April 12, 1958, sec. B, p. 4.

"a lack of parental control or supervision," "Crane Opens Legal Fight for Cheryl," *Los Angeles Times*, May 10, 1958, sec. B, p. 1.

Cupit, Jennifer

"She is a lying cruel killer," Paul Byrne, "I Close My Eyes and See Kathy Lying There Dying. All I Can Hear," *Daily Mirror*, February 27, 1999, p. 1.

Davis, Myra

"I know people make mistakes," "Jury Deadlocks on Life or Death for Convicted Murderer," City News Service, March 23, 2001.

"The chances are getting less ... you get diminishing

returns," "Prosecutors Settle for Life Imprisonment for Convicted Double-Murderer," Associated Press, September 7, 2001.

Dismukes, George

"I can be a good and caring neighbor ... I will take that choice away," Paul McKay, "Self-Appointed 'Vigilante' a Suspect in Bizarre Slaying," *Houston Chronicle*, January 6, 1992, p. 9.

Dunne, Dominique

"Bryan, please help me... Can't you see the marks on my neck," "Murder Trial Begins in Strangling of Young Actress," United Press International, August 16, 1983.

"Dominique was walking around the bedroom... She fell over the bed and on the floor," "Sweeney Breaks Down on Stand," Associated Press, September 1, 1983.

"but this is my house also," "Trial Begins for Man Accused of Murdering 'Poltergeist' Actress," Associated Press, December 13, 1982.

"I killed my girlfriend," "Actress Still in Coma after Strangling Attempt," Associated Press, November 1, 1982.

"If I die tonight, it was by John Sweeney," Dominick Dunne, *Justice: Crimes, Trials, and Punishments*, p. 5.

"When all the facts ... as little control as an electrical appliance with the plug pulled out," James J. Doyle, "Spurned Lover Pleads Innocent to Actress' Murder," United Press International, November 5, 1982.

"I just lost my temper ... at some point in time I dropped her," Linda Deutsch, "Sweeney Describes Strangling," Associated Press, August 31, 1983.

"justice was served ... not from our family, it wasn't...Too late then... You withheld important information ... about this man's violent behavior," Richard De Atley, "Sweeney Faces Six Years for Killing Actress; Family Outraged," Associated Press, September 22, 1983.

"I am convinced this was murder ... an act that is qualitatively not of manslaughter, but of murder," Aurelio Rojas, "Domestic News," United Press International, November 10, 1983.

Freaky Tah

"He checked their report cards ... I'll do the right thing,'" Henri E. Cauvin, "Rapper with Lost Boyz, Freaky Tah, Shot Dead," *New York Daily News*, March 29, 1999, p. 2.

Gaye, Marvin

"At least on this one day I can feel like I made Father proud," David Ritz, *Divided Soul: The Life of Marvin Gaye*, p. 162.

"If he touches me, I'll kill him," *Ibid.*, p. 328.

Hartman, Brynn

"Tell (them) that I love them ... she's just very sorry," Elizabeth Vargas, "The Night Phil Hartman Died: An Intimate Portrait of the Hartman Family," *20/20* (transcript), February 17, 1999.

Hedderel, Rivet

"I've got to get out of New Orleans ... I'm going to be murdered here," Lynne Jensen, "Actor Stabbed Dead in His N.O. Home," *New Orleans Times-Picayune*, August 20, 1996, sec. B, p. 1.

"just to talk ... to cuddle," Pamela Coyle, "Defense: Victim Sexual Predator; Prosecution: Killer was Thief," *New Orleans Times-Picayune*, January 16, 1998, sec. B, p. 1.

"I didn't know the guy was dead ... so he'd get off me," *Ibid.*

Holmes, John C.

"Go back to that house... Go!," Mike Sager, "The Devil and John Holmes," *Rolling Stone*, 554 (June 15, 1989):50–52, 54–55, 61, 150, 152 (p. 61).

"You will figure out who they are," Ted Rohrlich, "Drugs, Robbery Led to 4 Murders, Jury Told," *Los Angeles Times*, June 4, 1982, sec. C, p. 1.

"Thank God," Gene Blake, "Porn Star Holmes Acquitted in 4 Murders," *Los Angeles Times*, June 26, 1982, sec. A, p. 1.

Ince, Thomas H.

"I began this investigation because of the many rumors ... the liquor was secured," "Ince Inquiry Abandoned," *Los Angeles Times*, December 11, 1924, p. 1.

Jam Master Jay

"(Jason) helped to create this hip-hop nation ... people that have cried out across the world," Ronin Ro, *Raising Hell: The Reign, Ruin and Redemption of Run-D.M.C. and Jam Master Jay*, p. 318.

"They want to blame me for all the blood in rap," Michelle McPhee, "Convict Expects Charge in Jam Master Jay slay," *Boston Herald*, April 16, 2007 p. 5.

Jung, Paul

"a combination of an engineer and a gimmick builder," Irving Spiegel, "Star Clown of the Circus Slain in Hotel a Block from Garden," *The New York Times*, p. 1, April 22, 1965.

"It's that terrible New York City. It's like a jungle," "Who Killed the Clown?," *Newsweek*, 65 (May 3, 1965):34–35.

Kelly, George

"I am very unhappy ... I don't know what to do," "Drama of Love and Jealousy," *Daily Mail*, December 20, 1920, p. 5.

"Wish we could have fallen in love...," "Shot Dancer's Two Lovers," *Daily Mail*, December 23, 1920, p. 5.

Kelly, Paul

"I knew he was talking to Paul Kelly... Finally with one crushing blow Paul knocked Raymond out," "Maid Describes Beating," *Los Angeles Times*, April 20, 1927, sec. A, p. 2.

"Darling ... love you," "'Trump Card' Letter Runs Riot in Endearing Phrases," *Los Angeles Times*, May 14, 1927, sec. A, p. 8.

"take his punishment like a man ... when society's debt had been paid," "Kelly Drops Legal Fight," *Los Angeles Times*, July 6, 1927, sec. A, p. 15.

"I'm going straight to New York ... I'm going to hit it hard," "Kelly Freed from Prison," *Los Angeles Times*, August 3, 1929, p. 3.

King, Natel

"kind of weird ... I don't know, both," Bob Mitchell, "Man Admits Killing Model," *Toronto Star*, February 16, 2005, sec. B, p. 1.

"Cut with a knife ... death coming on slow," Ron Todt, "Photographer Charged in Murder," *National Post*, March 25, 2004, sec. A, p. 10.

Knight, Terry

"Critics don't count, the kids do," Pierre Perrone, "Obituary: Terry Knight," *The Independent* (London), November 10, 2004.

"How long are you going to put up with this," Robert Snell and Doug Pullen, "Knight's Last Days—In the End, Seclusion, Sex Charges, Poetry—and Murder," *The Flint Journal*, November 15, 2004.

Knox, Robert Arthur

"I'm coming to come back and someone's going to die," Richard Edwards, "Harry Potter Actor Stabbed to Death 'Defending Brother from Knifeman,'" *Daily Telegraph*, February 10, 2009, p. 15.

"carried knives like others carried pens in their pockets," Jon Clements, "Freed to Kill: Police Blunders Led to Potter Star's Murder," *The Mirror*, March 5, 2009, p. 25.

Kupcinet, Karyn

"You may die... One someone special cares," "Slain Actress Eulogized as 'Born to Be a Star,'" *Chicago Tribune*, December 4, 1963, p. 3.

"I'm no good... Why doesn't he want me," James Ellroy, "Glamour Jungle," *GQ*, 68(December 1988):288–300.

Lennon, John

"*The Catcher in the Rye* was the stove and the Lennon book was the fire," Jack Jones, *Let Me Take You Down: Inside the Mind of Mark David Chapman, the Man Who Killed John Lennon*, p.178.

"*This* is my statement. Holden Caulfield, The Catcher in the Rye," *Ibid.*, p. 22.

Longet, Claudine

"I am a fortunate woman ... live as Andy and I do," "Andy Stands by Claudine," *Los Angeles Times*, March 22, 1976, sec. A, p. 1.

"a crazy chick ... likes to ski fast and drive fast," John Hurst, "Crucial Testimony at Longet Trial Conflicts," *Los Angeles Times*, January 12, 1977, p. 3.

"more concerned with his own ambitions, than with justice," "Claudine Gets Jail, Raps DA," *Los Angeles Times*, January 31, 1977, sec. A, p. 1.

"malice, insult and a wanton and reckless disregard of Sabich's rights," "Claudine Longet Sued by Sabich Family," *Los Angeles Times*, May 18, 1977, sec. D, p. 2.

Mac, the Camoflage Assassin

"Mac come from the side ... I looked dead in his eyes," "Rapper Identified as Killer at Concert," *Times-Picayune* (New Orleans), September 19, 2001, p. 1.

"There's a kid who has never done anything wrong ... a little kid," "Rapper Convicted in Death of Teen," *Times-Picayune* (New Orleans), September 22, 2001, p. 1.

Menson, Michael

"an organization of producers, mixers, and DJs," Jay Rayner, "Who Killed Michael Menson? Racist Youths Get Away with Murder," *The Observer*, November 1, 1998, p. 15.

"Mario was just saying things ... so what, he was black," "Justice is Done at Last," *Daily Express*, December 22, 1999.

"Ossie lit a match and threw it at him... We didn't think he would go up," "Burned to Death, Just for a Joke," *Daily Express*, November 17, 1999.

"What they have done is really quite remarkable," "Justice is Done at Last," *Daily Express*, December 22, 1999.

"unprofessional, uncoordinated," T. M. Hall, "Police Won't Face Charges Over Race Murder Bungling," *Daily Mail*, May 17, 2003.

"I don't know why they are worried," Ibid.

"sufficiently willful or grave as to justify criminal proceedings," *Ibid.*

Milocevic, Milos

"If Barbara even looks at another man... We'll be in the headlines," William E. Gold, "Milos' Threats to Kill Revealed," *Los Angeles Herald-Examiner* (Latest ed.), February 1, 1966, sec. A, pp. 1, 4, 12.

"If it makes you unhappy ... even as a friend," Harry Tessel, "Rooney Unaware Conversation was Taped," *Los Angeles Herald-Examiner*, February 1, 1966, sec. A, p. 11.

Minor, Charlie

"someone Charlie had a physical relationship with a few times, maybe six or seven times," Daniel Jeffreys, "To Live and Die in L.A.," *The Independent* (London), July 2, 1996, p. 2.

"We will prove that Suzette was a victim," *Ibid.*

"I wish I'd known Charlie longer," Norma Meyer, "Stripper's Sentence in Record Mogul's Murder Ends Bizarre Case," Copley News Service, June 4, 1997.

Mr. Cee

"It was another case," Joel Selvin, "Fans Mourn RBL Posse's Mr. C," *San Francisco Chronicle*, January 14, 1996, sec. Sunday Datebook, p. 40.

Mitchell Brothers

"Hey Mr. Perfect ... I'm going to kill you first, motherfucker!," John Hubner, *Bottom Feeder*, pp. 373–374.

"Artie lived on the screaming edge of insanity, and that can never last for long," Burr Snider, "Blood Brothers: An Oral History," *San Francisco Chronicle*, May 5, 1991, sec. Image, pp. 16–25.

"The gravity of the crime ... compels me to impose a prison sentence," Diane Curtis, "Porn King Mitchell Gets 6-Year Sentence," *San Francisco Chronicle*, April 25, 1992, sec. A, p. 1.

"discipline-free ... did what he needed to do," Susan Sward, "Porn King Jim Mitchell Walks Out of Prison Today," *San Francisco Chronicle*, October 3, 1997, sec. A, p. 1.

Neal, Tom

"a little disturbed ... he could not live without her...," "Witnesses Say Neal Admitted Shooting His Wife," *Los Angeles Times*, April 16, 1965, sec. B, p. 15.

Ngor, Haing S.

"Dr. Ngor ... died on the cold payment," John Hiscock, "Killing Fields Actor Died for Photo of His Wife," *The Ottawa Citizen*, February 25, 1998, sec. A, p. 15.

Nixon-Nirdlinger, Fred G.

"We dined together ... while I retired to my bedroom," "Police Check Story of Killing in Nice," *The New York Times*, March 13, 1931, p. 9.

"My husband came into the bedroom ... he would have killed me," *Ibid.*

"Every quarrel was started by her husband ... they will find out how true she is," "Says Slain Husband Planned a Divorce," *The New York Times*, March 14, 1931, p. 10.

"She is too beautiful to be bad," "Too Beautiful to be Bad," *The New York Times*, May 21, 1931, p. 3.

Novarro, Ramón

"Oh, you punk liar ... you son of a bitch," Ron Einstoss, "Paul Ferguson Reviles Brother in Court, Throws Pen at Him," *Los Angeles Times*, September 5, 1969, p. 7.

Pappalardi, Felix

"All the clemency ... is not due one further bit of leniency," "Slain Rock Star's Wife Gets Four Years," United Press International, October 12, 1983.

Pasolini, Pier Paolo

"Pelosi had to play ... people who ordered the murder," WENN Entertainment, May 11, 2005.

Pastorius, Jaco

"brilliant goods in a damaged package," Bill Milkowski, *Jaco: The Extraordinary and Tragic Life of Jaco Pastorius, "The World's Greatest Bass Player,"* p. 213.

Peaklica, Piseth

"Her performances represent the entire nation ... killed the nation's soul," Ker Munthit, "Sobbing Cambodians Mourn Death of Murdered Actress," Associated Press, July 13, 1999.

Perez, Daniela

"Unfortunately, life has no value in Brazil," "Justice Decision to Release Actress's Murderer Sparks Resentment," EFE News Service, October 15, 1999.

Radin, Roy

"enjoyed shooting the big fat Jew," Linda Deutsch, "'Cotton Club' Witness Blurts Out Details of Confessions," Associated Press, June 2, 1989.

Ramirez, Israel

"Who the fuck are you ... I'm on parole, motherfucker," Kati Cornell Smith, "A Rhymes or Reason: Probers Eye Fitty

Pals in Video Shoot," *New York Post*, February 7, 2006, p. 6.

"Yo, man ... some shit might go down," *Ibid.*

"You don't talk to cops. If you do, your career tanks," Richard Schapiro, "Busta Move: Shuns Wake, Cops," *New York Daily News*, February 9, 2006, p. 8.

"It has nothing to do with you, just get out of the way," Kati Cornell Smith, *Ibid.*

Ross, Nat

"Oh, I just killed a guy. Better call the cops," "Twenty-five Women Witness Factory Foreman's Slaying," *Los Angeles Times*, February 25, 1941, sec. A, p. 1.

"Am I sorry ... I'm sorry I can't do it again," "Suspect in Man's Killing Quoted as Having No Regret," *Los Angeles Times*, March 5, 1941, sec. A, p. 2.

Salmi, Albert

"War of the Roses ... too bad you tripped in the final straightaway," Jeff Rovin, *TV Babylon II*, pp. 112–113.

Schaeffer, Rebecca

"I thought he was just lovesick ... but I didn't perceive it as violent," Associated Press, August 3, 1989.

"You came to my door again ... a callous thing to say to a fan," Valerie Kuklenski, "Bardo Re-enacts Shooting Actress," United Press International, October 21, 1991.

Scott, Walter

"She got off easy... It ain't fair," Marianna Riley, "JoAnn Williams Jailed for Role in Murder Case" *St. Louis Post-Dispatch*, April 27, 1993, sec. A, p. 3.

Shakur, Tupac

"for falsely representing them," Samuel Maull, "Shakur Sentenced to Maximum of 4 Years in Prison," Associated Press, February 7, 1995.

Silva, Fernando Ramos da

"doing in real life what he was portrayed as doing in the film," "Star of Brazilian Film Arrested for Fifth Time," *The Globe and Mail*, June 2, 1984, sec. E, p. 12.

Simpson, O.J.

"I'm not black, I'm O.J.," Jeffrey Toobin, *The Run of His Life: The People v. O.J. Simpson*, p. 49.

"She murdered my child," Susan Schindehette, "The Man with Two Faces," *People Weekly*, 42(July 4, 1994):32–39.

"He's going to kill me... You guys never do anything ... you never do anything," Toobin, p. 58.

"Please think of the real O.J. and not this lost person," *Ibid.*, p. 101.

"This case is about ... by any means necessary," *Ibid.*, p. 250.

"If it doesn't fit, you must acquit," *Ibid.*, p. 420.

"I didn't understand the DNA stuff ... carried absolutely no weight with me," Vincent Bugliosi, *Outrage: The Five Reasons O.J. Got Away with Murder*, p. 57.

"race card" (and) "bottom of the deck," Toobin, p. 438.

"There's never closure ... this monster is where he belongs, behind bars," Steve Friess, "After Apologies, Simpson is Sen-tenced to at Least Nine Years for Armed Robbery," *The New York Times*, December 6, 2008, sec. A, p. 9.

Smith, Jay R.

"He's cramping my style, so I think I'm going to get rid of him," Frank Curreri, "Police Capture Slaying Suspect," *Las Vegas Review-Journal*, October 25, 2002, sec. B, p. 1.

"It should not have happened ... it never will again," Frank Curreri, "Calls Mishandled, Coroner Says," *Las Vegas Review-Journal*, November 1, 2002, sec. B, p. 9.

"An incident occurred ... which only God's forgiveness has allowed me to partially overcome," Glenn Puit, "Killer of Former Child Actor Sentenced to Life in Prison," *Las Vegas Review-Journal*, February 25, 2005, sec. B, p. 4.

Soulja Slim

"I got some paperwork ... I get it in blood, nigga," Michael Perlstein, "DA's Decision Shocks Family of Slain Rapper," *Times Picayune* (New Orleans), March 22, 2004, p. 1.

"That's just their way... He was on artist-type time," Rich Rock, "Murdered Soulja Slim Suspected of Murder," www.sohh.com.

"It could have been jealousy ... the truth is going to come out," *Ibid.*

Spector, Phil

"I think I just killed somebody...," Mick Jones, *Tearing Down the Wall of Sound*, p. 399.

"You have to come here ... killed somebody," *Ibid.*, p. 400.

"the gun went off ... just gonna go to sleep," *Ibid.*, p. 402.

Stahl, Jennifer

"Take the money... Don't hurt anybody," Dan Barry, "A Fading Actress, a Pile of Drugs and 3 Slayings," *The New York Times*, May 12, 2001, sec. A, p. 1.

"like something out of *Law & Order* ... police horses in full gallop," Joe Williams, "3 Shot Dead in Midtown," *New York Daily News*, May 11, 2001, p. 5.

"I saw Sean ... in the back of their necks," Katherine L. Finkelstein, "Defendant Tells of Robbery Gone Wrong Above a Deli," *The New York Times*, June 14, 2001, sec. B, p. 4.

Stiles, Grady F., Jr.

"In spite of his deformities ... he did," Jesse Martinez, "Defense: Years of Abuse Drove Wife to Order Hit on 'Lobster Boy,'" Associated Press, July 12, 1994.

"now we don't have to worry ... the beatings and threats," Deborah Sharp, "'Lobster Boy' Trial Becomes a Sideshow Itself," *USA Today*, July 19, 1994, sec. A, p. 3.

"I am sorry. But my family is safe now," Marty Rosen, "'I am Sorry, but My Family is Safe Now,'" *St. Petersburg Times*, August 30, 1994, sec. B, p. 1.

Stratten, Dorothy

"That girl could make me a lot of money," Teresa Carpenter, "Death of a Playmate," *Village Voice*, 35(November 5–11, 1980):12–14, 16–17 (p. 12).

"A very sick guy saw his meal ticket slipping away ... made him kill her," *Ibid.*, p. 12.

"attacking behavior which he himself has done," Frank Sanello, "Hefner-Bashing," United Press International, August 21, 1984.

"confronting Hugh Hefner ... women who don't issue press releases," "Hefner Says Stroke Caused by Anxiety Over Book," United Press International, March 20, 1985.

"the happiest, most fulfilling and rewarding of her life because of *Playboy*," "Hefner, Bogdanovich Trade Stratten Charges," *San Diego Union-Tribune*, April 2, 1985, sec. E, p. 4.

"Our investigation demonstrated ... information has no basis in fact," "*Playboy*; Slander Suit Filed Against Hugh Hefner Voluntarily Dropped," Business Wire, August 29, 1985.

Tate, Sharon

"Only God could possess ... Susan "Honeybear" Atkins," "Former Charles Manson Disciple Wed in Prison Ceremony," Associated Press. September 2, 1981.

"My God is an amazing God," Linda Deutsch, "Ill Manson Follower Denied Parole," Associated Press, September 3, 2009.

"The mercy she is asking for is so minuscule... It's not like we're going to see her down at Disneyland," Richard Winton and Hector Becerra, "Panel Turns Down Manson Followers Request for Mercy," *Los Angeles Times*, September 3, 2009, pt. A, p. 3.

"likes to hang out... 'I drove the car, man,'" John Moore, "Prisons Have Lock on Manson, Most of Family," *Denver Post*, February 9, 2003, sec. A, p. 4.

Taylor, William Desmond

"Dey've kilt Massa! Dey've kilt Massa!," Kenneth Anger, *Hollywood Babylon*, p. 33.

van Gogh, Theo

"I'm deeply religious — I call him Allah," Toby Sterling, "Dutch Hold Memorial for Slain Filmmaker," Associated Press, November 9, 2004.

"Hey, it smells like caramel ... they must be burning diabetic Jews," Marc Perelman, "Slain Filmmaker Left Complex Legacy," *The Forward*, November 19, 2004, p. 2.

"now you know what's coming for you," Toby Sterling, "Alleged Killer of Filmmaker van Gogh Dreamed of Overthrowing Dutch Government, Prosecutors Say," Associated Press, January 26, 2005.

"I can't feel for you ... I would do it again," "Muslim Extremist Admits to Killing van Gogh, Tells Court He Would Do It Again," Associated Press, July 12, 2005.

Vicious, Sid

"Mr. Vicious scrawny and scowling, but in a somehow sweet and alluring way," John Rockwell, "Sex Pistols Make United States Debut," *The New York Times*, January 7, 1978, p. 12.

Wilson, Nathaniel ("Buster")

"Given the profound and unmistakable smell ... was acutely aware of Mr. Cavanaugh's condition," Sandra Chereb, "Judge OKs Suit Alleging Withheld Nev. Inmate Care," Associated Press, March 26, 2009.

Zapata, Mia

"He's a hunter ... his field of vision," Janet Burkitt, "Zapata Slaying Suspect Called 'Predatory,'" *Seattle Times*, January 14, 2003, sec. A, p. 1.

"I'm just glad ... a little freer lives," Tracy Johnson, "11 Years Later, Justice for Slain Singer Zapata," *Seattle Post-Intelligencer*, March 26, 2004, sec. A, p. 1.

"all the while Mia [was] in the ground," Tracy Johnson, "Singer's Killer Gets 37 Years," *Seattle Post-Intelligencer*, May 1, 2004, sec. B, p. 1.

Bibliography

Alexander, Frank, and Heidi Siegmund Cuda. *Got Your Back: The Life of a Bodyguard in the Hardcore World of Gangsta Rap*. New York: St. Martin's, 1998.

American Film Institute Catalog of Motion Pictures Produced in the United States. Berkeley: University of California Press, 1971–.

Andersen, Christopher P. *Michael Jackson: Unauthorized*. New York: Simon and Schuster, 1994.

Anger, Kenneth. *Hollywood Babylon*. San Francisco: Straight Arrow, 1975.

_____. *Hollywood Babylon II*. New York: Dutton, 1984.

Arnold, Chris. *A Vulgar Display of Power: Courage and Carnage at the Alrosa Villa*. Crystal River, FL: MJS Music, 2007.

Arraras, Maria Celeste. *Selena's Secret: The Revealing Story Behind Her Tragic Death*. New York: Simon and Schuster, 1997.

Atkins, Susan, and Bob Slosser. *Child of Satan, Child of God*. Plainfield, NJ: Logos, 1977.

Badger, Reid. *A Life in Ragtime: A Biography of James Reese Europe*. New York: Oxford University Press, 1995.

Barbieri, Paula. *The Other Woman — My Years with O.J. Simpson: A Story of Love, Trust, and Betrayal*. Boston: Little, Brown, 1997.

Bastfield, Darrin Keith. *Back in the Day: My Life and Times with Tupac Shakur*. New York: Ballantine, 2002.

Black, David. *Murder at the Met*. Garden City, NY: Dial, 1984.

Blanch, Tony, and Brad Schreiber. *Death in Paradise: An Illustrated History of the Los Angeles County Department of Coroner*. Los Angeles: General, 1998.

Bloom, Ken. *Hollywood Song: The Complete Film & Musical Companion*. New York: Facts on File, 1995.

Bogdanovich, Peter. *The Killing of the Unicorn: Dorothy Stratten (1960–1980)*. New York: W. Morrow, 1984.

Boteach, Shmuel. *The Michael Jackson Tapes: A Tragic Icon Reveals His Soul in Intimate Conversations*. New York: Vanguard, 2009.

Bresler, Fenton. *Who Killed John Lennon?* New York: St. Martin's, 1989.

Brown, Jake. *Ready to Die: The Story of Biggie Smalls, Notorious B.I.G., King of the World and New York City: Fast Money, Puff Daddy, Faith and Life After Death: The Unauthorized Biography*. Phoenix, AZ: Colossus, 2004.

Brown, Mick. *Tearing Down the Wall of Sound The Rise and Fall of Phil Spector*. New York: Knopf, 2007.

Bugliosi, Vincent, and Curt Gentry. *Helter Skelter: The True Story of the Manson Murders*. New York: Norton, 1974.

_____. *Outrage: The Five Reasons O.J. Got Away with Murder*. New York: W.W. Norton, 1996.

Buruma, Ian. *Murder in Amsterdam: The Death of Theo van Gogh and the Limits of Tolerance*. New York: Penguin, 2006.

Butt, Malcolm. *Sid Vicious: Rock 'n' Roll Star*, rev. and updated ed. London: Plexus, 2005.

CA v. Bardo. New York: Courtroom Television Network, 1993. (Videorecording, 110 min.)

Causey, Warren B. *The Stringbean Murders*. Nashville: Quest, 1975.

Chermak, Steven, and Frankie Y. Bailey. *Crimes and Trials of the Century*. 2 vols. Westport, CT: Greenwood, 2007.

Clark, Marcia, and Teresa Carpenter. *Without a Doubt*. New York: Viking, 1997.

Cochran, Johnnie L., and Tim Rutten. *Journey to Justice*. New York: Ballantine, 1996.

Coker, Cheo Hodari. *Unbelievable: The Life, Death, and Afterlife of the Notorious B.I.G.* New York: Three Rivers, 2003.

Crain, Zac. *Black Tooth Grin: The High Life, Good Times, and Tragic End of "Dimebag" Darrell Abbott*. Cambridge, MA: Da Capo, 2009.

Crane, Cheryl, and Cliff Jahr. *Detour: A Hollywood Story*. New York: Arbor House/William Morrow, 1988.

Crockett, Art, ed. *Celebrity Murders*. New York: Windsor, 1990.

Daggett, Dennis Lee. *The House That Ince Built*. Glendale, CA: Great Western, 1980.

Darden, Christopher A., and Jess Walter. *In Contempt*. New York: ReganBooks, 1996.

Dershowitz, Alan M. *Reasonable Doubts: The O.J. Simpson Case and the Criminal Justice System*. New York: Simon and Schuster, 1996.

Des Barres, Pamela. *Rock Bottom: Dark Moments in Music Babylon*. New York: St. Martin's, 1996.

Dictionary of American Biography. 22 vols. New York: C. Scribner's Sons, 1928–1944 (with additional supplements).

Donnelley, Paul. *Fade to Black: A Book of Movie Obituaries*, 3rd ed. London: Omnibus, 2005.

_____. *501 Most Notorious Crimes*. London: Barricade, 2009.

_____. *Marilyn Monroe*. Harpenden: Pocket Essentials, 2000.

Doyle, Billy H. *The Ultimate Directory of Film Technicians: A Necrology of Dates and Places of Births and Deaths of More Than 9,000 Producers, Screenwriters, Composers, Cinematographers, Art Directors, Costume Designers, Choreographers, Executives, and Publicists.* Lanham, MD: Scarecrow, 1999.

Dunne, Dominick. *Justice: Crimes, Trials, and Punishments.* New York: Crown, 2001.

Dyson, Michael Eric. *Mercy, Mercy Me: The Art, Loves, and Demons of Marvin Gaye.* New York: Basic Civitas, 2004.

Edberg, Mark Cameron. *El Narcotraficante: Narcocorridos and the Construction of a Cultural Persona on the U.S.–Mexico Border.* Austin: University of Texas Press, 2004.

Edmonds, Andy. *Frame-Up! The Untold Story of Roscoe "Fatty" Arbuckle.* New York: W. Morrow, 1991.

_____. *Hot Toddy: The True Story of Hollywood's Most Sensational Murder.* New York: Morrow, 1989.

Eells, George. *Final Gig: The Man Behind the Murder.* San Diego: Harcourt Brace Jovanovich, 1991.

Eliot, Marc. *Kato Kaelin: The Whole Truth, the Real Story of O.J., Nicole, and Kato from the Actual Tapes.* New York: Harper, 1995.

Ellenberger, Allan R. *Ramón Novarro: A Biography of the Silent Film Idol, 1899–1968; With a Filmography.* Jefferson, NC: McFarland, 1999.

Erlewine, Michael, ed. *All Music Guide to Country.* San Francisco: Miller Freeman, 1997.

Faragher, Scott. *Music City Babylon.* Seacaucus, NJ: Carol, 1992.

Fawcett, Anthony. *John Lennon: One Day at a Time: A Personal Biography of the Seventies.* New York: Grove, 1976.

Fine, Jason. *Michael.* New York: HarperStudio, 2009.

Fleming, E.J. *The Fixers: Eddie Mannix, Howard Strickling and the MGM Publicity Machine.* Jefferson, NC: McFarland, 2005.

_____. *Paul Bern: The Life and Famous Death of the MGM Director and Husband of Harlow.* Jefferson, NC: McFarland, 2009.

Frasier, David K. *Murder Cases of the Twentieth Century: Biographies and Bibliographies of 280 Convicted or Accused Killers.* Jefferson, NC: McFarland, 1996.

_____. *Suicide in the Entertainment Industry: An Encyclopedia of 840 Twentieth Century Cases.* Jefferson, NC: McFarland, 2002.

Fuhrman, Mark. *Murder in Brentwood.* Washington, DC: Regnery, 1997.

Gammond, Peter. *The Oxford Companion to Popular Music.* Oxford [England]; New York: Oxford University Press, 1991.

Garcia, Jessie B. *A Movie Album Quizbook.* Iloilo City, Philippines: Erehwon, 2004.

Garraty, John A., and Mark C. Carnes. *American National Biography.* 24 vols. New York: Oxford University Press, 1999.

Gilmore, John. *L.A. Despair: A Landscape of Crimes and Bad Times.* Los Angeles: Amok, 2005.

_____. *Laid Bare: A Memoir of Wrecked Lives and the Hollywood Death Trip.* Los Angeles: Amok, 1997.

Giroux, Robert. *A Deed of Death: The Story Behind the Unsolved Murder of Hollywood Director William Desmond Taylor.* New York: Knopf, 1990.

Golden, Eve. *Platinum Girl: The Life and Legends of Jean Harlow.* New York: Abbeville, 1991.

Goldman, Albert Harry. *The Lives of John Lennon.* New York: W. Morrow, 1988.

Grabman, Sandra. *Spotlights and Shadows: The Albert Salmi Story.* Boalsburg, PA: BearManor, 2004.

Graysmith, Robert. *The Murder of Bob Crane.* New York: Crown, 1993.

Guild, Leo. *The Fatty Arbuckle Case.* New York: Paperback Library, 1962.

Guiles, Fred Lawrence. *Legend: The Life and Death of Marilyn Monroe.* New York: Stein and Day, 1984.

_____. *Norma Jean: The Life of Marilyn Monroe.* New York: McGraw-Hill, 1969.

Guralnick, Peter. *Dream Boogie: The Triumph of Sam Cooke.* New York: Little, Brown, 2005.

_____. *Searching for Robert Johnson.* New York: Dutton, 1989.

Halperin, Ian. *Unmasked: The Final Years of Michael Jackson.* New York: Simon Spotlight Entertainment, 2009.

Harrison, Joel L. *Bloody Wednesday.* Canoga Park, CA: Major, 1978.

Harvey, Diana Karanikas, and Jackson Harvey. *Dead Before Their Time.* New York: MetroBooks, 1996.

Henderson, Jan Alan. *George Reeves: The Man, the Myth, the Mystery.* Hollywood: Cult Movies, 1995.

_____. *Speeding Bullet: The Life and Bizarre Death of George Reeves.* Grand Rapids, MI: M. Bifulco, 1999.

Higham, Charles. *Brando: The Unauthorized Biography.* New York: New American Library, 1987.

_____. *Murder in Hollywood: Solving a Silent Screen Mystery.* Madison, WI: Terrace, 2004.

Holmes, John C., and Laurie Holmes. *Porn King: The Autobiography of John C. Holmes.* Albuquerque, NM: Johnny Wadd, 1998.

Hubner, John. *Bottom Feeders: From Free Love to Hard Core: The Rise and Fall of Counter-Culture Gurus Jim and Artie Mitchell.* New York: Doubleday. 1993.

International Dictionary of Films and Filmmakers, 3rd ed. 4 vols. Detroit: St. James, 1997.

Jackson, Michael. *Moonwalk,* rev. ed. New York: Harmony, 2009.

Jacobson, Laurie, and Marc Wanamaker. *Hollywood Heartbreak: The Tragic and Mysterious Deaths of Hollywood's Most Remarkable Legends.* New York: Simon and Schuster, 1984.

Jeffers, H. Paul. *Sal Mineo: His Life, Murder, and Mystery.* New York: Carroll and Graf, 2000.

Jefferson, Margo. *On Michael Jackson.* New York: Pantheon, 2006.

Jones, Jack. *Let Me Take You Down: Inside the Mind of Mark David Chapman, the Man Who Killed John Lennon.* New York: Villard, 1992.

Kanfer, Stefan. *Somebody: The Reckless Life and Remarkable Career of Marlon Brando.* New York: Alfred A. Knopf, 2008.

Kashner, Sam, and Nancy Schoenburger. *Hollywood Kryptonite: The Bulldog, the Lady, and the Death of Superman.* New York: St. Martin's, 1996.

Katchmer, George A. *Eighty Silent Film Stars: Biographies and Filmographies of the Obscure to the Well Known.* Jefferson, NC: McFarland, 1991.

King, Gary C. *Murder in Hollywood: The Secret Life and Mysterious Death of Bonny Lee Bakley.* New York: St. Martin's, 2001.

King, Greg. *Sharon Tate and the Manson Murders.* New York: Barricade, 2000.

Kirkpatrick, Sidney. *A Cast of Killers.* New York: Dutton, 1986.

Konow, David. *Schlock-O-Rama: The Films of Al Adamson.* Los Angeles: Lone Eagle, 1998.

Lamb, Andrew, and Julian Myerscough. *Fragson: The Triumphs and the Tragedy.* Croydon: Fullers Wood Press/Music Hall Masters, 2004.

Lange, Tom, Dan E. Molden and Philip Vannatter. *Evidence Dismissed: The Inside Story of the Police Investigation of O.J. Simpson.* New York: Pocket, 1997.

Lasseter, Don. *Body Double.* New York: Pinnacle, 2002.

Lennon, Cynthia. *John.* New York: Crown, 2005.

Lentz, Harrison. *Western and Frontier Film and Television Credits 1903–1995.* Jefferson, NC: McFarland, 1996.

Long, Bruce. *William Desmond Taylor: A Dossier.* Metuchen, NJ: Scarecrow, 1991.

McCumber, David. *X-Rated: The Mitchell Brothers: A True Story of Sex Money, and Death.* New York: Simon and Schuster, 1992.

McDougal, Dennis, and Mary Murphy. *Blood Cold: Fame, Sex, and Murder in Hollywood.* New York: Onyx/New American Library, 2002.

McGilligan, Patrick, and Paul Buhle. *Tender Comrades: A Backstory of the Hollywood Blacklist.* New York: St. Martin's, 1997.

McIver, Stuart. *Murder in the Tropics.* Sarasota, FL: Pineapple, 1995.

McMillan, Jeffery S. *Delightfulee: The Life and Music of Lee Morgan.* Ann Arbor: University of Michigan Press, 2008.

McPhee, Colin. *A House in Bali.* Singapore; New York: Oxford University Press, 1979.

Mailer, Norman. *Marilyn, a Biography.* New York: Grosset and Dunlap, 1973.

Maltin, Leonard, and Richard W. Bann. *The Little Rascals: The Life and Times of Our Gang.* Updated ed. New York: Crown, 1992.

Manso, Peter. *Brando: The Biography.* New York: Hyperion, 1994.

Marill, Alvin H. *Movies Made for Television: The Telefeatures and the Mini-Series, 1964–1986.* New York: New York Zoetrope, 1987.

Marx, Samuel, and Joyce Vanderveen. *Deadly Illusions: Jean Harlow and the Murder of Paul Bern.* New York: Random House, 1990.

Milkowski, Bill. *Jaco: The Extraordinary and Tragic Life of Jaco Pastorius, "The World's Greatest Bass Player."* San Francisco: Miller-Freeman, 1995. (Includes music CD.)

Monroe, Marilyn. *My Story.* New York: Stein and Day, 1974.

Munn, Michael. *The Hollywood Murder Casebook.* New York: St. Martin's, 1987.

Ngor, Haing, and Roger Warner. *A Cambodian Odyssey.* New York: Macmillan, 1987.

Norman, Philip. *John Lennon: The Life.* New York: Ecco, 2008.

Oderman, Stuart. *Roscoe "Fatty" Arbuckle: A Biography of the Silent Film Comedian, 1887–1933.* Jefferson, NC: McFarland, 1994.

Palmer, Scott. *British Film Actors' Credits, 1895–1987.* Jefferson, NC: McFarland, 1988.

Parish, James Robert. *The Hollywood Book of Scandals: The Shocking, Often Disgraceful Deeds and Affairs of More Than 100 American Movie and TV Idols.* New York: McGraw-Hill, 2004.

_____. *The Hollywood Celebrity Death Book: From Theda Bara and Rudolph Valentino to Marilyn Monroe and James Dean.* Las Vegas, NV: Pioneer, 1993.

Parker, Alan. *Sid Vicious: No One Is Innocent.* London: Orion, 2007.

_____. *Vicious: Too Fast to Live.* London: Creation, 2004.

Patoski, Joe Nick. *Selena: Como la Flor.* Boston: Little, Brown, 1996.

Paytress, Mark. *Vicious: The Art of Dying Young.* London: Sanctuary, 2004.

Pearson, Barry Lee, and Bill McCulloch. *Robert Johnson: Lost and Found.* Urbana: University of Illinois Press, 2003.

Perchard, Tom. *Lee Morgan: His Life, Music and Culture.* London: Equinox, 2006.

Petrocelli, Daniel, and Peter Knobler. *Triumph of Justice: The Final Judgment on the Simpson Saga.* New York: Crown, 1998.

Pike, Jeff. *Death of Rock and Roll: Untimely Demises, Morbid Preoccupations, and Forecasts of Doom in Rock Music.* Boston: Faber and Faber, 1993.

Priesmeyer, Scottie. *The Cheaters: The Walter Scott Murder.* St. Louis: Tula, 1996.

Quinones, Sam. *True Tales from Another Mexico: The Lynch Mob, the Popsicle Kings, Chalino, and the Bronx.* Albuquerque: University of New Mexico Press, 2001.

Ragan, David. *Who's Who in Hollywood: The Largest Cast of International Film Personalities Ever Assembled.* 2 vols. New York: Facts on File, 1992.

Rajadhyaksha, Ashish, and Paul Wilson. *Encyclopaedia of Indian Cinema.* Rev. ed. Chicago: Fitzroy Dearborn, 1999.

Repsch, John. *The Legendary Joe Meek: The Telstar Man.* London: Woodford House, 1989.

Resnick, Faye D., and Mike Walker. *Nicole Brown Simpson: The Private Diary of a Life Interrupted.* Beverly Hills, CA: Dove, 1994.

Ribowsky, Mark. *He's a Rebel: Phil Spector — Rock and Roll's Legendary Producer.* New ed. Cambridge, MA: Da Capo, 2006.

Riccio, Thomas J. *Busted! The Inside Story of the World of Sports Memorabilia, O.J. Simpson, and the Vegas Arrests.* Beverly Hills, CA: Phoenix, 2008.

Richmond, Clint. *Selena! The Phenomenal Life and Tragic Death of the Tejano Music Queen.* New York: Pocket, 1995.

Riese, Randall. *Nashville Babylon: The Uncensored Truth and Private Lives of Country Music's Stars.* New York: Congdon and Weed, 1988.

Ritz, David. *Divided Soul: The Life of Marvin Gaye.* New York: McGraw-Hill, 1985.

Ro, Ronin. *Raising Hell: The Reign, Ruin, and Redemption of Run-D.M.C. and Jam Master Jay.* New York: Amistad, 2005.

Rooney, Mickey. *Life Is Too Short.* New York: Villard, 1991.

Rosen, Fred. *Lobster Boy.* New York: Kensington, 1995.

Rovin, Jeff. *TV Babylon.* Updated ed. New York: Signet, 1987.

_____. *TV Babylon II.* New York: Penguin, 1991.

Sager, Mike. *Scary Monsters and Super Freaks: Stories of*

Sex, Drugs, Rock 'n' Roll and Murder. New York: Thunder's Mouth; [Berkeley, Calif.], 2003.

Savage, Jon. *England's Dreaming: Anarchy, Sex Pistols, Punk Rock, and Beyond.* New York: St. Martin's, 1992.

Schessler, Kenneth. *This Is Hollywood: An Unusual Movieland Guide,* 6th ed. La Verne, CA: Ken Schessler, 1987.

Schickel, Richard. *Brando: A Life in Our Times.* New York: Atheneum, 1991.

Schiller, Lawrence, and James Willwerth. *American Tragedy: The Uncensored Story of the Simpson Defense.* New York: Random House, 1996.

Scoppa, Bud. *The Rock People.* New York: Scholastic, 1973.

Scott, Cathy. *The Killing of Tupac Shakur.* Las Vegas, NV: Huntington, 1997.

_____. *The Murder of Biggie Smalls.* New York: St. Martin's, 2000.

Seaman, Fred. *The Last Days of John Lennon: A Personal Memoir.* Seacaucus, NJ: Carol, 1991.

Shapiro, Robert L., and Larkin Warren. *The Search for Justice: A Defense Attorney's Brief on the O.J. Simpson Case.* New York: Warner, 1996.

Shevey, Sandra. *The Marilyn Scandal: Her True Life Revealed by Those Who Knew Her.* New York: W. Morrow, 1987.

Shulman, Irving. *Harlow, an Intimate Biography.* New York: Bernard Geis, 1964.

Siciliano, Enzo. *Pasolini: A Biography.* New York: Random House, 1982.

Simmonds, Jeremy. *The Encyclopedia of Dead Rock Stars: Heroin, Handguns, and Ham Sandwiches,* rev. ed. Chicago, IL: Chicago Review, 2008.

Simpson, O.J. *I Want to Tell You: My Response to Your Letters, Your Messages, Your Questions.* Boston: Little, Brown, 1995.

_____. *If I Did It: Confessions of the Killer.* New York: Beaufort, 2007.

Singular, Stephen. *Talked to Death: The Life and Death of Alan Berg.* New York: Beech Tree, 1987.

Smith, Carlton. *Reckless: Millionaire Record Producer Phil Spector and the Violent Death of Lana Clarkson.* New York: St. Martin's, 2004.

Smith, Ronald L. *Who's Who in Comedy: Comedians, Comics from Vaudeville to Today's Stand-Ups.* New York: Facts on File, 1992.

Soares, Andre. *Beyond Paradise: The Life of Ramón Novarro.* New York: St. Martin's, 2002.

Spector, Ronnie. *Be My Baby: How I Survived Mascara, Miniskirts, and Madness, or My Life as a Fabulous Ronette.* New York: Harmony, 1990.

Spence, Gerry. *O.J., the Last Word.* New York: St. Martin's, 1997.

Spoto, Donald. *Marilyn Monroe: The Biography.* New York: HarperCollins, 1993.

Steckles, Garry. *Bob Marley: A Life.* Northampton, MA: Interlink, 2009.

Steen, M.F. *Celebrity Death Certificates.* Jefferson, NC: McFarland, 2003.

Stenn, David. *Bombshell: The Life and Death of Jean Harlow.* New York: Doubleday, 1993.

Sullivan, Randall. *LAbyrinth: A Detective Investigates the Murders of Tupac Shakur and Biggie Smalls, the Implication of Death Row Records' Suge Knight, and the Origins of the Los Angeles Police Scandal.* New York: Atlantic Monthly, 2002.

Summers, Anthony. *Goddess: The Secret Lives of Marilyn Monroe.* New York: Macmillan, 1985.

Talevski, Nick. *The Encyclopedia of Rock Obituaries.* London; New York: Omnibus, 1999.

Taraborrelli, J. Randy. *Michael Jackson: The Magic, the Madness, the Whole Story, 1958–2009.* New York: Grand Central, 2009.

Thigpen, David E. *Jam Master Jay: The Heart of Hip Hop.* New York: Pocket Star, 2003.

Thompson, Dave. *Better to Burn Out: The Cult of Death in Rock 'n' Roll.* New York: Thunder's Mouth, 1999.

_____. *Wall of Pain: The Biography of Phil Spector.* London: Sanctuary, 2003.

Toobin, Jeffrey. *The Run of His Life: The People v. O.J. Simpson.* New York: Random House, 1996.

Tosches, Nick. *Country: The Biggest Music in America.* New York: Stein and Day, 1977.

Trintignant, Nadine. *Ma Fille, Marie.* Paris: Fayard, 2003.

_____. *Marie Trintignant.* Paris: Fayard, 2004.

Turner, Lana. *Lana—The Lady, the Legend, the Truth.* New York: Dutton, 1982.

Turner, Steve. *Trouble Man: The Life and Death of Marvin Gaye.* London: M. Joseph, 1998.

Vazzana, Eugene Michael. *Silent Film Necrology: Births and Deaths of Over 9000 Performers, Directors, Producers and Other Filmmakers of the Silent Era, Through 1993.* Jefferson, NC: McFarland, 1995.

Vibe, eds. *Tupac Amaru Shakur, 1971–1996.* New York: Crown, 1997.

Victor, Adam. *The Marilyn Encyclopedia.* Woodstock, NY: Overlook, 1999.

Wald, Elijah. *Escaping the Delta: Robert Johnson and the Invention of the Delta Blues.* New York: Amistad, 2004.

_____. *Narcocorrido: A Journey into the Music of Drugs, Guns, and Guerrillas.* New York: Rajo, 2001.

Waters, John. *Role Models.* 1st ed. New York: Farrar, Straus and Giroux, 2010.

Watson, Charles ("Tex"). *Manson's Right-Hand Man Speaks Out!* Jackson, CA: Abounding Love Ministries, 2003.

_____, and Ray Hoekstra. *Will You Die for Me?* Old Tappan, NJ: Revell, 1978.

Weaver, Tom. *Interviews with B Science Fiction and Horror Movie Makers: Writers, Producers, Directors, Actors, Moguls, and Makeup.* Jefferson, NC: McFarland, 1988.

Weller, Sheila. *Raging Heart: The Intimate Story of the Tragic Marriage of O.J. Simpson and Nicole Brown Simpson.* New York: Pocket, 1995.

West, Leslie, and Corky Laing. *Nantucket Sleighride and Other Mountain On-the-Road Stories.* Wembley: SAF, 2003.

White, Armond. *Rebel for the Hell of It: The Life of Tupac Shakur.* New York: Thunder's Mouth, 1997.

White, Timothy. *Catch a Fire: The Life of Bob Marley.* Rev. and enl. ed. London: Omnibus, 2006.

Wicks, Steve. *Bad Company: Drugs, Hollywood, and the Cotton Club Murder.* New York: St. Martin's, 1991.

Yallop, David A. *The Day the Laughter Stopped: The True Story of Fatty Arbuckle.* New York: St. Martin's, 1976.

Young, Robert. *Roscoe "Fatty" Arbuckle: A Bio-Bibliography.* Westport, CT: Greenwood, 1994.

Web Sites

www.adultfyi.com
www.allafrica.com
www.allhiphop.com
www.allmusic.com
www.armytimes.com
www.beausoleil.net
www.clown-ministry.com
www.deadpoetz.com
www.ejazznews.com
www.findagrave.com
www.hollywood.com
www.jacopastorius.com
www.jakibyard.org
www.lapdonline.org
www.luckydubemusic.com
www.mafikizolo.co.za

www.mansondirect.com
www.mansonfamilytoday.info
www.mary-miles-minter.com
www.mountaintheband.com
www.nasratparsamusic.com
www.nme666.com
www.palmspringslife.com
www.pappalardi.com
www.philadelphiaweekly.com
www.rapnewsdirect.com
www.robknox.co.uk/
www.sabcnews.com
www.salmineo.com
www.sohh.com
www.susanatkins.org
www.thegits.com
www.trutv.com

Index